D1599351

Dictionary

of

Philosophy

International Publishers, New York

Translated from the Russian

Edited by Murad Saifulin and the late Richard R. Dixon

© 1984 by Progress Publishers
First United States edition 1984 by International Publishers
All rights reserved
Printed in the Union of Soviet Socialist Republics

Library of Congress Cataloging in Publication Data
Main entry under title:

Dictionary of philosophy.

    Translated from Russian.
    1. Philosophy—Dictionaries. I. Frolov, Ivan
Timofeevich.
B41. D533 1984   103'.21   83-244
ISBN 0-7178-0604-9

PUBLISHERS' NOTE

The translation has been made from the fourth Russian edition produced by the Political Literature Publishers (Moscow) in 1980.

A uniform system of cross-references, and a number of abbreviations common for such publications, has been used. The word or words contained in the heading of each article are referred to by the initial letter or letters; in the article on Aristotle, for instance, the name of Aristotle is replaced by the letter A. If the heading of an article consists of several words, they are also referred to in the text by the initial letters. For instance, in the article on the Content and Form the full heading is replaced by C. and F; in the article on the Absolute and Relative Truth, A. T. means "absolute truth" and R. T. means "relative truth". References to books are given in italics; references to other articles are followed by the letters q.v. For instance, in the article on Anarchism we read: "The emergence of A. is connected with the names of Schmidt (Stirner, q.v.), Proudhon, Bakunin (qq.v.)." Where additional information on related subjects is supplied to explain some point cross-references are preceded by the word "see". This double system has been adopted because some of the headings contain a number of words and come alphabetically under the initial letters of the first, whereas the (q.v.) comes after the last word; (b) italics alone would not suffice because the editors have followed the usual British practice of printing the titles of books, foreign words and expressions, etc., in italics.

a

Abélard (Abailard), Pierre (1079-1142), French philosopher and theologian; in the dispute over the nature of universals (q.v.), which was characteristic of the medieval philosophy and in which the struggle between materialism and idealism (qq.v.) was expressed, he supported the ideas of conceptualism (q.v.) which are close to materialism. He also polemised against scholastic realism (see Realism, Medieval). His book *Sic et Non* which demanded that religious faith be restricted to rational premises and revealed irreconcilable contradictions in the utterances of church authorities, was of progressive significance. A.'s views were condemned by the Catholic Church as heretical.

Abilities, in a broad sense, the psychic properties of the individual which regulate his behaviour and serve as the condition of his activity. The most universal A. of the individual are his sensory capacities, which improve during the entire length of his phylo- and ontogenetic development. In the special sense, A. stand for the set of psychic properties that fit the individual for a definite, historically evolved type of professional activity. Their formation implies the acquisition by the individual of the forms of activity worked out by mankind in the course of its socio-historical development. Thus, man's A. depend not only on the activity of his brain, the inherited anatomic and physiological features, inclinations, skills and habits, but above all on the level of historical development attained by mankind. In this sense, man's A. are closely associated with the social organisation of labour and the system of education which corresponds to it. The qualitative level of A. is expressed by the concept of talent (a sum total of A. permitting to obtain an original, perfect, and socially significant product), and genius (the A. to effect fundamental changes in some sphere of creativity). The all-round development of man's A. for the purpose of giving every person access to a variety of professions and forms of activity is one of the principal tasks in the building of communism.

Absolute, the, a concept used in idealist philosophy to denote the eternal, infinite, unconditional, perfect and unchanging subject that has no dependence on anything else, contains within itself everything that exists and creates it. In religion the A. is God; in Fichte (q.v.) it is the ego; in Hegel (q.v.) it is the world reason (the absolute spirit); in Schopenhauer (q.v.) it is will; in Bergson (q.v.) it is intuition. Dialectical materialism rejects such concepts of the A. as unscientific.

Absolute and Relative, the, philosophical categories. The A. is independent, irrelative, complete in itself, unconditioned and immutable; the R. describes a phenomenon in its relations and connections with other phenomena and its dependence on them. On the whole, matter in motion is not conditioned and not limited by anything, it is eternal and inexhaustible, i.e., it is absolute. The infinite number of kinds and states of matter, the concrete forms of its motion that are constantly replacing each other, are temporary, finite, transitory, relative. Every thing is relative but it is a part of a whole and in that sense contains within itself an element of the absolute; that which is relative in one connection is absolute in another, etc.

Abstract and Concrete, the. The A., part of a whole, one-sided, simple, elementary, undeveloped. The C., many-sided, complex, developed, whole. Before Hegel (q.v.) the C. was understood mainly as the sensually perceived multiformity of individual objects and phenomena and the A. as the product of the mind alone (see Abstraction). Hegel was the first to make use of the categories of the A. and C. in that specific philosophical meaning which was later to be developed in Marxist philosophy—the C. is a synonym of dialectic interrelations, of dismembered wholeness; the A. is not metaphysically opposed to the C. but is a stage in the development of the C. itself; it is the unrevealed, undeveloped C. (Hegel compares the relation between the A. and the C. to that between the bud and the fruit, the acorn and the oak tree). According to Hegel, however, the C. describes only the "spirit", the thought, the "absolute idea". Nature and the social relations of people are "other-being", an abstract revelation of individual aspects or moments in the life of the absolute spirit. In Marxist philosophy the subject or vehicle of the C. is material reality, the universe of sensually perceived finite things and phenomena. The C. of an object is the objective interrelation of its aspects, determined by the essential, law-governed relation that underlines it; the C. of cognition is the reflection of this real interrelation in a system of concepts that reproduce the objective content of the object being cognised. The A. in real life is the expression of the non-whole, of the not fully unfolded, not fully developed and limited nature of any of the fragments of the whole, since the fragment is taken in isolation, divorced from its intermediary connections and from its subsequent history. Abstract knowledge, therefore, is counterposed to concrete knowledge because it is one-sided, expresses only one particular aspect of an object isolated from its connection with other aspects, isolated from that which determines the specific nature of the whole. Really scientific theoretical cognition consists of a thought process that proceeds from the sensual multiformity of the C. and achieves the reproduction of the object in all its complexity. The method for the theoretical reproduction of a whole object in the consciousness is the ascent from the A. to the C.; this is the universal form in which scientific knowledge unfolds; the systematic reflection of the object in concepts. The ascent from the A. to the C., being a means of linking up concepts in an integral system which reflects the objective dismemberment of the object of study and the unity of all its aspects, presupposes an original movement from the C. (perceived by contemplation) to the A. when concepts are formed which reflect individual aspects

and properties of the object that can themselves be understood only insofar as they are regarded as parts of the whole, determined by its specific content. It is, therefore, essential to distinguish the C. which is the object of study, the starting point of the investigation (the sensual C.) from the C. which is the end-product, the result of the investigation, the scientific concept of the object (the mental C.).

Abstraction, that aspect or form of cognition which mentally isolates properties of an object or connections between its properties from the others. Both the process and its result are called A. In the process of A. it is sometimes necessary to disregard certain of man's subjective possibilities. It is impossible, for instance, to "count" the entire series of natural numbers, but if we disregard that possibility we get the A. of actual (i.e., "counted", "completed") infinity. The various concepts and categories—matter, motion, value are the results of A. All cognition is inevitably associated with processes of A. Without them it is impossible to reveal the substance or penetrate into the "depth" of an object. The breaking down of an object, the singling out of its essential aspects and their all-round analysis in their "pure" form, all result from the mental work of abstraction. Lenin said the following about the significance of A. for cognition: "Thought proceeding from the concrete to the abstract—provided it is *correct*...—does not get away *from* the truth but comes closer to it. The abstraction of *matter*, of a *law* of nature, the abstraction of *value*, etc., in short *all* scientific (correct, serious, not absurd) abstractions reflect nature more deeply, truly and *completely*" (Vol. 38, p. 171). Practice (see Theory and Practice) is the criterion by which the true scientific nature of the Aa. introduced into science is judged. Dialectical materialism (q.v.) provides a scientific explanation of the process of A. and its results. Idealism often speculated on the difficulties connected with abstract thinking. Lenin warned that the possibility of idealism is inherent even in the most elementary A. The conversion of the products of A. (concepts, ideas) into the substance and the primary principle of the Universe is typical of idealist philosophy. Modern nominalism (q.v.) of a positivist hue denies the need of high abstraction for science, depriving it of essential means of reflecting reality, of its heuristic potentialities. In dialectical logic (q.v.), the concept of A. is also used to mean something one-sided and undeveloped as distinct from concrete (see Abstract and Concrete, the).

Academy of Plato, an ancient idealist philosophical school founded by Plato (q.v.) in 387 B.C. near Athens, which took its name from Academ, a hero of Greek mythology. It opposed materialism. At various stages of its long history it was influenced by different idealist schools. The influence of the Pythagoreans became great in the Older Academy (Speusippus and others, 4th-3rd centuries B.C.) which played an important part in the development of mathematics and astronomy. Plato's views were systematised on the basis of the mystic theory of numbers. The Middle Academy (Arcesilaus, q.v., and others, 3rd century B.C.) was influenced by scepticism (q.v.). The New Academy (Carneades, q.v., and others, 2nd-1st centuries B.C.) developed the scepticism of the Middle Academy and opposed the teachings of the stoics (q.v.) on the criterion of truth. In the later period the A. eclectically combined the teachings of the Platonic, stoic, Aristotelian, and other schools. In the 4th and 5th centuries the A. went over completely to the doctrine of Neoplatonism, q.v. (Plutarch of Athens). A. was closed in 529 by the Emperor Justinian. A.P. was founded once again in Florence and existed at the time of the Renaissance (1459-1521); it combatted from the Platonic position scholasticised Aristotle (q.v.) and translated and commented the writings of Plato (Marsilio Ficino).

Accident, a temporary, transient, non-essential property of a thing as opposed to that which is essential, substantial (see Substance). The term was first used by Aristotle (q.v.) and became widespread in scholasticism (q.v.) and in 17th- and 18th-century philosophy (Spinoza, q.v., and others).

Acosta (da Costa), **Uriel** (born in Portugal between 1585 and 1590, died 1640).

Dutch philosopher, rationalist; received education in Coimbra University. Fled to Holland in 1614, renounced Christianity for Judaism (q.v.). Soon opposed Jewish religious dogmatism and accused the Pharisees (rabbis) of distorting the Mosaic faith. In 1623 he wrote a treatise on *Sobre a mortalidade da alma do homen* in which he denied the immortality of the soul and life beyond the grave. Was twice excommunicated from the Sinagogue for his views (1623 and 1633). Persecuted by the rabbis and the Dutch authorities, he committed suicide. His *Exemplar humanae vitae* contained the idea of the natural law supposed to be inherent in man; this law joins people together by mutual love and serves as a basis for differentiating between good and evil (q.v.). A.'s ideas had an influence on Spinoza (q.v.).

Activity 1. In philosophy, a specifically human relation to the world, a process in the course of which man reproduces and creatively transforms nature, thereby making himself the subject of A. and the natural phenomena the object of his A. It is thanks to A., or labour (q.v.), that man raised himself out of the animal world and preserved and developed in the historical process all specifically human properties. In the course of A. man treats objects in accordance with their nature and properties, adapts them to his needs, and makes them the yardstick and basis of his A. In his interaction with nature man gradually includes it in his material and spiritual culture. Changes in the external world are only the premise and condition for the self-improvement of man. In the course of production men always reproduce themselves and are no longer the same as when they began it. According to Marx, they create "new powers and new conceptions, new modes of intercourse, new needs, and new speech" (K. Marx, F. Engels, *Pre-Capitalist Socio-Economic Formations*, p. 109). Thus, A. as a whole process also includes communication. The essence of A. is the social continuity of being, passed from generation to generation. The source of creative A. lies in its dynamics. Historically, the first stage of A. is the production of implements with the help of implements. A. exists in the form of man's potentiality to act and in the form of the embodiment of objects, being the process of constant transformation of the former into the latter and vice versa. Laws of history are in the final count laws of A., though in a class society, given the division of labour (q.v.) and its alienation (q.v.), they appear to govern people's behaviour in the guise of external alienated forces. Theoretical A., like the material and technical process of transforming an object, are only the relatively independent elements of whole A. as a system where the process of material transformation determines the ideal transformation. Theoretical A. is, thus, a socially creative process aimed at changing the world of human culture. The division of labour creates the illusion that "purely practical" and "purely theoretical" functions are A. as such. Only under communism, A. is a whole self-activity for each person, the aim and requirement of life (see Communist Labour). The philosophical concept of material A. is of considerable conceptual and methodological significance for all social sciences, notably for sociology, psychology (qq.v.), pedagogics, etc. 2. In psychology, A. is a concept connoting the function of the individual in his interaction with the surroundings. Psychic A. is a specific relation of a living body to its environment; it mediates, regulates, and controls relations between the organism and the environment. Psychic A. is impelled by need, aimed at the object which can satisfy this need, and effected by a system of actions. It presumes that the body has psychics (q.v.), but at the same time constitutes the basic cause for its origin and the motive force of its development. The elementary form of psychic A. should be distinguished from its highest form. The former is typical of animals and consists in the instinctive (see Instinct) adaptation of the body to its environment. The latter, which stems from the former and transforms it, is exclusively an attribute of man. The specifically distinctive feature of the highest form of A. is man's deliberate effort to transform his environment. The A. of man has a social complexion and is determined by the social conditions of life. Psychic A. of man may be external or

internal. The former consists of specifically human operations with existing objects effected by the movement of arms, hands, fingers, and legs. The latter proceeds in the mind, by means of "mental actions", wherein man operates not with existing objects and not through physical movements, but with their dynamic images. Internal A. plans external A. It arises on the basis of external A. and realises itself through it. Division of labour causes a differentiation between theoretical and practical forms of A. of man. According to the range of man's and society's needs, there also arises the range of concrete types of A., each of which usually embraces elements of external and internal, practical and theoretical A.

Actualisation, a concept denoting changes in being. This concept reveals only one aspect of motion—the transition of existence from a state of potentiality to a state of reality. In scholasticism (q.v.) and in Aristotle's (q.v.) philosophy explanation of A. was bound to lead to the recognition of the stationary source of motion external to real being—the prime mover, or God. The idea of the transition from the potential to the real is most fully expressed in the categories of materialist dialectics (see Possibility and Reality).

Adaptation, the process of a system's accommodation to the conditions of external and internal environment. A. is sometimes also called the result of this process, i.e., a system's adaptability to a factor of the environment. A wide spread of various adaptations in organic nature had long served as a basic argument of teleology (q.v.), which regarded them as results of "creative acts" or the action of internal spiritual principles (entelechy, q.v., and others). A rational interpretation of A. as the outcome of the struggle for existence and natural selection was first given in Darwin's (q.v.) theory of evolution. With the emergence of cybernetics (q.v.), which considers the negative feedback (q.v.) that ensures purposeful reaction of complex hierarchical (see Hierarchy) self-controlled systems to the changing conditions of the environment to be the mechanism of A., the concept of A. began to be applied, apart from biology, also to the study of social and technical systems. It should be noted, however, that in reference to man this concept has limited possibilities, as it mainly reflects responsive behaviour connected with the adaptation to the environment, rather than with its active and purposive transformation.

Additive and Non-Additive, concepts reflecting types of correlations between the whole and its constituent parts (see Part and Whole). The relation of additivity is often expressed as "the whole is equal to the sum of the parts", and the relation of non-additivity as "the whole is more than the sum of the parts" (superadditivity) or "the whole is less than the sum of the parts" (subadditivity). Any material object has A. properties, e.g., the mass of a physical system is equal to the sum of masses of the system's parts. However, many properties of complex objects are N.A., i.e., irreducible to the properties of the parts. For instance, society is characterised by some features which are impossible to explain proceeding from the properties of separate individuals. Methodologically, the principle of additivity presumes the possibility of an exhaustive explanation of the properties of the whole on the basis of the properties of its parts (or vice versa, the properties of the parts on the basis of the properties of the whole), while the principle of non-additivity, excluding such a possibility, requires the application of other grounds for explaining the properties of the whole (resp. the properties of the parts).

Adequate, the theory of knowledge (q.v.) regards as A. those images and that knowledge which correspond to the original object and are therefore authentic and represent objective truths. The problem of the degree of adequacy, i.e., the exactness, profundity, and fullness of the reflection of an object is connected with the problem of the correlation between relative and absolute truth, of essence and appearance (q.v.) and of the criterion of truth (q.v.).

Adorno, Theodor (1903-1969), German philosopher and sociologist of art who belonged to a Left radical orientation, a prominent representative of the Frankfurt school (q.v.). A.'s views took shape at the junction of German neo-Hegelianism (q.v.) and the vanguardist critique of culture. According to A.'s social philosophy, the history of West European culture, beginning with Homer, is a history of "abortive civilisation", a history of the "individualisation" of man, identical to his deepening alienation. The philosophical premises of A.'s conception are expounded in his *Dialectic of Enlightenment* (1947), written together with M. Horkheimer. In his *Philosophy of Modern Music* (1949) A. applied this conception to the development of modern European music. In his works *On Metacritique of the Theory of Knowledge* (1956) and *Negative Dialectics* (1966) the negativist, pessimistic philosophy of the history of the Frankfurt school followers is presented as a methodology of universal negation, and dialectics is interpreted merely as a method of disintegrating, destroying all that "is given". A.'s conception was popular in the West during the sway of "left" extremist, vulgar sociological and nihilist views in the 1960s, but lost its influence with the bankruptcy of the ideology of the New Left (q.v.).

Aenesidemus (1st century B.C.), Greek philosopher, a sceptic, one of the disciples of Pyrrho (q.v.) and those advocates of Plato's (q.v.) Academy (see Academy of Plato) who upheld scepticism (q.v.). A. claimed that true cognition of things is impossible, because every statement can be matched by another statement saying just the opposite. It is better to make no statements at all, for this is the only way to inner enjoyment. One should act as everybody else usually does, or as the necessity dictates. A.'s philosophy was a product of the decay of classical Greek philosophy.

Aesthetic and Ethical, the, aspects of man's relations with reality. Through the concepts of the good and the evil, justice and injustice, duty, responsibility (qq.v.), etc. the E. reflects moral relations, appraises the actions, behaviour of an individual or a group of individuals. The A. is the expression in objects and feelings of some aspects of objective social relations which promote or hinder the individual's harmonious development, favour or interfere with his creative work aimed at creating the beautiful, the sublime (qq.v.) and the heroic, at fighting the ugly (q.v.) and the base. The A. also includes a subjective aspect: man enjoys a free expression of his creative powers and admires the beauty of what has been created by people in all spheres of social and personal life (labour, social relations, everyday life, culture). Art (q.v.) is the fullest and most generalised form of expression of the A. The unity of the A. and the E. is a regularity which can be traced in both life and art, though in some works of art this unity may not be preserved. Modern bourgeois art, for example, allows the beautification of the ugly and advocacy of amoralism (q.v.). Socialist art, on the contrary, consistently puts into practice the principle of unity between the A. and the E. Positive characters, noble and beautiful, evoke respect, affection and sincere admiration. They are also a source of aesthetic feelings of pleasure and joy for readers and spectators. Negative images showing amorality of man's behaviour generate the feeling of moral disapproval which is closely linked with the aesthetic feeling of contempt for and aversion to the ugly and the base. Thus, the unity of the A. and the E. is the foundation for the art's educational and ideological mission in social life.

Aesthetic Feelings, an emotional condition arising in the process of aesthetic perception of phenomena of reality or works of art. A.F. are a kind of response to this perception which can be expressed through the feelings of the beautiful or the sublime, the tragic or the comic (qq.v.). Man's aesthetic experience is not limited to A.F., but it cannot exist without them. A.F. are a product of man's historical development. They reflect the level of society's aesthetic consciousness. Works of art which materialise the A.F. in images are an effective means of either ideological or emotional education. They are meant to be a source of human joy and inspiration.

Aesthetics, the science of the law-governed aesthetical assimilation of the world by man, of the essence and forms of creative work according to laws of beauty. A. originated about 2,500 years ago, in the period of slave-owning society, in Egypt, Babylon, India and China. It was greatly developed in ancient Greece and Rome. The materialist trend was encouraged by Democritus, Aristotle, Epicurus, Lucretius (qq.v.) and others who believed in the objective basis of beauty which they found in material qualities, links, relations and laws of reality, contrary to Plato's (q.v.) idealistic teaching, according to which beauty was an absolute, eternal, immutable and pretersensual idea, and sensibles created by art were but the reflection of this idea. Humanistic and realistic trends were developed in works by thinkers, writers and artists of the Renaissance (q.v.) who tried to combat the Western medieval mystic doctrines on "divine beauty" (see St. Augustine, Thomas Aquinas). In an attempt to overcome the ideas of aristocratic A., W. Hogarth, Diderot, Rousseau, Winckelman, Lessing, Herder (qq.v.) and later Schiller and Goethe (qq.v.), and their followers, affirmed that art (q.v.) is linked with real life. Kant (q.v.) set off beauty against utility, the perfection of artistic form against ideological content, thus contributing to the development of the formalistic A. The principles of historism and contradiction formed the basis for Hegel's (q.v.) explanation of aesthetic activity, this allowing him to compare aesthetic activity with the contradictory character of capitalist production and to snow the significance of labour for an understanding of the essence of the aesthetic. However, being an objective idealist, Hegel defined art as the first and imperfect form of the absolute spirit. Feuerbach (q.v.) tried to prove that the source of beauty is physical qualities of objects and phenomena and to deduce aesthetic feelings and tastes from biological laws and the nature of man. Pre-Marxian materialist A. has reached the peak of its development in the works by the Russian revolutionary democrats Belinsky, Chernyshevsky and Dobrolyubov (qq.v.), who formulated the laws of realistic art, the principles of ideological commitment and service to the people in works of art. A radical turn which took place in the history of A. is connected with its application to dialectical and historical materialism, the Marxist method of investigation. This formed a theoretical basis for comprehensive treatment of key problems of A., for the struggle against bourgeois, revisionist and dogmatic distortions in this sphere. Unlike the idealist and vulgar materialist theories, Marxist-Leninist A. holds that the objective basis for the aesthetical assimilation of the world is man's purposeful creative activity. In this activity man's social essence and creative powers aimed at transforming nature and society find their full application. The main aesthetic categories: the beautiful and the ugly (qq.v.), the sublime (q.v.) and the base, the dramatic, the tragic and the comic (qq.v.), the heroic, appear as specific manifestations of the aesthetic assimilation of the world in every field of social being, human life—in production, public and political activity, in attitude to nature, in culture, everyday life, etc. The subjective aspect of aesthetic assimilation, aesthetic feelings (q.v.), tastes, evaluations, experiences, ideas and ideals are regarded by Marxist-Leninist A. as specific forms of the reflection and embodiment of objective life's processes and relations. Marxist-Leninist A. is the theoretical foundation of the aesthetic education of people in a socialist society, of the formation of progressive, well-developed aesthetic feelings and tastes, of the educational work aimed at eliminating the influence of bourgeois survivals in the sphere of A. The arts and the process of artistic creation are part of A. and its most essential aspect. In analysing the essence of art and its laws, A. is intimately connected with all the special, theoretical and historical sciences, and sciences of the arts. A. is, however, a philosophical science. It studies the general principles of man's aesthetic attitude to reality, including art; as for art criticism it is concerned with the specifics of art as such. Being a world-view science, just like philosophy, Marxist-Leninist A. scientifically discloses the different aspects of the nature of art and the process of artistic creation: the origin of art, its

essence and relation with the other forms of social consciousness, partisanship and service to the people in art, its historical regularities, specific features of the artistic image (q.v.), interrelation between the content and form (q.v.) in art, the artistic method (q.v.) and style, fundamental principles of socialist realism (q.v.) and its socio-transforming role in building communism. The main tasks of Marxist-Leninist A. are a profound scientific analysis and generalisation of the aesthetic processes of today and active participation in tackling the problem of moulding the comprehensively and harmoniously developed man of communist society.

Aesthetics and Technology. The relations between these spheres of human activity can be considered in the following aspects: industrial A., technical A. and industrial design. In the USSR and other socialist countries, the aim of industrial A. is to organise production in keeping with the requirements of beauty and expediency, i. e., to create conditions most favourable for health maintenance and good spirits of the employees, for boosting labour productivity. Design of convenient and pleasant to the eye industrial buildings and tools, modelling of comfortable and nice clothes for work, interior decoration in industrial premises and places for recreation—all these are the sphere of industrial A., all these raise aesthetic culture, promote the harmonious development of working people and help develop a communist attitude to labour. Industrial goods of aesthetic perfection and, sometimes, of artistic value can be created in the process of design. Technical A. is a theory of industrial design. It prescribes technical and operational standards for industrial goods which combine expediency with beauty. Using data from many branches of knowledge, primarily those of ergonomics, the science that studies labour activity from the standpoint of technology, physiology, psychology, hygiene, etc., technical A. helps the designer to create items not only appropriate to a particular purpose but also having a certain aesthetic value. Finally, the interrelation between T. and art is manifested in the fact that the development of T. makes possible the appearance of new forms of art (cinema, television) and exerts influence on its most ancient ones (building equipment in architecture, new materials and new methods of their treatment in sculpture, new musical instruments, technical devices in theatre). T. plays a great role also in the dissemination of the arts (radio, television and printing industry).

Affection, an experience that is powerful and tempestuous in its action but differs from mood or passion (see Emotions) in being relatively brief—rage, horror, etc. A. is accompanied by jerky, expressive movements (specific mine and gesticulation) and vocal reactions (crying, shouting). Sometimes, on the contrary, numbness sets in. The outward expression of A. and its profundity depend to a great extent on individual peculiarities, in particular on the will and the typological features of higher nervous activity (q.v.). A person in a state of A. is in the power of whatever caused it; hence it interrupts the course of intellectual processes and weakens control over behaviour. A. can be overcome only by considerable willpower, and more easily in the early stages.

Affectivity, a term used by Kant (q.v.) to mean the property possessed by things to affect the sense-organs. The concept of A. expresses the materialist aspect of Kantianism: Kant considered that sense perceptions arise only as the result of the action of "things-in-themselves" on the sense-organs. This concept is counterposed in the Kantian system to the concept of transcendental apperception (q.v.). Nevertheless, Kant still insisted that things are unknowable. The concept was criticised by the neo-Kantians and all those who turned Kantianism into consistent idealism.

Agnosticism, a doctrine that completely or partially denies the possibility of knowing the Universe. The term was first used by the British natural scientist Thomas Huxley. Lenin laid bare the epistemological roots of A. and said that the agnostic separates substance from its appearance, that he does not go farther than sensations. The attitude of compromise adopted by A. leads its supporters to idealism. A. emerged in the form of scepticism (q.v.) in Greek philosophy (see Pyrrho) and was given its classic form in the philosophy of Hume and Kant (qq.v.). A variety of A. is the theory of hieroglyphs (q.v.). The champions of neo-positivism and existentialism (qq.v.) and of other trends in modern bourgeois philosophy attempt to prove the impossibility of knowing the world and the man. A. proceeds from their attempt to limit science, reject logical thought, and cognition of the objective laws of nature and, especially, of society. Practice (experience), scientific experimentation and material production are the best refutation of A. If people cognise certain phenomena and then deliberately reproduce them, no place is left for the "unknowable thing-in-itself". However, cognition is a complex process that may warrant doubt. Absolutisation of this brings some modern scholars to agnosticism.

Agrippa, Roman philosopher, representative of the latest scepticism, q.v. (1st-2nd centuries). There are no data on his life. To him philosophers ascribed five arguments (tropes, q.v.) on the unknowability of the Universe. A.'s tropes touch on problems of rational knowledge and contain elements of dialectics.

Ajivika, a non-orthodox theory in ancient Indian philosophy denying the existence of the soul. A. was originally connected with Buddhism (q.v.) of which it was probably a variant, since early Buddhists also rejected the existence of soul. The doctrine was fathered, according to tradition, by the wise man Markalideva, believed to have lived in the 6th-5th centuries B.C. In medieval Vedantic treatises A. was based on the atomistic theory which determined the other ideas and conceptions of the theory. According to A. there are four varieties of the atom, which make up the four elements of nature—earth, water, fire, and air; all atoms are able to combine. "Life" is not something atomic but is that which perceives and cognises combinations of atoms. The varieties of atoms and life constitute the five essences of which everything in existence is composed. Consciousness is a special aggregate of super-fine atoms that constitute the configuration of "life". Atoms are eternal, indivisible, were not created and cannot be destroyed. A. was a realistic and, in general, materialist theory that opposed the ancient Indian religions and the philosophy of Brahmanism (see Indian Philosophy). A. rejected the Brahmanist doctrines of *karma, samsara* and *moksha*. Sometimes this rejection took the form of ethical relativism (q.v.).

Akhundov, Mirza Fatali (1812-1878), Azerbaijanian writer, enlightener, and public figure. A.'s materialist world outlook was formed under the influence of progressive Russian social thought. A's theory of knowledge proceeded from a recognition of the knowability of the world; he also defended sensationalism (q.v.). A.'s materialism was combined with atheism (q.v.); he criticised Islam (q.v.), stressed the incompatibility of faith and knowledge and highlighted the reactionary role of religion in the history of society. A. was the founder of Azerbaijanian literature, dramaturgy, and theatre. He was a true patriot, a champion of the friendship of the peoples, and advocated the establishment of fraternal relations between the peoples of the Transcaucasus and the Russian people. A.'s main philosophical work was *Three Letters of the Indian Prince Kamal-ud-Daula to the Persian Prince Jamal-ud-Daula and the Latter's Answers to Them.*

Al Kindi (c. 800-870), Arab philosopher, astrologer, mathematician, and physician, honoured with the title of "The Philosopher of the Arabs". A.K. wrote commentaries to Aristotle's (q.v.) works (*Organon*, etc.) and a number of papers on metaphysics. A.K.'s world outlook was based on the idea of the universal causal connection due to which every thing, if completely understood, reflects the entire Universe as in a mirror. Orthodox believers in the Koran regarded A.K. as a heretic. Only fragments of A.K.'s numerous writings have been preserved.

Alberdi, Juan Bautista (1810-1884), Argentine statesman, writer, philosopher, and sociologist. His *Bases para la Organización Política de la Confederación Argentina* (1852) formed the basis of the country's Constitution. His book *El crimen de la guerra* was written under the impression of the horrors of the Paraguayan war (1864-70) and gave him a place in history as an impassioned exposer of war and champion of peace and fraternity on earth. He declared that aggressive wars were crimes. His understanding of war was influenced by the ideas of Grotius (q.v.). A.'s weakness was his approach to the problem of war from the standpoint of law and Christian morality.

Albert the Great (b. 1193-1207; d. 1280), German philosopher, naturalist, and theologian. He and his disciple, Thomas Aquinas (q.v.), revolted against the interpretation of Aristotle's philosophy in the spirit of Averroism (q.v.) and against the progressive scholastic schools; he used Aristotelian ideas to elaborate a single philosophical-theological system. Apart from his purely philosophical writings (*Summa Theologiae*, etc.), A.G. wrote a number of treatises on natural history.

Alembert, d', Jean Le Rond (1717-1783), French Enlightener, philosopher and mathematician. He attempted to expound the origin and development of human cognition and to classify the sciences mainly on the basis of F. Bacon's (q.v.) principles. Philosophically, A. was an exponent of sensationalism (q.v.) and opposed Descartes' (q.v.) theory of innate ideas (q.v.). However, his sensationalism was not consistently materialist. A. denied that thought is a property of matter and believed that the soul exists independently of matter. His views were thus dualistic. In contrast to other French Enlighteners, he maintained that morals do not depend on the social environment. He pronounced God to be the creative substance. Diderot (q.v.) criticised A.'s inconsistent sensationalism in his works. His main work: *Essai sur les éléments de philosophie* (1759).

Alexander, Samuel (1859-1938), British neo-realist philosopher, author of the idealist theory of emergent evolution (q.v.). Adhering to the idealist interpretation of the general theory of relativity, he regarded space-time as being the primary matter of the Universe and identified it with motion. A series of unforeseeable qualitative leaps cause the consecutive emergence of matter, life, the psyche, "tertiary values", "angels", and God from this space-time. Emergent evolution is guided by an ideal impulse which is perceived as a striving towards the new. A.'s views contradict modern science. His main work: *Space, Time, and Deity* (1920).

Alexandrian School of Philosophy (1st century B.C. to 6th century A.D.), the term occurs in literature in two different meanings. First, it is used to denote the Judaic philosophy of Philo of Alexandria who lived in Egypt in the 1st century B.C. and used the methods of stoic Platonism to interpret the Bible. This trend assumed Plato's ideas to be the basis of existence but understood them to be a creative fire that poured over the entire Universe, creating all living and inanimate things in it. Second, there has always been a wider conception of the A.S. in literature; it is made to include pagan neo-Pythagoreanism and the eclectic schools of the first centuries and also the whole of Neoplatonism (q.v.), although that trend was current in Rome, Syria, and Pergamum as well as in Alexandria itself and had pagan as well as Christian forms. It is more correct to use the term A.S. for the school of Philo and the Alexandrian Christian thinkers of the 2nd and 3rd centuries.

Algebra of Logic, a division of mathematical logic (q.v.) based on the application of algebraic methods in the study of logical objects—classes and statements (q.v.). Historically, A.L. came into being as the algebra of classes (see Boole) and was only later interpreted as the algebra of propositions. A.L. examines propositions exclusively from the standpoint of their truth-value and regards statements as equal if they have the same truth-value. A.L. uses symbols. In addition to the symbols used for the propositions themselves there are symbols for logical operations, with the aid of which

some expressions in A.L. are transformed into others. Today A.L. finds extensive application in the theory of electric and contact-relay systems.

Algorithm, a term that derives from the Latin transcription of al-Khuwarizmi, 9th-century Central Asian mathematician. A. is a rule of procedure for executing a system of operations in a certain sequence which will give the solution to all problems of a similar type. The simplest examples of A. are the arithmetic rules of addition, subtraction, multiplication, and division, the extraction of the square root, the finding of the greatest common measure for any two natural numbers, etc. We actually make use of A. whenever we master a means of solving a problem of a general type, i.e., one which can be used for a whole class with varying conditions. Since A., as a system of rules, is formal in character, a programme for a computer can always be evolved on the basis of it, and the problem solved mechanically. The solution of a large group of problems by A. and the elaboration of the theory of A. are vitally important in connection with the development of computer technology and cybernetics (q.v.).

Alienation, a concept describing both the process and the results of converting the products of human activity (both practical—products of labour, money, social relations, etc., and theoretical) and also man's properties and capabilities into something independent of them and dominating over them; also the transformation of some phenomena and relations into something different from what they are in themselves, the distortion in people's minds of their actual relations in life. The sources of the A. idea can be traced to French (see Rousseau) and German (see Goethe, Schiller) Enlighteners. Objectively, this idea expressed protest against the inhumane character of private property relations. The problem of A. was reflected in German classical philosophy. Hegel (q.v.) developed most fully the idealistic interpretation of A. The objective world appears as the "alienated spirit". The purpose of development, according to Hegel, is to overcome this A. in the process of cognition. At the same time, Hegel's understanding of A. contained rational surmises about some distinctive features of labour in an antagonistic society. Feuerbach (q.v.) regarded religion as A. of the human essence and idealism as A. of reason. By reducing A. merely to consciousness, he found, however, no real way for its elimination since he saw it only in theoretical criticism. Modern bourgeois philosophy and revisionist literature characterise A. as an inevitable phenomenon engendered either by technological and scientific progress or by such specific features of mankind's activity that are not conditioned by history. The theoretical foundation of this concept consists in identifying A. with objectification (see Objectification and Deobjectification), while in social essence it is apologetical. Marx analysed A. very closely. He proceeded from the fact that A. characterises contradictions at a definite stage in the development of society. He associated the appearance of A. with private property and division of labour (q.v.). Under such conditions social relations are formed spontaneously and are not controlled by men, while the results and products of human activity become alienated from individuals and social groups and appear to them as something imposed by other men or a supernatural force. Marx focussed attention on the A. of labour (q.v.), and with the help of this concept characterised the system of capitalist relations and the position of the proletariat. Recognition of A. of labour as the basis of all other forms of A., including ideological, made it possible to understand that distorted, false consciousness is a result of contradictions in real social life. At the same time, Marx held that A. would be eliminated in the process of the communist transformation of society.

All-Round Development of the Individual, assimilation of the wealth of social culture when the labour of every member of society becomes integral activity (see Communist Labour), and every person becomes self-acting and creative individual. It becomes possible only after the elimination of such social division of labour (q.v.) which cripples man turning him into a performer of narrow labour

functions assigned to him. Under capitalism the division and splitting of man's activity has given rise to numerous professional occupations devoid of creative initiative and even absurd in themselves. Such functions (e.g. bureaucratic) which arose due to the relations existing in society with antagonistic classes represent aspects of labour incompatible with the activity of the integral, communist man who is the subject and creator of social relations. Overcoming these aspects of human activity, turning it into a purposeful creative process do not at all mean that every person must necessarily know all and be able to do all the others know and do. This is in fact impossible: the developing productive forces give rise to ever growing specialisation. In communist society this will mean specialisation in which there will be no division into physical and mental work, into operatives' and managers' functions, into working and free (to be more precise, one's own) time, when there will be no gulf between intellectual, artistic and moral culture, and there will be no fixation of professional occupations. This will be achieved not through mechanical combination and concentration of all and sundry labour functions, specialities, etc., in one person, but through genuine all-round development of the individual which will remove all necessity for independent administration, control, distribution and security functions wielded over man. In the process of labour, the man himself masters these functions, includes them as auxiliary functions in his activity as a whole, thus becoming a universal and creative subject. As distinct from capitalist society, in which big industry, circulation of capital and other factors call for "the greatest possible development of his [the worker's] varied aptitudes" (Karl Marx, *Capital,* Vol. 1, p. 458), the communist system calls for man's integral, harmonious, not merely all-round, development. "The full and free development of every individual forms the ruling principle" of communism (ibid., p. 555).

Alogism, the rejection of logical thinking as a means of arriving at the truth; A. is the substitution of intuition, faith and revelation for logic. It is used by reactionary philosophers to justify irrationalism, mysticism, and fideism (qq.v.). A. is refuted by man's social experience and by the history of science.

Altruism, selfless service rendered to other people, readiness to sacrifice one's own interests for the sake of others. A. is the opposite of egoism (q.v.). The term was introduced into philosophy by Comte (q.v.). In bourgeois ethics, the concept of A. merges, as a rule, with the religious moral teachings of love for one's fellow-creature, forgiveness, etc. Under socialism the concept of A. retains its meaning in describing strictly personal relations among people; as for social relations, they are dominated by the principles of new, communist morality (collectivism, q.v., co-operation and mutual assistance, awareness of one's responsibility to society, etc.).

Amoralism, or immoralism, negation of any morality, conscious abandonment of the laws of morality, the urge to be "beyond good and evil" (see Nietzsche), "philosophical substantiation" of egoism (q.v.), inhumanity, scorn for conscience and honour preached by the most cynical advocates of the bourgeoisie.

Analogue, a term used in the theory of knowledge (q.v.) to mean an ideal object (concept, theory, research method, etc.) that adequately reflects some material thing, process, or law. In his *Dialectics of Nature* Engels wrote that for natural science (which is also true for socio-historical sciences) dialectics is the most important form of thinking, "for it alone offers the analogue for, and thereby the method of explaining, the evolutionary processes occurring in nature" (K. Marx and F. Engels, *Selected Works,* in three vols., Vol. 3, p. 60). In modern philosophical literature A. is also used to mean a material object (including the various forms of human material experience) which is a real basis for any theory, any law in the theory of knowledge or any rule of logic. For instance, the common-est, most usual relations between things constitute the objective basis for judgments, inferences (qq.v.) and other forms of thought. By finding A., the genesis of some ideal phenomenon is established, which is very important in the struggle against the various forms of idealism. The explanation of the specific nature of a methodological law, rule of logic, etc., presumes the all-round analysis of their functions in a definite system of knowledge. The term A. (which also applies to different models) is made more concrete in the analysis of the problems of reflection and modelling (qq.v.) (see Isomorphism and Homeomorphism).

Analogy, the establishment of similarity in certain aspects, properties and relations between dissimilar objects; deductions by A. are made on the basis of similarities in some other properties. The usual scheme of conclusion by A. is the following. Object B possesses the properties *a, b, c, d, e;* object C possesses the properties *b, c, d, e;* it is, therefore, possible that object C also possesses the property *a.* At the early stages of the development of science A. often took the place of systematic observation and experimentation, conclusions by A. being drawn, as a rule, from the external and secondary aspects. Most of the natural philosophical constructions were formed in this way up to the late Middle Ages. A. served as the starting point for establishing the similarity between the state and the human organism, and in the epoch of mechanism between the human mechanism and that of a clock, etc. In the course of further development of science, A. lost its significance as a means of explanation. It still retains, however, its role in advancing hypotheses, and continues to be a guide to the explanation of problems and to their solution. Ch. Huygens, when he discovered an A. in the behaviour of light and sound, got the idea of the wave nature of light; J. Maxwell extended the idea to the characteristics of the electromagnetic field. Viewed in isolation, A. is not proof, not only because the conclusions are mere probability but also because the degree of this probability can be small as a result of a fortuitous similarity or a fixation of the non-essential features of the objects compared. In modern science A. is widely applied in the theory of similarity and is also used in modelling (q.v.). Analogous modelling installations which can produce electrical analogues of the processes under study, mathematical modelling of the processes are widely used in scientific research and in management.

Analogy of Being, the central methodological concept of Catholic philosophy (see Neo-Thomism; Scholasticism; Thomism; Aquinas, Thomas). A.B. means that everything having existence (material object, phenomenon or idea) is similar to something else and at the same time unlike it. Catholic philosophy uses this principle to erect the hierarchic ladder of being. According to scholastic metaphysics (Thomas Aquinas and E. Przywara and others at the present time), insofar as similarity, uniformity, is primary and determining in A.B., only the outer, supernatural force, God, in whom all differences coincide, can be the cause, the primary source of the qualitative multiformity of being. In the concept of A.B., therefore, identity and similarity of objects and phenomena are made absolute and their qualitative differences are reduced to quantitative differences. This concept was introduced into medieval scholasticism. Modern scholastics declare A.B. to be the antipode of the dialectical unity of opposites.

Analysis and Synthesis, in the most general meaning, the processes of mental or factual breaking-down of a whole into its component parts and the reconstitution of the whole from the parts. A. & S. play an important role in the process of cognition and take place at every stage. In mental processes A. & S. occur as logical methods of thought that use abstract concepts and are closely connected with other mental operations—abstraction, generalisation (qq.v.), etc. Logically, A. consists in mentally dividing the object being studied into its component parts and is a method of obtaining fresh knowledge. A. takes on different forms according to the nature of the object of study. A multiplicity of A. is a condition for the all-round cognition of an object. The

breaking-down of the object into its component parts reveals its structure; the division of a complicated phenomenon into simpler elements enables the investigator to separate the essential from the non-essential and to reduce the complex to the simple; one form of A. is the classification of objects and phenomena. The A. of a developing process reveals its various stages, contradictory tendencies, etc. In the course of analytical activity, the mind advances from the complex to the simple, from the fortuitous to the necessary, from multiformity to identity and unity. The purpose of A. is the cognition of the parts as elements of a complex whole. On the other hand, S. is the process of uniting into a single whole parts, properties, and relations isolated by means of A. Going from the identical, essential, to the different and varied, S. combines the common and the individual, unity and variety, into a concrete living whole. S. complements A. and is in indissoluble unity with it. The dialectical-materialist conception of A. & S. is the opposite of the idealist conception of them as mere thought methods unconnected with the objective world and with man's experience. Metaphysicians isolate A. from S., counterpose them and make absolute either of these two indissolubly connected processes. In the history of philosophy the opposition of A. to S. goes back to the emergence of an analytical method in natural science and classical bourgeois political economy in the 17th and 18th centuries. By substituting the study of empirical reality for speculative constructions, this method then played a progressive role. The subsequent development of science showed that the analytical method was the historical forerunner of the synthetic method which is closely connected with it. From the point of view of their theoretical significance, once freed from their one-sidedness, both these methods become mutually conditioned logical processes satisfying the general requirements of the dialectical method.

Anarchism, a petty-bourgeois socio-political trend that is hostile to all authority and the state, and counterposes the interests of petty private ownership and small peasant economy to the progress of society based on large-scale production. A. has its philosophical foundations in individualism (q.v.), subjectivism, and voluntarism (q.v.). The emergence of A. is connected with the names of Schmidt (Stirner, q.v.), Proudhon, Bakunin (qq.v.), whose utopian theories were criticised in the writings of Marx and Engels. A. was widespread in France, Italy, and Spain in the 19th century. It does not go further than general phrases against exploitation and lacks an understanding of the causes of exploitation and of the class struggle as a means of achieving socialism. The anarchists' denial of the need to win political power by the proletariat objectively serves to subordinate the working class to bourgeois politics. In the struggle against A. the most important issue is the attitude of the revolutionaries to the state and the role of the state in general. The anarchists demand the immediate abolition of the state and do not admit the possibility of using the institutions of the bourgeois state to prepare the proletariat for the revolution and deny the role of the state in the socialist reconstruction of society. After 1917 A. in Russia turned into a counter-revolutionary trend and soon ceased to exist. A. had a certain influence in Spain in the 1930s. After the Second World War the ideas of the so-called communist A. (Kropotkin, q.v.) were widely disseminated in Eastern Asia and Latin America. Some youth movements in capitalist countries (the New Left, q.v.) are marked by anarchist sentiments.

Anaxagoras of Clazomenae (in Asia Minor), c. 500-428 B.C., Greek philosopher, inconsistent materialist, ideologist of the slave-owning democracy. He was accused of atheism and sentenced to death but left Athens to save his life. He recognised the infinite qualitative variety of the primary elements of matter, later known as homoeomeries (q.v.), various combinations of which make up all existing things. The motive force that conditions the union and division of elementary particles was the nous (q.v.), which he understood to be substance of the lightest and finest variety. A.'s cosmogony asserts that systems of celestial bodies emerge from the primary chaotic mixture of

substances as a result of their vortical rotation.

Anaximander of Miletus (c. 610-546 B.C.), Greek materialist philosopher, spontaneous dialectician, pupil of Thales (q.v.); author of the first philosophical work in Greece, *On Nature*, which has not been preserved. A. introduced the concept of *arché*, the "primary principle", or beginning of all things, which he considered to be the apeiron (q.v.). A.'s cosmological theory placed the Earth, which had the shape of a flattened cylinder, in the centre of the Universe. Three celestial rings, solar, lunar, and astral, surrounded the Earth. A. was historically the first to propound the idea of evolution; man, like all other animals, evolved from the fish.

Anaximenes of Miletus (c. 588-525 B.C.), Greek materialist philosopher, spontaneous dialectician, pupil of Anaximander (q.v.). According to his theory, all things evolve from the primary matter, air, and return to it. Air is infinite, eternal, and mobile. When it concentrates it first forms a cloud, then water, and lastly earth and rock; when it rarefies it turns into fire. Here A. gives expression to the idea of the transition from quantity to quality. The air embraces everything — it is the soul and it is the common medium of the endless worlds of the Universe. A. taught that the stars are fire but we do not feel their warmth because they are too far away (Anaximander placed the stars nearer than the planets). A.'s explanation of eclipses of the Sun and the Moon was close to the truth.

Anichkov, Dmitri Sergeyevich (1733-1788), Russian educationalist, philosopher; teacher of mathematics, logic, and philosophy at Moscow University since 1761; author of *Rassuzhdeniya iz naturalnoi bogoslovii o nachale i proisshestvii naturalnogo bogopochitaniya* (A Discourse from Natural Theology on the Beginning and Origin of the Natural Worship of God), 1769, in which he raised the question of the "natural" origin of religious beliefs. Like the 18th-century French Enlighteners, A. showed that religious beliefs arose when people were at the "barbaric" stage of development as a result of three causes: ignorance, fear, and imagination, when people were unable to explain the natural phenomena that surrounded them and ascribed everything incomprehensible to supernatural forces. A. ridiculed some biblical legends and for this was persecuted by reactionary professors and by the church. A. was the author of a number of papers on philosophy: *Slovo o svoistvakh poznaniya chelovecheskogo...* (An Essay on the Properties of Human Knowledge...), 1770, *Slovo o raznykh prichinakh...* (An Essay on Various Causes...), 1774, *Annotationes in logicam, metaphysicam et cosmologiam* (1782) and others. In these papers A. developed ideas of materialist sensationalism (q.v.) in the theory of knowledge and criticised the idealist theory of innate ideas (q.v.) supported by the followers of Descartes, Leibniz, and Wolff (qq.v.). A.'s materialism, however, was not consistent, it was wrapped up in a mantle of deism (q.v.); A. criticised the pre-established harmony (q.v.) theory of the Wolffians, but himself made concessions to religion, admitting the possible immortality of the soul.

Animism, belief in the soul and in spirits that allegedly affect the lives of people and animals, and exert an influence over the objects and phenomena of the surrounding world. Animist ideas emerged in primitive society. The chief reason for the emergence of A. was the extremely low level of development of the productive forces, the consequent small store of knowledge and man's inability to oppose the elemental forces of nature, which seemed alien and mysterious to him. At a certain stage of social development, the personification of natural forces was a form in which they were mastered. Animist conceptions formed the basis of later religions; in principle, A. is part of all religions.

Anselm of Canterbury (1033-1109), theologian and philosopher, early scholastic. Like St. Augustine (q.v.) A. maintained that faith must precede reason — one must believe in order to understand; faith, however, can be based on reason. For A. Christian dogmas were an indisputable truth; he, however, held that they

should be rationally understood, so as to strengthen the believer's faith. In this way his rationalism was subordinated to fideism (q.v.). In the dispute over universals (q.v.) A. professed extreme realism (see Realism, Medieval). He developed the "ontological argument" for God's existence (see Proof of the Existence of God).

Antagonistic and Non-Antagonistic Contradictions, the basic, qualitatively different contradictions typical of the development of society. Contradictions assume antagonistic nature when there is a conflict of the opposite irreconcilable material interests of various social groups or forces. A.C. are proper to all exploiting societies, and are caused by the same reasons as exploitation of man by man. It is typical of A.C. that they become more acute and profound as they develop and the struggle between them becomes a sharp class conflict, which is resolved by abolishing as a class one of the fighting sides during the class struggle and the social revolution that changes the given social order. The forms of resolving this conflict are determined by concrete historical conditions. A.C. permeate the entire mechanism of capitalist commodity production, including relations between the proletariat and the bourgeoisie, competitive struggle between capitalists and capitalist monopolies, and also contradictions between imperialist powers clashing in the struggle for markets and spheres of influence. The intensity of this type of contradictions can be demonstrated by the fact that they triggered off two world wars in the 20th century. A.C. have also been manifested in the national liberation struggle, which resulted in the abolition of the colonial system of imperialism. A.C. between the imperialist states and their former colonies striving not only for political but also for economic independence have not been removed, however. Marx wrote: "The bourgeois mode of production is the last antagonistic form of the social process of production — antagonistic not in the sense of individual antagonism of an antagonism that emanates from the individuals' social conditions of existence" (K. Marx, *A Contribution to the Critique of Political Economy*, p. 21). Under socialism alone antagonisms disappear, but contradictions remain. Development of socialist property ensures the unity of the basic interests of all classes and social groups of socialist society, which removes the objective basis for the existence of A.C. Given a correct policy N.C. may not involve a conflict and can be resolved in time in the interests of the whole society and not of some of its section, through a gradual and systematic transformation of the economic, social and other conditions that cause these contradictions. N.C., like any other, are also resolvable through the struggle of the new against the old, of the advanced against the backward, and the revolutionary against the conservative. Insofar as socialist society is interested in a conscious resolution of the N.C. that arise, it encourages the activity aimed at disclosing them (see Criticism and Self-Criticism), and at determining the ways and means of their resolution that are most optimal in given conditions. At the same time, socialist society is not excluded from the sphere of action of A.C., which are spearheaded in this case outside the respective country and may be expressed in its relations with the capitalist world. The nature of socialism is manifested here in its striving to regulate the action of A.C., prevent the germination of conflicts fraught with the danger of a nuclear holocaust, and ensure the peaceful co-existence of states with different social systems.

Antecedent and Consequent, see Implication

Anthropogenesis, the origination and development of man as a social being. Darwin (q.v.), Huxley, Haeckel (q.v.) showed that man descended from anthropoid apes of the tertiary period. The motive force in A., as Engels showed, was the social labour of primitive man which created specific social ties, culture, and formed man's body. This refutes the religious, idealist myths of the divine origin of man. The emergence and development of man is divided into a number of stages. The first stage is marked by the transition of the Australopithecus (the nearest ancestor of man—the South African fossil ape living

more than five million years ago) to the horde existence, omnivorous diet and the use of natural objects as tools (for hunting and utilisation of prey) and then to their improvement and occasional making. This comprehensively prepared the second stage, that of the emergence of a primeval horde out of representatives of the initial stage of A. (the most ancient people—the Pithecanthropus and Sinanthropus) who systematically made coarse stone, bone and wooden implements of various forms, hunted animals in common and could use fire. Their descendants, the Palaeoantropus or the Neanderthal man—made more complex tools, built first artificial structures and could obtain fire. The emergence of social production caused the appearance of consciousness and speech. The formation of man continued hundreds of thousands of years (South-East, South, and Anterior Asia and Africa). The third stage, conversion of the primeval horde into primeval society and of the Neanderthal man into modern man, occurred 35,000-40,000 years ago.

Anthropologism, a typical feature of pre-Marxian materialism which regarded man as the highest and the most perfect product of nature, the knowledge of whom provides the key to its secrets, since all its productive forces operate in the organic unity of man's bodily functions. The unity of man and nature was stressed in opposition to the idealist conception of man and against the dualist separation of body and soul. In the materialism of the 17th and 18th centuries, A. was one of the arguments in favour of the bourgeois revolution showing the incompatibility of the feudal social system and religion with the real nature of man. A. possesses the faults inherent in all pre-Marxian materialism, the chief of which is the failure to understand the social nature of man and his consciousness. A. regarded all truly human traits and qualities as abstractions inherent in man in general, i.e., apart from the historical forms of intercourse, in which man's activity takes place. A., in essence, is marked by a biological approach to the study of man. Such an approach inevitably leads to idealism in the conception of history, since social phenomena which arise as a result of the purposeful activity of men are only explained by the subjective psychological features of "natural individuals". A. is most fully developed in the works of Feuerbach and Chernyshevsky (qq.v.); some features of A. were overcome by the latter owing to his revolutionary attitude to reality. In modern bourgeois philosophy A. provides a basis for various forms of idealism which regard the objective world as something deriving from the nature of man. A. is an integral part of many trends in philosophy (existentialism, pragmatism, philosophy of life, philosophical anthropology, qq.v.), in sociology (anthroposociology, Social-Darwinism, qq.v.), and also in psychology (see Freudianism).

Anthropomorphism, the transfer of human shape and characteristics to the external forces of nature and attributing them to mythical beings (gods, spirits, etc.). Xenophanes (q.v.) realised that A. was a peculiarity of religion; the significance of A. in religion was revealed most fully and with great profundity by Feuerbach (q.v.). A. is connected with animism and totemism (qq.v.) and occurs in most modern religions; in Islam and Judaism (qq.v.) it occurs in a hidden form. In the 18th century attempts were made to purge religion of naive anthropomorphic conceptions (see Deism, Theism). A. is also typical of individual scientific concepts (e.g., power, energy, management, etc.). However, this "semantic" A. does not exclude their objective content.

Anthroposociology, a sociological theory that falsifies anthropological facts and establishes a direct connection between the social position of individuals and groups of individuals and the anatomical and physiological properties of man (size and shape of skull, height, colour of hair, etc.), and examines social phenomena from this point of view. It was founded by G. V. Lapouge (1854-1936) who accepted and developed the pseudo-scientific theory of J. Gobineau (1816-82) to the effect that the Aryans are the higher, aristocratic race, and that the nobility and the bourgeoisie belong to this race. He depicted the class struggle as a struggle between races, and the growth of

the workers' liberation movement as retrogression brought about by a reduction of the "Aryan element". According to him, eugenic measures (see Eugenics), capable of moderating the "restless masses" were essential. A. is one of the ideological weapons of racism (q.v.).

Anthroposophy, a mystical theory, a variation of theosophy (q.v.). A. is based on a conglomeration of religious and philosophical ideas borrowed from Pythagorean and Neoplatonic mysticism, gnosticism, cabalism, free-masonry, and German natural philosophy. Its central feature is the deification of man's nature, supposed to be revealed only to the initiated. A. was founded on the eve of the First World War by the German occultist R. Steiner (1861-1925). A. is still current in the Federal Republic of Germany and also in Britain and the USA.

Anticipation, preception, preconceived notion of something. The idea of A. was voiced by the Stoics and Epicureans; it signifies a general concept which appears in consciousness before the perception of concrete individual things directly from the logos (q.v.). In Kant (q.v.) the A. of perception appears as a principle of cognition which formally, a priori (q.v.) defines any experience. In modern philosophy, the term of A. is used in the meaning of prevision of possible experience, the supposition of the results of a study, and is elaborated in connection with the study of the categories "purpose" and "scientific prevision" (qq.v.). In psychology A. means expectation by the organism of a certain situation manifested in some pose or movement, and man's idea of results of his action prior to its performance. In logic A. is understood as temporary acceptance of a premise subject to further substantiation as proved.

Anti-communism, the chief ideological and political weapon of present-day imperialist reactionaries. Its main content is slander of the socialist system, the falsification of the policy and aims of the Communist parties and of the theory of Marxism-Leninism, open apologia for capitalism. In the economic sphere, A. is manifested primarily in a denial of the socialist nature of the economic system of the USSR and the other socialist countries, and in an attempt to present the economy of the socialist countries as state capitalism; in the political sphere, A. consists of slanderous inventions about Soviet "totalitarianism", violations of human rights and about "the aggressive nature" of world communism; in the ideological sphere, it is the repetition of the clumsy invention of the "standardisation of thought" under socialism. These distortions of facts are crowned by the conception that social relations are "dehumanised" under socialism, that man is turned into an instrument for the achievement of certain aims of the "leadership", and that the programme of scientific communism is "utopian". Hatred of communism which pervades all the aspects of bourgeois thinking is born of the fear of it, fear of social progress. The purpose of the mass propaganda of A. is to paralyse the revolutionary movement, sow distrust in the slogans and ideals of communism, and discredit and suppress all the genuinely democratic movements of the day. A. is not merely a totality of ideas. It is the actual political line of the most reactionary circles in the imperialist states.

Anti-Dühring, the name under which Engels' *Herr Eugen Dühring's Revolution in Science* has gone down in history; it contains an exhaustive exposé of the three component parts of Marxism—(1) Dialectical and Historical Materialism, (2) Political Economy, and (3) the Theory of Scientific Communism. Engels wrote the book to defend Marxist theory from the attacks of Dühring (q.v.), a petty-bourgeois theoretician whose views were supported by some members of the young German Social-Democratic Party. Marx read *A.D.* in manuscript and wrote the chapter on the history of political economy (Chapter X of Part II). The manuscript was published in book form in 1878, prohibited in that same year. *A.D.* consists of three parts: Philosophy, Political Economy, and Socialism. In Introduction, Engels describes the development of philosophy and demonstrates the inevitability of the emergence of scientific communism. Part I outlines dialectical and historical materialism; it provides a materialist answer to the fundamental question of philosophy (q.v.), postulates the material nature of the world, the fundamental laws of the cognition (q.v.) of the world, time and space (q.v.) as forms of all being and the unity of matter and motion (qq.v.). *A.D.* deals with the forms of motion of matter (q.v.) and with the classification of sciences (q.v.). Engels devoted considerable space to a description of dialectics (q.v.), its basic laws, and the relation existing between dialectical and formal logic. *A.D.* examines important problems in natural science from the standpoint of dialectical materialism—Darwin's (q.v.) theory, the role of the organic cell and the nature of life (q.v.), the cosmogonic hypothesis of Kant (q.v.). Engels also studied morality, equality, freedom and necessity (qq.v.), etc. In Part II Engels criticised Dühring's views on political economy, defined the subject-matter and method of political economy, outlined Marx's theory of the commodity and value, surplus value and capital, ground rent, etc. He criticised the idealist theory of force (q.v.) and showed the decisive importance of the economy in the development of society, explained the origin of private property and classes. Part III is a brilliant essay on the theory and history of scientific communism (q.v.), explains its attitude to utopian socialism (q.v.), provides a profound substantiation of the tasks and ways of the communist transformation of society, and outlines the Marxist theory on a number of basic questions of socialism and communism—on production and distribution under socialism and communism, on the state, the family (qq.v.), the school, the elimination of the antithesis between town and country (q.v.), between mental and manual labour (q.v.), etc. *A.D.* is a model of the consistent defence of the scientific world outlook and interests of the revolutionary proletariat, a model of Marxist implacability towards distortions in science and opportunism in politics. Engels' book is valuable as a textbook from which to study dialectical and historical materialism and as the ideological weapon of the working people in the struggle against bourgeois ideology and all departures from Marxism.

Antilogism, a formula in logic that expresses the incompatibility of the premises of a valid syllogism with the negation of its conclusion. The theory of A. is one of the variants of syllogistic (q.v.)

Antinomies, Semantic, antinomies (q.v.) which arise in propositions, whose object is expressions of a certain language (q.v.). Representative of one of the main types of S.A. is the liar antinomy which is credited to Eubulides of Miletus (4th century B.C.). It can be formulated as follows: [The sentence in square brackets on this page is false]. If this proposition is true, then it follows from its content that it is false. But if it is false then again it follows from its content that it is true. Thus, in violation of the logical law of contradiction, this proposition proves in any case to be both true and false. Antinomies of this kind arise in cases when the language in which the antinomy is constructed contains names for its own expressions and also predicates "true", "false" and the like. There are different methods for excluding S.A.: one of them consists in the strict definition of corresponding predicates in a metalanguage, q.v. (see Truth in Formalised Languages).

Antinomy, the appearance, in the course of reasoning, of two contradictory but equally well-founded inferences. The concept of A. was known in times of antiquity (Plato, Aristotle, qq.v.). Scholastic logicians devoted considerable attention to the formulation and analysis of A. Kant (q.v.) used A. in an attempt to justify the basic thesis of his philosophy, according to which the intellect cannot go beyond the bounds of sensory experience and cannot cognise the thing-in-itself. Kant said that such an attempt leads the intellect into contradictions, since it makes it possible to prove both the assertion (thesis) and its negation (antithesis) in each of the following "antinomies of pure reason": (1) the Universe is finite—the Universe is infinite; (2) every complex substance consists of simple parts—there is nothing simple in existence; (3) freedom exists in the world—there is no freedom in the world, only causality; (4) the primary cause of the Universe (God) exists—there is no

primary cause of the Universe. Hegel (q.v.) noted the vast importance of Kant's Aa. as a dialectical element of his views. Aa., i.e., contradictions, he asserted, exist in all objects, in all conceptions, concepts and ideas. Kant's Aa. are not the Aa. of modern formal logic, because the proof of the thesis and antithesis in them cannot be represented in the form of logically correct reasoning. Since the end of the 19th century investigations in logic and mathematics (see Set Theory) have led to the discovery of a number of real Aa. and this, in its turn, spurred on investigations in the foundations of logic and mathematics. Today they are usually subdivided into logical and semantic Aa. (see Antinomies, Semantic; Paradoxes). A. is not the result of an individual's subjective error; it is due to the dialectical nature of the process of cognition, and in particular to the contradiction between form and content. A. occurs within the framework of a certain formalisation (q.v.) of the process of reasoning (perhaps not clearly perceived but always assumed in fact); it is evidence of the limitation of that formalisation and shows the need for its rearrangement. The solution of A. means the introduction of a new and fuller formalisation, one that is more in accordance with the content being reflected. A. cannot be excluded from cognition once and for all; nevertheless each individual A. can be excluded by relevant changes in that method of formalisation within which it appeared. Today various ways of excluding A. have been evolved that permit a more profound description of the dialectic of cognition and the role of logical formalisation in it. Behind the A. that arises in the process of cognition of objective reality there are often hidden real dialectical contradictions of things whose reproduction in corresponding concepts allows one to more deeply understand the objective truth (q.v.).

Antisthenes of Athens (c. 435-370 B.C.), a pupil of Socrates (q.v.), founder of the school of cynics (q.v.) that developed the Socratic teachings and regarded as true only the knowledge of individual things. He criticised Plato's (q.v.) theory of ideas (as independently existing general concepts) and asserted that only individual things exist. Of greater importance was his cynic criticism of civilisation with all its achievements, his appeal to limit oneself to the most essential needs, contempt for social-estate and class differences, and resultant unity with the democratic elements of the society of that time.

Antithesis, a category expressing a stage in the development of contradiction (q.v.), which like difference (q.v.) can be both external and internal. External A. is the extreme degree of dissimilarity of aspects, objects or processes which have no internal connection between each other but at the same time possess some common features or properties. For example, the colour of two tables—black and white—is opposite and not connected of necessity with their existence as tables. Consequently, it is their external A. Internal A. (as well as internal difference) presupposes the existence of internal, necessary connection, i.e., internal unity between opposite aspects, objects and processes. External Aa. and differences are the prerequisites of internal Aa. and differences, which cannot exist without having connections with their external aspects. The A. is a more developed stage of the contradiction than the difference. At the stage of difference the old and the new coexist, whereas at the stage of A. they for the most part negate each other.

Antonovich, Maxim Alexeyevich (1835-1918), Russian materialist philosopher, publicist, and democrat; associated with Chernyshevsky and Dobrolyubov (qq.v.). His articles—"Contemporary Philosophy" (1861), "Two Types of Contemporary Philosophers" (1861), "The Philosophy of Hegel" (1861), "The Unity of Nature's Forces" (1865), etc.—gave expression to the materialist views upheld by the editors of the journal *Sovremennik* (The Contemporary). A. criticised Kant's (q.v.) apriorism and agnosticism, the Hegelians (Strakhov and Chicherin, q.v.), Grigoryev's Schellingism, the religious, idealist views of Yurkevich, Gogotsky (qq.v.), and others, the Slavophil theories and the eclectics of Lavrov and Mikhailovsky (qq.v.). On the basis of the anthropological principle propounded by

Feuerbach (q.v.) and Chernyshevsky, A. demanded an improvement in the living conditions of the working people, the spread of literacy, and the granting of political liberties; in the struggle against liberalism he showed the need for radical changes in the social system of Russia. He championed the aesthetic theory of Chernyshevsky and criticised the "art for art's sake" theory. After the suppression of *Sovremennik* (1866) A. continued his propaganda of materialism and natural science in the periodical press, using for this purpose the achievements of natural science (the works by Sechenov, Darwin, qq.v., and others). In 1896, he wrote the book *Charlz Darvin i yego teoriya* (Charles Darwin and His Theory). In 1909, A. opposed the Vekhism (q.v.) of writers and called for a resurrection of the traditions of the literary criticism of the 1860s (of Chernyshevsky and others). A. at times simplified and vulgarised the conceptions of his teachers, and his views were not as consistent as those of the revolutionary democrats. His materialism remained speculative and metaphysical. Although A. sympathised with Marxism, he did not understand it. He gradually retired from socio-political and literary activity and indulged in natural science.

Apathy, a state of indifference, absence of any inducement to act (frequently the result of disorders in the higher nervous activity, q.v.). In the ethical theories of the stoics (q.v.) A. is understood as impassibility, spiritual imperturbability, a state in which sensations do not interfere with the activity of the mind. It seems that Eastern religious and philosophical views, in particular the Buddhist and Jainist (qq.v.), on nirvana, or absolute tranquility as the highest state of the human soul, exercised an influence over the stoics.

Apeiron, a concept introduced by Anaximander (q.v.) to denote boundless, indefinite, qualityless matter in a state of constant motion. All the infinite multiplicity of objects, all worlds, came into being by the isolation from A. of opposites (hot and cold, wet and dry) and their struggle. The concept of A. was a step forward in the development of ancient Greek materialism, compared with the notions that identified matter with concrete substances (water, air). According to the Pythagoreans, A. is the amorphous, boundless concept, which, together with its opposite (the limit), is the basis of everything which exists.

Apodictic, that which is proved beyond all dispute, a term used to mean absolute truth which Aristotle (q.v.) used to denote a strictly essential proof deductively evolved from absolutely true premises. He regarded the syllogism as an instrument of apodictic knowledge. The term "apodictic" is used to differentiate a judgement of necessity from a judgement of possibility (problematic) and a judgment of reality (assertoric).

Apologetics, a branch of theology (q.v.) which defends and justifies a dogma by means of arguments addressed to reason. A. is included in the Catholic and Orthodox systems of theology, but Protestantism (q.v.) rejects it while proceeding from the primacy of faith over reason. A. includes proof of the existence of God (q.v.), the immortality of the soul, the teaching of the signs of divine revelation (including miracles and prophecies), an analysis of the objections to religion and its various dogmas. A. possesses the internal defect of appealing to reason and at the same time asserting that the basic religious dogmas cannot be grasped by reason, i.e., A. is rational in form but irrational in content. Typical of A. are its refined sophistry (q.v.), its extreme bias and dogmatism (q.v.), obscurantism and unscientific nature. A. of religion today is closely bound up with bourgeois A. and religious philosophy. It also means plausible defense or tendentious praise of somebody or something.

Aporia, in ancient Greek philosophy, a problem which is difficult to solve, owing to some contradiction in the object itself or in the concept of it. The arguments of Zeno of Elea (q.v.) on the impossibility of motion are called A. (he did not use this term himself). In the A. Dichotomy it is stated that before moving any distance it is necessary to cover half that distance, and before covering the half, a half of the

half, and so on, to infinity. From this premise the conclusion is drawn that motion is impossible. In the A. Achilles and the Tortoise it is said that the swift Achilles can never catch up with the tortoise because by the time the runner reaches the place where the tortoise was at the start, the tortoise has moved forward, etc. Zeno correctly noted the contradictory nature of motion but did not understand the unity of its contradictory moments and came to the conclusion that all motion is impossible. The term of A. first acquired a philosophical meaning in the works of Plato and Aristotle (qq.v.); the latter defined the term as "equality between contrary deductions". Kant's antinomies (qq.v.) are close to A.

A posteriori, the opposite of a priori (q.v.); it is used to qualify knowledge obtained by experience.

Appearance (semblance), external manifestation of the essence (q.v.) of things immediately perceived by the senses, more precisely, some aspects of the essence. A. has a subjective aspect; a thing may seem different from what it is (the break seen in objects partly immersed in water, the apparent movement of the Sun around the Earth, etc.). Yet A. in one way or another is connected with the objective essence, is its manifestation. The very fact of a wrong perception of the phenomenon's essence is due to objective factors. The task of cognition consists in reducing A. to essence, and in explaining how the latter is manifested in external forms, in phenomena (see Essence and Appearance).

Apperception, the dependence of every new perception on the previous experience of a man and on his psychic condition at the moment of perception. The term was introduced by Leibniz (q.v.) to mean self-consciousness as opposed to perception (q.v.).

A priori. In idealist philosophy, A. is used to qualify knowledge obtained prior to and independent of experience, knowledge which is inherent in consciousness from the beginning as opposed to a posteriori (q.v.) knowledge. This contraposing of the two terms is particularly typical of Kant's (q.v.) philosophy. Kant stated that knowledge obtained by means of sensory perception is untrue and contraposed to it as authentic knowledge the a priori forms of sensibility (space and time) and reason (cause, necessity, etc.).

Aquinas, Thomas (1225-1274), medieval Catholic theologian, Dominican monk, disciple of Albert the Great (q.v.); was canonised in 1323. He was named after his birthplace, Aquino near Naples. His objective idealist philosophy arose from a theological interpretation of Aristotle's (q.v.) teaching and its adaptation to Christian dogma. T.A. emasculated the materialist ideas of Aristotelian philosophy and accentuated its idealist elements (doctrine of the immobile world prime mover and others). The teaching of Neoplatonism (q.v.) also considerably influenced his philosophy. In the dispute about universals (q.v.) he held a position of "moderate realism" (see Realism, Medieval). The basic principle of the philosophy of T.A. is harmony of faith and reason; he held that reason is capable of proving rationally the existence of God and refuting objections to the truths of faith. Everything existing is fitted by T.A. in the hierarchic order created by God. His doctrine of the hierarchy of being reflected the organisation of the church in the feudal epoch. In 1879, the scholastic system of T.A. was officially proclaimed the "philosophy of Catholicism". It is used by the ideologists of anti-communism to combat the Marxist scientific world outlook. His main works: *Summa contra Gentiles* (1261-64), *Summa theologica* (1265-73).

Arcesilaus (315-241 B.C.), one of the founders of the Middle Academy (see Academy of Plato), a feature of which was the weakening of positive assertions of Plato and a transition from Plato's ideas towards scepticism (q.v.). All that remained of Plato was the tendency towards building various types of logical conceptions, which in this case boiled down to the destruction of dogmatic philosophy and the assertion of concepts of probability. In ethics also, A. was distinguished by the weakening of Plato's

enthusiastic theory which he reduced to imperturbability of the spiritual condition.

Areopagitics, a collection of four treatises ("Concerning Divine Names", "Concerning the Celestial Hierarchy", "Concerning the Ecclesiastical Hierarchy", and "Concerning Mystic Theology") and ten epistles which for a long time were ascribed to Dionysius the Areopagite (hence the name), first bishop of Athens (lst century A.D.), but later found by scholars to be a falsification. In the A. there is a strong influence of Neoplatonism (q.v.), although this trend did not exist in the lst century. It also contains a developed church doctrine which, again, could not have existed in the lst century. There are no references to this work in early Christian literature up to the mid-5th century. These arguments and others compelled scholars to date the appearance of the A. to the 5th century and to conclude that Dionysius the Areopagite was recognised as the author on account of his great authority in the early Christian Church. Some scholars attribute the authorship of the A. to Peter the Iberian, a Georgian bishop who was active in the East. A. is a systematically thought-out medieval Christian doctrine; the centre of all being is the uncognisable godhead from whom gradually diminishing light emanations radiate in all directions, through the world of angels and through the domain of the church right down to ordinary people and things. The strong pantheistic elements in the teachings were progressive in comparison with the church doctrine. For the whole thousand years preceding the Renaissance (q.v.), the A. was the most popular work of religious philosophy, and was one of the ideological sources of all medieval philosophy. The decay of medieval mysticism revealed in the A. elements of dialectics and some positive features in the doctrine on matter and form, which was successfully used in the struggle against medieval Aristotelianism and scholasticism (q.v.).

Argument 1. In logic—the statement (q.v.) (or system of statements) put forward in confirmation of the truth of some other statement (or system of statements); the premise of the proof (q.v.), also known as the basis of the proof; sometimes the proof as a whole is called the A. 2. In mathematics and mathematical logic, A. is the independent variable on the value of which the value of a function or predicate (qq.v.) depends.

Aristippus (c. 435-355 B.C.), Greek philosopher, disciple of Socrates (q.v.) and founder of the Cyrenaic (hedonist) school (see Cyrenaics). A. combined sensationalism (q.v.) in the theory of knowledge with hedonism (q.v.) in ethics. He regarded pleasure as the highest purpose of life but held that man should not be subordinated to pleasure, he should strive for the intellectual enjoyment which is his greatest blessing. Pleasure and suffering are the criteria of good and evil, truth and falsehood.

Aristotle (384-322 B.C.), Greek philosopher and encyclopaedic scientist, founder of the science of logic and a number of other branches of special knowledge. Marx called him the greatest thinker of antiquity. He was born at Stagira in Thrace and was educated in Athens at the school of Plato (q.v.). He criticised Plato's theory of disembodied forms ("ideas") but was unable to overcome Plato's idealism completely, wavering between idealism and materialism. He founded his own school (Lyceum) in Athens in 335 B.C. In philosophy A. distinguished (1) the theoretical aspect— dealing with being, its components, causes, and origins, (2) the practical— dealing with human activity, and (3) the poetic—dealing with creativity. Aristotle recognised four prime causes: (1) matter, or the passive possibility of becoming, (2) form (essence, the essence of being), the reality of that which in matter is only a possibility, (3) the beginning of motion, and (4) aim. A. regards all nature as successive transitions from "matter" to "form" and back. In matter, however, A. saw only the passive principle and attributed all activity to form, to which he reduced the beginning of motion and its aim. The ultimate source of all motion is God. Nevertheless, A.'s objective idealist theory of "form" is, in many respects, more objective than the idealism of Plato, hence Aristotle comes very close to

materialism. A.'s formal logic is closely connected with the theory of being, and the theory of truth, because in logical forms A. saw forms of being. In the theory of knowledge A. differentiated between the clearly established (see Apodictic) and the probable, which belongs to the sphere of "opinion" (dialectics). Nevertheless he connected these two forms of knowledge by language. Experiment, according to A., is not the last stage in the verification of "opinion", and the higher postulates of science are ascertained directly for their truth by the mind and not by the senses. However, the speculatively accessible higher axioms of knowledge are not inherent in our minds and presume activity—the collection of facts, the direction of thought towards facts, etc. The ultimate purpose of science is to define the object, and the condition for it is the combining of deduction and induction (qq.v.). In cosmology A. rejected the theory of the Pythagoreans (q.v.) and developed a geocentric system that gripped all minds until the days of Copernicus (q.v.), the creator of the heliocentric system. In ethics, A. regarded contemplation the highest form of mental activity. This was due to the separation of the physical labour of the slaves from mental leisure, the privilege of the free, that was typical of the slave-owning system in Greece. According to A., the model of morality is God, the most perfect of philosophers. In his theory of society A. showed that slavery had its roots in nature. The highest forms of state authority were those that precluded the selfish use of power and those under which the authorities served the whole of society. A.'s waverings in philosophy account for the duality of his later influence; the materialist tendencies played an important part in the development of progressive ideas in the philosophy of feudal society, and the idealist elements were expanded by medieval churchmen, who made A.'s theories a dead scholasticism. Lenin who studied A.'s *Metaphysics* (his basic work) greatly appreciated "the living germs of dialectics *and inquiries* about it...", "naive faith in the power of reason, in the force, power, objective truth of cognition".

Art, a specific form of social consciousness and human activity, which reflects reality in artistic images (q.v.) and is one of the most important means of aesthetical comprehension and portrayal of the world. Marxism-Leninism rejects the idealist interpretations of A. as a product and expression of the "absolute spirit", "universal will", "divine revelation" or subconscious conceptions and emotions of the artist. Labour (q.v.) is the source of artistic creation and also of the earlier process of shaping man's aesthetic sentiments and requirements. The first traces of primitive A. date back to the late Paleolithic epoch, approximately from 40,000 to 20,000 B.C. Among the primitive peoples A. bore an immediate relation to labour, but subsequently this relation became more intricate. Changes in the socio-economic structure of society underlie the subsequent development of A. A form of reflection of social being, A. has much in common with other manifestations of society's spiritual life: science, technology (see Aesthetics and Technology), political ideology (see Partisanship in Art) and morals (see Aesthetic and Ethical, the). At the same time A. has a number of specific features which distinguish it from all other forms of social consciousness (q.v.). Man's aesthetic relation to reality is the specific subject-matter of A. and its task is the artistic portrayal of the world. It is for this reason that man, his social links and relations, the life and activity of people in concrete historical conditions are always in the centre of any work of art. The subject-matter of art (life in all its multiformity) is mastered and presented by the artist in a specific form of reflection— in artistic images. The specific methods of reproducing reality and artistic tasks as well as the material means of portraying artistic images determine the specific types of art. Thus in literature the aesthetic reproduction of the world is made through the word, in painting—through the visual images of the colour wealth of the world, in sculpture—through plastic images and three-dimensional forms; in graphic art—through a drawing's line, stroke and chiaroscuro; in music— through sound intonations; in theatre and cinema—through the embodiment by ac-

tors of the characters' actions underlying dramatic conflicts. The object and form of reflection of reality in A. determine its specific function—to satisfy the aesthetic requirements of people through the creation of works which can bring man happiness and pleasure, enrich him spiritually and at the same time develop, awaken in him the artist, capable in the concrete sphere of his endeavour to create according to the laws of beauty. It is through this aesthetic function that A. displays its cognitive significance and exercises its ideological and educative influence. Marxism-Leninism has demonstrated the objective nature of artistic development, which is inseverably bound up with the development of society, with changes in its class structure. Although the general line of A. is the improving of methods for more profound artistic reflection of reality, this development is uneven. Thus, even in antiquity A. attained a high level and in a certain sense acquired significance of a standard. At the same time the capitalist mode of production, immeasurably higher than that of slave society, is hostile, to use Marx's expression, to A. and poetry, because it abhors lofty social and spiritual ideals. In capitalist society progressive A. is associated either with the period of the emergence of capitalism, when the bourgeoisie was still a progressive class, or with the activity of artists who are critical of this system. The highest aesthetic ideal is embodied in the A. of socialist realism (q.v.), which is established by the humane nature of socialist social relations.

Art for Art's Sake ("Pure Art"), a principle of idealist aesthetics, put forward in contrast to the realistic demand for ideological commitment and partisanship in art (q.v.). This principle, based on the divorcement of art from social life, spread in the 19th and 20th centuries, when in the struggle against realism bourgeois aestheticians advocated the internal "self-aim", "absolute nature" of art, which supposedly aims only at purely aesthetic pleasure. Denial of the cognitive, ideological and educative significance of art and of its dependence on the practical requirements of the age inevitably leads to the claim that the artist is "free" of society and bears no responsibility to the people, i.e., leads to extreme individualism (q.v.) and subjectivism. By declarations about "pure art" and its apolitical nature the contemporary bourgeois art masks its apologetic orientation. The Marxist-Leninist aesthetics contrasts the hypocritical bourgeois slogan that art is independent from society and the A.f.A.S. conceptions with the artist's conscious adherence to the interests of the people and to the ideals of communism.

Artistic Image, a form of reflection (reproduction) of objective reality in art proceeding from a certain aesthetic ideal (q.v.). The Marxist-Leninist theory of reflection (q.v.) is the epistemological basis for correct understanding of the essence of an A.I. Life, art's specific subject, is processed and assimilated in all its diversity and splendour, its harmony and dramatic collisions in an A.I. by creative imagination, talent and mastery of the artist. The A.I. is an unbreakable unity of intertwined opposites, such as the objective and the subjective, the logical and the sensory, the rational and the emotional, the abstract and the concrete, the general and the individual, the necessary and the accidental, the inner (inherent) and the outer, the whole and part, the essence and the appearance, the content and the form. The blending of those opposites in the course of a creative process into one whole, live image of art enables the artist to give a vivid, emotionally intense, poetically stimulating and at the same time deeply inspiring and highly dramatic portrayal of man's life, work and struggles, his triumphs and defeats, search and aspirations. Such blending, which is materialised by various means specific to each art (word, rhythm, colour, light and shade, proportions, scope, etc.), produces images bearing certain aesthetic ideas and emotions. It is through a system of A.Ii. that art is capable of performing its specific function, that is, to give profound aesthetic gratification to people, to awaken an artist in them, enable them to create in accordance with the laws of beauty and inject beauty into life. The educational value of art, its powerful ideological, political and moral influence upon people lie in that unique aesthetic function of art and are achieved through a system of A.Ii.

Artistic Method, a historically determined, specific way of reflecting reality and expressing man's aesthetic attitude to the world; a method of understanding and portraying reality in artistic images. A.M. is a means of embodying and asserting a definite aesthetic ideal (q.v.). The nature and trend of one A.M. or another, the degree of its capability to understand and mirror in artistic images the life of the people, the relationship between the individual and society, etc., depend on the socio-political and spiritual conditions of mankind's development at each given historical moment, on the objective role of one class or another in the life of society. Every A.M. is closely connected with a world outlook (q.v.) which exerts a positive or adverse influence on the work of the artist. But this is an intricate, dialectically contradictory relationship in which the artist, owing to the power of his realistic method, may overcome some of the limitations of his subjective views. Socialist realism (q.v.) is a qualitatively new A.M.

Asceticism, a principle of behaviour, a way of life, the basic features of which are extreme abstinence, "mortifying one's body", and the rejection of comforts for the achievement of a lofty moral or religious ideal. In ancient Greece the term of A. was first applied to exercises in the virtues. It was theoretically substantiated in religious dogmas of the ancient East, especially in Indian treatises and then in the works of Pythagoras. In the first centuries of Christianity, ascetic was the name given to those who spent their lives in solitude and self-mortification, in fasting, and praying. The early Christian and medieval ideal of A. underwent a change at the time of the Reformation (q.v.). Protestantism (q.v.) demanded "worldly asceticism". Early peasant and proletarian movements also called for A. as a form of protest against the luxury and idleness of the ruling classes. Marxist ethics regards A. as an irrational and unjustifiable extreme, as the result of incorrect conceptions of a moral ideal and the ways leading to it. It proceeds from the principle "Everything for the sake of man, for the benefit of man". Marxism, however, condemns the other extreme, lack of restraint in satisfying one's needs, unnecessary luxury, and the reduction of life to the pursuit of enjoyment.

Association, the nexus between elements of the psyche, which causes the appearance of any one of them to call forth, under certain circumstances, other connected elements. An example of A. in its simplest form is the repetition of the letters of the alphabet in proper sequence. A. emerges in the course of the interaction of subject and object as one of the elementary products of that interaction and reflects real connections between things and phenomena. It is a necessary condition for mental activity. The physiological basis for the existence of A. was discovered by I.P. Pavlov (q.v.); it is the mechanism of the formation of temporary neural nexus, i.e., of a nerve path between different areas of the cerebral cortex (in man and the higher animals) and the short-circuiting, of the excitations of those areas. A. is the basis of all the more intricate formations of man's psyche.

Association Psychology, various trends in psychology that use association (q.v.) as their main principle. The prehistory of the subject goes back to Hobbes, Locke and Spinoza (qq.v.); as a rule each of the trends is divided into materialist and idealist wings. Hartley and later Priestley (qq.v.), following Hobbes, developed the materialist tradition of associanism; they explained psychic activity by the general laws of association and maintained that such activity is conditioned by the brain processes. The idealist aspect of A.P.—the reduction of psychic activity to the association of subjective conceptions—is based on Hume's (q.v.) phenomenalism (Hume spoke of "clusters of impressions") and on Herbart (q.v.). A.P. took final shape mainly in Britain in the 19th century (Mill, q.v., James Mill) and combined the materialist and idealist wings through mechanism, q.v. (psychological atomism,

mental chemistry, etc.). In the 20th century A.P. is continued in behaviourism (q.v.), which greatly exaggerates the mechanistic tendencies inherent in it.

Astronomy, the science of the position, motion, structure and development of celestial bodies and their systems, and other forms of cosmic matter. A. is divided into a number of disciplines, each of which is again subdivided. Astrometry, for instance, includes spherical, geodesic, navigational, and other branches of practical A. and deals with the problems of measuring the positions and sizes of celestial bodies. Astral A. studies the laws of the spatial distribution and motion of stars and their systems. Radio astronomy studies various cosmic objects by observing the radio waves they emanate. Astrophysics studies, among other things, the physical properties of cosmic matter (bodies, dust, gas) and fields; cosmogony (q.v.) studies problems connected with the origin and development of space objects and cosmology (q.v.) studies the general laws of the structure of the Universe as a single connected whole, as an all-embracing system of cosmic forms of matter. A. extends to a tremendous degree in time and space the experimental field in natural science and human knowledge in general. Thanks to A. the human mind is able to penetrate milliards of light years into outer space and hundreds and thousands of millions of years in time into the past. A.'s objects are gigantic natural physical laboratories where the most varied processes are under way, processes that cannot yet be reproduced under terrestrial conditions, or, if they can, only on a tiny scale. Thermonuclear reactions, for instance, were first discovered in the stars and later reproduced on the Earth (so far only as uncontrolled explosions); particles in cosmic rays have energies that are not yet attainable in the most powerful accelerators; in space we can observe matter in a state of superdensity or rarefaction, gravitational and electromagnetic fields of enormous extent and power, explosions and blasts on a terrific scale, etc. A. extends the experimental field of physics, but itself relies first and foremost on physical sciences and their means and methods. Until quite recently

...gic (q.v.) studies idealised devices with several inputs by which the information is ...ed in and several outputs for the proces-...ed information. The processed informa-...on depends on the state of the given ...abstract" A. In an "abstract" A., like in ...real A., there can be only a finite ...umber of these states, i.e., its "memory" ...finite. Further abstraction involves the ...ransition from A. with memory of finite ...olume to A. with memory of infinite ...olume; an example of this is the Turing ...q.v.) machine abstraction, which plays an ...mportant role in the development of ...modern logic.

Autonomous and Heteronomous Ethics, ...ourgeois ethical theories. A.E. deduces ...norality from idealist notions of the ...nternally inherent, a priori moral duty ...q.v.). It proceeds from the principle that ...norality is allegedly based on the morally ...cting subject himself. Man himself pro-...uces moral law, under which he is quite ...ree from any external action. Kant (q.v.), ...pposing the ethics of 18th-century ...French materialists, developed ideas of ...A.E. in his *Critique of Practical Reason* ...n which he advocated the principle of the ...utonomy of moral behaviour. Opposed to ...A.E., H.E. deduces morality from the ...causes independent from the will of the ...cting subject. These external causes are ...considered to be the laws of states, ...eligious commandments, and also such ...notives as personal interest and wishes of ...good to other peoples. Among the var-...eties of H.E. bourgeois theoreticians ...ank ethical hedonism, eudaemonism, ...tilitarianism (qq.v.), which base their ...noral principles on the drive for pleasure ...nd happiness and on deriving benefit, ...nd some other systems. It is unscientific ...o distinguish A.E. from H.E. Attempts to ...o so are based on the negation of the ...conditionality of morality by objective ...aws, on the idealist principle of the will's ...utonomy, and on ignoring the subject's ...ctive role in society.

Avenarius, Richard (1843-1896), Swiss ...philosopher of the subjective idealist ...school, one of the first exponents of ...empirio-criticism (q.v.), professor of ...Zurich University. The central feature of ...his philosophy is the concept of experi-...ence which is supposed to reconcile ...opposites—consciousness and matter, ...psychic and the physical. A. criticised ...materialist theory of knowledge to wh... ...he opposed the idealist theory of "p... ...experience". He also supported the theo... ...of principal co-ordination (q.v.) of subje... ...and object, i.e., their absolute interdepe... ...dence. That A.'s views were groundle... ...and incompatible with the facts of natur... ...science was shown by Lenin in hi... ...*Materialism and Empirio-Criticism* (q.v.) ...A.'s major work is *Kritik der reine...* ...*Erfahrung* (1888-90).

Averroës, see Ibn Rushd.

Averroism, the teaching of Averroës ...(see Ibn Rushd) and his followers, a trend ...in medieval philosophy; its supporters ...held that the world is eternal and the soul ...mortal and upheld the theory of twofold ...truth (q.v.). A. was brutally persecuted by ...the church. A. acquired considerable in-...fluence in France (Siger de Brabant) in ...the 13th century as a progressive ...philosophical trend opposed to the ruling ...dogmatism of the church; it was also ...influential in Italy (the Padua school) from ...the 14th to 16th century.

Avicenna, see Ibn Sina.

Axiology, the philosophical study of ...the nature of values (q.v.). Bourgeois A. ...took shape at the turn of the 20th century ...in an attempt to solve some complex ...questions of philosophy that deal with the ...general "problem of value". Bourgeois ...philosophy assumes that these questions ...(the meaning of life and history, the ...object and basis of knowledge, the final ...aim and justification of human activity, ...relations between the individual and socie-...ty, and others) are not amenable to ...scientific analysis. The problem of value ...is thus reduced to disclosing all and ...sundry and to a special, extra-scientific ...study, a peculiar form of seeing the ...world. Moreover, values are considered ...extra-social phenomena. Bourgeois A. is ...represented by three types of axiological ...theories. Objective idealist theories ...(neo-Kantianism, q.v., followers of Husser-...lian phenomenology, neo-Thomism, in-...tuitionism, qq.v.) interpret value as ab-

astronomers were almost completely con-fined to observation and could not mount experiments. Since 1957, however, when the USSR launched the first artificial Earth satellite and paved the way for space exploration, the situation has changed radically. Extra-terrestrial obser-vation (measurements in interplanetary space, the atmosphere, and on the surface of other planets, etc.) has become possi-ble. A. is one of the oldest sciences and belongs to those branches of natural science which more than any other have served to elaborate and spread correct, materialist views of nature.

Ataraxia, a state of spiritual tranquility and imperturbability which, according to some Greek philosophers, was attainable by a wise man. The road to A., according to Democritus, Epicurus, and Lucretius (qq.v.), was through the cognition of the Universe, the overcoming of fear and liberation from alarm. The sceptics (Pyr-rho, q.v., and others) taught that A. is achieved by abstention from making judgements. The stoics (q.v.) developed their theory of apathy (q.v.) as indiffer-ence to what was going on, to joy and sorrow. Marxist ethics rejects the con-templative attitude to life, and, conse-quently, regards the individual's active position in life as an ideal.

Atheism, a system of views rejecting faith in the supernatural (spirits, gods, life beyond the grave, etc.); negation of all religion (q.v.). At every stage in history, A. reflected the level of knowledge reached and the interests of the classes and social groups that used it as an ideological weapon. A. is closely as-sociated with the materialist views of nature. A. took shape as a system of views in slave-owning society. There were considerable atheistic elements in the works of Thales, Anaximenes, Heraclitus, Democritus, Epicurus, Xenophanes, Luc-retius (qq.v.). They tried to explain all phenomena by natural causes, their A. was naive, speculative and inconsistent. In the Middle Ages, when the church and religion were dominant, A. made little progress. Bourgeois A., represented by Spinoza (q.v.), the French materialists of the 18th century, Feuerbach (q.v.) and others was instrumental in undermining the rule of religion. The exposure of the reactionary nature of the church by bourgeois atheists in European countries played an historic role in the struggle against feudalism and facilitated its aboli-tion. Bourgeois A., however, was incon-sistent and limited, was enlightening in character and was not addressed to the people at large but to a narrow circle. The Russian revolutionary democrats were militant atheists. A. acquired its most consistent form in Marxism-Leninism. The interests of the proletariat and its position and role in society coincide with the objective trends of social development owing to which Marxist A. is free from the class limitations that are typical of non-Marxist forms of A. The philosophi-cal basis of Marxist A. is dialectical and historical materialism. For this reason it acquires a scientific character for the first time in history. The subject-matter of scientific A. is elucidation of social and epistemological roots and causes of the origin and existence of religion, critique of religious doctrines from the angle of the scientific understanding of the world, an analysis of the social role of religion in society, and determination of the ways to overcome religious prejudices. Elimina-tion of the socio-economic and national oppression undermines the deep social roots of religion. Religious prejudices are very tenacious, however, and continue to exist among a section of the population. Both socio-economic reforms and active, flexible and purposive education are needed to overcome them. In the course of communist construction a new man is moulded, a man who is free from religious and other survivals of the past and has a scientific, atheist world outlook.

Atomic Fact, one of the basic concepts of logical atomism (q.v.). The A.F. is not divisible into components but consists of a combination of the things and objects of thought. Atomic facts are postulated as independent of each other, which means that the existence (or non-existence) of one A.F. is not proof of the existence (or non-existence) of another. Thus, mutual bonds (links) and the unity of the Uni-verse are denied, and the process of cognition is confined in practice to the description of the A.F. This metaphysical concept appeared as a result of the transfer to the external world of certain properties of the "atomic" (elementary) sentences that play an important part in mathematical logic.

Atomism, the theory of the discrete structure of matter (from atoms and other microparticles). A. was first formulated in the ancient Indian philosophical theories of *nyaya* and *vaisesika* (qq.v.), but was formulated more fully and consistently in the philosophy of Leucippus, Democritus, Epicurus, and Lucretius (qq.v.). Atoms were regarded as the ultimate, indivisible, tiniest, in substance infinitely small particles. They differ in number, weight, velocity and mutual disposition in bodies. These properties were regarded as the cause for the multiplicity of qualities in the world. Between the 17th and 19th centuries, A. was elaborated in the writings of Galileo, Newton, Lomonosov, Dalton, Butlerov, Mendeleyev (qq.v.), and others, and became the physico-chemical theory of the structure of matter. A. has almost always been the basis for materialist conceptions of the world. The old A., however, was to a considerable extent metaphysical, since the idea of discreteness was made absolute and the presence of an ultimate, unchanging state of matter, the "primary bricks" of the world edifice, was recognised. Modern A. recognises a multiplicity of molecules, atoms, elementary particles (q.v.) and other microobjects in the structure of matter, their infinite complexity and their faculty for conversion from one form into another. The existence of various discrete microobjects is seen by A. as a manifestation of the law of the transition from quantity to quality (q.v.): the reduction of distances in space changes qualitatively the forms of the structure of matter, its properties, connections between the elements in microsystems and laws of motion. Modern A. considers matter to be not only discrete but also continuous. The interaction between microparticles is carried out through the fields continuously distributed in space—gravitational, electromagnetic, nuclear, etc., which are inseverably connected with the elementary particles and form different bodies. Mod-

ern A. denies the existence of ultimate, unchanging matter and proceeds from the recognition of the quantitative and qualitative infinity of matter.

Attention, a mental state in which a person directs and concentrates his cognitive and practical activity on a definite object or action. Involuntary (unintentional) A. to an object (physiologically an orientative reflex) is aroused by the particular features of the object itself, such as novelty, changeability, contrast, forceful impact (e.g., bright light, sonority). Deliberate (intentional) A. is determined by consciousness of purpose. Deliberate A., which is peculiar only to man, was developed through labour activity.

Attribute, an inalienable property of the thing without which it cannot exist or cannot be conceived. Descartes (q.v.) regarded Aa. as the basic qualities of substance (q.v.). For this reason the A. of a corporeal substance is to him its dimension, while thought is the A. of a spiritual substance. Spinoza (q.v.) considered dimension and thought to be the Aa. of a single substance. The 18th-century French materialists regarded dimension and motion as the Aa. of matter, and some of them (Diderot, Robinet, qq.v.) added thought. The term is also used in modern philosophy.

Augustine, Saint (354-430), Bishop of Hippo (North Africa), Christian theologian and mystic philosopher, held views close to Neoplatonism (q.v.), and was a prominent patristic (see Patristics). His world outlook had a well-defined fideist character based on the principle "Where there is no faith there is no knowledge, no truth". His views constituted one of the sources of scholasticism (q.v.). In his *De Civitate Dei* A. developed the Christian conception of world history comprehended fatalistically, as pre-ordained by God. He counterposed his "City of God", the universal rule of the church, to *Civitas terrena,* the City of Earth, the "sinful" secular state. This doctrine played an important part in the struggle of the Papacy against the feudal lords. A. considerably influenced the subsequent development of Christian theolo-

gy. Augustinism is still widely used today by both Catholic and Protestant churches.

Authority, an ethical concept denoting the universally recognised importance, influence of an individual, a system of views or an organisation deriving from certain qualities or services performed. A. may be political, moral, scientific, etc., depending on the sphere or mode of influence. The political and legal authority of the state (q.v.) plays the main role in a class society. Moral A. plays an increasingly important part in the conditions of socialist construction, when the working people are involved to take an active part in the affairs of society. In modern bourgeois philosophy there are two opposite trends in interpreting A.: authoritarianism (preaching absolute infallibility of a bearer of A.) which is manifest in its extreme forms in the ideology of fascism (q.v.) (the cult of führer), or nihilistic denial of any A. and preaching "absolute freedom of the individual". Recognising the significance of various kinds of A., Marxism holds that it should be acquired through a selfless service to the people and the party, persistent work and profound knowledge of one's profession or trade. A. has nothing in common with the cult of the individual (q.v.). The notion of A. is based on the Marxist-Leninist theory of the role of the popular masses and the individual in history.

Automation, the performance of production, management, and other socially necessary processes without the immediate participation of man. A. is the highest stage in the development of technology and is marked by the appearance of automated lines of machine tools (in the 1920s); this was followed by automated shops and factories using (from the 1950s) modern computing and controlling machines. A. does not eliminate the human element which is necessary to give general guidance and exercise control over the work of the machine (adjustment, programming, feeding raw material, repairs), although as A. develops the machines will more and more perform these functions themselves. A. makes for a considerable increase in the productivity of labour and in the output of goods,

reduces costs and improves [...] trol over a number of process [...] power engineering, in space [...] etc.), can be done only a [...] Extensive A. in industry h [...] economic, political, and cu [...] quences. These differ radically [...] ent social systems. Under [...] leads to mass unemployment [...] of workers to jobs that r [...] skills and are lower paid; [...] economic depressions and [...] greatly aggravates the cont [...] bourgeois society. Under s [...] communism A. serves to [...] labour of man and create a [...] consumer goods, and leads t [...] improvement in living standa [...] ture and to the conversion of [...] primary necessity for man. A [...] tion processes is an essential [...] the creation of the material a [...] basis of communism.

Automaton, any technical [...] performs some process, actio [...] tion (e.g., a technological op [...] duction control, etc.) withou [...] participation of man. Very [...] were known in antiquity. [...] machine tools became wides [...] 19th and 20th centuries. Aa. [...] back (q.v.) and capable of m [...] process as required under cha [...] tions have been developed in [...] decades. The development of [...] (q.v.) and electronic computin [...] has led to the production [...] maintain a process under opt [...] tions. The development of r [...] shows that they are not only [...] replacing the muscular power [...] can undertake a number of [...] usually carried out by the hun [...] they can select the sequence a [...] of actions, carry out intricate [...] and draw logical conclusions, [...] information (q.v.), gather [...] "learn", and so on. This open [...] field for the automation of so [...] and processes of mental labou [...] ing from the technical charac [...] concrete Aa. leads to the [...] "abstract" A. The theory o [...] automata" created at the inters [...] theory of cybernetics and m [...]

solute essence outside space and time. Followers of subjective idealist theories (logical positivism, emotivism, linguistic analysis in ethics, qq.v.), regard value only as a phenomenon of consciousness and see it as a manifestation of psychological sentiment, of man's subjective attitude to the object he evaluates. The naturalistic theories of value (see Interest, Theory of; Ethics, Evolutionary; Cosmic Teleology, Ethics of) interpret it as an expression of man's natural requirements or laws of nature as a whole. The Marxist concept of value differs fundamentally from bourgeois A. The problem of value in Marxist interpretation is divested of universalism. Marxism views values as specifically social phenomena, as manifestations of social relations and normatively evaluative aspect of social consciousness. This aspect reflects the philosophical character of this consciousness rather than revealing it as a whole. In other words, world-view cannot be reduced to a particular axiological position. For example, Marxist world-view, though it is sometimes expressed subjectively as normative ideals, moral evaluations, etc., is basically a scientific understanding of the world and society that relies on the scientific knowledge of historical laws. On the whole, the Marxist axiological theory consistently upholds the viewpoint of historical materialism and subjects bourgeois A. to criticism from this position.

Axiom, a proposition in any scientific theory that is so constructed that it is taken as the starting point and does not have to be proved for that theory and from which (or from the totality of which) the remaining propositions of the theory are deduced in accordance with set rules (see Postulate). From times of antiquity to the mid-19th century Aa. were regarded as intuitively obvious or a priori true. This conception lost sight of the conventional nature of Aa. deriving from human practical cognitive activity. Man's practical activity requires the repetition of logical figures millions of times in the human mind so that these figures can become axioms. The present-day understanding of the axiomatic method (q.v.) requires that Aa. must satisfy one condition—all other

propositions of the given theory are derived from them and from them alone with the help of adopted logical rules. The truth of Aa. selected is determined by other scientific theories or when interpretations (see Interpretation and Model) of the given system are found: the realisation of a certain formalised axiomatic system in this or that field bears witness to the truth of Aa. accepted in it.

Axiom of the Syllogism, the basic principle of the syllogism which Aristotle (q.v.) formulated as "when one thing is predicated of another as the subject, all that is predicated of the predicate will be predicated also of the subject". Aristotle often used the term "belongs to" instead of the term "is predicated of", and considered the expression "A is predicated of B" to be identical with "B is included in A". Thus A.S. may be interpreted as content (intensively) and as volume (extensively). In traditional formal logic, the significance of A.S. is revealed in the reduction of all syllogisms to the first syllogistic figure (see Syllogistic). In modern formal logic, the problem of A.S. is handled in the context of a broader axiomatisation of syllogistic.

Axiomatic Method, a deductive method of building up a scientific theory in which (1) for a given theory a number of propositions acceptable without proof are selected (axioms, q.v.); (2) the concepts they contain obviously cannot be defined within the framework of the given theory; (3) rules are elaborated for the deduction and definition of the given theory, which allow to introduce new terms (concepts) into the theory and to deduce logically some propositions from others; (4) all the remaining propositions of the given theory (theorems, q.v.) are deduced from (1) on the basis of (3). The first ideas of the method appeared in Greece (Eleatics, Plato, Aristotle, Euclid, qq.v.). Later attempts were made to analyse various branches of science and philosophy axiomatically (Newton, Spinoza, qq.v., and others). These analyses were characterised by a substantial axiomatic construction of a given theory (and of no other), attention being paid mainly to the definition and selection of intuitively obvious axioms. Beginning with the second half of the 19th century, when there was an intensive elaboration of the problems involved in establishing the bases of mathematics and mathematical logic, the axiomatic theory came to be regarded as a sort of formal system (and since the 1920s-1930s as a formalised system) establishing the relation between its elements (symbols) and describing any number of objects that satisfied the theory. The attention was focussed on the non-contradiction of the system, its completeness and the independence of the system of axioms, etc. Since symbolic systems may be studied independently of their content or with due account of it, a distinction is to be made between syntactical and semantic axiomatic systems (only the latter represent scientific knowledge proper). This distinction made it necessary to formulate two types of basic requirements for them—syntactical and semantic (syntactical and semantic non-contradiction, completeness, independence of the axioms, etc.). An analysis of the formalised axiomatic systems led to the conclusion that they are limited in principle. One of these limitations is the one proved by Gödel (q.v.) that it is impossible to fully axiomatise the sufficiently developed scientific theories (e.g., arithmetic of natural numbers), which means that it is impossible to fully formalise scientific knowledge. Axiomatisation is only one of the methods of the organisation of scientific knowledge, but it can be used as a means of scientific discovery in a limited number of cases. It is usually carried out after the theory has been built up to a sufficient degree, and its aim is greater precision in expounding the theory, particularly in deducing all the consequences from the assertions that have been accepted. During the last 30 or 40 years great attention has been paid to the axiomatisation, not only of mathematical subjects, but also of certain branches of physics, biology, psychology, economics, linguistics, etc., including the theories of the structure and dynamics of scientific knowledge. In studying natural sciences (in general, any non-mathematical science) A.M. takes the form of the hypothetico-deductive method, q.v. (see Formalisation).

Axiomatic Theory, Completeness of, a logical and methodological requirement that in all axiomatically constructed theories the truth of each proposition should be proved (i.e., deduced from axioms) for the given axiomatic, formal system. In the process of investigating sufficiently rich axiomatic theories (arithmetic, for example) proof was found (Gödel, q.v., in 1931) that they were incomplete in principle, i.e., they contain propositions which are not capable of proof or disproof within their framework. Completeness is not an absolutely indispensable condition for successful axiomatisation: incomplete theories may have practical applications.

Axiomatic Theory, Non-Contradiction of, the logical and methodological condition of non-contradiction (q.v.) which must be fulfilled by axiomatic theories. There are two types of N.A.T.: the syntactic N.A.T. and the semantic N.A.T. A theory is syntactically non-contradictory if a proposition and its negation are not simultaneously deduced in it; a theory is semantically non-contradictory if it has at least one model, i.e., a certain sphere of objects, satisfying the given theory. Violation of the N.A.T. condition makes the theory invalid, because it becomes possible to prove any proposition in it.

Ayer, Alfred (b. 1910) British philosopher, a representative of neo-positivism (q.v.), professor of logic at Oxford University. Acquired recognition for his book *Language, Truth and Logic* (1936) in which he propagandises the ideas of the Vienna Circle (q.v.). In his later writings (*The Foundations of Empirical Knowledge*, 1940; *Thinking and Meaning*, 1947; *The Problem of Knowledge*, 1956, and others) he deviates somewhat from the orthodox form of logical positivism (q.v.) and comes strongly under the influence of linguistic philosophy (q.v.). In these books he attempts to investigate philosophical problems (the authenticity of knowledge, the relation between material objects and "sensory data", etc.) from the positivist position by analysing the relevant concepts and translating them into "logically clear" terminology.

b

Babouvism, the 18th-century French revolutionary movement for "a republic of equals"—an integrated national commune governed from a single centre. The movement took its name from its leader and most consistent theoretician, Gracchus Babeuf (1760-1797). B. signified the break-down of the alliance of exploited plebeians and the bourgeoisie that had taken shape in the course of the French Revolution. Politically and ideologically, B. reflected the early separation of the proto-proletariat from the general plebeian mass that had participated in the French Revolution. The Babouvists were the ideological heirs of French 18th-century materialism (q.v.), of the ideas of Mellier (q.v.) on the popular revolution, of the "rationalist" communism of Morelly (q.v.) and of the organisational and ideological experience of the most radical trends in the French Revolution. They were the first to attempt to convert socialism from a theory into the practice of the revolutionary movement. They put forward the idea of retaining the dictatorship of the working people after the victory of the revolution; they advanced the proposition that history is a struggle between the rich and the poor, patricians and plebeians, between masters and servants; between the sated and the hungry. Ideologically and organisationally, Babeuf and his companions contributed to the development of socialism from a utopia into a science.

Bachelard, Gaston (1884-1962), French philosopher. In the conditions of the crisis of neo-positivism (q.v.) and logical formalism B. tried to develop a new philosophy that would correspond to the "new scientific spirit", e.g., the spirit of non-classical science, by introducing into it specifically interpreted elements of dialectics. He called his teaching "applied rationalism", "dialectical rationalism" and even "technical rationalism". His works are of value for analysis of modern science and its role in society. At the same time the mixture of materialism and idealism, the understanding of science as a sum-total of constructions created by cognoscitive reason, bring his conceptions closer to those of Popper (q.v.), T. Kuhn and modern critical rationalists (q.v.). His works are: *La formation de l'esprit scientifique* (1934), *Le materialisme rationel* (1953), *Le rationalisme appliqué* (1962) and others.

Bacon, Francis (1561-1626), English philosopher, founder of materialism and experimental science in the period of modern history. Under James I attained the high position of Lord Chancellor. In 1620, published the famous treatise, *Novum Organum* (the title was a reference to Aristotle's, q.v., *Organon*), in which he evolved a new conception of the tasks of science and the foundations of scientific induction (q.v.). Declaring that the purpose of learning was to increase man's power over nature, B. maintained that this aim could be achieved only by learning which reveals the true causes of things. He, therefore, opposed scholasticism (q.v.). The early learning had suffered either from "dogmatism" in the sense that the scholar starting from concepts of his own invention, wove his system of propositions in the same way as the spider weaves its web, or else it suffered from "empiricism", i.e., mere enumeration of unrelated facts. On these grounds B. called for scepticism with regard to all previous learning. While admitting the possibility of acquiring true knowledge, he held that the method of doing so must be reformed. The first step towards this reform should be to cleanse the mind of the preconceptions and prejudices (Idols) by which it is constantly threatened. Having rid oneself of false conceptions one could then adopt the true method of the new learning. This learning, according to B., should be a rational reinterpretation of the facts of experience. The premises for the conclusions of the new learning *(media axiomata)* would be propositions based on concepts arrived at through methodical generalisation or induction. Induction was based on analytical comprehension of experiment. The one-sided development of Bacon's theory enabled him, and after him, Locke (q.v.), to shift the metaphysical approach, which had taken shape in the 15th and 16th centuries, from natural science to philosophy. In his theory of induction B. was the first to point to the importance of what were called "negative instances", i.e., cases contradicting the generalisation and calling for its revision as insufficiently vindicated. His contribution to the development of philosophy may be defined as follows: First, he restored the materialist tradition and reassessed the philosophical doctrines of the past from this standpoint; he praised early Greek materialism and revealed the errors of idealism. Second, he evolved his own materialist conception of nature, which he based on the idea that matter was a combination of particles, and nature a combination of bodies endowed with manifold properties. An essential quality of matter was motion, which B. did not confine merely to mechanical movement (he defined 19 types of motion). Bacon's views reflected the new demands made upon learning in England in the age of primitive accumulation of capital. But B. was not a consistent materialist. His political beliefs were reflected in the *New Atlantis* (1617), a utopia in which an ideal society flourished economically on the basis of rational learning and advanced technology, while the ruling and oppressed classes continued to exist.

Bacon, Roger (c. 1214-1292), English thinker of the Middle Ages, precursor of experimental science in modern history, ideologist of the town craftsmen. He exposed feudal customs, ideology, and politics. In 1277, B. was dismissed from teaching at Oxford University because of his views and was confined to a monastery by order of the church authorities. His world outlook was materialist but not consistently so. Condemning scholastic dogmatism and veneration of authority, he advocated the experimental study of nature and independent research and called for constant development of science. He upheld the method of cognition based on experiment and mathematics. He said the aim of all learning is to increase man's

power over nature. In spite of the traces of alchemist, astrological, and magical superstition that are to be found in his works, B. put forward a number of bold scientific and technical conjectures.

Baden School, an influential neo-Kantian school in the early 20th century. The name derives from Heidelberg and Freiburg universities, both in the Land of Baden, at which Professors Windelband and Rickert (qq.v.) taught the theory of the B.S. Basically it amounted to counterposing the historical method to the natural scientific method; history, they said, is the science of individual facts of development which have cultural value; natural science studies the general and recurrent regularities of natural phenomena. In both cases the concepts are not the reflection of reality, they are merely the conversion into thoughts that is subordinated to a priori principles; natural science is the cognition of the general, history, the cognition of the individual. The B.S., following Kant (q.v.), counterposes being to necessity. The denial of the laws of history, typical of the school, is associated with the theory of value. These theories were developed by H. Münsterberg (1863-1916) and E. Lask (1875-1915) and were applied to aesthetics by J. Cohn (1869-1947) and B. Christiansen, and to sociology by Weber (q.v.). In modern German sociology the ideas of the B.S. are being developed in a spirit of out-and-out subjectivism and voluntarism (q.v.), which is opposed to Marxism. This school of sociology in West Germany is represented by W. Theimer and G. Ritter.

Bakunin, Mikhail Alexandrovich (1814-1876), Russian petty-bourgeois revolutionary, ideologist of anarchism and Narodism (qq.v.). From 1836 to 1840, Bakunin lived in Moscow, where he studied Fichte and Hegel (qq.v.), interpreting the philosophy of the latter in a conservative spirit. In 1840, B. emigrated and joined the Young Hegelians (q.v.), evidence of which was his work *Reaktsiya v Germanii* (Reaction in Germany), 1842. He participated in the revolution of 1848-49 in Prague and Dresden. Returning to Russia, he was imprisoned in 1851 and in 1857 exiled to Siberia. In 1861, he escaped and spent the 1860s and 1870s in Western Europe, where he collaborated with Herzen and Ogaryov (qq.v.). He took an active part in organising the anarchist movement and fought against Marx in the First International, from which he was expelled in 1872. He was one of the most prominent theoreticians and leaders of Narodism in Russia in the 1870s. B.'s theory took final shape at the end of the 1860s (*Gosudarstvennost i anarkhiya* [Statehood and Anarchy], 1873, etc.). B.'s basic conception is that the chief oppressor of man is the state, which relies on the fiction of God. Religion is "collective madness", the ugly product of the consciousness of the oppressed masses. To lead mankind to the "kingdom of freedom" it is first necessary to "blow up" the state and exclude the principle of authority from the people's life. Its place is to be taken by a "free federation" of agricultural and factory-craft associations. B. believed implicitly in the socialist instincts and the inexhaustible spontaneous revolutionary spirit of the masses, mainly the peasantry and lumpenproletariat; he denied the need to prepare for revolution and plunged headlong into revolutionary adventures. Unable to grasp the significance of the theory of society, he opposed the Marxist teaching on the dictatorship of the proletariat. In the 1870s B.'s anarchist ideas were widespread among the revolutionary Narodniks of Russia and also in other economically poorly developed countries (Italy, Spain, and others). B.'s anarchist theories were severely criticised by Marx, Engels, and Lenin.

Basis and Superstructure, categories of historical materialism coined to characterise the basic structural elements of every socio-economic formation (q.v.). These categories are used to specify the fundamental question of philosophy (q.v.) as applied to society. Marxism-Leninism proves that the B. underlies ideas, institutions and organisations prevalent in a society. The B. is a totality of relations of production (q.v.) which is inherent in this society. The production relations are necessarily formed in accordance with a definite level of productive forces (q.v.). The S. is an interrelated system of social phenomena which are brought into being by the economic B. and actively influences it. The S. includes: 1) the totality of spiritual phenomena (thoughts, feelings, sentiments, ideas, theories, teachings) that are divided into political, legal, moral, religious, aesthetic and philosophical ones; 2) the totality of human relations which unlike material and production relations take shape independently of people's will and consciousness; these are called ideological because they are formed in accordance with the above-mentioned forms of ideological consciousness and appear as political, legal, moral and other social relations; 3) the totality of institutions and organisations: political (the state, parties), legal (courts of law), religious (the Church), etc. The concept of B. is correlated with the concept of S. The B. defines the given formation qualitatively, distinguishing it from other formations, while the corresponding S. characterises the social and spiritual life of every formation. Taken outside the concept of formation the B. and S. become dead like organs separated from the human body. The B. and S. are inherent in all formations and bear a specific nature in each formation. Living in a society and obeying the objective laws, people are entering material relations which constitute the B. of their social life. At the same time as conscious beings, they realise the demands of these laws. In other words, these demands are reflected in people's minds making them act. That is why material relations form of necessity the basis for certain ideology and corresponding relations, institutions and organisations, which make up the S. of this formation and serve to strengthen its B. With the appearance of a class society the state becomes the main institution of the S.; it provides the governing position in the system of the S. to the class (q.v.) that dominates the economy. As the given formation develops and its contradictions accentuate, the classes interested in its destruction create new ideas, institutions and organisations. These superstructural elements are not part of the dominant S., which seeks to suppress them or at least limit the sphere of their influence. In antagonistic formations the S. with all its ideas, ideological relations, institutions and organisations is the product, result and weapon of class struggle. The superstructural phenomena are relatively independent and can therefore actively influence all sides of social life, including the B. Revolutionary transition from one formation to another is first of all due to the substitution of one B. for another, in consequence of which a revolution takes place more or less quickly in the whole of S. The B. and S. are also subject to certain evolution within the limits of one formation, e.g., during the period of transition of socialist society to the stage of mature socialism. The development of capitalism is responsible for the more reactionary role played by the S. Only in socialist society where the economic B. is free of antagonisms, the S. becomes socially more homogeneous and serves the progressive development of society and its B.

Baturin, Pafnuty Sergeyevich (c. 1740-1803), Russian enlightener. His polemical philosophic work *Investigation...* made a critical analysis of the mystic ideas of L. Saint-Martin's book *Des erreurs et de la vérité ou Des hommes rappelés au principe universel de la science,* which had a programmatic character for free bricklayers. B.'s book was but the only one to expose their religious mysticism. Making use of the achievements of natural science of his day, B. gave a materialist explanation to natural phenomena, defending the heliocentric theory in cosmology, the law of conservation of matter and movement, the materialist theory of knowledge, assigning a considerable part to observation and experimental data. He denied the mystical concepts of "non-corporeal substance" or the "spiritual principles" of the objective world. His materialism was of a metaphysical, deistic character (see Deism). B. preached enlightenment and the development of natural science, and called for a "good" legal system and humanism.

Baumgarten, Alexander Gottlieb (1714-1762), German philosopher, disciple of Leibniz and Wolff (qq.v.). He introduced the term "aesthetics" to describe the study of man's sensory knowledge of the beautiful and its expression in artistic forms, as opposed to logic, which is concerned with knowledge acquired through reason. His unfinished *Aesthetica* (Vol. 1, 1750, Vol. 2, 1758) treats of the problems of knowledge acquired through the senses. Though B. cannot be regarded as the founder of aesthetics as a science, his concept fully corresponded to the needs of the aesthetic thought of the day and was widely recognised.

Bayle, Pierre (1647-1706), publicist, philosopher of scepticism, an early representative of the French Enlightenment. He held that religion and knowledge were incompatible and advocated religious toleration. Although he was never an atheist, the character of his indifference to religion was aptly described by Voltaire (q.v.), who remarked that though B. might not be an unbeliever himself, he made unbelievers of others. B. launched the critical study of Christian doctrine as a variety of pagan mythology. His arguments were based on scepticism (q.v.). B. suggested that ethical problems, instead of being associated with religion, should be approached from the standpoint of natural reason. He argued that it was possible for a society to be composed entirely of atheists. His writings, particularly his major work, the *Dictionnaire historique et critique* (1695-97), paved the way for French materialism and atheism in the 18th century.

Beautiful, the, a category of aesthetics (q.v.) reflecting and assessing phenomena of reality and works of art affording man the feeling of aesthetical enjoyment, embodying in an object-sensory form the freedom and fulness of man's creative and cognitive forces and capabilities in all fields of social life: labour, socio-political, and spiritual. The B. is the main positive form of the aesthetic assimilation of reality, in which the aesthetic ideal (q.v.) finds its direct expression. Since the B. takes shape while combatting the forces hostile to freedom and progress, the ugly (q.v.) and base, it may assert itself in life also through tragic circumstances and bear a tragic character. Idealists (Plato, Kant, Hegel, q.v.) regarded the B. as a property of the spirit, of consciousness (objective or subjective). Pre-Marxist materialism upheld the objectivity of the B., but not infrequently, owing to its contemplativeness (q.v.), reduced the B. to a pure natural quality (symmetry, harmony of the parts and the whole, man as a natural creature, etc.). The concept of the B. bears an historical character and has a different content for different classes. Dialectical and materialist aesthetics proceeds from the fact that the B. is a product of social and historical practice. It comes into being and develops when man as a social being realises more completely and freely in the given historical conditions his creative talents and capabilities, when he is the master of the objective, sensory world, enjoys labour as the play of his physical and intellectual forces. The B. finds a synthesised expression in works of art and artistic images. The B. in life and art, providing spiritual joy and pleasure, acquires a great cognitive and educational role in society. Capitalism is essentially hostile to art and man's aesthetical development. In contemporary conditions the truly B. arises only in the course of the struggle for the revolutionary remaking of society. Favourable socio-economic conditions to involve working people in creative work according to the laws of beauty can be created by communism alone.

Bebel, August (1840-1913), one of the founders of the German Social-Democratic Party, outstanding propagandist and theoretician of Marxism, an exponent of historical materialism. His study of the problem of the woman's place in society is of particular value. In *Die Frau und der Sozialismus* (1879) he showed that the position of the woman depends, in the final analysis, on social relations. The emergence of private property led to the humiliation and even contempt of women. Their emancipation is, therefore, an aspect of the problem of abolishing exploitation and social oppression. B. was an active opponent of bourgeois ideology and exposed Malthusianism (q.v.), idealism, and religion. His criticism of nationalism (q.v.) and chauvinism and defence of proletarian internationalism (q.v.) were of great importance. He was one of the first to realise that the views of Bernstein (q.v.)

were fundamentally hostile to the proletariat and to criticise revisionism (q.v.). Although he committed certain tactical mistakes and was wrong in some of his propositions, both his theoretical and practical work contributed enormously to the workers' struggle against social oppression.

Becoming, a philosophical category expressing the spontaneous changeability of things and phenomena—their continuous changeover and transformation into other things and phenomena. The classical representative of the conception of B. was Heraclitus (q.v.) whose understanding of reality may be summed up in the formula "all is flux". The category of B. is organically linked with the dialectical world outlook: it is based on the view that any thing or phenomenon is a unity of opposites—being and nonbeing; it is incompatible with the metaphysical idea of emergence and development as of simple quantitative increase or decrease.

Behaviourism, a trend in modern bourgeois psychology, based philosophically on pragmatism and positivism (qq.v.). B. was originated in 1913 by J. B. Watson (1878-1958) of Chicago University, the experimental material being provided by the research into the behaviour of animals carried out by E. L. Thorndike (1874-1949). Watson's theory was shared by K. S. Lashley (1890-1959), A. P. Weiss (1879-1931), and others. B. continues the mechanistic trend in psychology, reducing psychic phenomena to the reactions of the organism. B. identifies consciousness and behaviour the main unit of which it considers to be the stimulus-reaction correlation. Knowledge, according to B., is entirely a matter of the conditioned reactions of organisms (including man). In the 1930s Watson's theory was superseded by a number of neo-behaviourist theories, their leading exponents being C. Hull (1884-1952), E. Tolman (1886-1959), E. Guthrie (1886-1959) and B. Skinner (b. 1904). The neo-behaviourists (except Tolman) borrowed I. Pavlov's (q.v.) terminology and classification of forms of behaviour, substituted operationalism and logical positivism (qq.v.) for the materialist foundations of his theory. While making use of conditioned-reflex techniques, they ignore the role of the cerebral cortex in behaviour. Contemporary B. has modified the stimulus-reaction formula by inserting what are called "intermediate variables" (skill, excitation and inhibition potential, need, etc.). This does not, however, change the mechanistic and idealist nature of B. B. was criticised in I. Pavlov's article "A Physiologist's Answer to Psychologists", 1932. Skinner has approached the process of education from neo-behaviourist positions and developed the theory of linear programmed instruction, which was criticised by Soviet psychologists (A. N. Leontiev, P. Ya. Galperin and others).

Being 1. A philosophical concept denoting the objective world, matter (q.v.), which exists independently of consciousness. In reference to society the term "social being" is used. Regarding the materiality of the world and its B. as identical, dialectical materialism rejects the idealist conception of B. as something that exists before matter or independently of it, as well as idealist attempts to make B. a product of the act of consciousness (q.v.). On the other hand, it is not enough to stress only the objectivity of B., because in that case the problem of the material or ideal character of B. remains unsolved. While recognising B. as primary and consciousness as secondary, dialectical materialism nevertheless interprets consciousness as something more than a passive reflection of being, and regards it as an active force which influences B. 2. The most abstract concept denoting existence in general. In this sense B. must be distinguished from reality, existence, (qq.v.), which are more concrete and more profound characteristics of objective processes and phenomena.

Being, Social, a philosophical category denoting the primary position of historical forms of human relations and activities in relation to social consciousness. S.B. represents the concrete stages in the development of productive forces and corresponding relations which take shape of necessity between people in the process of production and other kinds of practical activity and which exist independently of human will and consciousness (see Social Being and Social Consciousness).

Belinsky, Vissarion Grigoryevich (1811-1848), Russian revolutionary democrat, literary critic, founder of Russian realist aesthetics. Ideologically, his works belong to the period when advanced Russian thinkers, taking into account the sad experience of the Decembrists, were only just beginning to seek new ways of fighting the autocracy and serfdom, and to evolve a scientific theory of social development. This explained the extreme complexity and intensity of B.'s ideological evolution. Between 1837 and 1839 he was an ardent supporter of Hegel (q.v.). In the early 1840s B. took up a materialist stand. Discussing the problem of the unity of the material and the ideal, he argued that the "spiritual" was "nothing but the activity of the physical". At the same time he stressed the active role played by consciousness in the process of interaction between man and his environment. While criticising the conservatism of the Hegelian system, B. perceived in his dialectics the basis for a method of scientific research, the seed of a genuine "philosophy of history". Objective law was defined by him as the necessity of social progress operating through human activity and its forms and expressing itself particularly in the actions of great men. B. maintained that it was unlikely that the new society could be established "by time alone, without violent upheavals, without bloodshed". However, he himself did not achieve a scientific perception of the inevitability of socialism. Hence his appeal to the ideas of primitive Christianity as the basis for the morality of the future. He acknowledged the progressive nature of the bourgeois system compared with feudalism, and considered that the immediate social tasks facing Russia were the destruction of the patriarchal, serf-owning forms of life (above all, serfdom itself) and the implementation of a number of bourgeois democratic reforms. With this as his point of departure B. ridiculed the Slavophile idealisation of Russia's patriarchal past from the position of revolutionary education and sharply criticised various liberal and revolutionary-utopian illusions (his polemics with Bakunin, q.v.). His revolutionary democratism found its most consistent expression in his "Letter to Gogol" (July 1847), his last will addressed to the posterity, and one of the finest works of the uncensored Russian democratic press in the 19th century. Historism was characteristic of his aesthetic judgments. Regarding it as the essence and specifics of art to reproduce the typical features of reality through imagery, B. inveighed against reactionary romanticism and didactic fiction and advocated the principles of realism underlying the work of Pushkin. Pointing to the connection between the concepts of kinship with the people and realism in art, he advanced important propositions on the social significance of literature being dependent on its ability to bridge the gap between educated "society" and the mass of the people, and on "sympathy with contemporaneity", i.e., with progress, as a quality essential to the true artist. B.'s views on art played a big role in the development of aesthetics.

Bell, Daniel (b. 1919), American bourgeois sociologist, one of the initiators of the "post-industrial society" theory which is widely used by bourgeois propaganda. Trying to outline the future society based on the principles of public utilities, "plural democracy" and meritocracy (q.v.), B. as a matter of fact suggests a renovated and idealised model of modern capitalist society. His sociological views are based methodologically on the assumed independence of social spheres, e.g., of economy, politics, culture (which, accordingly, are founded on the principles of efficacy, equality of opportunities and self-realisation). In the 1970s B. renounced his early theory of "the end of ideology" (see "Deideologisation" and "Reideologisation", Theories of, q.v.). He emphasised the importance of certain elements of ideology, religion in particular, for the development of modern man. His main works are *The End of Ideology* (1960), *The Making of the Post-Industrial Society* (1973) and *The Cultural Contradictions of Capitalism* (1976).

Bentham, Jeremy (1748-1832), English moralist and legal theorist. In his theory of ethics B. reduced all the motives of human conduct to either pleasure or pain, identifying morality with the utility of an action (see Utilitarianism). Morality could thus be calculated mathematically by balancing pleasure and pains that would accrue as the result of any particular action. This metaphysical and mechanistic approach to morality ("the felicific calculus") led him to defend capitalist society, since he declared the satisfaction of one's private interests ("the principle of egoism, q.v.") to be the means of providing for "the greatest happiness of the greatest number" (the principle of altruism, q.v.). He criticised the theory of natural law (q.v.). While rejecting "natural religion" with its concept of God based on an analogy with earthly rulers, he defended "revealed religion". As regards epistemology, he was a nominalist. His main work was *Deontology or the Science of Morality* (1834).

Berdyayev, Nikolai Alexandrovich (1874-1948), Russian bourgeois mystical philosopher, existentialist, founder of the so-called "new Christianity", ideologist of Vekhism (q.v.). He began as an exponent of "legal Marxism" (q.v.), but by 1905 his "critical appraisal" of Marxism had developed into direct opposition to revolution, while his neo-Kantian enthusiasm had led him to God-Seeking (q.v.) and mysticism. To the class struggle for the liberation of the workers B. counterposed an "inner", "spiritual" liberation of the personality by way of religion (*Filosofiya svobody* [Philosophy of Freedom], 1911; *Smysl tvorchestva* [The Meaning of Creativity], 1916, etc.). After the October Revolution of 1917, B. (now an émigré) set out to perfect the theory of "spiritual armament" that would repel wavering intellectuals from Marxism. Capitalism was declared by him an "inhuman system", the old Christianity a "weapon of exploitation". B. recognised the "truth of communism" to the extent that it rests on socialisation of production. At the same time B. claimed that Marxism could not solve the problem of the activity and freedom of the personality because it overshadowed the individual by the concept of class. This problem, according to

B., is solved by Christian existentialism or personalism (qq.v.). He maintains that the "existence" of the subject, whose creativity is based on "absolute freedom" is the only reality; the substance of this creativity is the so-called "dialectics of theo-humanity", the mystery of the "birth of God in man and man in God". B. placed the realisation of this "theo-human creativity" in the so-called "new Middle Ages", the after-life in the "fourth dimension", all earthly creative work being regarded as futile (*Ja i mir obyektov* [I and the World of Objects], 1934; *Opyt eschatologischeskoi metafiziki. Tvorchestvo i obyektivatsiya* [Experience of Eschatological Metaphysics. Creation and Objectivation], 1947, etc.). The reactionary nature of B.'s philosophy shows up most of all in his main work *Filosophiya neravenstva* (Philosophy of Inequality), 1918, published in 1923, in which social inequality was declared "beneficial and right", and war the basis of the creative movement of humanity.

Bergson, Henri (1859-1941), French idealist philosopher, representative of intuitionalism (q.v.). In 1900, he became a professor at the Collège de France, and in 1914, was elected to the Academy. The central concept of Bergson's idealism is "pure", i.e., non-material, "duration" (which should be distinguished from "time"), the basis and origin of all things. Matter, time, and motion are the various forms in which we conceive "duration". Knowledge of "duration" can be obtained only by intuition (q.v.), understood as direct, non-conceptual perception, in which the act of knowing coincides with the act that creates reality. To dialectics B. counterposed his doctrine of "creative evolution", based on the universalisation of concepts borrowed from biological idealism (see Vitalism). In his views on society B. justified the class rule, the oppression of one class by another as a "natural" condition, and war as an inevitable "law of nature". His philosophy is a vivid expression of irrationalism (q.v.) characteristic of bourgeois ideology in the epoch of imperialism. Main works: *Essai sur les données immédiates de la conscience* (1889), *Matière et mémoire* (1896), *L'évolution créatrice* (1907), *Les deux sources de la morale et de la religion* (1932), etc.

Berkeley, George (1685-1753), Irish philosopher, subjective idealist. Proceeding from the premise that man perceives nothing directly except his "ideas" (sensations), B. concluded that things exist only insofar as they can be perceived *(esse est percipi)*. According to B., ideas are passive. They are assimilated by an incorporeal substance, the soul. The latter is active and can perceive ideas (mind) and cause or influence them (will). In an effort to avoid solipsism (q.v.), B. recognised a multiplicity of spiritual substances, and also the existence of the "infinite mind", God. Ideas, he says, exist potentially in the mind of God, but actually exist only in the human mind. Later B. took up objective idealist positions close to Neoplatonism (q.v.) and acknowledged the eternal existence of ideas in the mind of God. In an attempt to disprove atheism and materialism, B. attacked the concept of matter as ridden with internal contradictions and useless in the quest for knowledge. The basis of his criticism of matter was idealist nominalism (q.v.). From this position he repudiated Newton's (q.v.) theory of absolute space and attacked his theory of gravitation as a doctrine on the natural cause of the motion of material bodies, whereas, according to B.'s own philosophy, only spiritual substance could be active. He disapproved of Leibniz (q.v.) and Newton's infinitesimal calculus, since to recognise the infinite divisibility of "real space" would contradict the basic postulate of his philosophy. In the latter part of the 19th century, attempts were made to revive B.'s philosophy, and it was borrowed by many idealist schools: the immanence school, empirio-criticism, pragmatism (qq.v.), and so on. His works are: *An Essay towards a New Theory of Vision* (1709), *A Treatise Concerning the Principles of Human Knowledge* (1710), *Three Dialogues Between Hylas and Philonous in Opposition to Sceptics and Atheists* (1713).

Bernal, John Desmond (1901-1971), British physicist, public figure, Lenin International Peace Prize winner (1953).

B. was member of the London Royal Society (since 1937) and the Academies of several countries, including the Academy of Sciences of the USSR (since 1958). In 1959-65 he was the executive president of the Presidium of the World Peace Council. Besides his research in physics, biochemistry, and crystallography, B. wrote various works (*The Social Function of Science*, 1939; *Science and Society*, 1953; *Science in the History of Society*, 1954), in which he gave a general summing-up of the achievements of science as a whole, revealing its philosophical significance and role in human history, the contradictions of its development in a society based on exploitation and its steady progress under socialism. His analysis of the history of science is based on dialectical materialism. In his book *World Without War* (1958), he discussed the prospects of the peaceful use of scientific discoveries for the benefit of humanity.

Bernstein, Eduard (1850-1932), German Social Democrat, founder of revisionism (q.v.) in the revolutionary working-class movement. In a series of articles entitled *Problems of Socialism* (1896-98) he revised the basic tenets of Marxism in philosophy, political economy, and the theory of scientific socialism. Proclaiming the slogan "Back to Kant", B. repudiated any consistent materialist solution of the fundamental question of philosophy (q.v.); treated Marxist and Hegelian dialectics as identical. He denied the very possibility of scientific socialism, and regarded socialism as a mere moral and ethical ideal. Rejecting the idea of the dictatorship of the proletariat (q.v.), he advocated the theory of the dying away of the class struggle and refused to recognise any goal for the working class except the winning of minor reforms within the framework of capitalism. Hence his well-known dictum: "The end is nothing, the movement is everything." Plekhanov (q.v.) did much to disprove B.'s revisionist ideas in philosophy. B.'s followers in Russia, the Economists and Mensheviks, and also the revisionists in the international movement, were exposed by Lenin.

Bertalanffy, Ludwig von (1901-1972), Austrian biologist and philosopher, founder of one of the first versions of the general theory of systems (q.v.). He generalised the principles of wholeness, organisation, equal finality (when a system reaches the same final state under different initial conditions) and isomorphism (see Isomorphism and Homeomorphism). Edited the *General Systems* yearbook (from 1956 to 1972). His main works are: *Theoretische Biologie* (Vol. 1, 1931; Vol. 2, 1951), *Das biologische Weltbild* (1949), *General Systems Theory. Foundations, Development, Applications* (1968).

Bhutavada (elementalism), a conception in ancient Indian philosophy, is mentioned in Upanishads (q.v.) and in the epos (Mahabharata). In some later sources it is regarded as a variety of the Lokāyata (q.v.). According to the doctrine of B., all qualitative differences between objects result from the different combination of the material elements of which they are formed. Consciousness is the result of a peculiar combination of material elements which, once it has occurred, can reproduce combinations similar to itself, but other combinations can never give rise to consciousness. Like the advocates of the Lākayata, the followers of B. were sensualists in epistemology and hedonists in ethics. The oldest texts of B. have not survived.

Biogenetic Law, a biological law which states that each organism in the course of its individual development (ontogenesis) repeats certain features and peculiarities through which its ancestors passed in the process of evolution (philogenesis). The term was introduced by Haeckel (q.v.) in 1866, although the fact had been remarked on earlier. As a rule, the B.L. is considered as a confirmation of the evolution theory (q.v.). Attempts to apply B.L. to the mental development of the individual (J. Baldwin, S. Hall, S. Freud, and others) were made in psychological and pedagogical literature. The individual was thought in his mental development to follow the main historical stages of world culture. However, the individual is not an organ of adaptation of species, he himself changes and creates new forms of culture through his communication.

Biological School in Sociology, a bourgeois sociological trend, popular in the second half of the 19th and the early years of the 20th centuries. Its basic postulates rest on the mechanical application of the laws of biology (struggle for existence, natural selection, cellular structure of the organism, etc.) to the life of human society; the B.S.S. also made use of the ideas of Malthusianism, eugenics, and racism (qq.v.). The attempt to explain social phenomena in terms of biology is unscientific. The class essence of this doctrine lies in the desire to overshadow the real laws of social life by treating man as a purely biological creature, supposedly endowed with "immutable instincts" of private ownership, individualism, and so on.

Biology, the study of life (q.v.). B. deals with life as a special form of the motion of matter, the laws of the development of living nature, and also with the manifold forms of living organisms, their structure, function, individual development, and interrelation with the environment. As a coherent system of knowledge, B. was known to the ancient Greeks, but it acquired a scientific basis only in modern times. In the 17th, 18th, and the first half of the 19th centuries B. was mainly descriptive. Ignorance of the material causes of biological phenomena and failure to perceive their specific features gave rise to idealist and metaphysical conceptions (vitalism, mechanism, qq.v., etc.). The discovery of the cellular structure of living creatures played an important part in establishing B. as a science. It was revolutionised by Darwin's (q.v.) evolution theory (q.v.), which revealed the basic factors and motive forces of evolution and proposed and substantiated the materialist view of the relative expediency of living organisms, thus undermining the former domination of teleology (q.v.) in biological theories. B. has made particularly rapid progress since the appearance of such branches as physiology, cytology, biochemistry, biophysics, and especially genetics (q.v.) which are concerned with the laws of the basic vital processes—nutrition, reproduction, metabolism, transmission of inherited characteristics, etc.

At the points where B. links up with other sciences (physics, chemistry, mathematics, etc.) it became possible to solve a number of important biological problems. The central problem of B. today is to reveal the essence of vital processes, to investigate the biological laws of the development of the organic world, to study the physics and chemistry of living things, to evolve various ways of controlling the vital processes, particularly metabolism, heredity, and the mutation of organisms. As a result, fundamental discoveries were made in various fields, primarily in genetics, where the material vehicles of heredity, genes, have been discovered, their structure and functions deciphered, and a general picture obtained of the mechanism of the doubling of biological structures and of the transmission of inherited characteristics. Over the past twenty years various methods of investigating the structure of proteins have been devised, and the simplest proteins have been synthesised. Biologists working in co-operation with chemists and physicists have made considerable progress in deciphering the mechanism of the biosynthesis of proteins. Darwin's conception of the causes of the variation of species has been made more precise by the elucidation of the nature of mutations on a molecular level. From the standpoint of modern B. mutations caused by the internal and external factors are the main factor in organic evolution, the principle motive force being natural selection. Progress in modern B. may be equalled to the utilisation of nuclear energy: it is making a key contribution to economic advance. Successes of molecular B. are of great philosophical importance, since they have introduced materialist views to that branch of science where vitalism reigned. The task of B. is to eliminate the negative impact of human activity on biosphere (q.v.) and to purposefully regulate the interaction of species and general processes of the rotation of substances on the earth.

Biosphere, that part of the Earth in which life exists and which is thus endowed with a special geological and physico-chemical organisation. The concept was introduced by E. Suess and developed by Vernadsky (q.v.). Vernadsky visualised the origin of life on the Earth and the formation of the B. not as the apearance of separate embryos at separate, isolated points, but as a powerful and unified process forming the "monolith" of life and encompassing every part of the planet where the appropriate conditions obtained. With the appearance of human society and the development of science and technology the B. evolves into the noosphere (q.v.).

Black Box, an object under study with unknown inner structure, whose functions can be deduced from its reactions to external stimulants. Inversely, a white box is an object with a thoroughly known internal structure, e.g., a man-made technical device (see Cybernetics).

Blanqui, Louis Auguste (1805-1881), French utopian communist, outstanding revolutionary. He took part in the revolutions of 1830 and 1848, was twice sentenced to death, and spent nearly half his life in prison. B.'s world outlook was formed under the influence of the philosophy of 18th-century Enlightenment, and also of utopian socialism (q.v.), particularly Babouvism (q.v.). Though a materialist in his general philosophical views, B. gave an idealist explanation to historical progress, regarding it as the dissemination of knowledge. He believed that history was essentially a movement from the absolute individualism of savages through various phases towards communism, a future society which would be the "crown of civilisation". At the same time B. was aware of the historical struggle between social forces, he sharply criticised capitalist society with its contradictions and supported social revolutions. His conspiratorial tactics was erroneous and led to the failure of the actions undertaken by his supporters. B. failed to realise that a revolution could be successful only if it was carried out by the mass of the working people led by a revolutionary party. Blanquism influenced the revolutionary movement in other countries, particularly in Russia (see Narodism). B. was praised for his revolutionary services by the classics of Marxism-Leninism, but his tactics was

criticised. His main work was *Critique sociale* (1885).

Boethius, Anicius Manlius Severinus (480-524), late Roman philosopher executed by Theodoric, formally a representative of Neoplatonism (q.v.). His philosophy was remarkable for its eclecticism and a leaning towards exact sciences; in its moral aspects it was close to stoicism. B. translated and interpreted the works by Aristotle, Euclid (q.v.) and Nicomachus. He also wrote a treatise containing a carefully elaborated theory of Greek music. The stoical *De Consolatione Philosophiae* is considered his main philosophical work. Some of his translations of Aristotle are now regarded as spurious.

Bogdanov (pseudonym of Malinovsky), **Alexander Alexandrovich** (1873-1928), Russian philosopher and economist, publicist, Social Democrat. He joined the Bolsheviks in 1903 but in 1909 was expelled from their party. He was a founder and leader of the Proletcult organisation (Proletarian Culture), set up in 1917. Describing B.'s philosophical views in 1908, Lenin noted four stages in his "philosophical wanderings". To start with, B. was a "natural-historical" materialist (*Fundamental Elements of the Historical View on Nature*, 1899). Shortly before the turn of the century he took up a doctrine known as energism, q.v. (see his book *Knowledge from the Historical Point of View*, 1901). Then he supported the philosophy of Mach (q.v.). Finally, his efforts to overcome the contradictions of Machism and create a "kind of objective idealism" brought him to empirio-monism, q.v. (*Empirio-Monism*, Vols. 1-3, 1904-06). Later he attempted to formulate what he called a "tectology", a universal organisational science, the aim of which was to describe the forms and types of any organisation, since he held that the whole world represented various forms of organisation of experience. He voiced a number of ideas (on systems studies, modelling, feedback, etc.), which were later elaborated by cybernetics and general theory of systems (qq.v.). In that period as well he tried to substitute tectology based on relativism and mechanism (qq.v.) for philosophy and opposed dialectical materialism. His works: *Filosofiya zhivogo opyta* (The Philosophy of Living Experience), 1913; *Vseobshchaya organizatsionnaya nauka (tektologiya)* (The Universal Organisational Science [Tectology]), 1913-21; *O proletarskoi kulture. 1904-24* (On Proletarian Culture, 1904-24), 1924.

Böhme, Jakob (1575-1624), German pantheist philosopher, whose work retained many elements of theology. A self-educated thinker, he created no consistent and coherent system. B. expressed his dialectical surmises on the contradictory nature of things and the world as a whole in a language of poetic images and symbols borrowed from Christianity, astrology and alchemy. In his works we find both simple paraphrases of Biblical myths, inspired by the power of his religious imagination, and some profound philosophical observations. God and nature, according to B., are one; nothing exists outside nature. Everything is contradictory, even God contains both good and evil. B. saw this dualism as the source of development of the world. Some modern bourgeois philosophers take interest in the mystical side of his teachings. His main work *Aurora oder die Morgenröte in Aufgange* (1612) was condemned as heresy. His ideas influenced the subsequent development of German philosophy (Hamann, Hegel, Schelling, qq.v., and others).

Bohr, Niels (1885-1962), Danish physicist, one of the authors of the quantum theory, Nobel Prize winner. His scientific interests lay at the juncture of physics and philosophy—in the sphere of analysis of the conceptual apparatus of physical theories. In order to overcome the methodological difficulties in quantum mechanics (q.v.) and its interpretation, he put forward and substantiated the principle of complementarity (q.v.), a method of description that was applied to various fields of knowledge in the analysis of alternative, contradictory situations. Overcoming positivism (q.v.) in his later years, B. tended towards a materialist and dialectical interpretation of a number of problems of quantum mechanics and the theory of

knowledge. The process of drawing science and politics closer together made B. realise that the atomic scientist must act both as a physicist and politician, must bear responsibility for the progress of science.

Bonaventura (Bonaventure), Giovanni di Fidanza (1221-1274), Catholic scholastic philosopher and mystic, general of the Franciscan Order, cardinal. Opposed the progressive ideas of his time, banned the publication of the works by R. Bacon (q.v.). He developed the teaching on the conditions and stages of God's contemplation in the spirit of St. Augustine's Neoplatonism (qq.v.). B. believed pious way of life and prayer to be the indispensable condition of learning the truth and the supernatural state of ecstasy that is experienced only by a person who receives God's blessing to be the highest degree of the contemplation of the truth. In the controversy over universals B. maintained a position of realism (see Realism, Medieval). As a representative of Catholic orthodoxy B. was canonised in 1482, and in 1587 proclaimed a Doctor of the Church.

Boole, George (1815-1864), English logician and mathematician, evolved the first system of mathematical logic (q.v.) known to history, which afterwards became known as the algebra of logic (q.v.). The idea of the analogy between algebra and logic determined the direction of all his researches in logic, which are contained in his two main works: *Mathematical Analysis of Logic* (1847) and *An Investigation of the Laws of Thought* (1854).

Boon, the most general philosophical concept to denote positive values, q.v. (as opposed by negative values, evil); an object or phenomenon meeting certain requirements, aims and interests of people. There are natural Bb. that are the result of natural processes, such as soil fertility, minerals (and, accordingly, natural evil, e.g., natural disasters, diseases, etc.) and social Bb.—products of human activity. In both cases, however, B. is socially useful in its nature. Bb. can be material or spiritual, depending on what type of man's needs they satisfy. Material Bb. are food, clothing, housing, etc., and the means of production; spiritual Bb. comprise knowledge, cultural and aesthetic values, moral good in people's actions, etc. This division is incomplete and conditional because many values do not fall into either of the given categories, or have the properties of both of them (achievements of historical progress, creative activity, social events, luxuries). Man himself, considered from the point of view of his creative potential, his ability to produce all other values, is the highest B. Antagonism between classes and social systems causes different evaluations of B.; for one class of society it can be good, while being evil for another one at the same time. That is why B. has both human and class character; it can also be of an individual character if it serves the person's requirements and interests. In this sense one should distinguish between the absolute (human and historical) and relative (historically limited, class, individual) sides of B.

Border-Line Situation, a concept of the philosophical teaching of Jaspers (q.v.). The B.L.S.—death, suffering, fear, guilt, struggle—places man on the border-line between being and non-being. Once in a B.L.S. man is free from all the conventionalities, standards of conduct and generally accepted views which bound him before and which characterise the sphere "Man" (q.v.). In this way man for the first time comprehends himself as the existence (q.v.). The B.L.S. enables man to pass from the untrue being to the true being, frees him from the bondage of everyday consciousness, which, the existentialists claim, cannot be achieved by the theoretical, scientific thought. In the B.L.S. man sees the entire surrounding world as illusory being, as the unreal world which allegedly separates him from the real being, the transcendental (q.v.) in relation to the empirical world. Thus, the B.L.S. enables man to establish contact with the transcendental, or God.

Botev, Khristo (1849-1876), Bulgarian poet and materialist philosopher. His world outlook embraced both revolutionary democracy and utopian socialism.

He was influenced by Herzen and Chernyshevsky (qq.v.), whose ideas he advocated in Bulgaria. Leader of the peasant revolution in Bulgaria and an ardent patriot, B. thought it would be possible to set up a socialist system in his country as soon as it was liberated from the Turkish feudal lords and the exploiters among his own countrymen. He held that the peasant commune was based on "socialist principles". Under the influence of Marx's *Capital* (q.v.) and the working-class movement in the West, B. came to the conclusion towards the end of his life that the proletariat would be the builder of socialism, but he was mistaken in regarding the poor in general as the proletariat. Philosophically, B. was a materialist and atheist who developed certain elements of dialectics. His understanding of social phenomena, however, was idealist and he regarded the historical process as a result of the perfection of reason in the people's struggle for liberation. Realism and revolutionary romanticism were organically merged in his poetry.

Brain, the central part of the nervous system. It consists of cerebrum and spinal cord. The uppermost sections of the cerebrum are directly connected with the psychic life of animals and man. They are the organ of control, i.e., the system which co-ordinates the activity of the various organs and regulates the relationships of the organism with the environment through psychical reflection. Throughout the history of philosophy and the sciences about man there was a struggle between the materialist and idealist trends over the problem of the nature of man's psychics, consciousness (qq.v.). However, the progress of biological studies of the structure and the activity of the central nervous system, and the cerebrum in particular, paved the way for the triumph of materialism in the solution of this problem. The ideas and works of Sechenov and I. Pavlov (qq.v.), which proved the reflectory nature of the psychical activity of animals and man, played a tremendous role. In addition to the first signal system which reflects reality and is common to both animals and man, a second signal system—speech—

was formed in man in connection with abstract vocal thought. While the experience of the species in animals is inherited in the form of instincts, in man, on the other hand, the historically-shaped forms of activity are assimilated in the process of the individual's development. Hence, particular human aptitudes, such as the ear for music and for speech, the capability for abstract thinking, etc., are functions not of morphological brain structures but of neuro-dynamic structures of relative stability. Man's psychic activity progressed not because of the morphological evolution of the B., as was the case in the animal world, but because of the development of the forms of human experience, of its storage, transmission, and processing as far as and including the creation of automatic instruments lightening mental work and enhancing man's creative possibilities. Thanks to the wide use of cybernetics, the study of the activities of the B. by the classical methods of the physiology of the higher nervous activity has been supplemented by the method of modelling, q.v. (see Cybernetics).

Bray, John Francis (1809-1895), English utopian socialist, economist, active figure in the working-class movement, self-educated worker. He held that the motive force of human development lay in man's material needs, and that the root of the workers troubles was the system of exchange. Value, he taught, could be created only by labour. The productive forces and labour must be socialised. He portrayed the future communist society in a manner close to the ideal of Owen (q.v.). His ideas influenced Proudhon (q.v.) and his school. An active figure in the Chartist movement, B. was well aware of the class contradictions in society and of the fact that only the working-class movement could bring communism into being. He held, however, that the road to communism lay through reform. In his books *Labour's Wrongs and Labour's Remedy* (1839) and *A Voyage from Utopia* (1841) he produced a devastating criticism of capitalism, taking Britain and the United States as examples.

Brentano, Franz (1838-1917), Austrian idealist philosopher. In opposition to Kant's criticism (q.v.) B. produced his own philosophical system of metaphysics permeated with the spirit of theism and Catholic scholasticism. His main interest was in psychology. He created an idealist doctrine of the "intentionality" of mental phenomena. According to this doctrine, mentality is always intentional, i.e., it always shows its attitude to something and is oriented to something, but its object is not necessarily real. Thus, B. drew a sharp borderline between physical and mental phenomena. B.'s views had a great influence on Husserl (q.v.) and other bourgeois philosophers and also on the development of psychology. Main works: *Psychologie vom empirischen Standpunkte* (1874), *Vom Ursprung sittlicher Erkenntnis* (1889), and *Die vier Phasen der Philosophie* (1895).

Bridgman, Percy Williams (1882-1961), American physicist and philosopher. Won Nobel Prize for work on the physics of high pressures (1946). In philosophy B. was the founder and leader of the subjective-idealist trend known as operationalism (q.v.). His philosophical views are expounded in his books *The Logic of Modern Physics* (1927) and *The Nature of Physical Theory* (1936).

Broglie, Louis Victor de (b. 1892), French physicist, professor of Paris University, foreign member of the Academy of Sciences of the USSR. One of the founders of the modern theory of the motion of microobjects—quantum mechanics (q.v.). His theoretical research, which established the extremely important law of nature that all microscopic material objects possess both corpuscular and wave properties, constitutes the basis of quantum mechanics today. B. studied relativist quantum mechanics, the theory of electrons, the problems of the structure of the nucleus, the theory of the distribution of electromagnetic waves in wave-conductors, etc. He is an exponent of a "causal" interpretation of quantum mechanics and maintains materialist positions in his interpretation of the microcosm phenomena.

Bruno, Giordano (1548-1600), Italian philosopher, opponent of scholasticism and the Roman Catholic Church, fervent advocate of the materialist world outlook, which he conceived in the form of pantheism (q.v.). After eight years' imprisonment he was burned at the stake by the Inquisition in Rome. His world outlook was formed under the influence of ancient classical philosophy (Neoplatonism, q.v., and Pythagoreanism, followed by the materialists Empedocles, Anaxagoras, Epicurus, and Lucretius, qq.v.), the Italian materialist free-thinkers of the Renaissance (q.v.), and the science of his day, particularly the heliocentric theory of Copernicus (q.v.). Consistently identifying infinite deity with nature, B. was even more persistent than Nicholas of Cusa (q.v.), by whom he had been influenced, in maintaining the infinity of nature itself. Using the discovery of Copernicus, B. strove to give concrete shape to the physical and astronomical implications of this philosophical principle and in so doing liberated the Copernican theory from its major defects: the traditional conception of a finite Universe, a closed sphere of motionless stars, and the idea that the Sun was stationary and constituted the absolute centre of the Universe. In the process B. deduced that the number of worlds in the Universe is infinite, and that some of them might be inhabited. He refuted the natural philosophical dualism of scholasticism (q.v.), asserting the physical homogeneity of the Earth and the celestial bodies, all of which, he maintained, consist of earth, water, air, fire, and ether. Under the influence of Neoplatonism he admitted the existence of a universal soul, which he understood as the principle of life, as a spiritual substance permeating all things and constituting their motive principle. In this B., like most of the ancient materialists, took up the position of hylozoism (q.v.). B. also developed a number of dialectical propositions: on unity, interdependence, and universal motion in nature, and on the coincidence of contraries both in the infinitely great and the infinitely small. His main works are the philosophical dialogues *Della Causa, Principio ed Uno* and *Del' Infinito, Universo e Mondi* (1584).

Buckle, Henry Thomas (1821-1862), English historian and positivist sociologist. Criticising the theological interpretation of history, B. set out to discover the laws of the historical process and show how they had operated in the various countries he took as examples. Following Comte (q.v.), he considered intellectual progress to be the main factor in historical development and denied the existence of moral progress. As a representative of geographical determinism B. attributed the peculiarities of the historical development of various peoples to the influence of natural factors (landscape, soil, climate, and also the type of food they ate). Main work: *History of Civilisation in England* (1857-61).

Buddhism, a world religion which preaches relief from suffering through the abnegation of desire and the achievement of the state of "supreme enlightenment" known as nirvana. B. originated in India in the 6th-5th centuries B.C. among numerous ethic heresies and was officially recognised in the 3rd century B.C. Today it is widespread in Sri Lanka, Japan, China, Nepal, Burma, Tibet (in the form of Lamaism), and other countries, where it has about 500 million adherents. In the period when large states were making their appearance, Siddhartha, the founder of B. called Buddha (Enlightened One), expressed the protest of the common people against the Brahman religion with its sacred caste distinctions, intricate rites of worship to the gods and sacrifice. He sought liberation from suffering only in moral perfection, which could be obtained by withdrawal from worldly life and submerging in nirvana. At first the ideas of Buddha were known in the form of parables, stories, legends, etc. Later, in the 3rd-1st centuries B.C., his idea of salvation was philosophically expressed in the doctrine that the world and human personality constitute a stream of elements of matter and consciousness—the *dharmas*—continually replacing one another. According to this doctrine, the path of salvation is seen in the suppression of the anxiety of the *dharmas*. In the early centuries A.D., the Buddhist religion assumed a completely different character. Simple reverence for the memory of the teacher was replaced by deification of

Buddha, and man's salvation was made dependent on the favour of the deity. This new religion became known as Mahayana (Great Vehicle), as distinct from the traditional trend of Hinayana (Little Vehicle) stemming from Buddha himself. The difference between these two types of Buddhism lies in their views on *dharmas*, which the Hinayana adherents considered real, and the Mahayana philosophers as unreal like the whole world. The doctrine of the unreality of the *dharmas*, or of Sunyata (void), was put on a logical basis by Nagarjuna (2nd century A.D.). His rationalism became the point of departure for Buddhist logic, which was represented by Dignaga and Dharmakirti (500-700 A.D.). Nagarjuna's teaching of the unreality of conceptual thought and of absolute intuitive knowledge became the basis of the later idealist schools and even of Zen Buddhism (q.v.). Currently the advocates of B. stress its "rationalistic" and "atheistic" character, name it a "religion without god". These new epithets are part of an attempt to propagate the modernised form of Buddhist religion.

Bulgakov, Sergei Nikolayevich (1871-1944), Russian economist and idealist philosopher, ideologist of Vekhism (q.v.). Emigrated in 1922. Professor of a theological institute in Paris (1925-44). A supporter of "legal Marxism" (q.v.), he criticised Narodism, q.v. (*O rynkakh pri kapitalisticheskom proizvodstve* [On Markets under Capitalist Production], 1897). His revisionist attempts to "test" Marx with Kant (q.v.) led him into conflict with historical materialism and the Marxist theory of progress (*Osnovniye problemy teorii progressa* [Basic Problems of the Theory of Progress], 1902). His evolution as a philosopher culminated in his recourse to a philosophy of religious mysticism, in which he attempted to "synthesise" science, philosophy, and religion, making them all ultimately dependent on faith, but avoiding the absurdities of pure religion. Besides the "absolute" (God) and the "cosmos", he introduced the concept of "sophia", a "third being", comprising both God and nature. According to B., Virgin Mary is the personification of "sophia", while the world is the manifestation of the absolute. Lenin called B.

"counter-revolutionary liberal" (Vol. 16, p. 377). Works: *Svet nevecherny* (Undying Light), 1917, *Tikhiye dumy* (Quiet Thoughts), 1918, and *O bogochelovechestve* (On Theo-Humanity), 1933-45.

Bureaucracy, a form of social organisation of society characterised by the separation of the administrative bodies from the people and also by the subordination of the organisation's rules and tasks to the aims of preserving and strengthening its ruling elite. B. necessarily emerges and develops in an exploiting class society, beginning from the early slave-owning states up to the modern state of monopoly capitalism where it develops to the full extent. In contrast to anarchism (q.v.), which refers all the state systems of administration to B., Marxism-Leninism makes disparate distinction between B. and statehood. In socialist society, the elements of B. being the survivals of the past, are condemned by the Communist party and consistently fought with. They are counterposed by a democratic social system organised along the lines of democratic centralism.

Butashevich-Petrashevsky, Mikhail Vasilyevich (1821-1866), organiser of the first socialist circle in Russia (see Petrashevsky's Group), compiler of *Karmanny slovar inostrannykh slov* (Pocket Dictionary of Foreign Words), 1845-46, where he expounded the ideas of utopian socialism (q.v.) and criticised the social system in tsarist Russia. He continued the line of revolutionary democracy upheld by Belinsky and Herzen (qq.v.), emphasised the necessity of political education for the masses of the people, and demanded the peasants' emancipation. Failing to see the forces capable of radically changing the social system based on serfdom, he pinned his hopes on reforms. His philosophy bore a materialist and atheistic character.

Butlerov, Alexander Mikhailovich (1828-1886), Russian chemist. His theory of chemical structure was a major contribution to world science. It underlies the modern conceptions of the nature of chemical compounds. This theory shows the existence of links between the properties of substance and the orderly chemical interaction of atoms in molecules, specific for each type of substances. This structural principle, which asserted itself in chemistry played an important role in overcoming mechanism (q.v.), contributed to the achievement of dialectical understanding of the systemic and structural character of objects. B.'s theory of chemical structure was instrumental in the organisation of the industrial production of substances with preset properties. The achievements of structural chemistry have promoted the broad dissemination and assertion of the ideas of the systems approach (q.v.) in other sciences.

C

Cabanis, Pierre Jean Georges (1757-1808), French materialist philosopher, enlightener, and physician. He held that consciousness depends mainly on man's physiological functions and the activity of his internal organs. C. claimed that the brain organically "secretes" thought, just as the liver secretes bile. Inclined towards vulgar materialism (q.v.), C. considered that the natural sciences provide the basis for the social sciences; that knowledge of the structure and activity of the human organism gives the key to understanding social phenomena and their changes. Towards the end of his life C. became a vitalist, recognising the independent existence of the soul. His main work is *Traité du physique et du moral de l'homme* (1802).

Cabet, Etienne (1788-1856), French utopian socialist. In his fantastic novel *Voyage en Icarie* (1840) and other works C. expounded ideas which became known as "Icarian communism". His utopia was marked by petty-bourgeois egalitarianism in consumption, preservation of religion in the society of the future, the idea of "reconciling" the poor and the rich. C. opposed the revolutionary struggle of the proletariat and advocated peaceful implementation of communism. In philosophical questions, especially in his views on history, C. adhered to idealism, combining the rationalism (q.v.) of the 17th century with Platonism and Neoplatonism (q.v.). Marx wrote that C. was a popular, although most superficial, proponent of communism.

Calculus, the system of rules for manipulating symbols, which extends the possibilities of thought in solving problems and proving statements expressed by means (in the "language") of the given C.

A characteristic feature of C. is that the material objects (figures, letters, and other symbols) dealt with in it do not practically change when the rules of the C. are applied to them. Historically, the C. arose and developed in mathematics (for example, differential and integral C., and others). Later, this method was extended to logic; various logical and logico-mathematical Cc. appeared, as a result of which the science and mathematical, or symbolic logic, came into being, in which logical forms (q.v.) are expressed by means of C. The presentation of certain spheres of knowledge, especially in the deductive sciences, in the form of C., based on methods devised in contemporary logic, is the most consistent method of formalisation (q.v.) of a relevant sphere of knowledge; the efficiency of such formalisation is confirmed by the practical application of modern computers and the development of cybernetics, q.v. (see Logistic Method).

Calvin, Jean (1509-1564), one of the leaders of the Reformation (q.v.) in France. Settled in Geneva in 1536 and became in fact dictator of the city (1541) by subordinating the secular authorities to the church. Calvinism, the system of Protestantism (q.v.), founded by C., expressed the demands of the most radical bourgeoisie. Calvinism is based on the doctrine that some are "saved" and others "damned" by divine predestination. This predestination, however, did not preclude man's activity, for although man does not know his fate, he can prove by his personal life that he is one of "God's elect". Calvinism justified bourgeois enterprise in the epoch of primitive accumulation. This was expressed in declaring modesty and frugality the greatest virtues and in advocating asceticism (q.v.) in life. C. was intolerant of all other religious beliefs. By his order, the scientist Michel Servet was burned at the stake (1553). C.'s main work is *Institution chrétienne* (1536).

Cambridge School, a trend in English 17th-century philosophy which revived the philosophy of Plato (q.v.). To the empirical materialism of F. Bacon and Hobbes (qq.v.) it counterposed the idealistic teaching of innate ideas (q.v.), interpreted in the spirit of the Platonic doctrine of knowledge and medieval realism (q.v.). R. Cudworth (1617-1688) held the eternal ideas of truth and good in the divine reason as criteria of man's judgments and his actions. External objects are only an occasion for cognition but not its source. Nature is a harmonious system implementing divine aims. An extremely mystic wing of the C.S. was represented by Henry More (1614-1687) who went over from Cartesian metaphysics to mysticism (q.v.). Members of the C.S. fought against atheism and materialism and defended religion. In bourgeois literature the C.S. is unfoundedly regarded as an element of the Renaissance.

Campanella, Tommaso (Giovanni Domenico, until taking monastic vows in 1582) (1568-1639), Italian philosopher, early utopian communist. C. shared the views of the natural philosopher Telesio (q.v.) and opposed scholasticism (q.v.), combined the ideas of sensationalism and deism (qq.v.), progressive for those days, with religious mystical views and enthusiasm for magic and astrology. Was persecuted by the Inquisition for his free-thinking. C. dreamed of the unity and welfare of mankind. In 1599, C. tried to raise a rebellion to liberate Italy from Spanish rule. The plot was uncovered and after brutal torture C. was kept in prison for 27 years. There he wrote in 1602 his utopia, *Civitas Solis* (published in 1623) about an ideal society in which there was no private property, universal labour guaranteed abundance and everyday life was strictly regulated, the rule of the priests being essentially theocratic. C. based his communist ideal on the dictates of reason and the laws of nature. *Civitas Solis* played a significant part in the development of progressive social ideas.

Camus, Albert (1913-1960), French writer and philosopher, representative of atheistic existentialism (q.v.), Nobel Prize winner (1957). His views were formed under the influence of Kierkegaard, Nietzsche, Dostoyevsky (qq. v.) and the German existentialists. The central theme of his philosophy was the meaning of human existence. From his study of the contem-

porary individual incorporated in the bureaucratic structure of bourgeois society, and his analysis of the contradictions in the spiritual life of the intellectual who harbours no illusions as to the meaning of his existence, C. concluded that man's existence is absurd and made the category of the "absurd" the basic principle of his philosophy. According to C., the senselessness of human life is personified by the mythological image of Sisyphus who, for his perfidy, is doomed forever to roll uphill a heavy stone, which always rolls down again. Unable to bear this senselessness man "revolts"; hence recurrent "riots" and revolutions, in which man spontaneously strives to find a way out of his "Sisyphean plight". C. considered "organised", "prepared" revolution as contrary to its concept just as he considered as illusory any hope that revolution is capable of actually providing a way out of the situation which has given rise to it. C.'s frame of mind was that of a hopelessly lonely man in the "absurd" world, a disposition expressing after its own fashion the inhumanity of modern capitalist society. His main works include *Le Mythe de Sisyphe* (1942) and *L'Homme Révolté* (1951).

Capital, the main work of Karl Marx, "the greatest work on political economy of our age" (V. I. Lenin, *Collected Works*, Vol. 2, p. 25), contains a profound scientific analysis of the economic laws of the movement of capitalism and proof of its inevitable demise and the victory of the communist formation. C. is therefore the fundamental substantiation of the communist world outlook. Marx called C. his life-work; he spent 40 years of tireless effort to create scientific political economy. Major landmarks on the way to this were his works written in the 1850s, in particular *Economic Manuscripts of 1857-1859*, and *A Contribution to the Critique of Political Economy* (1859), in which the foundations of the theory of surplus value were laid, detailed methodological principles for the study and criticism of bourgeois political economy were elaborated, and the basic principles of historical materialism were formulated, and his works of the 1860s (his extensive manuscript of 1861-63), in which the structure of *C.* was substantiated and the history of economic theories was thoroughly studied. Vol. I of *C.*, prepared by Marx himself, was published in 1867; subsequent volumes were published by Engels after Marx's death: Vol. II in 1885, and Vol. III in 1894; Vol. IV of *C.*, or *Theories of Surplus-Value*, was not published until early in the 20th century, by Kautsky (q.v.), who made substantial abridgements and arbitrary transpositions in the text. A complete scientific edition of Vol. IV of *C.* was first achieved in the USSR between 1955 and 1961. The significance of *C.* is not limited to its economic content, for it develops Marxist theory as a whole, in the unity of all its three component parts: philosophy—dialectical and historical materialism; political economy; and scientific communism. It is this work that most fully expressed Marx's two basic discoveries—the theory of surplus value and the materialist conception of history. The first revealed the secret of exploitation and substantiated the tenet on the historic mission of the working class as the grave-digger of capitalism and builder of the new, socialist society, which was decisive in transforming socialism from a utopia into a science. The materialist conception of history, which was turned, thanks to *C.*, from a hypothesis into a strictly proven theory, provided the theoretical and methodological basis for the theory of scientific communism. The materialist method of study used in *C.* essentially differs from the methodology of pre-Marxian thinkers. Substantiation of the proposition that it is in labour activity that people's social relations, and hence people themselves and their consciousness are formed and subsist made it possible to understand society as a self-moving organism, developing according to objective laws, and whose activity includes production of ideas, notions, and consciousness. Consciousness in its relation to being is therefore considered in *C.* not naturalistically, i.e., not as a relation of the already existing consciousness to the outside world, but from socio-historical positions, with knowledge of objects and the means of obtaining it being understood as a result of the process of practically mastering the outside world. This is the meaning of the principle of correspondence of thought to reality, which is developed in *C.* and according to which, the forms of thinking, of theoretical cognition of objects appear as laws of the latter's development. The content of these forms is revealed by dialectics (q.v.), which regards cognition as an aspect of man's practical activity, in the course of which general categories (q.v.) evolve, disclosing the essence of the development of both things and ideas. Dialectics, reproducing the objective logic of the motion of the real world, therefore appears both as a form of theoretical thinking (logic) and as a means of understanding reality (see Theory of Knowledge). *C.* developed all aspects of the dialectico-materialist method of investigation, disclosed the substance of the basic philosophical categories, substantiated the method of uniting them, by proceeding from the abstract to the concrete (see Abstract and Concrete, the), into a system which made it possible to reproduce the developing phenomenon theoretically (see Historical and Logical, the), and showed the role of contradictions in the development and cognition of any integral system. *C.* provides modern scientific knowledge with the methodology and logic of research, demonstrating the need for profound philosophical culture to solve the urgent problems of the day. Today *C.* continues to be a powerful weapon of the working class in its struggle for emancipation, manifesting the never-failing scientific and revolutionary power of Marxism.

Capitalism, the socio-economic formation that precedes socialism and communism (q.v.). Based on private ownership of the means of production and on the exploitation of wage labour. The aim of capitalist production and the source of capitalists' enrichment is appropriation of surplus value. The basic antagonistic contradiction of C. is that between the social character of production and the private form of appropriation. The main classes under C. are the proletariat and the bourgeoisie, between which there is an irreconcilable class struggle (q.v.). C. develops through various stages. Free competition, characteristic of the first stage of C., gradually leads to a high development of the productive forces, improvement of technology, concentration and socialisation of production, the formation of monopolies and to imperialism (q.v.), the epoch when the prerequisites are laid down for a socialist revolution. The Great October Socialist Revolution of 1917 in Russia and the First World War of 1914-18 led to the general crisis of C. (q.v.). At present the sphere of C.'s influence in the world has narrowed under the impact of the world socialist system. Typical of modern C. are a sharp growth of concentration and internationalisation of production, interstate regulation of the world capitalist economy (the Common Market, etc.), growth of the military-industrial complex, militarisation of the economy, the arms race, opposition of the monopolies to detente, a strengthening of state-monopoly capitalism (q.v.), and an upsurge of the democratic movement. At the contemporary stage the old contradictions are exacerbating and new forms of contradictions are arising within capitalist states. The system of state-monopoly regulation of the economy and anti-crisis policy are experiencing difficulties, contradictions are sharpening between the imperialist states and the developing countries, and the political, intellectual and ideological crisis is deepening. The system of exploitation is being further extended and refined as a result of the new forms of capitalist organisation and rationalisation of production. The social and class polarisation of capitalist society is developing, the incomes gap is widening, and the working class (q.v.) is growing numerically and changing in composition, becoming more and more qualified and coming to play a more important sociopolitical role; there is increasing proletarianisation of the middle classes and intellectuals. New social antagonisms are arising. C. still retains some possibilities for economic growth (one source of this growth being application of the achievements of the scientific and technological revolution, q.v.), but capitalist relations prevent the material and spiritual potential of society from being used in the interest of the whole population and make it necessary to replace them by socialist production relations. C. is incapable of rationally directing social development—a fact which refutes the various forecasts of a "post-industrial" society by which bourgeois ideologists attempt to justify and preserve C.

Carlyle, Thomas (1795-1881), British philosopher and historian. Advocated German idealist philosophy and reactionary romanticism (q.v.), was close to pantheism (q.v.). He applied to society Fichte's (q.v.) doctrine of man's activity as the creative element of the world. Hence the history of society was reduced to the biographies of great personalities and "hero worship". C. subscribed to the theory of historical cycle (q.v.). Modern bourgeois philosophers and sociologists use C.'s works in the struggle against Marxism-Leninism. Main works: *Heroes and Hero Worship, and the Heroic in History* (1840), *Past and Present* (1843), *History of the French Revolution* (3 vols., 1837), and *Latter-Day Pamphlets* (1850).

Carnap, Rudolf (1891-1970), philosopher and logician, a leader of neo-positivism (q.v.), active member of the Vienna Circle (q.v.), taught philosophy at Vienna and Prague universities. Since 1936 lived in the United States, was professor of philosophy at the University of California. C. denied the role of philosophy as a world-view science and reduced it to a "logical analysis of the language of science" based on mathematical logic (q.v.). In his understanding, the theoretical cognitive principles underlying this analysis represent a combination of empiricism (q.v.) and conventionalism (q.v.). In C.'s works, the philosophical conception of neo-positivism was intertwined with studies of the theory of logic and the logico-methodological analysis of science. C.'s views of the nature of the logical underwent an evolution in which two stages can be identified: (1) syntactic, when the logic of science was regarded as the logical syntax (q.v.) of the language of science, and (2) semantic, when not only the formal but also the sense-aspect of the language of science became the subject-matter of study. In the second stage C. tried to build up a single system of formal logic based on the initial concepts of logical semantics (q.v.). C.'s last works dealt with the possibility of evolving theoretical pragmatics (see Semiotic). His main works are *Logische Syntax der Sprache* (1934), *Introduction to Semantics* (1942-47), *Meaning and Necessity* (1947), and *Einführung in die symbolische Logik* (1954).

Carneades of Cyrene (214-129 B.C.), Greek philosopher, head of the so-called New Academy (see Academy of Plato), a sceptic who deepened the sceptic philosophy of his predecessor in the Academy, Arcesilaus (q.v.). C. himself wrote nothing and his lectures have not come down to us. Some meagre sources credit him with advocating sceptical views, typical of the Academy, that true knowledge is impossible and that any knowledge is at most probable assertion. Different degrees of this probability were analysed, but none was regarded as equal to truth. C. also criticised teleological proof of God's existence (see Proof of the Existence of God). In ethics C. advocated the usual sceptic doctrine of nature's blessings and of life conforming to nature without any active influence on it.

Cartesianism (from Cartesius, the Latin transcription of Descartes' name), the doctrine of Descartes (q.v.) and especially of his followers. The Cartesian school became especially widespread among philosophers of France and the Netherlands in the 17th and 18th centuries. It divided into two trends: the progressive one, which subscribed to Descartes' mechanistic materialist understanding of nature (M. Leroy, La Mettrie, q.v., and Cabanis, q.v.) and the reactionary one, which supported his idealistic metaphysics (see Occasionalism; Malebranche).

Cassirer, Ernst (1874-1945), idealist philosopher, one of the principal members of the Marburg school (q.v.) of neo-Kantianism (q.v.). Professor of philosophy at Berlin and Hamburg; after the establishment of the fascist dictatorship in Germany lived in Sweden and the United States (professor at Yale University). Applied the ideas of the Marburg school to the history of epistemology and of philosophy. In his *Substanzbegriff und Funktionsbegriff* (1910), he denied that scientific abstractions are a reflection of reality, dissolved the material world in categories of pure thought and substituted for its laws an idealistically interpreted functional dependence; subsequently sought to present scientific cognition as a form of "symbolic" thinking. C. wrote a number of works on the history of philosophy (antiquity, Renaissance, Enlightenment) and monographs about Leibniz and Kant (qq.v.). Main works: *Das Erkenntnisproblem in der Philosophie und Wissenschaft der neueren Zeit* (4 vols., 1906-57), and *Philosophie der symbolischen Formen* (3 vols., 1923-29).

Categorical Imperative, a philosophical term denoting a law in the ethics of Kant (q.v.). He called an "imperative" a statement in the form of a maxim. According to Kant, an imperative can be either hypothetical or categorical. The former expresses a maxim conditioned (as a means) by the desired aim; the latter expresses an absolute maxim. A C.I. orders everyone to act according to a rule which he would wish to become a universal law. The concept of C.I. is metaphysical, because in Kant's doctrine it expresses the absolute opposition of what should be to what is. This opposition reflects the practical weakness of the German burgherdom of Kant's time, which divorced the theoretical principles of ethics from the practical class interests underlying them and regarded these principles as purely ideological definitions of concepts and moral postulates.

Categories, terms expressing in concepts universal modes in man's relation to the world and reflecting the most general and essential properties and laws of nature, society and thought. The teaching of C. originated in the remote past. Great credit in developing philosophical C. is due to Aristotle (q.v.). He saw the problem of C. as one of correlating the content of statements about a being with that being itself. The doctrine of C. was developed by classical German idealists. For Kant (q.v.) C. are universal forms in which we conceive everything perceivable, a priori forms of contemplation and reason. Hegel (q.v.) understood C. as universal developing forms of the self-development and self-determination of the absolute spirit. According to Hegel, the interconnection of C. ultimately gives tone and rhythm to history, which becomes their embodiment. In modern bourgeois philosophy, particularly in neo-positivism (q.v.) C. are either ignored or considered to be purely subjective and "convenient" forms of the organisation of human experience, "receptacles" of experiential data, definite linguistic formations. Certain schools of idealist philosophy (neo-Thomism, personalism, qq.v., etc.) regard C. as purely spiritual transcendental substances. From the standpoint of Marxist philosophy C. were formed in the process of the historical development of cognition and social practice. They are based on the methods of man's concrete activity, and means of intercourse, and not on the activity of the spirit. The basic C. of dialectical materialism are matter and motion, time and space, quality and quantity, measure, the singular, particular and universal, contradiction, essence and appearance, content and form, necessity and chance, possibility and reality (qq.v.), and others. In their essential interconnection C. form a system reproducing the objective, historically developing interdependence of the universal forms of man's relation to the world, which reflect the forms of being of nature and social life. The basic principle for constructing a system of C. is unity of the historical and the logical (q.v.), movement from the abstract to the concrete, from the external to the internal, from appearance to essence. The C. of Marxist philosophy, as of any other science, do not constitute a closed, immutable system. With the development of man's activity, in the process of which he transforms the world and comes to know it, the number of C. increases, their content is enriched. As they express the essential connections of developing reality and the laws of the motion of nature, society and thought, they must be as mobile and flexible as the phenomena they reflect.

Catharsis, a concept of ancient Greek aesthetics describing the influence of art on man. The word C. was used by Greeks in many senses: religious, ethical, physiological, and medical. In the extensive literature on C. there is no concurrence on its essence. C. evidently included both physiological (relief after a big emotional strain) and ethical (ennobling of man's feelings) elements, synthesised in aesthetical emotions.

Catholicism, a variety of Christianity (q.v.) widespread chiefly in Western Europe and Latin America. The dogmatic distinctions of C. are: recognition of the procession of the Holy Spirit not from God the Father alone, but from God the Father and God the Son, the dogmas of purgatory, the supremacy of the Pope as the Vicar of Jesus Christ on earth, the infallibility of the Pope, etc. Cult and canonical distinctions of C. from Orthodoxy (q.v.) are celibacy of the clergy, a developed cult of the Virgin Mary, etc. The Vatican is the world centre of C. and is connected with the monopoly bourgeoisie ideologically, politically and economically. C. extends its influence to the Catholic parties, trade unions, youth and women's organisations, educational establishments, the press, publishing houses, etc. Modern C. attempts to corroborate its doctrine by data of natural science, and to influence socio-political life by proclaiming the Catholic "social doctrine". In recent years C. has displayed tendencies to strengthen its positions among the people by modernising Catholic dogmas and cult, by conducting services in the vernacular, by training priests from the local population in Asia, Africa and Latin America, by spreading the "depolitisation" of church slogan, etc. Taking into account popular feeling, many Catholic priests support social reforms and a sober, realistic political course, as shown, among other things, by certain encyclicals of the Popes, in particular in the first encyclical of Pope John Paul II "Redemptor hominis". The encyclical of Pope Leo XIII "Eterni patris" proclaimed neo-Thomism (q.v.) the official philosophy of C.

Causality, a philosophical category denoting the necessary genetic connection between phenomena, one of which (called cause) determines the other (called the effect, or consequence). There is a difference between the complete cause and the specific cause. The complete cause is the sum total of all the circumstances, the presence of which necessarily gives rise to the effect. The specific cause is the sum total of circumstances, the onset of which (in the presence of many other circumstances already existing in the given situation even before the appearance of the effect and providing the conditions, q.v., for the action of the cause) leads to the appearance of the effect. The establishment of a complete cause is possible only in comparatively simple cases, and usually scientific investigation is directed towards the disclosure of the specific causes of a phenomenon. Another reason for this is that the most essential components of the complete cause in a given situation are united into a specific cause, and the other components are only the conditions for the action of this specific cause. Materialism maintains the objectivity and universality of C., regarding causal relations as relations between objects themselves, existing outside and independent of consciousness. Subjective idealism either denies C. altogether, seeing in it only the ordinary sequence of human sensations (see Hume), or, recognising C. as a necessary relation, considers that it is introduced into the world of phenomena by the cognoscitive subject and that it has the a priori character (see Kant). Objective idealism may recognise the existence of C., independent of the cognoscitive subject, but it sees its roots in the spirit, in the idea, in the concept, which it regards as independent of the subject. Dialectical materialism not only recognises the objectivity and universality of C., it also rejects a simplified view of it, particularly the opposition between cause and effect which is characteristic of metaphysics, and regards them as the aspects of interaction by which the effect, determined by the cause, in turn influences the cause. Causal relations are multiform, and it is impossible to reduce them, as metaphysical materialism did, to any single form. The development of contemporary science, rejecting the absolutisation of the early known forms of cause-effect relations, discloses their variety, confirms, deepens and generalises the dialec-

tical and materialist understanding of C. The category of C. is one of the main categories of scientific investigation, which in the last analysis always leads to the discovery of the basic causal dependences (see Determinism and Indeterminism).

Cause, an essential condition which is the premise for, and explanation of, the existence of any phenomena (effects). The process of finding and studying C. as well as drawing conclusions from it is called substantiation. The history of philosophy and of the exact sciences is a chain of search for Cc. and of explanations of natural and social phenomena with their help. As a category within the system of dialectical logic (q.v.) C. was elaborated by Hegel (q.v.). After Hegel bourgeois philosophers regarded C. from the standpoint of general logic (see Schopenhauer, Wundt, Sigwart, Wittgenstein and others). The Marxist view of the dialectic of C. and its effect presupposes such analysis of reality which excludes subjectivism in the choice and interpretation of the facts and of purely formal Cc. which create the appearance of substantiation. The true C. of things is apprehended only by revealing their essence and their inner contradictions as the law of their movement and development (see Sufficient Reason, Principle of).

Chaadayev, Pyotr Yakovlevich (1794-1856), Russian thinker, public leader and politician. C. came from a noble family; took part in the war of 1812-1814 against Napoleon. In 1828-30, he wrote his famous series of *Philosophical Letters,* the first of which was published in the journal *Teleskop* in 1836. According to Herzen, it staggered intellectual Russia and aroused indignation of the monarchic circles. *Teleskop* was closed, its editor exiled, and C. was declared insane. In 1837, C. wrote "Apology of a Madman", and in the 1840s, together with Herzen and Granovsky (qq.v.), participated in the struggle of the Westerners (q.v.) against the Slavophiles (q.v.). A number of C.'s articles were circulated in manuscript form. Prior to 1823, C.'s world outlook was typical for the progressive-minded Russian nobleman of those days, brought

up on the ideas of the French encyclopaedists and the Russian 18th-century
enlighteners, opposed to serfdom. Later
C. shifted to the positions of Catholicism
(q.v.), although his new creed was in
effect a form of social utopia. Even in
that period C. remained opposed to the
autocracy, Orthodoxy and serfdom. C.'s
philosophy claimed the divine law was
supreme in nature and society. On the
whole, C. adhered to objective idealism
(q.v.), assimilating to some extent ideas of
the natural sciences. Man, according to
C., is incapable of conceiving the more
general laws of the world without divine
revelation. Applying this principle to the
philosophy of history, C. inferred that
divine revelation was a determining factor
of social development. He, therefore,
considered the religious education of mankind the main means for achieving the
"Kingdom of God" on earth. C. understood the future "Kingdom of God" as a
civilian society, in which equality, freedom and democracy would prevail. In this
connection, like Saint-Simon (q.v.), he
advocated the need for modernising
Catholicism. The religious form of his
views held him aloof from the general
advance of the Russian revolutionary
democratic movement and its ideology,
and he was inclined towards historical
pessimism. The contradictory nature of
C.'s world outlook was used by falsifiers
of Russian social thought as a pretext for
placing C., contrary to all truth, in the
camp of mystics alien to progressive
social interests and aspirations.

Chang Tsai (1020-1077), one of the
founders of neo-Confucianism. According
to C.T., everything existing in the world
is formed by primary matter, *ch'i* (q.v.),
which possesses the property of motion
and rest. Nature is the "root", and reason
is its product. The concentration or dispersal of *ch'i* determines the birth or
death of all phenomena and things. C.T.'s
philosophy attached great importance to
the *tao* (the way) concept, which designated the process of change and conversion of *ch'i*. The motion and change of
prime matter are determined by the interaction of two extreme opposites: the
positive, *yang* and the negative, *yin* (see
Yin and *Yang*). Their unity is what

makes *tao*, which C.T. also defined as
great harmony. Motion in nature is not
chaotic, it is determined by the law
inherent in the prime matter *ch'i*. The law
does not depend on the will of men. In his
theory of knowledge C.T. was not consistent. Sensations, he maintained, are the
source of knowledge, through them man
establishes contact with the external
world. But knowledge of *tao* is not based
on sense perception. C.T.'s teaching was
developed by the subsequent followers of
the neo-Confucian school.

Change, the most general form of
being of all objects and phenomena. C.
embraces every motion and interaction
(qq.v.), the passage from one state to
another. C. covers all movements of
objects in space, inner transformations of
the forms of motion, all processes of
development and also the appearance of
new phenomena in the world. C. embraces both a quantitative increase or
reduction in object characteristics and
their qualitative transformations. Historically, not only the specific properties of
objects undergo C., but also the laws of
the motion of matter itself. In philosophy
C. has always been contrasted to rest and
the stability of objects, but they are
relative, since they represent a specific
case and the result of the general motion
of matter.

Character, a combination of stable
psychic characteristics of the individual,
which depend on his specific genetic
features and are realised in connection
with and through the influence of life
conditions. Given the C., one can foresee
the individual's behaviour in various circumstances, and therefore control it,
thereby moulding socially valuable properties of his personality. C. finds expression
in the individual's attitude towards himself, to other people, to the job entrusted
to him, to things. C. is most amply
expressed through social and labour activity, through a pattern of human actions
and bears upon the entire individual's
behaviour. C. is socio-psychological in
nature and is influenced by the individual's world outlook, his knowledge and
experience, by accepted moral principles,
by guidance of other people and an active
interaction with them.

Charron, Pierre (1541-1603), French philosopher. He started as a lawyer, later became a priest, disciple and friend of Montaigne (q.v.). He was known for his sceptical views, close to those of Montaigne, which were chiefly set forth in his *De la sagesse* (1601). C. held that man could not guarantee the truth of any form of religion, because religion is not inherent in man, but is formed under the influence of education and the environment. Morality alone is primary in man. Hence, religion depends on morality. Therefore, one must live according to primary moral laws and profess that religion which is upheld by the authorities. C. hid his sceptical, antireligious views behind a formal recognition of orthodox religion. Theologians found in the treatise *De la sagesse* the reason to accuse C. of disbelief.

Chelpanov, Georgi Ivanovich (1862-1936), Russian psychologist, idealist philosopher, logician; founded the Moscow Psychological Institute in 1912. In philosophy C. was close to neo-Kantianism and positivism (q.v.). His *Brain and Soul,* published in 1900, and other works contained criticism of materialism. Engaged chiefly in experimental psychology, C. admitted self-observation as the only source of gaining knowledge of psychological phenomena, assigning experiments an auxiliary role. After the October Revolution of 1917, C. opposed the application of Marxism in Soviet psychology. C. was the author of textbooks on logic and psychology. His main works: *Problema vospriyatiya prostranstva v svyazi s ucheniyem ob apriornosti i vrozhdyonnosti* (The Problem of Perception of Space in Connection with the Doctrine of Apriority and Innateness), published in two volumes in 1896-1904; *Vvedeniye v eksperimentalnuyu psikhologiyu* (Introduction to Experimental Psychology), 1915.

Chernyshevsky, Nikolai Gavrilovich (1828-1889), Russian materialist philosopher and writer, critic and utopian socialist, leader of the revolutionary democratic movement in Russia in the 1860s, one of the outstanding predecessors of the Russian Social Democrats. A generation of Russian revolutionaries was brought up on his writings. C.'s world outlook was moulded under the influence of the ideas of Herzen and Belinsky (qq.v.) and also classical German philosophy, especially Feuerbach (q.v.). However C. went farther than Feuerbach in understanding the social role of philosophy. He fully subordinated his theoretical views to the struggle for the emancipation of the working people from serfdom and bourgeois slavery. In epistemology he adhered to materialist positions and sharply criticised the agnosticism of Kant (q.v.) and of others. C. saw the source or knowledge in the objective world, which acts on man's sense-organs. He attached great importance to practice, which he called the touchstone of any theory. Unlike Feuerbach, C. sought to reshape Hegel's (q.v.) dialectics in the materialist spirit. In a number of fields (political economy, history, aesthetics, art criticism) he furnished splendid examples of a dialectical approach to theoretical and practical problems. C.'s materialism was not free of some substantial shortcomings (anthropologism, q.v., limited understanding of practice, of the process of cognition, etc.). However, his revolutionary democratic views helped him to overcome many weaknesses of anthropologism. On a number of questions he came close to a materialist explanation of social life. This was evident above all in his understanding of the class nature of the contemporary society, in his recognition of the class struggle as a driving force of development, etc. C. also saw the connection between ideology and the consciousness of people with the economic conditions of their life; he emphasised that in the history of society the interests of the working people are of primary importance and regarded the masses as the chief maker of history. During the peasant reform, C. exposed the servility of the liberals to the feudal lords. C. dreamed of advancing to socialism via the old peasant community. He, like Herzen, was a founder of Narodism (q.v.). C. did not know and could not know that the proletariat is the only force capable of building up socialism. But of all the utopians C. was the closest in his theory to scientific socialism since he placed his hopes on revolution. C.'s utopian socialism was closely linked with his revolutionary democratic views. He understood that socialism could be built solely on the basis of developed technology and that only the masses themselves could build it. C. also worked fruitfully in the sphere of political economy. The main idea of his "political economy of the working people" was that of a "fully combining the owner and worker in one and the same person". Labour, he said, must cease to be a "commodity for sale". In his *Aesthetic Relation of Art to Reality* (1855) C. thoroughly criticised idealist aesthetics and formulated the basic principles of realistic art. C.'s critical essays, like the works of Belinsky and Dobrolyubov (q.v.), exerted great influence on the development of progressive Russian literature, painting and music; they have preserved their significance to this day. C. was a prominent writer, author of such works as *What Is to Be Done?* (1863) and *Prologue* (1867-69). His other main works: *Essays on the Gogol Period in Russian Literature* (1855-56), *Critique of Philosophical Prejudices Against Communal Ownership* (1858), *The Anthropological Principle in Philosophy* (1860), *Nature of Human Knowledge* (1855).

Ch'i, or **Yuoan Ch'i**, a basic concept of Chinese natural philosophy. Originally, it meant "air", "vapour", "breath". It acquired a very broad meaning: primary matter, nature's basic matter, etc. According to the ancient conceptions of natural philosophy, the world is formed of C., prime matter, the light and pure part of which rises upward creating the heavens, while the heavy and impure part settles down creating the Earth. Besides, there exist five *ch'i*, or five prime "elements" of nature: water, fire, wood, metal, earth. The flowering and death of *yin* and *yang* (q.v.) and the five elements occur through the succession of the year's four seasons. This natural philosophical scheme exerted an exceptional influence on the development of Chinese philosophical thought. It was widely utilised by Taoism, Confucianism and partially by Buddhism (qq.v.).

Chicherin, Boris Nikolayevich (1828-1904), Russian expert in the theory of law, historian and idealist philosopher, a leader of the liberal movement. C. was a Hegelian, who borrowed from Hegel chiefly his criticism of empiricism (q.v.) and his doctrine of the absolute idea. C. accepted dialectics, but distorted its meaning by moving to the forefront the idea of "agreement of the opposites" and adapted it to his own sociology aimed at justifying private property. According to C., the main part in society is played by law, i.e., the "free will" of the individual determined by legal rules. The legal and ethical elements merge in the state, which C. considered to be an "ideal" force uniting people into a single whole. C. founded the so-called legal, state school in Russian historiography, which considered the historical process above all as a succession of state legal relations. C. advocated constitutional monarchy, was opposed to the revolutionary movement and scientific socialism. His main works: *Nauka i religiya* (Science and Religion), 1879; *Mistitsism v nauke* (Mysticism in Science), 1880; *Sobstvennost i gosudarstvo* (Property and the State) in two volumes, 1882-83; *Polozhitelnaya filosofiya i yedinstvo nauki* (Positive Philosophy and the Unity of Science), 1892; *Filosofiya prava* (The Philosophy of Law), 1900; *Voprosy filosofii* (Problems of Philosophy), 1904.

Chiliasm, a religious doctrine about a thousand years-long "kingdom of God" on earth that is supposed to precede the end of the world. C. was intrinsic to Judaism (q.v.) and early Christianity (q.v.), where it was associated with the idea of the coming of the Messiah. The ideas of C. were attractive to the slaves and the poor. When established as the official religion of the Roman Empire, Christianity abandoned any attempts at changing the order of things on earth, concentrated on the idea of redemption in the next world, rejected C. as a false teaching. In the Middle Ages C. was revived in a number of heretic teachings, which were a religious cover for social protest by the peasantry and the townspeople against feudal exploitation. C. remains part of the ideology of some religious sects.

Chinese Philosophy has a long history. Its origins date from the beginning of the first millennium B.C. As early as the 8th—5th centuries B.C., C.P. had a widespread doctrine of the "primary sources", the Five Elements of nature: water, fire, wood, metal, and earth. The ancient Chinese thinkers taught that combinations of the Five Elements create the entire diversity of phenomena and things. There was also another system for revealing the primary sources of the real world. The *Yi King* (Book of Changes) named eight such primary sources, whose interaction formed different situations of reality. At the same time, the main tenets of the doctrine of the opposite and interconnected *yang* (active) and *yin* (passive) (q.v.) forces were being shaped. The action of these forces was regarded as the cause of motion and change in nature. They were symbols of light and darkness, the positive and negative, the male and female elements in nature. Ancient C.P. continued to develop from the 5th to the 3rd century B.C. It was in this period that the main Chinese philosophical schools emerged: Taoism, q.v. (Lao Tzŭ and Chuang Tzŭ), Confucianism (q.v.), Mo Ti (see Mo Tzŭ) and his followers. Many ancient Chinese thinkers sought to solve the logical problem of the relationship between the concept ("name") and reality. Mo Ti, Hsün Tzŭ (q.v.) and others held that concepts are reflections of objective phenomena and things. Kungsun Lun gave an idealist explanation of the problem. He was known for his statements resembling Zeno's (q.v.) aporias (q.v.) and for absolute abstraction of concepts and their divorce from reality. His doctrine of "names" has much in common with Plato's (q.v.) theory of "ideas". The ethical and political constructions of Confucius and Mêng Tzŭ (q.v.), the statements of other members of the Legalist school (see Fa Chia) about the state and law became widespread. That was the Golden Age of C.P. On questions of the philosophy of nature the struggle centred round the concept of *tien* (sky), regarded by some as nature (Hsun Chi), while others considered it the supreme, purposeful force (Confucius, Mêng Tzŭ); the concepts of *tao* (q.v.), the way

(natural law and the absolute); *te*, manifestations, qualities; *ch'i* (q.v.), the primary matter; the "elements" of nature, etc. In the sphere of ethics and morals, attention was devoted chiefly to the teaching on the essence of man. The views of Confucius led to the conceptions of Mêng Tzŭ about the innate goodness of human nature and of Hsun Chi about the innate evil of human nature. Yang Chu's (q.v.) theory of individualism and Mo Tzŭ's theory of altruism were widely known. The doctrine of the Five Elements, of the polar *yin* and *yang* remained the basis of numerous natural philosophical and cosmological constructions between the 3rd century B.C. and the 3rd century A.D. The concept of *ch'i* was interpreted materialistically in the deeply argumented system of Wang Chung (q.v.). The relationship of "being" to "non-being" became the central issue of struggle between materialism and idealism in the first centuries of our era. Buddhism (q.v.) began to spread in China in the 1st century. With Confucianism and Taoism it became a leading trend in Chinese thought. The 5th to 10th centuries was stamped by Buddhist mysticism. Struggle around the Buddhist teaching of the unreality of the world developed during that period. Many philosophers took a great interest in problems of the relationship between essence and appearance, being and non-being, body and soul. Philosophy flourished in China in the 10th—13th centuries as a result of the deep socio-economic changes. The further development of Confucianism, known as neo-Confucianism, came as a reaction to Buddhism and Taoism. Questions of ontology, the philosophy of nature and cosmogony were represented more widely in it. The central issue was the relation between the ideal element *li*, q.v. (law, principle) and the material element *ch'i* (prime matter). Early neo-Confucians approached some questions from the standpoint of materialism. Chu Hsi (q.v.) holds an important place in the development and generalisation of neo-Confucian constructions. Examining the interconnection of *li* and *ch'i*, Chu Hsi ultimately came to regard *li* as primary and *ch'i* as secondary. The questions of the relationship between *li* and *ch'i* was further developed in the 17th and 18th centuries;

it was resolved materialistically by Tai Chen (q.v.). The Opium War in 1840 marked the beginning of foreign penetration of China. The Chinese people reacted to the oppression of the feudal lords and foreign aggression by a powerful peasant rebellion, the Taiping movement, in which utopian ideas on the social reconstruction of society played no small part. Subsequently, China was turned into a semicolony. The best traditions and materialist ideas of C.P. were taken over and continued by progressive thinkers (Sun Yatsen, q.v., and others). A new stage in the development of socio-political and philosophical thought in China, that of the spread of Marxism, began with the May 4, 1919 movement under the influence of the Great October Socialist Revolution in Russia.

Christianity, one of the three world religions (besides Buddhism and Islam, qq.v.). It originated in the 1st century, in the eastern provinces of the Roman Empire as an expression of hopes and aspirations of the oppressed people who lost all hope to change their lot by themselves and who clung to the belief that the deliverance would come through the Messiah, a "divine saviour". C. stemmed from the moods of frustration especially acutely felt by the masses after the suppression of slave insurrections, unrest among the poor and the subjugated peoples against the Roman domination and the exploiting classes. The Christian doctrine was formed around the ideas of a number of Messianic sects with some elements borrowed from Graeco-Roman and Oriental religions and under the influence of the antique philosophers Philo of Alexandria and Seneca (q.v.). Central to C. is the belief in the redeeming sacrifice of the "Son of God", Jesus Christ, who is supposed to have been crucified by Pontius Pilate, governor of Judea, but later rose from the dead and ascended into heaven, thereby opening to his disciples a way for resurrection. The followers of C. believe in Christ's second coming upon earth in order to judge the living and the dead, bestow eternal bliss upon the righteous ones and infernal sufferings upon the sinners. The promise of happiness in the next world for the righteous ones and of a future bliss coming to those only who piously bear the brunt of life's hardships were the remedies with which C. meant to make the masses subservient and tolerant to an unjust social system. Throughout its entire history C. was evolving in an atmosphere of inner contradictions brought about by its diversified class composition, dissimilarity of class interests among its followers. These contradictions led to cleavages in its ranks, to formation of various trends and denominations. In 1054, two major Churches branched off: western (Catholicism, q.v.) and eastern (Orthodoxy, q.v.). Following Reformation (q.v.), a powerful anti-feudal and anti-Catholic movement in Europe in the 16th century, a third variety of C., Protestantism (q.v.), appeared. These Churches in their turn broke into smaller denominations arguing over interpretations of theological and cult issues, yet preserving the fundamental principles of C. intact. Today C. is the most widely spread religion in the world. It is represented by a multitude of churches and sects, whose distinct activities and political orientation are determined by the specific social conditions of their existence. The general crisis of religion, also involving C., compels the leaders of churches and sects to find new ways of retaining control over worshippers. They modernise their traditional dogmas, try to adapt their principles to the "spirit of the times". The social doctrines of churches, their attitude towards vital issues come under revision. C. is sometimes described as a "third way", supposedly the only one lending a solution to the most complex problems of man's being. Several Christian organisations and many believers condemn capitalism, uphold national and democratic freedoms. The Communist parties cooperate with Christians and with followers of other religions in their work for peace, social progress, fair relations among nations, while revealing the invalidity of Christian conceptions.

Chrysippus (281/78-208/05), a major representative of the stoic school. The stoics (q.v.) divided logic into rhetorics and dialectics. C. gave logic a precise definition of the sentence, rules for a systematic classification of all sentences into simple and complex, definitions of the correct and true argument (conclusion) and of the proof in propositional logic.

Chu Hsi (1130-1200), Chinese philosopher, an outstanding exponent of neo-Confucianism in the Sung epoch. C.H.'s doctrine is frankly idealist. It systematised the ideas of Confucianism (q.v.). According to C.H. the ideal substance *li* (q.v.) is primary, while the material substance *ch'i* (q.v.) is secondary. The ideal substance *li* is devoid of form and properties and is inaccessible to sense perception. There is constant alternation of motion and rest (see *Yin* and *Yang*) and in this process five prime material elements of the world arise: water, fire, wood, metal and earth. C.H. resolutely upheld the ethical and political doctrine of Confucianism. C.H. saw the foundation of social life in the strictest observance of Confucian ethical and political principles. Later on C.H.'s canonised teaching formed the basis for the traditional educational system in China.

Cicero, Marcus Tullius (106-43 B.C.), Roman orator, philosopher and politician. His philosophical works, written mostly in the form of dialogues, are eclectic. In his theory of knowledge C. leaned towards scepticism (q.v.), maintaining that there was no criterion to distinguish real perceptions from unreal ones. Central for C. were ethical problems delineated in his works *De Finibus Bonorum et Malorum* (45), *Cato maior, or De Senectute, Laelius, or De Amicitia* (44), *De Officiis* (43), etc. He discussed supreme welfare and virtues as the sole source of happiness and the conflict between moral obligation and personal gain, trying to give practical advice. C. urged to follow human nature, whose true essence is manifested only through man's practical philosophy. Meanwhile, one must strive for perfection. Four virtues support that effort: wisdom, justice, courage, moderation. In his political writings (*De Republica*, 54-51, *De Legibus*, 52) C. found it advisable to amalgamate monarchical, aristocratic and democratic principles in state activity and believed the Roman constitution to meet that requirement.

Circular Evidence, or vicious circle, a logical error arising out of the adduction of proof (q.v.) or evidence involving a premise proved with the help of the thesis to be proved. This error is occasionally encountered in scientific works. Marx demonstrated that A. Smith and other bourgeois economists reasoned in a vicious circle; the value of commodities results from the sum total of wages, profit, and rent, while the sum total of wages, profit, and rent is in turn determined by the value of commodities.

Civic Society, the term first used in the 18th century by pre-Marxist philosophers to denote social and, more narrowly, property relations, and also bourgeois society proper. A substantial shortcoming of the theory of C.S. propounded by the English and French materialists was that they failed to understand the dependence of C.S. on the mode of production. They inferred the origin of C.S. from the natural properties of man, from political tasks, forms of government and legislation, morality, etc. As the aggregate of social relations, the C.S. was regarded as something external to individuals, as a "medium" in which their activity unfolded. Hegel (q.v.) used the term to imply a system of requirements based on private ownership, property relations and relations of social estates, a system of legal relations, etc. Hegel's idealism came to the surface in that he regarded C.S. as dependent on the state, which he held to be the true form of the objective spirit. Marx used the term and concept of C.S. in his early works; for the first time, he used it in 1843 in his critique of Hegel. By C.S. Marx understood the family, social estate and class organisation, relations of property and distribution, and, in general, all the forms and modes of the existence and functioning of society, the conditions of man's actual life and activity of man. He stressed the groundlessness of counterposing the individual to C.S. Subsequently, Marx replaced this insufficiently clear term by strictly scientific concepts (economic structure of society, economic basis, mode of production, q.v., etc.).

Civilisation, combined material and spiritual attainments of a society.

Philosophical conceptions prior to Marxism treated the concept of C. as contextual in the analysis of the world historical process. The French Enlighteners considered a society civilised, when based on reason and justice, thereby emphasising the importance of factors ensuring integrity, social harmony. Kant introduced a distinction between the notions of C. and culture (q.v.). N. Ya. Danilevsky and Spengler (q.v.) conceived C. and culture as opposing notions. E.g., Spengler distinguished culture as a realm of the living and organic in contrast to C. as an assemblage of technical and mechanical elements. He therefore considered C. as a token of decline and ruin of society. Toynbee (q.v.) is notable for defining C. as a historical period artificially set off for analysis. The completeness of each period is what determines the points separating one C. from another. Modern bourgeois sociology views C. as an entity with three harmoniously blended components: technology, social structure and philosophy, technology being the pivotal component. Marxism historically relates C. with the advent of antagonisms between estates and classes, with the deepening division of labour (q.v.), with the emergence of laws reflecting the essence of class relations. Analysis of the antagonistic character of the pre-socialist types of C. depends on a class approach to the study of socio-economic formations (q.v.) as natural stages of the world historical process. Socialism and communism are the C. of a new, non-antagonistic type. The notion embraces the nature and level of material and spiritual development, the results of the social and cultural work of a new type of society, its role in solving modern global problems (q.v.), in mankind's social progress.

Clan, a form of community of people based on blood relationship, appeared in the primitive communities (q.v.) on the basis of economic relations. C. was the nucleus of the community and welded its members into a close-knit whole, guaranteeing reproduction of descendants able to work and maintain social relations by regulating marital and family relations, joint upbringing and care of children. C. relations often acted as a form of social link between community members, played a decisive part in production, distribution, religious rites, etc., and maintained the community character of administration (election of elders and chiefs from among the clan nucleus of the community, their rotation, etc.). Thus, C. and the community represented a social structure definable as the tribal system with social property in land, without property or social differentiation, and making participation in social affairs the right and duty of all adult members of the community. With the development of the primitive-communal system (q.v.) C. membership gradually increased. They merged into fraternities, the latter into tribes (q.v.) and the tribes into tribal unions. The progress of the productive forces, and the development of commodity-money relations among communities and families predetermined the decay of C. whose role decreased in the social life of a class society.

Class (in logic), finite or infinite totality, considered as a whole, of objects singled out according to a certain property. Objects forming a C. are called its elements. Not only individuals can be elements of a C. but also Cc. themselves. The theory of classes provides a systematic examination of Cc., their common properties and operations with them in logic.

Class Struggle, struggle between classes (q.v.) whose interests are incompatible or contradictory. The history of all societies, beginning with slave-owning society, was the history of the struggle between classes. Marxism-Leninism gave a scientific explanation of the C.S. as the driving force of the development of society divided into antagonistic classes and showed that the C.S. of the working class (q.v.) inevitably leads to socialist revolution (q.v.) and the dictatorship of the proletariat (q.v.), the purpose of which is to abolish all classes and create a classless, communist society. The main forms of the C.S. of the proletariat are economic, political, and ideological. Political struggle, the highest form of the C.S. of the proletariat, is the decisive condition for its emancipation from exploitation. In contemporary capitalist society, the C.S. of the proletariat is spearheaded against the omnipotence of the monopolies. In the course of this struggle all the main sections of the nation interested in preserving peace and implementing broad democratic reforms rally around the proletariat. The scientific and technological revolution (q.v.), far from leading to a waning of the C.S. in capitalist society, as reformists and revisionists claim, on the contrary, increasingly sharpens all the old antagonistic contradictions of the capitalist system and gives rise to new ones. This is proved, e.g., by the growth of the strike movement of the workers. With the establishment of dictatorship of the proletariat the C.S. assumes new forms. Proceeding from the experience of the young Soviet Republic, Lenin named five such new forms: (1) suppression of the resistance of the exploiters, (2) civil war as the extreme form of the C.S. between the proletariat and the bourgeoisie, (3) struggle to gain leadership over the peasantry and other non-proletarian working masses, (4) struggle for the utilisation of bourgeois specialists, (5) struggle to educate people in a new, socialist labour discipline. Depending on the concrete historical conditions the C.S. can assume more or less acute forms. The victory of socialism eliminates the grounds for conflicts between classes within the country, and promotes socio-political and ideological unity of society (q.v.). The steady growth of socialism into communism takes place in conditions when all social groups—workers, peasants, and the intelligentsia—are interested in the victory of communism and purposefully work for it. But there remains the necessity to struggle against survivals of the past (q.v.), against the ideological resistance of the old world. The C.S. persists in relations with the capitalist world. Strengthening socialism, fighting for peace, supporting the world liberation movement, the peoples of the socialist countries headed by the working class wage a C.S. against the imperialist forces.

Classes (social). "Classes are large groups of people differing from each other by the place they occupy in the historically determined system of social production, by their relation (in most cases fixed and formulated in law) to the means of production, by their role in the social organisation of labour, and, consequently, by the dimensions of the share of social wealth of which they dispose and the mode of acquiring it. Classes are groups of people one of which can appropriate the labour of another owing to the different places they occupy in a definite system of social economy" (V. I. Lenin, *Collected Works*, Vol. 29, p. 421). The existence of C. is associated only with historically determined modes of production. The emergence of C. is determined by the development of the social division of labour (q.v.) and the appearance of private ownership of means of production. In every class society, besides the basic C.—slaveowners and slaves in slave society, landowners and serfs under feudalism, capitalists and proletarians in bourgeois society—there also exist non-basic C.; the latter are associated either with remnants of the old mode of production (in bourgeois society, the peasantry) or with the emergence of a new mode (the bourgeoisie, which arose in feudal society). Abolition of the exploiting C. and the overcoming of class antagonisms become possible only as a result of the socialist revolution (q.v.), abolition of private ownership of the means of production, and its replacement by public ownership. The victory of socialism radically changes the character of the working class and draws the workers and peasants nearer to each other. Under socialism the working class (q.v.) can no longer be called the proletariat; it is free of exploitation and, together with the entire people, owns the means of production and does not sell its labour power. Under socialism the peasantry (q.v.) does away for ever with farming based on private property, with the disunity inherited from capitalism and backward and primitive implements and farming methods. It farms on the basis of collective socialist ownership. The intelligentsia (q.v.) also radically changes. The distinctions between workers, peasants, and intelligentsia are effaced in the course of transition from socialism to communism. This process is based on the gradual obliteration of the essential distinctions between town and country (q.v.), between mental and physical labour (q.v.). The socio-political and ideological unity of society (q.v.) achieved under socialism is consolidated and the social homogeneity of society is extended. The indissoluble alliance of the workers, peasants and intelligentsia constitutes the social basis of the USSR. The further strengthening of this alliance, with the working class playing the leading role, is of decisive political and socio-economic significance for the building of communism. A classless structure of society will take shape mainly within the historical framework of mature socialism.

Classical German Philosophy, the stage in the development of philosophy, represented by the teachings of Kant, Fichte, Schelling, Hegel and Feuerbach (qq.v.). C.G.P. is an ideological expression of the views of the progressive bourgeoisie in the epoch of breaking up of feudal relations in the 18th-first half of the 19th centuries. It was a specific generalisation of the experience of the bourgeois revolutions which by that time had already passed the peak of the highest revolutionary activity (the English and French revolutions). This explains the clearly marked compromise tendencies of C.G.P., heightened by the conditions of Germany of that time (feudal disunity, relative weakness of the bourgeoisie, etc.), the striving to find solution of many vital problems within the limits of either a theoretico-spiritual or an abstract-sensory field. The theoretical sources of C.G.P. include the largest achievements of the previous spiritual experience of mankind, in particular, the ideas inherited from the French and German Enlightenments; the rationalism of Descartes, Spinoza, Leibniz (qq.v.); the materialist line in philosophy (F. Bacon, Hobbes, Spinoza, Gassendi, qq.v., and others). C.G.P. is represented by all the main trends in philosophy: dualism (Kant), subjective idealism (Fichte), objective idealism (Schelling, Hegel), and materialism (Feuerbach). For all the diversity of the main philosophical positions, C.G.P. is an integral, relatively independent stage in the development of philosophy, because all its systems logically follow from one another. For exam-

ple, the inner contradiction of Kant's philosophical system, the admission of objectively existing "things-in-themselves" and negation of the possibility of their cognition, caused an attempt by Fichte to overcome this contradiction within the framework of subjective idealism, and later of the objective idealism of Schelling and Hegel, whose idealist schemes were based on the principle of the identity of subject and object, the ideal and the real. According to Hegel, reality already corresponds to its concept, categories and laws taken in their movement and self-development, which allowed him to divine the dialectics of objects in the dialectics of concepts. Meanwhile, Hegel's idealism, his absolutisation of thought and its history, i.e., closing of thought on itself, eventually gave rise to the fundamental fault of his system—the dialectical development turned essentially into a circular movement. Feuerbach, who levelled criticism against Hegelian idealism, rejected the absolute idea and the dialectic of spiritual development of mankind. He reduced thought, consciousness to sense contemplation, and the human essense— to the natural sensuous basis. Feuerbach's abandonment of the idea of development, contemplativeness (q.v.) of his materialism determined his inconsistency, which revealed itself in an idealist interpretation of history. The whole development of C.G.P. shows that the most complete, fundamentally scientific and philosophical comprehension of the world and man is possible only on a materialist basis with the use of all the achievements of C.G.P., especially its dialectics (q.v.). It is precisely this circumstance that made C.G.P. one of the sources of Marxism.

Classicism, artistic method and aesthetic theory characteristic of European art in the heyday of absolutism (17th-18th centuries). The aesthetic programme of C., most fully formulated in N. Boileau's treatise in verse: *L'Art poétique* (1674), held up the artistic works of classical antiquity as models of art. But the old forms were given a new ideological content, namely, extolment of the national interests and regard for man's psychology. The realistic trends that arose in C. on the basis of this aesthetic programme entered into conflict with C.'s other principles, which were determined by the narrow class character of the aristocratic culture of the royal court, in particular by complete disregard for "earthy" life of the lower estates. This reduced the art of C. to abstract rationalism and schematism. C. was most consistent in France (Corneille, Racine, Molière, Poussin, and others). In the late 18th century (e.g., in the period of the French Revolution) within the framework of C. the revolutionary art ("new classicism") of the young bourgeoisie developed and found its fullest expression in the work of J.-L. David).

Classification, a specific division of the extension of the concept (q.v.), representing a sum total of divisions (division of concepts into species, division of these species, etc.). C. is designed for constant use in science or practical activity (for example, C. of animals and plants, socioeconomic formations or C. of books in a library). Usually features essential to the given objects are taken as a basis for C. In this case, C. (called natural) singles out the essential similarities and differences between objects and is of cognitive significance. In other cases, when the purpose of C. is merely to systematise objects, features convenient for this purpose but not essential to the objects themselves (for example, in alphabetical catalogues) are taken as a basis. Such C. is called artificial. The most valuable are Cc. based on knowledge of the laws of connection between species and the transition from one species to another in the process of development. Such, for example, is the C. of chemical elements made by Mendeleyev (q.v.). Classification effected according to the essential features is called typology; it is based on the concept of type as a unit of division of the reality being analysed, a concrete ideal model of historically developing objects (biological, linguistic, culturological and other typologies). Every classification is the result of a certain rough demarcation of the real boundaries between types, for they are always conventional and relative. With the development of knowledge Cc. are altered and made more precise.

Classification of Sciences, the interconnection of the sciences, their place in the system of knowledge determined by definite principles which reflect the properties of and the connection between the objects studied by the different sciences and also the method of their study. C.S. can be formal (based on the principle of co-ordination) and dialectical (based on the principle of subordination). In his *Dialectics of Nature* (q.v.) Engels developed a classification which removed the one-sidedness of the earlier classifications of sciences (Saint-Simon and Comte, qq.v., on the one hand, and Hegel, q.v., on the other). Engels understood the C.S. as a reflection of the interconnections and transitions of the forms of motion of matter (q.v.) studied by the particular sciences, and their material bearers (types of matter). Engels suggested the following series: mechanics—physics—chemistry—biology. Further, the labour theory of anthropogenesis (q.v.), elaborated by Engels, opens the transition from nature to man, to history and, accordingly, from the natural to the social sciences and sciences of thinking. Mechanics opens the transition to mathematics. Engels devoted his attention chiefly to transitions between the separate sciences (corresponding to the forms of motion), on the principle that the essence of a higher form of motion is revealed through cognition of its connection with the lower forms from which it historically arose and which it contains as subordinated ones. Later the differentiation of the sciences determined their increasing integration, their combination into a single whole through the appearance of intermediate sciences between the formerly disunited ones and the more general ones which penetrate other sciences. The technical sciences stand between the natural and the social sciences; mathematics (q.v.) stands between the natural sciences and philosophy, with mathematical logic (q.v.) on the boundary between mathematics and logic. Psychology (q.v.) is linked with the main spheres of knowledge (with the natural sciences, through zoopsychology and the theory of higher nervous activity; with the social sciences, through linguistics, pedagogy, social psychology, etc.; with the sciences of thought, through logic and the theory of knowledge). Cybernetics (q.v.) holds a special place, being a section of the technical and mathematical sciences which deeply penetrates other sciences. Correlated to it are method-sciences such as systems analysis and modelling (q.v.). The contemporary development of science has introduced radical changes in Engels' original scheme of C.S.: an entirely new science of the microcosm has emerged (sub-atomic physics—nuclear, quantum mechanics); intermediary sciences (biochemistry, biophysics, geochemistry, and others, e.g., bionics) have been formed; old sciences have divided (for example, into sciences which study the macro- and microcosm). As a result the C.S. can no longer be unilinear but is a complex ramification with the division of special sciences into more general, abstract and more concrete sciences. All special sciences are embraced by dialectical materialist philosophy as a general science.

Clericalism, a socio-political trend in capitalist countries seeking to strengthen the position of religion and the church in different spheres of social life. According to its objective class role C. serves to reinforce the domination of the bourgeoisie, to prevent the working people from adopting the communist world outlook and the ideals of communism. C. creates its own parties, trade unions, peasant, youth, women's, and other mass organisations to reinforce the influence of the church on the masses. Making use of these organisations, church leaders spread ideas of "social peace". C. enjoys influence in Italy, West Germany, Spain, and a number of other countries.

Club of Rome, an international non-governmental organisation of scientists, political and public figures of many countries, founded in 1968 on the initiative of the Italian economist, public figure and businessman, A. Peccei who is the organisation's President. C.R. is legally registered in Switzerland. Its members do not officially represent the interests of any country or organisation. The Executive Committee organises and co-ordinates all its activities. C.R. holds annual meetings, symposia, seminars and meetings with political leaders and businessmen. Its basic aims are to study global problems (q.v.) of today, to understand the difficulties of mankind's development and influence public opinion. A number of research projects were carried out on its initiative whose results were published as reports. They include *The Limits to Growth*, 1972 (directed by D. Meadows); *Mankind at the Turning Point*, 1974 (directed by M. Mesarovic and E. Pestel); *Reshaping the International Order*, 1976 (J. Tinbergen); *Goals for Mankind*, 1977 (E. Laszlo); *No Limits to Learning*, 1979 (J. Botkin, M. Elmandjra, M. Malitza); *The Third World: Three Fourths of the World*, 1980 (M. Guernier); *Road Maps to the Future*, 1980 (B. Havrylyshyn). C.R.'s positive activities include global modelling (q.v.), construction of the first computer models of the world, criticism of negative tendencies of capitalist civilisation, search for ways and means of humanising the world and man, disapproval of the arms race, a call to world public to combine efforts to prevent a thermonuclear war, to protect the environment, to raise people's well-being and to improve the "quality of life". On negative side is the application of conclusions drawn from separate, particular observations to the more general laws of scientific, technical and social development; examination of the crisis processes and contradictions of contemporary capitalist society as a worldwide crisis; recommendations on the spiritual renovation of bourgeois society without its radical transformation; utopian programmes for the humanisation of the world and of man, and social philosophy proclaiming a new "global community", which in substance represents a capitalist variant of mankind's development. These negative aspects of C.R. theoretical activity have led to some scientifically and methodologically incorrect evaluations and socially unpromising recommendations.

Cognition, a socio-historical process of men's creative activity designed to shape their knowledge (q.v.), which, in turn, underlies men's aims and motives of their actions. Throughout the history of class antagonistic societies, where there was an antithesis between mental and physical labour (q.v.) and where creative activity was socially opposed to monotonous, routine work, C. was, as a rule, a special function of those who were professionally engaged in spiritual production, q.v. (scientific, aesthetic, ethical, religious, moral and other activity). For this reason the theory of knowledge was elaborated as a theory of specific, exclusively spiritual activity alienated from practice (see Theory and Practice). This engendered agnosticism and idealism in the understanding of C. The dialectico-materialist theory of knowledge views practical activity as a basis of C. and a criterion of true knowledge. C. begins with man's action on nature, with the processing of natural substances and utilisation of objects and their properties for the needs of production. Practical activity of men is at the same time a means of their communication. When men cut stones or smelted metals, etc., the essential properties of these objects were reflected and fixed in their thought. Stones or metals ceased to be for man just a sum total of their external properties perceived by his sense-organs. Seeing an object, man, as it were, superimposed on it the historically shaped habits of processing and utilising it; thus this object becomes the aim of his actions. Living perception becomes, consequently, an element of man's sensuous-practical activity. Living perception takes place in such forms as sensation, perception, notion (qq.v.), etc. The properties and functions of objects, their objective value fixed in man's signal-speech activity become the meaning and the sense of the words with whose help man creates definite notions of the objects, their properties and manifestations thanks to his ability of abstract thinking. The logical activity of thought is effected in various forms: notion and judgment, inference, induction and deduction, analysis and synthesis (qq.v.), construction of hypotheses and theories. But only when socio-productive practice confirms the coincidence of ideas and hypotheses with reality, it can be said that they are true. Lenin wrote: "From living perception to abstract thought *and from this to practice*—such is the dialectical path of the cognition of *truth,* of the cognition of objective reali-

ty" (Vol. 38, p. 171). The truth of knowledge is practically verified, not only in an isolated special experiment. Socio-productive activity as a whole, the entire social being defines, deepens and verifies knowledge throughout its history. Inasmuch as it is definite enough to distinguish objective truth from error, to confirm the truth of our knowledge, practice is at the same time a developing process, which is limited at every given stage by the potentialities of production, its technical level, etc. This means that it is also relative, as a result of which its development does not allow truth to be transformed into a dogma, into an immutable absolute (see Truth, Absolute and Relative). The revolutionary remaking of the old and the building of the new society is only possible given the true knowledge of the objective laws governing nature and social development.

Cognitum, aspects, properties and relations of objects, fixed in experience and included into the process of practical human activity, and investigated with a definite purpose in the given conditions or circumstances. Dialectical materialism recognises the influence of the object on the subject of cognition and the latter's active role. Through the cognitive activity of the subject, carried out on the basis of and for the sake of practice and verified by it, the investigated object becomes the object of cognition. The latter cannot be totally reduced to the investigated object. The motion or development of the object conditions the change and development of C. At the same time the latter develops together with the development of cognitive activity. Since cognition has become an independent branch of knowledge, C. is distinguished from the object of practical activity. With the development of science the object of scientific (empirical and theoretical) investigation also reveals its identity. The development of C. is reflected by the logical and historical method (see Historical and Logical, the), by the movement of knowledge from the abstract to the concrete in unity with the movement of knowledge from the concrete to the abstract (see Abstract and Concrete, the). C. also develops in this process.

Cohen, Hermann (1842-1918), German philosopher, professor in Marburg, founder of the Marburg school (q.v.). In the 1870s, he undertook to revise Kant's theory of experience, his ethics and aesthetics in a spirit of idealism more consistent than that of Kant: he rejected the "thing-in-itself" as the real cause of sensations and regarded it only as the limited concept of experience. Proceeding from Kant, he constructed a system of philosophy embracing logic, ethics, aesthetics, and the philosophy of religion. Philosophy, according to C., for the first time matures to be a science only when it takes as its subject-matter not things and processes, but the facts of science. The soul of philosophy is the idealist method modelled on mathematical infinitesimal calculus. By satisfying the requirements of knowledge, concepts give rise to new requirements, to which neither philosophy nor science give final answers. Philosophical consciousness is cognising consciousness; even religious belief rests on the clarity of systematic knowledge. His main works are *Kants Theorie der Erfahrung,* 1871, and *System der Philosophie,* 3 vols., 1902-12.

Coherence, Theory of, a neo-positivist theory of truth, developed by O. Neurath and Carnap (q.v.) in the course of their polemic in the Vienna Circle (q.v.) against Schlick (q.v.). While Schlick imparted a "realistic" tinge to his idealist understanding of truth, his opponents, by introducing the T.C., actually went over to positions of open subjectivism. According to this theory, truth is based on internal harmony of the propositions in a definite system. Any new proposition is true if it can be introduced into a system without upsetting its internal non-contradictoriness. To be true means to be an element of a non-contradictory system, a system being taken to mean a language structure deductively developed from the sum total of initial axioms. T.C. assumed a purely conventionalist character (see Conventionalism).

Collective and the Individual. The concept of the C. has the following features: a) unity of individuals on the basis of common tasks; b) joint action and mutual assistance;

c) constant contact; d) a certain organisation. The I. (see Individual and Society), who is a part of any C., stands in definite relations to it. The character of these relations depends on the social environment in which the given C. functions, and on the type and nature of its activity. There is an essential difference, for example, between production C. at a capitalist enterprise and socialist production C. Relationships within C. in capitalist society are determined by the conflict between personal and collective interests, which cannot be eliminated within the framework of that society. Hence the view that genuine freedom is incompatible with membership of any C., and that man can only display his individuality outside C. Hence also a false understanding of the interests of the C. (corporativism, the theory of "human relations",q.v.) and those of the I. (individualism, anarchism, qq.v.). The socialist social structure creates a favourable atmosphere for establishing relations between C. and the I. on the basis of their common interests and aims. The principle and practice of combining public and private interests, which are inherent in socialist society, are in evidence in all Cc. regardless of the type of their activity. The well-known Marxist postulate that the I. can get the means for an all-round development of his abilities only in C. and consequently that personal freedom is possible only in C., is equally applicable to all Cc. in socialist society. But the practical implementation of this postulate depends largely on subjective factors, such as the personal composition of C. and the interests of its members, how principled and sincere they are in their mutual relations, and such qualities of C.'s leader as competence, impartiality, respect for the opinion of the C.'s members, and rational use of his administrative powers.

Collectivism, a principle of living and working together as a group, diametrically opposed to individualism (q.v.). C. has a number of historical forms. In primitive society it was embodied in the joint struggle for existence. Communal ownership formed its basis. In slave-owning and feudal societies C. was ousted by individualism bred by the domination of private ownership of the means of production. C. was preserved only in some residual forms (for example, joint communal ownership of land). Capitalism is entirely dominated by bourgeois individualism. At the same time a new form of C. is born, of which the proletariat becomes the vehicle. The social nature of production and work at factories and in large groups determine the formation of proletarian collectives and the moulding of collectivist views among the workers. In socialist society C. becomes a general principle in people's relations, a most important demand of communist morality (q.v.), an essential feature of the socialist way of life (q.v.). Expressing socialist relations of production, C. has its social basis in social ownership of the means of production and absence of exploitation of man by man, and its political basis in the equality of all citizens. C. presupposes such relations between society and the individual in which the development of society as a whole creates favourable conditions for the development of the individual, and the latter in its turn is a condition for the progress of the whole of society. The main requirements resulting from the principle of C. are: comradely mutual assistance, social awareness and fulfilment of duty to society, combination of personal and social interests, equality in the collective, respect for the collective and its decisions, awareness of responsibility to the collective for one's actions and for the behaviour of one's comrades. The collective cares for man, cares for the satisfaction of his requirements and the full development of his gifts and capabilities. The principle of C. does not involve abolition of the personality of man. On the contrary, it is only in a collective that man develops and displays his gifts and abilities to the full. Communism signifies the highest form of C.

Combinatorial Logic, a school in mathematical logic (q.v.) which analyses concepts that are accepted without further study within the framework of classical mathematical logic. Such concepts are those of variable and function.

Comic, the, an aesthetic category which holds up to ridicule the historically conditioned (complete or incomplete) irrelevance of a social phenomenon, human action or behaviour, moral standards or customs to objective development and the aesthetic ideal (q.v.) of the progressive forces of society. Its origin, nature and aesthetic function confer a social character upon C. Its source lies in the objective contradictions of social life. The aspects of C. are varied: they may reflect incompatibility between the new and the old, between form and content, or the end and the means, the action and the circumstances, a man's real nature and his opinion of himself. C. may depict the ugly (q.v.), historically doomed and inhuman in a hypocritic effort to pass for the beautiful, progressive and humane. In such a case C. arouses either angry laughter or a satirically negative reaction. The absurd urge to hoard for the sake of hoarding is comic inasmuch as it contradicts the ideal of a harmoniously developed individual. C. is a powerful tool of revolutionary criticism in the fight against all that is withering away. The various aspects of C. are satire, humour, etc.

Commodity Fetishism, see Fetishism.

Common Sense, sum total of views, habits and forms of thought used by man in his everyday practical activity. This term is used in philosophical literature primarily in contrast to scholastic doctrines divorced from practice. In the works written by materialists the term of C.S. was opposed to idealism, although the defenders of idealism (e.g., Berkeley and Fichte, qq.v.) tried to refer to C.S. The C.S. was declared to be essentially correct, though limited by outward aspects of phenomena. Results of philosophical and scientific discourse were regarded as a detailed explanation and sometimes even as a rigorous proof of C.S. arguments accepted by intuition. The broader ties of science with production and the spread of scientific views change the characteristics of C.S., bring it to a certain extent closer to scientific knowledge.

Communication, a category of idealist philosophy denoting intercourse in which the self is revealed in another. C. finds its fullest expression in the existentialism of Jaspers (q.v.) and in modern French personalism (q.v.). Historically, the doctrine of C. originated as a refutation of the theory of social contract (q.v.), which has its origins in the age of Enlightenment (q.v.). The adherents of the C. theory (Jaspers, O. Bollnow, E. Mounier) emphasise that the social contract is essentially a contract or transaction, the parties to which are bound by mutual obligations; mutual perception and cognition is achieved solely in the light of such obligations, i.e., in an abstract or impersonal manner. The contract is a bond based on the practical dissociation of individuals. C. is considered to be a consciously established interdependence as opposed to the contract. C. is stated to be established by discussion in the course of which individuals become convinced that their dissociation is caused by the accepted patterns of thought, whereas they are brought closer together by that wherein they differ and by that which constitutes their unique individuality. The "individually unique" actually consists of carefully concealed subjective fears, cares and worries in which people, in the final resort, experience (each in his particular way) merely their own actual membership of some group of modern bourgeois society. Seen in this light, discussion is merely a means of clarifying this membership, and the doctrine of C. as a whole is a refined form of protection of caste and corporate bonds. Objectively, the doctrine of C. is counterposed to the Marxist conception of the collective. The term of C. is also used in a broad sense to mean intercourse (q.v.).

Communism, see Socialism and Communism.

Communist Education, a process of all-round transformation of man and his very essence, enabling him to become the subject of communist relations proper; the process by which man acquires harmonious, integral development and aspires to creative activity regardless of any profit and reward. It is C.E. which provides the aim and continuously operating humanistic criterion of the whole aggregate of social, technical, economic, and ideological transformations, which overcome class antagonisms, alienation and dehumanisation, for the only purpose of changing the conditions is ultimately to elevate man, to develop to the utmost his creative forces, his personality. C.E. is not a passive result of changed "environment", it affects above all and most deeply man's activity itself, which it transforms from partial (see Division of Labour) into integral activity incorporating practical creativity, morality, artistic skill, ideological integrity and culture of human intercourse. In this activity no achievement, no model of education can be taken as final, for the practice of C.E. itself will infinitely enrich its content and its norms. This enrichment unites and blends creation of new forms with ever fuller assimilation of the entire history of culture. C.E. demands that cultural values be made a treasure accessible to the individual, not an object of no interest to him. C.E. therefore means a revolution in motivation: the communist attitude to work is a desire to be active for the benefit of all working people. C.E. is oriented towards the ideal of fraternal collectivism implying full respect for the particular path to perfection chosen by each, in accordance with the principle: the free development of each is the condition for the free development of all. The basic task of C.E. is to form conscientious, harmoniously developed people free from any survivals of the past (see All-Round Development of the Individual). In this connection such aspects of educational work can be singled out as forming the scientific, Marxist-Leninist world outlook, the communist attitude to work, making the norms and principles of communist morality habitual norms of behaviour, educating aesthetic taste, and physical development. The core of the entire system of C.E. is the guiding activity of the Communist Party, and its basis is Marxist-Leninist ideology. Success of educational work depends on its comprehensiveness, on close unity of ideological and political, labour and moral education.

Communist Labour, (1) in a narrow and strict sense, C.L. is labour in mature communist society, which has become free, vital activity and therefore a prime necessity for all people; labour "with no quota set by any authority or any state", "labour performed not as a definite duty, not for the purpose of obtaining a right to certain products, ... voluntary labour, irrespective of quotas, labour performed without expectation of reward..." (V. I. Lenin, *Collected Works*, Vol. 30, pp. 286, 517). The prerequisite for this is maximum development of man's productive forces and overcoming of the division of his activity (see Division of Labour). In his everyday work man acts in these conditions as a social agent, as the creator of all norms and objectives, for the need to provide himself with the means of livelihood no longer dominates him. The necessity for activity is no longer external, imposed from without, but acquires inner meaning. On this basis "begins that development of human energy which is an end in itself, the true realm of freedom" (K. Marx, *Capital*, Vol. III, p. 820). C.L. overcomes the contradiction between working and leisure time and becomes the source of aesthetic satisfaction. (2) In a broad sense, C.L. is the sum total of the elements of labour under socialism whose development promotes the transition to C.L. proper. This is a tendency to make labour a creative process, a tendency to remove the distinction between paid and unpaid, voluntary labour, and a growth of the real responsibility of the individual. These tendencies are based not only on changes in consciousness, but above all on changes in reality itself, changes in the social essence of labour.

Communist Public Self-Government is a form of society's organisation under communism which will be established once a mature communist society has been achieved. A distinguishing feature of C.P.S.G. is that its organs and functions will be no longer political, nor social management a special profession. Preconditions for the establishment of C.P.S.G. are: creation of the material and technical base of communism; development of communist social relations and formation of the new man, i.e., attainment of so high a level of consciousness in all members of society that the norms of

law and morality merge into a single code of conduct for all members of the communist society. The main trend in the emergence of C.P.S.G. is further development of socialist democracy and participation of all citizens in social management. This requires continuous improvement of the material and cultural standards of living; perfection of the forms of popular representation and the democratic principles of the electoral system; extension of the practice of nationwide discussion of important problems of communist construction and of draft laws; the widest possible extension of people's control over the activities of administrative bodies; and gradual extension of the electivity and accountability principles to cover all high officials of state and social organisations. Involving as it does the transformation of organs of state power into public self-government bodies, the development of C.P.S.G. also implies expansion of the activities of all existing social organisations. "The supreme goal of the Soviet state is the building of a classless, communist society in which there will be public, communist self-government" *(Constitution of the Union of Soviet Socialist Republics).*

Community, the main economic cell of the primitive-communal system (q.v.), a closed formation based on public property in the means of production, on the collective work with the natural division of labour between men and women, between adults and children, and collective distribution and consumption of the products of labour. The development of C. was characterised by a further complication and diversification of labour performed by members of the C., and by a strengthening of the connection between the forms of labour (especially during the transition to agriculture and cattle-breeding in the Neolithic period) and the increasing economic independence of the families in the C. Economic, familial, religious and ritual life of C.'s was usually determined by the consolidation of a group of blood relatives with common ancestors and bearing a common tribal name. That is why a tribal C. was the most widespread form of primitive C. Owing to exogamy some blood relatives stayed in the tribe only temporarily and quit it after marriage. The permanent group found partners outside their own tribe. Intercommunity connections in different spheres of material and spiritual life, serving as the foundation of the tribal system and as the origin of tribal organisation, developed on the basis of family ties and conjugal relations. With the appearance of metal tools, of the social division of labour (q.v.) and constant trade between Cc., a process of differentiation began between the latter into rich and noble families and poor, subordinate ones, and, indeed, within the C. between propertied families and unpropertied exploited ones, C. gradually turning into rural communities (q.v.).

Comparison, a juxtaposition of two or more objects to find similarities or differences (or both) between them. It is an important prerequisite of generalisation (q.v.) and forms the basis of judgments by analogy (q.v.). Judgments expressing the result of C. serve to determine the content of the concepts of the objects compared. In this sense, C. is a device supplementing, and sometimes replacing, definition (q.v.).

Complementarity, Principle of (or complementary method of description), a methodological principle suggested by Bohr (q.v.) to interpret quantum mechanics. It may be formulated as follows: to reproduce the wholeness of a phenomenon at a certain "intermediate" period of its cognition, use must be made of mutually exclusive "complementary" and mutually limiting classes of concepts, which can be used separately, depending on specific (experimental, etc.) conditions, but only taken together cover all definable information. With the help of P.C. Bohr hoped to solve one of the "paradoxes" of quantum mechanics, which revealed the inadequacy of the old, classical concepts, though it could not get by without them in the early stages. P.C. helped to bring out the dual, wave-corpuscular nature of minute phenomena. P.C. established the equivalence of two classes of concepts describing contradictory situations. Thus, Bohr's methodological conception contained elements of

dialectical thinking. In the works of several representatives of the group known as the Copenhagen school (P. Jordan, Frank, q.v., and other advocates of extreme positivist views) the P.C. was used to defend idealist and metaphysical views. The necessity of using "complementary" concepts was inferred not from the objective nature of minute objects, but from the peculiarities of the cognitive process, and was associated with the arbitrary intervention of the observer. In recent Marxist philosophical studies, attempts have been made to give P.C. a dialectico-materialist interpretation.

Comte, Auguste (1798-1857), French philosopher, founder of positivism (q.v.). Secretary and associate of Saint-Simon (q.v.) in 1818-24. The basic thesis of C.'s "positive philosophy" was his demand that science limit itself to a description of the outward appearance of phenomena. C. attempted to synthesise the vast body of data provided by natural science, but owing to his philosophical stance (subjective idealism and agnosticism, qq.v.) his attempt led to a falsification of science. C. described the cognition of nature in terms of three stages, each of which corresponded to a definite type of world outlook: the theological, the metaphysical, and the positive. In the first, theological, stage man attempted to attribute the various phenomena to supernatural powers, or God. The metaphysical world outlook, according to C., is a modification of the theological; in his view, the basis of all phenomena is to be found in abstract metaphysical essences. The theological and metaphysical world outlooks were followed, according to C., by the "positive method", which rejected "absolute knowledge" (i.e., materialism first of all, and also objective idealism). C.'s three-stage formula distorted the actual history of science and philosophy. For instance, an entire period in the development of human thought—the epoch of antiquity—was left out. In the final analysis it was an uncouth imitation of the dialectical triad borrowed from Saint-Simon. C. applied his three-stage formula to a classification of sciences and a systematisation of civil history. In his sociology (a term proposed by C.) he used an unscientific biological approach in an attempt to explain society. The principal idea of his sociological doctrine was the assertion that it is useless to seek to change the bourgeois system by revolutionary means. Capitalism, according to C., crowns the history of man's evolution; and social harmony could be achieved by propaganda of a "new" religion which substituted belief in an abstract supreme being for faith in a personal God. C.'s most important work is the *Cours de philosophie positive* (1830-42).

Concept, one of the forms of reflection of the world at the stage of cognition associated with the use of language (q.v.), a form (method) of generalising objects and phenomena. C. also denotes thought which generalises objects of a certain class according to their specific attributes. Moreover, the objects of one and the same class (atoms, animals, plants, socio-economic formations, etc.) can be generalised to form Cc. according to different aggregates of attributes. The more essential are the attributes that comprise the content of the objects and according to which they are generalised, the higher the scientific value of the C. The C. becomes a definite system of knowledge as other general attributes of objects, generalised in a C., are inferred from the attributes which comprise the basic content of C. Progress of knowledge signifies above all the development of C., a passage from one C. (of a given object) to another, fixing the deeper essence of objects and, therefore, representing their reflection more adequately. Cc. impart the sense (see Denotation and Sense) to the words of a language. One of the logical functions of C. is to single out in thought by definite attributes the objects which interest us from the point of view of practice and of cognition. Thanks to this function Cc. link up words with definite objects, which makes it possible to determine the exact meanings of words and to operate with them in the process of thought. The identification of the classes of objects and their generalisation in C. are an indispensable condition for the cognition of the laws of nature. Every science operates with definite Cc., in which the knowledge accumulated by

science is concentrated. The formation of C., the transition to it from sensory forms of reflection, is a complicated process that sees the application of such methods of cognition as comparison, analysis and synthesis (qq.v.), abstraction, idealisation, generalisation, and more or less complex forms of inference (q.v.). At the same time, scientific Cc. are often created initially solely on the basis of hypothetical assumptions concerning the existence of objects and their nature (that is how, for example, the C. of atoms emerged). On the basis of knowing laws and trends of development, the C. of some objects may be formed before the emergence of objects or phenomena themselves (C. of communism). Thus, the formation of Cc. is a manifestation of the active and creative character of thought, although the successful use of the Cc. created depends entirely on the precision with which objective reality is reflected in them. Every C. is an abstraction, which makes it appear to be a deviation from reality. As a matter of fact, with the help of a C. a more profound knowledge of reality is obtained by singling out and investigating its essential aspects. Moreover, the concrete which is incompletely reflected in particular Cc. may be reproduced to a certain degree of completeness by an aggregate of Cc. reflecting its various aspects. To reflect reality as accurately as possible, Cc., to quote Lenin, "must ... be hewn, treated, flexible, mobile, relative, mutually connected, united in opposites, in order to embrace the world" (Vol. 38, p. 146). This tenet is one of the most essential aspects of the teaching of dialectical logic (q.v.) on the C. The dialectical materialist approach to the C. is corroborated by the development of the whole of modern science and serves as a method of scientific cognition.

Concept, Extent and Content of, two interconnected sides of a concept (q.v.). Extent is a class of objects generalised in a concept; content is the sum total of (usually essential) properties, according to which objects are generalised and singled out in the given concept. By formulating the content of a concept we single out the identical (general) in objects of the given class; a characteristic of volume, i.e., differentiation of elements (objects which are carriers of the properties comprising the content) and parts (specifying subclasses of the given class) brings out the difference between objects of the given class. There is a connection between content and extent expressed in formal logic by the law of inverse relation.

Conceptualism, a theory of scholastic philosophy, mainly connected with the names of Abélard (q.v.), John of Salisbury and others. In the debate on universals (q.v.) the conceptualists denied the doctrine of realism (see Realism, Medieval) and the real existence of the universal apart from particular objects, as did the nominalists (see Nominalism), but unlike the latter they admitted the existence of general a priori concepts as a special form of knowledge of reality. Locke (q.v.) held views close to C.

Concrete Sociological Investigation, study of social relations in different spheres of social reality (economics, politics, culture, everyday life, etc.), of the trends and regularities of their development and functioning by combining theoretical and empirical methods of investigation (see Methods of Concrete Sociological Investigation). C.S.I. considers any social process or phenomenon from the standpoint of their structure and dynamics being determined by specific features of the economic, socio-political and spiritual life of society, including the regularities established by other social investigations, with economic regularities being determinative in these processes. The theoretical basis of C.S.I. is general sociological theory, i.e., historical materialism (q.v.) and particular sociological theories worked out on its basis, which perform the function of the scientific methodology of investigation and make possible an objective approach in analysing facts of social reality. C.S.I. is an important instrument for analysing social tendencies, and combining the theory and practice of socialist construction. It serves as a means of actually (empirically) substantiating scientific theoretical conclusions concerning the regularities of social development and hence is a necessary link in adopting

decisions concerning the regulation of social processes and their management in socialist society. A distinction should be made between C.S.I. aimed at scientific analysis of social processes, and the so-called applied investigation of narrow practical significance and analysis of current information (e.g., specialised public opinion polls). C.S.I. is widely practised in the USSR. Soviet sociologists study the trends of changes taking place in society's social structure, the dynamics of the requirements of different population groups and the various forms of people's activity in the labour, socio-political, spiritual and other spheres of life. Marxist C.S.I. differs radically from bourgeois empirical sociology (q.v.) of the positivist type, which rejects general sociological theory and confines itself to a scrupulous study of so-called microproblems and particular social phenomena. Insofar as it replaces analysis of the objective trends in social life by a study of people's subjective reactions to the conditions of their life activity, empirical sociology is unable to discover the deep-down sources of social processes that do not depend on consciousness. Since the mid-1960s bourgeois sociologists have been actively discussing the critical state of theoretical models of investigation which cannot be overcome without resorting to the materialist conception of the laws of social development.

Concreteness of Truth, an attribute of truth (q.v.), deriving from the consideration and generalisation of specific conditions of the existence of some fact; the dependence of truth upon definite conditions of time and space, etc. Thus, the truth or falsity of a proposition cannot be established unless the relevant conditions are specified. The proposition "The sum of the angles of any triangles is equal to two right angles" is true only in Euclid's geometry and is false, e.g., in Lobachevsky's (q.v.) geometry. Therefore, truth is never abstract, it is always concrete. A concrete historical approach and consideration of circumstances of time and space are important in analysing social development, which proceeds unevenly with new phenomena constantly emerging.

Condillac, Etiènne Bonnot de (1715-1780), French encyclopaedist (see Enlightenment). Born at Grenoble, he became a Catholic priest, but through his works sought to undermine the ideology of the church. He was a follower of Locke (q.v.) in respect of the theory of knowledge, but, unlike him, denied the existence of "reflection" as a source of knowledge second to sensation. His failure to understand the nature of the relationship between sensations and external objects, and his exaggeration of their subjectivity led C. to conclusions close to subjective idealism (q.v.). Sensations, according to C., are produced by external objects, with which, however, they have nothing in common. Inasmuch as sensation is the sole link between the world and the reason, the latter has for its object the sum total of sensations, rather than the objective world. Nevertheless C.'s sensationalism (q.v.) was opposed to the idealism of Leibniz (q.v.) and to any speculative philosophy. His influence on the French 18th-century materialism (q.v.) was considerable. His main works include: *Le Traité des systèmes, où l'on en démèle les inconvénients et les avantages* (1749), and *Le Traité des sensations* (1754).

Condition, a philosophical category expressing the relationship of an object to phenomena around it, and without which it cannot exist. The object itself is something determined, while C. represents the diversity of the objective world external to the object. As distinct from the cause, which directly engenders phenomena or processes, C. is the environment, the atmosphere in which they emerge, exist, and develop. By learning the laws of nature, men are able to create Cc. favourable to their activity and eliminate unfavourable Cc. While influencing phenomena and processes, Cc. themselves are subject to their influence. Thus, the socialist revolution, arising in definite Cc., subsequently changes the Cc. of society's material and spiritual life.

Conditionalism, a philosophical teaching which substitutes the concept of a complex of conditions for the concept of cause. It was founded by M. Verworn

(1863-1921), a German physiologist, holder of idealist views in the spirit of Machism in philosophy. The concepts of C. have supporters among theoreticians in the West.

Condorcet, Jean Antoine (1743-1794), French philosopher and encyclopaedist. In economic matters he was a follower of the physiocrats (see Turgot). His criticism of religion was based on deism (q.v.) and bourgeois enlightenment (q.v.). He called for the abandonment of superstitions and for a development of scientific knowledge. In his most important work, *Esquisse d'un tableau historique des progrès de l'esprit humain* (1794), C. viewed history as a product of human reason, and declared the bourgeois system to be the apex of reasonableness and "naturalness". He divided history into 10 periods on the basis of chance attributes, and undertook to prove that capitalism implied endless progress. C. opposed the system of social estates, fought for political equality. At the same time, he considered property inequality beneficial to society.

Conformism, a concept signifying time-serving passive acceptance of the existing order of things, of prevailing opinions, etc. Unlike collectivism (q.v.), which implies active participation of the individual in taking group decisions, conscious assimilation of collective values and the consequent conformity of one's behaviour to the interests of the collective and society and, if necessary, subordination to the latter, C. means failure to form one's own opinion, unprincipled and uncritical following of whatever exerts the greatest influence (opinion of the majority, acknowledged authority, tradition, etc.). Marxism sees the social roots of C. in the historically traditional lack of political rights of the people in class antagonistic societies. Revolutionary transformation of society is impossible unless C. is overcome.

Confucianism, one of the leading philosophical schools in ancient China, founded by Confucius (551-479 B.C.), whose views were expounded by his followers in the *Lun Yü (Analects)*. According to Confucius, the fate of man is ordained by "Heaven"; all men are unalterably either "noble" or "base". The younger must humbly submit to their seniors, subordinates to their superiors. A prominent follower of Confucius was Mêng Tzǔ (q.v.), or Mencius, who attributed social inequality to the "will of Heaven". Another Confucianist of note was Hsün Tzǔ (q.v.), who propounded a materialist doctrine according to which Heaven formed part of nature and lacked consciousness. A man who has attained knowledge of the laws (*tao*, q.v.) of things should use those laws to advance his own interests. The central tenet of C. was justification of the supremacy of the privileged classes and glorification of the "will of Heaven", which formed the basis for the orthodox Confucian doctrine of Tung Chung-shu (2nd century B.C.). In the 11th and 12th centuries, Chu Hsí (q.v.) and others introduced neo-Confucianism, which implied the existence of two elements in things — *li* (q.v.), the rational creative principle, and *ch'i* (q.v.), passive matter. *Li* generates virtue in men, whereas *ch'i* produces vice, surrender to sensual temptation. C. was for many centuries the leading ideology in feudal China.

Conjunction, a logical operation forming a composite proposition out of two propositions united by the logical connective "and". The composite proposition is true when and only when all the propositions it contains are true and is false in all other cases.

Conscience, an ethical category expressing the highest form of a personality's ability to moral self-control. As distinct from the motive (the sense of duty, q.v.), C. also includes an appraisal by the person concerned of his past actions, based on an understanding of his responsibility (q.v.) to society. C. compels man, not only to act in a way that is likely earn him respect, as, say, the sense of honour and personal dignity, but fully to give himself up to the service of society, an advanced class, mankind. In addition, C. presupposed the individual's ability to be critical of his own and others' opinions in accordance with the objective needs of society, as well as his responsibility not only for his own actions but for all that is going on around him. C. is an ability that can be instilled in man by society. It is determined by the measure of his historical development, and his social position in the objective conditions in which he has been placed. C. may manifest itself both in the form of man realising the moral significance of his actions, and in a complex of emotions (being consciousstriken). The cultivation of C. in every person is an important aspect of the work to form communist morality.

Consciousness, the highest form of reflection of objective reality inherent only in man. C. is the sum total of mental processes which actively participate in man's understanding of the objective world and of his personal being. It takes its origin in the labour, socio-productive activity of people and is inseparably linked with language (q.v.), which is as old as C. Man is born into the world of objects created by previous generations, and is formed as such only in the process of learning how to use them to a definite end. The mode of his relation to reality is not determined directly by his bodily organisation (as is the case with the animals), but by the habits of practical activity acquired solely through communication with other people. In communication, man's own vital activity is perceived by him also as the activity (q.v.) of others. Therefore, he assesses every action of his by the social standard he holds common with other people. It is precisely because man treats objects with understanding and knowledge, that the mode of his attitude to the world is called C. Without understanding, without knowledge, which is a result of man's sociohistorical activity and human speech, there is no C. either. Any sensuous image of an object, any sensation or notion (qq.v.), is part of C. inasmuch as it possesses definite denotation and sense (q.v.). Knowledge, denotation and meaning, preserved in language, direct and differentiate man's sentiments, will, attention, and other mental acts, combining them into a single C. Knowledge accumulated by history, political and legal ideas, morality, religion, social psychology, and the achievements of art constitute the C.

of society as a whole (see Social Being and Social Consciousness). But C. must not be identified solely with knowledge and thinking in terms of language. There is no thinking outside man's vital, sensuous and will-governed mental activity. Thinking involves not a mere processing of information; it is an active, sensuous and purposeful transformation of reality in conformity with reality's own essence. Thinking in terms of language—the changing of the meaning of words, signs, symbols, etc.—is only one form of man's thinking. On the other hand, the concepts of C. and the psychics (q.v.) must not be identified, i.e., one must not consider that every mental process at every given moment is included in C. A number of mental emotions can be for a definite time "beyond the threshold" of C. (see Subconscious). Absorbing historical experience, knowledge, and methods of thinking elaborated by preceding history, C. masters reality in idea, setting itself new aims and tasks, designing tools for the future, and directing all practical activity of man. C. is shaped by activity and, in its turn, influences this activity, determining and regulating it. As they realise their creative plans, people transform nature and society and thereby transform themselves. The problem of C. and its relation to matter has been the basic keen issue of the ideological struggle in science through the ages. A materialist understanding of history enabled Marxists to solve this problem and thereby create a truly scientific philosophy.

Consequential Ethics, a type of ethical theories which define the moral value of an act according to its practical consequences (see Utilitarianism; Hedonism; Eudaemonism), regardless of its motives and the general principles of morality. Adherents of C.E. hold that morality serves to satisfy certain requirements of society and man or at least formally recognise its expedience. Marxist ethics notes the inadequacy of the principles of C.E. and considers it necessary to assess the moral value of an act as a whole, including motives, attitude of the moral subject to it and its more remote consequences, in relation to the advanced social ideal.

Conservation of Energy, Law of, one of the most important conservation laws (see Conservation Principles), according to which energy neither disappears, nor is created anew, when changing from one kind into another. The processes of conversion from one form of energy into another are regulated by constant numerical equivalents. The L.C.E. was discovered by R. Mayer, J. Joule, Helmholtz (q.v.) and others in the mid-19th century, its discovery being preceded by conjectures propounded by Descartes, Leibniz, and Lomonosov (qq.v.) on the conservation of matter and motion. Engels regarded the discovery of the L.C.E. as one of the three great discoveries comprising the scientific foundation of the dialectico-materialist understanding of nature. The L.C.E. reflects the unity of the material world. Contemporary physics is providing massive fresh proof of the L.C.E.

Conservation Principles, a special class of scientific principles reflecting the constancy of the fundamental properties and relations in nature. In the structure of physical theories, the C.P. are formulated as conservation laws and the principles of invariance (q.v.). Currently, we know the following C.P.: the law of conservation of energy (q.v.), the law of conservation of mass, the law of conservation of momentum, the law of conservation of the moment of momentum, the law of conservation of spin, etc. The special theory of relativity (q.v.) formulates the principle of invariance of natural laws in relation to systems which are in uniform and straight motion in respect of each other. The physical theory includes the fundamental constants: h—Planck's constant in quantum mechanics (q.v.), c—the constant of the velocity of light in the theory of relativity. The constancy of these quantities may be regarded as a special type of C.P. Thus, the types of C.P. are diverse. This diversity can be compared with the diversity of the forms of motion of matter. In the study of complex, particularly biological, systems great importance attaches to the concept of structure (q.v.), and the C.P. aquire here the form of structural principles. The C.P. control the mutual transformations of material objects. They provide the basis for the essential law-governed causal nexuses in nature. Being the most general laws in any scientific theory, they have a great heuristic value. The C.P. reflect one of the aspects of the dialectical contradiction inherent in nature, viz., the contradiction between conservation and change.

Constructive (Genetic) Method, one of the methods of deductive construction of scientific theories (see Deductive Method). The idea of C.M. was conceived at the beginning of the 20th century and developed (in the works of Hilbert, q.v., L. Brouwer, A. Heyting, A. N. Kolmogorov, A. A. Markov, and others) in an attempt to deal with the difficulties of providing an axiomatic basis for mathematics and logic (for example, to solve the paradoxes, q.v., of the set theory, etc.). Unlike the axiomatic method (q.v.), the constructive method of developing a theory strives to reduce to a minimum the primary, non-demonstrable within the framework of the theory statements and undefinable terms and pays special attention to their profound substantiation. At present the C.M. is applied solely to the formal sciences—mathematics and logic (constructive logic, q.v.). There is no apparent reason, however, for denying the possibility of using this method in building up knowledge in the field of natural science as well.

Conta, Basile (1845-1882), Romanian materialist philosopher. He drew his conclusions from data furnished by the natural sciences, largely basing them on the theories of J. Lamarck, Darwin and Haeckel (qq.v.). C. considered infinite matter as endlessly developing in time and space. He classified all laws according to different forms of matter, while refusing to accept the concept of chance and asserting that all laws operate fatally. He considered the cognitive capacity of the human mind to be unlimited, just as reality itself. Knowledge is verified by practice, by which C. meant laboratory experiment and personal experience. Being an atheist, C. attributed the origins of religion to primitive man's ignorance and fears of the unknown forces of nature. In the field of social science, C. adhered to idealism.

Contemplativeness, the main shortcoming of pre-Marxian materialism in the theory of knowledge, implying that cognition (q.v.) is viewed as a passive process of perception, contemplation, in which the external world acts on man's sense-organs, while man himself only perceives it. Moreover, the objective world and human activity were one-sidedly regarded as opposites. Reality was seen only as an object and not considered subjectively, i.e., not as depending on the activity of the subject, not as transformed by man's social activity. Practice itself was understood by pre-Marxian materialists solely as man's individual activity, aimed at satisfying his personal needs. That practice is activity which creates both man and the world at large he lives in could not be grasped by the old materialists. Actually, in the process of cognition man deals, not so much with nature as such, as with a "humanised" world, i.e., a world drawn into the process of production in one way or another; and it is the practical transformation of the world that reveals to man its laws and essence. Therefore, cognition is not passive contemplation but energetic activity which is inseparably linked with the practical transformation of the world. Another feature of C. is that the subject of knowledge is seen as an abstract individual ("epistemological Robinsonade"), as a purely natural being, all of whose cognitive abilities were formed biologically. In the theory of knowledge C. inevitably leads to metaphysics and makes it impossible fully to refute idealism. Marxism has overcome C. and thereby revolutionised epistemology.

Content and Form 1. Philosophical categories reflecting the interconnection between the two sides of natural and social reality; a specifically ordered sumtotal of elements and processes which constitute an object or a phenomenon, i.e., the C., and the mode of existence and expression of this C., its various modifications, i.e., F. The concept of F. is also used to denote the internal organisation of C., and in this meaning it is further developed in the category of structure (q.v.). In pre-Marxist philosophy, especially in idealist philosophy, F. was reduced to structure, and C. was equated with some disordered sum-total of elements and properties ("matter"), which was conducive to the idealistic notions about the primacy of F. over C. gaining ground and persisting for a lengthy historical period. In materialist dialectics, structure, internal organisation is viewed as an indispensable component of C. As the structure changes, the object's C., its physical and chemical properties also undergo a considerable change. As it fixes the diverse modifications of the C., the modes of its existence and manifestation, the F. also has a definite structure. The interaction of C. and F. in the process of development always includes both the impact of different elements of the C. on the F., and the impact of different elements of the F. on the C. in accordance with the objective subordination of the C. and the F. In the combination of C. and F., C. is the leading and determining side of the object, while F. is that side which is modified and changed following changes in the C. and the concrete conditions of its existence. In its turn, being relatively independent, the F. exerts an active reverse influence on the C.: a F. which corresponds to the C. speeds up its development, whereas a F. which has ceased to correspond to the changed C. retards its further development. Interrelation between C. and F. is a typical example of relations between dialectical opposites, characterised as they are both by unity of C. and F. and by contradictions and conflicts between them. The unity of C. and F. is relative and transient; conflicts and contradictions inevitably emerge between them in the process of development. As a result, there appears a discrepancy between C. and F., which is ultimately resolved through the "shedding" of the old F. and the appearance of a new one that corresponds to the changed C. The emergence, development and overcoming of contradictions between C. and F., the struggle between them (transitions of C. into F. and vice versa, the "filling" of the old F. with a new C., the reverse influence of the F. on the C., etc.) are important components of the dialectical theory of development. Especially complex and dialectically contradic-

tory is the interrelation between C. and F. in the development of society. The contradictions between C. and F. in the mode of production, basis and superstructure, economy and politics (qq.v.) are one of the most important motive forces of social development. 2. In thinking C. and F. are fundamental concepts of the science of logic. In materialist dialectics as logic (see Logic, Dialectical), the C. of thinking means natural and social reality as the object of scientific and theoretical thinking, i.e., as a sum-total of concepts, ideas, theories, various abstractions and idealisations shaped in the course of the historical development of cognition. The F. of thinking covers manifold methods whereby the social subject acts on the object on an ideal plane so as to reproduce the regularities and properties of objective reality in the C. of thinking (categories, q.v., movement from the abstract to the concrete, diverse kinds of inference, etc.). The sum-total of the Ff. of thinking arranges the cognitive C. according to a definite pattern and directs the subject's thinking in acquiring new knowledge. 3. In the arts C. and F. are mutually conditioned aspects of art as a whole, or of individual works of art, with C. playing the leading role. The C. of art is multiform reality in its aesthetic particularity, chiefly man, human relations, the life of society in all of its concrete manifestations. F. is the inner organisation, the concrete structure of a work of art, which is created through specific expressive means to reveal and embody the C. The main elements of C. of a work of art are its theme and idea. The theme reveals a range of the phenomena of life which are reflected and interpreted in this particular work. The idea expresses the essence of the phenomena and conflicts of reality reproduced, gives an artistic and emotional assessment of these from the point of view of the aesthetic ideal (q.v.), thereby inviting definite aesthetic, moral and political conclusions. The artistic F. of a work of art is multifaceted. Its main elements are the plot, composition, artistic language, material expressive means (word, rhyme, rhythm, sound intonation, harmony, colour, colouring, line, design, chiaroscuro, dimension, tectonics, pas, staging, mounting, etc.). As opposed to formalism (q.v.) which divorces C. from F., and naturalism (q.v.), which equates these, Marxist aesthetics considers the integral unity between C. and F. and conformity of C. to F. a basic criterion of artistic value.

Continuity, the objective and necessary connection between the old and the new in the process of development, one of the main features of the law of the negation of the negation (q.v.). As opposed to metaphysics, materialist dialectics turns to the investigation of the processes of progressive development in nature, society, and thought. The very genesis of the forms of the motion of matter shows that every higher form of motion, succeeding lower ones, does not annul them but includes them in and subordinates them to itself, raising them to a new qualitative level. A dialectical understanding of negation presupposes not only the liquidation of the old but also the conservation and further development of the progressive and rational in what was achieved in previous stages, without which the movement forward, whether in being or in knowledge, would be impossible. A correct understanding of the processes of C. is of particular significance in analysing the laws governing social development, progress of science and art, and in fighting both the uncritical attitude to the achievements of the past and the nihilist negation of cultural heritage.

Contradiction, a category expressing the inner source of all motion and development (qq.v.). C., understood only as external, cannot be such a source. It is the recognition of internal C., of the unity of the internal and the external C. that distinguishes dialectics from metaphysics (qq.v.). In other words, dialectics is distinguished from metaphysics not only by recognising C. in general but, precisely, by recognising C. in the very essence (q.v.) of objects, i.e., essential, internal and necessary Cc. Dialectical Cc. must be distinguished from the so-called logical Cc., which manifest confusion and inconsistency in thinking. Dialectical C., as a source of motion, is itself in the process of motion or development. The stages of development of C. in the essence of

objects include identity, difference, antithesis (qq.v.) and C., or C. proper. Hence, the category of C. characterises all the stages of the development of C. in the essence of objects and its highest stage. Identity is already an embryo of C., since the old, essentially identical to itself, contains the prerequisites of the new, i.e., elements that distinguish it from itself, though they are subordinate to the identity. Difference is also an undeveloped C., because the new has come into being within the old and continues to grow from it and in connection with it, despite the fact that the coexistence between the old and the new comes to the foreground. In antithesis, Cc. develop to a still greater extent, with negation of the old by the new predominating; here the new also emerges from the old and reveals its internal ties with the latter: the new asserts itself by negating the old. At the highest stage of C., or at the stage of the C. proper, the new completes the negation, transformation of the old and includes it, in a sublated, transformed shape, as its own element. Now the connection between, or the internal unity of, aspects, objects, etc., takes shape. At the stage of C. the main thing is not negation of one aspect of C. by another but the fact that during this process they engender one another as mutually distinctive. By negating one another the opposite aspects pass into one another, become identical, and this is a culminating stage of C. When an object reaches the highest stage of C., the prerequisites for its disappearance become ripe, for this stage of C. signifies the object's negation of itself within itself through its own development. According to Marx, dialectics includes "in its comprehension and affirmative recognition of the existing state of things, at the same time also, the recognition of the negation of that state, of its inevitable breaking up; because it regards every historically developed social form as in fluid movement, and therefore takes into account its transient nature not less than its momentary existence; because it lets nothing impose upon it, and is in its essence critical and revolutionary" (K. Marx, *Capital,* Vol. I, p. 20). Dialectical C. is universal, it exists in nature, in society, and in thinking, consciousness.

Contradiction, Law of, a law of logic, according to which two propositions negating (see Negation) each other cannot be simultaneously true. The first formulation of the L.C. was given by Aristotle (q.v.). This law may be formulated as follows: a proposition cannot be simultaneously false and true. Judgments or scientific theories become inconsistent when they contain formal contradictions. The L.C. is the reflection in thought of the qualitative definiteness of objects, of the simple fact that, if abstraction is made of a change in the object itself, it cannot simultaneously possess properties which exclude each other.

Contraposition, Law of, a law of logic according to which if proposition (q.v.) B follows from a proposition A, negation of proposition B follows from negation of proposition A.

Control, a function of organised biological, technological, and social systems ensuring the preservation of their structure and regimen and the realisation of their programme and purpose. Social C. is a conscious influence on society with the purpose of organising, preserving, improving and developing its specificity. It is determined by the systems nature of society, the social nature of labour, the need to communicate in the course of human activity, in the process of exchanging the material and cultural products of human activity. The main stages in the process of C. are: collection and processing of information; its analysis, diagnosis and prognosis, systematisation (synthesis), and target-setting; decision-making to attain the target; step-by-step concretisation of the general decision through planning, programming, projecting and working out concrete (partial) management decisions; organisation of activities for target realisation; supervision over these activities (including the selection and placement of personnel); collection and processing of information concerning the outcome of this activity, and a new cycle of this, ideally non-stop, process. In reality we observe two kinds of social C., spontaneous and conscious (planned). The former involves influencing society by the interplay of various social factors (market, traditions, habits, etc.), while the latter presupposes a special mechanism of C., functioning in accordance with a programme. The scientific, planned C. of social processes is typical of socialist society. It is based upon active knowledge of the laws of development and a target-oriented programme of action. Under socialism, social C. is based on the principle of democratic centralism and is gradually developing into communist public self-government (q.v.). Social C. comprises state administration, management of production, technological C., etc.

Conventionalism, philosophical conception according to which scientific concepts and theoretical constructions are basically products of agreements among scientists. These agreements stem from considerations of habitualness, convenience, simplicity, etc. Consistent C. leads to subjective idealism (q.v.), as it implies negation of the objective content of scientific theoretical knowledge. The theoretical principles of C. were elaborated by Poincaré (q.v.), who nevertheless tried to defend the objective value of scientific theories. Elements of C. are to be found in positivism, pragmatism, and operationalism (qq.v.). These present theoretical thought as something subjective and account for the scientists' using some systems of concepts and certain mathematical constructions by their desire to reach mutual understanding. This viewpoint is, however, refuted by historico-scientific research and epistemological analysis. The former demonstrates that theoretical devices used in science are historically conditioned, and the latter proves that these devices are merely a form in which the objective world is reflected and cannot therefore be simply a product of agreement.

Convergence, Theory of, a basic conception in modern bourgeois ideology, according to which economic, political and ideological differences between the capitalist and socialist world systems are gradually evening out and tend to disappear completely in the future. The founders of T.C. (J. Galbraith, P. Sorokin, J. Tinbergen, R. Aron, and others) claimed in various forms that socialist elements are gaining strength under modern capitalism and bourgeois elements in socialist countries, pointing in fact to a synthesis of the two world systems on a capitalist basis. In the 1950s and 1960s, C.T. was widely current in the West among various groups of intellectuals, from conservatives to progressives. From the late 1960s onwards, the theory became considerably less popular owing to the developments on the world scene, but it still plays a certain role in the ideological struggle even today. The theory of scientific communism (q.v.), which reveals the essence of today's processes of internationalisation of social life, provides a comprehensive criticism of T.C.

Copernicus, Nicolaus (1473-1543), Polish astronomer, founder of the heliocentric theory of the Universe. In the history of science C.'s theory was a revolutionary act signifying that research in the realm of nature would hence forth be independent of religion. His theory of the Earth's revolution round the Sun and its diurnal rotation upon its own axis meant a break with the geocentric theory originated by Ptolemy and the religious views founded thereon of the special favour bestowed upon the Earth by God. This theory further discarded the contraposition of the movements of heavenly bodies to those of earthly bodies, expounded by Aristotle (q.v.) and adopted by scholasticism (q.v.); undermined the church's story of the creation of the world by God; and prepared the ground for the later appearance of theories concerning the natural origin and development of the solar system. C.'s discoveries became the object of a violent struggle. Although they were condemned by the church, progressive thinkers of his age and later times proclaimed them their militant banner and developed them further, eliminating, e.g., such erroneous propositions in C.'s system as locating all stars in a single "sphere" and the Sun in the centre of the Universe. C.'s principal work *De Revolutionibus Orbium Coelestium* (1543) shows that C. was familiar with the achievements of ancient atomism and the hypotheses of ancient astronomers (see Heliocentricism and Geocentricism).

Corporate State, the most reactionary fascist type of bourgeois dictatorship developed after the First World War amid the general crisis of capitalism (q.v.) and characterised by: dissolution of workers' organisations and enforced grouping of the population in corporations (e.g., capitalists', workers', and office employees' corporations); dissolution of the elective body, i.e., parliament, and substitution of "corporate representation" for it. This results in the workers' deprivation of all civil rights and in their exploitation by the monopolies with the aid of the corporations. Fascist Italy and Portugal were declared C.Ss. The principal purpose of the C.S. is to disguise the dictatorship of monopoly capital and to give the fascist state the appearance of a "class partnership" and "harmony of interests" within the corporate framework.

Corpuscular-Wave Dualism, a specific property of microobjects described by quantum mechanics (q.v.) and expressed in the presence of opposite corpuscular and wave properties in these objects. C.W.D. was first formulated exactly in De Broglie (q.v.) equations, which described the "waves of matter". C.W.D. expresses the relationship of the macrocosm and microcosm (q.v.) and their specific unity. In interpreting C.W.D. and revealing the mechanism of the relation between these opposite properties quantum mechanics faced great difficulties that have not been fully surmounted up to this day. The mechanistic view separated the opposite corpuscular and wave properties, regarding them as characteristic of different objects. The dialectical approach, on the other hand, stresses the objectivity of corpuscular-wave properties which are inherent in microobjects, but expressed differently, depending on different experimental conditions; it stresses the need to cognise these opposite properties in their unity and interconnection. This interpretation of C.W.D. was developed by Langevin (q.v.), V. A. Fok, S. Vavilov (q.v.), and other scientists.

Correctness and Truth, categories of logic and the theory of knowledge: C. (logical) is a quality of logical operations (see Inference; Proof; Definition; Classification) independent of the concrete content of cognitive acts where they are used, particularly of the concrete content of statements and concepts—objects of these operations. Conditions of the C. of operations (formulated usually as certain rules) are determined by their purposes and the laws of logic. T. is a quality characterising the content of the results of cognition (statements, theories, etc.) and means their conformity to cognisable reality (see Truth). However, the concept of C. also characterises the relation of thought to the objective world, for the forms of logical operations, based on the laws of logic, reflect the more general features and relations of the objective world. These concepts are closely interrelated in the process of cognition. C. is a necessary condition of attaining the set goal, which called for the use of a certain logical operation, and in the final analysis a *sine qua non* of true results of cognition. Idealist logic and philosophy (particularly Kantianism, logical positivism, q.v., etc.), denying the objective origin of the forms and laws of logic, incorrectly interpret the C., seeing its basis to be laid in the mind itself or in the consensus of people regarding the use of certain linguistic forms (see Conventionalism).

Correspondence of Production Relations to the Character and Level of Development of Productive Forces, Law of, an objective economic law which determines the interaction of the productive forces and relations of production (qq.v.) in all socio-economic formations (q.v.). The productive forces are the determining, the most revolutionary and mobile element of production, while relations of production are a more stable element. That is why at a certain stage in society's development a contradiction arises between the relations of production and the character (quality aspect) and the level of development (quantity aspect) of the productive forces. The former begin to hinder the development of the latter and bring about its destruction. The need for developing productive forces sooner or later leads to the removal of the lag of relations of production behind the productive forces and brings them into correspondence with the character and level of development of the

latter. Both correspondence and non-correspondence of the production relations to the character and level of the productive forces is never, nor can there be, absolute, for otherwise their interaction would be impossible. The law of correspondence means that production relations conform to the character and level of the productive forces. But this unity includes elements of non-correspondence, which are augmenting to prevail over the elements of correspondence as the productive forces develop; a contradiction ensues, which is resolved through eliminating the old and establishing new production relations corresponding to the developing productive forces. In a society divided into antagonistic classes, the contradiction between the old relations of production and the developed productive forces always culminates in a conflict which is resolved through a social revolution (see Revolution, Social). Under socialism, the social ownership of the means of production affords the full scope for the accelerated development of productive forces. In socialist society contradictions sometimes arising between the productive forces and the relations of production do not reach the point of conflict, since there are no classes interested in preserving the obsolete production relations. That is why it is possible to notice in time the growing contradictions and take steps to eliminate them by improving the production relations. The law of correspondence of production relations to the character and level of development of the productive forces determines the replacement of one socio-economic formation by another.

Correspondence Principle, one of the basic methodological principles governing the development of science. Philosophically, it expresses the dialectic of cognition, the movement from relative to absolute truth, ever more complete truth. This principle was formulated by Bohr (q.v.) in 1913, at a time when the basic precepts of classical physics were breaking down. According to the C.P., the succession of one natural science theory by another reveals, not only a difference between them, but also a continuity which can be expressed with mathematical precision. In replacing the old theory, the new one does not merely deny the former but retains it in a certain form. This allows of reverse transitions from the later theory to the preceding one, or their coincidence in a certain extreme sphere where the differences between them became insignificant. The operation of the C.P. may be traced in the history of mathematics, physics and other sciences. The natural concatenation of old and new theories follows from the inner unity of the qualitatively different levels of matter. This unity not only determines the integrity of science but also demonstrates the untenability of relativism (q.v.).

Cosmic Teleology, Ethics of, a trend in bourgeois moral philosophy current in the first half of the 20th century in the USA and Britain; it contains elements of ethical naturalism (q.v.) and objective idealism. According to E.C.T., morality can only be understood from the viewpoint of the evolutionary development of the Universe, supposedly based on some world purpose. Each stage in that development is preordained and is effected by adapting the existing means to that purpose. Adherents of E.C.T. hold that man is part of nature and the cosmos and that his moral purpose is to continue to create nature. Thus, E.C.T. attributes to man's moral activity an extra-social, cosmic and biological meaning. The conception of morality as man's serving some preordained purpose brings E.C.T. close to the religious ethics of "natural law" (see Neo-Thomism).

Cosmogony, a branch of astronomy (q.v.), treating of the origin and development of heavenly bodies and their systems. Conventionally it may be divided into planetary C. and astral C., though they are mutually interrelated. The findings of C. are based on data furnished by other branches of astronomy, by physics, geology and other branches of science dealing with the Earth. Like cosmology (q.v.), C. is closely related to philosophy and has been the venue of a violent struggle between materialism and idealism, between science and religion. The difficulties of cosmogonic problems stem from the fact that the processes of development of the heavenly

bodies have been going on for thousands of millions of years, by comparison with which astronomical observations and even the entire history of astronomy embrace infinitesimal periods of time. The difficulties of planetary C. are further enhanced by the fact that we have thus far been able to observe directly but one planetary system. Scientific C. dates back some 200 years, when Kant (q.v.) advanced the hypothesis of the development of the planets from nebulae which at one time surrounded the Sun. The hypotheses of Kant (1755) and Laplace, q.v. (1796) (see Nebular Hypothesis) failed to explain certain significant structural peculiarities of the solar system. Factual data are now being consistently accumulated and generalised, but no solution of the problem has as yet been found. A very substantial contribution to planetary C. has been made by Soviet scientists (O. Yu. Schmidt, V. G. Fesenkov, and others). The nature and interior structure of stars were established only in the 20th century. The nature of stellar evolution is now known in its essentials, but all hypotheses of the origin of stars still remain debatable. The C. of the metagalaxy (q.v.) is usually dealt with in cosmology.

Cosmology, a branch of astronomy (q.v.), a science which views the Universe (q.v.) as an integral whole, and the part of the Universe which is under astronomical observation as a part of that whole. The first naive cosmological ideas appeared in antiquity as a result of man's efforts to discover his place in the Universe. Accumulated observation data and the certainty, suggested by ancient philosophy, that behind the apparently confused movement of the planets there must be a real law-governed pattern, led to the geocentric conception of the Universe, which was superseded, as a result of a violent struggle against the church and scholasticism, by the conception of a heliocentric system (see Heliocentricism and Geocentricism). Following the discovery of the law of universal gravitation by Newton (q.v.), the cosmological problem could be treated as the physical problem of an infinite system of gravitating masses.

This, it was discovered, gave rise to serious difficulties known as cosmological paradoxes resulting from extending to the Universe as a whole the physical laws established for a finite part of it. These difficulties are resolved by modern cosmological theory based on the theory of relativity (q.v.). At present the models constructed by the Soviet physicist A. A. Friedman in the 1920s on the basis of the general theory of relativity are almost universally recognised in science. The real value of modern cosmological models lies in the fact that they give an idea of the general laws that govern the structure and development of the metagalaxy (q.v.) and thus constitute a necessary stage in the process of getting to know the endless material world.

Cosmopolitanism, a bourgeois theory calling for a repudiation of patriotic sentiments and national culture and traditions in the name of the "unity of mankind". In the form professed by modern bourgeois ideologists C. reflects the ambition of imperialists to achieve world supremacy. The propaganda of C. (the idea of a world government, etc.) impedes the peoples' struggle for national independence and national sovereignty. C. is incompatible with internationalism (q.v.).

Cosmos, the Universe as a whole, matter in motion in its entirety, including the Earth, the solar system, our galaxy (q.v.), and all other galaxies. Since the development of cosmonautics, C. is usually understood to mean the small part of the Universe adjacent to but not comprising the Earth.

Counter-culture, a form of spiritual protest against modern bourgeois culture (q.v.) by young people in the West in the 1960s and 1970s. It signifies outright rejection of the social values, moral norms and ideals of consumer society, of the standards and stereotypes of mass culture, the way of life (qq.v.) based on the desire for respectability, social prestige and material well-being. C. may be regarded as an attempt to create a culture opposed to the spiritual atmosphere in modern bourgeois society. However,

being a particular form of escape from social reality, it is at the same time endemic in the existing bourgeois system, and is a usual consumer product of "mass society" and of commercial enterprise with all its inherent utilitarian values, which C. so "resolutely opposes". Symptomatically, many leaders and adepts of C. have subsequently abandoned their ideals.

Cousin, Victor (1792-1867), French idealist philosopher, eclectic. C. maintained that any system of philosophy could be formed on the basis of the "truths" contained in various doctrines. C.'s philosophy is an eclectic combination of such "truths" drawn from the idealistic system of Hegel (q.v.), Schelling's (q.v.) "philosophy of revelation", the monadology of Leibniz (q.v.), and other idealistic doctrines. Being an opponent of materialism, C. shared the view that God was the creator of the Universe, believed in the existence of after-life, and urged a reconciliation of philosophy and religion. C.'s theories influenced the subsequent development of idealistic philosophy in France. His most important work is the *Cours d'histoire de la philosophie* (1815-29) in eight volumes.

Creationism, an idealist doctrine holding that the world and nature, animate and inanimate, were brought into being by a single act of creation. The view of Linnaeus and Cuvier (qq.v.) concerning the supernatural origin of all species of animal and plant life is a modified version of C. in biology. Science furnishes proof of the complete unsoundness of C.

Creative Work, the process of human activity in which new material and spiritual values are created. C.W. is a human ability, which appeared in the process of labour, to create (from the material supplied by nature and on the strength of the knowledge of the laws of the objective world) new reality that satisfies the multiform requirements of society. All types of C.W. are determined by the nature of creative activity: the C.W. of an inventor, organiser, scientist or artist, etc. Idealists regard artistic C.W. as divine obsession (Plato, q.v.), as synthesis of the conscious and the subconscious (Schelling, q.v.), as a mystic intuition (Bergson, q.v.), and as a manifestation of instincts (S. Freud). According to Marxist-Leninist theory, C.W. is a process in which all the spiritual powers of man take part, including imagination (q.v.), and also the skill which is acquired by training and practice and required to realise a creative design. The possibilities for creative work depend on social relations. Communism puts an end to alienation of work and human abilities, which exists in a society based on private property, and creates conditions for the development of all types of C.W. and the creative abilities of every individual.

Criterion of Truth, any means of judging an assertion, hypothesis, theoretical proposition, etc., as to its truth or falsity. Social practice (see Theory and Practice) is the C.T. Definitive verification scientific theories undergo in practice, i.e., in material production, in the revolutionary activities of the masses aimed at reorganising society. Successful application of a given theory in practice is proof of its correctness. Methods of verifying ideas by practice may vary. Thus, in the field of natural science a proposition may be verified by experiment (q.v.) involving observation, measurement (qq.v.), and mathematical treatment of the results obtained. Verification of scientific theories in practice does not, nevertheless, make them absolute truths: they continue to develop and become enriched, gaining in scope and exactitude, some of their propositions are dropped in favour of new ones (see Truth, Absolute and Relative). This is due to the fact that social practice undergoes a process of continuous development, and therefore the methods of comparing scientific theories with reality through practice are constantly perfected. Only the developing practice of society is capable of fully confirming or completely refuting the ideas produced by man. Practice as a C.T. was first included in the theory of knowledge by Marxism. Modern bourgeois philosophy either denies practice as a C.T., or else provides a distorted interpretation of it (see Pragmatism).

Critical Rationalism, a trend in modern European and American philosophy whose main principles were formulated by Popper, q.v. (he also coined the term C.R.). C.R. is not a clearly defined philosophical doctrine and is often designated by other terms, such as critical empiricism, criticism, or falsificationism. Some of its adherents (e.g., P. Feyerabend) passed from active support to sharp criticism of it, while others (e.g., I. Lakatos), though adhering to its principles, want to be formally outside it. C.R. claims to have evolved the principles of the rational explanation of knowledge, human actions, social ideas and institutions, etc., by criticising and perfecting them. In social philosophy C.R. is a variety of bourgeois reformism (q.v.). C.R. strives to oppose its main principles to the traditional philosophical positions: unlike scepticism and dogmatism it advances the principle of fallibility, i.e., recognises the basic hypotheticalness of any scientific knowledge; unlike the urge to justify and substantiate the formal truth of scientific knowledge, it formulates the idea of methodological rationalism, i.e., the possibility to define, on the basis of critical analysis, to what extent some hypotheses are preferable to others; and finally, unlike instrumentalism, C.R. asserts that scientific knowledge can describe reality. C.R. reflects the realisation by some modern bourgeois philosophers that the formal structural approach to science is inadequate. Stressing the integrality of scientific knowledge, the interdependence between the levels of observation and theory, and organic penetration of science into culture, its permeation by philosophical and axiological principles, representatives of C.R. try to build interdisciplinary models of scientific knowledge, regarding it as a continuous critical dialogue between various types of scientific theories, between science and non-science. At the same time C.R., being a form of post-positivist philosophy, cannot emerge from the framework of bourgeois philosophical consciousness. The basic principles of C.R. led its representatives to give up defining objective truth and its criteria and to recognise pluralism and relativism (qq.v.). This means that C.R. has failed to work out criteria for distinguishing the rational and the irrational, the scientific and the unscientific.

Critical Realism (in philosophy), 1) a school in US bourgeois philosophy of the 1920s and 1930s. (A. Lovejoy, Santayana, q.v., R. Sellars and others). It originated by way of a reaction to neo-realism (q.v.). The neo-realist thesis of the direct "interjection" of the object in consciousness has been countered by the critical realists with their theory of the structure of the act of cognition, which comprises three elements: subject, object and "datum", or "essence". This "essence" is alleged to be the content of our consciousness. The "essences", according to C.R., unlike the object, are conveyed to us with direct certitude. C.R. attempts to present these "essences" as something objectively existing, like the universals (q.v.) of medieval realism. The "essence" possesses a reality of its own, different from physical reality; it cannot be measured by a spatio-temporal criterion. "Essences", according to C.R., are by no means images or copies of things. Like neo-realism, C.R. opposes the materialist theory of reflection (q.v.). C.R. recognises the existence of reality, this recognition being founded on instinct and "animal faith" (Santayana) in reality. The epistemological source of this alleged "realism" lies in its false interpretation of the difference between the material and ideal, the objective and subjective, and in metaphysically regarding consciousness as opposed to the objective world. 2) The name "C.R." is also given to a school which formed towards the end of the 19th century in Germany (E. Becher, H. Driesch, A. Wenzl, and others). This school gives a theological interpretation to modern natural science, striving to reconcile knowledge with faith and to prove the "unsoundness" and "limitations" of science.

Criticism and Self-Criticism, a method of discovering and correcting errors and removing shortcomings widely used in the social life of the socialist countries and in the activities of the Marxist parties and other workers' organisations. Marx pointed out that the proletarian revolution engages in self-criticism in the interests of its own development, this being its peculiar characteristic. With the victory of the socialist revolution C.&S. become one of the mainsprings of social development.

C.&S. are a special method of revealing and resolving the non-antagonistic contradictions of socialism. Self-criticism is a most important principle in the work of the Communist Party of the Soviet Union. The creative role of C.&S. is seen with particular clarity in socialist emulation, which is a form of the people's active participation in building communism. C.&S. afford the people full scope for initiative in building the material and technical base of communism, serve to draw the masses into social management, aid in educating men and women worthy of communist society, and help overcome everything conservative, backward, hindering the progressive development of society.

Critique of the Gotha Programme, written by Marx in 1875, published in 1891, is a critical analysis of the draft programme of the German Social-Democratic Party. Marx called this programme the capitulation of the German Social-Democrats before the ideas of Lassalle (q.v.). Marx vigorously criticised the Lassallean assertion that in respect of the working class all the other classes are but "one reactionary mass", and demonstrated that this assertion denies the alliance of the proletariat and the peasantry. Marx further showed the reactionary nature of the Lassallean "iron law of wages", according to which the proletariat was condemned to perpetual poverty. The *C.G.P.* revealed the main problems of scientific communism (q.v.). Marx developed the tenet of the inevitability of the socialist revolution and the establishment of the dictatorship of the proletariat, and presented a scientific analysis of the communist society of the future. The *C.G.P.* was the first to advance the tenet of the necessity of a transition period in the process of the replacement of capitalism by communism and of a revolutionary dictatorship of the proletariat as the essence of state in that period. No less substantial a contribution to scientific communism was Marx's definition of socialism and communism (q.v.) as two phases of the communist socio-economic formation, as two stages in the economic maturity of communism. Marx stated that only at the higher phase of communism would society be free from the "birth-marks" of capitalism; an end would be put to man's subjection to the enslaving system of division of labour (q.v.); work would be transformed from a means of livelihood into a prime necessity of life; productive forces would reach so high a level of development that there would be an abundance of products and society would be able to proclaim the principle "From each according to his ability, to each according to his needs".

Croce, Benedetto (1866-1952). Italian bourgeois philosopher of the neo-Hegelian school. Towards the end of the 19th century C. came out with a criticism of the philosophical and economic theories of Marxism. C.'s philosophy is that of abso-lute idealism. His aesthetic ideas exercised a strong influence on the bourgeois theory of art. He contrasted art as intuitive cognition of the singular, embodied in sense images, with logical reasoning as a rational process of knowing the general. C.'s ethical doctrine strove to cover up the social roots and class character of morality. C.'s ethics propounded the principle of subordinating the individual to the "universal", that is, to the dominant exploiter system. C. was a prominent ideologist, a political leader of the Italian liberal bourgeoisie, and an opponent of fascism. His most important work is *Filosofia dello spirito* (1902-17).

Cult of the Individual, unquestioning deference to the authority of a statesman or public figure, an exaggerated evalua-tion of his actual merits, fetishistic rever-ence of the name of a historical personage. C.I. is theoretically based on an idealistic and voluntaristic interpretation of history, according to which the course of history is determined by the desires and will of great men (soldiers, heroes, outstanding ideolog-ists, etc.), rather than by objective laws or the activity of the masses. The role of outstanding personalities in history is ele-vated to an absolute by the various schools of idealistic philosophy (see Voluntarism; Young Hegelians; Narodism). By its nature C.I. is alien to Marxism, which views the role of the individual, the leader, as closely linked with the objective course of class

struggle, the history-making activity of the masses. The experience of no matter how great a leader cannot be substituted for the collective experience of millions. Marxism-Leninism censures any C.I. and superstiti-ous worship of authority. Success in the struggle against the C.I. within socialist society and in the Communist parties is guaranteed by the fullest possible develop-ment of democracy and the observance of the Leninist principles of government and party activities. The struggle of the CPSU against the C.I. found its expression, in particular, in the resolute condemnation of the cult of Stalin and in the overcoming of its consequences.

Cultural Cycles, Theory of, a doctrine holding recurrence to be inevitable in the process of historical and cultural develop-ment, evolved out of the crisis of the historico-comparative method (q.v.). At the turn of the century the problem of establishing criteria for comparative analysis required urgent solution. It was becoming increasingly clear that historical comparisons and analogies were generally concerned merely with the pattern of historical processes rather than their con-tent. The T.C.C. offered an artificial way of overcoming these difficulties. The ex-ponents of this theory (Spengler, Toyn-bee, qq.v.) maintained that historical analogies do not require rationalisation, being self-evident. The recurrence, syn-chronism, and cyclic nature of historico-cultural processes were regarded as the sole evidence of the existence of universal historical laws. The social bias of this theory is revealed in the teaching of Spengler, who urged that historical action be based on conscious imitation of the past. What this philosophy means in practice was seen in the ideology of fascism, which adopted the basic principles of Spengler's "historicism".

Cultural-Historical Approach, a form of idealistic substantiation of the inner unity and integrity of the historical process. It was suggested towards the close of the 19th century by K. Lamprecht (1856-1915), a German historian of liberal views. He challenged the individualisation method prevalent in bourgeois historiography, i.e., the reduction of history to a description of the lives of outstanding personalities (L. Ranke and his school). According to Lamprecht, the concept of culture (q.v.) facilitates a synthesis of the various aspects of social life. Culture is seen as a spontaneous consciousness expressed in a people's mode of existence, daily life and collectivity. C.H.A. is a half-hearted attempt to overcome the crisis of bourgeois historicism by a purely eclectic combination of individual aspects of social life in the concept of culture and by recognition of material and economic relationships as merely one of the factors of spiritual evolution. Nevertheless, its insistence on regarding history as a science about the laws of social development was a distinct merit of the C.H.A. as compared with the other methods of bourgeois historiography. In contemporary Western literature on the philosophy of history the C.H.A. has been ousted by outright subjectivist theories.

Cultural Revolution, radical changes in the spiritual life of society taking place during the building of socialism and communism. C.R. is possible only on the basis of political and economic transformations in the process of the socialist revolution (q.v.), which provides all the necessary prerequisites for it, and primarily as a result of the take-over of power by the people and the transfer of all material and spiritual values into their hands. In the period of transition from capitalism to socialism the C.R. has the following main tasks: to reconstruct the system of education within a reasonably short time and to make the best achievements of culture available to the masses, thereby assuring their direct participation in managing economic, social, and political affairs, creating a socialist intelligentsia, and forming a new, socialist culture. These tasks hold good for all countries building socialism whatever may be their specific features. The C.R. in the USSR where most of the population were illiterate made possible a tremendous leap from illiteracy and ignorance towards the summits of culture. The task of mature socialist society is to create the spiritual prerequisites for the victory of communism, a truly rich spiritual culture, and

possibilities for all-round development of the individual. Upon the solution of this task largely depends the growth of the productive forces; the progress of technology and organisation of production; the increased public activity of the masses; the development of the democratic principles of self-government and the reorganisation of daily life.

Culture, all the material and spiritual values (q.v.) created or being created by society in the course of history and characterising the historical stage attained by society in its development. More specifically, it is customary to distinguish material C. (i.e., production experience, machinery and other material wealth), and non-material, spiritual C. (i.e., achievements in the realm of science, art, literature, philosophy, ethics, education, etc.). C. is a historical phenomenon, and its development is determined by the succession of socio-economic formations. Unlike idealistic theories, which sever spiritual C. from the material basis and consider it to be the spiritual product of the "elite", Marxism-Leninism sees production of material goods as the basis and source of spiritual C. Hence, C. is directly or indirectly the product of the activities of the masses. Although basically determined by material circumstances, spiritual C. does not automatically follow changes in its material basis, being characterised by relative independence (continuity of development, reciprocal influence by the cultures of various peoples, etc.). In any class society C. assumes a class character both as to its ideological content and its practical aims. Under capitalism, every national C. is split into two cultures, comprising the dominant C. of the bourgeoisie and the more or less developed elements of democratic and socialist C. of the working masses. Socialist C., assimilating as it does all the progressive achievements of the past, differs radically from modern bourgeois C. as regards both ideology and social function, reflecting the superiority of the socialist system over the capitalist. Socialist C. cannot be created without a socialist revolution, which provides all the necessary conditions for a cultural revolution (q.v.). Characteristic of socialist C. are: its kinship with the people, communist ideology and partisanship, scientific world outlook, socialist humanism, collectivism, socialist patriotism, and internationalism. The leading role in the creation and development of socialist C. belongs to the Communist party, which influences the entire cultural and educational activity of the socialist state. Under socialism, C. is national in form and socialist in content, internationalist in character; interchange of material and spiritual values among nations becomes increasingly intensive; the cultural treasure-house of each nation is increasingly enriched with values of an international character. This facilitates the shaping of the C. common to all humanity, the communist society of the future.

Cusa, Nicholas of (1401-1464) (his real name was Nicholas Crebs or Chrypffs; his name derives from his birthplace—Cusa on the Mosel), a German philosopher, scientist, and theologian of the transitional period from scholasticism (q.v.) to humanism and a new science in early capitalist society. Under the influence of Neoplatonism (q.v.) he refashioned the concepts of Christian philosophy in the teaching of God, who was supposed to stand above the opposites. All opposites coincide in God: finite and infinite, the smallest and the greatest, single and multiple, etc. Despite its mystic idealist content, the theory of N.C. on the concordance of opposites in God *(coincidentia oppositorum)* contains a number of fruitful ideas. These are criticism of the limitations of rational opposites; anticipation of the subsequent concept of infinitesimals; formulation of the question concerning the limits of applying the law of contradiction in mathematics, etc. His main work: *De docta ignorantia*, 1440.

Custom, repeated, conventional mode of people's behaviour in certain situations. C. includes generally accepted methods of work, interrelationships between people in everyday life and within the family, diplomatic and religious rituals and other actions reflecting the specific features of the life of a tribe, a class, a people. Morality (q.v.) of society is also

manifested in customs. Customs take shape in the course of history. Their origin and character are influenced by the features of a nation, its economy, the natural climatic conditions, the social position of individuals, religious views, and so on. Customs have the force of a social habit and influence the behaviour of people. That is why they can be morally evaluated. Some customs are closely connected with the interests of earlier classes and can therefore be considered survivals of the past (q.v.).

Cuvier, Georges (1769-1832), French naturalist, founder of comparative anatomy and palaeontology. Through studies of fossil organisms he came to the conclusion that their structure gradually improved if seen during the transition from ancient strata to new ones. However, as a supporter of creationism (q.v.), he explained qualitative differences in the geological strata by the "catastrophe theory", according to which the history of the Earth had witnessed upheavals which destroyed entire faunae and florae and gave rise to new ones of higher organisation. Though C. promoted the working out of the evolution theory (q.v.), he resolutely opposed the views of the early evolutionists—Lamarck and Geoffroy Saint-Hilaire (q.v.), who did not have the requisite data to substantiate the idea of the evolution of organisms.

Cybernetics, the science of the common features of processes and control systems in technological devices, living organisms and human organisations. The principles of C. were first set forth by Wiener (q.v.). The emergence of C. as a science was prepared by a number of technological and scientific achievements in the theory of automatic control; radioelectronics, which made possible the construction of fast-action scanning and programme-controlled computing machines; the theory of probability (q.v.), notably its applications in investigating problems of transmission and processing of information (q.v.); mathematical logic (q.v.) and the theory of algorithms (see Algorithm); the physiology of nervous activity and homeostasis (q.v.). As distinct from devices that transform energy or substance, cybernetic systems engage in processing information. In the study of control systems C. combines the macroscopic with the microscopic approach. The macroscopic approach is employed when the internal structure of a system is not known. It helps establish the main flows of information and the ultimate functions of the control system. This type of problems is known as the "black box" (q.v.) problem. The microscopic approach assumes a certain knowledge about the internal structure of the control system and involves the determination of its basic elements in their interrelationship, their algorithms of work and the possibility of synthesizing a control system out of these elements. One of the central problems of C. is that of the structure of self-organising (self-adjusting) systems. These are complex systems capable of maintaining or attaining certain states against external factors tending to disturb or hinder those states. The most perfect self-organising systems have developed as a result of evolutionary processes in animate nature. That is why C. makes use of analogies between control functions in living organisms and technological devices. The importance of C. is seen primarily from the opportunities it opens up for automation of production and all types of formalised human mental activity, the investigation of biological control and regulation systems (hormonal, neural, hereditary mechanisms) by the method of modelling (q.v.), and the development of new types of medical apparatus. Another promising field is the application of cybernetic methods to economic studies and other spheres of organised human activity. This great diversity of applications of cybernetic methods is not due to any subjective whims and wills; its objective foundation is the existence of certain common features in the functions and structures of living organisms and man-made devices susceptible of mathematical description and investigation. Being in this respect a synthetic discipline,

C. offers a striking example of a new type of interaction of sciences and provides abundant material for the philosophical investigation of the forms of motion of matter, the theory of reflection and the classification of sciences (qq.v.). The development of C. sparked off discussion of a number of methodological problems, viz., the analogies between human thinking and the working of cybernetic mechanisms, the essence of what is called organised, purposeful, and living, and other problems of an indubitably philosophical nature around which a struggle between dialectical materialism and idealism has developed. Thus, idealist philosophy, which rejects the possibility of objectively investigating psychic activity, denies the findings of C. which contribute to an understanding of certain important aspects and mechanisms of such activity. While recognising the objective soundness of cybernetic analogies, dialectical materialism at the same time emphasises that it is erroneous to identify man with the machine and human intelligence with the functioning of cybernetic systems.

Cynics, a school of Greek (Socratic) philosophy (4th century B.C.), followers of Antisthenes (q.v.). Diogenes (q.v.) of Sinope was the most prominent C. The C. voiced the views of the democratic sections of slave-owning society. They considered contempt for social standards, renunciation of wealth, glory, and all sensuous pleasures the foundation of happiness and virtue.

Cyrenaics, a school of Greek (Socratic) philosophy (North Africa, 5th century B.C.), founded by Aristippus (q.v.) of Cyrene. It preached hedonism (q.v.), according to which pleasure is the highest good. C. expounded the ideology of the slave-owning aristocracy.

d

Dalton, John (1766-1844), English chemist and physicist. His discoveries helped to convert atomism (q.v.) from a natural philosophical conjecture into a scientific theory and promoted the materialist approach in natural science. Engels described D. as the father of chemistry.

Darwin, Charles Robert (1809-1882), English natural scientist, founder of evolution theory (q.v.). He generalised contemporary biological knowledge and farming practices, augmented them with copious factual material obtained on his round-the-world voyage (1831-36), and deduced the evolution of living nature by means of natural selection. In *The Origin of Species by Means of Natural Selection, or the Preservation of Favoured Races in the Struggle for Life* (1859) he set forth the basic propositions of his theory. In 1868 D. explained the origin of domestic animals and plants by artificial selection in *The Variation of Animals and Plants Under Domestication*. In *The Descent of Man and Selection in Relation to Sex* (1871) he offered a scientific exposition of the origination of man from animal ancestors. However, D. failed to reveal the social causes which set man apart from the animal world, these being labour and social consciousness. D.'s teaching won recognition after a long and bitter fight with the enemies of the theory of evolution, with clericals and idealists. D.'s theory ranks among the outstanding natural science achievements of the 19th century, which contributed greatly to the emergence of dialectical materialism. D.'s theory retains its general methodological and philosophical relevance, and is now being developed and modified on the basis of factual and theoretical data supplied by genetics (q.v.), biocybernetics, and other sciences.

David the Philosopher (Dawith Anjalth) (the Unconquerable) (end of the 5th-first half of the 6th century), Armenian philosopher, representative of neoplatonism. While developing the legacy of the philosophy of antiquity, q.v. (Plato, Aristotle, qq.v., Neoplatonist Porphyrios, c. 233-304 and others), D.A. created his own system of logic, expressed some valuable ideas in the sphere of astronomy and mathematics, and opposed scepticism and relativism (qq.v.). D.A. regarded successively philosophy as a science of being, as a science of divine and human things, as an art of the arts, as a science of sciences, and as love of wisdom. According to him, its aim was to release the soul from the "dungeon" of the body, and to achieve intellectual perfection. His main works: *Definitions of Philosophy* and *Analysis of Porphyrios' "Introduction"*.

Davydov, Ivan Ivanovich (1794-1863), Russian idealist philosopher and linguist, professor of Moscow University (1822-47). At first he eclectically combined different philosophical ideas, such as sensationalism (q.v.) and Schellingian idealism, as set out in his *Nachalniye osnovaniya logiki* (Rudimentary Basis of Logic), 1819-20. His *Vstupitelnaya rech o vozmozhnosti filosofii kak nauki* (Introductory Speech on the Possibility of Philosophy as a Science), 1826, also espoused Schellingian idealism. In his article "Could Russia Accept German Philosophy?", 1841, D. attacked Hegel from a Rightist's position and expounded the Slavophile (see Slavophiles) notion of the national distinctiveness of Russian philosophy.

Decembrists, Russian revolutionaries, mostly aristocrats, who organised an uprising against tsarist autocracy and serfdom in December 1825. The D. and Herzen (q.v.) were the most outstanding leaders of Russia's liberation movement at its aristocratic stage. The movement of the D. was prompted by the discontent of the people, who opposed serfdom. The D. intended to destroy tsarist autocracy, abolish oppression and serfdom, and establish democratic freedoms. But owing to their aristocratic limitations they feared a popular revolution. Their tactics were hesitant during the uprising. Many among the D. (P. Pestel, K. Ryleyev) were for a republic; others (N. Turgenev, G. Batenkov) for a constitutional monarchy, which found expression in N. Muravyov's *Draft Constitution.* Lenin noted the republican tradition which the D. introduced in progressive Russian social thought. The projects and ideas of the D. testified to the bourgeois orientation of their movement. They defined the purpose of philosophy as "finding the truth", enlightening the mind, purifying it of prejudice, and animating love of country and humanity. The D. were influenced by the materialism of Lomonosov and Radishchev (qq.v.), and the ideas of the French materialist philosophers. The D. opposed the ideology of serfdom, religion, mysticism, and idealism. The materialists among the D. were I. Yakushkin, N. Kryukov, P. Borisov, I. Gorbachevsky, V. Rayevsky, and others. Their materialism was based on natural science. The materialists attacked Descartes' dualism (q.v.) and the idealist German philosophers, and opposed the idealists in their own ranks (Y. Obolensky, V. Kyukhelbeker, and others). The materialist outlook and knowledge of natural science prompted some D. to adopt atheism. The D. considered religion to be rooted in the yearning of the oppressed to mitigate their misery and their hope of a better life in the other world. Although the philosophy of the D. was progressive for its time, it was contemplative and tainted with metaphysics. D. approached social matters from an idealistic standpoint and attributed prime importance in the life of society to education. Many D. sided with the theories of natural law (q.v.) and social contract (q.v.). Their movement strongly influenced the succeeding generation of Russian revolutionaries, the revolutionary democrats.

Decidability, Problem of, one of the main problems arising in connection with the construction of formalised deductive theories. Positive or negative decision for each specific formalised theory depends on the existence or absence of some general method (or algorithm, q.v.) whereby through a finite number of operations,

it is possible to find out whether the arbitrary formula of the theory in question is provable (true) in a given system. P.D. is positively decided, for instance, in propositional calculus (q.v.) and formalised Aristotelian syllogistic (q.v.). However, there is no general decision of the problem in the case of predicate calculus (q.v.). The impossibility of finding a general method of decision for any formalised theory does not rule out a search of such decisions for separate classes of formulae of this theory.

Deduction, a method of inference (q.v.) and research. Broadly, D. denotes any conclusion in general, in a more specific and generally accepted sense—authentic proof or inferring a conclusion (effect) from one or several earlier premises on the basis of the laws of logic. In a deduced conclusion the effects are concealed in the premises and have to be inferred by methods of logical analysis. The modern concept of D. is a far-reaching generalisation of the Aristotelian interpretation of D. as a conclusion drawn from the general to the particular, and thus demonstrates its one-sidedness.

Deductive Method, a method of scientific inference based exclusively on deductive techniques (see Deduction). Attempts have been made in philosophy to draw a line of distinction between the D.M. and other methods (such as the inductive) and to define deductive reasoning as excluding experience and laying excessive stress on deduction in science. In fact, deduction and induction (q.v.) are interconnected, and deductive reasoning is determined by many centuries of man's practical and cognitive effort. D.M. is one of the valid methods of scientific inference, used, as a rule, to systematise empirical data after they have been accumulated and theoretically interpreted, in order to infer all pertinent effects more strictly and consistently. This also yields new knowledge—in the form of a great number of the effects of deductive theory and as an aggregate of possible interpretations of a deductively formulated theory. The general scheme of the deductive systems (theories) includes: (1) basic premises, that is, the aggregate of basic terms and propositions; (2) the devices of logic (rules of deduction and definition) used; (3) an aggregate of propositions obtained from (1) by applying (2). Examination of such theories involves an analysis of the interrelation of their specific components abstracted from the genesis and development of knowledge. Deductive systems are divided into axiomatic (see Axiomatic Method) and constructive (see Constructive Method). When applied to knowledge based on experience and experiment, D.M. is more precisely termed as a hypothetico-deductive method (q.v.). Analysis of the D.M. of inferring scientific knowledge began in antique philosophy by Plato, Aristotle, Euclid, stoics (qq.v.), and was dealt with at length subsequently by Descartes, Pascal, Spinoza, Leibniz (qq.v.), and others. However, the principles of the deductive organisation of knowledge were not formulated conclusively and definitely until the turn of the 20th century (with extensive use of mathematical logic, q.v.). Up to the end of the century D.M. was applied almost exclusively in mathematics and logic. In the 20th century attempts were also made to apply D.M. (including the axiomatic method) to non-mathematical knowledge—physics, biology, linguistics, sociology, etc.

Definition 1. A brief logical description of a thing or the meaning of a word, stating its essential distinctive properties and determining its content and boundaries. 2. A logical method making it possible to distinguish, find or build some object, formulate the significance of a newly introduced term or specify the significance of a term existing in science. The diversity of kinds of D. is determined by what is defined, the tasks, the logical structure of D., etc. With the help of D. objects are singled out by their specific characteristics (properties and relations). Often they assume the form of D. through a genus and specific distinction. For example, "oxygen is an element (genus), whose atomic weight is equal to 16 (specific distinction)". Definitions are subject to rules: the rule of proportion between what is defined and what is defining, the rule banning a vicious circle, and so on.

"Deideologisation" and "Reideologisation", Theories of, specific interpretations of ideology (q.v.) in bourgeois sociology, spread in the 1960s-1970s. The T."D." is linked with the names of R. Aron, Bell (q.v.), S. Lipset and others. According to the T."D.", ideology is a false consciousness essentially opposed to science and used by a social group to justify its actions and to stake its social claims. The T."D." is also regarded by their proponents as a product of a technologically undeveloped society with unsolved economic and socio-political problems. The advocates of T."D." hold that the developed capitalist countries have passed the social stage requiring an ideology and have entered a new, "non-ideological" era. They declare the "end of ideology". The T."D.", in fact, expresses the scientifically-technocratic illusion that all problems in capitalist society can be solved by purely "technical" means, without the masses, the class struggle, etc. This bourgeois-ideological conception is spearheaded against socialism, against the Marxist-Leninist ideology, which the T."D." declares unscientific and obsolete. Nevertheless, the acute class struggle, the youth and other social movements of the late 1960s in major capitalist countries showed that "technical" means are hardly enough to cope with the ailments of capitalist society. The T."D." is attacked by bourgeois theoreticians, who consider that it is disarming bourgeois society in its fight against the communist ideology. Thus, there appeared the seemingly contrasting conception of T."R.", which stresses the need to substantiate the social values of bourgeois society and their significance for the bourgeoisie. Basically, the two conceptions are not opposed, both being in essence bourgeois-apologetical and anti-communist.

Deism, belief in the existence of God as an impersonal prime cause of the world. From the deistic point of view, the world, having been created, was abandoned to the operation of its own laws. Herbert of Cherbury, 17th-century English philosopher, was "the Father of Deism". D. differs from theism (q.v.) which acknowledges the connection of God with the world and man, from pantheism (q.v.) which dissolves God in nature, and from atheism (q.v.) which denies the existence of God. Where feudal religious conceptions dominated, D. was often a surreptitious form of atheism—a convenient device of the materialists for discarding religion. Exponents of D. in France were Voltaire and Rousseau (qq.v.), in England Locke, Newton, Toland and Shaftesbury (qq.v.), and in Russia Radishchev (q.v.). Idealists, such as Leibniz and Hume (qq.v.), and dualists also donned the garb of D. At present, D. is used to justify religion.

Dembowski, Edward (1822-1846), Polish philosopher, a leader of the revolutionary democratic group in the Cracow uprising of 1846. In his philosophical discourses, D. continued the progressive traditions of the late 18th-century Polish materialists, H. Kollataj and S. Staszic. He wrestled with Hegelian idealism and opposed the metaphysical materialism of the French Enlighteners, calling for a "philosophy of creation" or "philosophy of the future" based on the needs of the people, on the facts of practice. He believed that dialectics should justify the overthrow by the peasants of landowner oppression and the necessity for establishing a communist order. D. attacked Hegel (q.v.) for "reconciling" with the existing evil, for trying to press the new into the service of the old. D. was an atheist and denounced religion and the Catholic Church as an instrument of feudal reaction. However, his view of society was distinctly idealistic. He rejected Feuerbach's (q.v.) naturalism and considered human reason the motive force of history.

Demiurge, in Plato's (q.v.) idealist philosophy and the Neoplatonic mystics, the creator of the Universe, or deity.

Democracy, a form of power that officially proclaims subjection of the minority to the will of the majority and recognises the freedom and equality of citizens. In its definition of D. bourgeois science usually confines itself to these merely formal attributes and considers them in isolation from the socio-economic conditions prevailing in society and from the actual state of affairs. As a result, there emerges the conception of so-called pure democracy, also propounded by opportunists and reformists. As a form of political organisation of society every D. is ultimately determined by the relations of production in a given society. It is, therefore, essential to weigh the historical development of D. and its immediate dependence on the change of socioeconomic formations (q.v.) and on the character and degree of acuteness of the class struggle. In the antagonistic class formations, D. exists practically for the members of the dominant class. In bourgeois society, for example, D. is a form of the dictatorship of the bourgeoisie. As compared with the feudal system, bourgeois D. was a historically progressive stage in the development of society. Up to a point, the bourgeoisie wants D. as an instrument of its political rule. It frames a constitution, forms a parliament and other representative bodies, and introduces (under pressure from the people) universal suffrage and formal political liberties. But the people's possibilities for utilising all these democratic rights and institutions are curtailed in every way. The bureaucratic machinery of a bourgeois republic is so patterned as to paralyse the political activity of the working people and keep them out of political affairs. The political rights are proclaimed formally and are not guaranteed and representative bodies are more often than not an instrument of the policy of the ruling class. With the capitalist countries entering the imperialist stage, the pressure of monopoly capital has brought about a turn from D. to political reaction. The fight of the working people and all progressive forces for D., for democratic rights, therefore acquires major significance as a condition and component of the proletariat's struggle for the socialist transformation of society. Socialist D. is the highest form of D., genuine D. for the majority of the people, for the working people. Economically, it is based on social ownership of the means of production. Truly universal, direct and equal suffrage by secret ballot was introduced for the first time in history in the socialist countries. All citizens, irrespective of sex, nationality and race, enjoy equal rights in political, economic and cultural affairs. The main feature of socialist D. is the drawing of the masses in the administration of all state and social affairs. A pride of place in the system of socialist D. belongs to the organs of people's control in whose work millions of people take part. The Constitution of the USSR records all the rights and freedoms of citizens and provides material guarantees for them. For example, in socialist society the right to labour is not simply proclaimed, but legislatively sanctioned and effectively secured by the abolition of exploitation, eradication of unemployment, absence of crises in production, etc. Therein lies the basic difference between socialist D. and bourgeois D. The all-round improvement of socialist D. is the main direction of the development of the state of the whole people and the entire political system of socialism in the process of building communism. This will eventually lead to the replacement of the state by communist public self-government (q.v.).

Democratic Socialism, official ideology of modern reformism (q.v.) set out in the declaration of the Frankfurt Congress of the Socialist International, "Goals and Tasks of Democratic Socialism" (1951), in opposition to the ideology of Marxism-Leninism. The theoretical roots of D.S. go back to neo-Kantianism (q.v.) and its notions of ethical socialism (q.v.). Socialism, it says, is not a natural product of historical development, but a moral ideal equally acceptable to all sections of society. D.S. infers that the socialist reconstruction of society is basically a moral problem, a problem of the re-education and education of people in a socialist spirit. It rejects class struggle and socialist revolution. Socialism, it contends, emerges "democratically", i.e., from an aggregate of social and, in particular, cultural and educational measures effected within the framework of the bourgeois state by bourgeois governments, and exists as a "democracy", i.e., as a harmonious unity of all social strata and groups, the capitalists included. These reformist conceptions are reflected in the policy documents of the Social Democratic parties of Austria and Federal Germany and the British Labour Party. Objectively, D.S. is designed to perpetuate the foundations of bourgeois society.

Democritus of Abdera (c. 460-370 B.C.), Greek materialist philosopher, disciple of Leucippus (q.v.). Lenin described D. as the brightest exponent of materialism in antiquity. A founder of atomism (q.v.), he believed in two prime beginnings: atoms and vacuum. The atoms, he contended, being indivisible particles of matter, are immutable, eternal and in continuous motion, differing only in shape, size, position, and order. They do not have other properties, such as sound, colour, taste, etc., and exist conditionally, "not by the nature of the things themselves". This point of view contains the embryo of the teaching on the primary and secondary qualities (q.v.) of things. A combination of atoms produces bodies, while their dissolution brings about the end of bodies. An infinite multitude of atoms is eternally in motion in infinite vacuum, which is divisible and "atomised". When moving in different directions the atoms sometimes collide, producing vortices of atoms. There is an infinite multitude of worlds "born and dying", created not by God, but arising and being destroyed of necessity in a natural way. D. identified causality and necessity and denied chance, which he considered the outcome of ignorance. In his theory of knowledge he assumed that bodies emit thin shells ("idols", or images) of things which react on the senses. Sense perception is the main source of cognition, but yields no more than a "dim" knowledge of things. It is transcended by another, "bright", more subtle knowledge, knowledge by reason, which leads to the cognition of the essence of the world—atoms and vacuum. Thereby D. raised the problem of the relation of the senses to reason in cognition. In his political views he gravitated towards antique democracy. He opposed the slave-owning aristocracy. D.'s materialism was continued by Epicurus and Lucretius (qq.v.).

Demography, the study of population (q.v.), its structure (break-down by sex, age, occupation, nationality, region) and dynamic balance (birth-rate, mortality, migration, etc.). Quantitative characteristics of demographic processes derive from the operation of biological, social, cultural, ethical, ethnical, socio-psychological and other factors. Marxism highlights the leading role of the economic relations, the mode of production (q.v.). Marx wrote that "under various social modes of production there exist various laws of the growth of population and overpopulation" (K. Marx, *Grundrisse der Kritik der Politischen Ökonomie. Entwurf,* Moscow, 1939, p. 498). Population, in turn, influences the mode of production, being the subject of production and consumption. A global problem of the present day is the accelerated growth of population due, to a considerable extent, to declining mortality rates (in particular infant mortality) in the developing countries. Better medical care and sanitation, on the one hand, and family traditions and the old ways of life impeding birth control and effective employment of population in industry, on the other, account for the fact that the population grows faster than the productive forces. One of the tasks is to work out a demographic policy as a system of measures involving not only medical and economic solutions, but a whole series of social and cultural factors, bearing in mind that population growth influences the economy, social structure and territorial distribution of manpower. Marxism rejects Malthusian (see Malthusianism) and neo-Malthusian conceptions which divorce the problem of population growth from the socio-economic relations. Marxism shows that only a socialist society, in the course of its development, creates the necessary prerequisites for solving demographic problems, for substituting conscious regulation of demographic processes for spontaneous, uncontrolled demographic behaviour at the societal as well as family level.

Denotation and Sense 1. Denotation of a thing is its objective function which it performs in people's activity and which is presented to people either by the thing itself or by some means of communication. Since historical methods of man's objective activity are at the same time the methods of communication among people, all various objects of activity (and, consequently, knowledge) play the part of a

universal means of communication and, as a result, possess D. Thus, D. of a thing is determined by its objective essence and performs only those functions which correspond to its own nature. In language, the practical significance of things is preserved in the D. of words. S. is a specification of the D. of a thing in relation to the D. of words or to an objective situation. The relationship of Dd., which gives rise to their S., is determined either by objective factors of reality and the objective logic of reasoning or by subjective factors: the wishes, aspirations, social (also class) and personal aims and motives of man. Theoretical understanding of a thing, reproducing in its development real contradictions of the process which gave birth to it, and, first of all, social practice, as an implementation of this concept in reality, bring this or that S. into conformity with the essence of real things and phenomena. They cast aside subjectivist distortions and fix the diversity of senses which reproduces the real diversity of concrete things. 2. In linguistics, D. (lexical meaning) is understood as the S. of the word. Words as a rule have different denotations and also various senses. Hence, the D. of words greatly depends on the context and situation in which words are used. 3. The concepts of D.&S. in linguistic expressions which denote objects are made more exact in logical semantics (q.v.). The D. of a linguistic expression is usually understood as the object or class of objects which denotes (names) the given expression, and the sense of the expression is understood as its connotation, i.e., the information contained in it which makes it possible to assign the given expression to one object or another. Thus, "the Evening Star" and "the Morning Star" have as their D. one and the same object, the planet Venus, but their connotation, their S., differs. In contemporary logic, the differentiation between D. and S. dates to Frege (q.v.). Questions related to criteria of equality of S. (synonymics) of linguistic expressions are studied by logical semantics (see Name).

Deontology, a branch of ethics that deals with duty, moral requirement and normative, and the notion of obligation in general as a social necessity specific for ethics. The term was introduced by Bentham (q.v.) to denote a theory of ethics. Later D. was distinguished from axiology (q.v.)—the study of value (q.v.), in general, the theory of good and evil. Obligation (something that must be accomplished or carried out) expresses the requirements of social laws, including the needs of the individual and of society as a whole. Obligation assumes diverse forms, as in a particular command, general norm, general principles of behaviour, moral or social ideal (q.v.). These forms and their correlation are the subject of D. The Marxist theory of ethics is opposed to bourgeois theories (intuitionalism, q.v., etc.) which sever obligation from value. Marxist ethics establishes the close connection between the two, views them as two aspects of a single moral attitude. That is why Marxist ethics does not regard D. as a special theoretical discipline or an independent sphere of ethics, and sees it as a specific field of the study of ethics possessing its own special tasks. In a narrower sense, D. is the professional ethics of medical workers, directed to securing the maximum benefit of treatment with the help of psychotherapy, observance of medical ethics, etc.

Descartes, René, latinised as Renatus Cartesius (1596-1650), French philosopher, mathematician, physicist, and physiologist. After army service he settled in Holland, the foremost capitalist country of his time, where for twenty years he devoted himself to secluded scientific and philosophical research. Persecuted by Dutch theologians, he moved to Sweden (1649), where he died. D.'s philosophy is linked up with his mathematics, cosmogony, and physics. He is one of the founders of analytical geometry. In mechanics he noted the relativity of motion and rest, formulated the general law of action and counteraction. In cosmogony he postulated the novel idea of the natural development of the solar system. He contended that vortices of particles were the main form of motion of cosmic matter, and that they determined the structure of the world and the origin of the heavenly bodies. His hypothesis gave impetus to a dialectical understanding of nature, although with him development was still a mechanistic conception. Dualism (q.v.) invaded D.'s materialistic physics. The common cause of motion, he averred, is God. God created matter together with motion and rest, and maintains the same quantity of motion and rest in matter. D.'s doctrine of man was equally dualistic. He contended that a soulless and lifeless bodily mechanism combined in man with rational soul. Body and soul, which are heterogeneous, interact by means of a special organ. In physiology D. established a scheme of motor reactions, this being one of the earliest descriptions of reflex actions. However, D.'s materialist physiology conflicted with his idea of the immaterial soul. In contrast to the body, whose essence lies in extension, the essence of the soul lies in thought. D. considered animals to be no more than elaborate automata devoid of soul and mental capacity. Like F. Bacon (q.v.), D. defined the ultimate end of knowledge as man's mastery of the forces of nature, discovery and invention of technical devices, perception of causes and effects and improvement of the nature of man. To attain this end, one must refuse to believe anything until it is proved completely. This doubt does not imply that all existence is not cognisable; it is a method of finding the unconditionally authentic beginning in knowledge, which D. defined as *"Cogito: ergo sum"* ("I think, therefore I am"). D. employed this formula to deduce the existence of God and then the reality of the outer world. In epistemology, D. was the founder of rationalism (q.v.), which sprang from his one-sided understanding of the logical nature of mathematics. D. believed that the universal and necessary character of mathematical knowledge derived from the nature of the mind. He, therefore, attributed exclusive power in the act of cognition to deduction (q.v.), based on valid intuitively comprehended axioms. D.'s doctrines of the immediate validity of self-consciousness, of innate ideas, q.v. (among which he included the idea of God, and of the spiritual and corporeal substances) influenced subsequent idealist schools and were strongly attacked by materialist philosophers. On the other hand, D.'s basically materialist teaching on nature, his theory of the development of nature, his materialist physiology and his mechanistic method, which was inimical to theology, influenced the materialist philosophy of his times. His main works: *Le Discours de la méthode* (1637) and *Principia philosophiae* (1644).

Deschamps, Léger-Marie (1716-1774), materialist philosopher, Benedictine monk. His main work is *La Vérité ou le vrai système*. In his philosophical views D. combined rationalistic tendencies gravitating towards Spinozism with peculiar dialectical ideas. The pivotal concept of his system, the universal whole, postulates unity of all physical bodies. He described the universal whole as a hypersensous essence perceptible to reason, but not to the senses. D. contended that the concept of God is manmade and believed atheism to be the privilege of a limited circle of enlighteners.

Description, a stage of scientific study which consists in recording the data of an experiment (q.v.) or observation (q.v.) with the help of a definite system of designations accepted in science. D. is made both by means of the usual language and figures and by special means comprising the language of sciences (symbols, matrixes, diagrams, etc.). D. is a preparatory stage of transition to a theoretical study of an object (see Explanation) in science. D. and explanation are closely connected. Without a D. of facts it is impossible to explain them; on the other hand, D. without an explanation is not enough for science. Interpreting the nature of scientific study from positions of extreme phenomenalism (q.v.), the positivists (Mach, Pearson, qq.v. and others) declared the only task of science to be "pure description of facts".

Desnitsky, Semyon Yefimovich (1740-1789), Russian enlightener, jurist, sociologist; educated at Moscow and St. Petersburg universities, later at Glasgow University, where he took his master's degree (1767). On returning to Russia he was professor of law at Moscow University. His works— *Slovo o pryamom i blizhaishem sposobe k naucheniyu yurisprudentsii* (About the Immediate Method of Teaching Jurisprudence), 1768, *Yuridicheskoye rassuzhdeniye o nachale i proiskhozhdenii supruzhestva* (Legal Discourse on the Beginning and Origin of Marriage), 1775, *Yuridicheskoye rassuzhdeniye o raznykh ponyatiyakh, kakiye imeyut narody o sobstvennosti* (Legal Discourse of the Different Concepts of Nations About Property), 1781—were prominent in the development of Russian social thought. D. referred to four stages (hunting, animal husbandry, land cultivation, and commerce) in the development of mankind. He was one of the first men in Russia to speak of the historical origin and development of property and the family (marriage). He shared the views of Anichkov (q.v.) on the origin of religious beliefs, opposed serfdom and worked out a draft of a new Russian "legislative, judicial, and punitive authority", which, however, was rejected by the tsarist government.

Determinism and Indeterminism, opposite philosophical conceptions of the place and role of causality (q.v.). D. is a doctrine on the universal causative origin of all phenomena. Consistent D. postulates the objective character of causality. I. denies the universal nature of causality, while its extreme variety goes to the length of denying causality as such. Deterministic notions first appeared in ancient philosophy and were most clearly postulated by antique atomism (q.v.). The conception of D. was substantiated and developed by natural science and materialist philosophy in the epoch of modern history (by F. Bacon, Galileo Galilei, Descartes, Newton, Lomonosov, Laplace, Spinoza, qq.v., and the French 18th-century materialists). Their D. was necessarily mechanistic and abstract, in conformity with the level of contemporary natural science. They believed the forms of causality to be absolute and governed by the strictly dynamic laws of mechanics, identified causality and necessity, and denied the objective character of chance. Laplace defined this point of view more conclusively than other philosophers (hence Laplacian D., the other name of mechanistic D.). Laplace held that the co-ordinates and impulses of all particles in the Universe at a given instant unequivocally determine its state at any past or future instant. This brand of D. leads to fatalism (q.v.), assumes a mystical complexion and, in effect, merges with belief in divine predestination. Scientific developments refuted Laplacian ɳD. not only with reference to organic nature and social life, but also to physics. The discovery of the correlation of uncertainties in quantum mechanics (q.v.) proved Laplacian D. puerile, but it was at once interpreted by idealist philosophers in the spirit of I. (conclusions about the "free will" of the electron, absence of causality in micro-processes, etc.). Dialectical materialism overcomes the limitations of mechanistic D. It recognises the objective and universal character of causality and does not identify it with necessity. Neither does it reduce its operation to the purely dynamic type of laws (see Laws, Statistical and Dynamic). The long-standing controversy between D. and I. has become more acute in natural and social science. In contemporary bourgeois sociology, I. is presented as voluntarism and empiricism (qq.v.). Though not rejecting D. as such, some bourgeois sociologists view it in a vulgar light (biological theories of social development, vulgar technicism, etc.). It is historical materialism which first introduced genuine D. in social research.

Development, essential, required motion, change in time. Transference in space is D. insofar as it retains change in time in a transformed shape. Motion as a means of the existence of matter neither arises nor disappears; it exists perpetually and sempiternally, at the same time, motion is always directed to something from something, i.e. it exists as the motion of various objects, processes, etc., which have a beginning and an end. The direction of motion cannot be a characteristic of motion as a means of the existence of matter, as an infinite. The direction of motion is a characteristic of finite motion. D., like motion, is infinite insofar as it is material; at the same time, D. exists every time as a separate finite process. D. may be ascendant or descendant, may go from the

external to the internal and vice versa, from the old to the new and vice versa, from the simple to the complex and vice versa, from the lower to the higher and vice versa, from the accidental to the necessary and vice versa, and so on. The D. of inorganic systems, the living world and human society, is governed by the general laws of dialectics. D. occurs in the form of a spiral, in the unity and conflict of opposites, as transition of quantity into quality and vice versa. Each separate process of D. has stages, those of preparation of the premises for its formation, i.e. chiefly external motion (this stage may be called the beginning of the process of D.); emergence, i.e. the transition to internal motion; formation, i.e. the transformation by the new process of D. of those conditions from which it has emerged; D. proper, or maturity of the process of D., i.e. its existence on its own basis; death, decay of the process. D. as a finite process from the very beginning contains in concealed form the tendencies leading from the lower to the higher and from the higher to the lower. Direction is not only necessary in any separate process of D., but also develops together with it. For this reason the tendencies of D. which are concealed at the beginning, take form and develop, reaching the highest stage of their existence and manifestation at the highest stage of D. of a separate process. Only then do the signs of the higher contained in the lower and their theoretical reflection develop in full as well. D. is reproduced in a theoretical form by means of dialectical logic (q.v.).

The Development of the Monist View of History, the work written by Plekhanov (q.v.) who published it in 1895 under the pseudonym of N. Beltov. Lenin described it as "a book which has helped to rear a whole generation of Russian Marxists" (Vol. 16, p. 269). It thoroughly analyses pre-Marxist philosophy and sociology, critically examines the views of the French 18th-century materialists, French bourgeois historians of the Restoration period, utopian socialists, and idealist German philosophers. Plekhanov revealed the class limitations of these theories and demonstrated that it was Marx and Engels who had created a scientific materialist philosophy, that only Marxism furnished a genuine science of society and discovered the materialist basis of social development. Besides the exposition of Marxist philosophy the book gives a profound critique of the Narodniks. This criticism of their unscientific views was especially important in Russia at that time. Today, too, it is one of the best works for studying the philosophy of Marxism.

Dewey, John (1859-1952), American idealist philosopher; considerably influenced bourgeois philosophy, sociology, aesthetics, and pedagogics in the USA; founder of the Chicago school of pragmatism (q.v.). A Hegelian in the early period, D. passed on to positivism (q.v.) and eventually came up with a new version of pragmatism which he called "instrumentalism" (q.v.). D. went to great lengths to disguise the subjective-idealist and agnostic essence of his philosophy which was contrary to materialist theory of reflection. In his works on sociology D. showed himself an advocate of bourgeois liberalism (regulated freedom and equal opportunities) and individualism (q.v.). He set off co-operation of classes and improvement of society by way of educational reforms against class struggle and socialist revolution. The essence of the "experimental method" of D.'s system of education is development of individual initiative and enterprise inherent in "human nature". His main works: *School and Society* (1899), *Democracy and Education* (1916), *Reconstruction in Philosophy* (1920), *Logic: The Theory of Inquiry* (1938), *Problems of Men* (1946).

Dézamy, Théodore (1803-1850), French revolutionary utopian communist, member of secret revolutionary societies (Société des Saisons, Société Républicaine Centrale, and others). In the 1848 revolution he championed the demands of the workers. D.'s utopian theory drew on the ideas of Morelly (q.v.), Babeuf (see Babouvism) and Fourier (q.v.). He opposed the "peaceful" brand of Cabet's (q.v.) communism and the Christian Socialism of F. de La Mennais. Philosophically, D. was a materialist and atheist, and a follower of Helvétius (q.v.). His main work: *Code de la communauté* (1842).

Dialectical Theology, a trend in Protestant theology which has spread chiefly in West Germany and the USA. D.T. appeared in Germany in the 1920s as an attempt to ascribe the crisis of bourgeois society to the "spiritual crisis of man". Its ideological roots go back to the mystical religious teaching of Kierkegaard (q.v.) and to German existentialism (q.v.). Its founder, the Swiss theologian K. Barth, contrasted "faith" with indefinite content to "religion" as a sum total of theological and cult manipulations. Barth supported the thesis that human nature is inherently sinful and base, and rejected the ideas of social or individual progress. The German theologian P. Tillich, on the other hand, allowed for the possibility of religious consecration of all walks of life, within the framework of D.T., by the "theology of culture", the "oecumenical synthesis" of all religious denominations. R. Niebuhr, a follower of D.T. in the USA, criticised the ideas of "social gospel" and its hopes of reforming society in accordance with the norms of Christian morality. D.T. has had a considerable influence on the contemporary versions of Protestant theology.

Dialectics, science of the more general laws governing the development of nature, society, and thought. The scientific conception of D. was preceded by a long history of development and the very concept of D. emerged through revising, even overcoming, the original meaning of the term. Originally, the term (*dialektikē téchnē*—art of dialectic) denoted: a) the art of debate by means of questions and answers, and b) the art of classifying concepts, dividing things into genera and species. In antiquity philosophers strongly stressed the mutability of all the existent and considered reality as a process, postulating change of every property into its opposite. Take Heraclitus (q.v.), some of the Milesian philosophers, and the Pythagoreans. But the term D. was not as yet used. Aristotle (q.v.) believed that D. had been invented by Zeno of Elea (q.v.), who analysed the conflicting aspects in the concepts of motion and plurality. Aristotle differentiated D., the science of probable opinions, from analytics, the science of proofs. Plato (q.v.) defined true being as identical and immutable, yet gave credence to the dialectical conclusion that the higher genera of the existent can each be conceived only as being and not being, as equal to themselves and not equal to themselves, as identical to themselves and as passing into "something else". Therefore, being contains contradictions: it is single and plural, eternal and transient, immutable and mutable, at rest and in motion. Contradiction is the necessary condition for prompting the soul to reflection. This art, according to Plato, is the art of D. In scholasticism (q.v.), the philosophy of feudal society, the term of D. was used to denote formal logic as opposed to rhetoric. In the epoch of Renaissance (q.v.), dialectical ideas on the "coincidence of opposites" were enunciated by Nicholas of Cusa and Bruno (qq.v.). Later, despite the prevalence of metaphysics (q.v.), Descartes and Spinoza (qq.v.) produced specimens of dialectical thought. In the 18th century in France, a wealth of dialectical ideas was produced by Rousseau and Diderot (qq.v.). Rousseau examined contradiction as a condition of historical development. Diderot went a step further and investigated contradictions in the contemporary social consciousness. The most important pre-Marxian stage in the development of D. was classical German idealism which, in contrast to metaphysical materialism, considered reality not merely as an object of cognition, but also as an object of activity. However, ignorance of the true, material basis of cognition and activity of the subject limited and distorted the dialectical notions of the German idealists. The first to make a breach in metaphysics was Kant (q.v.). He noted the purpose of opposite forces in the physical and cosmogonic processes and followed Descartes by introducing the idea of development into cognition of nature. In his epistemology, Kant developed dialectical ideas in his teaching of antinomies. Yet he described D. of reason as an illusion which evaporates as soon as thought recedes within itself, bounded by the cognition of phenomena proper. After Kant, Schelling (q.v.), too, developed a dialectical appreciation of the processes of nature. The idealistic D. of Hegel (q.v.) was the summit in the development of

pre-Marxian D. "For the first time the whole world, natural, historical, intellectual, is represented as a process, i.e., as in constant motion, change, transformation, development; and the attempt is made to trace out the internal connection that makes a continuous whole of all this movement and development" (F. Engels, *Anti-Dühring*, pp. 31-32). The result of Hegel's D. transcended by far the significance which the author himself ascribed to it. Hegel's teaching on the necessity with which all things arrive at their own negation, contained an element which revolutionised life and thought, for which reason the foremost thinkers of the time regarded his D. as the "algebra of revolution" (Herzen). A truly scientific appreciation of D. was given by Marx and Engels. They discarded the idealistic content of Hegel's philosophy and based D. on their materialistic understanding of the historical process and the development of knowledge, on their generalisation of the real processes taking place in nature, society and thought. Scientific D. organically combines the laws governing the development of being and the laws of cognition, these two being identical and differing in form only. For this reason, materialist D. is not only an "ontological", but also an epistemological teaching, a logic which regards thought and cognition equally as being in a state of becoming and development, inasmuch as things and phenomena are what they are becoming in the process of development and contain as a tendency their own future, or what they will become. In this sense the theory of knowledge (q.v.), too, is considered by materialist D. as a generalised history of cognition; and every concept, every category is, therefore, historical in nature, despite its extremely general character. Contradiction (q.v.) is the chief category of materialist D. In the teaching on contradictions it reveals the motive force and source of all development. It contains the key to all the other categories and principles of dialectical development— development by passage of quantitative changes into qualitative ones, interruption of gradualness, leaps, negation of the initial moment of development and negation of this very negation, and repetition at a higher level of some of the features and aspects of the original state. It is precisely such understanding that distinguishes D. from every kind of vulgar-evolutionist views typical of present-day bourgeois and reformist theories. Materialist D. is a philosophical method of investigating nature and society. None but the correct dialectical approach will yield an understanding of the complex and contradictory emergence of objective truth, the connection, at every point in the development of science, between the elements of the absolute and the relative, the stable and the changeable, and the transition from one set of forms of generalisation to other, deeper forms. The revolutionary substance of materialist D., which does not tolerate the slightest stagnation or immobility, makes it an instrument for the practical reconstruction of society and helps to assess objectively the historical requirements of social development, the discrepancy between old forms and new content, the necessity of transition to higher forms stimulating the progress of mankind. The strategy and tactics of the struggle for communism are framed to conform fully to the dialectico-materialistic world outlook (see Logic, Dialectical).

Dialectics of Nature, an unfinished work by F. Engels, first published in the USSR (1925), consists of notes (1873-86) treating the key problems of the dialectics of natural science. Engels held that the philosophy of dialectical materialism should be based on exhaustive knowledge not only of the social sciences but also of the natural sciences and that the natural sciences, in turn, could not develop fruitfully, unless based on dialectical materialism (q.v.). *D.N.* contains a profound philosophical investigation of history and the most important questions in natural science, and criticises mechanistic materialism, the metaphysical method, and idealistic and agnostic conceptions in natural science. Deeply versed in contemporary science, Engels demonstrated how the metaphysical conception of nature is exploded from within by scientific progress and compelled to give place to the dialectical method. He showed, too, that natural scientists are forced to abandon the metaphysical approach and adopt the dialectical one. Engels developed the dialectico-materialistic teaching on the forms of motion of matter (q.v.). In keeping with this teaching, he worked out the principles for classifying the natural sciences, suggesting a concrete classification, on which he based his work. Engels made a detailed philosophical study of the basic laws of natural science and revealed their dialectical nature. Showing the true purport of the law of the preservation and conversion of energy, Engels examined the second principle of thermodynamics and demonstrated the fallacy of the conclusion that the Universe was steadily approaching thermal death. Engels made a thorough analysis of Darwin's (q.v.) teaching on the origin of species and showed that its main point, the theory of development, agreed in full with materialist dialectics. Engels delved into the role of labour (q.v.) in the emergence and development of man. He also showed how mathematical concepts and operations reflect the relation of things and processes in nature, where they have their real prototypes, and noted that the introduction of variables signified the penetration of dialectics into mathematics. Engels investigated the relation between chance and necessity, and revealed that the mechanistic and idealistic approaches to this problem were both erroneous. He used Darwin's teaching to show how natural science confirms and specifies the propositions of dialectics. To be sure, some particulars related to special problems in natural science, treated by Engels in his book, have grown obsolete as a result of the immense scientific progress since achieved, but his dialectico-materialistic approach to analysis of natural science and its philosophical generalisation is entirely valid to this day. Many propositions laid down in *D.N.* anticipated scientific developments by decades. The book is a model of dialectical thinking on complex problems of natural science.

Dictatorship of the Proletariat, a scientific definition of the essence of state power of the proletariat, established after abolition of the capitalist system and destruction of the bourgeois machinery of state. Lenin called the D.P. a major idea of Marxism regarding the state (q.v.). The D.P. is the main content of socialist revolution (q.v.) and the necessary condition for its victory. The revolutionary D.P. is the state of the period of transition from capitalism to socialism. The proletariat uses its political power to suppress the resistance of the exploiters, to consolidate the victory of the revolution, and to combat aggressive actions of international reaction. However, the D.P. is not only coercion, and not chiefly coercion. Its main function is creative and constructive. Dictatorship serves the proletariat to win over the mass of working people, to rally them around it and to draw them into socialist construction. The basis and supreme principle of the D.P. is the alliance of the working class and the peasantry (qq.v.) under the leadership of the former. The D.P. is, therefore, the highest form of democracy (q.v.)—real democracy for the working people, whose aim is to enlist the ever broader masses in governing state and public affairs. The Communist Party, the vanguard of the working class, is the leader and guiding force in the system of the D.P. The system of the D.P. comprises various mass organisations of working people: representative bodies of the people, trade unions, co-operatives, youth and other associations, which serve as the link between the Party and the masses. The D.P. can be of various forms; the form of the D.P. depends on the given conditions; the concept "dictatorship" as such explains neither the form nor the political regime of the state. The Paris Commune (1871) was the first D.P. in history. It enabled Marx to surmise the shape of the state of the D.P. that should replace the destroyed bourgeois machinery of state. The Soviets are a new form of the D.P., which Lenin discovered by studying the experience of two revolutions in Russia. The later revolutionary experience gave rise to one more form of the D.P.— People's Democracy (q.v.). The parliamentary republic, too, is theoretically possible as a state form of the D.P. It is contrary to the principles of Marxism-Leninism either to reject the need for the D.P. in the period of transition from capitalism to socialism or to absolutise the D.P. and spread it over the whole period

of socialism. With the abolition of exploiting classes and the building of socialist society there no longer exists an object for class oppression inside the respective country, with all social groups adopting the political and ideological platform of the working class; therefore, the D.P. ceases to be indispensable as far as the tasks of internal development are concerned. Upon the building of socialism the D.P. gradually develops into a state of the whole people (q.v.), an essential stage on the road to future communist public self-government (q.v.).

Diderot, Denis (1713-1784), French philosopher and Enlightener, editor and publisher of the *Encyclopédie,* man of letters and art critic. Voltaire (q.v.) and D. exercised an enormous influence on contemporary social thinking. In philosophy, D. quickly passed from deism (q.v.) and ethical idealism to materialism (in the teaching on nature, psychology, and the theory of knowledge) and atheism (q.v.). To his mechanistic materialist outlook on nature, which he shared with La Mettrie and Holbach (qq.v.), D. imparted some elements of dialectics, such as ideas on the connection of matter and motion, connection of processes proceeding in nature, and the eternal change of forms in nature. D. dealt with the concept of the universal sensibility of matter to explain how mechanistic motion of material particles may give birth to the specific content of sensations. In developing this view, D. outlined a materialist theory of the psychic functions, thus anticipating the later teaching on reflexes. According to his theory, men and animals are instruments endowed with an ability to feel and with memory. In epistemology, D. rejected the idealist notion of spontaneity of thought. All reasoning is rooted in nature, and all we do is register phenomena known to us from experience, between which there is either a necessary or conventional connection. It does not follow with D. that our sensations are mirror-perfect copies of things; the resemblance between most of the sensations and their external causes is never greater than between conceptions and their denotations in language. He developed F. Bacon's (q.v.) belief that knowledge, which originates from experience, is not prompted by the sole urge of perceiving the truth, but by the aim of perfecting and increasing man's might. In so doing, D. noted the role of technology and industry in developing thought and cognition. According to him, experiment and observation were the methods and guides of cognition. It is through them that thought is able to acquire knowledge which, though not entirely authentic, is highly probable. Compilation of the *Encyclopédie* (see Encyclopaedists), became D.'s lifework. Progressive in content, the *Encyclopédie* was militant in tone. Dissemination of new ideas went hand in hand in it with criticism of inert views, prejudices, and beliefs. Despite enormous difficulties, D. succeeded in completing the publication of the *Encyclopédie*. He was the author of many works on art and art criticism, developed a new aesthetics of realism, defending the unity of the good and beauty. He attempted to embody the principles of his aesthetics in his novels and dramas. The classics of Marxism acclaimed the works and teaching of D. Engels noted "masterpieces of dialectic" in D.'s writing (*Anti-Dühring*, p. 28). Lenin pointed out that D. "came very close to the standpoint of contemporary materialism" and that he "drew a clear distinction between the fundamental philosophical trends" (Vol. 14, pp. 35 and 38). But for all this, D. was an idealist in his views of social phenomena. In combatting feudal despotism, he advocated the political system of enlightened monarchy. His main works: *Pensées sur l'interpretation de la nature* (1754), *Entretien entre d'Alembert et Diderot* (1769), *Principes philosophiques sur la matière et le mouvement* (1770), and *Eléments de physiologie* (1774-80).

Dietzgen, Joseph (1828-1888), worker, tanner, "one of the most eminent German Social Democratic philosophical writers" (V. I. Lenin, *Collected Works*, Vol. 19, p. 79). A self-educated philosopher, D. was strongly influenced by Feuerbach's (q.v.) materialism and independently discovered materialist dialectics. He lived and worked in Germany, Russia, and the United States. His main works are *Das Wesen der menschlichen Kopfarbeit* (1869) and

Das Akquisit der Philosophie (1887), which are devoted to epistemology. According to D., consciousness is an ideal product of eternally existing and moving matter, the "universum". The brain, which is part of the world whole, is the bearer of consciousness. Natural and social being is the content of consciousness. Cognition proceeds in sensory and abstract forms. It is a process of motion from relative to absolute truth. D. rejected Kant's (q.v.) agnosticism (q.v.) and asserted that in both sensory and abstract forms man's cognition is an image of the outer world verified by experience. He considered the "universum" in motion, and saw the source of development in contradiction. However, D. failed to mould dialectics into a scientific system; he did not succeed in making an exhaustive exposition of dialectics as a theory of knowledge (though he expressed a number of profound ideas in this field, too). This led him to make concessions to relativism and vulgar materialism (qq.v.), and to confuse the material and the ideal. D. was a militant atheist, an ardent propagandist of the teaching of Marx and Engels.

Difference, a category expressing one of the aspects of the development of contradiction (q.v.). D. is a necessary attribute of development (q.v.), of the self-motion of matter and the dialectical bifurcation of the whole. D. does not exist without identity (q.v.). Like identity, D. may be external and internal. External D. is the D. of things, processes, etc., insofar as they are not internally related, or mutually connected, but are similar, identical. The internal D. is the D. of uniform things, processes, etc., internally related to each other. It means that a given thing (process, etc.) originates from something different and turns into something different, while remaining what it is for the time being. Internal D. is possible only in conjunction with external D. All things, processes, etc., differ internally because the nature of any thing, process, etc. "retracts" its specific relationship to other things, processes, etc. D. characterises one of the first stages in the development of contradiction when the latter is not yet a fully developed contradiction. With the help of D. the process of development is reflected more deeply in thought than by identity. D. records the stage of a thing when the latter, having come into being as something different from what it originated from, contains identity with the latter as a subordinate feature.

Dignity, a concept of morality expressing the degree of value or esteem of a person, an ethical category reflecting a person's moral attitude towards oneself and of society towards a person. Sense of D. is the individual's form of self-control lying at the basis of the demands he makes upon himself. In this respect demands imposed upon him by society assume the form of specifically personal demands (to behave so as not to abuse one's sense of D.). Thus D. is, like conscience (q.v.), a mode of man's realisation of his duty and responsibility (qq.v.) to society. The person's D. is regulated by the attitude towards him on the part of people around him, of society as a whole, who claim respect for and acknowledgement of, his rights. In both cases D. is an important aspect of man's social and moral freedom. Idealist ethics looks for a source of D. in the non-social essence of the personality (divine, natural, or "inherent in human nature") and opposes the D. of the person to the laws, requirements and rights of society. Marxist ethics views D. as a socially conditioned and historical relation that arose in the period of the disintegration of the primitive-communal system simultaneously with the emergence of the personality; in a class society its manifestations are contradictory. Under feudalism, D. took shape chiefly as the honour of the nobility; under capitalism it is, in fact, also determined by the class a person belongs to. D. becomes an equal right of every person in the absence of social inequality. A person becomes aware of this right and claims it individually in accordance with the level of his social or moral development and consciousness.

Dilemma, a form of inference, q.v. (conditional-disjunctive syllogism) that contains two premises—conjunctive affirmation of two hypothetical propositions and a disjunctive premise (see Disjunc-

tion) containing the grounds for or effects of the hypothetical propositions. Also describes a situation involving a choice between equivalent alternatives.

Dilthey, Wilhelm (1833-1911), German idealist philosopher, exponent of the so-called philosophy of life (q.v.). D.'s ideas pivoted on the notion of a living spirit, which develops in historical forms. D. rejected the knowability of the laws of the historical process, claiming that philosophy could only be a "science of sciences", i.e., a "teaching on science". D. divided the world of science into sciences of nature and sciences of the spirit, the object of the latter being social reality. Philosophy should start with an analysis of consciousness, because it alone offers the means by which we can arrive at the substance of natural and spiritual life. Psychology, D. averred, is the most fundamental of all the sciences of the spirit; he meant descriptive, not explanatory psychology, which is based on causality. In his study of the imaginative arts, D. stressed the role of fantasy, with whose assistance the poet elevates the accidental to the level of the substantial and by which he depicts the typical as the basis of the individual. According to D., the "science of interpretation", or "hermeneutics" (q.v.), comprises the link between philosophy and historical sciences. His main works: *Einleitung in die Geisteswissenschaften* (1883), *Die Entstehung der Hermeneutik* (1900).

Diogenes, Laertius, Greek writer of the first half of the 3rd century. His voluminous work, *Lives and Opinions of Famous Philosophers* in ten books, is the only existing summary compilation of the antique epoch on the history of philosophy. It contains biographical information and the teachings of the Greek philosophers up to Sextus Empiricus (q.v.). D. is noteworthy as a compiler of various statements and information, often of a whimsical nature. D. adopted a critical attitude towards the stoics (q.v.) and displayed sympathy for the sceptics and Epicurus (q.v.).

Diogenes, the Cynic (404-323 B.C.), Greek philosopher of Sinope, disciple of Antisthenes (q.v.) who founded the Cynic school of philosophy (see Cynics). He carried the notions of his teacher to their extreme. Like Antisthenes he rejected everything but the particular and criticised the teaching of Plato (q.v.) that ideas are general essences. He rejected all the accomplishments of civilisation and called on men to limit themselves to the necessary requirements. He also disavowed polytheism and all religious cults, which he described as superfluous, purely human contrivances. D. attacked social-estate differences and advocated asceticism (q.v.). He is said to have been bold and independent in confronting rulers and potentates and to have scorned the accepted standards of social behaviour, and is reputed to have lived in a barrel. However, this excessively colourful description of the outspoken cynic is doubtful, all available information being highly conflicting.

Discreteness and Continuity, essential characteristics which reflect the antithetical but interconnected properties of material objects. D. is an attribute of the discrete conditions of matter (planets, bodies, crystals, molecules, atoms, nuclei, etc.)., the degree of its differentiation in the form of separate stable elements of different systems, qualitatively defined structures. It is also expressed in the leap-like nature of the process of development, of change. C., on the other hand, is revealed in the wholeness of the systems consisting of separate discrete elements, in the infinity of their relations, the gradualness of change of conditions, the smooth transition from one state to another. Isolated investigation of D.&C. was typical of metaphysical materialism. It was based in particular on the postulates of classical mechanics, which considers D. inherent only in certain types of material elements (from planets to atoms), and C. only in the wave processes. Dialectical materialism stresses not only the antithesis, but also the interconnection, the unity of these attributes, confirmed by contemporary physics, which has proved, for example, that light, like substance possesses both wave (continuous) and corpuscular (discrete) properties. The interconnection of D.&C. expresses the essence of motion (q.v.), its contradic-

tory character. Motion is thus the unity of discrete and continuous changes of the object's state and position in space and time. The dialectics of D.&C. affords the possibility of comprehending scientifically the specific features of material objects, their properties and relations (space and time, motion, interconnection of field and matter, etc.).

Discursive, the, rational, mediate, logical, demonstrative, as distinct from sensory, immediate, and intuitive. The differentiation between the immediate (intuitive) and mediate (based on proof) truths is made by Plato and Aristotle (qq.v.). Metaphysicians either rejected the role of D. thinking (Jacobi, q.v., and others) or exaggerated it (Wolff, q.v., and others). Marxist philosophy recognises the vast importance of the D. aspect of cognition.

Disjunction, a logical operation forming a compound sentence by combining two sentences by means of the connective "or". Classical mathematical logic (q.v.) differentiates between two types of D.: the inclusive (conjunctive) and exclusive (disjunctive). An inclusive D. forms a complex sentence, which is true if at least one of its predicates is true, and false if all its component predicates are false. Exclusive D. forms a compound sentence which is true only if one of its members is true.

Distinction, act of the consciousness reflecting the objective difference between things or the elements of consciousness itself (sensations, concepts, etc.). In logic, D. is a method which replaces the definition (q.v.) of concepts (e.g., hydrogen differs from oxygen, for it burns but does not sustain combustion). The term of D. was introduced in the Middle Ages. The scholastics used it to denote an objective difference (real D., essential D., causative D., etc.) and differences in thought (D. of reason, subjective, formal, etc.). The term of D. is also used in our time.

Division of Labour 1. In a broad sense, a system of different interdependent forms of labour (q.v.), of production functions and occupations in general, and also a system of social links between them. The diversity of activities is analysed by economic statistics, the economics of labour, the branches of economics, demography, and so on. Territorial, including international, D.L. is described by economic geography. In Marxist-Leninist literature, the term "distribution of labour" is preferred in defining the relationship between different production functions in terms of their material result. 2. As distinct from specialisation social D.L. as human activity (q.v.) is a historically transient social relation. Specialisation of labour is the division of labour into different forms by the subject; this division expresses and promotes progress of the productive forces (q.v.). The diversity of such forms corresponds to the degree to which man masters nature, and increases with man's development. In class societies, however, specialisation breaks up man's activity into partial functions and operations which do not by themselves have the character of activity and do not serve as a means of reproduction of social relations by man, of his culture, spiritual wealth, and of his personality. These partial functions are devoid of intrinsic meaning and logic; their necessity derives merely from the external requirements of the system of D.L. Such is the division into material and spiritual (mental and physical) labour, executive and administrative labour, practical and ideological functions, etc. Social D.L. is manifested in the division into material production, science, art and other spheres, and in the division of each of these spheres as well. Historically, D.L. inevitably grows into class division. This is due not so much to the fact that D.L. makes specialisation so narrow and deformed and that it ties the individual to a specific profession, but to the fact that the individual enters social intercourse as a bearer of certain function, as labour power of certain quality. The individual acts as a character cast in a role imposed on him from outside. Capitalism aggravates the contradictions implicit in D.L. and its consequences to their extreme (see Alienation). These contradictions are gradually solved in the course of building socialism and communism (q.v.). Communism ultimately eliminates the D.L. that splits man himself through further specialisation and development of man's diverse

aptitudes, i.e., by means of the all-round development of the individual (q.v.).

Dobrolyubov, Nikolai Alexandrovich (1836-1861), Russian revolutionary thinker, materialist, critic, and publicist, associate of Chernyshevsky (q.v.). Joining the monthly *Sovremennik* in 1856, he ran the department of criticism and bibliography from 1857 to 1861. His numerous articles over this period dealt with pedagogics, aesthetics, philosophy, and art, the most important being: "The Importance of Authority in Education" (1857), "The Organic Development of Man in Connection with His Mental and Moral Activities" (1858); "Robert Owen and His Attempts at Social Reform" (1859); "What Is Oblomovshchina?" (1859); "Realm of Darkness" (1859); "When Will the Real Day Come?" (1860); "Features for Characterisation of the Russian Common People" (1860); "A Ray of Light in the Realm of Darkness" (1860). In his treatment of various philosophical problems D. defended the principle of the genetic community of nature and man, and the materialist idea of the unity of mental and physiological processes in the human organism, challenged the philosophy of dualism (q.v.), and opposed agnosticism and scepticism (qq.v.) in epistemology. Relying on the data supplied by contemporary natural science, he conducted a polemic against separation of "soul" from body, a dogma of the Christian religion. D. considered Feuerbach (q.v.) to have originated the study of man as a whole and integral being. By referring to social problems and showing that human actions are socially conditioned, D., however, exposed the inadequacy and limited character of Feuerbach's anthropological principle. He strove to achieve historism and defended the principle of development in nature and society. Though by comparison with Chernyshevsky he paid less attention to the elaboration of socialist theory, he adopted basically the same positions as his teacher and worked for the development of Russia along socialist lines. D. made an important contribution to aesthetics. Following Belinsky (q.v.), he insisted that it was the social duty of literature and art to portray the "unnaturalness of social relations" in the life as it was then, to define the "natural aspirations" of the people and to seek for an ideal in social life. The writer's greatest virtue, according to D., is the truth with which he portrays life. Regarding as his main purpose the striving to awaken and develop Russian self-consciousness, D. also assumed that only revolution, revolutionary action by the masses themselves, could radically change the existing system, pull down the autocratic machine and put an end to the "realm of darkness"—to serfdom. D. exposed the pseudo-radical character of liberal literary criticism. His ideal was a society in which "a man's worth would be judged by his personal qualities" and in which "each man would receive his share of material wealth in strict proportion to the amount and value of his labour".

Dogmatism, a term indicating a way of thinking based on unalterable concepts and formulas regardless of the new data of practice and science and the specific conditions of space and time, i.e., ignoring the principle of creative development and of the concreteness of truth (q.v.). The source of dogmatism is to be found in the development of religious conceptions, the demand for faith in church dogmas, which are asserted as indisputable truths, above criticism and sacred to all believers. The supporters of antique scepticism (q.v.) classed as dogmatic all positive doctrines concerning the world. In contemporary philosophy D. is connected with anti-dialectical conceptions which deny the mutability and development of the world, and also with the failure to understand that the dialectical laws of development manifest themselves differently in different historical conditions, in different objects and processes. In politics D. leads to sectarianism, the rejection of creative Marxism, to subjectivism, and to loss of contact with practice. Under present-day conditions D., along with revisionism (q.v.), is a great danger to the international working-class movement. Dogmatists do not take into account the changed conditions in the world and hang on to old formulas laid down for different conditions. Dogmatists indulge in "left" phrase-mongering and advance "ultra-revolutionary" slogans, which, however, result in far from revolutionary policies in practice. Marxism-Leninism is vigorously opposed to all forms of D.

Dostoyevsky, Fyodor Mikhailovich (1821-1882), Russian realist writer and thinker. His first novel *Poor People* (1846) showed that he was a humanist "aching for the people" (Dobrolyubov). Belinsky (q.v.), whose ideas had influenced D. at that period, appreciated *Poor People* as "the first attempt at a social novel". D. joined Petrashevsky's group (q.v.) in 1847—its radical wing, headed by N. Speshnev; he was arrested in 1849 and sentenced to death, the sentence being commuted to four years of penal servitude. In Siberia, his outlook evolutionised: he came to reject revolutionary methods of fighting social inequality, arrived at the idea that the destinies of Russia and the West were contrary, that the ideas of tsarist autocracy and religion were associated in the consciousness of the masses. At the same time, D. remained true to the humane ideals of the brotherhood of peoples and social harmony based on individual perfection and happiness. D.'s views found expression in a back-to-the-soil conception, much like that of Slavophilism (including some features of Westernism) which D. developed together with M. Dostoyevsky, N. Strakhov and A. Grigoryev when he came back to St. Petersburg in 1859. D. substituted the idea of a peaceful fusion of the upper classes with "the soil" (i.e., the Russian people) for that of socialism and revolution. According to D., the Russian people, thanks to the Christian ideal of "universal conciliation" and "humanity" which it had preserved, could assimilate the fruits of European civilisation, while avoiding the strife between classes characteristic of Western societies. In the full realisation of this ideal D. saw the historic mission of the Russian people. The project aimed at eliminating social antagonisms was obviously conservative and utopian. In his literary works D. censured the "egoism, cynicism, servility, alienation, and commercialism" of bourgeois civilisation; he was distressed by the "ethical devastation" (A. V. Lunacharsky) in Russia after the abolition of serfdom. In his writings D. concentrated on problems connected with the moral and spiritual strivings of the individual: the meaning of life, freedom and responsibility, man and God, good and evil, inclination and duty, reason and morality, etc. D. saw man as a personality possessing a free will and responsible for his actions (and not as an object for manipulation) and demanded that in any life's situation man be guided by the lofty and stern principle: "be a *human being* among people and remain so forever". According to D., freedom of the individual is a source of good as well as of evil. Unrestricted freedom and individualist revolt against the existing relations lead to despotism, alienation of men, moral ruin of the personality, even to death. The way to improvement and to a perfect society, as D. saw it, lay in humility and suffering, which helps man to overcome the moral crisis and to freely choose the ideal of uniting in Christ, the ideal of theo-humanity (or else the principle of permissiveness, would triumph and the world would sink into chaos). D. wanted to believe that his religious ideal was feasible, but reality suggested other conclusions, generating insuperable contradictions in his mind. The antinomianism of D.'s outlook is expressed in his treatment of religious, socio-ethical, historical, and aesthetic problems, but the essence of his thinking was humanism. Through a character in one of his novels D. said that he did not want to and could not believe that evil was a normal state of people. His humanism, compassion for "the insulted and humiliated", and hatred of social and spiritual oppression have endeared him to progressive mankind. D.'s works made an era in the history of realism and made a visible impact on the development of world literature and the outlook of many philosophers. Bourgeois ideology today (especially existentialism, personalism, and Freudianism, qq.v.) crudely distort D.'s views. To be able to understand D.'s views correctly, one must read not only his novels (*Crime and Punishment*, 1866; *The Idiot*, 1868; *The*

Devils, 1871-72; *The Adolescent*, 1875; *The Karamazov Brothers*, 1879-80), but also his letters and his *Diary of a Writer*.

Dramatism, an aesthetic category reflecting and generalising contradictions and conflicts in human life and man's inter-relations with the social milieu and the natural environment. Realistic art truthfully depicts reality and its contradictions and complexity, probes the D. of life, people's destinies and emotional experience. Dramatic conflict as a specifically aesthetic form of expressing contradictions in life, as a form of reproducing in art sharp collisions of opposite human deeds, ideas, aspirations, and emotions, is the most complete and concentrated manifestation of D. In real art, the dramatic conflict is profound and has significant ideological and social content; it is sharp and tense, and is expressed in a perfect artistic form, thereby securing the desired aesthetic impact.

Dualism, a philosophical doctrine which, in contrast to monism (q.v.), regards material and spiritual substances as first equal principles. D. is often invoked in attempts to reconcile materialism and idealism, and the dualistic separation of consciousness from matter leads ultimately to idealism. D. is a prominent feature of the philosophies of Descartes and Kant (qq.v.). It forms the philosophical basis of the theory of psychophysical parallelism (q.v.).

Dühring, Eugen Karl (1833-1921), German philosopher and economist, professor of mechanics. In philosophy he was an eclectic, who tried to combine positivism (q.v.), inconsistent mechanistic and even vulgar materialism (q.v.), and outspoken idealism (q.v.). In political economy and sociology he expressed the ideology of the petty bourgeoisie. He opposed Marx and Engels during the period when the German Social Democratic Party, which had been formed out of two previously independent parties (Lassalleans and Eisenachers), was rallying its ranks, and when theoretical issues had acquired special importance. D.'s muddled and harmful views on philosophy, political economy, and socialism found support among some of the Social Democrats. Realising the danger D.'s writings represented for as yet immature German working-class movement, Engels attacked them in his well-known book *Anti-Dühring* (q.v.). D. subsequently descended to anti-semitism and racism. His main works: *Kursus der Philosophie* (1875), *Kritische Geschichte der Nationalökonomie und des Sozialismus* (1875).

Duns Scotus, John (1265/66-1308), a Franciscan monk, a prominent representative of medieval scholasticism (q.v.). In the words of Marx, D.S. forced theology itself to preach materialism. He sharply criticised Thomism (q.v.). Unlike Thomas Aquinas (q.v.), he strove to separate philosophy and theology, arguing that it is impossible to find rational grounds for the idea of creation from nothing and admitting that reason is dependent on the will. In his view, God is absolute freedom. In the medieval controversy over the universals (q.v.) he advocated nominalism (q.v.). He introduced the concept of intention in logic and was the first to contrast concrete meaning (the term is his) with abstract meaning.

Durkheim, Emile (1858-1917), French sociologist and positivist philosopher, follower of Comte (q.v.). D. maintained that sociology should study society as a particular kind of spiritual reality whose laws differed from those of the individual psyche. Every society, according to D., is based on commonly understood collective ideas; the scientist is concerned with social facts, collective ideas (law, morality, religion, sentiment, habit, etc.), which are forced upon the human consciousness by the social environment. D. attributed social development to three factors: density of population, development of means of communication, and collective consciousness. Every society is characterised by social solidarity. In primitive society, solidarity was "mechanical", since it was

based on blood relationship. In the modern world, solidarity is "organic", since it is based on the division of labour, i.e., on class co-operation for acquisition of the necessities of life. D. considered religion to be an important factor in the life of society. According to D., society deified itself in religion. His main works: *De la division du travail social* (1893), *Les règles de la méthode sociologique* (1895), *Les formes élémentaires de la vie religieuse* (1912).

Duty, an ethical category denoting a special moral relation. Moral obligation, applied to all people (see Moral Norms), assumes the form of D. when it becomes a personal task assumed by the individual in a specific situation. Here the individual is an active subject of morality, assumes and carries out the moral obligation in his activity. While non-Marxist ethics sought the source of D. in the will or reason of God (see neo-Thomism; neo-Protestantism), a priori moral law (see Kant; Intuitionalism), extra-historical human nature, or laws of outer nature (see Naturalism). Marxist ethics sees the source of D. in the laws of history which manifest themselves in the requirements and tasks of society and classes. D. is based not on the authority of the society (group of people, an individual), but on the objective source of this authority. The individual, therefore, is not to conform to the principles formulated by somebody or established spontaneously but to be aware of their social origin and of the effects for his personal or common activity. This is one of the indispensable principles of communist morality, raising man to the level of conscious (and hence self-motivated and self-grounded) service in the interests of mankind and history-making. In the period of the developed socialist society, which is tackling the world historic task of building communism, the supreme D. of the individual is to contribute to the achievement of this goal and to see behind any specific social task the general historical perspective.

e

Eclecticism, a deliberate confusion of different, very often diametrically opposed ideas, philosophical views, theoretical premises, political assessments, etc. It shows up in various attempts to marry materialism to idealism, in revisionists' aspirations to combine Marxism and empirio-criticism, dialectical materialism and Kantianism, and so on. E. is also typical of modern bourgeois philosophy. The chief methodological defect of E. is its inability to identify the principal connections of an object, or of a phenomenon, in their concrete historical conditionality, from the sum total of connections and relations of the objective world, a mechanical combination of different qualities and properties of objects or phenomena. In practice and politics E. brings about errors and miscalculations, because it hampers the search for the main link in a chain of events and prevents the planning of appropriate measures to solve the most topical problems in a concrete historical period.

Ecology, a branch of biology that embraces the interrelations between organisms and between the latter and their environment. The term of E. was first introduced by Haeckel (q.v.) in 1866. Modern E. is concerned with a number of above-organismic levels of the organic world, such as populations, biocenoses, biogeocenoses, and biosphere (q.v.) as a whole. E. is also understood as a science (or complex of sciences) called upon to study the interaction between society and nature (see Social Ecology).

Economic Materialism, a vulgar materialist conception considering the economy in isolation from real individuals and their activity. It rejects or underestimates the significance of politics, political institutions, ideas and theories in the historical process. Actually, E.M. perpetuates alienation (q.v.), and the state brought about by the results of people's activity. E.M. appeared as a vulgarised form of the materialist understanding of history. In the West, it was upheld by Bernstein (q.v.) and others and in Russia, by the proponents of "legal Marxism" and economism (qq.v.).

Economics and Politics. E. means relations of production (q.v.), that is relations between people in the process of production, exchange, distribution and consumption of material wealth. Economic relations determine all other social relations and form the economic basis. P. belongs to the superstructure over the economic basis (see Basis and Superstructure). The superstructure appears with the emergence of classes; it exists in a class society and disappears with the disappearance of classes and class distinctions. Consequently, P. is a concentrated expression of E., it is ultimately determined by E., but at the same time it exerts a great retroactive influence upon the latter. Political struggle is mainly the struggle for fundamental economic class interests. The state (q.v.) is the most important means of political struggle which allows a certain class to establish and maintain its economic rule. No class can establish its lasting economic rule without a seizure and maintenance of political power. In this respect, P. has precedence over E. The relation between E. and P. does not remain unchanged. On the one hand, P. constantly experiences a determinative influence of E. and preserves its unity with E., on the other hand, the development of classes and class antagonisms leads to a greater isolation of P. from E., its greater relative independence and its increased retroactive influence on E. P. attains the greatest degree of its relative independence under capitalism when the social character of production increases on a gigantic scale, thereby creating the material precondition for abolishing the rule of the capitalist class; the need for intensified political struggle by the working class grows, state intervention into E. as well as the influence of all other political levers upon E. sharply increases.

The possibilities of political influence upon E. are, however, limited by the dominance of private ownership. Under socialism, the role of P. is particularly important and entirely different from that under capitalism, for it effects the socialist transformation of society. In contrast with the E. of the antagonistic formations, socialist E. does not emerge and develop spontaneously but as a result of the purposeful activity of the working people led by the working class; the appearance and development of social ownership requires a centralised economic management. In conditions of struggle against antagonistic classes, in the transition period from capitalism to socialism and already under socialism where class distinctions still exist, economic management bears a political character and is effected by the socialist state. Improvement in the state economic management in the USSR is one of the most important tasks to be solved by the Communist Party of the Soviet Union within the whole period of society's socialist development.

Economism, an opportunist trend in Russian Social-Democracy at the turn of this century. Its proponents wanted to limit the tasks of the working-class movement to economic struggle (improving labour conditions, higher wages, etc.). They held that political struggle should be waged by the liberal bourgeoisie alone. The Economists (S. N. Prokopovich, Y. D. Kuskova, and others) denied the leading role of the working-class party, its revolutionary theory, and preached spontaneity in the labour movement. Being a variety of revisionism (q.v.), E. served as a vehicle of bourgeois influence upon the proletariat. The dissemination of E. hampered the creation of a centralised proletarian party. Lenin's newspaper, *Iskra*, greatly contributed to revealing the insolvency of E., and Lenin's *What Is to Be Done?* (1902) routed it ideologically.

Economy of Thought, Principle of, a subjective and idealist concept according to which the criterion of truth (q.v.) of any knowledge consists in achieving the maximum knowledge with the minimum means of cognition. The concept was introduced by Mach (q.v.) (*Das Prinzip herhaltung der Arbeit*, 1872), and Avenarius (q.v.) (*Philosophie als Denken der Welt gemäß dem Prinzip des klensten Kraftmaßes*, 1876), and it has its supporters among contemporary bourgeois philosophers. Lenin in his *Materialism and Empirio-Criticism* (q.v.) severely criticised P.E.T. as idealist, because the truth of scientific propositions is not determined by the "economy" of thought but by their correspondence to the objective world.

Ego (in philosophy), the spiritual centre of human personality in his active relation to himself and the world at large. The individual who regulates his behaviour and is capable of displaying initiative possesses E., the self. In the history of philosophy, idealist conceptions saw E. as an ideal principle, and completely disregarded the concrete, historical nature of human E. In such conceptions E. was often treated as a point of departure in the construction of philosophical systems. In Descartes (q.v.) E. exists as a thinking substance, as the intuitive principle of rational knowledge and thereby asserts its independence. The viewpoint of an isolated individual and contemplativeness (q.v.) within the framework of idealism led to solipcism (q.v.), and within the framework of metaphysical materialism—to the reduction of man to a passive object that submits to the external course of history. The psychologically individualist interpretation of E. proper to English empiricism (q.v.) was discarded by classical German philosophy. But the latter separated E. from the living social man and transformed it into a "transcendental subject". Fichte (q.v.) considered such E. a substance that posits not only itself but all that exists as its non-ego. Objective idealism, which developed dialectics, treated the social essence of human E. as an alienated force standing above specific people—world reason (Hegel, q.v.). In a bourgeois society, irrationalism (q.v.) produced the perception of the individual who faces the negation of his "ego" in this society. Irrationalist treatment of the individual only perpetrates the situation of alienation (q.v.). Freudianism (q.v.) expressed the idea of split personality under capitalism, presented the biologisation of urges as the submersion of E. into the kingdom of blind inclinations and the distorted perception by the individual of his own social essence as a result of control on the part of the super-E., which is hostile to him. In antagonistic class formations the splitting and alienation of activity in fact leads to a dispersonalisation of the individual, to a loss by him of his E. The false conceptions of E. may be overcome through the real struggle for man's assertion of himself as an active creator of social relations and norms of social life. The most free and full manifestation of the human E. in each man as an active subject will be possible in a communist society, in condition of an all-round development of the individual (q.v.).

Egoism, a principle of life and a moral quality which characterise a person from the standpoint of his attitude to society and people. Egoistic person is guided only by self-interest disregarding the interests of society and other people. E. is one of the forms of individualism (q.v.). It is more typical of the relations based on private ownership. Although in the period of struggle against the hierarchical, social estate organisation of the feudal society it played a certain positive role in vindicating the right of every individual to happiness, in the history of human morality E. was normally regarded as a negative quality. Capitalist relations established, anti-social tendency became ever more pronounced in the theories advocating E. (see Stirner), later the theories acquired even reactionary slant (see Nietzsche). Those who consciously upheld E. as a pseudo-moral principle ended in amoralism (q.v.). Resolutely condemning E. in all its forms, communist morality confirms principles of collectivism (q.v.) and conscientious labour for the good of people and society.

Einstein, Albert (1879-1955), German physicist, founder of the theory of relativity (q.v.) and a number of other physical theories, which led to new notions of space, time, motion, substance, light and gravity. In 1905, he advanced a theory on particles of light, quanta of light, or photons. That same year he published his first article on the special theory of relativity and in 1916 E. formulated the general theory of relativity. Nazi terror forced him to leave Germany. He settled in Princeton (USA). In the 1930s and 1940s, E. tried to develop the unified field theory and explain the nature of the field of gravitation and other fields. The main principles of his world outlook were an absolute denial of the existence of God, denial of any non-material substance, conviction that the world is objective and knowable, and that there is causal interdependence of all processes in nature. E. argued against Kant's (q.v.) apriorism and the views of Poincaré (q.v.) and others who claimed that the scientific truth was "conditional". At first, E. shared Mach's (q.v.) views but then he resolutely rejected Machism and in 1920 he called Mach "a poor philosopher". No less negative was his attitude towards logical positivism (q.v.) and positivist treatment of quantum mechanics (q.v.). In his public and political views E. opposed social and national oppression, militarism and reaction, and voiced his protest against the use of atomic energy for military purposes.

Eleatics, exponents of an ancient Greek philosophical school which shaped in the town of Elea (Southern Italy), 6th and 5th centuries B.C. The idealistic trend inherent in the philosophy of E. developed with the school. Its main representatives were Xenophanes, Parmenides, Zeno of Elea (qq.v.). The Eleatic school put forward the teaching on the immutable essence of true being and the illusory nature of all visible changes and differences to counter the spontaneous dialectical views of the Milesian school (q.v.) and Heraclitus (q.v.) on the changeable primary basis of things. This position involved a certain belittling of sense experience as a basis of knowledge and served later as one of the sources of Plato's (q.v.) idealism. The arguments of the E. against dialectics, notwithstanding their metaphysical character, played a positive role in the subsequent development of dialectics. They posed the problem of expressing in logical concepts the contradictoriness of motion.

Element, a concept of an object being an integral part of a certain system and considered indivisible in the framework of this system (for example, atom in the system "molecule", or electron in the system "atom", etc.). "The indivisible" in one system, however, turns out to be divisible in another. The concept of E. is bound to arise in the process of historical cognition of nature. The ancient Greek materialists considered that the single cosmic element was either water (Thales, q.v.) or air (Anaximenes, q.v.) or fire (Heraclitus, q.v.). Democritus (q.v.) and later Epicurus (q.v.) put forward the teaching on atoms as the smallest indivisible particles of matter. In the development of the science of matter there has always been a contradiction between the desire of natural scientists to find the simplest elements of matter and the absence of such particles in nature because of the infiniteness and inexhaustibility of matter. The great natural science discoveries at the end of the 19th century undermined the prevalent ideas on the existence of primary and structureless atoms. Modern physics has shown the intricacy of the structure of electrons, neutrons and other particles considered as elementary, and thus confirmed the view according to which there are no absolutely simple and indivisible elements in nature.

Elementary Particles, the simplest microobjects known today, which interact as an integral entity in all known processes. All other types of matter—atoms, molecules, macroscopical bodies and cosmic systems—consist of E.P. Today we know more than 200 varieties of E.P., but the overwhelming majority of them are unstable, appear as a result of the interactions of great energy and disintegrate shortly after. Almost every particle has its corresponding anti-particle, which differs in electric charge and some other quantum qualities. Matter is characterised by the unity of discreteness and continuity (q.v.) in structure, space distribution and motion. The development of the physics of E.P. brought to light some new aspects of the infinity of matter. Today priority is given to the creation of a unified E.P. and field theory, which will allow a better understanding of their qualities and types of interaction.

Elida-Eretrian School, one of the Socratic schools which existed during the 4th and 3rd centuries B.C., founded, according to Plato (q.v.), by Phaedo of Elida, Socrates' (q.v.) favourite. Later the school was transferred to Eretria. No original works of this school are extant. We know about it mostly from the works of Cicero and Diogenes (qq.v.). The E.E.S. was very close to the Megarian school (q.v.). Followers of the E.E.S. studied mainly ethical problems, claiming that all the different virtues are one in their foundation and, therefore, can all be reduced to one single good, which is truth, comprehended by reason.

Elite, Theories of, theories of an exceptional mission and active participation in social, political and intellectual life of the society's privileged strata (elites) and passiveness of the other people (masses). The bases of these theories differ. Biological theories (R. Williams, E. Bogardus) lay emphasis upon biological and genetic features which allegedly form the basis for people's division into outstanding and common, into active and passive, superior and inferior; psychological theories (G. Gilbert, B. Skinner) stress psychological factors determining exceptional qualities of some and commonplace features of the others; psycho-analytical theories (Freudianism, q.v.) accentuate the ability of sublimating sexual energy and the aspiration to power or submissiveness; socio-psychological theories (Fromm, q.v.) emphasise the existence of different types of characters determined both by psychological features of each individual and social factors of his life; technocratic theories (J. Galbraith) give priority to organisational functions of people involved in management, who occupy an eminent position in "technostructure" due to their know-how; scientocratic theories (Bell, q.v., and others) concentrate on the factor of scientific knowledge and the role of contemporary scientists as the leading force which promotes scientific, technological and social progress in "post-industrial" society. Although these theories slightly differ in interpreting certain problems, they are all united by the following postulates: natural inequality of people predetermines society's division into the elite and the masses; the elite is necessary as a driving force of scientific, technological and social progress; some must rule, others submit; the ruling minority that exerts its power over the majority is legitimate and enjoys full rights; the masses are passive and amorphous, they do not have any positive influence on the historical process, moreover, they allegedly possess some destructive power which can be turned against the achievements of civilisation. In contrast to T.E., the Marxist-Leninist teaching exposes the true causes for social inequality in society, for people's division into exploiters and the exploited, oppressors and the oppressed. These causes are private ownership of the means of production and antagonisms in the social relations generated by it. Under socialism, the role of both the people's masses and individuals constantly grows, all members of society unite in their endeavour to further scientific, technological and social progress, and to help each individual develop his abilities to the full.

Emergent Evolution, an idealistic theory of development; it spread in modern Anglo-American bourgeois philosophy, particularly among the representatives of neo-realism (q.v.). Chief exponents of E.E. are: Alexander (q.v.), C. Lloyd Morgan and C.D. Broad. E.E. appeared in the 1920s to counter materialist dialectics. Its aim is to idealistically explain development by leaps and bounds, the emergence of the new. The theorists of E.E. interpret the process of change as irrational acts, logically incomprehensible, and finally admit the existence of a deity. This theory leads to a denial of natural and historical laws, and the role of the quantitative stage of change in the process of development.

Emerson, Ralph Waldo (1803-1882), American philosopher, publicist and poet, leader of the transcendentalists (q.v.). His views were contradictory. He was greatly influenced by Plato (q.v.) and Neoplatonists, Goethe, Carlyle (qq.v.) and Oriental mystics. According to E., the "eternal problem" of philosophy consists in the relation of spirit and matter. He solved this problem as an idealist, regarding nature as a symbol of the spirit. The highest synthetical principle of being is the oversoul, God. In epistemology, E. was close to intuitionalism (q.v.); contemplation, intuition (q.v.) and ecstasy were regarded as the best means of penetrating into the essence of things. Great men play the decisive role in history; they promote social progress, which consists in the moral perfection of the individual. E. saw the eternal struggle and antagonism of interests between the rich and the poor on earth, and his sympathies were for the poor. His social and ethical ideal was an utopian dream about a solid individual, universal well-being and equality for all based on labour and a fair distribution of private property. He criticised the bourgeois system, opposed slavery in the USA and condemned predatory wars. His main works: *Nature* (1836), *Essays* (1841-44), *Representative Men* (1850).

Emotions, man's feelings expressing his attitude towards the surrounding world (towards people, their actions, phenomena) and towards himself. Brief feelings (joy, sorrow, etc.) are sometimes called E. in the narrow sense of the word as distinct from stable and lasting feelings (love, hatred, etc.). E. are a specific form of reflecting reality, they reflect relations of people to one another and to the objective world. Man's E., though genetically inborn, are shaped by society; they play a tremendous part in his behaviour and his practical and cognitive activity. E. indicate success or failure of man's efforts, conformity or non-conformity of objects and phenomena to man's interests and needs. E. can be active (sthenic), with a positive emotional tone—satisfaction (joy, etc.), and passive (asthenic), with a negative emotional tone—dissatisfaction (sorrow, etc.). Sthenic E. intensify man's vital activity, asthenic ones reduce it. There are specific types of E.: moods, affections (intense, turbulent emotions: fury, dread, etc.), passions. Mood is a prolonged (as compared to affection) emotional state (joyous, depressive, etc.), which imparts a definite emotional tone and colouring to all other feelings and also to man's thoughts and actions. Passion is a powerful, deep-seated E. holding a man in a long-lasting grip. Another special group are E. of a higher order: moral (feeling of collectivism, q.v., sense of duty, q.v., of honour, q.v., etc.), aesthetic (sense of the beautiful, q.v.), intellectual (E., associated with the satisfaction of cognitive interests, with the solution of intelligible problems, etc.).

Emotivism, a subjectivistic bourgeois theory of morality which consistently applies the methods of logical positivism (q.v.). The main exponents are Ayer, Carnap, Reichenbach (qq.v.) and C. Stevenson. Having established through investigations that moral judgments and terms cannot be verified by experience (see Verification, Principle of), the emotivists concluded that these judgments and terms bear no information, have no sense, and, therefore, are neither true nor false. Ethical utterances are purely "emotive", i.e., they are only used to express speaker's moral emotions, to stir similar emotions in listeners and induce them to act accordingly. E. explains the existence of people's different stands on morality through differences in their individual and collective emotions, and draws the conclusion that everybody is free to choose any point of view in morality, that contrary moral views do not logically contradict each other. Therefore, any view cannot be proved or refuted rationally but only psychologically, through subconscious suggestion. E. is a nihilistic and sceptical theory of morality. In an attempt to establish an absolute freedom of choice in morals E. practically justifies arbitrariness in behaviour and moral views, and deprives the individual of his ability to take a stand on moral problems independently and consciously.

Empedocles (c. 490-30 B.C.), a Greek materialist philosopher from Agrigentum, Sicily, ideologist of slave-holding democracy. In his philosophical poem *On Nature* he reduced the whole diversity of things to four elements of nature: earth, water, air and fire. This doctrine was retained for many years in ancient and medieval philosophy. The union and division of the elements were explained by the action of two opposing forces: attraction and repulsion. E. explained the different stages of the development of the Universe by the prevalence of one or another of these forces. E.'s assumption that the law-governed evolution of living beings is brought about by natural selection of the more viable combinations had great historic significance.

Empirical Sociology, one of the main trends in modern bourgeois sociology, deals chiefly with particular aspects of social life and their description. It was widely disseminated during and, particularly, after the Second World War, notably in the USA (A. Lundberg, S. Dodd, Mayo, q.v., etc.). The study of individual social phenomena by means of concrete sociological investigation (q.v.) is a significant contribution to science, only if it is based on a scientific theory that examines society as one whole developing according to law. The exponents of E.S., however, reject the objective laws of society's development, refuse to penetrate into the essence of social phenomena and often regard society as a mechanical aggregate of separate social phenomena, which they merely describe and list, investigating only the relationship between different factors. E.S. applies the following methods: questionnaires, interviews, statistical material and mathematical means (for example, the set theory, q.v., the theory of games). All these methods, however, lack a reliable methodological foundation—a scientific theory of the social process as a whole. E.S. is characterised by a profound differentiation of social investigations, which resulted in the emergence of individual branches: urban sociology, rural sociology, family sociology, industrial sociology, sociology of alcoholism, sociology of advertisement, sociology of mass media, etc. E.S. studies are often used by corporations, the government and the military to camouflage exploitation and intensify it, to increase profits and step up war preparations. Certain bourgeois sociologists, acknowledging the crisis in E.S., try to exceed its limits and sometimes turn to Marxist methods. Others make attempts at elaborating comprehensive sociological theories to be able to solve the most urgent problems of today and to resist historical materialism. These attempts, however, fail.

Empiricism, a teaching in the theory of knowledge (q.v.), which holds that sense experience is the only source of knowledge and affirms that all knowledge is founded on experience and is obtained through experience. Idealist E. (Berkeley, Hume, Mach, Avenarius, Bogdanov, modern logical empiricism, qq.v., etc.), limits experience to the sum total of sensations or notions, denying that the objective world underlies experience. Materialist E. (F. Bacon, Hobbes, Locke, French 18-century materialists, qq.v.) holds that the objectively existing outer world is the source of sense experience. However, the basic antithesis between E. and rationalism (q.v.) does not follow from the origin or source of knowledge: some rationalists agree that nothing exists in reason which has been lacking previously in the senses. The main point of disagreement is that E. deduces the general and necessary character of knowledge not from reason, but from experience. Under the influence of rationalism, some empiricists (like Hobbes and Hume) arrived at the conclusion that experience cannot impart to knowledge any necessary and general meaning. E.'s shortcomings are: metaphysical exaggeration of the role of sense cognition, experience, underestimation of the role of scientific abstractions and theories in knowledge, and denial of the active role and relative independence of thought.

Empirio-Criticism ("criticism of experience"), or Machism, a subjective-idealistic trend, founded by Avenarius and Mach (qq.v.). Considering "economy of thought" (see Economy of Thought, Principle of) as the basic law of knowledge, E.C. "purifies" the understanding of experience from the concepts of matter (substance), necessity, causality, etc., as "a priori apperceptions" (rational concepts) which, according to E.C., are wrongly introduced to experience. As a result, E.C. advances the concept of the world as the sum total of "neutral elements", or sensations. By introducing the doctrine of the principal co-ordination (q.v.), i.e., the inseverable connection between subject and object, E.C. was transformed into a system of subjective idealism. E.C. was a revival of the doctrines of Berkeley and Hume, disguised by the demand for neutrality in philosophy. E.C. was also connected with the crisis in physics, with the school of physical idealism (q.v.). Criticising E.C. in his *Materialism and Empirio-Criticism* (q.v.), Lenin showed the reactionary social role played by this philosophical trend, its connection with fideism (q.v.). E.C. appeared as a variety of positivism, q.v. ("second positivism"). Proponents of E.C., besides Avenarius and Mach, were J. Petzoldt, F. Adler, Bogdanov (q.v.), V. Bazarov, etc. The "anti-metaphysical" doctrine of E.C. was continued by neopositivism (q.v.).

Empirio-Monism, the name given by Bogdanov (q.v.) to his philosophy, a variety of empirio-criticism, or Machism. E.M. is built upon Mach's (q.v.) subjective-idealistic view on the neutrality of the elements of experience (i.e., sensations). In Bogdanov's view, the philosophy of Avenarius (q.v.) and Mach is dualistic because it admits that the psychical and physical elements of individual experience are independent of each other, and the experience must be interpreted monistically. This explains the name of his theory, "empirio-monism". According to E.M. everything is organised experience (understood as a totality of sense data, i.e., idealistically). The physical world, objective, is experience organised socially and collectively, and the psychical world, an integral part of the latter, is experience organised individually. E.M. holds that the Universe with its space, time and causal nexus (including man and his consciousness) is a continuous chain of complexes of elements different both in a degree and a form of organisation. Analysing psyche from the standpoint of energism (q.v.), E.M. attributed essential significance to biological adaptation of the organism to its surroundings. E.M. puts the sign of equality between social being and social consciousness and defends idealism in history. E.M. was criticised by Lenin in his *Materialism and Empirio-Criticism* (q.v.), and by Plekhanov.

Empirio-Symbolism, a term used by the idealist Yushkevich (q.v.) to denote his variety of empirio-criticism (q.v.). The main idea of E.S. is that concepts (truth, being, essence, etc.) are only symbols and they do not reflect anything real. This idea was taken from Poincaré and Mach (qq.v.) who considered, for example, that matter is only a logical symbol. Yushkevich tried to prove that the objective world is but an aggregate of empirio-symbols (i.e., symbols of idealistically interpreted experience). Yushkevich claimed that a choice of one or another system of symbols is dictated by a convenience of interpreting experience (here the influence of pragmatism and conventionalism, qq.v., on E.S. is evident). In *Materialism and Empirio-Criticism* (q.v.), Lenin showed that E.S. is subjective idealism, which regards the outside world and its laws only as symbols of man's capacity for knowledge.

Encyclopaedists, compilers and authors of the *Encyclopédie, ou dictionnaire raisonné des sciences, des arts et des métiers* (1751-80). This work played a great role in the ideological preparation of the French bourgeois revolution at the end of the 18th century and gave a systematic summary of the scientific achievements of the time. Up to 1772, Diderot (q.v.), assisted by d'Alembert (q.v.), was at the head of the *Encyclopédie*. Other E. were Montesquieu, Rousseau, Voltaire, Helvétius, Holbach (qq.v.). The materialists of the *Encyclopédie* were the most consistent fighters against feudal ideology; the moderate members of the E. came out against the Church interference in science, declaring themselves to be the defenders of social progress, criticised despotism and advocated emancipation of man from class oppression.

Energism, a philosophical conception which appeared at the end of the 19th century among some natural scientists. The followers of E. explain all phenomena of nature by changes in energy (q.v.) which is devoid of materiality. W. Ostwald, Mach (q.v.), and other followers of E., while developing the energetist interpretation of natural science, denied the scientific value of the atomistic theory. Later, influenced by the success of the

atomistic theory of the 20th century, they had to recognise the existence of the atoms. The ideas of E., however, reappeared but in a less systematic form in connection with new data provided by nuclear physics and the physics of elementary particles (q.v.). In particular, the discoveries of the mass defect, and of the possibility of transforming pairs of particles into a field, and vice versa, were interpreted as mere transformations of matter into energy and vice versa. These arguments were supported by references to the law of the interconnection of mass and energy, which was explained as a theoretical foundation of this possibility. The epistemological roots of E. are to be found, on the one hand, in the successes achieved by natural science and, on the other, in the difficulties facing the contemporary theory of the structure of matter. E., as a philosophical trend, revives whenever science is confronted with the task of penetrating deeper into the structural levels of matter.

Energy, the common measure of the various forms of the motion of matter. Qualitatively different forms of the physical motion of matter have the property of being converted into each other, this process of conversion being controlled by strictly defined quantitative equivalents. This makes it possible to establish the common measure of motion—E. as such. In the system of physical theory E. is expressed in various forms: mechanical, thermal, electromagnetic, nuclear, gravitational, etc. Each form of E. determines the essential characteristics of a given physical form of motion in terms of its convertibility into any other form of motion, the quantity of motion remaining invariable.

Engels, Frederick (1820-1895), a leader and teacher of the working class, who together with Marx created the Marxist doctrine, the theory of scientific communism, dialectical and historical materialism. From his youth E. strove to take part in the struggle for transforming the existing social relations. E. joined the Left wing of the Young Hegelians (q.v.) and subjected to his brilliant and profound criticism Schelling's (q.v.) reactionary-mystical views (*Schelling and the Revelation*, 1842, and others). At the same time he criticised Hegel (q.v.) for his conservative conclusions and the contradictions in his idealist dialectics. Engels' views took a radical turn when he came in contact with the life of the working class in the then most developed capitalist country, England. He gave much thought to the causes of the unbearable economic conditions of the proletarians, their deprivation of political rights. He studied the shortcomings which the Chartist movement revealed in its ideology and its utopian idea about the capitalists voluntarily giving up their power. The result of the study were his works: *A Contribution to the Critique of Political Economy* (1844), which Marx called a brilliant contribution to the critique of economic categories and *The Condition of the Working-Class in England* (1845). In these works E. laid the theoretical basis for the historic mission of the proletariat and showed that the latter was not only a suffering class but also a class struggling for its emancipation. In England he became a socialist. Soon he left England, and in 1844, he met Marx in Paris. This meeting marked the beginning of their deep friendship, which was based on their common ideas and joint struggle for the emancipation of the proletariat from capitalist enslavement. During the years 1844-46 they jointly wrote *The Holy Family* and *The German Ideology* (qq.v.) The aim of these works to reinterpret critically the then dominating philosophical views of Hegel, Feuerbach (q.v.) and their followers, and to elaborate the foundations of dialectical and historical materialism. In 1847, E. wrote the draft programme of the Communist League — *Principles of Communism*. On the basis of this Marx and E. wrote the *Manifesto of the Communist Party*, q.v. (1848), proclaiming the birth of the integral teaching of Marxism, the scientific ideology of the working class. E. got his baptism of fire fighting on the side of the revolutionary forces in Germany during the events of 1848-49. The following years, living in emigration, E. generalised the experience of the German revolution in his works: *The Peasant War in Germany* and *Revolution and Counter-Revolution in Germany*. These works disclosed the role of the peasantry as the proletariat's ally and exposed the treachery of the bourgeoisie. Having moved to England, where Marx had also settled, E. actively participated in the workers' movement, in the creation of the First International and in the struggle against petty-bourgeois opportunistic and anarchistic views. Since then E. helped Marx in every way with the latter's work on *Capital* (q.v.). He himself edited and published the second and the third volumes after the death of his great friend. In the process he did a great deal of research. E. continued to work hard on the comprehensive substantiation of dialectical and historical materialism. His contribution to Marxist philosophy is tremendous. Such works of E. as *Ludwig Feuerbach and the End of Classical German Philosophy, Anti-Dühring, The Origin of the Family, Private Property and the State* (qq.v.), etc., are a classical presentation of the essence and significance of Marxist philosophy. E. rendered particularly great service in applying the ideas of dialectical materialism to natural science. Many people realised the depth of his ideas dozens of years later (for example, the idea of the indissolubility of matter and motion, and the consequent teaching on the unity of time and space; the inexhaustibility of the forms of matter and the complex structure of atoms; the idea of life as a form of the motion of matter that arose at a certain stage of development of inorganic nature, etc.). E.'s versatility enabled him to work out a harmonious system for the classification of sciences (q.v.), basing the distinctions of disciplines on the objective forms of the motion of matter. Proceeding from this, E. categorically refused to impose upon philosophy the inappropriate role of science of sciences and emphasised its methodological value. E. provided philosophy with a means of orientation among the innumerable schools and systems of the past, formulated the fundamental question of philosophy (q.v.), and disclosed its class character. His contribution to the development of the theory of knowledge and his criticism of agnosticism (q.v.) are of great importance. His formulation and elaboration of certain problems of dialectical logic (q.v.) are of everlasting value. While elaborating the fundamental problems of historical materialism (q.v.), he devoted much attention to a critique of vulgar conceptions of the materialistic understanding of history. E. proved that the determinative role of the economic conditions in which people live does not in any way detract from the role of ideas or the role of the individual in history. He fought against the mechanistic views of the connections and interrelations between the economic basis and the superstructure, etc. E. took a great interest in the revolutionary movement in Russia, foretelling the imminent Russian revolution and placing great hopes in it. To the very end of his life he participated in the political life of many European countries and, together with Marx, was a recognised leader of the working-class movement.

Enlightenment, a socio-political trend, the representatives of which tried to correct the shortcomings of the existing society, to change its morals and manners, politics and way of life by spreading the ideas of goodness, justice, and scientific knowledge. At the base of E. lay the idealistic assumption that consciousness plays a decisive role in the development of society, the desire to account for social vices by men's ignorance and lack of understanding of their own nature. The Enlighteners did not take into account the decisive significance of the economic conditions of development and hence could not reveal the objective laws of society. The Enlighteners addressed their preachings to all classes and strata of society, but mainly to those in power. E. was widespread in the period of the preparation of bourgeois revolutions and expressed bourgeois and petty-bourgeois ideology. Among the Enlighteners were Voltaire, Rousseau, Montesquieu, Herder, Lessing, Schiller, Goethe, (qq.v.), and many others. Their activities considerably helped to undermine the influence of the clerical and feudal ideology. The Enlighteners struggled resolutely not only against the church, but also against religious dogmas, against the scholastic methods of thinking. E. exerted considerable influence upon the formation of sociological views in the 18th century. The ideas of E. made a great impression on the utopian socialists and Russian Narodniks.

Entelechy in Aristotle's (q.v.) philosophy and scholasticism (q.v.), purposefulness as a driving force (see Teleology), end in itself, or the active principle that converts possibility into reality. The concept of E. was used by Leibniz (q.v.) in his monadology. It is also connected with the idealistic interpretation of biological phenomena (see Vitalism).

Enthymeme, in traditional formal logic, a deductive inference in which one of the parts, either a premise or a conclusion, is not explicitly stated. For example, in the E. "all Marxists are materialists, therefore this man is also a materialist", the minor premise of the syllogism ("this man is a Marxist") is left out.

Entropy, one of the main concepts of classical physics, introduced into science by R. Clausius. According to the macroscopic point of view, E. expresses the convertibility of energy (q.v.); the greater the E. of a system the less its energy is able to convert. It is the concept of E. that allows us to formulate one of the fundamental laws of physics, the law of the increase of E., or the second principle of thermodynamics, which determines the direction of the conversion of energy. E. cannot decrease in a closed system. The achievement of maximum E. signifies the onset of a state of balance, in which no further conversion of energy is possible— the entire energy has been transformed into heat and a state of thermal balance has set in. The authors of the second principle of thermodynamics R. Clausius and W. Thomson, applied it to the Universe as a whole and arrived at the erroneous conclusion that "thermal death" of the Universe is inevitable. Subsequent development of physics deepened the content of E. The growth of E. is not absolute, it only expresses the most probable development of processes. For systems consisting of an infinitely great number of particles (the Universe or the world as a whole) the concept of the most probable state loses its meaning (in infinitely large systems all states are equally probable). By taking into account the role of gravitation, cosmology arrives at the conclusion that the E. of the Universe grows without tending to any maximum (the state of thermal balance). Modern science proves the complete groundlessness of the conclusions on the allegedly inevitable thermal balance and "thermal death" of the world.

Epicheirema, a syllogistic conclusion whose premises are enthymemes (q.v.).

Epictetus (c. 50-138 A.D.), an exponent of Roman stoicism born in slavery. His teaching was recorded and so the *Discourses of Epictetus* and other works have come down to us. E.'s teaching is divided into physics, logic, and ethics. The keynote of his teaching is his ethics, particularly his preaching of inner freedom. He argued that the master can be a slave to his passions, and the slave is free in his inner spiritual idependence; this freedom, however, cannot be obtained by changing the world. Not things themselves but the notions of them make him happy; the good and the evil are not inherent in things, but lie in our attitude towards them. That is why to be happy is a matter of will. The philosophy of E. expressed the passive protest of the oppressed classes against the system of slavery. This philosophy influenced Christianity (q.v.).

Epicurus (341-270 B.C.), Greek materialist philosopher and atheist of the Hellenic period. E. denied the gods' interference in the affairs of the world and recognised the eternity of matter as an inner source of motion. E. revived the atomism of Leucippus and Democritus (qq.v.), adding his own changes. He introduced the idea of spontaneous (internally conditioned) "deviation" of atoms from their course to explain the possibility of collisions between atoms moving in empty space with equal speed. This was the basis of a deeper view of the interrelation of necessity and chance (q.v.), a step forward, compared with Democritus' mechanistic determinism. In the theory of knowledge E. was a sensationalist. Sensations are true by themselves, because they proceed from objective reality; mistakes arise from the interpretation of sensa-

tions. The origin of sensations was explained by E. in a naively materialist manner: a continuous flow of minute particles is emitted from the surface of bodies to penetrate the sense-organs and produce images of things. The purpose of knowledge is to free man from ignorance and superstition, from the fear of gods and death, without which happiness is impossible. In ethics E. justified joys of the mind based on the individualistic ideal of evading suffering and attaining a quiet and joyful state of the soul. The most rational state for man is not activity but complete peace, ataraxia (q.v.). The materialist doctrine of E. was distorted in idealistic philosophy (e.g., by Hegel, q.v.).

Epiphenomenon, a term used to describe consciousness as a passive reflection of the material (or ideal) content of the world. It is used by the exponents of natural-scientific materialism (Th. Huxley, F. Le Dantec) and by some idealist philosophers (E. Hartmann, Nietzsche, Santayana, q.v.).

Epistemological and Class Roots of Idealism, the causes accounting for the origin and existence of idealist philosophy. Idealism (q.v.) derives from live human knowledge owing to the complex and contradictory nature of the latter. In the process of cognition there is always the possibility that man's sensations and concepts may become dissociated from real things and that fantasy may transcend objective reality. This possibility becomes reality whenever one of the aspects or facets of cognition is exaggerated, inflated to the proportions of an absolute divorced from matter and from nature, and even idolized. Objective idealism (q.v.) exaggerates, and makes an absolute of the role of concepts and abstract reasoning, while subjective idealism (q.v.) exaggerates the role of perceptions and sensations, counterposing them to the objective world. The class roots of idealism lie in the domination of the exploiting classes and in the isolation and counterposition of mental and physical labour (q.v.). This gives rise to a rift between knowledge and the practical activity of the working people and to monopolisation of ideological activity by the ruling classes, leading to the appearance and spread of illusions about the absolute independence and special creative role of the intellectual, ideal side of human activity. All this lies behind the incorrect notion that ideas and concepts are primary, and also behind the idealist approach to matter, nature and being. The theoretical and epistemological roots of idealism are closely associated with its class roots, which not only give birth to the idealist world outlook, but also assert it in the interests of the exploiting classes.

Epistemology, a theory of knowledge (q.v.), gnoseology. The term of E. is used in English, American and, more rarely, in French and German bourgeois philosophy. The introduction of this term is attributed to the Scottish philosopher J.F. Ferrier (*Institutes of Metaphysic*, 1854), who divided philosophy into ontology (q.v.) and E.

Equality 1. A concept denoting the identical condition of people in society, but having different contents in different historical epochs and among different classes. In bourgeois understanding E. means the equality of the citizens before the law, while the exploitation of man by man, property and political inequality and the actual absence of rights for the working people remain intact. Petty-bourgeois theories of E. proceed from the right of every man to own private property, though on more or less equalitarian principles. In either case, the main thing—relation to the means of production (q.v.)—is not taken into account. Marxism proceeds from the fact that economic E. (in the sphere of production, distribution, and consumption of material wealth), political E. (in the sphere of class, national and interstate relations) and cultural E. (in the sphere of production, distribution and consumption of cultural values) are impossible without abolition of private ownership of the means of production and liquidation of exploiting classes. Real E. in respect of the means of production appears only as a result of the victory of socialism. The socialist system retains some elements of social inequality owing, among other things, to the inadequate development of material production,

the survival of substantial distinctions between mental and physical labour, between town and country (qq.v.), and the application of the principle of distribution according to the quantity and quality of work done. Complete E. is created only under communism. However communism does not signify any equalisation of all men, but, on the contrary, opens up unlimited possibilities for every man freely to develop his capabilities and needs, according to his individual qualities and tastes. 2. In logic E. coincides with identity (q.v.). From the properties of E. follows, in particular, a well-known axiom: two quantities, each equal to a third quantity, are equal to each other.

Equilibrium, Theory of, a vulgar mechanistic and anti-dialectical theory which holds that equilibrium is a natural and "normal" condition, while movement, development is a temporary, transient condition. This theory sees the source of movement in external contradictions, denying the existence of inner contradictions in general and in particular their being the source of development. T.E. claims that the development of society depends chiefly on its relation with the surroundings, with nature; that society's external contradictions with nature, not the class struggle, are the motive force of development of an antagonistic society. T.E. was propounded by Comte, Kautsky, Bogdanov, (qq.v.) and others. Now it is shared by many idealists, bourgeois sociologists and economists. On the strength of T.E. the ideologists of opportunism build their anti-Marxist dogmas concerning the "peaceful growth" of capitalism into socialism, the "harmony" of class interests, ultra-imperialism, etc. In the period of building socialism in the Soviet Union it was used as a philosophical substantiation of the practice of Right opportunism. One of its postulates is that opposites (for instance, classes) must neutralise and balance each other, that this is allegedly the only way of making society stable. In reality, however, the opposites are in a state of conflict, and this conflict inevitably leads to the removal of the antithesis, to the resolution of concrete contradictions in society and to the transformation of society.

Equivalence (in logic), an operation which consists in the use of connectives like "if and only if" in logical conclusions and spoken language. E. is expressed through implication and conjunction (qq.v.).

Equivalence Relation (in logic), a relation between two propositions (judgments, sentences or formulas) showing that the two propositions are either true or false. The term of E. R. has a broader meaning, to be used to describe all kinds of relations based on equality. The following examples can be cited: similar or equal in size geometric figures, equipotent sets (see Set Theory), isomorphic systems (see Isomorphism and Homomorphism), and parallel straight lines and planes.

Erasmus Desiderius (a pen-name of Gerhard Gerhards, 1469-1536), a Netherlandish philosopher, humanist, scholar, fighter against scholasticism (q.v.) and the forerunner of the Reformation (q.v.). He considered the renaissance of ancient sciences and arts absolutely necessary for "true" Christianity. He was the first to study the Gospels philologically. From the standpoint of humanism he criticised both Catholicism and Protestantism (qq.v.), which was taking shape at the beginning of the 16th century. Fanaticism and violence, national narrow-mindedness and religious hatred, hypocrisy and ignorance were portrayed by the talented satirist in his well-known book *Praise of Folly* (1509). His criticism exerted a profound influence on the humanistic tradition in Europe.

Erigena, Johannes Scotus (810-877), philosopher of Irish birth who lived in France. On the basis of Neoplatonism (q.v.) E. created his mystic doctrine, the essence of which is expounded in his work *De Divisione naturae*. E. divided being in four natures: 1) a non-created but creating, God being the source of all things, the only non-created creator of everything; 2) created and creating—divine ideas existing as the primary causes; the ideal world was created by God, out of himself, and exists eternally; 3) created but not creating—the world perceptible by the senses, manifesting a single ideal world in the multiplicity of different things; 4) uncreated and uncreating—God, perceived as the ultimate end of all things. The second and the third natures have no independent existence and do not differ in their essence; they are but different manifestations of the single divine essence which exists in everything. E. associated the creation of things with the time, when man falls from grace. After a while, however, comes the atonement and all things return to God. In its essence E.'s system was pantheistic (see Pantheism) and was condemned by the Catholic Church.

Eristic, the art of dispute, particularly popular among sophists (q.v.) in ancient Greece. E. appeared as a means of searching truth through dispute, soon it fell into dialectics and sophistry (qq.v.). Dialectics was developed by Socrates (q.v.) in his method, and sophistry, whose sole aim was to get the upper hand over the opponent in dispute, reduced E. to a sum total of devices which helped to prove or refute any statement with equal success. Therefore, even Aristotle made no difference between E. and sophistry.

Error, a distorted perception of reality conditioned at each given moment by restricted socio-historical practice. E. should be distinguished from falsehood (q.v.), which is a conscious distortion of truth, and from mistakes arising from the incorrect behaviour of the individual. This or that understanding of E. depends on the initial principles of the theory of knowledge (q.v.). The contemplative character (see Contemplativeness) of the pre-Marxist philosophy resulted, e.g., in identifying E. with mistake, which stems from the imperfection of man's cognitive capabilities. Surmises about the nature of E., about the correlation of truth (q.v.) and error arise only in the course of the formation of a dialectical approach to cognition. Thus, Hegel (q.v.), considering truth as a process, regarded E. not as an abstract opposite of truth but as its moment, as an historically limited ("finite") form of the movement of human consciousness towards truth. In Marxist philosophy E. is considered to be a result of limited practice or of its comprehension, which in the actual course of cognition appears as absolutisation of the results of the assimilation of reality's separate aspects, of the elements of truth. That is why E. is not just illusion, it fixes attention upon the surface of phenomena; the historically limited characteristics of these phenomena are thus turned into "natural", and, consequently, eternal and absolute. In this case E. forms the basis for the behaviour of individuals, who are included into the historically limited forms of practical activity, and becomes a prejudice. All this impedes the critical understanding of reality, and in the social sciences serves to reconcile man with the existing order of things. To overcome such Ee. it is necessary to change social conditions which gave birth to them. This presupposes a critical approach to the existing order of things from the positions of practice, taken in its historical development, tendencies and prospects.

Eschatology, a religious doctrine on the ultimate fate of the world, mankind, the end of the world, and doomsday. It is based on the ancient notions of occult, active powers in nature, the struggle between the good and the evil, the punishment of sinners and the reward of righteous after death. The E. ideas are to be found in their developed form in Christianity, q.v. (Apocalypse) and in Judaism (q.v.). Eschatologic moods were widely spread during social and political crises, as in Judea in the 1st century A.D., in Germany in the 15th and 16th centuries, in England in the 16th and 17th centuries, and in Russia at the turn of the 17th century. Even today clergymen and sectarians make use of E. Contemporary theologians falsify data obtained by natural science to strengthen the position of E.

Esoteric and Exoteric. The term esoteric is used to name an idea or theory meant only for initiates, understandable only to experts. The term exoteric, on the contrary, is used in the meaning of popular, clear even to laymen. The terms are also used to qualify essential inner (esoteric) and external (exoteric) connections of phenomena.

Essence, the meaning of a given thing, that which is in itself, in contradistinction from all other things and in contrast to the states of a thing changing under the influence of various circumstances. The concept of E. is of great importance for any philosophical system, and for drawing a distinction between systems from the standpoint of how the relationship between E. and being and between the E. of things and consciousness is viewed. Objective idealism takes being, reality, and existence (q.v.) as dependent on the E. of things, which is regarded as something independent, indisputable, and absolute. In that case, the E. of things constitute a specific ideal reality which produces all things and guides them (see Plato; Hegel). Subjective idealists take E. to be the product of the subject, who projects E. in the form of things. The only correct view is to recognise the reality of the objective E. of things and its reflection in the mind. E. does not exist outside of things, but in and through them, as their main common property, as their law. Human knowledge gradually delves deeper and deeper into the E. of the objective world. This knowledge is used for reciprocal action on the objective world for the purpose of its practical transformation (see Essence and Appearance).

Essence and Appearance, philosophical categories reflecting universal and essential aspects of all objects and processes in the world. E. is a sum total of latent ties, relations and internal laws determining the main features and trends in development of a material system. Aa. are individual phenomena, properties or processes expressing outward aspects of reality, a form of manifestation and revelation of some E. The categories of E. and A. are always inseparably linked. There is no E. that would not make any outward appearance and lend itself to cognition, and there is no A. that would contain no information about E. However, the unity of E. and A. does not mean that they are identical, since E. is always hidden behind the surface of A., and the deeper it lies the more difficult and lengthy is its cognition in theory: "...All science would be superfluous if the outward appearance and the essence of things directly coincided" (K. Marx, *Capital,* Vol. III, p. 817). E. can be cognised by abstract thinking and through the creation of a theory of the process under investigation. This cognition is a qualitative leap from the empirical to the theoretical level of knowledge, and implies the discovery of the determinative in objects, the laws of their change and development. This is concurrent with the transition from the description (q.v.) of Aa. to their explanation (q.v.), to the discovery of their causes and grounds. The E. may be considered as cognised if, among other things, there is the exact wording of the laws governing movement and development of the objects, if the forecasts made on the basis of these laws and the conditions of their operation are confirmed, if, in addition, we know the causes of the emergence and the sources of development of the object under consideration, if we have revealed the ways of its formation or technical reproduction, and if we have created, in theory or in practice, its adequate model (see Modelling), the properties of which are identical with those of the original. The knowledge of E. permits to separate the true objective content of A. from its outward aspects, and to rid the research of distortion and subjectivism. The tasks of cognition are not confined to revealing E. They call for a theoretical explanation and substantiation of the laws that have been formulated earlier, the sphere of their application, their correlation with other laws, and the like. This involves cognition of deeper structural levels of matter, or else the discovery of a system of more general ties and relations of which the phenomenon under consideration constitutes an element. To do this, it is necessary to cognise more general and fundamental laws of being, with the laws and processes discovered earlier as their particular manifestations. A transition is made to deeper E. on new structural levels of matter. The dialectic of the unity and diversity reveals itself in the relations between E. and A. One and the same E. may have many different appearances, while any sufficiently complex A. may be determined by several Ee. related to different structural levels of matter. E. is always more stable than concrete Aa., but in the long run the essences of all systems and processes in the world are subject to ultimate change in accordance with the universal dialectical laws governing the development of matter. Any science can achieve maturity and perfection only when it reveals the E. of the Aa. it studies, and is capable of predicting future change in the sphere of both E. and A. Agnosticism (q.v.) groundlessly separates E. from A., and regards E. as an unknowable "thing in itself" which is not manifested in A., and does not lend itself to cognition. Idealists ascribe ideal, divine origin to the E. of things and contend that it is primary in relation to the material things.

Etatism, a conception in bourgeois political science which implies active intervention by the state (q.v.) in a country's economy and politics. It is in contrast with the ideas of state non-intervention in the economy which were typical of pre-monopoly capitalism. The theories of E. are also widespread in developing countries. They claim that the state alone can be a motive force of economic development, can ensure modernisation of production, overcome ethnic disunity, tribalism and separatist trends, secure the unity of the nation and strengthen the country's independence.

Eternity, infinite duration of the existence of the world resulting from the uncreatability and undestructibility of matter, and the material unity of the world. E. is inherent only in all matter as a whole. Every concrete formation in the world is transient in time. E. is not reducible to an unlimited homogeneous existence of matter in one and the same state or to an endless succession of historical cycles but presupposes constant qualitative transformations of matter and its assuming new states.

Ethical Relativism, a methodological principle of interpreting morality based on the assumption that moral ideas and standards are mere conventions. E.R. negates the possibility of creating scientific ethics. Its advocates do not realise that morality is dependent on the social background; moreover, they do not understand the essence of the objective historical laws that determine it. E.R. was prominent in the doctrine of the sceptics (Pyrrho, q.v., and others), later it was upheld by the followers of Mandeville, q.v. (see Moral Sense, Theories of). It is also inherent in certain modern trends in bourgeois philosophy: neo-positivism, existentialism and pragmatism (qq.v.). Ayer and Carnap (qq.v.), for example, considered it impossible even to raise the question of the correctness or incorrectness of a moral judgment. E.R. logically results in justifying amoralism (q.v.).

Ethics, one of the most ancient theoretical disciplines that studies morality (q.v.). E. appeared in the early stage of slave-owning society and singled out from the spontaneous moral consciousness of society as one of the principal integral parts of philosophy and, unlike purely theoretical knowledge of reality, gave practical recommendations on how to behave. Later E. was divided into theoretical and practical, into philosophical and normative E. (q.v.). In modern bourgeois E. this historically justified division has resulted in alienation between science and morality (see Linguistic Analysis in Ethics; Logical Positivism; Metaethics). In the history of E., theory was traditionally set off against practice, and this caused certain difficulties to the solution of its key problem—what the source and basis of moral ideas is. Attempts were often made to find the source of moral ideas in "extra-historical" principle: God, nature of man, cosmic laws (see Naturalism; Ethics, Theological), some a priori principle or self-developing absolute idea (see Kant and Hegel), or some authority (see Ethics, Approbative). In the 20th century, the crisis of these traditional theories has found its reflection in the statement on the impossibility of theoretical substantiation of moral ideas made by bourgeois E. and in the latter's split into two opposing trends (irrationalism and formalism, qq.v.). Marxism alone bridges the antithesis between theory and practice by explaining their social and historical nature and proves scientifically that the sources of moral ideas are the historically developing modes of production, the structures of social life logically replacing one another and progress made by material and spiritual culture of society. Marx-

ism alone sheds light upon the nature of morality, its place in social life and the specific reflection of social being in moral consciousness. Accordingly Marxists solve the question of the subject-matter and the tasks of Marxist E. which embraces a number of spheres of investigation. One of the tasks is to study the development of human morality that takes the form of a struggle between moral ideas of different socio-economic formations and classes with their subsequent change, and also the form that reflects this process—the history of ethical doctrines. Today the task of E. is to substantiate historically the highest form of human morality, communist morality (q.v.), to criticise bourgeois morality and E. Thus, conclusions made in the historical theory of E. find their natural development in normative E., and the latter ceases to be a self-sufficient teaching opposed to theoretical E. Moral principles are not established by individual philosophers, proponents of one or another trend, but are elaborated in the process of social practice, reflecting the experience of many generations, of the whole people as well as that of individual classes. Marxist E. also analyses the nature and mechanism of morality, studies it as one of the forms of man's social activity, and a special form of social relations and consciousness. In the period of communist construction both the theoretical tasks and significance of Marxist E. grow immensely. It generalises and systematises the principles of communist morality formulated by working people in the process of building a new society and puts them on a scientific foundation; it serves as a scientific basis for the moral education of working people, helps them to adhere to a firm stand on key problems of today and to take an uncompromising attitude to any violation of the norms of communist morality.

Ethics, Approbative, idealist theories of morality in which good is defined as that which someone has approved or ordered. According to who does the approving (God, man's moral sense, society), A.E. is subdivided into theological, psychological, and social approbative theories. An example of the first is the ethical doctrine of neo-Protestantism (q.v.) which considers God's absolute will the supreme law of morality. Conceptions of the second type were called theories of moral sense. Social approbative ethics was founded by French sociologists Durkheim and Lévi-Brühl (qq.v.). According to their theory of "collective notions", moral evaluations and instructions are deprived of any objective and cognitive meaning whatsoever, and based solely on having been sanctioned by society. It is therefore supposedly useless to try to prove their truth scientifically. The psychological and social approbative conception of the phenomena of morality brought them subsequently to their sceptical and nihilistic interpretation (see Logical Positivism; Emotivism). On the whole A.E. denies objective assessment criteria in morality, which results in renunciation of man's rationally critical attitude to his own or society's moral notions and in their adoption through blind faith or subjective bias.

Ethics, Evolutionary, a trend in bourgeois ethics founded by Spencer (q.v.) and developing in the framework of ethical naturalism. In the 20th century, E.E. was upheld by J. Huxley, C. Waddington (Britain), E. Holt, R. Gerard (USA), Teilhard de Chardin, q.v. (France) and others. E.E. regards man's moral behaviour as a function of his adaptation to the environment. The criterion of morality is the process of development (evolution) embracing the whole living world; everything that promotes it is good, everything that hampers it is evil. Man produces moral ideas and concepts to have his bearings in natural and social phenomena. Society is but the highest form of the natural association of living beings of the same species. Recently attempts have been made to put E.E. on a genetic foundation, this is evident from socio-biological theories (E. Wilson and others) which inflate the significance of evolutionary and genetic prerequisites of ethics. By and large, E.E. has serious methodological drawbacks, because a biological interpretation of society and morality cannot be considered scientific; it is always fraught with anti-social and amoral conclusions.

Ethics, Normative, the ethics which studies the problems of the meaning of human life and the designation of man, the content of good and evil (q.v.), and of moral duty (q.v.). N.E. gives a theoretical substantiation of moral principles, ideals and norms. It considers theoretically the problems which spontaneously arise and are solved in the moral consciousness of this or that society or class. Any ethical conception, reflecting the moral ideal of certain social groups, is in the final analysis normative. To solve the contradiction, which allegedly exists between the scientific truth and morality, neopositivists attempt to create a "scientific" ethics by eliminating from it the normative questions (see Metaethics). Marxism, however, believes that it is possible to give a scientific theoretical substantiation of moral ideas only through cognition of the laws of history and that these ideas reflect the objective logic of the development of society. The morality of the working class does not only answer this condition but is also the basis for the formation of general human morality in a classless society. The limitations of idealist and other unscientific views on N.E. can be overcome not through separation of theory from practice, from the struggle of the classes and their moral outlooks, but through the realisation of the historical prospects of this struggle. N.E. becomes truly scientific by virtue of a strict objective analysis of the entire history of human morality and a study of its social prerequisites. As a substantiation of norms and principles of communist morality, N.E. is closely connected with all the other branches of Marxist ethics.

Ethics, Theological, ethics founded on some theological system. The most influential trends in T.E. were and still are the ethical doctrines of the three main religions: Christianity, Islam, and Buddhism (qq.v.). The source of morals in T.E. is God. God is the embodiment of moral good and virtue, while evil and amorality in society are due to the "original sin". Moreover, God is the only criterion of what is moral. An action is either good or bad depending on whether it conforms or does not conform to the will of God. And, finally, God gives a moral sanction, i.e., is the only authority in evaluating the morality of an action. T.E. is anti-social in its aim, since it negates the right of society to produce moral evaluations. A great place in it is taken up by the doctrine of the reward of the righteous and the punishment of sinners, which theologians associate with the end of the world (see Eschatology). The complete triumph of the good and the just is ascribed either to life-after-death or to the advent of the "kingdom of God". Hence, submission, humility, non-resistance to evil and remission are elevated to the rank of virtues.

Euclid (4th century-beginning of the 3rd century B.C.), Greek mathematician, author of the famous *Elements*, in which ancient geometry and the theory of numbers were given systematically, according to the axiomatic method (q.v.). The famous (fifth) postulate of E. is logically equivalent to the statement: through a given point *P* not on a given line *L* there passes at most one line, in the plane of *P* and *L*, which does not intersect *L*. Geometry, based on this postulate, is called Euclidean geometry. Attempts to prove the parallel postulate led in the 19th century to the discovery of non-Euclidean geometries (see Lobachevsky). E. was strongly influenced by Plato's and Aristotle's (qq.v.) philosophy. His *Elements* were a model for deductive science. Euclidean geometry was the basis of some philosophical conclusions on the nature of space and the notions of real space.

Eudaemonism, a methodological principle of ethics, close to hedonism (q.v.). It has already been fully developed in the ethical theories in antiquity (Democritus, Socrates, Aristotle, qq.v.). The desire for happiness, either personal (individualist E.) or public (social E.), is considered the main criterion of morality and the chief motive of human behaviour. The French materialists of the 18th century (Helvétius, Diderot, qq.v.) also upheld E., claiming that happiness is the chief end of any society and of any useful human activity. More active and humane in its call for happiness on earth and not in the hereafter, eudaemonistic ethics stands incomparably higher than Christian ethics.

The adherents of E. regard happiness as a concept common to all mankind and all epochs, although there is not and cannot be any common understanding of man's mission in a society with antagonistic classes. This mission is always conditional upon the social environment. Therefore, eudaemonistic interpretation of morality cannot be considered scientific.

Eugenics, in bourgeois science the term is used to denote a doctrine similar to racialism and Malthusianism (qq.v.), which, distorting Darwin's (q.v.) teaching, explains social inequality through psychological and physiological disparities between human beings. The eugenists advocate artificial selection in order to create "a new breed" of people. Nowadays eugenics is being regenerated in the form of neo-eugenics, which seeks to rely on the achievements of modern genetics (q.v.), gene engineering, etc. The problem of heredity and its improvement can be scientifically solved only within the bounds of man's genetics.

Europocentrism, in philosophy and culture, a conception according to which genuine science, art, philosophy and literature are developing only in Europe. The sources of E. can be seen in the contraposition of the Graeco-Roman civilisation to the Barbarians. In the Middle Ages E. was maintained by the ideologues of Catholicism (q.v.), who considered Rome and Papacy as the intellectual centre of the world. Early bourgeois E. also had a religious basis and often served to camouflage the colonialist aspirations of the European capitalist countries. The ideas of E. were shared, among others, by Hegel, who saw the Prussian empire as a stronghold of freedom and true culture and by J. Michelet, who ignored non-European culture. Theories of Spengler and Toynbee (qq.v.) to a certain extent reflect the ideas of E. They deny succession and existence of connections between autonomous cultures. From the ideological point of view E. serves to protect "European", i.e., capitalist civilisation, to praise the bourgeois way of life and to justify neocolonialism. "Eastcentrism", which maintains that European culture has borrowed much from the

Eastern culture, and the theory of Negritude, the proponents of which regard the African culture as standing above all other cultures, can be considered a peculiar response to E. Progressive thinkers of Europe, beginning with the Enlighteners, disapproved of the E. and suggested the idea of universal human and cultural history common to all peoples. The line of Montesquieu, Voltaire, Herder, Goethe (qq.v.) and others in the question of universal cultural progress is continued by Marxism-Leninism, which strongly criticises both E. and other conceptions of the cultural exclusiveness of certain peoples or regions.

Evolution and Revolution, concepts used to describe different aspects of development. In the broad sense of the word E. implies changes in being and consciousness, both quantitative and qualitative. In this meaning it is close to the concept of development (q.v.). The relation between quantitative and qualitative changes manifests itself in the correlation of the two concepts—E. (in the narrow sense of the word) and R. Accordingly, the term E. stands for rather gradual quantitative changes, while R. implies radical, qualitative, leap-like transformations. The E. and R. correlation is expressed in the law of transition from quantity to quality (q.v.). The complexity of this correlation becomes evident when we analyse the emergence of something new. Clearly, the new cannot grow out of nothing as a product of supernatural creation (see Creationism), it is always the result of previous states. At the same time previous states cannot by themselves produce the new, because the emergent new is something entirely different from those states. Within the framework of metaphysics this contradiction cannot be solved, because the two aspects of the contradiction are treated separately, with one aspect being raised to an absolute. As a result, development is understood either as a mere E. (see Spencer) or as a sum total of causeless and independent of the previous development leaps (see Cuvier, Emergent Evolution). A one-sided approach of this kind is particularly harmful when applied to social development because the result is either the denial of the revolutionary transformation of society (see Reformism) or the leftist ideas about unconditioned "R.", about direct "revolutionary" violence as a means of solving any problem, and about "the export of R." (anarchism, q.v.). Marxist philosophy understands development as a solution of the contradiction inherent in a developing phenomenon. Therefore, the negation of a phenomenon emerges in the phenomenon itself, when necessary conditions are created in the process of E. The emergence of the new, however, is only possible as an interruption of gradual development, as a leap (q.v.). Thus, E. and R. are the necessary aspects of any development: E. prepares R., and the latter crowns the former. This is also true of social Rr.

Evolution Theory, the doctrine of living nature elaborated chiefly by Darwin (q.v.). The E.T. summed up the results of many centuries of selective practice, the achievements of biology, geology and paleontology, and Darwin's observations in a round-the-world trip. Darwin believed that the main factors in the evolution of living creatures are mutation, heredity and selection (artificial in domestic conditions, natural in nature). In the struggle for existence in varied environmental conditions only the fittest of living creatures survive and procreate. Natural selection continuously improves the structure and functions of organisms, develops their adaptability to the environment. E.T. first provided a scientific explanation to a great variety of biological species and their development, and became the basis of modern biology. E.T., together with the natural scientific theories of Kant (q.v.) and J. Lamarck, showed the fallacy of the metaphysical way of thinking. It also delivered a blow to the idealistic views on living nature, and formed the natural and historical basis of the dialectico-materialist outlook. Further development of E.T. is connected with discoveries in the genetic mechanism of hereditary variation, with the studies of species populations, and etc.

Excluded Middle, Law of, a law of logic, according to which of the two propositions, one of which denies what the other affirms, one is necessarily true. It was first formulated by Aristotle (q.v.). Thus, of the two statements: "The sun is a star" (A is B) and "The sun is not a star" (A is not B) one is necessarily true. Having in view such statements, traditional formal logic formulated the L.E.M. as follows: either A is B or is not B. No third is possible (tertium non datur). The L.E.M. is often used in the process of proof (q.v.), for example, by the rule of contraries.

Existence 1. the whole diversity of mutable things in their concatenation and interaction. The E. of things cannot be reduced either to their inner essence, or to their being. Those philosophical theories are wrong, which rate the essence, cause (qq.v.) of things above their E., regarding the latter as something base, accidental, and short-lived. But it is just as wrong to rate the E. of things above their essence, regarding the latter either as non-existent, or as something unfathomable and beyond human cognition and practice. The correct view is that just as essence is inconceivable without E. (in which case there is a realm of immobility, which has nothing in common with real life in nature and society), so E. is inconceivable without essence (in which case, only the external, the restless, and the accidental are registered). An understanding of all existing phenomena can be gained only from a unity of E. and essence, being and becoming (qq.v.). 2. one of the main concepts in existentialism used to describe the way of being of human personality. Kierkegaard (q.v.) was the first to use the term E. in this meaning. Existentialists maintain that E. is the kernel of human "ego" thanks to which this latter does not exist as a separate individual or something general (human) but as a concrete unique personality. One of the main characteristics of E. is that it cannot be objectified. Man can objectify his abilities, knowledge and know-how practically—in the form of external objects; he can, furthermore, analyse his psychic actions, his thinking, objectifying them theoretically. Only E. cannot be objectified by man either practically or theoretically, cannot be cognised and, therefore, is beyond his power. The

theory of E. is directed both against the rationalist understanding of man, according to which human essence lies in man's mind, and the Marxist understanding of human essence as a totality of social relations.

Existentialism, a philosophy of existence, an irrational trend in bourgeois philosophy which appeared in the 20th century in an attempt to create a new world outlook corresponding to the frame of mind of bourgeois intellectuals. E. has its ideological roots in the philosophy of life (q.v.), Husserl's phenomenology (qq.v.) and mystico-religious teachings of Kierkegaard (q.v.). E. is subdivided into the religious E. (Marcel, Jaspers, Berdyayev, qq.v.) and the atheistic E. (Heidegger, Sartre, Camus, qq.v.). E. reflects the crisis of superficial optimistic world-view and belief in progressive development of bourgeois society inherent in bourgeois liberalism which gave way under the pressure of the present turbulent century. Having emerged as a pessimistic world outlook, E. tried to answer the question how a man should live after his liberal illusions had been shattered by historical disasters. E. is a reaction to the rationalism of the Enlightenment and classical German philosophy, to Kantianism and positivism widespread at the turn of this century. The existentialists maintain that the essential feature of rational thought is that it proceeds from the principle of antithesis of subject and object (q.v.). As a result the rationalist considers all reality, including man, only as an object of investigation and practical manipulation, and for this reason such approach is "impersonal". E. must be an antithesis to impersonal scientific thought. Thus, philosophy is set off against science. Heidegger, for example, believes that subject-matter of philosophy is "being", while subject-matter of science is "existing". "Existing" is everything that belongs to the empirical world and should not be confused with "being" itself. The latter is comprehended by man not indirectly (through rational thinking) but directly, through his being, his personal existence (q.v.). It is the existent that incarnates the unbreakable unity of subject and object, which cannot be comprehended by either rational-scientific thinking or speculative thinking. In everyday life man is not always aware of himself as existence, for this he must find himself in a border-line situation (q.v.), for example, in the face of death. When he has realised himself as existence, man gains freedom for the first time. According to E., freedom means that man should not be a thing that is being shaped under the influence of natural or social necessity but he should mould himself by his every act or deed. Thus, a free man takes responsibility for what he has done and does not try to justify himself by "circumstances". Sense of guilt for what is going on around him is the sense of a free man (Berdyayev). The existentialist conception of freedom reflects the protest against conformism (q.v.) and time-serving typical of a bourgeois philistine who believes that as a screw in the gigantic bureaucratic machine he is unable to change anything in the chain of events. That is why E. constantly emphasises that man is held responsible for everything that happens in history. However, the explanation of freedom by E. is subjectivist because it discusses freedom in a purely ethical and not in a social plane. While rejecting rational cognition as improper for the subject-matter of philosophy, E. offers the method of immediate intuitive cognition of reality, basing mainly on Husserl's theory and partially on Bergson's (q.v.) intuitionism. Many of the existentialists (Heidegger in his later period, Marcel, Camus and others) believe that by its method of cognition philosophy is closer to art than to science. It is not accidental that E. is exerting profound influence on Western art and literature, and through them on the frame of mind of a large section of the bourgeois intelligentsia. Social and political views upheld by various groups of E. are dissimilar.

Expediency, a property of processes or phenomena conducive to a certain result, to a purpose (q.v.) in a broad or a conventional sense of the term. E. is specific in organic life, social systems, human activity. E. assumes a different shape in each of those realms: in organic life it finds its expression in the adaptability and regulatory properties of organ-

isms, in the orderly character of the development process; in social life it is expressed in the decay of the obsolescent social structures and the origination of new ones promoting further social progress, in the purposeful actions of people, etc. Facts of organic E., employed in teleology (q.v.), were given scientific interpretation in Darwin's (q.v.) theory of natural selection, E. of forms of social life—in Marx's economic theory and historical materialism (q.v.). The highest form of E. is the E. of human activity (q.v.), whose cause-and-effect sequence includes conscious purpose as its most important link. All man's actions conforming to a certain purpose are "expedient" in a broader sense. In a narrower sense, only such activity is expedient that follows the overall trend of development and is based on known objective laws and developmental requirements, rather than just suitable to current conditions.

Experience, in the traditional philosophical sense, sensuous empirical reflection of the external world. The view that E. is the only source of knowledge is widespread (see Empiricism; Sensationalism). Materialism recognises the external objective source of E., independent of consciousness. The contemplativeness (q.v.) of pre-Marxian materialism is reflected in its view that E. is merely the result of passive perception of the external world. But sense E. does not by itself give universal and necessary knowledge; it merely grasps the outward, superficial side of phenomena of the objective world. As a reaction to the shortcomings of contemplative materialism in interpreting the concept of E. there arose rationalism (q.v.), on the one hand, and the subjective idealist and agnostic understanding of E., on the other. The latter reduces E. to various states of the subject's consciousness (emotions, sensations, perceptions, verbal statements, theoretical constructions of thinking), while its source is either ignored or declared to be unknowable in principle. Kant (q.v.) held a special position on this question, considering that the chaotic influence of the object ("thing-in-itself") on consciousness becomes E. only when systematised by a priori forms of reason. But in Kant's presentation of the question, notwithstanding its idealism, there is rational meaning, namely, the idea of active thinking by the subject engaged in cognition. Contemporary positivism (q.v.), reducing E. to sensations, to sensory emotions of man, etc., in effect denies the possibility and necessity for raising and solving the question of what stands behind this E., i.e., the existence of a real world, independent of consciousness. Utilising the achievements of preceding philosophy and continuing the traditions of materialism. Marxism overcame contemplativeness in interpreting E. Acknowledging experience to be secondary, derivative, in relation to objective reality, Marxism defines it not as the passive content of consciousness but as man's practical action on the external world. In the process of this action the necessary connections, properties and laws of phenomena are discovered, rational methods and means of activity are explored and tested, etc. E. is thus understood both as an interaction of the social subject with the external world and as the result of such interaction. In such an understanding E. merges with the sum total of society's practical activity. E. is a primary means of enriching science and developing theory and practice. Scientific experiment and observation (qq.v.) also come under the head of E.

Experiment, an investigation of phenomena by actively influencing them through creating new conditions in keeping with the investigator's purposes or through altering the process in the required direction. E. is an aspect of man's social and historical practice, and is, therefore, a source of knowledge and a criterion of the truth of hypotheses and theories. As science and technology develop the sphere of E. expands, embracing ever greater number of objects in the material world. E. is to define the object of the investigation, to create the necessary conditions, including the removal of interfering factors, to exert material influences on the object, and to apply requisite technical devices. E. must not be confused with simple observation (q.v.), which does not involve active influence upon the object, or with "mental" E., which is a form of theoretical modelling

(q.v.) of processes and systems impracticable at the given moment for technical or other reasons. A special form of E. today is the investigation of complex processes or systems designed with the help of technical models. It can be supplemented with a theoretical modelling of processes with the help of computers. In contrast with apriorism (see A priori) dialectical materialism regards E. and observation as a source of theoretical conceptions. Their connection with E. can be direct if they are drawn up directly from the experience or indirect if they are deduced as a result of the analysis of the effects of laws or propositions established earlier through direct E. Theory (q.v.) is a qualitatively new level in cognition as compared to E. It shows that the thought moves from phenomena to essence, to a still deeper knowledge of laws. Today complex forms of E. are calculated and designed on a theoretical basis.

Explanation, an important function of human knowledge, notably scientific research (and, correspondingly, that stage of the latter where this function is fulfilled). It consists in revealing the essence (q.v.) of the object studied. In the practice of a researcher E. is secured by showing that the object that is being explained obeys a certain law (q.v.) or laws. E. is closely connected with description (q.v.), is usually based on it, and is itself a basis for scientific prevision (q.v.).

Explication 1. A stage of investigation intended for revealing the essence of an object or phenomenon, explanation (q.v.). 2. Unfolding, a process as a result of which the contents of a certain unity are uncovered, and its components become independent and may be differentiated from one another. The term of E. is widely used in this meaning in idealist philosophy. For example, Neoplatonism (q.v.) regards the world and individual things as E., "self-unfolding" of God, in whom from the very beginning they exist in unity. Hegel (q.v.) held reality to be the self-unfolding of a concept into a plurality of its definitions. 3. Logico-methodological method of substituting an exact scientific concept for a well-known out inexact notion or idea. It is widely used in logical semantics (q.v.) where the term of E. assumed the latter meaning.

Extent, one of the main characteristics of space, expressing its dimensions. In the concept of E. is reflected the relative stability and constancy of a definite type of relations between objects and phenomena. It is precisely this stability that makes it possible to compare the dimensions of bodies. Metaphysical materialism, divorcing space from matter in motion, regarded it as pure E. Thus, the ancient atomists, assuming the existence of void as a necessary condition of the movement of atoms, attributed to space the only property—that of E. In the philosophy of the 17th-18th centuries the view of space as pure E. was more prominently expressed by Descartes (q.v.). Leibniz (q.v.), criticising the Cartesian conception of space, correctly showed that from E. one may conclude only the geometrical properties of space. To explain E. we need a body, without it E. would be vain abstraction. In mathematics, a clear distinction between such geometrical properties of space as E. and form and its physical properties was drawn only after non-Euclidean geometries (q.v.) had been discovered. By defining space as a form of the existence of matter, dialectical materialism at the same time affirms that the spatial properties of bodies, in particular their E., depend upon the properties of matter in motion.

External and Internal, the. 1. Aspects of an object or process differing by their place and role in the structure of the whole. The category of the external reflects the superficial aspect of the object immediately perceived by the senses, or the reality existing outside the object. The category of the internal expresses the essential aspect of the object. This internal aspect cannot be immediately perceived and is known through the external, through its manifestations. The external aspects of the object are determined by its internal aspects, by law (q.v.), by the essence (q.v.) through which they are revealed and known. Investigation of the internal nature of the object leads to an understanding of its contradictions, the source of its development, and the external forms in which it manifests itself. 2. Aspects of reality, which are defined as the external and internal worlds. In this sense, the internal is the spiritual world, while the external is the world of nature, objective processes taking place in society. The actual connection between the external and the internal, the objective and the subjective was elucidated in the history of sciences and philosophy through the struggle of materialism against idealism and agnosticism.

f

Fa Chia (legalists), a leading ideological trend in ancient China. Shang Yang (390-338 B.C.) and Han Fei Tzu (288-233 B.C.) were its most prominent exponents. The followers of F.C., expressing the interests of the new nobility which had become rich with the development of exchange relations, resolutely fought against the survivals of the gentile system and the communal-patriarchal traditions and stood for the unification of the country and strictly centralised administration. Thus, Shang Yang carried out a number of reforms in the state of the Chin period and thereby facilitated the founding of the first empire in China in the late 3rd century B.C. Han Fei Tzu provided the philosophical basis for the economic and political views of F.C. He held that natural laws determine the development of things. Human society must also have its own laws which would serve as the criterion of men's actions. These laws are the chief instrument of the state in the struggle against various socio-political forces, for consolidating the country's might and prosperity by despotic means. Han Fei Tzu and other proponents of F.C. opposed Confucianism (q.v.).

Fact. We distinguish objective and scientific Ff. An objective F. is an event, phenomenon or fragment of reality that is an object of man's practical activity or knowledge. A scientific F. is the reflection of an objective F. in human consciousness, i.e., its description in a definite language. Scientific Ff. are the basis for theoretical constructions which would be impossible without them. As an individual phenomenon or event the F. is necessarily connected with other Ff. through various relations. Scientific knowledge should therefore give as full a picture as possible of Ff. with all their interrelations and interconnections. An aggregate of scientific Ff. forms a scientific description (q.v.). A scientific F. is inseparable from the language it is expressed in and, consequently, from the terms in which the concepts are formulated. An idealistic interpretation of the F., going from Hume (q.v.) and empirio-criticism (q.v.) to neo-positivism (q.v.), treats Ff. as something existing only in man's sensations. According to this conception, the world is seen as an aggregate of isolated, "atomistic facts", elements of sense experience connected with each other through the subject.

Factors, Theory of, a positivist sociological conception which has gained wide currency in the West and in Russia since the late 19th century (Weber, Kovalevsky, qq.v.). Its principal feature is denial of monism (q.v.) in sociology and recognition of the mechanical interaction of many diverse equal factors (economics, religion, morality, technology, culture, and others). Being an expression of pluralism (q.v.) in sociology, the T.F. denies the objective laws of social development, the internal links between social phenomena, and has slipped into subjective idealism. The proponents of this theory, unable to elaborate a scientific theory of society, hold that the main task of the social and historical sciences is to describe social, technological, cultural, and other factors in their external interaction. Pointing to some positive elements in this theory (attempts at a concrete analysis of the facts of social, scientific, technical, and cultural realities), Marxism-Leninism has demonstrated its complete theoretical unsoundness, its mechanistic methodology, and hence its inability to grasp the essence of social phenomena. A modified form of the T.F. exists in our time, too. Some modern bourgeois sociologists single out as the determining factors of social development technology and industry (e.g., R. Aron's "industrial civilisation", Bell's (q.v.) "post-industrial society" theory, and some futurological conceptions) and sometimes the economy as a whole. New concepts have been introduced into the T.F. owing to recognition of the role of important spheres of material production such as technology and industry, and also of concrete socio-economic and cultural processes connected with present-day scientific and technical progress. But the role of these factors is patently exaggerated. Modern varieties of the T.F. have their epistemological roots in neo-positivist and vulgar-materialist views on society.

Faith, recognition of something as true without proof. Blind F. in the supernatural (God, angels, devils, etc.) is a part of any religion (q.v.). In this sense there is no difference between F. and superstition (q.v.). Religious F. stands at the opposite pole to knowledge. Nevertheless many idealist philosophers try to reconcile F. with knowledge or to pass it off as knowledge (see Fideism). In its usual connotation F. means conviction of the truth of scientific hypotheses and suppositions which at the moment cannot be proved either in theory or by experiment.

Falsehood, a statement distorting the actual state of things. In epistemology F. was defined by Aristotle, q.v., who considered everything that contradicted reality a F.: if a judgment connects what is disconnected in reality and vice versa, it is false. F. must be distinguished from nonsense or absurdity. Psychologically and ethically we must differentiate between deliberate and unintentional F. (see Error).

Falsification, a means of verifying theoretical assumptions (hypotheses, theories) through their refutation by comparing them with experimentally obtained data. F. is based on the postulate of formal logic which says that a theoretical proposition is disproved if its refutation logically follows from a multitude of mutually compatible statements based on observation. Proceeding from this logical postulate, Popper (q.v.) countered the neo-positivist principle of verification (see Verification, Principle of) with the principle of F., which he interpreted not as a means of determining the comprehensibility of a scientific proposition, but as a method of distinguishing between the scientific and non-scientific. According to Popper, only statements that can in principi-

ple be falsified are scientific; those that are not susceptible of falsification are not. The Marxist conception of logic and methodology of science considers F. a particular means, subordinate to practice, of verifying scientific theories.

Family, a nucleus (small social group) of society, the most important form of organisation of individual everyday life, based on matrimony and kinship, i.e., multilateral relations between husband and wife, parents and children, brothers and sisters and other relatives who live and keep house together. The life of the F. is marked by various material (biologic, economic) and spiritual (moral, legal, psychologic, aesthetic) processes. Its social role is determined by its direct participation in the reproduction of man, in procreation of the human race. The F. is a historical category. Its forms and functions depend on the character of existing relations of production, and social relations as a whole, as well as the level of society's cultural development. For its part, the F. exerts its influence on the life of society (procreation, socialisation of children and teenagers, housework, influence on the physical, spiritual, moral and aesthetic development of its members). There are two viewpoints on the origin of the F. Most specialists hold that at early stages of the primitive-communal system haphazard sexual relations were the predominant form of intercourse, which were later replaced by group matrimony. This was supplanted by pair marriage, which formed the basis first of the large maternal family, and then of the large paternal family-community, or, respectively, matriarchy and patriarchy (qq.v.). Latest research has led some scholars to the conclusion that the pair F. was the primordial form, which existed on the basis of both matriarchy and patriarchy, and traced its descent and kinship both through the mother and the father. The rise of monogamy was concomitant with the enslavement of woman by man. She gradually became property, the slave of her husband and lord. Accumulation of wealth and its transfer to legitimate heirs became the main purpose of the F. Given the sway of private property relations, legitimate prostitution came to be a complement to matrimony. Private property in great measure determines the nature of intra-family ties in bourgeois society. Here gross material considerations and the commercial advantage of marriage play a tremendous part. The proletariat has originated and developed matrimonial and family relations which are free from these distortions, based as they are on love, friendship and mutual trust. This is a result of the massive involvement of women in production and social activities. The victory of socialism has opened wide scope for the equality of men and women in all spheres of social life, including the F. Love, mutual respect, the upbringing of children, concern of grown-up children for their parents are important moral principles of the F. in socialist society. According to the Constitution of the USSR, "the family enjoys the protection of the state". In the course of communist construction family relations undergo steady improvement: the legal relations in the F. will gradually die away as the social need in them disappears; the significance of economic and consumer relations will decrease; moral, aesthetic and psychological relations will come to the fore and will be perfected in line with the harmonious development of the individual.

Fantasy, imagination (q.v.) distinguished by the power, vividness and unusualness of the ideas and images it conceives.

Fascism, overt terroristic dictatorship of the most reactionary, chauvinistic elements of finance capital. The establishment of F. reflects the inability of the ruling bourgeoisie to maintain its power by usual "democratic" methods. F. heads the forces of anti-communism (q.v.) and strikes its main blow against the Communist and Workers parties and other progressive organisations. The fascist system was established first in Italy (1922) and then in Germany (1933) and in other countries. In Germany F. was masked under the name of National-Socialism. F. was the striking force of international reaction; the fascist states, Hitlerite Germany in the first place, unleashed the Second World War. The Soviet Union

rendered the whole of progressive mankind the historic service of acting as the decisive force in routing German fascism. Notwithstanding the complete rout of the fascist states in the Second World War, reactionary elements in some imperialist countries are trying to revive F. The ideology of F. is irrationalism (q.v.), extreme chauvinism and racism (q.v.), obscurantism, and inhumanity.

Fatalism, an anti-dialectical philosophical conception according to which all processes in the world were initially predetermined and ruled by necessity to the exclusion of freedom and creative endeavour. Originally F. developed in mythology as the idea that people and even gods were inevitably ruled by blind, senseless, purposeless fate. In philosophy F. was given various interpretations. The stoics (q.v.) taught that inexorable Fate governs the Universe, and that after periodically recurring world conflagrations everything is repeated over again. According to Leibniz's (q.v.) doctrine of pre-established harmony (q.v.), the interaction between monads is pre-ordained by God. In Schelling's (q.v.) objective-idealist system, the gap between freedom and necessity deprives real individuals of the possibility to act freely. Hegel (q.v.) maintained that in the final analysis the individual is but an instrument of the Absolute Spirit. The metaphysical materialists (Hobbes, the French 18th-century materialists, qq.v., and others) denied objective chance and identified causality and necessity, which also led to F. Theological F. claims that historical events and human lives are predetermined by the will of God. Within it the struggle has been waged between the conceptions of absolute predestination (Augustinianism, Calvinism, Jansenism, q.v.) and the views seeking to conciliate the omnipotence of Providence and the free will of man (Catholicism, Orthodoxy, qq.v.). In Marxist philosophy the action of the laws of social development and people's free activity are organically connected, and understanding of the dialectics of necessity and chance, freedom and necessity (qq.v.) has been achieved. Marxism sees the class roots of F. in the interests of definite social forces, and shows that only a radical transformation of society can gradually remove the historical grounds for fatalistic views.

Fate, the religious, idealist conception of a supernatural force predetermining all the events in the life of men. In ancient Greek mythology, the fate of men and even of gods depended on the Moerae (the Parcae among the Romans). As time went on, F. came to be regarded as a supreme justice ruling the world. In Christianity (q.v.), F. is a divine Providence, a supreme power. All modern religions regard F. as divine predestination (see Fatalism). Some religions (like Catholicism and Orthodoxy, qq.v.) try to reduce the fatalism of the idea of F. through an eclectic combination of the idea of divine predestination and free will. F. is sometimes used by laymen to denote the concurrence of circumstances in the life of individuals or nations.

Feedback, a fundamental concept characterising systems of control (q.v.) (regulation) in animate nature, society and technology and denoting the reverse action of the regulated process on the regulating organ. F. is positive when the results of the regulated process strengthen that process, and negative when the results of the regulated process weaken it. The concept of F. is needed to analyse the functioning and development of complex control systems in animate nature and society, and to reveal the structure of the material unity of the world. Herein lies its methodological significance (see Cybernetics).

Fetishism, a social relation (economic, ideological, etc.) and the corresponding conception which attributes specifically social qualities to things in themselves and regards properties resulting from human culture as something natural. Metaphysical materialism held that F. was due only to deception, while Marxism disclosed its objective content. Historically, the earliest form of F. was due to the extremely low cultural level of primitive man, who attributed to objects (fetishes) magical power to influence his life (see Magic; Totemism). Elements of F. survive in almost all modern religions. Commodity,

especially capitalist, production makes F. a feature of everyday practice. Its most elementary form is fetishisation of a commodity, which means its personification and the simultaneous reification (q.v.) of its producers. The latter regard their relations not as direct social relations between individuals at work, but as material relations between persons and social relations between things. F. is manifested in the worship of money, gold, in attributing to capital the power to increase of itself, independently of labour, in a fanatical reverence towards symbols of power and political institutions, and in ascribing magical powers to ideological conceptions and slogans. In all these cases the results of human activity (either material or cultural) are attributed a mystical independence and power over people. The roots of F. lie in the objective distortion and inversion of the relation between subject and object, in alienation (q.v.) and reification of social relations, i.e., in reducing man to the level of a thing or performer of the functions of things. In the building of socialism and communism all the sources and forms of F. are being overcome and relations established between people as personalities.

Feudalism, the socio-economic formation that follows the slave-owning system (q.v.) and precedes capitalism (q.v.). The economic system of F., for all the variety of its forms in different countries and at different times, has one typical feature: the principal means of production, the land, is in monopoly ownership of the ruling class of feudal lords (which sometimes merges almost entirely with the state), while the economy is run by the small producers, the peasants, using their own implements. The main economic relation of F. is manifested in feudal rent, i.e., the surplus product that is collected by the feudal lords (or the state) from the producers in the form of labour, money, or payment in kind. The system of feudal relations necessarily includes the town, for without marketing agricultural produce in the towns F. would not have known money rent. The antagonism of feudal society, based on the exploitation of the peasants by the feudal lords (an exploitation not confined to economic coercion alone), gave rise to various forms of social conflict. The most acute forms were popular uprisings and peasant wars. The ideology of F. gravitates towards speculative conceptions poorly grounded in positive knowledge, and world religions (Christianity, Islam, Buddhism, Confucianism, qq.v., etc.). The political structure of feudal society differs at various stages of its development: from separate tiny states to highly centralised absolute monarchies. So-called nomadic F. was a specific form of F., although its main distinctive features are the same. The later period of F. saw the growth of manufactory production, the embryo of capitalist relations. In Western Europe that was the time when the first bourgeois revolutions matured and were carried out.

Feuerbach, Ludwig (1804-1872), German materialist philosopher and atheist, taught at Erlangen University, from which he was removed in 1830 for his atheistic views. F. spent the last years of his life in the countryside. In 1870 he joined the Social Democratic Party of Germany, although he did not accept Marxism. In his struggle against religion F.'s views evolved from the ideas of the Young Hegelians (q.v.) to materialism. His proclamation and defence of materialism greatly influenced his contemporaries. Criticism of Hegel's (q.v.) idealistic understanding of man's essence and his reducing it to self-consciousness (q.v.) was the initial point of F.'s philosophical evolution. Renunciation of this view inevitably led to renunciation of idealism in general. One of F.'s services was that he emphasised the connection between idealism and religion. He sharply criticised the idealist nature of Hegelian dialectics. This opened the way to utilising the rational content of Hegelian philosophy and in this respect facilitated the establishment of Marxism. But F. himself simply cast aside Hegel's philosophy and that is why he failed to notice its main achievement, dialectics. The basic content of F.'s philosophy was the defence of materialism. Anthropologism (q.v.) made itself felt here in the problem of man's essence being placed in the foreground. He saw the essence of man as the one and only, universal, and supreme subject-matter of philosophy. But F. did not pursue a consistently materialist line on this question because he took man as an abstract individual, as a purely biological being. In the theory of knowledge F. applied the viewpoint of empiricism and sensationalism (qq.v.) and resolutely opposed agnosticism (q.v.). At the same time he did not deny the importance of thought in cognition, tried to examine the object in connection with the activity of the subject and voiced suppositions about the social nature of human knowledge and consciousness. But on the whole F. did not overcome the contemplative nature of pre-Marxian materialism because in his understanding of history he remained entirely on idealist positions. Idealist views of social phenomena followed from his desire to apply anthropology as a universal science to the study of social life. F.'s idealism was especially evident in the study of religion and morality. He regarded religion as the alienation of human traits: man, as it were, is doubled and contemplates his own essence in God. F. saw the reason for such doubling in man's feeling of dependence on the spontaneous forces of nature and society. Of special interest are F.'s surmises about the social and historical roots of religion. But he was unable to find effective means of combating religion (he sought them in education) and even advocated the need for a new religion. Not understanding the real world in which man lives, F. deduced the principles of morality from man's intrinsic striving for happiness. Its achievement is possible, provided every man rationally limits his requirements and loves other men. The morality constructed by F. is abstract, eternal, and the same for all times and peoples. Some present-day idealists reproduce F.'s ideas of anthropologism in a frankly idealist interpretation. His main works: *Zur Kritik der Hegelschen Philosophie* (1839); *Das Wesen des Christenthums* (1841); *Vorläufige Thesen zur Reform der Philosophie* (1842); *Grundsätze der Philosophie der Zukunft* (1843).

Fichte, Johann Gottlieb (1762-1814), German philosopher; second figure after Kant (q.v.) in classical German idealism, professor of Jena (dismissed on being accused of atheism) and Berlin universities. He criticised the social estate privileges and advocated German unity and abolition of feudal disunity; he emphasised the importance of "practical" philosophy, of justifying morality, the state and legal system, but reduced "practice" to the mere activity of moral consciousness; considered the scientifically elaborated theoretical system, namely, the science of science, to be a prerequisite for "practical" philosophy. Subjective idealism (q.v.) underlies his *Wissenschaftslehre* published in 1794. F. discarded Kant's doctrine of the "thing-in-itself" and sought to deduce all the diversity of forms of knowledge from only one, subjective-idealist principle. F. posited the existence of some kind of absolute subject with boundless activity which created the world. His method, in which some features of idealist dialectics are developed, is called "antithetical", because the antithesis as such is not deduced by F. from the thesis but is placed alongside it as its opposite. F. regarded direct contemplation of truth by the mind, as the organ of rational knowledge. Besides subjective idealism, which was basic to F.'s doctrine, his philosophy also evinced a leaning towards objective idealism (q.v.) which increased in the last years of his life. The question of freedom became central for F. in ethics. Interest in it was heightened by the French Revolution. Like Spinoza, F. saw in freedom not a causeless act, but an action based on the recognition of necessity. In contrast to Spinoza, however, F. made the degree of freedom accessible to people depending not on individual wisdom but on the historical epoch to which an individual belongs. Unable to overcome the illusions engendered by Germany's backwardness in his day, F. elaborated a utopian project for a German bourgeois society in the form of *"der geschlossene Handelsstaat"* (closed merchant state). The project reflected specific elements of Germany's bourgeois development and was marked by a number of reactionary features, including nationalist German exceptionalism. The founders of Marxism-Leninism made a profound assessment of the progressive and reactionary features of F.'s doctrine.

Fideism, a reactionary doctrine that seeks to subordinate science to religion and to use scientific knowledge for defending religious dogma. F. is based on the assertion that science gives only knowledge of phenomena, facts, secondary (physical) causes, and cannot disclose the primary (supernatural) causes, or explain the deeper sources of being. By limiting the field of operation of science the fideists claim that scientific knowledge cannot reveal the whole truth; they deny the existence of objective truth in order to make way for religious faith. The aim of fideists' teaching on the limits of knowledge is also to deprive science of its broad philosophical and methodological significance. They maintain that religion alone provides the true explanation of how and for what purpose the Universe exists, and gives meaning and purpose to human life, while science merely provides some means to achieve the desired aim. F. is the ideological basis of the alliance between bourgeois philosophy and theology. Many trends in contemporary bourgeois philosophy contain obvious fideistic elements (personalism, neo-Thomism, existentialism, qq.v., etc.). On the other hand, theologians use the ideas of these and other bourgeois philosophical trends (on the power of irrational forces over man, on the existence of things that cannot be rationally explained, etc.) for a more sophisticated defence of religion.

Finitism 1. A philosophical conception which denies the objectively real content of the category of the infinite (see Infinite and Finite) and proceeds from the assumption that there can be no infinity in the Universe, the microcosm, or man's thinking. F. accounts for this by the fact that in his experience man always deals with finite things and their properties. Metaphysically counterposing the finite and the infinite, F. ignores their dialectics and fails to see that knowledge of the finite leads to the infinite. 2. In analysing formal systems in metamathematics (q.v.), F. means the application only of those methods that are free from ambiguity or doubt.

Florensky, Pavel Alexandrovich (1882-1943), Russian religious thinker and scholar. He developed Solovyov's (q.v.) philosophy of the "all-embracing being", trying to substantiate it not only with religious and philosophical theses, but also with scientific postulates taken from physics, mathematics, philology, etc. F.'s views testify to the unsoundness of his attempts to combine scientific truths with religious belief, to trace the origin of culture to religious worship, to preserve and defend Orthodox dogma by means of science and philosophy. Nowadays, in the time of religious crisis, Orthodox theologians resort to F.'s philosophical legacy to uphold religious dogma.

Force, Theory of, an idealist theory claiming that social inequality is the result of the use of force by some people against others. T.F. gained currency chiefly among bourgeois ideologists. Dühring (q.v.) associated the appearance of classes with the use of force by one part of society against the other (internal force). Kautsky (q.v.) and others regarded the enslavement of a weaker tribe by a stronger one (external force) as the decisive cause of the appearance of classes and the state. Marxism does not deny the role of force in history and views it as the application of different forms of compulsion by a social group with regard to other social groups for the purpose of preserving or changing the social order. Revolutionary force is not an end in itself, it is used to break up the resistance of the classes being overthrown. T.F. is utilised by the ideologists of the imperialist bourgeoisie to defend neo-colonialism, justify the policy "from strength" and the escalation of the cold war.

Formal and Conceptual, the, concepts used in philosophy, logic and the methodology of science in the following principal meanings; 1) as referring to the categories of content and form (q.v.) in their general philosophical meaning. In this case, the term of F. is applied to rules and methods used primarily to study the form (structure, q.v.) of an object or phenomenon (mathematical, systems, structural, functional, etc., methods). All the other rules and methods are regarded as conceptual; 2) as referring to the concepts of content and form of thinking. In this case the F. is applied to the study of cognitive and logical structures in their relative independence, first from the concrete content of thinking, and, second, from the properties and interconnections of natural and social phenomena as their objective basis. The study of cognitive and logical forms in an organic link with the historically shaped sum total of concepts, models and abstractions relating to the subject-matter of a given science, and with universal aspects and relations of reality expressed through philosophical categories, is referred to as the C.; 3) in modern formal logic and the foundations of mathematics, syntactic operations and methods are called F. when they take into account only the type and order of symbols of linguistic expressions. Semantic operations and methods that deal with denotation and sense (q.v.) of these expressions are called C. The difference between the F. and the C. is relative. In one system of assumptions and idealisations the F. can function as the C., and in another system, vice versa. The relation of the F. to the C. is that of one content to another (relatively immature and abstract to a more developed and concrete). The C. means and methods play the decisive role in cognition, while the absolutisation of the F. components of research leads to formalism (q.v.).

Formalisation, a method of ascertaining more precisely the content of knowledge by comparing in a definite way the objects or phenomena being studied with relatively stable material constructions; this makes it possible to disclose and fix the essential and law-governed aspects of the examined objects. As an epistemological method F. helps to establish and specify content by ascertaining and fixing its form. Every F. necessarily gives a rough picture of living, developing reality. But this "rough picture" is an essential aspect of the process of cognition. Historically, F. arose simultaneously with thought and language. An important step in the development of F. is associated with the appearance of written language. Later, as science, especially mathematics, developed, special signs were added to the natural languages. Together with formal logic there appeared the method of logical F., which consists in revealing the logical form of conclusion and proof. The creation of calculuses using letters in mathematics and the appearance of the idea of logical calculus, q.v. (see Leibniz) were an important stage in developing F. methods. The construction of logical calculuses, which began in mathematical logic (q.v.) in the mid-19th century, made it possible to apply its methods to formalising entire branches of science. Spheres of knowledge formalised by means of mathematical logic acquire the character of formal systems. F. of knowledge does not eliminate the dialectically contradictory relationship between content and form (q.v.), characteristic of knowledge as a whole. The results of modern logic show that if a theory with sufficiently rich content is formalised it cannot be fully reflected in a formal system: something in the theory always remains not disclosed and not formalised. This non-conformity between F. and the formalised content acts as an internal source for developing the formal logical means of science and is usually manifested in the discovery of propositions which cannot be solved in the given formal system. Another form in which this contradiction is manifested is the antinomy (q.v.). This situation can be remedied by constructing new formal systems in which the part not covered in the preceding Ff. is formalised. Thus, ever deeper F. of content is effected but its absolute completeness is never achieved.

Formalised Language, a calculus (q.v.) to which interpretation is ascribed (see Interpretation and Model). The syntactic part of the F.L. (see Logical Syntax), or the calculus itself, is constructed in a purely formal way (see Logistic Method). A calculus becomes a F.L. by adding the semantic rules which impart meaning (see Denotation and Sense) to properly constructed propositions of the calculus. In addition to purely logical axioms, a F.L. may also contain some propositions of a non-logical nature (for example, some laws of biology, axioms of arithmetic, and others); then a F.L. deductively describes the corresponding content. Thanks to its

deductive means a F.L. makes it possible to carry on a strict process of reasoning and receive new deductive conclusions not contained directly in the accepted axioms. Thus, F.L. is an instrument for conclusion and proof in formalised scientific subjects. The role of F.L. has been enhanced by attempts to automate scientific reasoning through electronic machines (see Cybernetics).

Formalism 1. A method in art based on absolutising, aestheticising form; it is the opposite of realism (q.v.). F. emerged at the turn of the century and included various trends and schools in art (futurism, cubism, abstract art, surrealism, expressionism, etc.). All these trends, notwithstanding their distinctions, have common features: they counterpose art to reality, divorce artistic form from idea-content, and proclaim the autonomy and primacy of form in works of art. F. proceeds from the erroneous idea that artistic endeavour is completely beyond the control of reason, and from an idealist conception of aesthetic pleasure, which, it alleges, has nothing to do with social ideas, vital interests, and the aesthetic and social ideal. Though some formalistic trends protest against the ugliness of capitalist society, the content of the majority of formalistic works depends entirely on bourgeois and petty-bourgeois ideology, or have no content whatsoever (abstract art, tachism, etc.). The divorcement of form from content inevitably leads to its destruction, although it is claimed to be "form-creation" (see Content and Form). F. reflects the crisis of bourgeois culture and art in the epoch of imperialism and in its extreme forms (pop-art, op-art, etc.) is hostile to art in general. 2. A trend in mathematics (q.v.) which tries to solve problems concerning the foundation of mathematics by means of formal axiomatic constructions. F. arose at the beginning of the 20th century. In contrast to intuitionism (q.v.), Hilbert (q.v.) sought a way out of the crisis concerning the foundations of mathematics in a strictly elaborated formalised axiomatic method (q.v.). 3. In ethics, F. is the underlying principle of ethical theories in which the formal logical aspects of research prevail in some way or other over analysis of the content and social nature of morality. This is typical, in particular, of the ethics of Kant (q.v.) who believed that all meaningful moral principles and solutions applicable to different social conditions and life situations can be deduced from a certain abstract and formal absolute principle (categorical imperative, q.v.). In reality, the formula of this imperative (act in such a way that your rule of behaviour may be at the same time a law for all people) can have only a methodological meaning, being a criterion of relating one's position to morality proper, since any sufficiently consistent system of morality is subject to this demand of universality. F. in ethics is a major trend in the modern bourgeois philosophy of morality. As such it has a somewhat different meaning: the task of ethics is considered to be the study of only the epistemological aspect and logical form of ethical ideas, whereas their concrete content is not subject to analysis (see Intuitionalism in ethics; Logical Positivism in ethics; Linguistic Analysis in ethics). Such an understanding of the subject-matter of ethics leads not only to unjustified limitation of its tasks, but also to a number of scientifically unsound conclusions. Philosophical ethics (metaethics, q.v.) is counterposed to normative ethics (q.v.), science to moral consciousness, facts and knowledge of them to values, q.v., (moral judgments). The formalists exclude analysis of moral problems from the tasks of ethics: their solution by means of theory is declared impossible and in the final analysis irrational. This deprives ethics of social content and world-view significance, and diverts it from tackling ideological and practical problems of our day.

Forster, Georg (1754-1794), German materialist thinker, naturalist and revolutionary. His views were shaped under the influence of French 18th-century materialism (q.v.). F. criticised Kant's (q.v.) apriorism from the standpoint of materialist sensationalism (q.v.) and rejected the irrationalism of Jacobi (q.v.). He supported the theory of social contract (q.v.) from which he inferred the right of the people to overthrow despotism and feudal order by a revolution. Revolution,

F. held, is at the same time a means for reviving morality and freeing people from their vices. He was an ardent champion of national sovereignty and bitterly condemned colonial slavery. He was an active participant in the revolutionary events in Germany and France in 1792-93. Engels regarded him as a true democrat and ranked him among the best patriots of Germany. His main work: *Über die Beziehung der Staatskunst auf das Glück der Menschheit* (1794).

Fourier, François Marie Charles (1772-1837), French utopian socialist. F. sharply criticised bourgeois society, revealing the contradictions between the ideas voiced by the ideologists of the French Revolution and reality, the antagonism between poverty and wealth. In justifying the socialist system, he proceeded from the tenets of the French materialists on the decisive part played by environment and education in moulding the personality. All human passions and strivings as such are good. The fault is not with man but with the society he lives in. Hence, it is necessary to create a social system which would promote full satisfaction and development of the human passions. The *phalange*, consisting of several production units, was to be the main cell of the future society, as F. saw it. Each member of the *phalange* had the right to work. Narrow professionalism, which warps man, was eliminated in the *phalange*; in the course of a day each member of the *phalange* passed from one type of work to another, spending $1^1/_2$—2 hours on each. This turned labour into a necessity and an object of pleasure. As a result, society attained a high level of labour productivity and material abundance. Distribution in the *phalange* was proportioned to labour and talent. Lack of understanding of the historic mission of the proletariat and denial of revolution as a means for remaking the society was characteristic of F., as of other utopian socialists. He expected to achieve his aims by peaceful propaganda of socialist ideas even among the capitalists. His main works: *Théorie des quatre mouvements et des destinées générales* (1808); *Théorie de l'unité universelle* (1822); *Le Nouveau Monde industriel* (1829).

Frank, Philipp (1884-1966), physicist and philosopher, specialising in mathematical physics. He was an active member of the Vienna Circle (q.v.) and, together with Schlick (q.v.), played a big part in shaping the positivism of his time. Typical of F. as also of some other neo-positivists (q.v.) was eclectic combination of empiricism with apriorism and recognition of the pretersensual aspect of some categories (space, time, and others). His main work: *Philosophy of Science. The Link between Science and Philosophy* (1957).

Frankfurt School, a trend in Left radical socio-philosophical thought in the West, a variety of so-called neo-Marxism, which claims to "discover anew", to restore the "true ideas" of Marx, but it in fact attempts to distort and falsify Marxism. The F.S. arose in the 1930s on the basis of the Frankfurt Institute of Social Research. The formal head of the school, M. Horkheimer (1895-1973), was a Left radical neo-Hegelian influenced by the German revisionist K. Korsch (*Marxismus und Philosophie*, 1923, etc.) and also by Freudianism (q.v.). The most widely known representatives of the F.S. are Adorno, Marcuse and Fromm (qq.v.). After the Second World War there appeared the "intermediate" generation of Frankfurters (J. Habermas, A. Schmidt, O. Negt, and A. Wellmer). The 1960s saw the emergence of the youngest and most extremist generation (H.-J. Krahl and others). The F.S. evolved from the "critical theory of society" (as presented in the works of Horkheimer and Marcuse in the latter half of the 1930s) to a pessimistic philosophy of history. The chief tendency of this evolution was to "remove" all that is natural and objective in social relations, which are identified with commodity-money relations (extended to the whole history of human civilisation). In the final account, this led to a vulgar-sociological interpretation of social relations. The popularity of the F.S. grew with the spread of the New Left (q.v.) movement in the West, and decreased when this movement declined.

Franklin, Benjamin (1706-1790), scientist of encyclopaedic knowledge, representative of American Enlightenment, publicist and ideologist of the national liberation movement. He took an active part in the struggle of the American people for independence. F. censured slave ownership and defended the rights of national minorities. He saw the principal task of philosophy in protecting science from interference on the part of theology and in fighting religious prejudices. He regarded the spreading of knowledge and the preaching of religious tolerance and freedom of conscience as most important factors of social progress. F. rejected in a moderately deist (see Deism) form the religious dogma of divine intervention in nature and society. He did not completely reject Christian morality but held that ethical norms and rules of behaviour had no need of coercive religious sanction, were intrinsic in man's nature and human reason. F. approached the origin of social institutions (private property, the state, etc.) from the positions of natural law (q.v.) and the theory of social contract (q.v.). In his study of economic problems F. was among the first to advance the thesis that labour creates value. His main philosophical works: *A Dissertation on Liberty and Necessity, Pleasure and Pain* (1725), *The Way to Wealth...* (1758).

Freedom and Necessity, philosophic categories expressing the interrelation between human activity and the objective laws of nature and society. Most idealists regard F. and N. as incompatible notions and interpret F. as free will, as the possibility to act in accordance with a volition which is not determined by external causes. They hold that the idea of determinism, which asserts that human actions are decreed by necessity fully relieves man of responsibility and makes impossible the moral evaluation of his actions. According to them, it is only unrestricted and unconditional F. that can be the basis of human responsibility and, therefore, ethics. An extremely subjectivist interpretation of F. is given, among others, by the proponents of existentialism (q.v.) (see Sartre; Jaspers). A diametrically opposite, but also incorrect, view is held by the adepts of mechanistic determinism. They deny free will, maintaining that man's actions are always determined by external circumstances over which he has no control. This metaphysical conception tends to absolutise objective N. and leads to fatalism (q.v.). The scientific interpretation of F. and N. is based on the recognition of their organic interconnection. The first attempt to substantiate this point of view was made by Spinoza (q.v.) who defined F. as recognised N. A detailed conception of dialectical unity of F. and N. was given, from idealist positions, by Hegel (q.v.). The scientific, dialectico-materialist solution of the problem of F. and N. is based on recognition of objective N. as primary, and man's will and consciousness as secondary and derivative. N. exists in nature and society in the shape of objective laws. Unknown laws manifest themselves as "blind" N. At the dawn of history, man, being unable to grasp the mysteries of nature, was a slave of unknown N. and hence unfree. The more man learned the objective laws, the more conscious and free became his activity. Apart from nature, man's F. is also restricted by his dependence on the social forces, which dominate him under certain historical conditions. In a society divided into antagonistic classes, the social relations stand opposed to people and dominate them. Socialist revolution (q.v.) destroys class antagonisms and frees people from social oppression. With the socialisation of the means of production, anarchy in production gives way to a conscious and planned organisation of it. In the course of building socialism and communism, the conditions of life which hitherto dominated people as alien, elemental forces, come under man's control. A leap from the realm of necessity into the realm of freedom takes place (Engels). All this enables people consciously to use objective laws in their practical activity, to direct the development of society in a rational and systematic manner, and to create all necessary material and spiritual prerequisites for an all-round development of society and every individual, i.e., for the implementation of genuine F. as an ideal of communist society.

Free Time (leisure), that part of non-working time which is left after indispensable functions (sleep, eating, travel to work and back, everyday self-service,

etc.) and is spent on recovery of strength and on physical and spiritual development. F.T. embraces study and self-education, acquisition of culture (reading, theatre- and cinema-going, etc.), social and political activities, non-professional research and designing, amateur activities, attendance to children, hobby-sharing contacts, etc., but it can also include passive rest ("idleness") and even antisocial pastimes (e.g., indulgence in alcohol). The social value of F.T. under the concrete historical conditions obtaining in a specific social system is determined by its extent and content. Over recent decades, the extent of F.T. has grown several times over and now the main problem facing the socialist countries is that of improving its structure and reducing the time spent on everyday needs (getting to work and home, housework, etc.). Changes in the structure and content of F.T. are mostly due to the fact that, as the society advances to communism, working time and F.T. cease to be opposites, since work done during working hours becomes creative and free, while F.T. is increasingly devoted to creative activity. Under capitalism, the increase in F.T. is accompanied by negative social phenomena, and this prompts some bourgeois sociologists to question the prospects for the Western "leisure society".

Frege, Gottlob (1848-1925), German logician, mathematician, and philosopher. His works opened a new stage in mathematical logic (q.v.). F. was the first to effect the axiomatic construction of the logic of propositions and predicates and laid the foundation for the theory of mathematical proof (q.v.). F. constructed a system of formalised arithmetic with the intention of proving that most of mathematics is reducible to logic (see Logicism). The subsequent development of logic is largely connected with the development of F.'s legacy, in particular with overcoming the contradiction discovered in his system. F. opposed the subjectivist "psychological" trend in logic. His views of logic are stamped by elements of materialism. At the same time F.'s treatment of the problem of the universal contained features of objective idealism in the spirit of Plato (q.v.). F. founded that part of logical semantics (q.v.) which is connected with the concepts of denotation and sense (q.v.) of linguistic expressions.

French Historians of the Restoration (1820s)—A. Thierry, F. Mignet, F. Guizot, A. Thiers. Influenced by the experience of the French Revolution and the ideas of Saint-Simon (q.v.), these bourgeois scholars went further than the French 18th-century materialists in explaining social development. They considered the history of feudalism up to the establishment of bourgeois society as the history of a struggle of classes, which they treated as the struggle of the third estate led by the bourgeoisie against the nobility. They saw the causes of the class struggle in the differing material interests of the social classes. But, reducing social life to property relations, these historians failed to see its basis—the dialectics of the productive forces and the relations of production. They adhered to idealist positions on the question of the origin of classes, and ascribed the decisive role to violence, conquest and wars. As ideologists of the liberal bourgeoisie, the historians of the Restoration denied the existence of contradictions within the third estate which, in their opinion, included the entire people except the nobility and clergy. Viewing the class struggle as natural and progressive in the past since it was waged against feudalism for the triumph of the bourgeoisie, they either ignored the class struggle of the proletariat or considered it a violation of the natural order. They advocated class peace and claimed that capitalism would last for ever.

Freudianism, the theory and method of psychoanalysis (q.v.) so named after S. Freud (1856-1939), Austrian physician, neuropathologist, and psychiatrist. Studying the causes of pathological mental processes, Freud resolutely rejected vulgar materialistic attempts to explain changes in mental acts by physiological causes. He regarded psychic activity as something independent, existing side by side with material processes (see Psychophysical Parallelism), and governed by special, eternal psychic forces lying outside consciousness (see Unconscious). Dominating man's psyche, like fate, are immutable psychic conflicts between the unconscious striving for pleasure (see Libido) and the "principle of reality" to which the mind adapts itself. Freud subjected all psychic conditions, all actions of man, and also all historical events and social phenomena to psychoanalysis, i.e., interpreted them as manifestations of unconscious, above all sexual, impulses. Eternal conflicts in the depth of the human psychics are, according to Freud, the source and content—concealed from direct comprehension—of morality, art, science, religion, the state, law, wars, and so on (see Sublimation). Neo-Freudianists (see Neo-Freudianism), exponents of the schools of "cultural psychoanalysis" (K. Horney, A. Kardiner, F. Alexander, and others), preserved untouched the main logical line of Freud, renouncing only the tendency to see a sexual undercurrent in all phenomena of human life and some other methodological features of classical F. The Freudianist conception has exerted and continues to exert great influence on various spheres of bourgeois culture, particularly on the theory and works of art. F. has now less influence in neurology and psychiatry.

Fromm, Erich (1900-1980) German-American philosopher, sociologist, representative of the neo-Freudian school of "cultural psychoanalysis" (see Freudianism). Compared with Freud, F. was less inclined to biologise the essence of man and more of a "socio-psychologist". He tried to solve an important problem: to grasp the mechanism of interrelations between the psychological and social factors of social development. However, in his analysis of the "social environment", F. ignored class differences and regarded the essence of man and of the historical process as a whole from an abstract psychological viewpoint. At the same time he correctly noted the vices of modern bourgeois society (man's transformation into a "thing" as a result of alienation, q.v., the irrationality and meaninglessness of existence, etc.). Capitalism, in his view, is a mentally ill, irrational society. But he saw the way out of the situation in a "humanistic psychoanalysis", in curing "individual pathology". F. tried to "synthesise" Freudianism and Marxism. His main works: *Escape from Freedom* (1941), *Man for Himself* (1947), *Marx's Concept of Man* (1961), *The Revolution of Hope.* *On Humanistic Technique* (1968), *The Crisis of Psychoanalysis* (1973).

Function, an outward manifestation of the properties of objects in a given system of relations, e.g., the functions of the sense-organs, the functions of money, the functions of the state, etc. A number of idealist trends seek to reduce science to a description of the functions of objects, denying not only the possibility of knowing the essence and laws of things but also their existence (see Machism; Behaviourism, etc.).

Functional Dependence, a form of stable relation between objective phenomena or magnitudes reflecting them, in which a change in some phenomena causes a definite quantitative change in others. Objectively, F.D. is manifested in laws and relations which have precise quantitative definiteness. F.D. presupposes that the phenomena subordinated to it are distinguished by definite parameters, constants, concrete conditions and quantitative laws. F.D. is not identical to a causal connection. Side by side with phenomena in which the causal connection is expressed through objective functional relations, there are F.Dd. between properties of bodies or mathematical magnitudes which are not causal nexuses. Following Mach (q.v.), neo-positivism (q.v.) tries to replace the concept of causality by the concept of F.D. without analysing the objective content of a process or phenomenon. These views were criticised by Lenin in his *Materialism and Empirio-Criticism* (q.v.).

Functional School in Sociology, a school in modern bourgeois sociology (B. Malinowski, Merton, q.v., Parsons, q.v., P. A. Sorokin). The F.S.S. regards society as a single, interconnected "social system", each element of which performs a definite function. The basic feature of such a system is the interaction of its

components and the absence of a single determining basis. Marxist philosophy and sociology criticise the F.S.S. for its metaphysics, displayed in its maintaining that the social system is absolutely stable and ignoring its qualitative changes and contradictions, and for its anti-historical and idealist approach (see Structural-Functional Analysis).

Futurology, ideas about the future of humankind, a branch of knowledge dealing with the prospects of social processes. The term of F. was proposed in 1943 by the German sociologist O. Flechtheim who meant by it a supra-class "philosophy of the future" opposed to ideology and utopia. In the early 1960s this concept gained wide currency in the West in the sense of "history of the future", the "science of the future", whose purpose was to reveal the forecasting functions of all scientific disciplines. Since the prospects of social processes are studied by many sciences, the term of F., being polysemantic and rather vague, was replaced in the late 1960s by the concept of "research into the future", which covers the theory and practice of prognostication (q.v.). Bourgeois F. includes apologetic, reformist, Left Radical and other trends. The apologetic trend, which prevailed in the 1960s, advanced the theory of "post-industrial society", q.v. (Bell, q.v., H. Kahn, R. Aron, and B. de Jouvenel). The reformists proceeded from the theory of convergence, q.v. (F. Baade, F. Polak). Left Radicals sought to prove that a catastrophe of "Western civilisation" was inevitable under the scientific and technological revolution, q.v. (A. Waskow and others). Since the late 1960s bourgeois F. has been going through a crisis, which brought forth a trend which tries to demonstrate the inevitability of a "global catastrophe", given the present tendencies of social development. The leading influence in this complex, essentially apologetic trend has gone to the Club of Rome (q.v.), which initiated the so-called global modelling of mankind's prospects based on computer calculations. The varied and contradictory conceptions of bourgeois F. are opposed by the Marxist-Leninist teaching on the future of mankind, scientific forecasting based on dialectical and historical materialism, and the theory of scientific communism.

Fyodorov, Nikolai Fyodorovich (1828-1903), Russian thinker whose contradictory world outlook contained idealist and reactionary utopian elements (recognition of the creation, Slavophile views) and a number of original hypotheses on the possibility of regulating natural phenomena by scientific and technical means, on the union of theory and practice, and on the necessity of exploring space. His works: two volumes of articles, notes and letters published by his followers in 1906-13 under the title *Filosofia obshchego dela* (Philosophy of the Common Cause).

g

Galaxy, the Milky Way, a cosmic system of more than 100,000 million stars, of which the Sun is one. The star clusters, gas and dust nebulae, of which it is composed, are knit by gravitation into a single complex system with a variety of forms of motion. Distances between neighbouring stars of G. are of the order of a few light years; the diameter of G. is about 100,000 light years. Cosmic systems resembling G. and numbering from a few thousand million to several hundred thousand million stars each, and including gas (chiefly hydrogen) and dust, are also known as galaxies. Together, they form the metagalaxy (q.v.).

Galich, Alexander Ivanovich (1783-1848), Russian philosopher, aesthetician and psychologist; objective idealist. In his lectures (St. Petersburg University, 1817-21) and his *Kartina cheloveka* (Picture of Man), 1834, G. maintained that individual thinking is conditioned by objective reality. He stressed the prominence of sensations in the process of cognition, held that cognition developed by stages (hypothesis-concept-idea) and associated thinking with physiology; he substantiated the anthropological philosophy of history, which included social utopia. In his *Istoriya filosofskikh sistem* (History of Philosophical Systems) (1818-19) he attempted to formulate objective laws governing the development of philosophy; opposed materialism, but commended the methodology of the experimental sciences. In his *Opyt nauki izyashchnogo* (An Essay on the Science of the Beautiful), 1825, he was one of the first in Russia to advocate the aesthetics of romanticism (q.v.).

Galileo Galilei (1564-1642), Italian physicist and astronomer; defied blind worship of Aristotle (q.v.) and attacked dogmatic scholasticism (q.v.); he was the first to apply scientific experiment (q.v.) as a mathematical, and especially geometrical modelling (q.v.) of natural phenomena. G.G.'s main achievement in mechanics was the discovery of the law of inertia and the principle of relativity, according to which uniform and rectilinear motion of a system of bodies does not affect the processes within the system. G.G.'s astronomical discoveries, which corroborated the heliocentric system of Copernicus (q.v.), delivered the death blow to religious dogma. G.G.'s world outlook was distinctly progressive. He believed the world was infinite, matter eternal and nature single, and maintained that nature was governed by the rigorous causality of immutable atoms obeying the laws of mechanics. Observation and experience (qq.v.) were for G.G. the points of departure in the cognition of nature. He considered cognition of intrinsic necessity of phenomena to be the highest level of knowledge. G.G. was the father of so-called exact induction (q.v.) and one of the founders of experimental science but was unable to shake off the influence of religious prejudice and acknowledged divine origin. His principal work: *Dialogo dei due massimi sistemi del mondo* (1632).

Gandhi, Mohandas Karamchand (1869-1948), leader of the Indian national liberation movement, founder of the ideology and tactics known as Gandhism. Philosophically, G. was an objective idealist, his system was based on identification of God and Truth, the latter being apprehended through moral self-improvement. His ethical views were based on the "law of love", "law of suffering" (see Jainism), and the abstention from self-indulgence, etc. Gandhism's typical feature is its ethical treatment of socio-political problems, its "moralisation" of political acts. G.'s socio-political ideas are embodied in his conception of *Satyagraha* (literally, persistent seeking of truth), the main forms of which were non-co-operation and civil disobedience (under British imperialist colonial rule). G. opposed expropriation of the exploiting classes and denied the possibility of any radical revolutionary reorganisation of society. He held that social progress lay not in the growth of people's requirements, but in their voluntary restriction. He advocated Hindu-Muslim unity, abolition of "untouchability", emancipation of women, a national system of public education, etc. G. was given the title of *mahatma* (great soul). Gandhism is the official ideology of the ruling Indian National Congress.

Gassendi, Pierre (1592-1655), French materialist philosopher, physicist, astronomer, priest, and professor of a number of universities. G. campaigned strongly against scholasticism (q.v.) and its perversion of Aristotle's (q.v.) teaching, and against Descartes's (q.v.) theory of innate ideas (q.v.); revived the materialism of Epicurus (q.v.), on which he based his own doctrine. In his basic work, *Syntagma philosophicum* (1658), he divided philosophy into three parts: (1) logic, in which he analysed the problem of the authenticity of knowledge and criticised scepticism and dogmatism; (2) physics, in which he expounded the atomistic theory and inferred the objectivity, uncreatability and indestructibility of time and space; (3) ethics, in which he attacked the ascetic moral code of the church and echoed Epicurus in maintaining that every pleasure is a blessing in itself and every virtue is a blessing so long as it provides "serenity". G. made many important observations and discoveries in astronomy (the passage of Mercury across the sun disc, the discovery of five of Jupiter's satellites in addition to the previously known four, ·etc.) and is the author of a book on the history of science. In the specific conditions of the 17th century, G. was progressive as a philosopher and scientist, but his materialism was inconsistent, for he reconciled himself to religion and the church, recognised God as the creator of atoms and held that in addition to the materialistically conceived "animal soul", man also had a pretersensual "rational soul".

General Crisis of Capitalism, the process of disintegration of the world capitalist system embracing all areas of bourgeois society: economy, politics and ideology. The theory of G.C.C. was elaborated by Lenin in connection with the teaching on imperialism (q.v.) being the final stage of capitalism (q.v.), and was enriched in theoretical documents of the CPSU and other Communist parties. G.C.C. is generated by the immanent laws of imperialism. Its main feature is the narrowing of the sphere of domination of the world capitalist system and its disintegration expressed in the formation of the socialist system and the break-up of colonialism, and the aggravation of the economic and political contradictions of imperialism. Underlying the capitalist system as a whole, G.C.C., however, allows for the possibility of capitalist development in productive forces, science, etc. There are periods when growth in capitalist countries may reach a high level. But growth of capitalism means simultaneous growth of all its contradictions. Attempts to use state-monopoly capitalism (q.v.) to overcome G.C.C. only aggravate this process and prepare the material basis for the revolutionary transformation of society. G.C.C. has passed through three main stages, in each of which G.C.C. has characteristic traits. The first stage, which began during the First World War and the October 1917 Revolution in Russia, was characterised by the formation of the world's first socialist state and the beginning of the crisis of colonialism. The second stage of G.C.C., which began during the Second World War, was characterised by the breaking away from capitalism of more countries (see People's Democracy) and the formation of the world socialist system (q.v.), and the disintegration of the colonial system. The third stage of G.C.C. is characterised by a further aggravation of all capitalist contradictions and a narrowing of its sphere of influence. Its special feature is that it is not the result of any world war. This shows that a war by itself, without the contradictions being ripe, is not a necessary condition for the development of G.C.C. The beginning of each of its new stages is defined by the qualitative change of the place and role of capitalism in the world. And this is connected above all with the further strengthening of the socialist countries and the growth of their economic and political influence on world development. G.C.C. is a complicated process of capitalism's contradictory development over a long period characterised by a global tendency to crises afflicting a whole range of economic and social spheres and intensifying the general instability of capitalism. The anti-imperialist orientation of the national liberation movement is getting to be more distinct, and the working-class movement is growing stronger. Each stage of the uneven development of G.C.C. has its specific manifestations. Of late, for example, capitalism is racked by a currency fever, inflation, structural crises, rising prices of raw materials, declining rates of profit, internationalisation of capital, and so on. The contradictions between the imperialist powers, and between developing and neo-colonialist countries, are more acute. One of the specific features of modern capitalism is its ability to adjust to the new situation in the world (use of more disguised forms of exploitation and readiness, in some cases, to carry out partial reforms). However, this accommodation does not signify stabilisation of capitalism as a system. G.C.C. is continuing to grow more intensive.

Generalisation, a logical process of transition from the particular to the universal, from less general to more general knowledge, e.g., the transition from the concept of "heat" to the concept of "energy", from the geometry of Euclid (q.v.), to the geometry of Lobachevsky (q.v.), and also the result of this process: a generalised concept, judgment (qq.v.), law of science, and theory (q.v.). The obtaining of generalised knowledge signifies deeper reflection of reality and insight into its essence. In formal logic, generalisation of a concept is understood to mean transition from a specific to a generic concept. At the same time, the content of a generic concept is narrower, because specific features are excluded from it (see Concept, Volume and Content of). In proceeding from the concept "oak" to the concept "tree", for example, the specific features of the oak are discarded. The process opposite to G. is restriction.

Genesis, the term that appeared originally, in Greek myths. Later, it was taken up by philosophers (Thales, Heraclitus, Kant, Hegel, qq.v., etc.) and spread to the natural sciences (the Kant-Laplace cosmogonic hypothesis, Darwin's evolution theory, qq.v., etc.). In Marxist philosophy, G. most often denotes the emergence of prerequisites for the new within the old and the appearance of a new object (or phenomenon) on the basis of these prerequisites (see Genetic Method).

Genetic Method, a method of investigating natural and social phenomena, based on analysing their development (q.v.). It came into existence when the idea of development took precedence in science (17th century), viz., differential calculus in mathematics, the theory of evolution in biology, etc. The G.M. was also adopted in mathematics and logic as a method of substantiating the axiomatic method (q.v.). According to the G.M. we must determine (1) the initial conditions of development, (2) the main stages of development, and (3) the basic tendency or line of development. The chief purpose is to establish the connections between phenomena in time and to examine the transitions from lower to higher forms. However, the G.M. fails to reveal all the complexities of the development process. If used as an absolute method, unsupported by other methods, it leads into error, distorts reality, simplifies the development process and is reduced to vulgar evolutionism. In modern science, the G.M. is used in combination with structural-functional analysis (q.v.), systems analysis, the historico-comparative method (q.v.), etc.

Genetics, a science dealing with the laws of heredity and mutability of organisms. G. is one of the main branches of biology and studies the genotype, whose function is to regulate a living system. G. as a science dates back to Mendel (q.v.) who discovered the laws of heredity (1866); in 1900 these laws were "rediscovered" by H. de Vries, K. Correns and E. Tschermak. Later the chromosome theory of heredity was expounded and the materialist conception of the gene elaborated (Th. Morgan, q.v. and others). The gap formed at G.'s beginnings between it and Darwin's evolution theory (qq.v.) was later filled by population genetics, whose foundations were laid by S. S. Chetverikov (1926). A progressive development in G. was the break with certain mechanistic principles in the chromosome theory of heredity such as exaggeration of the stability of the gene, disregard of its complex links with other components of the cell, and underestimation of external factors, of the integrity of the genotype and the phenotype and of the link between them in their individual and historical mutability. This was considerably promoted by the discovery of the mutagenic effect of X-rays (G. S. Filippov, H. Muller), and by work on the chemically induced mutation (V. V. Sakharov, M. Ye. Lobashov, I. A. Rapoport and others). As he engaged in practical selection in agriculture, N. I. Vavilov (q.v.) discovered quantitative and qualitative possibilities of mutation in natural conditions. I. V. Michurin developed the principles for actively changing the living nature by remote hybridisation methods. Attempts to discover the internal structure of the gene proved successful. A. S. Serebrovsky and N. P. Dubinin advanced the centre theory of the gene (1928-29) showing that the latter is divisible into separate units in linear arrangement. Subsequent numerous experiments showed that it is the deoxyribonucleic acid (DNA) found in the chromosomes that provides the chemical basis of the specific qualities of the gene, and that has the hereditary (genetic) information "written into" it for regulating the molecular synthesis and, eventually, the self-reproduction of the cell and the organic nature as a whole. The molecular structure of the material basis of heredity was further elucidated by N. K. Koltsov's research (1927), by J. Watson and F. Crick's discovery of the "double spiral" molecular model of DNA (1953), etc. In recent decades, G. has been evolving increasingly intense links with the other biological sciences, practical agriculture, medicine, microbiology and space biology. Scientific exploration in G. has been accompanied by a heated philosophical contention between materialism and idealism, dialectics and metaphysics. However, progress in G. has always been based on materialism, as the study of the objective properties of heredity has led geneticists to a spontaneous

materialist outlook. With the rapid progress in G. mechanistic limitations have been overcome and a growing need has been felt for a dialectical methodology, as conditions have matured for solving the problem of the part and the whole (relation of the gene and the genotype), of determinism (relation of the gene and its characteristics, of the genotype and the phenotype, of mutation and evolution), and also for awareness of the systems character of methods used in genetic analysis by the particular branches of science. Another concomitant of the advance in G. was the latter's increasingly progressive, humanistic, social and moral content. This is particularly important in human G., medical G., and genetic engineering, in which man becomes not only the subject, but also the main object of cognition. The Marxist approach to G. lies in its ability to reveal the unscientific nature of bourgeois ideological speculations regarding the cognition of man by means of natural science (racism, q.v., neo-eugenics, etc.). The dialectico-materialist principles in theoretical modelling of the process by which man is formed in his integral entity provide a philosophical and methodological basis for a comprehensive study of man as a single complex of his social and biological (including genetic) aspects.

Genius, the highest degree of creative mental endowment; a person of such endowment. Considering the relative difference between G. and talent, works of genius may be defined as having extraordinary novelty, individuality and historic importance for the development of human society, for which reason they are preserved for all time in the memory of mankind. G. is not a mystical being, a superman (as some idealist philosophers believe), but one who by virtue of his extraordinary endowment and labour is able to contribute to the progress of mankind.

Gentile, Giovanni (1875-1944), Italian philosopher, Minister of Education in Mussolini's government. He attacked Marxism in his work *La filosofia di Marx* (1899), revised the doctrine of Hegel (q.v.), and created a system of "actualism", a subjective idealist variety of neo-Hegelianism (q.v.). G. described all the existent as the fruit of the thinking mind in motion. Thought, he contended, is always actual and active, and its creative activity is not restricted by space or time. The matter which it produces is dead and inert, although it is in unity with thought. Reality, he contended, is not identical with the conceptions of the individual mind, but is the pure thought of a supra-personal transcendental entity in the Universe, which overcomes all opposites in the process of becoming. G.'s socio-political views evolved from liberalism to fascism (q.v.). His main work: *La riforma della dialettica hegeliana* (1913).

Geoffroy Saint-Hilaire, Etienne (1772-1844), French zoologist-evolutionist. While elaborating the classification of the animal world he arrived at the conclusion that all vertebrates possess common features. He came out in favour of the idea of changeability of organisms but erroneously saw the reason for it only in the influence of the environment on the development of the embryo. His ideas played a big role in preparing the way for the evolution theory (q.v.).

Geographical Environment, the aggregate of things and phenomena of animate and inanimate nature (the earth's crust, lower layers of the atmosphere, water, soil, flora and fauna) involved at any given time in the process of social life and constituting the objectively necessary medium for the existence and development of society. The development of society also changes and widens the G.E. In the distant past men used mainly natural sources of livelihood (wild plants and animals, fertile land, etc.). In the course of time, natural wealth comprising means of labour, i.e., mineral and power resources, acquired increasing importance. The G.E. considerably affects the life of society, tending to retard or accelerate the development of countries and nations, and often exerting a decisive influence on the growth of specific economic branches. In their natural state the elements of the G.E. do not necessarily satisfy the growing requirements of production. For this reason, man transforms or changes them, and therefore acts

as the most powerful agent in the transformation of the G.E. But the extent, nature and forms of change depend on the level of technology and the social system. The anarchy of production and the competition prevailing in capitalist society more often than not stand in the way of rational influence on nature and cause changes in the G.E. which are harmful to society. The building of the material and technical base of communism proceeds from the effective and planned utilisation of all the elements of the G.E. for the good of the people (see Ecology; Global Problems).

Geographical School in Sociology (Geographical Determinism), a bourgeois school in sociology which holds that the geographical environment (climate, soil, rivers, etc.) is the chief factor in social development; an essentially naturalist and idealist approach to history. First advanced by ancient thinkers, Plato, Aristotle (qq.v.) and others, in opposition to religious and mythological views. G.D., which took shape as a distinct school of thought in the 18th century under the influence of Montesquieu (q.v.), was progressive so long as it opposed the church-sponsored feudal ideology which preached the divine preordination of social phenomena. In the mid-19th century it lost its progressive message (Buckle, q.v., K. Ritter). Buckle used G.D. to account for the persisting social inequality and to justify colonial expansion. Closely related to the geographical school was the theory expounded by Mechnikov (q.v.), who argued that social development leads inevitably from tyranny to anarchy. The geographical school paved the way for the appearance, in the imperialist epoch, of geopolitics (q.v.).

Geometrical Method in Philosophy, a widely used but inaccurate name for the axiomatic method (q.v.) of setting out philosophical theories; Spinoza (q.v.) was its most prominent exponent. He modelled his chief work, *Ethics,* on Euclid's (q.v.) geometry, in the sense that he first presented the necessary definitions and axioms (q.v.) and then proceeded to prove the resultant theorems (q.v.). In our time these theorems appear artificial, but it was Spinoza's purpose to stress the necessary interconnection between the parts of the Universe, whose knowledge is provable. Descartes (q.v.), whose *Discours de la méthode* is clearly influenced by geometry, set a high value on the G.M. He went so far as to postulate that clarity and obviousness, both notable features of geometrical axioms, are criteria of the validity of all knowledge.

Geopolitics, a bourgeois doctrine justifying imperialist expansion on alleged grounds of economic and political geography. Theoretically, G. is a modern variety of bourgeois fetishism (q.v.). It presents as properties of the Earth itself specific qualities which geographical space acquires only as an element of economic policy. G. was propounded by F. Ratzel, a German geographer, shortly before the First World War; he viewed states as organisms struggling for *Lebensraum*. Its other proponents were H. Mackinder (Britain) and Admiral A. Mahan (USA). The term G. was first used by R. Kjellén, a Swedish scholar, who, in his *Staten som Lifsform* used the arguments of Malthusianism and Social-Darwinism (qq.v.) to justify the imperialist approach to geographical space. In 1923-27 a study group organised by the German journal *Geopolitik* proclaimed G. a special science distinct from conventional political geography. K. Haushofer and E. Obst, the leaders of this group, used G. to promote the political aims of nazism. After the Second World War, G. won adherents in the United States, Canada, and particularly in Federal Republic of Germany (C. Schmitt, H. Grimm, A. Hettner, A. Grabowski, and others). Today, G. argues the need for inter-state imperialist blocs and seeks to prove the geographical causes of the rift between the East and the West (the "continental" and "maritime" types of civilisation). In addition to the previous Malthusian rhetoric, adherents of G. widely use arguments from cultural psychology and comparative history of culture. Prominent among the contemporary geopolitical conceptions is the so-called global approach to political geography which, as a rule, reflects imperialist claims to world domination.

The German Ideology, an early philosophical work of Karl Marx and Frederick Engels written in 1845-46, criticising the idealism of the Young Hegelians (q.v.) and the limited nature of Feuerbach's (q.v.) materialism. The book was not published during the lifetime of Marx and Engels; it appeared for the first time in 1932 in the Soviet Union. Developing further the ideas expounded in *The Holy Family* (q.v.), Marx and Engels showed that idealism is the ideology of the classes hostile to the proletariat. Criticising the metaphysical character and the contemplative nature of Feuerbach's materialism, Marx and Engels showed that in his view of history Feuerbach was an idealist and, therefore, like the Young Hegelians, was unable to understand the driving forces of social development. The work presents a profound critique of bourgeois individualism and anarchism (qq.v) of Stirner (q.v.) and also of the reactionary, so-called "true socialism" (q.v.) of Karl Grün, Hess (q.v.), and others. Marx and Engels developed the theory of scientific communism and proved that the proletariat based its activity on the objective laws of social development. They saw in the proletariat's struggle against the bourgeoisie, in the victorious communist revolution and the inevitable establishment of the communist system the necessary result of the economic laws which operate independently of man's will. The work gives the first detailed exposition of the materialist understanding of history: of the question of the socio-economic formations, the productive forces, and relations of production, qq.v. (the latter term was not used yet), the relationship between social being and social consciousness (q.v.), etc. In their work Marx and Engels expounded their world outlook, which by that time was, in the main, clearly formed. This book is a model of militant philosophical critique of ideology hostile to the working class.

Gestalt Psychology, an idealist sensationalistic trend in psychology; originated in Germany in 1912. The term "G.P." was first introduced by Ch. von Ehrenfels (1859-1932); its most prominent exponents were M. Wertheimer (1880-1944), W. Köhler (1887-1967) and K. Koffka (1886-1941). Philosophically, G.P. is based on the ideas of Husserl and Mach (qq.v.). In contrast to association psychology (q.v.), G.P. considers what it styles psychic structures, "organised wholes", or *"Gestalts"*, rather than sensations, to be primary and basic in the workings of the mind. Their formation, according to G.P., is subject to the intrinsic psychic faculties of individuals to create simple, symmetrical and closed figures. This theory assumes the individual's isolation from his environment and his own practical activities. Ultimately, the *Gestaltists* ascribe the wholeness of the psychic structures to immanent subjective "laws"; this leads them to idealism. Subsequently, the ideas of G.P. (particularly the concept *"Gestalt"*) were applied to physical, physiological and even economic phenomena. Theoretically, G.P. was disproved by Pavlov (q.v.) and many other materialist psychologists (L. S. Vygotsky and others).

Ghose, Aurobindo (1872-1950), Indian idealist philosopher, founder of the so-called integral Vedānta (q.v.). In the early 20th century he was a leader of the radical wing in the Indian national liberation movement, the so-called extremists; founded a religious community in 1922. His chief philosophical works are *The Life Divine*, *The Human Cycle*, and *The Ideal of Human Unity*. In these books elements of the different trends of the Vedānta interweave with those of idealist Western schools, particularly Hegel (q.v.) and F. Bradley. G. believed that in human history there is a transition from "subconsciousness" to consciousness and "superconsciousness" and that the solution of the riddle of history and the achievement of man's aspirations lie in the attainment of mystical "superconsciousness". G. claimed to have discovered a "third way" of social development, distinct from capitalism and socialism. He was in effect a bourgeois ideologist. Whereas defence of the right of nations to independent development, criticism of the feudal past and of imperialist policy, etc., constituted an important part of his philosophical teaching between 1914 and

1920, in later years the reactionary aspects of his teaching, religious propaganda and criticism of socialism occupied a prominent place.

Global Problems, a set of problems facing the world as a whole, or some areas or countries. The most important of these are prevention of a world thermonuclear war and creation of favourable conditions for international relations to develop on a peaceful basis; worldwide social development and economic growth; elimination of hunger and poverty, the most glaring manifestations of social injustice; rational and comprehensive use of natural resources; elaboration and implementation of active demographic policies and strategies for the protection of the environment; development of international co-operation in scientific research to make use of the achievements of the scientific and technological revolution (q.v.); problems of education, health protection, etc. The solution of G.P. requires concentrated effort in various spheres of activity, including philosophy, which determines the ideological and methodological approach to the study of G.P. and appraises them in terms of humanity. The general human character of G.P. does not mean that they have no concrete socio-class content as maintained by bourgeois ideologists. Even the most advanced science and technology cannot ensure the adoption of correct decisions if they are not based on concrete social reality or are used in support of false socio-political conceptions. It is because of this that bourgeois society gives rise to all sorts of pessimistic forecasts and "disillusionment in progress" (R. Aron), on the one hand, and on the other, to attempts to find an "optimistic" solution by suspending the development of mankind, as proposed by D. Meadows and his co-authors, who set "limits to growth" by suggesting to contain the growth of production, population, etc. When Marxists analyse the ideas and theories involved in G.P. and devise strategies for their practical implementation, they take into account both their dialectical interconnection and their comprehensive, systemic character. In doing so, they single out the sociopolitical (including international legal), scientific and technological, cultural and historical, as well as moral and humanistic aspects of the G.P. They study these problems as they stand today in the context of the main contradiction of our epoch—between capitalism and socialism, and as they may stand in the future under communism. Being clearly aware of both the historical origins of G.P. and of the role played in their aggravation by the development of production, science and technology, Marxists also clearly realise that these problems will not necessarily lead to disaster, that they can be solved. Yet, their complete and final solution can only be possible on an adequate social basis in communist society. Despite the still limited material, scientific and technological possibilities, the socialist countries are already doing as much as they can to solve G.P. in keeping with the humane character of the new society. Yet, G.P., by their very nature, require concentrated effort not only on a national or regional but on a world scale. That is why the socialist countries develop active co-operation with all countries, including the capitalist ones, in solving the G.P.

Gnostics, adherents of a philosophico-religious school who combined Christian theology with the religions of the Orient, Neoplatonism (q.v.) and Pythagoreanism. The G. believed in an unknowable arche which manifests itself in emanation and is counterposed to matter, the source of "evil". The two leading G. were Valentinus of Egypt (2nd century) and Basilides of Syria (2nd century).

God, imaginary conception of a supernatural omnipotent being, which is supposed to have created the world and to be ruling it; in Judaism (q.v) Jehovah, in Islam (q.v.) Allah, in Christianity (q.v.) the Holy Trinity (God the Father, God the Son and God the Holy Ghost), etc. Conceptions of a god form the basis of modern forms of religion, whereas in the early stages of the development of religion this conception did not exist (see Animism; Fetishism; Totemism). The conceptions of tribal and national gods came into existence with the collapse of the primitive-communal system, the development of tribal associations, and the emergence of classes and the state. The conception of a single and omnipotent Almighty God, deity, the Lord of Heaven, took shape as a "copy of the single oriental despot" (Engels). Theology (q.v.) resorts to idealism to prove the existence of God philosophically, to embellish and cloak this idea, to present God as an absolute idea, a universal will, a kind of impersonal rational principle. That the idea of God and all attempts to defend it are groundless was made perfectly clear by Marxism and corroborated by the whole development of the natural and social sciences. "God is," wrote Lenin, "(in history and in real life) first of all the complex of ideas generated by the brutish subjection of man both by external nature and by the class yoke—ideas which *consolidate* that subjection, *lull to sleep* the class struggle" (Vol. 35, p. 128).

God-Building, a religious-philosophical trend in Russia which arose after the defeat of the revolution of 1905-07. Among its leaders were Lunacharsky (q.v.), V. Bazarov, Yushkevich (q.v.); Maxim Gorky was also associated with the God-builders for a time (*Confession,* 1907, and *Destruction of the Personality,* 1909), but broke with the movement under the influence of Lenin. The aim of G.B., which was closely linked with the "collectivist philosophy" of Bogdanov (q.v.) was to create a so-called religious atheism, i.e., a religion without God, whose place would be taken by a community of people and cosmos. The advocates of G.B. discussed "exuberant growth of socialist religious consciousness" and regarded Marxism chiefly as a system of religious and philosophical views showing the people the road to a new life. They thought that Marxism would be easier mastered by the masses in a religious clothing and thereby be more effective for their organisation. The ideas of the trend were much advocated in the school which Bogdanov and others set up on the island of Capri in 1909. Although the God-builders belonged to the Russian Social-Democratic Labour Party and opposed God-Seeking (q.v.), their theories had nothing in common with Marxism. Lenin and Plekhanov were sharply critical of G.B. "... Both in Europe and in Russia," Lenin wrote, "*any,* even the most refined and best-intentioned defence or justification of the idea of God is a justification of reaction" (Vol. 35, p. 128). By the outbreak of the First World War G.B. had already ceased to exist as a trend.

God-Seeking, a religious-philosophical trend in Russia that set out to prove that the aim of social development was to realise the ideals of a "new", properly understood Christianity. The ideas of G.S. became particularly popular among bourgeois intellectuals in Russia after the defeat of the Russian revolution of 1905-07. The advocates of G.S. included such philosophers and decadent writers as Berdyayev (q.v.), D. Merezhkovsky and others. They called for a "new attitude" to the Christian gospel and preached a "religious reformation"; they tried to revive religion in the masses, to give it a new foundation. They maintained that the aim of life was to seek God, that the purpose of history was the realisation of God in humanity, the creation of a theo-humanity, i.e., a social organisation founded on religious principles. In contrast to traditional Christianity with its other world's kingdom, the advocates of G.S. believed that the religious ideals (eternal life, "holy society", etc.) could have been achieved on earth. They upheld irrationalism (q.v.), considering mystical knowledge, revelation the most reliable means of discovering the truth. After the October Revolution of 1917 most of them left Russia and opposed the Soviet Government.

Gödel, Kurt (1906-1978), Austrian mathematician and logician. He worked on problems of metamathematics and mathematical logic (qq.v.). His most important achievement was that he proved (1931) the incompleteness of the formal systems as they contained propositions which could be neither proved nor refuted within the framework of those systems. G.'s exposition stimulated research into the limitations of the formal systems by A. Church, S. Kleene, Tarski (q.v.), A. Mostovsky, P. Novikov, and others and affirmed that complete formalisation (q.v.) of scientific knowledge is philosophically impossible. In the 1930s, G.'s philosophical views were strongly influenced by neo-positivism (q.v.); subsequently, he was critical of subjectivism.

Godwin, William (1756-1836), English political thinker and novelist; exponent of petty-bourgeois egalitarian utopianism. He was a protestant preacher as a young man and became a consistent rationalist in the early 1780s. G. gave primacy to the influence on man of the social environment and morals. He advocated abolition of the right of property and state power. His ideal was a society of independent small producers organised in communities. He favoured the communist principle of distribution according to requirements. However, his views were anti-social. G. influenced anarchistic doctrines.

Goethe, Johann Wolfgang von (1749-1832), German poet, naturalist and thinker. G. championed the idea that theory and experience are one. "First came the cause" is the basic principle of his approach to the world and cognition. He was convinced of the objectiveness of the laws of nature, which itself contains the motive principle of its development. G. sought to supplement Spinoza's (q.v.) conception, which he interpreted pantheistically (see Pantheism), with the idea of development. Interaction of the positive and negative ("ascents" and "polarities"), G. held, is inherent in every phenomenon; this interaction gives rise to new qualities. G. considered motion the basic form of the existence of matter. However, unable to explain the multiplicity of forms of motion, he arrived at hylozoism (q.v.) and acknowledged "an eternal vital power". Although G.'s views were inconsistent and often contradictory, they were close to materialist. G. supported the evolution theory (q.v.) and stressed the idea of the unity of the world. He regarded labour as a transforming power in society and culture. In aesthetics, he posed the problem of correlation between the natural and the human, the universal and the particular, the whole and the part, and resolved it from the standpoint of creative artistic activity.

Gogotsky, Sylvestr Sylvestrovich (1813-1889), Russian idealist philosopher. G. deliberately adapted his philosophical views to suit his advocacy of Orthodoxy (q.v.). He attacked materialism as a doctrine leading to atheism, and considered it the purpose of philosophy to represent the idea of God as the rational and creative prime cause of the natural and moral world. G. believed knowledge of God to be innate and attainable through faith. He held that the idea of God is inseparable from human cognition, which is secondary and derives from faith. Antonovich and Pisarev (qq.v.) demonstrated the unscientific essence of G.'s writings. His *Filosofskii leksikon* (Philosophical Lexicon) (4 vols., 1857-73) is of informative value as one of the earliest attempts to compile a philosophical encyclopaedia in Russia.

Good and Evil, ethical categories which express a moral appraisal of the conduct of people (groups, classes) and of social phenomenon from definite class positions. G. is what society (or a given class) considers moral and worthy of imitation, the reverse being true of E. The metaphysicians present G. and E. as eternal and universal conceptions. Idealists look for the source of G. and E. in the commandments of God or the absolute spirit. According to the ethical theory of Kant (q.v.), G. is what conforms to the moral law, which is inherent in every rational being and does not depend on the conditions in which a man lives (see Categorical Imperative). Pre-Marxian materialists held that the source of G. and E. lay in abstract human nature, in a man's desire to enjoy and to be happy (see Hedonism; Eudaemonism). Even those among them who connect morality with man's conditions of life and upbringing also claimed that the notions of G. and E. are eternal and immutable. The "extra-historical human nature", in fact, always stood for the socially conditioned features common to representatives of certain large groups or classes. That is why definitions of G. and E. invariably expressed the morality of a definite class. The characteristic features of present-day bourgeois ethics are its attempts, on the one hand, to present the conceptions of G. and E. prevailing in the official morality of capitalist society as eternal and universal and, on the other hand, to deny the objective criteria of G. and E. Marxist

ethics gave the first scientific substantiation of G. and E. "The conceptions of good and evil have varied so much from nation to nation and from age to age that they have often been in direct contradiction to each other" (F. Engels, *Anti-Dühring*, p. 109). But these variations are not the result of arbitrary rule; they do not depend on the individual's opinion alone. They are rooted in social conditions of life and for this reason bear an objective character. Men's actions may be appraised as G. or E., according to whether they promote or hinder the satisfaction of the historical needs of society as a whole, i.e., the interests of a given progressive class expressing these needs. In the communist code of morals the conceptions of G. and E. find expression in the aggregate of concrete moral requirements determining the norms of the kind of behaviour that is instrumental in the liberation of the working masses from exploitation, in the building of socialism and communism, the cause of peace and social progress.

Gorgias (c. 483-375 B.C.), Greek sophist of Leontini, Sicily, a proponent of slave-owning democracy. Supplemented the relativism (q.v.) of Protagoras (q.v.) with rationalistic agnosticism (q.v.). His postulates have come down to us in the rendering of Plato (q.v.) and other authors. G. advanced three propositions: anything is not real; if anything were real, it would still be unknowable; if anything were knowable, it would still be inexpressible.

Gramsci, Antonio (1891-1937), Marxist theoretician, founder of the Italian Communist Party; sentenced by a fascist court in 1928 to 20 years' imprisonment for his revolutionary activities. G. played a prominent part in exposing mechanistic philosophy, the ideological basis of Rightwing deviationism, widespread in some of the Communist parties of Europe in the 1920s. His main writings are contained in the *Quaderni del Carcere*. In philosophy, G. concentrated on problems of historical materialism; he examined the relations between the basis and the superstructure (q.v.), between the proletariat and the intelligentsia, and made a profound analysis of the relative independence of ideology (philosophy, the arts, ethics, etc.). Of great interest are his studies of Italian culture, his criticism of Catholicism, and of idealist theories in philosophy (Croce, q.v.) and sociology.

Granovsky, Timofei Nikolayevich (1813-1855), Russian historian and sociologist, a prominent exponent of Westernism (see Westerners, Slavophiles). His views on history in general were strongly influenced by Stankevich, Belinsky and Herzen (qq.v.); he also assimilated the fundamentals of classical German philosophy, particularly Hegel, whose logical scheme, however, he rejected. According to G., the historical process including revolutions in society is rigorously governed by objective laws. He defined objective law as an ideal, a rational and moral goal, in the attainment of which not only peoples but also personalities play a great role. Hence, he denounced fatalism (q.v.) which he described as a doctrine that relieves individuals of moral responsibility. G.'s views on historical development (containing elements of dialectics) evolved from idealism towards naturalism. He believed that history should borrow the methods of research employed in natural science. His explanations of social phenomena attached considerable weight to material, mostly geographical, conditions. G. was an advocate of constitutional monarchy. He opposed serfdom in Russia from the position of liberal education. He exercised a beneficial influence on Russian society and

Russian historiography. G. expounded his views in *O sovremennom sostoyanii i znachenii vseobshchei istorii* (On the Modern Condition and Significance of General History), 1852.

Grotius, Hugo (1583-1645), Dutch jurist, historian and statesman; a prominent exponent of the bourgeois theories of natural law and social contract (qq.v.). G. believed that law and the state are of earthly rather than divine origin. The state, he said, came into being as a result of an agreement among men. His teaching helped to free the theory of the state and law from the tutelage of theology and medieval scholasticism (q.v.). His main work: *De Jure Belli et Pacis* (1625).

Gurvitch, Georgi Davydovich (1894-1965), French sociologist, was born in Russia, emigrated to France after the October Revolution of 1917. In sociology, he founded so-called dialectical hyperempiricism, which claims to examine comprehensively all aspects of social reality in all its "strata", "levels", "dimensions and aspects", and all its "contradictions". G.'s conception is unhistorical, extremely formal and idealistic, because it rejects the concept of a single determinative basis of society, objective sociological laws, and the concepts of society and progress. G. was associated with the World Peace Movement. His main works: *La vocation actuelle de la sociologie* (1950) and *Déterminismes sociaux et liberté humaine* (1955).

h

Habits, actions which become automatic as a result of prolonged repetition. The physiological mechanism of H. is represented by the dynamic stereotype. The H. of animals are unconscious and are formed in the course of their adaptation to the environment. Similar H. are formed in man, too. These are automatic actions timed for concrete specific situations. Some habits are of practical value, but as long as they are not recognised they cannot be transmitted to another person through the modern forms of education. The highest form of H. is man's H. whose components are apprehended in advance, consciously divided and united into systems which correspond to the general specific features of the objective situation in which the H. are formed. This being the case, man in the process of automating H. and their functioning retains the possibility of consciously controlling his actions and he can adjust them with relative ease should the need arise. H. are included in all kinds of actions, both external (e.g., motor H.) and internal (e.g., automatic mental actions). H. are not only a result but also a requisite for man's creative activity.

Haeckel, Ernst (1834-1919), German biologist, known for his defence of Darwin's evolution theory (qq.v.) and natural-historical materialism (q.v.). H. took Darwinism a step farther in a number of his theoretical propositions, such as the biogenetic law (q.v.) and the theory of phylogenesis, the idea of the natural inception of life (q.v.) from inorganic matter. H. developed Darwin's conception of natural selection as a factor of organic evolution. H. won popularity with his book, *Die Welträtsel* (1899) in which he attacked the idealist religious outlook and advocated the materialist approach to nature. The book roused opposition from idealist philosophers, the church, and idealist naturalists. Progressive scientists ranged themselves behind him. Lenin highly commended the book (Vol. 14, p. 334). H. publicly renounced religion and the church, but was not always consistent in his views. He departed in some matters from his materialism and atheism, and, among other things, suggested replacing official religion with belief in the divine powers of nature in the spirit of Spinoza's (q.v.) pantheism.

Hamann, Johann Georg (1730-1788), German idealist philosopher; exponent of the teaching on immediate knowledge (q.v.); H. opposed enlightenment and rationalism (qq.v.); believed in the creative powers of mystic intuition. Yet he expressed the notion of the unity of opposites as a general law of being and thereby influenced the idealist dialectics of Fichte, Schelling and Hegel (qq.v.). The most notable of his writings is *Kreuzzüge des Philologen* (1762).

Hamilton, William (1788-1856), Scottish idealist philosopher and logician; denied objective truth and gravitated towards agnosticism. H. held that "absolute", i.e., material reality, is cognisable through supernatural revelation only. He ranged himself beside Kant (q.v.) in accepting apriorism and moral postulates as the foundation of religious faith. He introduced into logic the doctrine of the quantification of the predicate, thus attempting to reduce judgment to equation and logic to calculus. H. was a forerunner of the exponents of modern mathematical logic (q.v.). One of his best-known works is *Metaphysics and Logic* (lectures edited and published posthumously in four volumes, 1859-60).

Hartley, David (1705-1757), English physician, materialist philosopher and a founder of association psychology (q.v.). According to H., the action of external objects on the sense-organs produces in sensory nerves vibrations of the tiny particles which, propagated through the nerves to the brain, produce there according to their order, direction, number and frequency corresponding sensations and

ideas of a "spiritual nature". H.'s
mechanistic materialism considerably influenced the views of Priestley (q.v.) and
J. Mill. Main work: *Observations on Man,
His Frame, His Duty, and His Expecta-
tions* (1749).

Hartmann, Eduard von (1842-1906),
German idealist philosopher; a forerunner
of the contemporary schools of irrationalism and voluntarism (qq.v.). Of his
works, *Philosophie des Unbewußten*
(1869) has had the greatest influence. Like
Schopenhauer (q.v.), H. believed the unconscious spirit was the basis of being.
The idea of the unconscious also pervades
H.'s ethics. The desire for happiness, H.
held, is the source of unhappiness, and
the rejection of all desires is the way to
freedom from suffering, this being the
only form of and the only substitute for
happiness. To achieve freedom from suffering, H. averred, man had to renounce his
three dominant illusions—that of earthly
happiness, that of happiness in the hereafter and that of happiness attainable by
reorganising and perfecting society. H.'s
doctrine denies any possibility of attaining
happiness through social progress and is,
therefore, reactionary not only in the
philosophical, but also in the socio-
political sense.

Hartmann, Nicolai (1882-1950), German idealist philosopher, belonged to the
neo-Kantian Marburg school (q.v.), then
dissociated himself from it, being dissatisfied with its subjective idealistic rationalism. Developed an objective idealist teaching on being, the categories of being and of
cognition. H.'s "critical ontology" is
based on a hierarchy of layers of being:
inorganic, organic, soul and mind. His
philosophy contains traces of irrationalism
and agnosticism (qq.v.), proclaiming as
mysterious and uncognisable all the basic
forms of being present in all its layers. On
the basis of his ontology H. constructed
a philosophy of nature, a philosophy of
objective mind, a system of ethics and a
theory of "values", an aesthetics and a
theory of knowledge. Main works: *Ethik*
(1925), *Zur Grundlegung der Ontologie*
(1935), *Philosophie der Natur* (1950), and
Ästhetik (1953).

Hedonism, the principle that substantiates moral requirements, the theory which
defines the good as that which yields
pleasure or relief from suffering and the
evil as that which causes suffering.
Theoretical H. is a variety of naturalism
(q.v.) in ethics. It is based on the idea that
pleasure is man's main principle inherent in
his nature and determining all his actions.
Hedonistic theories have been held since
the antiquity. In Greece the hedonists
adhered to the ethics of Aristippus (q.v.).
H. reached its peak in the ethics of
Epicurus (q.v.), and was pivoted in the
utilitarianism (q.v.) of Mill and Bentham
(qq.v.). In modern bourgeois theories, H.
can be found only as a methodological
principle for defining the good, though
most bourgeois ethicists hold that to define
the good by pleasure is a vulgar simplification of moral problems.

Hegel, Georg Wilhelm Friedrich (1770-
1831), a German objective idealist, exponent of classical German philosophy
(q.v.), taught at Jena University since
1801 and at Berlin University since 1818.
The young philosopher was a radical,
welcomed the French Revolution and
opposed the feudalism of the Prussian
monarchy. On the whole, H.'s philosophy
reflected the contradictory development of
Germany on the eve of the bourgeois
revolution; it was affected by the dualism
of the rising German bourgeoisie, of which
H. was the ideologist. Hence the progressive, even revolutionary tendency of his
philosophy as an expression of the ideological preparation of a bourgeois revolution in
Germany, and at the same time his
conservative, reactionary ideas, reflecting
the inconsistency and cowardice of the
German bourgeoisie and its tending to
compromise with the reactionary Junker-
dom. H.'s dualism is evident in all his
writings. In *Die Phänomenologie des
Geistes* (1807), H. examined the evolution
of human consciousness from its first
awakening to its conscious mastering of
science and scientific methodology
(phenomenology—doctrine of phenomena
[manifestations] of consciousness in their
historical development). Analysing the
category of alienation (q.v.), H. grasped,
albeit idealistically, the essence of labour,

i.e., important aspects of man's objective activity (q.v.) and conceived man and his history as the result of his own work and consequently formed some ideas about certain real laws of history. As the point of departure for his philosophy H. chose the identity of being and thinking, i.e., the conception of the real world as a manifestation of an idea, a concept, or spirit. This identity he regarded as the historically developing process of the absolute idea's cognizing itself. When developed the content of H.'s objective idealism (outlined in *Enzyklopädie der philosophischen Wissenschaften in Grundrisse*, 1817) is that all phenomena in nature and society are based on the absolute—the spiritual and rational principle, the "absolute idea", "world reason", or "world spirit". This principle is active, and its activity consists in thinking or, more precisely, in self-cognition. The absolute idea passes three stages: (1) development of the idea in its own bosom, in the "element of pure thinking"—Logic, wherein the idea reveals its content in a system of logical categories which are related and grow out of one another; (2) development of the idea in the form of the "other-being", i.e., in the form of nature—Philosophy of Nature. Nature, H. averred, does not develop: it is merely the external manifestation of the self-development of the logical categories that constitute its spiritual essence; (3) development of the idea in thought and history (in the "spirit"), i.e., Philosophy of Mind. At this stage the absolute idea withdraws within itself and conceives its content in the different forms of human consciousness and activity. However, the idealistic principle of identity of thought and being serves to substantiate the unity of the laws governing the external world and thinking; it is directed against Kant's agnosticism (qq.v.). H.'s dialectics (q.v.), set out exhaustively in *Wissenschaft der Logik* (1812-16), was a most valuable contribution to philosophy. In it H. analysed the major laws and categories of dialectics, substantiated the thesis on the unity of dialectics, logic and the theory of knowledge, and elaborated for the first time in the history of thought a system of dialectical logic (q.v.). H. made an exceptionally valuable contribution to the theory of knowledge. Of particular importance is his

profound critique of contemplativeness (q.v.) and of Kant's dualism of the "things-in-themselves" and phenomena. Important also are *Grundlinien der Philosophie des Rechts* (1821), *Vorlesungen über die Geschichte der Philosophie* (1833-36), *Vorlesungen über Aesthetic* (1835-38) and *Vorlesungen über die Philosophie der Geschichte* (1837). He left a profound imprint on all the branches of philosophy in which he applied dialectics and profoundly analysed topical problems of science. However, H.'s dialectics was shrouded in mysticism. The idealism of his philosophy and his bourgeois limitations were at variance with his own dialectical ideas: he claimed that the development of the world and of cognition had run its course to completion, injected mysticism into dialectics, applied the principle of development solely to phenomena in the realm of the ideas, made a number of categories of logic stereotyped and artificial and presented their system as a closed one. He was unable and reluctant to draw any consistent social conclusions from dialectics and reconciled himself to the status quo, which he justified, proclaiming the Prussian monarchy the crowning of social development, tolerating nationalist prejudice, etc. H.'s philosophy played a great role in the formation of Marxism, which preserved its most valuable element, dialectics, moulding it into a scientifically strict teaching on the development of nature, society and thought. Marxism acclaims H.'s opposition to agnosticism, his historical approach, his faith in the powers of human reason, and his science of logic, in which he traced the connections of the real world and the most important objective laws governing theoretical and practical activity.

Hegelianism, see Young Hegelians and Old Hegelians.

Heidegger, Martin (1889-1976), one of the founders and the main representative of German existentialism (q.v.). In his rectoral address at Freiburg University in 1933, he accepted the ideology of National-Socialism. The basic category of H.'s idealist philosophy was "temporality" understood by him as man's inner experience. "Mood", a form of spontaneous, undeveloped consciousness, was considered primary by H. The a priori forms of human personality, according to H., are care, dread, concern, etc. These forms constitute man's subjective being. The theory of a priori forms was developed by H. as the theory of existence. In order to comprehend the "essence of existence", man must deny himself any considerations of aim or practicality, realise his "mortality", "frailty". It is only through a permanent realisation of being "faced with death" that man can, according to H., visualise the validity and substantiality of each moment of life and get rid of aims, "ideals", "scientific abstractions". H.'s philosophy combined the irrationalist tendencies of Kierkegaard, philosophy of life, and Husserl's phenomenology (qq.v.). His main works: *Sein und Zeit* (1927); *Kant und das Problem der Metaphysik* (1929); *Einführung in die Metaphysik* (1953).

Heine, Heinrich (1797-1856), German poet, revolutionary democrat, a friend of Marx; he was the first to reveal the underlying revolutionary complexion of classical German philosophy (q.v.) and, in particular, the dialectics of Hegel (q.v.) which, he said, paved the way to revolution. H. maintained that the history of philosophy was a history of the struggle between spiritualism and sensationalism, and declared himself a champion of the latter trend (*Zur Geschichte der Religion und Philosophie in Deutschland*, 1834). The poet associated his criticism of religion and idealism with the fight against feudalism, monarchism and philistinism. He advocated a democratic revolution and socialism, which he conceived in the spirit of Saint-Simon (q.v.). He held the future of mankind depended on the implementation of the people's right to satisfy their material requirements and interests.

Heisenberg, Werner (1901-1976), German theoretical physicist, one of the founders of quantum mechanics (q.v.). In 1927 H. formulated the uncertainty principle (q.v.). Discussing philosophical problems in his books, H. gradually departed from the positivist outlook of the so-called Copenhagen school to the objective ideal-

ism of Plato, q.v. (*Philosophic Problems of Nuclear Science*, 1953).

Heliocentrism and Geocentrism. The geocentric theory maintained that the Earth was immobile and constituted the centre of the Universe, that the Sun, Moon, planets and stars revolved round the Earth; based on religious conceptions and the writings of Plato and Aristotle (qq.v.), G. was expounded most completely by Ptolemy, a 2nd-century Greek scholar. The heliocentric theory maintained that the Earth, while revolving on its axis, is one of many planets orbiting round the Sun. This theory was supported by Aristarchus of Samos, Nicholas of Cusa (q.v.) and others, but Copernicus (q.v.) is rightly considered as its true father, for he produced an exhaustive exposition of H. and substantiated it mathematically. Subsequently, the Copernican system was elaborated upon. The Sun, it was shown, is the centre not of all the Universe, but only of the solar system. Much was done by Galileo Galilei, Kepler and Newton (qq.v.) to substantiate H. Progressive scientists, who championed the heliocentric system, refuted the church-sponsored geocentric theory.

Helmholtz, Hermann (1821-1894), German naturalist. His physico-chemical methods of examining living bodies refuted the doctrine of vitalism (q.v.) and stimulated the development of materialist views in biology. H. made notable physiological discoveries (change of the speed of excitation in nerve fibres, physiological studies of the sense-organs and the laws governing the perception of space, etc.). In his works on theoretical physics and other natural sciences H. expounded spontaneously materialist views, but inclined at times towards Kantianism while departing from materialism. He erroneously inferred from the theory of the specific energy of sense-organs that sensations are not subjective images of the objective properties of real things, but mere symbols, or "hieroglyphs" bearing no resemblance to these properties (see Hieroglyphs, Theory of). In his *Materialism and Empirio-Criticism* (q.v.)

Lenin criticised H. for his inconsistent philosophical views.

Helvétius, Claude Adrien (1715-1771), an exponent of French 18th-century materialism (q.v.). H.'s philosophy was based on Locke's sensationalism (qq.v.), which he purged of its idealistic elements. According to H., objectively existing matter is cognised through sensations. He considered memory as another instrument of cognition. He had a simplified approach to thought, which he conceived as a mere combination of sensations. He stressed the part played by the social milieu in developing the human character, using it to prove the necessity of substituting capitalist for feudal relations, but held that human consciousness and passion played the dominant role in social development. Marx gave a profound analysis of H.'s philosophy. "The sensory qualities and self-love, enjoyment and correctly understood personal interest are the bases of all morality. The natural equality of human intelligences, the unity of progress of reason and progress of industry, the natural goodness of man, and the omnipotence of education, are the main features in his system" (K. Marx and F. Engels, *Collected Works,* Vol. 4, p. 130). H.'s idea of the harmonious combination of personal and social interests and his conception of the original mental equality of individuals cleared the way for utopian socialism (q.v.). Main works: *De l'esprit* (1758), *De l'homme* (1769, published in 1773).

Heracleides Ponticus (4th century B.C.), Greek philosopher, disciple of Plato (q.v.), tended to atomism. H. assumed that atoms were formed by a world reason, nous (q.v.). His conception of the soul was atomistic and clearly influenced by Pythagoreanism. H.'s astronomical views inclined towards heliocentrism, while his musical theories were influenced by Aristotle (q.v.). None of his many works have survived.

Heraclitus of Ephesus (c. 544-c. 483 B.C.), Greek materialist philosopher and dialectician born in an aristocratic family. His philosophical work *On Nature,* of which only fragments survive, was extolled in the antique world for its profundity. The mysterious presentation of his views earned him the name of "The Obscure". Fire, H. held, was the prime material in nature, for it was the most capable of change and motion. The world as a whole, separate things and even souls, originated from fire. "The world, an entity out of everything," H. maintained, "was created by none of the gods or men, but was, is, and will be eternally living fire, regularly becoming ignited and regularly becoming extinguished." Lenin described this aphorism as "a very good exposition of the principles of dialectical materialism" (Vol. 38, p. 349). All things derive from fire in accordance with necessity, which H. named "logos", yet the world process is cyclical: all things again turn into "fire". Everything in nature is in continuous flux. All things and all properties change into their opposites: cold becomes hot, hot becomes cold, etc. Since everything is constantly changing and being renewed, one cannot step into the same river twice because the second time one steps into new water. In human affairs this conversion of everything into its opposite is not a simple change, but a struggle. Struggle is universal. But the struggle of opposites reveals their identity: the road up and the road down, life and death, etc., are all one and the same. The universality of change and the conversion of every property into its opposite make all qualities relative. Sensations are the basis of knowledge, but only thinking can lead to wisdom. If something were concealed from the light which is perceived by senses, it would not, all the same, succeed in concealing itself from the light of reason. H. opposed his world outlook to that of most of his contemporaries and compatriots. His aristocratic conceptions of society blended with a few progressive views: he opposed the traditional unwritten law championed by the aristocrats, and advocated law established by the state, which, he held, men should guard as closely as the walls of their native city.

Herbart, Johann Friedrich (1776-1841), German idealist philosopher, psychologist and teacher. H. believed all existence to be based on *reals,* which are essences eternal, immutable, spiritual (like Leibniz's monads, qq.v.) and uncognisable (like Kant's, q.v., "things-in-themselves"). The "soul" is the most perfect of the *reals*, giving birth to all psychic phenomena. In education, he departed from the democratic principles of his teacher, Pestalozzi.

Herder, Johann Gottfried (1744-1803), German philosopher of enlightenment, writer and literary critic. He denounced Kant's (q.v.) "critique" of reason and opposed to it the "physiology" of cognitive faculties and the teaching on the primacy of language over reason. H. deduced his concepts of time and space from experience and championed the unity of matter and the forms of cognition. Proceeding from the concept of progress in nature he developed the teaching of progress in history and of society's advancement towards humanism. H. stressed the originality of the spiritual cultures of the various peoples, in particular the Southern Slavs, whose poetry he held in high esteem. He voiced a number of conjectures on the role of production (the crafts) and science in the development of society and anticipated the teachings of Schelling and Hegel (qq.v.) on the disparity between the subjective purposes of individual human acts and their objective historical results.

Heresies, various departures from official religious doctrines, opposite or hostile to them. The first Christian H.— montanism, Judeo-Christianity, gnosticism—arose in the 2nd and 3rd centuries and opposed the established Christian dogmas. Arianism, Nestorianism, and Monophysitism date from the 4th and 5th centuries, when Christianity (q.v.) became the official religion of the Roman Empire. H. reached their peak in the Middle Ages, when the Catholic Church was most closely connected with the exploiting classes of feudal society and was at the height of its power (Bogomils, Waldenses, Albigenses, Beggards, Lollards, Taborites, etc.). In many cases H. were the religious form in which the popular masses protested against the ruling classes of feudal society, supported by the Catholic Church. H. prepared the collapse of the feudal system in some countries of Western Europe. The peasant-plebeian H.,

which provided the slogans for peasant rebellions and inspired the common people, played a particularly prominent role in this respect. With the rise of capitalism H. lost their militancy and declined into religious sectarianism.

Hermeneutics, the science and theory of interpretation whose object is to explain a text proceeding from its features, both objective (grammatical meaning of words and their historical variations), and subjective (the author's intention). It first appeared in the Hellenic period in connection with the study and publication of classical texts (e.g., Homer). It then developed as exegesis of the Scriptures. The 19th century saw the development of "free" H. not confined to any subject or the meaning of a text. With Dilthey (q.v.) H. became a specific method in social sciences designed to ensure "understanding" of events in the life of society through the subjective intentions of historical figures. He opposed "understanding" to "interpretation" in natural science involving abstraction and establishment of the general, or law (q.v.). In the 20th century, H. gradually became one of the basic methodological procedures in philosophy, first in existentialism, q.v. (see Heidegger) and then in philosophical H. proper. As a result, philosophy becomes confined within language, which makes H. something akin to neo-positivist "language analysis". In the Frankfurt school, q.v., (J. Habermas and others) H., viewed as "criticism of ideology", is designed to reveal through language analysis "an instrument of rule and social power" serving "to justify relations of organised coercion". Habermas regards H. as a means of consolidating the different trends in modern bourgeois philosophy. Hermeneutic procedures can be used in history, jurisprudence, and other disciplines which analyse objectified results of conscious human activity.

Herzen, Alexander Ivanovich (1812-1870), Russian revolutionary democrat, materialist thinker, writer; founder of Narodism (q.v.); he founded in England the Free-Russian Printing Press (1853), which put out *Polyarnaya zvezda* (The Polar Star) from 1855 to 1862, *Kolokol*

(The Bell), a revolutionary Russian language newspaper, from 1857 to 1867, and other publications. H.'s ideological development was complex, but a basic goal was always evident in his highly contradictory theoretical search: proceeding from the highest accomplishments of social and philosophical thought, he wanted to create a new, "realistic", scientific theory to serve as a groundwork for the coming social revolution. H. critically revised the ideas of French utopian socialism, with which he became first acquainted in 1832, the romantic historiography of the Restoration, and 19th-century classical German philosophy (q.v.) and in the early 1840s produced an original atheistic and materialistic world outlook whose main value lay in its materialist interpretation of Hegel's (q.v.) dialectics. Later, he called it "the algebra of revolution". H. "came right up to dialectical materialism" (V. I. Lenin, *Collected Works*, Vol. 18, p. 26). The main accent in his philosophical searchings lay in proving the identity of being and thinking, practice and theory, society and the individual. H. wanted to find and formulate a method of cognition adequate to reality. In the philosophy of history, H. studied social law, which he ultimately conceived as a combination of the spontaneous process of history (the unconscious life of nations) and the conscious activities of individuals (the development of science). In socio-political sphere the notion of the unity of theory and practice prompted H. to work for the revolutionary enlightenment of the masses, to prepare them for socialist revolution. He approached this complex but intrinsically connected range of problems from different angles at different stages of his ideological development. The revolution of 1848-49 in several West European countries, whose defeat was a personal tragedy to H., did much to correct his socio-philosophical views. Not finding in West European reality any coincidence of the historical process with the development of human thought, which had advanced and elaborated the socialist ideal, H. became pessimistic and sceptical of the prospects of a social revolution in the West. He attempted to overcome his pessimism by preaching a "Russian", peasant socialism, considering the Russian peasant community the real embryo of the socialist future. H. pictured the further progress of Russian history as emancipation of peasants from all feudal and autocratic trammels and fusion of the peasants' patriarchally collective way of life with socialist theory. He not only called for a radical solution of the peasant question in Russia, but postulated the possibility of by-passing the capitalist stage of development. But events in the mid-1860s convinced him that the "bourgeois plague" was spreading in Russia. He did not succeed in overcoming his pessimism until shortly before his death, when he broke with the anarchist Bakunin (q.v.) and acclaimed the reviving working-class movement in Western Europe led by the First International as an earnest of the victory of socialism. Bourgeois historians distort the meaning of H.'s social and philosophical evolution, describing him either as a religious searcher (Bulgakov, q.v., V. Zenkovsky, V. Pirozhkova, and others) or as an opponent of revolution and socialism (Struve, q.v., G. Kon, I. Berlin, and others). His chief philosophical works include: *Dilettantism in Science*, 1842-43; *Letters on the Study of Nature*, 1845-46; *From the Other Shore*, 1847-50; *Robert Owen* (1860); *Letters to the Opponent*, 1864; *To an Old Comrade*, 1869.

Hess, Moses (1812-1875), German petty-bourgeois publicist and philosopher. H. was at first close to the Young Hegelians, q.v. (*Europäische Tetrarchie*, 1841). He did much for the formation of philosophical communism (q.v.). Proceeding from the teachings of Hegel (q.v.) and mostly of Feuerbach (q.v.) and French utopian socialism, he criticised the existing society whose main evil he saw in alienation of "the true essence" of man. A social revolution was needed, he said, in order to eliminate this alienation caused by private property, the coercive character of labour, etc. However, H. saw this revolution in isolation from the class struggle of the proletariat, and in the final account reduced it to spiritual emancipation and the assertion of the principles of abstract humanism and altruism. These ideas were further developed in "true socialism" (q.v.). Towards the end of his life, H. tried to find a scientific basis for his socialist views.

Heuristics, a science concerned with the process of creation; methods used to discover the new and in education. Heuristic methods, the other name of H., make it possible to accelerate the process of finding solutions to problems. Considerable attention is focussed on these methods thanks to the possibility of solving certain problems (identification of objects, proof of theorems, etc.), for which man failed to obtain a precise algorithm (q.v.) with the help of technical devices. The aim of H. is the construction of models for the process of solving some new problem. There are the following types of models: a model of a blind search based on the so-called method of trials and errors, a laboratory model which treats a problem as a labyrinth and the process of searching a solution as a wandering in the labyrinth, and a structurally semantic model which is considered most significant today and reflects semantic relations between objects covered by a problem. H. is connected with psychology (q.v.), physiology of the highest nervous activity, and cybernetics (q.v.).

Hierarchy, a type of structural relations in complex multi-level systems, characterised by orderliness and the organised vertical interaction between different levels. The concept of H. is widely used in various spheres of modern science due to the spread of ideas and principles of cybernetics and systems approach (qq.v.). The hierarchical relations are present in numerous systems (q.v.) which are characterised both by structural and functional differentiation, i.e., the ability to perform a certain number of functions, moreover the functions of integration and co-ordination at higher levels. The necessity for hierarchical structures of complex systems is explained by the fact that control (q.v.) in them is related to the processing and utilisation of a large mass of information (q.v.), at the lower level more detailed and specific information being used by covering only certain aspects of system functioning, while more general information characterising the conditions of the functioning of the whole system reaching higher levels and decisions regarding the whole system being taken there. In real systems the hierar-

chical structure is never absolutely strict, since H. is combined with a greater or lesser autonomy of lower levels in respect of the higher ones and the possibilities of self-organisation typical of each level are used in control.

Hieroglyphs (or symbols), **Theory of,** an epistemological conception, according to which sensations are not images reflecting attributes of objects and phenomena, but symbols, signs, hieroglyphs, which have nothing in common with the objects and their properties. The term of hieroglyph in its epistemological meaning was introduced by Plekhanov (q.v.). T.H. was developed by Helmholtz (q.v.) on the basis of the so-called law of the specific energy of sense-organs, which was formulated by the German physiologist J. Müller, who believed that sensations are the organism's reaction to the condition of his nerves and the specifics of sensations depend not on outside factors but on the features of the sense-organs. (For instance, any irritation of the organ of sight brings the sensation of light.) Such viewpoint introduces an element of agnosticism (q.v.) into epistemology. The sensations which appear during the organism's interaction with the objective world also depend on the specific organisation of the sense-organs. This organisation, however, is, in the final analysis, determined by those objective factors (electromagnetic, air waves, etc.) which are used by the organism in the process of its active orientation. For this reason sensations are a subjective image of the objective world. They link us with reality and do not represent an insurmountable gap separating man's consciousness and the objective world. The criticism of T.H. is contained in Lenin's *Materialism and Empirio-Criticism* (q.v.).

Higher Nervous Activity, aggregate of the complex processes forming temporary associations in the cortex of the cerebral hemispheres. Pavlov's (q.v.) teaching and the modern theory of H.N.A. reveal the specific function of nervous activity, which enables highly developed organisms to adapt themselves to the changing conditions of their environment. H.N.A. is based essentially on conditioned reflexes acquired by an organism in the course of individual experience. The H.N.A. of animals is limited to immediate reflection of external influences through the first signal system (q.v.). Man, on the other hand, makes use chiefly of the higher, second signal system, in which reflex activity is mediated by speech (q.v.). The spoken word, speech affords man a more profound, generalised reflection of reality in the form of abstract concepts (q.v.) and complex inferences (q.v.). The teaching on H.N.A. reveals the physiological basis and laws governing psychic activity. This facilitates knowledge of the origin and development of human consciousness and confirms the proposition of materialist philosophy that consciousness is a function of highly organised matter, the brain.

Hilbert, David (1862-1943), German mathematician and logician; founder of the Göttingen mathematical school. H. worked on the theory of algebraic numbers and the foundations of mathematics and mathematical logic (q.v.). In his *Grundlagen der Geometrie* (1899) he reduced Euclidean geometry to a rigid system of axioms, which largely predetermined further work on the axiomatisation of knowledge (see Axiomatic Method). H. produced important works on the propositional calculus and predicate calculus (qq.v.). At the beginning of the 20th century H. formulated a new approach to the foundations of mathematics, which led to the appearance, on the one hand, of the conception of formalism (q.v.) and, on the other, of metamathematics (q.v.), a new branch of mathematics (theory of proof).

Hinduism, a system of religious conceptions, customs, cult rituals and socio-domestic institutions typical of the majority of India's population (a Hindu is considered any person who has at least one Indian parent and worships no other religion). The roots of H. go back to Brahmanism, the ancient Indian religion; genetically, this connection is manifested, for example, in the fact that the most revered Hinduist gods are the Brahmanic triad: Brahma (the creator), Vishnu (the preserver), Śiva (the creator, preserver and destroyer at the same time). H. is

manifested in many specific ways and is in many ways connected with different aspects of man's life and activities. Though H. does not have a coherent doctrine compulsory for all its adherents and a church organisation, nor does it have one administrative centre or institute which would busy itself with problems of religious character, though H. tolerates deviations from the religious dogmas to a certain extent, its requirements in the domain of socio-domestic traditions are very strict. H. is highly intolerant to any violations of the many restrictions and taboos in the sphere of social, family and private life. The above are different for the various groups, castes and subcastes into which H. divides the population, the barriers between them being considered inviolable in certain cases. Adherents of H. believe that the eternal individual soul *(atman)* aspires to fuse with the world soul *(brahman)*. And the flow of constantly changing, final manifestations of material natural being prevents the fusion. On the way to the ultimate "salvation" Atman undergoes constant transmigrations, each form of which is determined by karma, the fate, shaped by each person's actions. The main trends of H. are: Vishnuism, Śivaism, Shaktism (Shakti is Brahma's female consort). "Professional saints" who often proclaim salvation systems of their own enjoy popularity with their adherents. R. Tagore, Gandhi (q.v.) and other leaders of India's national liberation movement tried, within the limits of the above systems, to reform H., to create on its basis a religion free from fanaticism and obscurantism. In spite of the fact that law prohibits caste discrimination, the survivals of caste antagonism are still preserved in India today.

Historical and Logical, the, the philosophical categories characterising the process of development and also the relationship between the logical development of thought and the real history of an object. The H. expresses the structural and functional processes of the origin and formation of the given object; the L. expresses the relationship, the laws, connection and interaction of its aspects, which exist in the object's developed state. The H. is related to the L. as the process of development to its result, in which the connections successively shaped in the course of history attain complete maturity. The H. and L. are in dialectical unity, including an element of contradiction. Their unity is expressed, first, in the H. containing within it the L. to the extent to which every process of development contains its own objective orientation, its own necessity, which leads to a definite result. Although at the beginning of the process the L., as an expression of the developed structure of the object, is still absent, the sequence of the phases undergone during the process on the whole coincides with the relationship (logical connection) between the components of the developed system; the process, as it were, carries its own result. Secondly, the unity of the H. and L. is expressed in the specific reflection, by the relationship and interdependence between the sides of the developed whole, of the history of this whole, its emergence and the formation of its specific structure. The result contains in itself the process of its emergence: the L. contains within itself the H. Although the unity of the H. and L. is of decisive significance for understanding the relationship between the history of the object and its developed form, the two coincide only in sum and substance, because all the accidental and transient, all the zigzags of development which are inevitable in the real process are obviated and lost in the object which has reached complete maturity. The L. is the "corrected" H., but this "correction" is made according to the laws which the actual historical process itself provides. Hence the difference between the logical and historical ways of reflecting reality in thought. Because in reality itself the process and results of development do not coincide, although they are in unity, the historical and logical methods of study must differ in content. The purpose of historical study is to reveal the concrete conditions and forms of the development of phenomena, their sequence and transition from certain historically necessary stages to others. The purpose of logical study is to reveal the role which separate elements of the system play in the developed whole. But since the developed whole preserves only the conditions and

features of its development, which express its specific nature, the logical reproduction of the developed whole proves to be the key to revealing its real history. At the same time the facets distinguishing these two methods of study are conditional and mobile, because ultimately the L. is the selfsame H. released from its concrete form and presented in a generalised, theoretical way; and vice versa, the H. is the selfsame L. vested in concrete historical development. The dialectics of the H. and L. expresses the essential aspect of dialectical logic (q.v.) that reveals the general laws of cognition of the objective processes of development.

Historical Cycle, Theory of, an idealist theory elaborated by Vico (q.v.), according to which society endlessly passes through the same stages. In the 19th and 20th centuries, bourgeois philosophers and sociologists rejected the positive elements of Vico's theory—the idea of historical progress, law-governed social development, and highlighted the reactionary idea of mankind's constant return to its point of origin (see Nietzsche; Spengler). Of late, the main adherents of this theory were P. Sorokin and Toynbee, q.v. (see Progress and Retrogression). The theory of historical cycle raises into an absolute and thereby distorts certain aspects of the historical process (idea of recurrence, continuity, etc.).

Historico-Comparative Method, a method of investigating and explaining phenomena which infers genetic kinship, i.e., common origin, by assertaining similarity in form. When applied to culture the H.C.M. reproduces and compares the oldest elements common to various spheres of material culture and knowledge. W. Humboldt and, particularly, Comte (qq.v.) were chiefly responsible for the development of the H.C.M. in this field. The H.C.M. was developed further by the 19th-century protagonists of comparative linguistics, J. Grimm, A. Pott, A. Schleicher (Germany), F. de Saussure (Switzerland) and the Russian linguists I. A. Baudouin de Courteney, A. N. Veselovsky, A. Kh. Vostokov, F. F. Fortunatov, and others. The H.C.M. strongly influenced linguistics and ethnography and prompted deep-going studies of myths and popular beliefs. However, the H.C.M. concentrated on the outward resemblances of cultural and ideological forms, while neglecting the material and social relations behind them. This is one of its limitations. In modern research, the H.C.M. is employed in combination with other methods (experiment, q.v., etc.).

Historism (or Historicity), the principle of cognition of things and phenomena in the process of their becoming and development (qq.v.), in connection with the conditions determining them. H. implies an approach to phenomena that considers how they arose and developed, how they will look like in the future. As a definite method of theoretical research H. is a fixation not of any and every (even qualitative) change, but only of that which reflects the formation of specific properties and connections of things, determining their essence and specifics. H. presupposes recognition of the irreversible and successive nature of changes of things. H. has become a major principle of science, enabling it to give an objective picture of nature and discover the laws governing its development (for example, Darwin's evolution theory, qq.v.). Thanks to H., which constitutes an integral side of the dialectical method, Marxism was able to explain the essence of such intricate social phenomena as the state, classes, etc., to foresee the historically transient nature of capitalism and its inevitable replacement by socialism. Denial of the principle of H., struggle against it or attempts to emasculate it of its materialist and dialectical content are characteristic features of contemporary bourgeois philosophy, sociology and logic.

Hobbes, Thomas (1588-1679), English materialist philosopher. At the time of the English bourgeois revolution he emigrated to Paris where he wrote *De Cive* (1642) and *Leviathan* (1651). In 1652 he returned to England. H. developed the doctrine of mechanistic materialism and systematised F. Bacon's (q.v.) materialism. Marx pointed out that H.'s materialism was one-sided. "Knowledge based upon senses," Marx wrote, "loses its poetic blossom, it passes into the abstract ex-

perience of the *geometrician*. *Physical* motion is sacrificed to *mechanical* or *mathematical* motion; *geometry* is proclaimed the queen of sciences" (K. Marx and F. Engels, *Collected Works*, Vol. 4, p. 128). According to H. the world is the sum total of bodies governed by the laws of mechanical motion. H. also reduced to motion and effort the psychic life of man and animals. These, he held, are complex mechanisms completely governed by outside effects. H. denied the objectiveness of the qualitative multiplicity of nature, believing that it was a property of human perception based on the mechanical differences between things. In his doctrine on knowledge H. attacked Cartesian theory of innate ideas (q.v.). While H. held that experience or knowledge of isolated facts furnishes no more than probable truths about the connections of things, he admitted that valid general knowledge is possible, being conditioned by language. In his doctrine of law and the state, H. rejected the theories of the divine origin of society and defended the theory of social contract (see Social Contract, Theory of). H. considered absolute monarchy the best form of state, but his numerous explanations and reservations left room for revolutionary principles. His idea centred not on the monarchistic principle as such, but on the unrestricted character of state power. Powers of the state, he pointed out, were compatible with the interests of those classes who in the mid-17th century carried out the bourgeois revolution in England. His theory of society and the state contained embryos of the materialist understanding of social phenomena.

Holbach, Paul Henri Dietrich (1723-1789), French materialist philosopher, and atheist. Born a German baron, he spent most of his life in France. His most important book, *Le Système de la nature* (1770) was publicly burned by order of the Paris Parliament. His other works are *Le Christianisme dévoilé* (1761), *Théologie portative* (1768), and *Bon Sens, ou idées naturelles opposées aux idées surnaturelles* (1772). H. attacked religion and idealist philosophy, particularly the doctrines of Berkeley (q.v.). He described idealism as a chimera opposed to common sense, and attributed the origin of religion to ignorance and to the fear of some and the deceit of others. Matter, H. held, is everything that acts in one way or another on our senses; it consists of immutable and indivisible atoms whose main properties are extent, weight, shape and impenetrability. He believed that motion, another attribute of matter, was simple mechanical movement of bodies in space. Man, H. stated, was part of nature and subject to its laws. He advocated determinism, but interpreted causality mechanistically. He denied the objective existence of chances and defined them as phenomena, the causes of which were unknown. In epistemology, H. leaned towards sensationalism (q.v.) and opposed agnosticism (q.v.). In politics, he favoured constitutional monarchy, but in specific cases advocated enlightened absolutism. An idealist in his approach to society, H. said that "opinions rule the world". He attributed the decisive role in history to legislators. He saw education as the means for man's emancipation. Ignorance of their own nature, H. averred, put the human race under the sway of governments. He considered the developing bourgeois society a realm of reason.

Holism, an idealist "philosophy of wholeness", ideologically close to the theory of emergent evolution (q.v.), the notion introduced by the South African Field-Marshal J. C. Smuts in his *Holism and Evolution* (1926). While advancing an idealist interpretation of the fact that a whole can never be understood as a sum total of its parts, Smuts insisted that the world is governed by a holistic process, one of a creative evolution, of formation of new wholes. In that evolutionary process the forms of matter continuously multiply and renew. The holistic process, according to Smuts, denies the law of the preservation of matter. "The factor of wholeness" is considered by H. nonmaterial and non-cognisable and of a mystical nature. The ideas of H. were also developed by J. S. Haldane (*The Philosophical Basis of Biology,* 1931) and A. Meyer-Abich (*Ideen und Ideale der biologischen Erkenntnis,* 1934).

The Holy Family, or Critique of Critical Criticism (1845), an early philosophical work of K. Marx and F. Engels directed against Young Hegelians (q.v.). "The Holy Family" is a facetious nickname for the Bauer brothers, the philosophers, and their followers. They "preached a criticism which stood above all reality, above parties and politics, which rejected all practical activity, and which only 'critically' contemplated the surrounding world and the events going on within it. These gentlemen, the Bauers, looked down on the proletariat as an uncritical mass. Marx and Engels vigorously opposed this absurd and harmful tendency" (V. I. Lenin, *Collected Works,* Vol. 2, p. 23). *The H.F.* gives a profound critique of the idealism of Hegel (q.v.) and the Young Hegelians and continues the elaboration of dialectical and historical materialism. In it Marx and Engels arrived at a major idea in the materialist understanding of history, the idea of the social relations of production (q.v.). They sharply criticised the personality cult upheld by the Young Hegelians and showed that the struggle of the working people against the exploiters constituted the main content of history. They put forward the idea that the proletariat is the grave-digger of capitalism. *The H.F.* gives a profound outline of the history of philosophy, particularly the history of materialism in Britain and France. It was a landmark in the creation of scientific communism, in the struggle against idealism, against anti-proletarian, petty-bourgeois ideology.

Homeostasis, a type of dynamic equilibrium characteristic of a complex self-regulating system (q.v.) and consisting in maintenance within permissible limits of the parameters essential to that system. As a concept, H. was introduced by the American physiologist W. Cannon who described a number of homeostatic processes in biological organisms. Later, H. was extended to cybernetics, psychology, sociology and some other sciences. To study homeostatic processes it is necessary to single out: 1) those parameters whose considerable change would disrupt the normal functioning of the system, such as temperature in higher animals; 2) the limits of permissible changes in these parameters under the influence of the internal and external environment; 3) all the specific mechanisms that begin to operate as soon as the variables go beyond these limits. Each of these mechanisms registers change in the essential parameters and acts to restore the disrupted equilibrium.

Homoeomeries, a term used by Anaxagoras (q.v.); though not in surviving fragments of his works it was passed down by his later commentators. Anaxagoras believed that all things were an infinite number of particles of different qualities, each of these being divided into an infinite number of like particles. According to Anaxagoras, H. are the qualitatively like particles or qualitatively original particles containing an infinity of smaller particles. This, he inferred, is why they bear the name of the thing which possesses similar or like particles. In modern mathematical terms H. may be defined as an infinity given to an infinite degree.

Homogeneity and Heterogeneity. According to the principle of homogeneity postulated by Kant (q.v.) the specific concepts must have something in common, this common quality classing them under a common generic concept. The principle of heterogeneity, on the other hand, requires that special concepts classed under the same generic concept should differ. The modern interpretation of homogeneity forbids the classification of heterogeneous principles within the framework of one theory. Violation of this principle leads to eclecticism (q.v.).

Honour, a concept of moral consciousness and ethical category expressing both the individual's recognition of his own social significance and admission of that significance by society. By its content and the nature of the moral attitude reflected in it H. is similar to the concept of dignity (q.v.). Being a form of manifesting the attitude of the individual towards himself and of the society towards the individual, H., like dignity, in some way controls man's behaviour and his evaluation by people around him. However, unlike dignity, H. does not proceed from the principle of moral equality of all people, but rather from their differen-

tiated evaluation (depending on the person's social standing, class, nationality, professional or collective allegiance or reputation). The criterion of that evaluation and demands made on man, associated with his H., evolved historically. In socialist society, H. is national, professional and, to a certain extent, class (based exclusively on man's labour input), and also collective and individual. The latter rests on man's personal merits premised on his actual services to other people and society. Nobody enjoys exclusive privileges, while arrogantly hostile attitudes to representatives of other nations, professions, and so on are condemned. Eradication of the vestiges of old H. (exclusiveness attributed to some social estate, stratum or community, snobbism, conceit in any form, etc.) is part of the overall effort to assert communist morality in people's relations.

Hsün Tzŭ (c. 313-238 B.C.), a Chinese materialist philosopher. Critically assimilated and used in his teaching the ideas of many philosophical schools and trends in ancient China; produced a coherent doctrine of nature. He saw the heaven as a sum total of natural phenomena, rather than a mystical supreme lord; he denied the existence of the Creator. The emergence and change of all phenomena and things are cyclic, and can be explained by the interplay of two forces: the positive *yang* and the negative *yin* (see *Yin* and *yang*). According to H. T., cognition is prompted by sense data. But it is only through meditation on these that man can aquire true and comprehensive knowledge. H. T.'s theory that evil qualities are innate in human nature was widely popular. Man aquires his best qualities through education. H. T.'s teaching had a profound influence on the subsequent development of Chinese philosophy (q.v.).

"Human Relations", Theory of, a modern bourgeois sociological theory dealing with the principles and tasks of management at capitalist enterprises and attempting to picture the relations between the exploiters and the exploited as "human relations" based, as it were, on Christian commandments. In effect, it sets forth a programme of measures for camouflaging capitalist exploitation and distracting the workers from the class struggle (workers' share in monopoly profits and the buying of shares by them, group insurance, visits of workers' homes by employers, the presentation of holiday gifts, joint consultations of workers and management, some improvement of working conditions at automated enterprises, and so on). The employers cover the expenses for these measures by means of intensifying labour. Under the pressure of the scientific and technological revolution (q.v.), "T.H.R." aims at increasing labour productivity, overcoming dissatisfaction with labour and aversion to it on the part of those employed in capitalist production, alleviating class antagonisms. Employers in the USA, France, Italy and other countries base their policies on "T.H.R."

Humanism, a system of views based on respect for the dignity and rights of man, his value as a personality, concern for his welfare, his all-round development, and the creation of favourable conditions for social life. H. is the opposite of fanaticism, rigorism, intolerance, and disrespect for the views and knowledge of others. It grew into a distinct ideological movement at the time of the Renaissance (q.v.) from the 15th to 16th century, when it figured prominently as an element of bourgeois ideology opposed to feudalism and medieval theology. H. was closely associated with progressive materialist views; it proclaimed freedom of the individual, opposed religious asceticism (q.v.), vindicated man's right to pleasure and the satisfaction of earthly requirements. Some of the most prominent humanists of the Renaissance, such as Petrarch, Dante, Boccaccio, Leonardo da Vinci, Erasmus Desiderius (q.v.), Bruno, (q.v.), F. Rabelais, Montaigne (q.v.), Copernicus (q.v.), Shakespeare, F. Bacon (q.v.), and others, helped to mould mundane views. Bourgeois H. reached its zenith in the works of the 18th-century Enlighteners, who put forward the slogans of liberty, equality and fraternity and proclaimed men's right freely to develop their "natural essence". However, even the finest manifestations of bourgeois H. have the shortcoming of basing humanistic ideals on private property and individualism (q.v.). Hence the contradiction, which the bourgeoisie cannot resolve, between the slogans of H. and their actual implementation in capitalist society. In their reasoning, bourgeois ideologists as a rule seek to conceal the actual vices of capitalism and its inhuman essence. Almost from the very start, a trend emerged within H. whose exponents—More, Campanella, Münzer (qq.v.), and later other advocates of utopian socialism (q.v.) expressed the interests of the working masses. They saw the anti-humanistic nature of society, attacked its vices and demanded equality in property. But, not knowing the objective laws of history, they were unable to discover effective ways and means for achieving a just society. Socialist H. is fundamentally different. It is based on Marxist-Leninist philosophy and the theory of scientific communism, which postulate liberation of the working people from social oppression and the building of communism as an essential condition for the all-round and harmonious development of all men and genuine freedom of the individual. Therefore, socialist H. is genuine, being based on the necessity for struggle by the working class and other working people against the exploiter classes and for communism, which creates the conditions essential for the triumph of man's humanistic ideals. By abolishing private ownership and exploitation, socialism establishes truly humanistic relations, based on the principle that man is to man a friend, comrade and brother. Communism is the supreme embodiment of H., for it eliminates all surviving traces of inequality and establishes the principle "from each according to his ability, to each according to his needs", providing the essential conditions for the all-round development of the individual (q.v.). The term of H. is also used to describe the culture and ideology of the Renaissance.

"Humanitarian" Ethics, a trend in bourgeois moral theory current in the USA since the 1920s. I. Babbitt and other advocates of this trend named their theories "humanitarian" on the grounds that they deduce ethics from "specifically human" phenomena, whereas, in fact, they are derived from phenomena of individual psychology. Such a limited basis for morality leads the advocates of "H".E. to an extremely individualistic and subjectivist understanding of morality. They reduce the criteria of morality to consciousness of one's actions and readiness to abandon any previously set goal, to an internal human concentration and abandonment of external expansion (Babbitt), to wisdom, and, finally, to reasonable behaviour. These criteria are purely formal, and do not reveal the specific content of morality, as they are arbitrarily taken out of the complex system of moral relations between the individual and society. The advocates of "H".E. reject the significance of general principles in ethics, even though these apply to all people; each individual, in their view, is the sole judge of his actions. Man need not respect the interests of those who cannot defend themselves. Thus, "H".E. has nothing to do with genuine humanism, and its frank individualism at times turns into an apology of egoism (q.v.).

Humboldt, Alexander von (1769—1859), German philosopher and naturalist. He considered matter endowed with intrinsic activity to be the only cosmic substance. He believed that motion, space and time are the universal and fundamental properties of matter and insisted on the dialectical interpretation of motion as unity of the universal interconnection and development of phenomena. He opposed Kant (q.v.), the natural philosophies of Schelling and Hegel (qq.v.) and Comte's (q.v.) positivism, and attached great importance to the union of science and materialist philosophy. His ideas on philosophy and natural science helped to refute various metaphysical views. He recognised the unity of sensationalism and rationalism (qq.v.), and advocated a poetical appreciation of reality which, he averred, makes cognition socially useful and humane. H. believed that cognition is possible through experimental communion with nature. This was a strong point in his epistemological system. He expressed the interests of the radical wing of the German bourgeoisie and sympathised with the French Revolution. His main works: *Ansichten der Natur*

(1808) and *Kosmos* (5 vols., 1845-59).

Humboldt, Karl Wilhelm (1767-1835), German philosopher, linguist and statesman; brother of Alexander von Humboldt (q.v.). H. accepted Kant's (q.v.) philosophical doctrine and sought to concretise and develop it by basing it on social history, though he inclined towards objective idealism on a number of points. According to H.'s theory of historical knowledge, world history is the result of the activity of a spiritual force that transcends cognition. He therefore believed that the history of mankind cannot be understood from the causative point of view. History as a science may to a certain degree be replaced by aesthetics. H. suggested the comparative historical method in linguistics which proved highly valuable. His anti-feudal views did not go beyond the aim of educational reform and the idea of German unity. His main works: *Ideen zu einem Versuch, die Grenzen der Wirksamkeit des Staates zu bestimmen* (1792), *Über die Aufgabe des Geschichtsschreibers* (1821).

Hume, David (1711-1776), English idealist philosopher, psychologist and historian. H. believed that the task of knowledge does not lie in the comprehension of being but in its ability to be a guide in practical life. To him, the only objects of authentic knowledge were those of mathematics. All other objects of study concern facts which cannot be proved logically and can only be deduced from experience. All opinions on existence also proceed from experience, which H., however, understood idealistically. Reality, to him, was only a stream of "impressions" whose causes are unknown and unknowable. He considered insoluble the problem of the existence or non-existence of the objective world. One of the fundamental relations established by experience is the relation of cause and effect. If one phenomenon precedes another it cannot be deduced that the former is the cause and the latter the effect. Even the most frequent repetition of the concatenation of events in time does not give knowledge a hidden force with the help of which one object produces the other. Thus, H. denied the objective character of causality (q.v.). The stream of our impressions, according to H., is not absolute chaos: some objects appear to us as bright, vivid and stable, and H. maintained that this was quite sufficient for practical life. It was only necessary to understand that the source of practical certitude is not theoretical knowledge but faith. In ethics H. developed the theory of utilitarianism (q.v.) and declared utility to be the criterion of morality; in the philosophy of religion he admitted that the causes of the order in the Universe have some analogy with reason, but denied all the theological and philosophical doctrines of God, and, turning to historical experience, he acknowledged the evil influence of religion on morality and civil life. H.'s scepticism (q.v.) was the theoretical foundation of the utilitarian and rational world outlook of the bourgeoisie. H.'s agnosticism (q.v.) greatly influenced contemporary idealism: it served as one of the main ideological sources of neo-positivism (q.v.). His main work: *An Enquiry Concerning Human Understanding* (1748).

Husserl, Edmund (1859-1938), German idealist philosopher, founder of the so-called phenomenological school (see Phenomenology). His philosophy is based on the teachings of Plato, Leibniz, and Brentano (qq.v.). In his first works H. sought to turn philosophy into a strictly defined science and to lay theoretical foundations of scientific knowledge. For this purpose, he believed, categories of scientific thinking had to be defined in their pure form. He held that they could be revealed by cleansing what was "given" of the accretions introduced by culture, history and personal factors. Analysis of the world of phenomena not susceptible of any arbitrary interpretation led H. to conclude in the spirit of Plato's idealism that there exist levels of phenomena and a special sphere of essences. On the whole, H.'s views were subjectively idealist, inasmuch as he held that the object of cognition does not exist outside the consciousness of the subject focussed upon it. The object is revealed (and created) in this way. Later H. abandoned his attempts to turn philosophy into a strictly defined science

and studied the "living world" representing the result of the mental and emotional activity of individual subjects. From this position he criticised science and scientific thinking, which he declared to be incapable of studying this subject. H.'s ideas strongly influenced the subsequent development of bourgeois philosophy. Elements of H.'s objective idealism were developed by N. Hartmann (q.v.) and the neo-realistic schools in the USA and Britain. His subjective idealism became to a large extent the foundation of German existentialism (q.v.), particularly that of Heidegger (q.v.). His main works: *Logische Untersuchungen* (1900, 1901), *Die Krisis der europäischen Wissenschaften und die transzendentale Phänomenologie* and *Erste Philosophie*, published posthumously, the former in 1954 and the latter in 1956-59.

Hylozoism, a teaching that all matter is animate. The early Greek materialists, Bruno (q.v.) and some French materialists (Robinet, q.v.), were hylozoists. The term was first employed in the 17th century. The teaching attributes sensations (q.v.) and mental faculties to all forms of matter. In fact, however, sensations are a property only of highly developed organic matter.

Hypostatisation 1. In the general sense, conversion of a property of something into a self-subsistent object or substance. 2. In the more common usage, idealist attribution of self-subsistent reality to abstract concepts.

Hypothesis, a deduction based on a series of facts from which we infer the existence of an object, or the relation or cause of a phenomenon without actual proof. The corresponding judgment or conclusion is called hypothetical. The need for H. arises in science when the connection between, or the cause of, phenomena is unclear, although many of the circumstances preceding or accompanying these phenomena are known; H. is also used when a picture of the past has to be restored from some characteristics of the present or a conclusion has to be drawn about the future development of a phenomenon on the strength of the past and present. But the formulation of H. on the basis of definite facts is only the first step. Being no more than probable, H. calls for verification and proof (q.v.). After verification, H. becomes either a scientific theory (q.v.) or, if the result is negative, is revised or rejected. The main rules governing the formulation and verification of H. are: 1. H. must agree or at least be compatible with all the pertinent facts (q.v.). 2. Of many conflicting Hh. formulated to explain a series of facts, the H. which unequivocally explains the largest number of those facts is preferable. So-called working Hh. may be formulated to explain individual facts of the series. 3. The least possible number of Hh. should be formulated to explain a connected series of facts, and their connection should be as close as possible. 4. When formulating H. it should be borne in mind that H. is essentially no more than probable. 5. Hh. contradicting each other cannot both be true unless they explain different aspects and connections of one and the same object. Modern positivists, empiricists and the like believe that science should record and register the facts and should not formulate Hh. on the laws governing the objective world. They hold that Hh. play no more than a working role and are of no objective significance. However, instances of Hh. becoming scientifically proven theories demonstrate the reverse. As H. is always based on certain objective data, it can always be developed into a theory. A close scrutiny of this stage in scientific thinking becomes increasingly imperative in view of the character of modern science, and the more complex mechanisms of observations and experimentation.

Hypothetico-Deductive Method, a methodological device by which certain propositions are advanced as hypotheses (q.v.) and subjected to verification by deducing effects and comparing them with the facts (q.v.). The initial hypothesis is evaluated on the basis of such a comparison by a rather complex and step-by-step procedure, as only a long testing of a hypothesis can lead either to its substantiation and adoption or its rejection.

Hypothetico-Deductive Theory, a form of logical arrangement of knowledge in the natural sciences. H.D.T. is a concrete concept of the deductive, or axiomatic theory (employed in mathematical methodology), applied to the specific nature of natural science which is based on experiment and observation (qq.v.). In addition to the rules governing deductive systems in general, the H.D.T. presupposes a possible empirical verification of its propositions.

Hyppolite, Jean (1907-1968), French existentialist philosopher. His main works are devoted to Hegel (q.v.). H. maintained that Hegelian philosophy has the same importance for our age as the philosophy of Aristotle (q.v.) had for the Middle Ages. He regarded the main philosophical trends as a continuation of the individual parts of the Hegelian system. From this point of view, Hegel's teaching must become the basis for knowing human existence. He thus turns Hegel into an existentialist. Proceeding from his false conception, H. claimed that Marx was a Hegelian and tried to find elements of idealism in Marxism.

i

Ibn Rushd Muhammad (Averroës in Lat. transcription) (1126-1198), Arab philosopher and scientist who lived in Spain during the Caliphate of Cordova. Without breaking with the Muslim religion, he tried to prove the eternity and uncreatability of matter and motion, denied the immortality of the individual soul and after-life. Founded the doctrine of twofold truth (q.v.). His comments on the works of Aristotle played a great part in acquainting European philosophers with ancient philosophy. His teaching (see Averroism) was persecuted by orthodox Muslims and Christians. His main works: *Destructio destructionis* and *Discourse About Decision on Ties between Philosophy and Religion.*

Ibn Sina, Abu-ali (Avicenna in Lat. transcription) (980-1037), Tajik philosopher, natural scientist and physician; lived in Bokhara and Iran. Although faithful to Islam, q.v., played a considerable role in spreading among the Arabs and, through them, in Europe, the philosophical and scientific heritage of the ancient world. I.S. did much to assert rational thinking and propagate natural science and mathematics. In his philosophy preserved both the materialist and idealist tendencies of Aristotle (q.v.), deviating on some questions from Aristotelianism towards Neoplatonism (q.v.). I.S. developed Aristotle's logic, physics and metaphysics, recognised the eternity of matter, considering it the cause of diversity of individual things, and opposed astrological and other superstitions. His main work, *Danesh-name* (Book of Knowledge), gives a concise exposition of his views on logic and physics. His *al-Shifa* (Book of Recovery) and *Canon of Medicine* are known throughout the world.

Idea, a philosophical term denoting "sense", "meaning", "essence", and closely connected with the categories of thinking and being. In the history of philosophy, the category I. is used in different senses. When the I. is regarded only as existing in the mind it denotes: (1) a sensory image that arises in the mind as a reflection of sensory objects (see Realism, Naive); (2) "sense" or "essence" of things reducible to sensations and impressions of the subject or to the creative principle which gives being to the Universe (see Idealism, Subjective). In some philosophical systems I. also denoted the materialist principle. Democritus, for example, called his atoms "ideas". In the systems of objective idealism (q.v.) the I. is the objectively existing essence of all things (see Objective Idea). In Hegel's (q.v.) philosophy, for example, the I.— the sense and creator of all things— developing purely logically, passes through three stages: objective, subjective, and absolute. Proper understanding of the relation of thinking to being helps solve the question of the I. This question has been scientifically and consistently elaborated only in dialectical materialism, which regards the I. as a reflection of objective reality. At the same time it stresses the reverse influence of the I. on the development of material reality with the object of transforming it. The I. is also understood as a form of cognition, the purpose of which is to formulate the general theoretical principle explaining the essence, the law of phenomena. For example, such are the ideas of the materiality of the world.

Ideal 1) social I., a conception of the most perfect social system corresponding to the economic and political interests or some social group, the ultimate aim of its activity and aspirations. In the history or social consciousness there were both progressive Ii., which corresponded to some extent to the objective trend of social development and served as the ideological basis of revolutionary movements, and reactionary Ii., which reflected the interests and views of obsolescent classes, ran counter to social progress and were therefore untenable. Many progressive Ii. of the past were utopia (see Socialism, Utopian). Marxism turned socialism from utopia into a science and pointed to the real ways of attaining communism, the social I. of the working class (q.v.) and all working people; 2) moral I., a conception of moral perfection, more often than not expressed in the image of the individual who embodies such moral qualities that can provide the highest moral example. It reflects the socio-economic position of a class and corresponds to its criterion of morality and social I. Individualism, egoism (qq.v.), calculation, and striving to attain one's own mercenary motives by any means—such is the content of the moral I. of the bourgeoisie. The proletarian I., on the contrary, presupposes such features in the fighter for communism as collectivism (q.v.), comradely mutual assistance, internationalism (q.v.), humaneness, high consciousness of public duty (q.v.), truthfulness, unpretentiousness, etc. The aim of moral education is to come as close as possible to the moral I.; 3) aesthetic I.—the historically most consummate, harmonious unity of subject and object, man and the social whole (and also nature), expressed in a free and universal development of human creative powers as an end in itself. Forming the basis of creativity in any field of endeavour, aesthetic I. is also a criterion of assessing the beautiful (q.v.) in life and art (q.v.). The aesthetic I. of past epochs (ancient Greece, Renaissance) contained, alongside the historically hidebound aspects, also the general human elements as a measure of realising the integrity of human personality. The modern bourgeoisie has forfeited the aesthetic I., in consequence of which bourgeois art is increasingly degenerating, sometimes taking perverted, ugly forms. The aesthetic I. of communism, based on the all-round, integral development of the creative powers of every man who would harmoniously combine spiritual wealth, moral purity and bodily perfection is the highest and qualitatively new stage in the aesthetic development of humankind.

Ideal, the, a subjective image of objective reality, appearing in men's purposeful activities; "the ideal is nothing else than the material world reflected by the human mind and translated into forms of thoughts" (K. Marx, *Capital,* Vol. I, p. 19). In pre-Marxian materialist philosophy objects were regarded as something external, opposed to the subject as an object of contemplation and not of activity. Idealists, as a rule, stressed the pretersensual character of spiritual activity, viewing the I. as a manifestation of special immaterial substance, "universal reason", etc. They absolutised the role played by the I. in man's activity, seeing it as a starting point, the universal beginning of the latter (classical German idealism). From the point of view of Marxist philosophy the I. is the forms (images) of being independent of man and all multiplicity of their social meanings which form the goals and motives of his conscious activity. These images do not only reflect the objectively existing objects, phenomena but also bear the imprint of human relations, skills and modes of their activity and communication. Although consciousness functions only with the help of certain material means and processes (society's practical activity, the physiology of the central nervous system, signal means of communication through language, etc.) it is not reduced to any of them. The I., operating not with material things themselves, but only with their images, meanings and senses, which act as substitutes of things and of their models, can study objective laws and, basing itself upon them, create projects of the future. It can also produce illusory ideas and concepts which distort objective reality. For this reason the process of activity is always accompanied by the comparison of images with the objects themselves to ascertain how exactly and fully they reflect their objective nature. The I. is the images created by mankind's history not only to understand but also to change the world.

Idealisation, an act of thought in the course of which some abstract objects are formed that cannot be realised or created in practice experimentally. Idealised objects are marginal cases of certain real objects; they serve as a means for the scientific analysis of the real objects and a basis for constructing a theory about them; they ultimately act as reflections of objective things, processes and phenomena. The following concepts are examples of idealised objects: "point", "straight line", "actual infinity" in mathematics, "absolutely solid body", "ideal gas", "absolutely black body" in physics; "ideal solution" in physical chemistry. Together with abstraction (q.v.), with which it is closely associated, I. is a powerful means of cognising the laws of reality.

Idealism, a philosophical trend diametrically opposed to materialism (q.v.) in the solution of the fundamental question of philosophy (q.v.). I. proceeds from the principle that the spiritual, non-material, is primary and the material is secondary, which brings it closer to the dogmas of religion on the finiteness of the world in time and space and its creation by God. I. regards consciousness in isolation from nature, as a result of which it inevitably mystifies human consciousness and the process of cognition and, as a rule, advocates scepticism and agnosticism (qq.v.). To materialist determinism consistent I. counterposes the teleological point of view (see Teleology). Bourgeois philosophers use this term in various senses and consider the trend itself as truly philosophical. Marxism-Leninism has shown the insolvency of this point of view, but in contrast to metaphysical and vulgar materialism, which regards I. merely as an absurdity and nonsense, stresses the existence of epistemological roots in any concrete form of I. As theoretical thinking develops, even the most elementary abstraction (q.v.) offers the possibility of I.—the divorcement of concepts from their objects. I. arises as a pseudo-scientific continuation of the fantastic concepts of mythology and religion. In contrast to materialism, I. is usually rooted in the world outlook of the conservative and reactionary sections and classes interested neither in the correct reflection of being, nor in a radical reconstruction of social relations. I. turns into an absolute the inevitable difficulties in the development of human knowledge and thereby retards scientific progress. At the same time some idealist philosophers, by raising new epistemological questions and seeking to study the forms of the process of cognition, gave an impulse to the elaboration of a number of important philosophical problems. In contradistinction to bourgeois philosophers who insist that there are many independent forms of I., Marxism-Leninism divides all the varieties of I. into two groups: objective idealism (q.v.), which takes as the basis of reality a personal or impersonal spirit, some kind of superindividual mind; subjective idealism (q.v.), which construes the world on the basis of individual consciousness. But the difference between subjective and objective I. is not absolute. Many objective idealist systems contain elements of subjective I.; on the other hand, subjective idealists, in an effort to get away from solipsism (q.v.) often adopt the position of objective I. Objective idealist doctrines first arose in the East (Vedānta, Confucianism, qq.v.). The philosophy of Plato (q.v.) was a classical form of objective I. A close connection with religious and mythological ideas was typical of Plato's objective I. and of ancient I. in general. This connection was reinforced at the beginning of our era, during the crisis of ancient society, when Neoplatonism (q.v.) developed. The latter became closely intertwined both with mythology and extreme mysticism (q.v.). This feature became even more pronounced during the Middle Ages, when philosophy was completely subordinated to theology (see St. Augustine; Thomas Aquinas). After Thomas Aquinas, the main concept of objective idealist scholastic philosophy became the concept of the non-material form, treated as the purposeful element which fulfils the will of preternatural God who wisely planned the world, finite in space and time. Beginning with Descartes (q.v.), subjective I. increasingly developed in bourgeois philosophy as individualistic motives grew stronger. The epistemology of Berkeley's (q.v.) system and Hume's (q.v.) philosophy became the classical expression of subjective I. In the philosophy of Kant (q.v.), the materialist assertion of the independence of "things-in-themselves" from the subject's consciousness was combined, on the one hand, with the subjective idealist thesis of a priori forms of consciousness, a thesis providing a basis for agnosticism, and, on the other, with the objective idealist recognition of the superindividual nature of these forms. Subsequently, the subjective idealist tendency prevailed in the philosophy of Fichte (q.v.), while the objective idealist tendency, in the philosophy of Schelling (q.v.) and especially Hegel (q.v.), the author of an all-embracing system of dialectical I. The evolution of I. after the disintegration of the Hegelian school was the result of the bourgeoisie abandoning its progressive social role and fighting against dialectical materialism. Bourgeois philosophers began to identify I. only with its most pronounced spiritualistic form. There appeared many teachings standing allegedly "between" or even "above" materialism and I. (see Positivism; Neo-Realism). Agnostic and irrational trends, the mythologisation of philosophy, disbelief in human reason and the future of mankind grew stronger. Reactionary pseudoatheism (Nietzscheism, fascist philosophical conceptions, some forms of positivism, etc.) was on the rise. Capitalism's general crisis has led to the spread of such forms of I. as existentialism and neo-positivism (qq.v.) and of a number of schools in Catholic philosophy, neo-Thomism (q.v.) in the first place. These were the three main trends of I. in the mid-20th century, but the further fragmentation of I. into small epigonic schools continues to this day. The main social causes for the "diversity" of forms of contemporary I. (phenomenology, critical realism, personalism, pragmatism, philosophy of Life, philosophical anthropology, conceptions of the Frankfurt school, qq.v.) are the growing disintegration of bourgeois consciousness and the desire to consolidate the illusory "independence" of idealist philosophy from the political forces of imperialism. On the other hand, an opposite process is under way, the rapprochement and even "hybridisation" of various trends of I. on the basis of the common anti-communist stand of bourgeois ideology in the 20th century. The scientific groundwork for a critique of the contemporary forms of I. was laid by Lenin in *Materialism and Empirio-Criticism* (q.v.), in which he gave a Marxist analysis both of the Machist variety of positivism and of the main content of all bourgeois philosophy in the epoch of imperialism.

Idealism, Objective, one of the main varieties of idealism (q.v.). It holds that the spirit is primary and matter secondary, derivative. As distinct from subjective idealism (q.v.), it regards as the prime source of being not the personal, human mind, but some objective other-world consciousness, the "absolute spirit", "universal reason", etc. O.I. regards concepts as primary to material objects and thereby obfuscates the real relations between them. Plato (q.v.), for example, considered general concepts as existing eternally in the "world of ideas", while material objects were pallid reflections or shadows of these ideas. The "absolute spirit" of Hegel (q.v.) is, in fact, an absolutised concept divorced from and opposed to matter. In contemporary bourgeois philosophy O.I. is represented by neo-Thomism, personalism (qq.v.), and other schools. O.I. as a rule merges with theology (q.v.), and furnishes a peculiar philosophical basis of religion.

Idealism, Physical, the name given by Lenin in his *Materialism and Empirio-Criticism* (q.v.) to subjective-idealist views capitalising on the achievements of modern physics. The break-up of old physical ideas associated with the discoveries at the turn of the century (see Relativity, Theory of) led to a crisis in physics and brought to the fore two factors in the development of this science: its mathematisation and the principle of relativity of knowledge. The incorrect understanding of these factors was responsible for the spread of P.I. among scientists who, not having a broad worldview of the new phenomena, could not generalise the laws governing the historical progress of scientific knowledge and, because of their socio-political position, denied, in particular, dialectical materialism. The possibility of describing the simple objects of physics in abstract mathematical terms led to the erroneous conclusion that "matter vanished" and only mathematical equations remained. The collapse of customary conceptions, coupled with ignorance of the dialectics of absolute and relative truth (q.v.), led scientists to assert the "relativity" of man's knowledge, to deny objective truth and ultimately to postulate idealism and agnosticism. P.I. denied the objectivity of knowledge and thereby is an obstacle to the development of science.

Idealism, Physiological, a subjective idealist theory current among biologists and physicians in the mid-19th century. It was founded by J. Müller. Feuerbach (q.v.) was the first to use the term of P.I. The untenability of this doctrine arises from its overestimating the dependence of the content of sensations on the neuro-physiological properties of the sense-organs. Sensations were regarded not as an image of the objectively real world, but as a symbol of it. According to Müller, the colour spectrum, the timbre of sound, and the distinctions of taste and smell are determined only by the functional features of the corresponding sense-organs. Supporters of P.I. raised to an absolute the relative independence of a number of physiological reactions in the organism of the intensity and quality of external stimuli. Theories close to P.I. (holism, q.v., and others) are now current among some bourgeois natural scientists.

Idealism, Subjective, a philosophical trend denying the existence of the objective reality independent of the will and consciousness of the subject. S.I. holds that the sum total of the subject's sensations, experiences, feelings and actions make up the world in which the subject lives and acts, or at the least believes that they are an integral, essential part of the world. Consistent S.I. leads to solipsism (q.v.). Classical S.I. is represented by Berkeley, Fichte, Hume (qq.v.); a number of ideas of S.I. was developed by Kant (q.v.). In the 20th-century S.I. has many varieties, including various schools of positivism, q.v. (Machism, operationalism, logical empirism, linguistic philosophy, qq.v., etc.), pragmatism, philosophy of life, qq.v. (Nietzsche, Spengler, Bergson, qq.v.), and its outgrowth, existentialism, q.v. (Sartre, Heidegger, Jaspers, qq.v. and others). The exponents of present-day S.I., above all, neo-positivists, tend to discard obvious subjectivism, psychologism and relativism (q.v.), and seek for some criteria to bring out the "universal truths". In this way the formerly distinct border-line between subjective and objective idealism is being erased and they merge, e.g., in various trends of neo-realism (q.v.). Present-day S.I. more and more often appears in the guise of "realism". At the same time it often displays growing tendencies to irrationalism, q.v. (especially in the philosophy of existentialism). The absolutisation of the subject's cognitive and practical activity forms the theoretical and cognitive basis of S.I. Dialectical materialism shows that this activity is not arbitrary; it does not contradict the existence of the objective world and its laws independent of man's consciousness; moreover, it presupposes their existence. The subjective form of cognition does not obviate its objective source and content. Moreover, the very forms of cognition reflect the most general traits of the objective world and practice. Therefore, the contraposition of the subjective and the objective is only possible within the framework of the fundamental question of philosophy (q.v.).

Idealist Conception of History, understanding of the historical process based on recognition of the primary character of social consciousness as compared with social being. It absolutises and mystifies the subjective factors in history. The epistemological roots of the I.C.H. lie in the difficulty of distinguishing the objective factors of history hidden deep in the process of material production from the striking role of ideas and the conscious activities of outstanding personalities in historical events. The class roots of the I.C.H. lie in class interests, which stimulate the creation of theories for the benefit of exploiters, for they justify their aims and policies. Since ancient times the dominant view was that historical events are determined by the will of gods, by Providence, and fate. To oppose these theological views French Enlighteners and materialists put forward ideas on the conscious activities of people who establish social orders of their own will (see Social Contract, Theory of), at the same time pointing to the social consciousness of people in the given epoch as the determinative force of history. According to Hegel (q.v.), the determinative force of history is man's cognitive and creative activity mystified in the form of the "Absolute Idea" or "universal reason". Anthropological theories, both progressive (see Feuerbach, Chernyshevsky) and subjectivist, voluntarist (see Young Hegelians; Narodism) spread later. The development of industry and natural science gave rise to conceptions which apply biological laws to society (see Comte; Spencer), drew attention to some of the material conditions of social life—the geographical environment (see Geographical School in Sociology), and the population (see Malthusianism). In the epoch of imperialism, a combination of the most reactionary ideas of voluntarism (q.v.) with the distorted role of individual factors led to utterly reactionary, misanthropic conceptions—neo-Malthusianism, geopolitics, racism, and fascism (qq.v.). At the same time eclecticism (see Factors, Theory of) and agnosticism (q.v.) spread in the bourgeois philosophy of history. Today technocratic ideas, absolutisation of the role of technology in historical development (the theories of industrial society, stages of economic growth, "post-industrial society", q.v.) have become dominant in I.C.H.

Identically True Statements, propositions, expressions or formulas of the logical calculi (q.v.), which are true given any truth-values of their variables. All the laws of formal logic are true. Accordingly, identically false propositions or formulas are false given any truth-values of their variables.

Identity, a category denoting the equality of an object of phenomenon with itself or the equality of several objects. Objects A and B are identical if and only if all the properties (and relations), which characterise A, also characterise B, and vice versa (Leibniz's, q.v., law). But since material reality undergoes a constant change, there cannot be objects absolutely identified with themselves even in their essential, basic properties. I. is concrete, not abstract, i.e., it contains inherent distinctions, contradictions which are eliminated and recreated in the process of development. The very identification of objects requires that they be distinguished from other objects beforehand; on the

other hand, various objects often need to be identified (for instance, with a view to classifying them). This means that I. is inseparably connected with difference (q.v.) and is relative. Every I. of things is temporary and transient, while their development and change are absolute. The exact sciences, however, make use of the abstract I., i.e., abstracted from the development of things, in conformity with the afore-mentioned Leibniz's law, since idealisation and simplification of reality are possible and necessary in certain conditions during the process of cognition. The logical law of identity (q.v.) is also formulated with similar limitations.

Identity, Law of, a law of logic, according to which every meaningful expression (concept, judgment, qq.v.) must be used in reasoning in the same meaning. The premise of its decidability is the possibility to identify or distinguish between the objects which are the subject of judgment. In actual fact, however, this identification and this distinction are not always possible (see Difference; Identity). For this reason L.I. implies some idealisation of the actual character of the objects which are discussed in a given judgment (abstraction from their development and change), this being determined by the relative stability of phenomena in the objective world.

Ideology, a system of political, legal, ethical, aesthetical, religious and philosophical views and ideas. I. is part of the superstructure (see Basis and Superstructure) and as such ultimately reflects economic relations. In a society with antagonistic classes, ideological struggle corresponds to the class struggle. I. may be scientific or unscientific, a true or false reflection of reality. The interests of reactionary classes nurture a false I., the interests of progressive, revolutionary classes help shape a scientific I. Marxism-Leninism is a truly scientific I., expressing the vital interests of the working class and the overwhelming majority of mankind striving for peace, freedom and progress. Views on incompatibility of ideology with a scientific approach to reality became widespread among bourgeois philosophers in the 1950s and

1960s. They considered I. as something subjective that expresses the interests of some groups, parties, etc. Hence their striving to make the difference between science and I. absolute and to oppose science to I.; their attempts to achieve "deideologisation" of philosophy and science, which in practice are reduced to the isolation of science and philosophy from the class struggle and to diminishing the role of Marxism-Leninism—the only I. providing a strictly scientific, objective analysis of reality. In the 1970s, bourgeois ideologists, while pursuing this goal, began positing "reideologisation" by opposing Marxism to their "new" I. (see "Deideologisation" and "Reideologisation", Theories of). For this reason the struggle against bourgeois I., anticommunism (q.v.) and anti-Sovietism, with the right and "left" revisionism (q.v.) is a necessary prerequisite for the successful development of science and the ideological unity of the international communist movement. The development of I. is ultimately determined by the economy, but I. possesses a certain relative independence. This is expressed, in particular, in the impossibility of directly explaining the content of I. by economics and also in a certain unevenness in economic and ideological development. Moreover, the relative independence of I. is manifested more in the operation of the internal laws of ideological development and also in the ideological spheres most removed from the economic basis. The relative independence of I. is due to the fact that ideological evolution is affected by a number of extra-economic factors: internal continuity in the development of I., the personal role of individual ideologists, the mutual influence of various forms of ideology, etc.

Illusions, a distorted perception of reality. We distinguish two types of I. One is caused by unusual external conditions in which the objects are perceived; in such cases the physiological mechanisms function normally. The other is determined by the pathological functioning of physiological mechanisms taking part in perception. Idealist philosophers frequently utilise I. as an argument to prove that our perception of the objective

world is inadequate. But the very fact that we are able to single out I. as a separate class of phenomena and oppose them to adequate perceptions attests to the falsity of the agnostic "conclusions". Ii. should be distinguished from hallucinations which, unlike Ii., arise in the absence of external objects.

Imagination, the ability to create new sensuous or thought images in the human consciousness, based on the conversion of impressions received from reality. A man acquires I. through work, which without I. could be neither purposeful nor fruitful. Psychology classifies I. according to the degree of deliberateness (voluntary and involuntary I.), of activity (reproductive and creative I.), and of generalisation (concrete and abstract I.), according to the type of creative activity (scientific, inventive, artistic, religious, and other I.). The scientist's I. helps him to know the world by evolving hypotheses, model conceptions, ideas for experiments. The role of I. is particularly important in the arts. Here it serves not only as a means of generalisation, but as a force that calls to life aesthetically significant images, artistically reflecting reality. Unlike fantastic dreams that lead man away from reality, I. associated with the needs of society is a most valuable quality which helps us to know life and change it.

Immanent, the, an inner feature (regularity) characteristic of an object, phenomenon or process. The term of I. is borrowed from Aristotle (q.v.). Kant (q.v.) developed the present understanding of I. As distinct from the transcendental (q.v.) I. means the being of something in itself. The I. critique is the critique of an idea or a system of ideas based on the prerequisites of this idea or system. I. history of philosophy is the interpretation of philosophy in idealist terms, as a process determined exclusively by its own laws, in disregard of the influence of economics, class struggle and various forms of social consciousness on the evolution of philosophical thought.

Immanent School in Philosophy, a subjective idealist trend in philosophy at the end of the 19th century. Its most out standing proponents were W. Schuppe, R. Schubert-Soldern, J. Rehmke and A. Leclair. Mach and Avenarius (qq.v.) admitted their affinity with this trend. This school had its followers in Russia (see Lossky). The immanentists criticised Kant's (q.v.) "thing-in-itself" (so-called criticism from the right). They demanded a reversion from Kantianism to Berkeley and Hume (qq.v.). The main postulate of this philosophy is: "only that exists which is the object of thought". To avoid solipsism (q.v.), the immanentists (with the exception of Schubert-Soldern who openly admitted adherence to the positions of "theoretico-cognitive solipsism") introduced the concept of "consciousness in general", or "generic consciousness" supposedly existing independently of the human brain. In *Materialism and Empirio-Criticism* (q.v.) Lenin gave a profound criticism of I.S.P. and its direct connection with religion. The immanentists' rejection of the theory of reflection was subsequently taken up by neo-realism (q.v.). By the beginning of the 20th century, this school had broken up into many small trends.

Immediate Inferences, inferences (q.v.) in which the conclusion follows immediately from one premise alone. I.I. include conversion, transformation, and others. I.I. are contrasted to implicative inferences, which consist of two or more premises.

Immediate Knowledge, knowledge gained without proof, a direct contemplation of truth, as distinct from discursive (q.v.) knowledge, which is always mediated not only by data of experience, but also by logical reasoning. There are two kinds of I.K.: sensitive and intellective, which in metaphysical doctrines are sharply opposed to each other. Prior to Kant (q.v.) sensitive I.K. was always regarded as knowledge arising from experience. Kant asserted that in addition to I.K., which results from experience, there are also a priori forms of sensitive I.K. (space and time). Kant rejected the possibility for the human mind to have intellective I.K., admitting, however, its possibility for a more perfect mind than human. Intellective I.K. was recognised in anti-

quity by Plato and Plotinus (qq.v.); in the 17th century by the rationalists Descartes, Spinoza and Leibniz (qq.v.); at the turn of the 19th century, by the German idealists and philosophers of romanticism Fichte, Schelling (qq.v.); in the 20th century by Husserl (q.v.). Under intellective I.K. they understood the ability of the mind to see the truth with the "eyes of the mind", directly, without proof; for example, axioms (q.v.) of geometry were regarded as such truths. Hegel (q.v.) criticised the earlier theories of I.K. as undialectical. He saw in I.K. the unity of immediate and mediated knowledge. But Hegel wrongly considered the self-developing thought as the basis of this unity. Dialectical materialism considers that the unity of immediate and mediated knowledge is based on material practice: the truths, mediated by practice and thinking conditioned by it, become directly authentic by virtue of repeated reproduction.

Imperialism, monopoly capitalism, the highest and last stage of capitalism (q.v.), the eve of the socialist revolution. The scientific theory of I. was developed by Lenin who established that at the turn of the century the capitalist mode of production acquired some new important features: in the development of productive forces—a high level of concentration of production leading to the formation of capitalist monopolies; in the sphere of production relations—the establishment of domination by these monopolies. According to Lenin, "domination, and the violence that is associated with it" (Vol. 22, p. 207), which was introduced by monopolies into the economic relations of capitalism, caused in its political superstructure a turn from bourgeois democracy to reaction (up to the establishment of fascist regimes). All this enabled Lenin to draw the conclusion that capitalism had entered a special, imperialist stage of development: "imperialism is capitalism at that stage of development at which the dominance of monopolies and finance capital is established; in which the export of capital has acquired pronounced importance, in which the division of the world among the international trusts has begun, in which the division of all territories of the globe among the biggest capitalist powers has been completed" (Vol. 22, pp. 266-67). Monopolisation of economy determines the historical place of I. as the highest and last stage of the development of capitalism, as decaying, parasitic and dying capitalism. It determines the peculiarities of functioning of all economic laws of capitalism at this stage, including the law of uneven economic and political development of capitalist countries. This unevenness is sharply increasing and acquiring spasmodic, conflicting character, which in the conditions of complete division of the world among the imperialist states generates world wars. The imperialist countries pursue aggressive foreign policies, which reflect the striving of monopolies for world domination. Within the country this policy is accompanied by growing militarisation of the economy. Monopolisation leads to an ever increasing socialisation of production and thereby to still sharper aggravation of class antagonisms, thus creating objective prerequisites for the victory of socialism. The Great October Socialist Revolution signified the beginning of the general crisis of capitalism (q.v.)—the historical process of replacing capitalist mode of production by the socialist one. The creation of the world socialist system (q.v.) and the collapse of the political system of colonialism signify the further aggravation of this crisis. In the conditions of confrontation with socialism the ruling classes of capitalist countries as never before dread a transformation of the class struggle into mass revolutionary movement. For the sake of consolidating its positions, increasing the effectiveness and rate of economic growth, for intensifying the workers' exploitation, the monopolies make a wide use of the achievements of the scientific and technological revolution and of state-monopoly capitalism (q.v.). However, the latter is unable to solve the main contradiction of capitalism; it is a specific form of the movement and aggravation of this contradiction, thus testifying to the historical doom of imperialism.

Implication, the logical operation which forms a complex proposition from two propositions through a logical connective conforming to the conjunctive "if ... then". In an implicative proposition we distinguish the antecedent preceded by the word "if" from the consequent which follows the word "then". Classic mathematical logic (q.v.) proceeds from the concept of material I. which is determined through the function of truth-value. I. is false only if the antecedent is true and the consequent is false, and true in all other cases.

Indeterminism, see Determinism and Indeterminism.

Indian Philosophy. In India philosophy arose on the basis of one of the oldest human civilisations; its traditions, dating back to the 15th-10th centuries B.C., have been preserved to our days. I.P. is usually divided into four periods: (1) the Vedic period; (2) the classical period, or Brahman-Buddhist period, from the 6th century B.C. to the 10th century A.D.; (3) post-classical, 10th-18th centuries; (4) new and current I.P. The very first monuments of Indian thought, the Vedas (q.v.) together with hymns to the numerous gods, contain the concept of a single world order. The Upanishads (q.v.), religious philosophical commentaries to the Vedas, contain ideas which largely shaped the subsequent development of I.P. (unity of the integral spiritual substance and the individual soul; immortality of the soul which is reincarnated according to the law of karma, or retribution). Like the religious idealistic doctrines the Upanishads reflected the views of the materialists and atheists who denied the authority of the Vedas and the life of the soul after death and regarded one of the material elements as the primary foundation of the world. In the classical period, I.P. developed under the strong influence of the Vedas and Upanishads. Since the early Middle Ages it has become a tradition to divide all philosophical schools into orthodox, which recognised the authority of the Vedas, and non-orthodox, which rejected the infallibility of the Vedas. The Mimamsā, Sānkhya, Yoga, Nyāya, Vaisesika, and Vedānta (qq.v.) are the principal orthodox schools. The non-orthodox schools include the Buddhist, Jainist and numerous materialist and atheist schools, the most widespread being the Chārvākas (see Lokāyata). Although this division has historical grounds, it conceals the true mainspring of philosophy: the struggle between materialism and idealism. Both Buddhist and "orthodox" sources denounce above all the materialist schools. Shankara, the most outstanding Vedanta philosopher, vehemently attacked both the materialist ideas of the Sānkhya school and the empiricism of the Nyāya and Vaisesika. He dissociated himself from the common sense of the Nyāya and was close to the idealist and mystic schools. Within the bounds of Buddhism (q.v.) the idealist schools fought against the materialist teachings of the Theravdins and Sarvāstivādins. Bitter conflicts between different philosophical schools brought into being the art of dispute and the science of the sources of knowledge and authentic knowledge—logic. First information about Indian logic may be gleaned from early Buddhist sources (3rd century B.C.); subsequently, logic was developed in the Nyāya school and later in the treatises of Buddhist logicians Dignāga, Dharmakīrti, and others. Towards the end of the classical period, Jainism (q.v.) was losing its influence, while Buddhism was assimilated by Hinduism (q.v.). In this period the Vishnu and Śiva systems of Hinduism were developed. They taught that the Brahman of the Upanishads is the God Śiva, or Vishnu. Tantrism (q.v.) and Shaktism spread since the 5th-7th centuries. Under the influence of Islam (q.v.), monotheistic doctrines arose in the 10th century. In the 19th century philosophy in India developed under the influence of the people's national liberation struggle against British domination. The nature of new I.P. was determined by the fact that the movement for national liberation was headed by the Indian bourgeoisie, whose ideologists followed the road of reviving national religious and philosophical traditions. As a result, there arose modernised theism, Brahma Samāj and Ārya Samāj, pantheism and idealism, the doctrines of R. Tagore, Gandhi and Ghose (qq.v.). Contemporary Indian philosophers advocate a merger of Western science and technology with the spiritual values of the East. After the Great October Socialist Revolution the ideas of Marxist-Leninist philosophy have been gaining ground in India.

Indirect Proof, a form of logical proof (q.v.) distinguished by its method of rationalising a proposition. Unlike direct proof, the truth of the proposition to be proved indirectly is rationalised by demonstrating the falsity of certain premises. The latter stand in such a relationship to the proposition to be proved that their falsity necessarily implies the truth of the proposition.

Individual 1. Man as a social being, the individual as a member of society. The scientific interpretation of the term rests on the Marxist conception of man as a biosocial being whose essence is the aggregate of social relations. Each human being is an I. in so far as the social has become an aspect, a feature, a property of his or her individuality (personality). The very existence of man as a social being necessarily presupposes human mutual relations, not only the influence of social conditions and other people on a given man but also his influence on social conditions and other people. Man's development as a personality necessarily presupposes and depends on the existence of the innate features of the human individual, but it takes place mainly in society, in which each man is both object and subject of activity. Thus, every man is an I. But the I. may develop variously. Every individual finds the objective conditions of his development as an I. in the historical form of society in which he lives. The scope and depth of man's development as an I. are the scope and depth of his assimilation of the social and the transformation and creation of the social itself. The historical forms and types of society are at the same time the historical forms and types of the I. In primitive communal society, people live mainly to find means of subsistence and produce instruments for that purpose; they are in a considerable degree in immediate natural unity with one another and with the natural conditions of their existence, and therefore do not single themselves out from nature or from one another as social beings. In class antagonistic societies, a gap appears and widens between the natural conditions of human existence, the conditions of production and human existence proper. The gap widens between people and nature, between different classes and between different individuals; man grows apart from nature and from other people; he begins to regard himself more and more as a separate I. The development of the I. in a society based on antagonistic classes is antagonistic. A society based on private property cramps and distorts the development of the I., above all of the majority who belong to the exploited classes. With the destruction of capitalism and the building of socialism essentially new prospects for the development of the I. open out. As a result of the creation of the material and technical base of communism, in the process of development of communist social relations and education of the new man with the I.'s active attitude to life, the I.'s integral, harmoniously developed I., spiritually rich, morally pure and physically perfect I. is formed. Gradually all members of society become conscious creators of history, consequently, profoundly developed Ii. The I. is studied by different sciences; e.g. ethics studies the moral consciousness and behaviour of the I., pedagogy deals with problems of education, etc. 2. In psychology, the personality of the social individual as the subject of psychic activity (see Psychics). Each human being has his individual peculiarities of character, intellect, and emotional make-up proper to him. These qualities in their aggregate form the psychics of the I. The psychological make-up of the I. remains relatively stable in the changing psychic condition of the I. (emotional experiences, motives of behaviour, etc.), owing to the relative stability of his conditions of life and nervous system. Changes in the I.'s psychic make-up take place in the course of activity as a result of changes in his being. The I.'s psychic make-up presupposes definite innate features but the decisive role in the development of the I.'s psychics is played by social conditions and changes in them. In socialist society, the I. is formed in conditions which ultimately define the content of his thoughts, emotions and moods. Nevertheless, human personality can be manifested and developed only in the process of purposeful vital activity.

Individual and Society, a socio-philosophical problem that shows what conditions each historically concrete S. presents for the formation and development of the I., to what degree the activity of the I. influences S. and how the interests of the I. and S. are linked. Pre-Marxist social theories were based on the idea that antagonism between the I. and S. will always exist and cannot be resolved; that the I. and S. are independent, self-contained entites. Thus, in slave-owning S. alongside the theories of Plato and Aristotle (qq.v.), who sought to prove the need for inevitable subordination of the I. to the political whole—the state, there were current theories of the stoics, sceptics, and Epicureans who regarded the power of the state as a repressive force hostile to the I. In feudal S. the status, rights and obligations of the I. rigidly fixed by the social estate and caste structure of S. were reflected in the undivided sway of religious ideology with its vindication of hierarchy, its preaching of submission to God, etc. Emerging capitalism destroyed the unity of the man with the community, social estate, caste, guild and established the viewpoint of the separate individual, who was faced by S. as an aggregate of formally equal private owners whom it must have provided with the best opportunities to display their abilities and energy. In the 17th-18th centuries there appeared the theories of the social contract (q.v.), according to which the social and state system is the product of a contract between individuals and can be changed if it ceases to serve the good of the people, i.e., violates the contract. However, the establishment and development of capitalism, especially in the epoch of imperialism, showed that the emancipation of the I. proclaimed by its ideologists was in actual fact the I.'s enslavement by commodity and money relations. The dehumanisation and depersonalisation of man embraces not only the sphere of labour but also of intellectual activity, the bureaucratic administration and even leisure and entertainment. This process is reflected in bourgeois philosophy, which is unable to reveal the fact that the conflict between S. and the I. arises from the private-property relations and which makes it a lasting and unsolvable antagonism. Marxism showed that the development and succession of socio-economic formations is at the same time an historical process of formation and development of the I., connected the contradiction between S. and the I. with the existence of antagonistic social relations, and disclosed the concrete character of its manifestation and the ways by which it will inevitably be overcome. The liquidation under socialism of antagonistic classes and historically inherited forms of the division of labour provides the conditions for the formation of highly developed and creatively active Ii. As early as the stage of developed socialism there are growing possibilities for the harmonious combination of social and individual interests, when, on the one hand, S. does everything for the I. and his well-being, and on the other, members of S. consciously serve the interests of S., raise their professional skill and cultural level, social responsibility, organisation and discipline, i.e., develop as socially rich Ii.

Individual, Particular, and Universal, the philosophical categories formed in the course of the development of practice and cognition and expressing different objective relations in the world, and the degree to which we can know these relations. Each object at first appears before us as something individual. Practical experience, however, shows that individual objects may have certain recurrent features in common, which makes it possible to include them in definite groups. General features may belong either to a restricted group of objects, in which case they are merely particular, or they may be found in all objects, in which case they are universal. The solution of the problem of the relation of the individual, particular and universal in consciousness and objective reality, especially the problem of the correlation of general concepts and individual and real objects, designated by such concepts, has given rise to great difficulties in the history of philosophy. The naive conception of the U. has not as yet raised the question of the origin or cause of similarity. This position was held by the materialists of ancient Greece. Thales (q.v.) conceived the basis of all things to be water; Heraclitus (q.v.) conceived it as fire; Democritus (q.v.) as atoms. Most of the idealist philosophers

of the ancient world also regarded the U. as objective, but in their view it was detached from material reality and became a special world of ideal essences (see Plato). Aristotle (q.v.) did not regard the U. as a special essence isolated from the I., from the objects of the real world. For him the U. was primarily the abstractions of the human mind, but also the essence of individual objects, the aim for the sake of which these objects exist. In this he was close to Plato's conception of the U. His teaching became the groundwork for the controversy between nominalism (q.v.), and realism (see Realism, Medieval). Experimental science which emerged in modern history from the struggle against theology and scholasticism (q.v.), raised a protest against the idealist interpretation of the U. Following this tendency, Locke (q.v.) interpreted the U. as a purely abstract, verbal expression of the similarity of phenomena. This interpretation was in accord with the natural science of his time, particularly with the attempts to classify phenomena. The further development of theory reveals the one-sided nature of Locke's understanding of the U. This understanding of the U. was criticised by Kant (q.v.) and particularly by Hegel (q.v.), who drew a distinction between the "abstract universal", as the verbally expressed sameness of phenomena (their mere resemblance) and the real "concrete universal", understood as the inner essence, the law of existence and change. According to Hegel, however, only the spiritual—the concept, the idea—is the real universal. Marxism regards the categories of the I., the P. and the U. as a means of reflecting the objective links of being. "The form of universality in nature," wrote Engels, "is *law*" and again "the form of universality ... is the form of self-completeness, hence of infinity; it is the comprehension of the many finites in the infinite" (*Dialectics of Nature*, p. 234). Revealing the objective links between different objects and phenomena in the world by means of the categories of the I., the P. and the U. materialist dialectics maintains that the U. embodies all the richness of the I., that the I. does not exist without the U., and vice versa, that under certain conditions the I. is not only connected with the U., but also turns into it. Theoretical analysis and reconstruction of these links with the help of their concepts are of tremendous importance for practice, in which people, confronted with individual objects in specific conditions, are guided by the knowledge of universal laws which manifest themselves in these objects as a tendency and take into account the peculiarities determined by concrete conditions. Thus, in the process of building socialism and communism it is necessary to reveal the correlation between the universal laws of the process and the peculiar features of development in this or that country, which are determined by the specificity of their historical development, their economy and culture.

Individualism, a moral principle especially typical of bourgeois ideology and morality. The theoretical foundation of I. is the recognition of the autonomy and the absolute rights of the individual in society. Theorists of exploiting classes hold that I. is inherent in "immutable human nature". In actual fact, I., as a principle setting the individual in opposition to the collective and subordinating the social interests to the personal, emerged with the appearance of private property and the division of society into classes. In the epoch of the emergent bourgeois relations the conceptions of I. played their positive role in the struggle for the liberation of the individual from the fetters of feudalism and the Catholic church (see Humanism); but with the establishment of the bourgeoisie as a ruling class the advocacy of I. acquires an increasingly unhumane character and eventually serves as an ideological justification of capitalist exploitation. I. was most fully expressed in the philosophy of Stirner (q.v.) and, in the epoch of imperialism, in the philosophy of Nietzsche (q.v.), whose doctrine of the "élite" and "superman" was taken over by fascism. The survivals of I. in people's consciousness in the conditions of socialist society are in sharp conflict with collectivism (q.v.), the principles of communist morality. Overcoming the survivals of I., socialist society defends the true interests of the individual and creates real conditions for the flourishing of man's individuality and the development of his abilities.

Induction, one of the types of reasoning and a method of study. Questions pertaining to the theory of I. are already found in the works of Aristotle (q.v.), but they began to command special attention with the development of empirical natural science in the 17th-18th centuries. A big contribution to elaborating problems of I. was made by F. Bacon, Galileo Galilei, Newton, and Mill (qq.v.). As a form of reasoning I. makes possible the transition from single facts to general propositions. Usually three main types of inductive inferences are distinguished: complete I.; I. through simple enumeration (popular I.); scientific I. (the latter two types are an incomplete I.). Complete I. represents a general proposition concerning a class as a whole to be concluded on the basis of examining all its elements; it gives a true conclusion, but its sphere is limited because it is applicable only to classes all the members of which can be easily observed. In popular I. the presence of a feature in some of the elements of a class warrants the conclusion that all elements of the class possess that feature. Popular I. has an unlimited sphere of application, but its conclusions form only probable propositions that need subsequent proof. Scientific I. also represents a conclusion concerning a whole class based on a number of the elements of that class, but here the grounds for conclusion are provided by the discovery of essential connections between the elements studied, which show that the given feature must be possessed by the whole class. Hence, methods of disclosing essential connections are of prime importance in scientific I. In cognition I. always appears in unity with deduction (q.v.). Dialectical materialism regards I. and deduction not as universal self-sufficient methods, but as aspects of dialectical cognition of reality which are closely interconnected and interdependent; it is therefore opposed to the one-sided exaggeration of the role of any one of them.

Inductive Definition, one of the ways of defining objects of mathematical and logical systems. It indicates: a) the primary or elementary objects of the system; b) the rules or operations by which it is possible to form new objects of a system from already available objects. This is how a natural number (in arithmetic), properly constructed and demonstrable formulas (in logical calculus, q.v.) and others are determined. I.D. must be complete, i.e., it must be used to determine all the objects of a given system and only such objects.

Inference, the process of reasoning in the course of which from one or several propositions called premises an I., a new proposition is deduced (called conclusion or consequence) which logically follows from the premises. The transition from the premises to the conclusion is always made according to some rule of logic. I. is a form of thought in which (alongside a concept, q.v., proposition, and other forms of thinking and methods of reasoning) cognition of the external world is effected at the stage of abstract thinking. Every proper I. must meet the following condition: if its premises are true, its conclusion, too, must be true. This condition is met if in the course of I. the laws of logic and rules of inference are not violated. In the actual process of thinking some of the premises of I. are often omitted and the rules of inference and laws of logic underlying it are not formulated. This makes errors possible in I. Logic lays down methods of distinguishing a valid I. from an invalid one and thereby helps to prevent and correct logical mistakes (q.v.). Usually, the process of reasoning and proof makes up a purpose of Ii., in which the conclusion of a preceding I. becomes the premise of a subsequent I. For a proof (q.v.) to be valid it is necessary for its initial premises — the basis of proof — to be true, and each I. within it must be correct. Depending on their form, Ii. are divided into several types. Their most common division is into deductive and inductive (see Deduction; Induction).

Infinite and Finite, categories denoting the two inseparably connected opposite aspects of the objective world. In its application to the objective world I. characterises: (1) the existence of the world in space, infinite variety of space structures of matter and the essential non-exclusiveness of all material systems; (2) the existence of the world in time, the uncreatability and indestructibility of matter, the eternity of its existence; (3) the quantitative inexhaustibility of matter in depth, the infinite variety of its qualities, interrelations, forms of existence, and tendencies of development; (4) the qualitative heterogeneity of the structure of matter, the existence of innumerable qualitatively different levels of the structural organisation of matter, which possesses at each level different specific properties and is subject to different laws. The theoretical understanding of I. develops with the progress of scientific knowledge. Initially in the history of science more attention was paid to the quantitative aspects of I. that were studied by mathematics: infinite or infinitesimal quantity, infinite set, etc. Dialectical materialism takes into consideration both quantitative and qualitative aspects of I. of the existing world, connected with its structural heterogeneity and infinite qualitative variety of material systems. F. represents every object limited in space and time. Every specific quality in the world is finite, exists within definite limits. But F. is indissolubly connected with I. Every finite object is inexhaustible in terms of its structure; matter that gives birth to finite objects is uncreatable and indestructible, exists for eternity, and merely changes from one form to another. Thus, F. includes I., just as I. is composed of innumerable finite objects and phenomena. The contradictory unity of I. and F. makes it possible to know I. through revealing the universal and absolute in the properties and laws of matter's motion. "All true knowledge of nature is knowledge of the eternal, the infinite..." (F. Engels, *Dialectics of Nature*, p. 234) (see Infinity, Bad; Eternity).

Infinity, Bad, metaphysical conception of the infinity of the world, based on the assumption of a monotonous, unceasing repetition of the same specific qualities, processes, and laws of motion on any scale of space and time. Applied to the structure of matter, B.I. implies recognition of the unlimited divisibility of matter, each smaller particle possessing the same qualities and obeying the same specific laws of motion as the macroscopic bodies. Applied to the structure of the Universe, it assumes an infinite hierarchy of mechanical systems with identical qualities and laws of existence. Applied to the development of nature, it implies recognition of infinite cycles of matter constantly returning to the same starting points. The concept of B.I. was introduced by Hegel (q.v.), who, however, believed the true infinity to be the property of the Absolute Spirit, not matter. Dialectical materialism rejects B.I. It proceeds from the recognition of the inexhaustibility and heterogeneity of the material world and of the existence of countless numbers of qualitatively different levels in the structural organisation of matter of the eternal self-development and qualitative change of matter and the forms of its motion.

Information, a) the sum total of certain knowledge or data; b) one of the fundamental concepts of cybernetics (q.v.). The scientific concept of I. largely detracts from the meaning of messages and deals with their quantitative aspect. Thus, the concept of measurement of information is introduced, being defined as a quantity inversely proportional to the degree of probability of the event mentioned in the message. The more probable the event, the less the amount of I. that is carried in a message about its occurrence, and vice versa. The development of the scientific concept of I. has revealed a new aspect of the material unity of the world and made possible a uniform approach to many processes that had previously been thought to have nothing whatsoever in common, e.g., the transmission of messages along technical communication channels, the functioning of the nervous system, computer operations, various control processes, etc. In all of these we deal with processes involving the transmission, storage, and processing of I. Here the concept of I. has played a part similar to that of the concept of energy in physics by providing an opportunity to describe the most diverse physical processes from a common point of view. The theory of I. is closely connected with reflection (q.v.). If changes occur in the object that reflect the impact of another object, one can say that the first object becomes the bearer of I. about the second object. In cybernetic systems the changes in the object (B) caused by the influence of another object (A) are not merely some characteristics of B., but become the factor of functioning of the cybernetic system precisely as the bearers of I. about A. The relative I. turns from the potential I. as it appears in the precybernetic systems (systems of the inorganic nature not connected with control, q.v.) into the actual I., i.e., the passive reflection in the precybernetic systems becomes an active reflection. From this point of view man's brain is an exceptionally complex cybernetic system that stores and processes relative actual I. that comes from the outside world. The brain's ability to reflect and perceive the outside world is seen as a link in the development of processes associated with the transmission and processing of I. That is why one finds in modern information theory an embodiment of Lenin's thesis, according to which all matter possesses a quality akin to perception, namely, reflection.

Innate Ideas, concepts which, according to idealism, are primordially inherent in the human mind and independent of experience. They include axioms in mathematics and logic and the primary principles of philosophy. The teaching of I.I. was founded by Plato (q.v.). Some philosophers believed these I.I. to be bestowed by God (Descartes, q.v.); others, believed them to be inclinations or dispositions of the mind whose development is promoted by sense experience (Leibniz, q.v.). Despite the above difference, all theories of I.I. contain an element of apriorism, i.e., knowledge preceding, and independent of experience. Epistemologically, the theories of I.I. originated from an unhistorical, undialectical approach to the origin of general concepts and principles, to the relation between the mediate and the immediate, between the sensory and the rational elements in cognition and between individual and socio-historical experience.

Inspiration, condition particularly conducive to various forms of man's creative activity. It is characterised by total concentration of the individual's spiritual energy on what he is creating, and by emotional elation that makes work exceptionally productive. In contradistinction to the idealist conception of I. as "divine madness", mystical intuition and sudden revelation (Plato, Schelling, Hartmann, qq.v., S. Freud, H. Read, and others), materialism denies that I. has any supernatural character and regards it as a mental phenomenon determined by the social and individual incentives to create, and also by the process of work itself.

Inspirationism, an idealist theory about the mystic, religious character of knowledge, according to which truth is revealed not in a rationally logical way but all of a sudden, without any preparation, solely through inspiration, i.e., an idea born by inspiration, prompted to man from above in the form of divine suggestion. In a pure form I. can be found in rare cases, chiefly in theological doctrines. In fact this principle is shared by irrationalism (q.v.)

Instinct, a form of psychic activity, a type of behaviour. In a broad sense, I. is counterposed to consciousness. Instinctive behaviour is characteristic of animals; it is based on biological forms of existence developed in the process of adaptation to the environment. On the other hand, conscious behaviour is expressed in the purposeful changing of nature by man and is based on his knowledge of nature's laws. In a more specific sense, I. is a type of behaviour inborn in a given species of animals and fixed by biological heredity. According to I. Pavlov (q.v.), I. is a chain of unconditioned reflexes. I. is most distinctly expressed in animals of relatively low organisation (insects, fishes, birds). With evolutionary development, the role of intricate reflectory activity resting on individual experience becomes more and more important. Ii. are also a feature of man, but in humans they do not play a decisive role, because specifically human activity originates and develops as a consequence of socio-historical processes and is prompted chiefly by social, not biological motives.

Instrument, a means of cognition used for observation and registering different kinds of measurement (q.v.). In contemporary scientific knowledge I. is a sort of intermediary between scientists and objects under study and amplifies human sense-organs, allowing the investigation of material objects that are inaccessible to direct perception. Modern scientific installations consist of an aggregate of Ii. fulfilling various functions: some of them isolate or single out the object of study and in that sense prepare it for investigation, others record information on its state and properties, still others register in a certain way the results of the I.'s interaction with the object (by means of light or sonic effects or photographic means, etc.). Erroneous interpretation of the enhanced role of Ii. in cognition, its subjectivisation, gave rise to so-called "instrumental idealism". Its exponents (P. Jordan and others) maintain that the subject creates the physical reality (object) by means of Ii.

Instrumentalism, a subjective idealist doctrine of the American philosopher Dewey (q.v.) and his followers, a variety of pragmatism (q.v.). The distinctions between subject and object, thoughts and facts, psychical and physical, are, according to Dewey, merely differences within "experience", elements of a "situation", aspects of an "event". Such ambiguous terms and also references to the "social nature" of experience are used to disguise the idealism of this philosophy. According to I., concepts, scientific laws and theories are merely instruments, tools, keys to the situation, "plans of action" (hence the name of this form of idealism). Recognising cognition as a vital function of the organism, I. denies that its importance lies in its ability to reflect the objective world; it regards truth in subjectivist terms, as something justified, which ensures success in the given situation. Dewey and his supporters do not recognise the reality of social classes, resort to metaphysical abstractions of society, the individual and the state "in general". The instrumentalist "theory" of progress holds that progress does not imply the attainment of definite aims by society but the process of movement itself. In fact, this theory resurrects the old opportunist slogan of Bernstein "the final goal is nothing, the movement is everything". Dewey's chief followers (S. Hook, J. Childs, M. Mead) are active opponents of Marxism.

Intellectualism, a philosophical doctrine which places cognition through the intellect in the foreground and metaphysically divorces it from sense knowledge and practice. I. is akin to rationalism (q.v.). In ancient philosophy I. was represented by Eleatics (q.v.) and Platonists. In new philosophy I. opposed the one-sidedness of sensationalism (q.v.) and was represented by Descartes (q.v.) and the Cartesians and to some extent by Spinozism. In modern bourgeois philosophy, with a considerable admixture of agnosticism (q.v.), I. is advocated by logical positivism (q.v.). Dialectical materialism recognises the unity of sense and intellectual knowledge (see Cognition; Theory and Practice).

Intelligentsia, a social group of people, professionally engaged in brainwork. It includes engineers, technicians, doctors, lawyers, actors, teachers, scientific workers, a great part of office workers. The I. appeared already in the slave-owning and feudal societies, but reached its peak development (in pre-socialist formations) under capitalism. The I. has never been and cannot be a separate class as it draws on various classes and does not hold any special place in the system of social production. As a social layer it is incapable of pursuing independent policies, its activities being determined by the interests of those classes that it serves. In capitalist society, a large part of the I. has to serve the bourgeoisie. Scientific and technological progress increases the numbers of the I. and enhances its role in society. At the same time capitalism increasingly manifests its hostility towards genuine culture and limits the scope of the intelligentsia's creativity. This contradiction compels a large part of the I. to apply to the working class (q.v.) with whom many of representatives of the I. become close friends by virtue of their position. After a socialist revolution the working class faces an acute problem of how to use the old and to create the new I. Under socialism there is no longer antithesis between mental and physical work

(q.v.); there are only essential differences between them, which are being overcome during communist construction. This is accompanied by the process of rapprochement between the working class, the peasantry and the I. Under the conditions of the scientific and technological revolution (q.v.) in socialist countries the growth rate of the scientific and technical I. exceeds that of all other social groups. The socialist I., together with the workers and peasants, takes an active part in the construction of communist society. The development of creative work and the elimination of the after-effects of the old division of labour would ultimately result in the I. ceasing to be a separate social layer in the future communist society.

Intelligible, the philosophical term denoting an object or phenomenon perceivable only by reason, or intellectual intuition (q.v.). The term of I. is contrasted with the term "sensible" denoting an object perceived with the help of the sense-organs. The concept of I. was widely used in scholasticism (q.v.) and in the philosophy of Kant (q.v.).

Interaction, the process of mutual influence of bodies on one another, the more general, universal form of changing their states. I. determines the existence and structural organisation of any material system, its properties, its union with other bodies in a system of a larger order. Without the capacity for I. matter could not exist. In any integral system I. is accompanied by mutual reflection by the bodies of each other's properties, as a result of which they may undergo change. There exist in the objective world many other forms of I. (see Universal Connection of Phenomena, Motion, Change, Functional Dependence).

Intercourse, a mode of mutual relations specific for individuals, a mode of the being of man in his interconnection with other people. I. is an integral part of the objective activity of man. The productive forces (in as much as they are primarily the essential forces of man) are forces of intercourse. Social relations, especially production relations, find their concrete manifestation in I. The availability of mass communication (q.v.) media does not guarantee wider I., and can even worsen its quality, destroy its uniqueness, if they are not woven into the sphere of man's integral activity, if man's alienation (q.v.) has not been overcome. The process and forms of I. are studied by psychology, sociology (qq.v.), ethnography, linguistics, and other sciences.

Interest 1. A concept characterising something objectively important for an individual, a family, a group of people, a class, a nation, society as a whole. Consequently, individual and common interests are distinguished: family, group, class, national, social. I. is the product of objective social conditions which determine the appropriate orientation of people's will and action. Common I. is always the I. of people who are part of some social or historical entity (a class, a nation), some collective or association (a political party, a trade union, a co-operative, etc.). Every association comes into being on the basis of choice made by the individuals joining it. Being part of a social or historical community (class, nation) is not the result of the people's self-determination. It is conditioned by the unity of Ii., which are determined by the social nature of each such community and the conditions of its existence. Being objectively an I. of each member of such a community it is not always recognised by all of them. Thus, the class I. of the proletariat is objectively the I. of each individual worker; however, individual groups of workers may lose the awareness of their class Ii. under the influence of an alien class ideology, and even act contrary to them. This explains why Marxist-Leninist parties should wage a struggle to make all proletarians conscious of the Ii. of their class. In the antagonistic class societies there is always a struggle between the forces of progress and the forces of reaction. Therefore social Ii. can never be homogeneous or similar for all members of a society. Under socialism all social groups—workers, peasants and intellectuals—are united by their common communist ideal (q.v.) whose realisation they are striving for. This means that under socialism the Ii. of society become objectively common for all its members.

This does not eliminate, however, the task of educating people in the spirit of understanding their social I. (see Individual and Society). 2. In psychology I. is manifested in a positive emotional attitude to an object and in the concentration of attention upon it. A temporary, situational interest arises in the process of performing a given action and vanishes with its completion. A stable I. is a relatively constant trait of the individual and is an important requisite of man's creative attitude to his activity, helping to broaden his horizon and enrich his knowledge.

Interest, Theory of, a trend in modern bourgeois axiology (q.v.) and ethics which appeared in the 1920s within naturalism (q.v.) and which is close to pragmatism (q.v.). Its proponents R. Perry (USA), F. Tennant (Britain) and others determine the significance of objects and phenomena of reality for man (their value, q.v. including moral value) not on the basis of their objective role in society, but on the basis of man's subjective attitude to them, of his interest. The interest itself is understood purely psychologically, as a desire, disposition, inclination, sympathy, love (or, on the contrary, disgust, antipathy, hatred) felt by people. Strictly speaking, they ignore social dependence of interests on the mode of man's activity, on the objective laws of historical development. This results in a subjectivist interpretation of the nature of values. Morality is understood in a liberal bourgeois way, as a means of co-ordination and reconciliation of private interests, the good—as something that agrees with the sum total of individual interests; the duty—in the spirit of utilitarianism (q.v.)—one is to act in such a way as to satisfy the greatest number of wishes and aspirations of this society. Thus, the historical purpose of morality, which is the overcoming of the clash between interests by restructuring society and satisfying the vital interests of all mankind, is brought down to the level of a political programme of compromise and opportunism and replaced by the task of mitigating contradictions, of mutual agreement between competitors.

Internationalism (proletarian, socialist), one of the basic principles of the ideology and policy of the working class and its party, which expresses the international solidarity of working people of different countries in their struggle against capitalism, for their social and national emancipation, for building socialism and communism. I. is based on the community of class interests of the proletariat and the final goal of its struggle, irrespective of the affiliation of its representatives to any state and nationality. I. came into being at the dawn of the international communist movement and initially found its expression in workers' minds in the form of social feelings and slogans of international solidarity. Scientific communism (q.v.) provided a theoretical basis for I. The *Manifesto of the Communist Party* and other works of Marx and Engels illustrate the objective necessity of the unity of workers of different countries in their struggle against capital, formulate the main ideas of I. and proclaim its famous slogan "Workers of All Countries, Unite!". The principle of I. means mutual support and co-operation of the working people of different countries in their struggle against the international bourgeoisie, recognition of equality of all nations and irreconcilability to any oppression of one nation by another, presupposes a combination of international and national interests. For this reason I. is opposed to bourgeois nationalism (q.v.), great-power chauvinism, and the ideology of racism (q.v.) and colonialism. It is also radically opposed to cosmopolitanism (q.v.), which under the mask of neutrality conceals relations of national and political inequality, imperialist domination and oppression. For the first time in history the ideas of I. found their practical implementation in the process of building socialism in the USSR where the national question (q.v.) has been solved, a multinational state of equal nations has been formed, and inter-national relations of a new type—free from class and national antagonisms—have developed. This provides the basis for the transformation of proletarian I. into *socialist* I.: the growing social basis for I. and for its conversion into the ideology of the whole society. I. is organically related to socialist patriotism (q.v.). The emergence of the world socialist system (q.v.) have made the principles of I. the groundwork for the relations between socialist states and between the peoples of socialist countries and the working people of capitalist countries and the peoples fighting for their national liberation.

Interpretation and Model, semantic concepts which play an important role in metamathematics and metalogic (qq.v.) as well as in science in general. In a broad sense, I. is the assigning of meanings to initial propositions of a calculus (q.v.), as a result of which all properly constructed propositions of the given calculus acquire sense (see Denotation and Sense; Name; Logical Semantics). An interpreted calculus is, therefore, a formalised language, in which various propositions having sense are formulated and demonstrated. A formal definition of I. can be given by utilising the concept of M. Let us take a certain class of propositions of some calculus; if we replace all constants in these propositions by variables of corresponding types (see Types, Theory of), we shall obtain a class of propositional functions (see Predicate). Any set of objects which will discharge each of the propositional functions of this class is called M. of the given class of propositions and of the corresponding calculus. The concept of M. of calculus helps to introduce the concept of I. Being either extracted or specially constructed M. is called the I. of calculus. In its turn, the concept of I. is used to determine the logical and factual truth (q.v.) and analytical and synthetical propositions. The theory of models of logical systems has been developed in the works of Tarski, Carnap (q.v.), the Soviet mathematician A.I. Maltsev, and others. In the natural sciences, the term of M. is used in a different sense, based on the concepts of isomorphism and homeomorphism (qq.v.) of the systems "being modelled" and "modelling" ones (see Modelling).

Introjection, a concept introduced by Avenarius (q.v.) for the interpretation and criticism of naturalistic and contemplative (metaphysical) materialism, in contradistinction to which he put forward the theory of principal co-ordination. According to Avenarius, I. is an impermissible "incorporation" in individual consciousness of a specifically spiritual image, of the ideal (q.v.), which leads to dualism (q.v.). Dialectical materialism avoids I. and dualism by revealing the socio-practical nature of the ideal instead of reducing it to the state of individual consciousness, and regarding it as the reflection of the material. The theory of I. was criticised by Lenin in his *Materialism and Empirio-Criticism* (q.v.).

Introspection, observation of one's own psychic phenomena, self-observation. I. is associated with the development of the higher form of psychic activity, i.e., with man's understanding of reality around him and with the crystallisation of his world of inner emotions and the formation of his inner plan of action. Only that which is perceived by consciousness can be the object of I. The results of I. can be expressed in the form of statements by people about their thoughts and emotions. Idealist psychology holds that I. is the only or the main method of studying psychic phenomena, and that it enables us to penetrate their essence directly. Materialist psychology holds that the data of I. do not go beyond directly sensitive knowledge, and that strictly objective methods are necessary for the study of the essence of these data. For scientific psychology, I. is, therefore, both a method and one of the objects of psychological study.

Intuition, ability to understand truth directly. In pre-Marxist philosophy I. was considered a special form of cognitive activity. Descartes (q.v.), for example, held that the deductive form of proof rests on axioms; the latter are understood purely intuitively, without any proof. According to Descartes, I. in combination with the deductive method serves as a universal criterion of complete truth. I. also holds a big place in the philosophy of Spinoza (q.v.), who considered it the most fruitful and important knowledge grasping the essence of things. In contemporary bourgeois philosophy and psychology I. is regarded as a mystical ability of cognition, incompatible with logic and vital practice (see Intuitionalism). Dialectical materialism regards I. as immediate knowledge

(q.v.), as living contemplation in its dialectical connection with the mediated knowledge (see Cognition) and rejects any attempts to treat it as a superrational, mystical cognitive ability. I. must not be considered as a kind of fundamental deviation from the usual ways of knowing the truth; it is a natural form of their manifestation based on logical thinking and practice. Behind the ability "suddenly" to grasp the truth, are, in reality, accumulated experience and knowledge acquired before. The psychological mechanism of I. is not studied enough, but the available experimental data make it possible to hold that it is based on the individual's ability to reflect the side (uncognised) product alongside the direct (cognised) one in the process of its interaction with the surrounding world. Under certain conditions this (still uncognised) part of the result of an action becomes a key to the solution of a creative task. In due course the results of intuitive cognition are logically proved and verified by practice.

Intuitionalism 1. An idealistic trend which has gained great influence in bourgeois philosophy in the epoch of imperialism. I. counterposes to rational knowledge the immediate perception of reality based on intuition (q.v.), which is understood as a special ability of the mind, irreducible to sense experience and discursive (q.v.), logical thought. I. is directly associated with mysticism (q.v.). Bergson and Lossky (qq.v.) were the main proponents of I. **2.** A trend in 20th-century bourgeois ethics, which gave rise to modern formalism (q.v.) in ethics. Intuitional ideas in ethics were first formulated by the Cambridge school (q.v.) in the 17th-18th centuries and later developed by contemporary bourgeois proponents of ethics. The main proposition of I. in ethics is that the more general moral concepts (good and evil, q.v.) are entirely "unique", that they cannot be reduced to any other qualities, that they cannot be denied or explained, that they are "self-evident", need not any proof and can be cognised only by intuition. These ideas convince the proponents of I. that normative ethics (q.v.) cannot base its conclusions on the data of other sciences, and is a special sphere of knowledge. They hold that the main moral conceptions have no roots in history and are absolute. This point of view objectively serves to justify the universal nature and immutability of bourgeois morality.

Intuitionism, a trend in the philosophical foundations of mathematics (along with logicism, formalism, qq.v., and effectivism), which arose in the early 1920s in connection with polemics over the theoretical principles of mathematics. According to I., the exact mathematical thought is based on rational intuition (q.v.), which includes the process of logical construction of all mathematical objects. According to I., all mathematics is based on such intuition and, therefore, mathematical objects do not exist apart from their logical counterparts. To avoid paradoxes (q.v.), mathematical proof must be based not on strict logic, but on the intuitive clarity: it is true if one intuitively understands its every stage, beginning from the points of departure and the rules of reasoning. That is why the applicability of logical laws and rules must be ultimately judged by intuition as well. But I., as distinct from intuitionalism (q.v.), does not oppose intuition to logic. I. believes that mathematics cannot rely on logic and develops its own understanding of logic as part of mathematics, viewing the logical theorems as mathematical theorems of the most general character.

Invariance, the property of magnitudes, equations and laws to remain invariant, unchanged under certain transformations of co-ordinates and time. During the transition from an old theory to a new one the old property of I. either remains or is generalised, not discarded. I. follows from the material unity of the world, from the fundamental homogeneity of physical objects and their properties.

Irrational, uncomprehensible by reason, thought, not expressible in logical concepts. In irrationalism (q.v.) the I. represents the forces void of reason, which allegedly underlied human spirit and even being itself.

Irrationalism 1. A philosophical doctrine which declares that the cognitive power of reason, thinking is limited and that the main method of cognition is intuition (q.v.), feeling, instinct (q.v.), etc. I. considers the world to be chaotic, devoid of regularity, depending on game of chance and unconscious will. Irrationalist teachings appear, as a rule, at turning points of society's development and are usually put forward not as logical, coherent systems but as separate ideas and moods formulated as aphorisms. The end of the 19th and beginning of the 20th century saw the revival of I. At that time capitalism grew into imperialism, and liberal bourgeois and reformist ideals collapsed and the hopes to "improve" capitalism by rationalising it and by using natural-scientific and technical knowledge floundered. A number of irrationalist teachings appeared in that period, the philosophy of life (q.v.) being one of them. Another variation of I.— existentialism (q.v.)—appeared in the 1930s. Irrationalist ideas were also clearly manifested in Freudianism (q.v.). As an anti-scientific trend I. was a breeding ground for reactionary, fascist theories which denied scientific knowledge and advocated the prophecies of the leader, the führer, and the voice of "blood and race". In some form or other I. is widespread in contemporary bourgeois philosophy, sociology and psychology. 2. In ethics, I. is a method of explaining the nature of morality typical of many bourgeois theories of morals. At present I. unites a number of schools, among them existentionalism, neo-Protestantism, "humanistic" ethics, the ethics of self-realisation (qq.v.), in a separate trend, which exists along with ethical formalism and naturalism (qq.v.). I. declares that any moral situation or condition of every individual are specific. This warrants the conclusion that it is impossible to formulate general principles of morality or to justify them by means of rational thought and science, which are seemingly not applicable to morality, as they see only the abstract and the general in a multitude of things. Irrationalists declare as untrue the purposeful morality of society that serves some practical needs. In their view, the true morality, as man's existence as a whole, cannot be defined and generalised, as it is not subject to laws of nature and society. In morality man establishes himself as an absolutely free being as opposed to the realm of objective dependence. Thus, I. comes to the extreme relativist and voluntarist understanding of morality, to the denial of any objective meaning in man's choice of his moral position. Although some trends in I. criticise the apologetic nature, dogmatism and utilitarianism of bourgeois morality they, irrespective of their proponents' intentions, confuse individuals in the course of the struggle between the two world outlooks.

Irreversibility, a quality which makes reversion to the original state impossible, determining the passage into a qualitatively new stage. I. is inherent, to a greater or lesser degree, in all processes in the world. This is determined by the infinity of matter, the inexhaustible complexity of its structure, and its countless potentialities for change, which cannot be fully realised in any finite period of time. That is why every cyclical process includes an element of irreversible change, which is expressed in the general irreversible run of time from the past to the future. I. cannot be reduced to some kind of change in one direction. Development along an ascending line or, the reverse, the degradation of a system with its subsequent demise, are specific cases of I. Change in one direction can occur only in finite systems. In the infinite Universe I. presupposes changes in the most diverse directions and never-ending emergence of fundamentally new possibilities of development.

Irritability, the quality of living matter to react to the influence of internal and external environments. I. is one of the general biological forms of reflection (q.v.) of matter. The most elementary form of I., inherent in the protozoa, is the movement to the source of irritation (light, smell, etc.) or away from it. In the process of historical development I. gives rise to excitability. As living creatures become more complex and the nervous system develops, the biological forms of reflection also become more complicated, conditioned and unconditioned reflexes (q.v.) make their appearance. The process of

metabolism and the functioning of albuminous components form the basis of I. The theory of I. provides abundant factual material in support of the Marxist theory of reflection (q.v.).

Islam, or Mohammedanism, one of the world religions, widespread chiefly in the Middle East, North Africa, and South-East Asia, in the USSR—among the believers in the Central Asian republics, North Caucasus, Transcaucasia, the Tatar and Bashkir Autonomous Republics. I. arose in the 7th century in Western Arabia in the period of the Arab peoples' transition from the primitive-communal system to a class society and their unification in the feudal-theocratic state of the Arab Caliphate. I. was an ideological reflection of these processes. The creed of I. is expounded in the "holy" book of the Muslims, the Koran; it is compounded of elements of primitive religions and also of Judaism, Christianity and Zoroastrianism (qq.v.). It is based on the belief in the Almighty God (Allah). The pivot of I. is the doctrine of divine predestination, according to which the fate of every man is predestined by Allah. Advocating man's impotence in face of God, I. urges the faithful to be patient, to submit to Allah and his envoys on earth. The religious duties prescribed by the Koran link with I. the believers' life, designs and behaviour. In return they are promised heavenly bliss in the other world. At the same time the unruly are intimidated by future sufferings in hell. The believers have to kneel in prayer daily, to keep the fast, to pay tax and make a pilgrimage to the Muslim Holy places. Two main branches in I.—the Sunnites and the Shiites—differ primarily in the interpretation of some Muslim dogmas, which at times led to clashes between them and were used by certain circles to instigate national strife. I. has always played an important role in those countries of the East where it is spread. This role has intensified in the present epoch of the rise of the national liberation struggle, in the process of which Muslim leaders seek to use I. as the ideology of liberation movements. They put forward, for instance, the theory of "Islamic socialism", which tries to define a "special path" to socialism on the basis of converging it with the Muslim religion. At the same time the most reactionary ideologists of I. advocate hostility towards communism and state that socialism is unacceptable for the Muslims. This contradictory approach results from the class heterogeneity of I. proponents and, consequently, of their differing class interests, although they use the same system of dogmas. And for this reason it is important to make a concrete analysis of the views of the wide strata of Muslims and their leaders who give different interpretations to the religious dogmas, depending on their class positions. History corroborates the correctness of the CPSU's policy in the national question, this being manifested in the socialist transformations in the Soviet republics where I.'s influence has been traditionally strong. The drawing of Muslim working people into the process of socialist construction helps to develop their class consciousness, liberate them from religious survivals and to enable them to understand the true ways of society's transformation.

Isomorphism and Homeomorphism, the concepts characterising the correspondence between the structures (q.v.) of objects. Two systems considered apart from the nature of their component elements are mutually isomorphic when to every element of the first system corresponds only one element in the other and to every operation (connection) of the first system corresponds only one operation (connection) of the other, and vice versa. This one-to-one correspondence is called I. Full I. is possible only between abstract, ideal objects, for example, between a geometric figure and its analytical expression in a mathematical formula. I. is related not to all but only few fixed properties and relations of objects compared in the act of cognition, which in their other properties and relations may differ. H. is a general case of I. when the identity is true only one way. For this reason, the homeomorphous image is an incomplete, approximate reflection of the original structure. Such, for example, is the relation between the map and the terrain, between the sound recording and its original-sound oscillation of the air. The concepts of I. and H. are widely applied in mathematical logic, cybernetics, physics (q.v.), chemistry and other fields of knowledge. In the theory of knowledge both concepts are extensively applied in the analysis of similarity (correspondence) between the image and the object, between theory and object and in the analysis of information (q.v.) transformation. I. and H. are closely related to the concepts "model" (see Modelling), "signal", "image" (see Reflection; Ideal, the).

j

Jacobi, Friedrich Heinrich (1743-1819), German idealist philosopher, a friend of Goethe's. He criticised rationalism (q.v.) and justified the so-called philosophy of feeling and faith. The philosophy of Jacobi is an attempt to define metaphysically and counterpose immediate knowledge, which he identified with faith, and mediated knowledge. For him the only true knowledge is sense experience, the activity of reason never transcending the limits of sense experience. Reason, dealing with subjective concepts, is powerless to prove the existence of things. The reality of the surrounding world can be guaranteed only through faith that underlies sense experience. Religious feeling, which, according to Jacobi, forms the foundation of philosophy, cannot be understood from the point of view of rationalism. This led J. to conclude that rational philosophy was linked with atheism. Some elements of J.'s philosophy were further developed in the philosophy of life and existentialism (qq.v.).

Jainism, a heterodox system of Indian philosophy and religion, a system of ontological pluralism, which emerged about the 6th century B.C. J. is based on the doctrine of the essences, the primary material of which the world is built; it is also the fundamental truth of which knowledge is built. The two chief essences are *jīva* (the soul), whose basis is consciousness, and *ajīva* (all that is not soul). Matter is a variety of *ajīva* possessing the properties of tactility, sound, smell, colour, and taste. Matter is atomistic, perceptible to the sense-organs, subject to change, has no beginning and no end, and is not the result of divine creation. In addition, there is also subtle matter, which conditions the connection between soul and body. There is no single soul or supreme God: there are very many souls in the world which are either embodied or not in living creatures. Like matter, the souls have not been created by anybody and have always been in existence since the very beginning. Every soul is potentially omniscient, all-permeating, and omnipotent, but its possibilities are limited by the concrete body in which it lives. The ethics of J. is based on the doctrine of refraining from doing injury to any living being. The philosophical system of J. is the basis of religion of the same name, believed to have been founded by a mythical sage Mahāvīra (or Jina), who is said to have lived in the 9th-8th centuries B.C. The cult of J. includes worship of Mahāvira and other sages.

James, William (1842-1910), US psychologist and idealist philosopher, prominent exponent of pragmatism (q.v.). Opposed the materialist, scientific world outlook. Conscious of the fallacies of the metaphysical method, J. nevertheless rejected dialectics and professed irrationalism (q.v.). His analysis of psyche, which J. described as a stream of consciousness, laid emphasis on the volitional and emotional elements. J. substituted the pragmatic principle of utility and interest for objective understanding of the truth. J. advocated the right to believe what cannot be proved or reasoned. J.'s radical empiricism is, in effect, a subjective reduction of reality to pure experience, to consciousness. His neutral monism defines the material and the spiritual as two different aspects of one and the same "experience". J. championed religion and was active in a special organisation he founded in New York for the "examination" of mystical "experience". His main works are *The Principles of Psychology* (1890), *The Varieties of Religious Experience* (1902), and *Pragmatism* (1907).

Jansenism, a politico-religious trend that was widespread in France and in the Netherlands in the 17th and 18th centuries. Its principal tenets were laid down by the theologian Cornelius Jansen (1585-1638) who developed the teaching of St. Augustine (q.v.). Being a variety of

Catholicism (q.v.), J. had same features in common with Protestantism (recognition of predestination, negation of free will). Speaking in social terms, J. was the ideology of those sections who were dissatisfied with the domination of the Catholic Church, which consecrated the absolutist-feudal orders. Jansenist communities were engaged in religious and educational activities, setting up primary schools with a comparatively comprehensive programme of instruction, based on the principles of conscious assimilation of knowledge, use of visual methods, etc. J. was repeatedly condemned by the Roman Catholic Church as heresy. In the mid-18th century it had lost its influence in France with the rise of revolutionary bourgeois ideology. In Holland it became an independent denomination.

Japanese Philosophy. The formation of the first philosophical doctrines in Japan began in the epoch of feudalism. J.P. developed under the influence of the natural philosophical ideas of ancient China, the ethico-political teachings of Confucianism, Buddhism (qq.v.) and later of neo-Confucianism. The founders of neo-Confucianist idealism in Japan were Fujiwara Seika (1561-1619) and Hayashi Razan (1583-1657). Their school ("Shushi gakuha") propagated the doctrine of the Chinese philosopher Chu Hsi (q.v.). The Japanese neo-Confucianists thought that the "Great Ultimate" rules the Universe. It is a universal transcendental force, without qualities and forms, and beyond man's perception. The mystical absolute is the foundation of the ideal principle *ri* (*li*, q.v.); which is connected with the material principle *ki* (*ch'i*, q.v.) and is able to create the physical nature of things and man. The neo-Confucianists justified the dogmas of Confucianism about the eternal relations of subjection (the son to the father, the subject to the emperor, the wife to the husband, and so on). The schools of classical Confucianism and those of the followers of the subjective idealism of the Chinese philosopher Wang Shou-jên (Wang Yangming) were also active during that period. The materialist views of Muro Kyuso (1658-1734) and Yamagata Shunan (1687-1752) were formed in defiance of the then

dominant idealist trends in J.P. The materialist philosopher and atheist Ando Shoeki was active in the epoch of feudalism (end of the 17th and beginning of the 18th centuries). He discarded the neo-Confucian idea of the "limitless" ideal principle and defended the principle that uninterrupted formation is the real law of nature. According to Ando Shoeki, the world consists of five infinite material elements. He was a resolute enemy of the feudal regime, and propagated the advanced ideas of enlightenment. He denied the idea of the inborn inequality of men and considered private ownership the source of social evil; his demands in the social sphere, however, were utopian. The incomplete bourgeois revolution of 1867-68 was an important factor influencing the development of J.P. in the second half of the 19th century. Philosophical ideas developed during this period in the struggle between the philosophers of *kanryo gakusha* (scientists of the bureaucracy) and of *minkan gakusha* (scientists of the people). The representatives of the *kanryo gakusha* were Nishi Amane (1826-1894) and Kato Kiroyuki (1836-1916). They thought their mission was to "develop culture according to the plans, tastes, and efforts of the top layers". They attempted to combine the elements of Confucianism and the ideas of West European idealist philosophy (Mill, Bentham, Comte, Spencer, qq.v., and others). Nishi was the first to introduce the term "tetsugaku", or "philosophy". Fukuzawa Yukuchi (1834-1901), a prominent exponent of *minkan gakusha*, denied the Social-Darwinist ideas of Kato Hiroyuki and preached social equality. An ideologist of the Japanese monarchical regime, idealist and eclectic Inoue Tetsujiro (1855-1944) opposed English empiricism (q.v.) and tried to synthesise the ideas of Confucianism, neo-Confucianism, Shintoism (q.v.), Buddhism with the ideas of classical German philosophy (especially Hegel, q.v.), E. Hartmann and empirio-criticism (qq.v.). His eclectical doctrine became the philosophical basis of the ideology of Japanism. Inoue's philosophy and all idealism in general was opposed by the materialist and atheist philosopher Nakae Chomin (1847-1901), who had a great influence upon Japanese progressive scientific and social thought. With Japan's transition to imperialism idealist philosophical schools were getting increasing support. At that time special chairs instituted in universities spread the ideas of classical German philosophy and latest idealism (phenomenology, philosophy of life, pragmatism, and existentialism, qq.v.). The most widespread was the philosophy of Nishida Kitaro (1870-1945), who tried to express the ideas of Zen Buddhism (q.v.) in the concepts of West European idealist philosophy. The Great October Socialist Revolution of 1917 in Russia, the general crisis of capitalism and the successes scored by the workers' movement promoted the rise and spread in Japan of the Marxist philosophy, associated with Sen Katayama (1859-1933) and his followers, who actively propagated this philosophy in the country.

Jaspers, Karl (1883-1969), a leading exponent of German existentialism (q.v.). He started as a psychiatrist, and this determined in many ways his conception of philosophical problems. J. saw in psycho-pathological phenomena (*Allgemeine Psychopathologie*, 1913) not the expression of individual disintegration, but man's intensified search for his individuality. Considering this morbid search as the core of real philosophising, J. came to the conclusion that any rational picture of the world can be regarded as something allegorical, as a "rationalisation" of emotional desires which can never be realised completely and which always need interpretation. According to J., the main task of philosophy is to show that all conscious manifestations of man (science, art, religion, etc.) are based on the unconscious activity of the existence (q.v.), that the irrational dominating the world is the source of supreme wisdom (*Vernunft und Existenz*, 1935). J.'s existentialism figures most prominently in his doctrine of border-line situations (q.v.). According to J., the real meaning of existence becomes clear to man only during periods of deep shock (illness, death, unatonable guilt, etc.). Precisely at this moment man becomes free from the burden of everyday cares and of his ideal interests and scientific views of reality. He faces a profoundly intimate existence (*Existen-*

zerhellung) and his true experience of (transcendental) God (*Philosophie*, 1932). The doctrine of border-line situations was used by J. to defend the cold war (*Die Atombombe und die Zukunft des Menschen*, 1958). In the 1950s, J. showed himself an open enemy of communism and a defender of reactionary regimes. His later works (*Wohin treibt die Bundesrepublik?*) testified to certain changes in his political views: J. began speaking against the authoritarianism and diktat of ruling parties, and against the introduction of emergency laws in Federal Republic of Germany.

Joliot-Curie, Frédéric (1900-1958), French physicist, Communist, Chairman of the World Peace Council (1951-58), member of the Paris Academy of Sciences, Corresponding Member of the Academy of Sciences of the USSR. His name is associated with major research into a new field of physics—the microcosm. His chief discovery (together with Irène Curie) was the phenomenon of artificial radioactivity; he also investigated the conversions of electron-positron pairs; and when the neutron was discovered he was one of the first to indicate the possibility of splitting atomic nuclei and making practical use of atomic energy. He was an adherent of dialectical materialism. The life and activities of Joliot-Curie may serve as an example of how important it is to master the up-to-date philosophical methods in order to promote scientific progress and to realise the scientist's social responsibility.

Judaism, religion of the Jews. It arose out of the pagan polytheism of the ancient Jewish tribes and became a monotheistic religion in the 7th century B.C. The characteristic features of J. are: belief in one god, Jehovah, belief in the Messiah (saviour), the dogma that the Jews are the chosen people and a multitude of ritual injunctions, covering almost all spheres of believers' daily life. The sources of J. are the Old Testament (also recognised by the Christians) and the Talmud (an intricate scholastic system of commentaries on the Old Testament). The church of J. is the synagogue. J. is the state religion of Israel. The religious philosophy of J. is imbued with messiahnistic mysticism. Some postulates of J. (the idea of the Jews being the chosen people, etc.) are used by Zionism, a reactionary nationalist movement of the Jewish bourgeoisie.

Judgment, an idea expressed in the form of a declarative sentence, which makes some assertion about objects and which is objectively either true or false. Examples of J.: "All planets revolve around the Sun", "If a number is divisible by 10, it is also divisible by 5", "Smith will pass his exam with excellent marks". The first two Jj. are true, whereas the third may prove to be true or false (depending on Smith's marks), although the speaker may have assumed that he was expressing a truth. A hypothesis (q.v.) is also a J. and may be objectively either true or false, although it is not yet proved or disproved. The laws of science are Jj., the truth of which has been proved. Ideas which cannot be characterised as true or false are not Jj. (questions, orders, requests, etc.). Jj. may be divided into simple and complex. Simple Jj. are those which within the limits of a logical system cannot be reduced to other Jj. Complex Jj. are made up of simple ones through various logical connectives, e.g., conjunctions "and" (see Conjunction), "if ... then" (see Implication). The truth or falsity of complex Jj. is the function of the truth or falsity of simple Jj.: by knowing the value of simple Jj., we can determine the value (truth or falsity) of complex Jj.

Justice and Injustice, normative concepts of morality (q.v.), which play a great part in socio-political consciousness. An actual or imaginary situation is described in terms of J.&I. as either proper and conforming to man's essence, rights and requirements, or as conflicting with them and, therefore, due to be eliminated. As distinct from the concepts of good and evil (q.v.), J.&I. are assessed, not merely as an individual phenomenon as a whole, but as a combination of several phenomena considered from the point of view of how good and evil are distributed among people. This concerns, in particular, the correlation between the role individual people (classes) play in society and their social position, between the work done and remuneration, deed and recompense, crime and punishment, people's merits and their social recognition, between rights and duties, etc. The content of the concepts of J.&I. is historically conditioned. Marx and Engels held that although the working masses share the concepts of J.&I., this is not tantamount to a conscious understanding of the objective historical laws. Therefore, the scientific theory of the history of society cannot base its conclusions on the concepts of J.&I. Nevertheless, these concepts reflect an elemental and instinctive awareness of the operation of these laws: for instance, the fact that the working masses come to see capitalist society as unjust serves as an indication of this system being historically outdated.

k

Kant, Immanuel (1724-1804), German philosopher and scientist, founder of classical German idealism. Founder of "critical" or "transcendental" idealism (q.v.). In the "pre-critical" period (prior to 1770) K. formulated his cosmogonic hypothesis, according to which the planetary system arose and developed out of a prime "nebula". At the same time K. advanced the hypothesis about the existence of a Great Universe of galaxies outside our Galaxy, developed the theories of the retardation of the Earth's rotation by tidal friction and the relativity of motion and rest. These studies, united by the materialist idea of natural development of the Universe and the Earth, played an important part in shaping dialectics (q.v.). In the philosophical works of the "pre-critical" period under the influence of the empiricism and scepticism of Hume (q.v.), K. noted the difference between real and logical causes, introduced in philosophy the concept of negative magnitudes and ridiculed the predilection of his contemporaries for mysticism and "spiritualism". In all these works the role of the formal deductive methods of thinking is restricted in favour of experience. In 1770, K. went over to the views of the "critical" period. His *Kritik der reinen Vernunft* appeared in 1781 and was followed by *Kritik der praktischen Vernunft* in 1788 and *Kritik der Urteilskraft* in 1790. In them K. consistently expounded: the "critical" theory of knowledge, ethics, aesthetics, and the doctrine of purpose in nature. In his works of the "critical" period K. proved the impossibility of constructing a system of speculative philosophy ("metaphysics" in the terminology of those days), without a preliminary study of the forms of cognition and the bounds of man's cognitive abilities. This study led K. to agnosticism (q.v.), to the assertion that the nature of things as

they exist of themselves ("things-in-themselves") is in principle inaccessible to human knowledge. Knowledge is possible only of "phenomena", i.e., the means through which things reveal themselves in our experience. True theoretical knowledge is available only in mathematics and natural science. According to K., an irrepressible striving for absolute knowledge is inherent in reason. Under the pressure of this striving, man's reason seeks to solve the problem of the finity or infinity of the world in time and space, the possibility of the existence of indivisible elements of the world, the nature of the processes taking place in the world, and of God as the absolutely essential being. K. held that opposite solutions can be equally demonstrable: the world is finite and is infinite; indivisible particles (atoms) exist and there are no such particles; all processes are causally conditioned, and there are processes (actions) that occur freely: an absolutely essential being exists and does not exist. Thus, reason is by its nature antinomic, i.e., is divided by contradictions. But these contradictions, according to K., are merely seeming. A solution of the enigma lies in limiting knowledge in favour of faith, in differentiating between "things-in-themselves" and "phenomena", in recognising that "things-in-themselves" are unknowable. Thus, man is simultaneously not free (as a being in a world of phenomena) and free (as a subject of the unknowable pretersensual world); the existence of God is undemonstrable (for knowledge), and at the same time it is the necessary postulate of faith, on which our conviction of the existence of moral order in the world rests, etc. This teaching on the antinomic nature of reason, which served K. as the basis for the dualism (q.v.) of the "things-in-themselves" and "phenomena" and for agnosticism, gave an impetus to the development of positive dialectics in classical German idealism. On the other hand, in the understanding of knowledge, behaviour, and creative effort this teaching remained a captive of dualism, agnosticism, and formalism (q.v.). For example, in ethics K. proclaimed as the basic law the categorical imperative (q.v.) which demands that man be guided by a rule which, being absolutely independent of the moral content of an action, could become a universal rule of behaviour. In aesthetics he reduced the beautiful (q.v.) to a "disinterested" pleasure which does not depend on whether the object depicted in a work of art exists or not and is determined solely by form. But K. was unable to apply his formalism consistently: in ethics, contrary to the formal nature of the categorical imperative, he put forward the principle of the self-value of each individual, which must not be sacrificed even for the good of society as a whole; in aesthetics, contrary to the formalism in understanding the beautiful, he declared poetry the highest form of art because it is able to portray the ideal. K.'s doctrines of the role of antagonisms in the historical process of social life and the need for eternal peace were progressive. He considered international trade and contacts with their mutual benefit for different states as a means of establishing and maintaining peace. Though abounding in contradictions, Kantianism considerably influenced the subsequent development of scientific and philosophical thought. In their criticism of K. the founders of Marxism-Leninism demonstrated that the social causes of his delusions, contradictions, and inconsistencies were rooted in the backwardness and weakness of the German bourgeoisie of that period. Bourgeois philosophers of the end of the 19th and in the first half of the 20th centuries, exploited K.'s inconsistencies and borrowed a number of his erroneous propositions to justify their own reactionary doctrines (see Neo-Kantianism; Socialism, Ethical; Marburg School; Baden School).

Karinsky, Mikhail Ivanovich (1840-1917), Russian logician and philosopher. Gravitated in his views towards materialism: *Yavleniye i deistvitelnost* (Phenomenon and Reality), 1878; *Logika* (Logic), 1884-85; and others. In his Doctor's thesis *Klassifikatsiya vyvodov* (Classification of Inferences), 1880, K. analysed syllogistic and inductive trends in logic and expressed original views on this question. In his *Ob istinakh samoochevidnykh* (Self-Evident Truths), 1893, K. criticised the dogmatism and apriorism of Kant's (q.v.) theory of knowledge. He repeatedly at-

tacked neo-Kantians (q.v.) including Vvedensky (q.v.) and also subjective idealists of the Berkeley (q.v.) type. K. is the author of a few works on the history of philosophy: *Lektsii po istorii drevnei filosofii* (Lectures on the History of Ancient Philosophy), 1885; *Lektsii po istorii novoi filosofii* (Lectures on the History of New Philosophy), 1884, etc.

Kautsky, Karl (1854-1938), German historian and economist; a leader and theoretician of the German Social-Democrats and the Second International, an ideologist of Centrism. At first K. was influenced by the ideas of Lassalle, anarchism (qq.v.) and the philosophy of positivism (q.v.). From the late 1870s K. actively contributed to the Social-Democratic press, and sided with Marxism, especially after his acquaintance with Marx and Engels in 1881. K. wrote a number of works — *Karl Marx ökonomische Lehren*, 1887; *Vorläufer des neueren Sozialismus*, 1895; *Die Agrarfrage*, 1899, *Der Ursprung des Christentums*, 1908; and others, which played a big part in spreading the ideas of Marxism. As Lenin put it, K. knew how to be a Marxist historian. But already then K. made opportunist errors and distorted Marxism, for which he was criticised by Engels. In 1910, K. formed a "central group" in the German Social-Democratic Party and after that openly opposed revolutionary Marxism, denying partisanship in Marxist philosophy. His work *Die Diktatur des Proletariats* (1918) was described by Lenin as a model of philistine distortion of Marxism and foul betrayal of it in deeds, while hypocritically recognising it in words. K. is the father of the anti-Marxist theory of "ultra-imperialism". Hostile to the socialist revolution in Russia, K. conducted anti-Soviet propaganda till his death. K.'s betrayal was condemned by Lenin in *The Proletarian Revolution and the Renegade Kautsky*. In his philosophical views K. was an eclectic, combining elements of materialism and idealism. In his *Die materialistische Geschichtsauffassung* in two volumes, 1927-29, K. distorted the theory of dialectical and historical materialism, in particular the question of classes and the state.

Kavelin, Konstantin Dmitriyevich (1818-1885), Russian idealist philosopher, historian, and politician. In his youth was a Westerner (q.v.) and an admirer of Belinsky and Herzen (qq.v.). In the 1850s became a liberal, which led to his break with the editors of the *Sovremennik* (The Contemporary) and Herzen. Turned to philosophy in the 1860s to substantiate his political and ethical views. In his *Zadacha Psikhologii* (The Aim of Psychology), 1872, and *Zadachi Etiki* (Aims of Ethics), 1885, tried to accommodate psychology in order to justify Christian ethics. Philosophy, in his opinion, should become the science of the individual human soul, the psychology which explains the moral, spiritual world regardless of the material carrier. K. supported the idea of freedom of will (q.v.). The unsoundness of K.'s theory was demonstrated by Sechenov (q.v.) in his remarks on K.'s *Aim of Psychology*.

Khomyakov, Alexei Stepanovich (1804-1860), Russian writer and idealist philosopher, one of the founders of Slavophilism. K. opposed materialism and criticised classical German idealism. He adhered to objective-idealist views which assumed the form of religious mystical voluntarism (q.v.). He regarded the ideal, rational, and free element as the prime principle of all that exists. This element could not be cognised with man's usual means of knowledge, sensations and reason, but with the help of religion. As regards society, K. adhered to the doctrine of providentialism (q.v.) and advocated the union of individuals congregated in the name of God and love. An ideologist of the Russian liberal nobility, K., though criticising to some extent the Russian social order and welcoming the abolition of serfdom through reforms, held that autocracy was indispensable for the preservation and development of Russia.

Kierkegaard, Sören (1813-1855), Danish religious philosopher, precursor of existentialism (q.v.). A disciple of the German romanticists, K. eventually opposed both romantic sentiment, which he called "aesthetic", and German idealist philosophy, above all that of Hegel (q.v.). He considered Hegel as the head of the school of speculative philosophers who reasoned from the viewpoint of the universal—mankind, people, the state—and excluded the ontological significance of the personal principle. The latter, according to K., cannot be understood if viewed from the standpoint of philosophy which takes society as the starting point, as was the case with Hegel, for then we lose what is most essential, what constitutes the basis of the personality, its existence (q.v.). Genuine philosophy, K. held, can be only "existential", i.e., have a profoundly personal character. Regarding man as an "existence", K. introduced such concepts as "fear", "despondency", and "resolution", which were subsequently developed by the existentialists. K. recognised three modes of existence of the individual, or three types of existence, aesthetic, ethical and religious, and considered the last as the highest. The basic category of K.'s religious doctrine is "paradox". Since, according to K., the divine world and the human world are in principle incommensurable, faith implies rejection of logical thinking and introduces one into the sphere of "paradoxes", which are absurd from the angle of human logic and ethics. K. severely criticised any attempt at combining these two spheres or compromising between them; this caused his conflict with the official church in the last years of his life. K.'s ideas not only served as a source of existentialism; his religious doctrine also influenced K. Barth's dialectical theology (q.v.) and the teachings of other Protestant and Catholic philosophers. Main works: *Euten-Eller* (1843), *Furcht und Zittern* (1843), *Begrebet Angst* (1844), and *Sygdommen til Doden* (1849).

Kinship with the People in Art, an aesthetic category used to describe the specific quality of art (q.v.) of being a reflection of creative activity of the people, their artistic tastes and emotional experience. Directly or indirectly, true art embodies the aesthetic ideals of the people, their understanding of justice and beauty and the fervour of the people's revolutionary struggle for freedom and happiness. It is a historical concept and its content is determined by the specific conditions and stages of social development, the place and role of art in society. Artistic endeavour is an important sphere of the working people's activities. The collective creative endeavour of the people is the basis and inexhaustible source of professional art. K.P.A. in artistic endeavour stems from the wisdom of the people and reflects their struggle for emancipation. By their creative work artists help the people in their struggle often without being aware of it. Marxist-Leninist aesthetics considers K.P.A. in unity with the principle of partisanship (q.v.) in art. An artist, aspiring to K.P.A. in his works, is bound to take a definite ideological-aesthetical stand, i.e., to join the class or political party which is most consistent in voicing the interests of the people.

Kireyevsky, Ivan Vasilyevich (1806-1856), Russian publicist and idealist philosopher, one of the founders of Slavophilism (see Slavophiles); was close to the circle of Lovers of Wisdom (q.v.). Edited the journals *Yevropeyets* (The European), 1832, and *Moskvityanin* (The Muscovite), 1845. According to K., who adhered to an antirationalist, religious and intuitionist theory of knowledge, the life of individuals, nations, and groups of nations, for example, the Slavs, West Europeans, etc., is founded on religion, which determines the education and the entire life of a nation. Since the Orthodox religion professed by the Slavs, chiefly the Russians, is the true religion, the future belongs only to the Slavs. The other peoples could make progress only if they accepted the Orthodox Christian civilisation. Otherwise civilisation would disintegrate (in K.'s opinion, this is what happened in Western Europe). K. regarded non-resistance to evil, the absence of class stratification, and communal life in the village (which he idealised) as distinctive features of the Russian people. Though he criticised certain aspects of European philosophy (e.g., its metaphysical nature) and bourgeois civilisation (e.g., self-interestedness, egoism), on the whole K.'s views were utopian-conservative both in sociology and politics.

Knowledge, a product of social material and intellectual activity of people; an ideal reproduction in sign form of objective properties and connections in the world, of the natural and the human. K. can be either pre-scientific (everyday) or scientific. The latter is divided into empirical and theoretical. Moreover, there exists in society mythological, artistic, religious and other K. The essence of K. cannot be understood without revealing the dependence of man's activity on his socio-historical conditions. Man's social power is accumulated, crystallised and objectivised in K. This fact has furnished the basis for objective idealist theories about the primacy and self-sufficient character of man's intellectual activity. Pre-Marxist philosophers contraposed to the idealist mystification of K. their own understanding of K. as a result of individual cognitive efforts, of individual experience. But such a view could not explain the fact that man begins the process of cognition in the context of real social relations, possessing a "ready-made" apparatus of concepts and categories elaborated by society. It is a direct function of K. to convert scattered concepts into a theoretically systematised universal form, retaining in them that which may be preserved, passed on to others and developed successively as a stable basis for man's activity.

Komensky, Jan Amos, or Comenius (1592-1670), Czech pedagogue, humanist, and philosopher, opponent of the scholastic system of education, leader of a group of the Moravian Brothers, a sect formed in the course of the anti-feudal movement and national struggle against the German feudal lords and the Catholic Church. He was a Protestant close to pantheism (q.v.). There were considerable materialist tendencies in his sensationalist theory of knowledge. Cognition, according to K., is an active process closely connected with rational education. All people, he asserted, are capable of knowledge and education. The ordinary people should be given access to knowledge. For the first time in the history of pedagogics K.

created a system of didactics as a special science. His didactic principles (visual presentation, gradation, imitation, exercise) demanded deep knowledge of the laws of nature and rationally organised assimilation of knowledge. K.'s progressive views exerted great influence on the subsequent development of pedagogics. His main works are *Janua linguarum reserata*, 1631, and *Didactica Magna*, 1657.

Konissky, Georgi (Grigory Osipovich) (1717-1795), writer and philosopher, Orthodox Church leader in Byelorussia, opposed Uniatism. Studied and later taught at the Kiev-Mogilyanskaya Academy, a major scientific and cultural centre of the Ukraine, Byelorussia and Russia (1632-1817) where he delivered a course of lectures "General philosophy, divided into four sections comprising logic, physics, metaphysics and ethics...", which, alongside Aristotelian principles, contained elements of the philosophy of the postmedieval period. In his works advocated unity of Byelorussia and Russia, defended the principle of toleration. Leaning towards deism (q.v.), K. opposed submission of reason to faith, and at the same time acknowledged the ontological proof (q.v.) of the existence of God. He considered reason to be the criterion of moral behaviour and believed that man's aim was to strive for happiness. In his views of society K. championed enlightened absolutism.

Kovalevsky, Maxim Maximovich (1851-1916), Russian sociologist, historian, jurist, and politician. K. was a supporter of classical positivism (q.v.) and one of the organisers of the Moscow Psychological Society (1884). K. was familiar with the ideas of Marx and Engels, as can be seen in his works and in the interest he took in the history of landownership and the economic development of Europe: *Obshchinnoye zemlevladeniye. Prichiny, khod i posledstviya yego razlozheniya* (Communal Landownership. Causes, Course and Consequences of Its Disintegration), 1879; *Ekonomichesky rost Yevropy do vozniknoveniya kapitalisticheskogo khoziaistva* (Economic Growth of Europe up to the Rise of the Capitalist Economy), 1898-1903. Engels positively assessed K.'s studies on the history of the family. In his historical works, which contained extensive factual material, K. elaborated the historico-comparative method (q.v.). He analysed sociological doctrines in his books: *Sovremenniye sotsiologi* (Contemporary Sociologists), 1905; *Sotsiologiya* (Sociology), 2 vols., 1910. K. was a proponent of the theory of social progress, which he saw in the development of solidarity between peoples, classes and groups. This solidarity, according to K., arises by virtue of numerous causes (economic, social, political), among which it is impossible to single out the main and determining factor. A historian should limit himself to recording the interaction and co-relationship in the development of social phenomena. K. was largely influenced by theories which biologised social progress and also by bourgeois socialism of the chair (q.v.). Denial of revolutionary methods of reconstructing society was their common feature. K. sought to justify Russian liberalism and conciliation of democracy with the monarchy. His political activities were criticised by Lenin.

Kozelsky, Yakov Pavlovich (c. 1728-1794), Russian enlightener and philosopher; author of *Filosoficheskye predlozheniya* (Philosophical Propositions), 1768; *Rassuzhdeniya o chelovecheskom poznanii* (Discourse on Human Knowledge), 1788. He advocated materialist ideas and criticised medieval scholasticism (q.v.) and mysticism, separated philosophy from theology and held that philosophy should give "general knowledge of things and human deeds". In his view of nature K. developed the ideas of 18th-century mechanistic materialism. Declaring nature the "universal mother of all things", K. proved that nature consists of four material elements and that matter and motion are indestructible. He considered sense perceptions the initial element in the theory of knowledge, assigning a big role to experience and the activity of reason. He divided all knowledge into historical, philosophical, and mathematical, and the truths obtained by people into natural, ethical, and logical. K. criticised the religious mystical aspects of the theory of monads, pre-established harmony (qq.v.) and Christian non-resistance to evil. He criticised serfdom, idleness, and parasitism and extolled labour, a modest mode of life, and a humane attitude to people.

Krause, Karl Friedrich (1781-1832), a German idealist philosopher, close to the Freemasons, who purported to unite people on the principles of religious brotherhood and love. His philosophy claimed to have overcome the "extremes" of materialism and idealism. According to K., the world was created by God and rests in God, without merging, however, with Him. The most perfect part of the world is man, who combines the natural and rational principles. The individual is the basis and part of the family, people and mankind. The life of these communities is regulated by natural law, whose motive principle is moral progress of mankind. Hence the need for a world alliance of nations. K.'s philosophy was not popular in his country, but was widespread in Belgium, Spain and Latin American countries, where representatives of so-called Krausism fought against the Catholic church and for the development of education. His works are *Das Urbild der Menschheit* (1811), *Entwurf des Systems der Philosophie* (1828) and others.

Kropotkin, Pyotr Alexeyevich (1842-1921), Russian theoretician of anarchism (q.v.) and geographer. In the 1870s, K. joined the Narodnik movement (see Narodism). During the First World War K. was a chauvinist, opposed Marxism and the dictatorship of the proletariat, but at the end of his life acknowledged the historical significance of the October Revolution. He developed the theory of so-called anarchist communism, which allegedly could be introduced in a stateless form immediately after the destruction of the old order in the course of a social revolution; he considered the latter to be a natural phenomenon in the historical process. For K., the society of the future was to be a federation of free productive communities (communes) in which the individual freed from guardianship by the state would have unlimited opportunities for development. K.'s philosophical views were a blending of positivism (q.v.) and mechanistic materialism. Contrary to the Marxist conception of history, K. proclaimed the conception of abstract solidarity and mutual aid, which he deduced from the biological and psychological conditions in which organisms exist and considered to be the corner-stone of social and moral progress. Repudiating dialectics, K. considered the inductive-deductive method of natural science to be the only scientific method of thinking. He was considerably influenced by the theories of Proudhon and Bakunin (qq.v.) and the positivism of Comte and Spencer (qq.v.). Main works: *Khleb i Volya* (Bread and Freedom), 1892; *Vzaimnaya pomoshch, kak faktor evolyutsii* (Mutual Aid as a Factor of Evolution), 1902; *Velikaya Frantsuzskaya Revolutsia* (The Great French Revolution), 1909; *Sovremennaya nauka i anarkhia* (Modern Science and Anarchy), 1913; *Etika* (Ethics), 1922 and others.

1

Labour is, in the first place, a process in which man of his own accord starts, regulates, and controls metabolism between himself and nature (K. Marx, *Capital*, Vol. I, p. 177). Man purposefully acts on the objects of nature and changes them. His attitude to nature is one aspect of L. By changing external nature, man also changes his own nature. The adaptation of objects to man's requirements (q.v.) implies, above all, the change of external nature. L. consists of the following elements: (1) man's purposeful activity, or L. proper; (2) the object of L.; (3) means of L. L. aimed at the transformation of nature comes to a head when all its elements are created by L. and are not given in a ready-made form. The development of L. is a historical process. It cannot be considered completed if it is performed in society chiefly to sustain physical existence. L. becomes completely mature when it is caused by the very need of L., while the sustenance of physical existence becomes its necessary prerequisite. As a means of changing external nature L. is the main condition of the specifically human existence. Its becoming was a fundamental process of man's emergence from the animal world, the formation of a modern biological type of man and of man as a social being. The other aspect of L. is the social character of people's attitude to each other regarding the conditions, process, and result of L. attitude towards nature. This aspect of L. develops on the basis of, and in harmony with, the first one, but is not reduced to it. The unity of the aspects is realised in the co-operation and division of L. (q.v.). Throughout history the interconnection between these aspects has been changing, and the ideas about L. have been changing accordingly. L. appears in different forms in different types of historical development (pre-class, class and classless) and in different socio-economic formations (q.v.). In the primitive-communal system (q.v.) L. is communal, and property (q.v.) in the means of production and its fruits is also communal. Under this system, there is no exploitation of the labour of others. In all the antagonistic class societies L. develops through the development of antagonistic contradictions. The transition from the less to more developed forms of L.—from the L. of slaves in slave-owning society to the L. of serfs under feudalism, and to wage labour under capitalism—was also the transition to more developed forms of exploitation. The development of human culture was accompanied by the more and more developed, subtle and refined spiritual and physical mutilation of man. Only socialist revolution (q.v.) liberates working people from exploitation, and abolishes it. Only under communism, especially in its higher phase, L. will be developed to the full extent; while remaining the source of subsistence, L. will become mainly the process of satisfying the inner need of every individual for free and all-round development, which is a condition for the free and comprehensive development of all people (see Communist Labour; Mental and Physical Labour).

Labriola, Antonio (1843-1904), first Italian Marxist; writer and philosopher. L. became a Marxist after having rejected bourgeois democratism and the idealism of Hegel. He asserted that with the advent of historical materialism communism had ceased to be a "doubtful hypothesis" and could now be regarded as the inevitable "final result and outcome of the class struggle of our times". L. regarded the publication of the *Manifesto of the Communist Party* as a revolution in the social sciences. He criticised the theories of Nietzsche, E. Hartmann, Croce, and neo-Kantianism (qq.v.). His philosophical and sociological views are not free from errors (elements of agnosticism, q.v., underestimation of dialectics, etc.). His best work, *Saggi intorno alla concepzione materialistica della storia* (1895-98; 1925—posthumous edition), greatly influenced the thinking of A. Gramsci and P. Togliatti.

Lafargue, Paul (1842-1911), French socialist, active in the international working-class movement, disciple of Marx and Engels. His main work was in philosophy and political economy, the history of religion and morals, literature and language. Lenin said that L. was one of the most gifted propagators of the ideas of Marxism. Having become a member of the First International in 1866, L. freed himself of Proudhonist and positivist views. He took a prominent part in the activity of the Paris Commune; later associated with Jules Guesde, both of them becoming leaders of the French Workers' Party. L. fought anarchism and the opportunist theory of capitalism "growing peacefully" into socialism and criticised the reformist and nationalistic errors of Guesde. In his major philosophical work *Le déterminisme économique de Karl Marx* (1909) L. stressed the objective nature of the laws of history and revealed the interconnection between the economy and the superstructure of society. He opposed revisionist attempts to "synthesise" Marxism with the doctrine of Kant and "reconcile" materialism with idealism. He also opposed social-Darwinism and other bourgeois theories. His book *Das Problem der Erkenntnis* (1910) was a profound and witty repudiation of agnosticism. L.'s anti-religious pamphlets *La religion du capital* and others exposed religion as a defender of capitalism. His reminiscences of Marx, giving a picture of the great fighter and thinker, are of considerable interest. L.'s works, despite a number of defects (simplification of certain problems, underestimation of the active part played by the superstructure, failure to fully comprehend the specific features of the imperialist stage of capitalism, etc.) played an important part in the struggle against bourgeois ideology.

La Mettrie, Julien Offroy de (1709-1751), French materialist philosopher and physician. L.'s teaching was based on the physics of Descartes (q.v.) and the sensationalism of Locke (q.v.). L. regarded the world as an internally active material substance possessing extent and sensation. The forms of matter were the inorganic, vegetable and animal kingdoms (man being included in the animal kingdom). L. understood the thinking process, proper to man alone and resulting from his complex organisation, as the comparison and combination of conceptions arising on the basis of sensation and memory. An exponent of mechanism (q.v.), L. moved nearer to the theory of evolution. He held that the enlightenment and the actions of outstanding individuals are the main causes of historical development and advocated enlightened absolutism. Though an atheist, and persecuted as such, he nevertheless considered it necessary to preserve religion for the common people. Main works: *L'homme machine* (1747) and *Le Système d'Epicure* (1750).

Langevin, Paul (1872-1946), French physicist, public figure, Communist, advocate of dialectical materialism. Author of several major researches on the ionisation of gases, the theory of magnetism, etc. In 1939 he founded *La Pensée* journal in order to propagate the "ideas of modern rationalism". L. criticised positivist theories, indeterminism, and subjectivist interpretations of the uncertainty principle (q.v.).

Language, a sign-system fulfilling the cognitive and communicative functions (see Intercourse) in the process of human activity. L. can be natural and artificial. Natural L. is the L. of everyday life, a means by which human beings convey thoughts and communicate with each other. Artificial L. is created by people for some narrow needs (as mathematical symbols, systems of signalisation, etc.). L. is a social phenomenon arising in the course of development of social production and is its indispensable aspect—a means of co-ordination of human activity. From the point of view of physiology L. is the second signal system (see I. Pavlov). As a form of existence and conveying thoughts L. plays an essential role in forming consciousness (q.v.). The L. sign, conventional in relation to what it designates by virtue of its physical nature, is nevertheless in the final count conditioned by the process of cognition of reality. Information is accumulated, preserved and passed on from generation to generation with the help of L. L. is instrumental in the development of abstract thought and its generalisation. However, L. and thought are not identical. Once it has arisen, L. is relatively independent and obeys its own specific laws, the laws that differ from the laws of thought. Therefore, there is no identity between word and concept, sentence and judgment. Furthermore L. is an organised system of signs with its own peculiar structure, outside of which the nature and meaning of a L. sign cannot be understood. Due to the growing scope of theoretical research in recent decades more interest is shown in the study of artificial, formalised languages, of their logical syntax and logical semantics (qq.v.). For this reason L. has become the object of study of linguistics, logic and semiotic (q.v.). Contemporary neo-positivism (q.v.) absolutises the role and significance of these studies and tries, incorrectly, to reduce the problems involved in philosophical studies to a logical analysis of L.

Laplace, Pierre Simon de (1749-1827), French scientist, mathematician and astronomer. His philosophy was mechanistic materialism, atheism. Proved that the Solar system was stable and consequently needed no periodical interference of a creator to restore its equilibrium. He made an important contribution to the development of materialism and atheism by proving mathematically that the Solar system had its origin in a primary nebula. L. gave a classical definition, often called Laplacian, of mechanistic determinism (q.v.), developed some propositions of the theory of probability, etc. Main works: *Exposition du Système du Monde* (1795), *Théorie analytique des probabilités* (1812).

Lassalle, Ferdinand (1825-1864), prominent figure in the German working-class movement, founder of the Lassallean trend in opportunism. He took part in the revolution of 1848. L. was one of the organisers of the General Association of German Workers in 1860. His agitation for workers' unity played a positive role, but on the whole L. repudiated the class struggle. Being an idealist, he regarded the state as a supra-class organisation. He interpreted Hegel scholastically, using his philosophy to justify his own opportunist political line and actual agreement with the

Prussian monarchy. In sociology L. adhered to the views of Malthusianism (q.v.) and was one of the authors of the anti-scientific "iron law of wages", according to which any struggle of the workers for wage increases was considered futile. L.'s views were criticised by Marx in his *Critique of the Gotha Programme* (q.v.) and by Lenin in the *Philosophical Notebooks* (q.v.). Main works: *Die Philosophie Herakleitos des Dunklen von Ephesos* (1858), *System der erworbenen Rechte* (1861).

Lavrov, Pyotr Lavrovich (1823-1900), theoretician of Narodism (q.v.), founder of the Russian "subjectivist school" in sociology, and writer. He participated in the work of illegal revolutionary organisations such as Zemlya i Volya (Land and Freedom) and Narodnaya Volya (People's Will). He was a member of the First International. While in London, he became acquainted with Marx and Engels. L. wrote and spoke on problems of philosophy, sociology, ethics, the history of social thought, and art. L.'s chief interest lay in the ways of the revolution in Russia. Admitting that the Marxist theory of socialist revolution was valid for the developed capitalist countries of Europe, L. was sceptical about its applicability to the conditions prevailing in Russia. His socio-political doctrine (influenced by Herzen, q.v.) rested on two interdependent ideas: (1) the socialist nature of the Russian peasant community, and (2) the special role of the intelligentsia in the Russian emancipation movement. These ideas determined L.'s whole philosophico-historical conception. According to L., "the critically thinking individuals" are the vehicles of civilisation. The measure of the critical enlightenment of human consciousness (primarily moral consciousness) is the criterion of progress. Social development implies the growth of the individual's consciousness and of the solidarity between individuals. Philosophically, L. was eclectic, combining materialism and idealism. Influenced by positivism and agnosticism (qq.v.), he gravitated to subjective idealism. Main works: *Istoricheskiye pisma* (Historical Letters), 1869; *Tsel i znacheniye klassifikatsii nauk* (The Purpose and Importance of the Classification of Sciences), 1886; *Zadachi positivisma i ikh resheniye* (Tasks of Positivism and Their Solution), 1886; *Vazhneishiye momenty v istorii mysli* (Essential Moments in the History of Thought), 1899.

Law 1. An inner essential and stable interconnection of phenomena which conditions their requisite development. Knowledge of L. makes it possible to foresee the process. The concept of L. is close to the concept of regularity, which is a totality of laws interrelated in terms of content and ensuring a stable tendency or direction in the changes of the system. But at the same time L. is an expression of one side of the essence (q.v.), the cognition of which in theory coincides with the transition from empirical facts to the formulation of laws governing the processes under study. There are many types of Ll. in the objective world. Some of them express functional interconnections between the properties of the object (e.g., the L. of interconnection of mass and energy), others demonstrate the mutual relations between material objects in large systems (e.g., the L. of electromagnetic and gravitation interrelations), between the systems themselves or between various states or stages in the development of systems (e.g., the L. of transition from quantity to quality, q.v.). Laws are also classified by the degree of their community and the sphere of operation. Particular, or specific, laws express relations between concrete physical, chemical or biological properties of bodies. General laws characterise relations between universal properties and attributes (q.v.) of matter. They manifest themselves on all known structural levels of matter and are studied by dialectical materialism, physics, cybernetics, biology, etc. All phenomena obey certain laws, everything is determined and conditioned by objective laws. There are different forms and laws of determination. If the former states of a system predetermine its development only in one direction, then the changes of such system are subject to dynamic Ll., to unambiguous determination. If in a complex system the former states predetermine the latter ones in many ways, then the changes taking place

in such a system are subordinated to the probabilistically statistical Ll. In nature, Ll. operate objectively, independent of people's consciousness, as a result of the objective interaction of material bodies. In society, all social Ll. are applied purposefully by consciously acting people, the subjective factor. The application of this or that L. depends on the corresponding conditions. The creation of the latter makes possible the transition of the consequences of a given L. from the probable into the real sphere. People, however, do not invent Ll., they only restrict or extend the scope of their operation according to their needs or interests. As for Ll. as such, they exist objectively, independently of the consciousness of people, as an expression of the essential, inner relations between properties of things or different tendencies of development. 2. The will of the ruling class given the statutory force and determined by the material conditions and interests of that class. L. is institutionalised as a system of rules and standards of behaviour, established or sanctioned by state authority. The fulfilment of legal rules is forcibly ensured by the state (q.v.). Being part of the superstructure, L. is determined by the given society's dominant relations of production, which it sanctions and gives embodiment to together with other social relations based on them. The historical type of L. corresponds to the relevant socioeconomic formation (q.v.). The common feature of slave-owning, feudal and bourgeois L. is the consolidation of the master and subordinate relations, the relations of exploitation, based on private property. Slave-owning and feudal L. overtly fixed the rule of minority over majority and the privileged position of the dominant classes. Bourgeois L. is hypocritical for it embodies and consolidates the actual rights of capitalists, giving the working people formal rights. With the advent of imperialism the bourgeoisie more and more often resorts to extralegal methods of subjugation, abandoning rule of law it had established. In an antagonistic class society, the class struggle exerts influence on the existing laws and they, to some extent, reflect the alignment of class forces. The concessions won by the working people from the ruling class do not change the class content of L. A qualitatively new type of L. is socialist L., which legally embodies production relations based on socialist property and characterised by friendly co-operation and mutual aid and which is instrumental in the building of communism. Socialist L. is the will of the people given the statutory force; for the first time in history it establishes and really guarantees truly democratic liberties. It differs from bourgeois L. in that it provides the working people with genuine rights, guaranteed by all the means at the disposal of the state.

Laws, Statistical and Dynamic, forms of law-governed connection between the preceding and subsequent states of the systems. D.L. is a form of causal connection as well as connection between the states, in which the given condition of the system determines unequivocally all of its subsequent conditions. Due to this, knowledge of the initial conditions permits accurately to predict the further development of the system. D.L. is operative in all autonomous systems composed of a relatively small number of elements and dependent little on outside influences. It determines, e.g., the nature of the motion of planets in the solar system. S.L. is a form of causal connection, in which the given condition of the system determines all of its subsequent conditions, not unequivocally, but with a definite degree of probability, which objectively indicates to what extent the constitutional propensity for change may be realised. S.L. is operative in all non-autonomous systems composed of a very large number of elements and dependent on ever changing external conditions. There is only a relative difference between S.L. and D.L., for, strictly speaking, each D.L. is a S.L. possessing the occurrence probability close to one. This is caused by the fact that each material system is inexhaustible, consists of innumerable elements of matter, has a variety of external ties, and, as time goes on, is subject to qualitative change.

Leap, a radical change in a thing or phenomenon, when its old quality is changed into a new one as a result of

quantitative changes (see Transition from Quantity to Quality). In comparison with the preceding, evolutionary stage of development, the L. represents more or less apparent, relatively quick changes. Any qualitative change can be brought about by a L. only. But the L. may take on exceptionally diverse forms, depending on the character of the phenomena and on the conditions in which it develops. Essentially, every phenomenon assumes a new quality in a way of its own. But all these transitions can be divided into two relatively definite types: sudden and gradual Ll. (which often combine in one and the same process). The former take place in such a manner that the old quality is fully changed at once (e.g., the change-over of certain elementary particles into others; in social life, a social revolution may serve as an example of a sudden, abrupt leap). The latter takes place in such a way that a thing or phenomenon changes by parts, by individual elements, until, as a result of gradual mutation, it is transformed as a whole. In nature this is predominantly the way in which qualitative changes occur in animal and plant species. In social life, the first type of L. is characteristic of antagonistic formations, in which the dominant class is an obstacle to the historically urgent transition from the old to a new system. Such a transition (for instance, from capitalism to socialism) can be accomplished only by a political revolution. The second type of L. is principally typical of non-antagonistic systems, in which all the main social forces are interested in society's progressive development. This is what Marx had in mind when he foretold that in a classless society social evolution would cease to be a political revolution. The CPSU proceeds from the fact that gradual qualitative change is a law of communist construction. The creation of the material and technical basis of communism, the obliteration of class and other distinctions, the withering away of the state, the education of the new man, are all decisive revolutionary steps in the development of socialist society, which do not take place at once and all of a sudden, but gradually and continuously. Nevertheless, the gradual transition from socialism to communism does not preclude quick, sudden Ll. in some fields, for instance, in technology and science.

"Legal Marxism", a reflection of Marxism to be found in bourgeois literature, a liberal-bourgeois distortion of the actual doctrine. It arose in the 1890s, when Marxism was becoming a leading trend in Russian social thought. Some bourgeois intellectuals became temporary "fellow travellers" of the working-class movement. Their writings were published in legal newspapers and journals, i.e., publications appearing with the sanction of the government, such as *Novoye Slovo* (New Word), *Nachalo* (The Beginning) and others, and they thus became known as "legal Marxists". They used certain Marxist propositions to criticise the Narodniks. For the "legal Marxists" the break with Narodism meant going over from peasant socialism not to proletarian socialism but to bourgeois liberalism. Struve, Berdyayev (qq.v.) and others were prominent representatives of "L.M.". They attempted to adapt the workers' movement to the interests of the bourgeoisie, lavished praise on the bourgeois system, and advocated learning from capitalism. "L.M." repudiated the principal Marxist tenets (the doctrine of the class struggle and proletarian revolution and the dictatorship of the proletariat). Lenin showed the anti-Marxist essence of "L.M." and made a profound criticism of bourgeois objectivism, to which he counterposed the partisanship of revolutionary Marxism. In philosophy the "legal Marxists" usually adopted neo-Kantian positions (see Vekhism).

Leibniz, Gottfried Wilhelm (1646-1716), German philosopher, scientist and public figure, made a great contribution to mathematics (he was one of the inventors of the differential calculus) and physics (he anticipated the law of the conservation of energy); he was also a geologist, biologist, historian, linguist and the author of several technical inventions. His philosophical evolution began with mechanistic materialism. But dissatisfied with the passive character of substance (q.v.) in terms of this world outlook, he went over to objective idealism, which found its expression in the theory of monads (q.v.) (*Monadologie*, 1714). According to L., matter cannot be substance, as it is extensive and divisible while substance must be absolutely simple. The monads are the indivisible, spiritual substances, of which the whole Universe is composed. Infinite in number, all monads are percipient, mobile and self-active. This is the dialectics of his teaching, but his dialectics was idealistic and theological. The monads, in his view, cannot have any physical influence on one another and yet they form a single developing and moving world, which is regulated by a pre-established harmony (q.v.) depending on the supreme monad (the absolute, God). The concept of pre-established harmony formed the most reactionary part of L.'s philosophy. L.'s theory of knowledge—idealist rationalism—was aimed against the sensationalism and empiricism of Locke (q.v.). Not sharing Locke's view that the mind is but a blank sheet *(tabula rasa)* and denying that sense experience is the source of the universality and necessity of knowledge, L. contended that only reason can be that source (*Nouveaux essais sur l'entendement humain*, 1704). In effect, L. modified the Cartesian doctrine of innate ideas (q.v.), which he described as residing in the mind. L. held that the criterion of truth is clarity of knowledge, the absence of contradictions in it. Accordingly, to test the truths of reason it was enough to apply the logic of Aristotle (the laws of identity, contradiction, and the excluded middle); while the law of sufficient reason was needed to test "truths of fact". L. is considered the founder of modern mathematical logic (q.v.). In his opinion, it would be ideal to create a universal language (see Calculus) and formalise all thinking. In his socio-political activity he tended to compromise between the German bourgeoisie and the feudal class.

Lemma, something taken for granted or assumed in logic, a preliminary assumption (premise of a syllogism). Depending on the number of conditional statements in the major premise, the L. becomes a dilemma (q.v.), trilemma or multilemma. The most common form of L.

is the dilemma, implying the need to choose between two alternatives (q.v.).

Lenin, Vladimir Ilyich (1870-1924), continuator of Marx and Engels, leader of the Russian and international proletariat, founder of the Communist Party of the Soviet Union and the Soviet state. Born in Simbirsk (now Ulyanovsk). After finishing the Gymnasium (secondary school) in 1887, he entered the law faculty of Kazan University, but was arrested for his activities in the student movement, exiled and placed under police surveillance. In 1891, he graduated as an external student at St. Petersburg University. In Kazan (1888-89) and Samara (1889-93) L. studied Marxism and became a Marxist, organising the first Marxist circle in Samara. Went to St. Petersburg in 1893 and became leader of the local Marxists. In 1894, he wrote his first major work *What the "Friends of the People" Are and How They Fight the Social-Democrats*, in which he proved the insolvency of the theory and tactics of Narodism and showed the working class of Russia the true path of struggle. In 1895, he united the Marxist groups of St. Petersburg in the League of Struggle for the Emancipation of the Working Class. Soon afterwards L. was arrested and imprisoned, then banished to Siberia. Early in 1900, he emigrated. Abroad he founded *Iskra* (The Spark), the first all-Russian Marxist newspaper, which played an enormous part in forming a Marxist party of a new type and working out its first programme, and in the struggle against reformists and opportunists. The Second Congress of the RSDLP in 1903 saw the inauguration of the Bolshevik Party, which under Lenin's guidance led the proletariat and the toiling peasantry in the struggle to overthrow the tsarist autocracy and replace it by a socialist social system. The milestones in this struggle were the bourgeois-democratic revolution of 1905, the February bourgeois-democratic revolution of 1917, and the victorious October Socialist Revolution in 1917. The great service Lenin rendered was that he creatively developed the Marxist teaching with reference to the new historical conditions, and gave it a concrete form on the basis of the practical experience of the Russian revolutions and the international revolutionary movement since the death of Marx and Engels. In *Imperialism, the Highest Stage of Capitalism* (1916) Lenin continued the analysis of the capitalist mode of production which Marx had made in *Capital* (q.v.) and discovered the laws governing the economic and political development of capitalism in the era of imperialism. The creative spirit of Leninism was expressed in his theory of the socialist revolution (q.v.). He proved that in the new conditions socialism could be victorious at first in one or several countries. He evolved the doctrine of the party of the proletariat as a leading and organising force of the nation without which there could be no dictatorship of the proletariat or building of communist society. L. became head of the first proletarian state, which was able to survive in the struggle against internal and foreign enemies and to begin building socialism. Developing the ideas of Marx and Engels, L. drew up a concrete programme of socialist construction in the USSR, which became a guide for the Communist Party and the whole Soviet people. L.'s name is associated with a new stage in the development of all the components of Marxism; philosophy (dialectical and historical materialism); political economy; and scientific communism. From the outset he paid great attention to the further development of dialectical and historical materialism. Marxist philosophy was his means of solving every problem that confronted the working class and its Party in the new age, and he enriched that philosophy with many new ideas. In 1908, he wrote his fundamental philosophical work *Materialism and Empirio-Criticism* (q.v.) in which he gave a profound analysis of the latest achievements of natural science in the light of dialectical materialism and developed the basic principles of Marxist philosophy, particularly its theory of knowledge. His criticism of Machism has lost none of its significance today and teaches Marxists how to fight reactionary philosophy. With an urgency unprecedented in this field L. posed the question of partisanship (q.v.) in philosophy and demanded that Marxists fight consistently against any and every type of idealism or metaphysics. He worked particularly hard to develop and perfect materialist dialectics. He showed the versatility of dialectics as a theory of development and substantiated the extremely important postulate on the unity of dialectics, logic, and the theory of knowledge. L. put forward a host of valuable ideas, which may be regarded as a programme of further work on dialectics (see *Philosophical Notebooks*). His works covering the most diverse fields of economics, politics, strategy, and tactics provide unsurpassed models of the application of dialectics to real life. In his article "On the Significance of Militant Materialism", q.v. (1922), L. outlined important tasks that must be undertaken for the further development of Marxist philosophy, including the struggle against the religious view of the world, which retain their importance even today. L. considered the materialist understanding of history the greatest achievement of Marxist philosophy. He regarded the theory of historical materialism as a scientific basis for getting to know the laws of social development and revolutionary struggle for the socialist transformation of society. His creative study of the economic, political, and spiritual development of society in the new age developed all aspects of Marxist sociology. Of particular importance are his investigations of the problems of the classes and the class struggle, the state and revolution (see *The State and Revolution*), the role of the masses in the epoch of socialist revolution and the building of communist society, his ideas concerning the new forms taken by the general laws of social development during socialist construction, on the relationship between economics and politics, on culture and the cultural revolution, and on socialist morals and the principles of socialist art. L also had valuable ideas in the field of Marxist historico-philosophical science and gave us penetratingly accurate assessments of many philosophers of the past (the philosophers of antiquity, the French materialists, classics of German idealist philosophy, and others). He highly valued the work of the Russian revolutionary-democratic thinkers (Belinsky, Herzen, Chernyshevsky, qq.v.), and what he had to say about them and of the revolutionary movement and social thought in Russia, form a theoretical basis for the scientific history of Russian materialist philosophy. Leninism, as a continuation and development of Marxism, Marxism-Leninism as a single and undissoluble entity, has become in our day the watchword of progressive people all over the world who are fighting for peace, democracy, and socialism.

Leontyev, Konstantin Nikolayevich (1831-1891), Russian writer, literary critic and sociologist. Representative of the neo-Slavophiles (q.v.). He distinguished three stages in the development of the social organism: primary simplicity (when elements of the whole are only outlined), flourishing complexity and unity (when they are extremely individualised and included in a strict hierarchy) and secondary simplification (when they lose individuality and the whole disintegrates). From these same positions L. assessed the society of his time, assuming that the West, with its formal bourgeois equality and simplified social relations, had entered the stage of decline, while Russia had not yet gone through the stage of "flourishing complexity". According to L., bourgeois philistinism, democratism and socialism (which he identified) led to the formation of an irreligious man, and destroyed the beauty of individuality and creativity; hence he rejected revolutionary-democratic and humanistic ideas and movements from both the religious and the aesthetic points of view. It was Russia first and foremost that could resist these trends if she strengthened her "Russo-Byzantine social ideal" with its autocracy and ascetic Christianity, which denied the possibility of achieving happiness on earth, and its social estates. L.'s ideas are used by contemporary bourgeois philosophers to fight the socialist ideology. Main works: *Vostok, Rossiya i slavyanstvo* (The East, Russia and Slavs), in two vols., 1885-86. *Sredny yevropeyets kak ideal i orudiye vsemirnogo razrusheniya* (The Average European as the Ideal and Weapon of Universal Destruction), 1884.

Lesevich, Vladimir Viktorovich (1837-1905), Russian positivist philosopher. Till

1877, he was a supporter of Comte, q.v. (see his *Ocherk razvitiya idei progressa* [Essay on the Development of the Idea of Progress], 1868). He then moved to the position of the neo-critical German school (Alois Riehl, Avenarius, q.v., Joseph Petzoldt, and others), which he considered the highest stage of positivism (q.v.). According to L., this school supplemented Comte's philosophy with a fully elaborated theory of knowledge constructed on an interpretation of "pure experience", i.e. on the basis of empirio-criticism (q.v.) and neo-Kantianism (q.v.). Denying that philosophy could be a world outlook, L. declared that it "united" concepts produced by particular sciences. He explained the life of society from an idealist standpoint borrowing many ideas from Lavrov and Mikhailovsky (qq.v.). According to L., social progress is determined mainly by the results of the "mental activity" of mankind. Rejecting the elitist conception of culture, L. advocated the propagation of knowledge in the conditions of the freedom of speech and of the press, criticised the representatives of the religious-idealist trend in Russian philosophy (Solovyov, q.v., and others) from the positivist standpoint. Main works: *Opyt kriticheskogo issledovaniya osnovonachal pozitivnoi filosofii* (Critical Investigation of the Basic Principles of Positivist Philosophy), 1877; *Chto takoye nauhnaya filosofiya?* (What Is Scientific Philosophy?), 1891.

Lessing, Gotthold Ephraim (1729-1781), German enlightener and philosopher, publicist, playwright, critic, and art theorist. He was an active opponent of feudal policy and ideology and worked for the free and democratic development of the German people and their culture. In his philosophical work *Erziehung des Menschengeschlechts* (1780) L. dreamed of a future society free of all coercion, in which religion would give place entirely to enlightened reason. In his philosophical play *Nathan der Weise* (1779) L. proclaimed both the idea of religious tolerance but also the right of free thought, asserting the equality of nations and appealing for friendship among them. While reflecting the contradictory nature of the German movement for enlightenment, his world outlook remained idealistic, though it contained some materialist trends as well. In his *Laokoon* (1766) and *Hamburgische Dramaturgie* (1767-69), which constituted a landmark in the development of world aesthetic thought, L. upheld the principles of realism in poetry, drama, and acting and demolished the classicist theory and practice of the nobility. L. limited the sphere of the fine arts by reducing it to the beautiful. He strove to define the objective laws of composition in various types and genres of art, but could not see the historical character of these laws. Always an enemy of vain moralising, L. defended the moral and educative function of art, particularly in the theatre. His writing for the theatre heralded the emergence of German classical literature, and his aesthetic views exercised a beneficial effect on its development.

Leucippus (c. 500-440 B.C.), a contemporary and associate of Democritus (q.v.), with whom he founded the system known as atomism (q.v.). Owing to the almost complete lack of L.'s texts and of information concerning the man himself, it was at one time suggested that L. was a literary myth. The latest data have refuted this assumption. L. contributed three new concepts to science: (1) absolute vacuum; (2) atoms moving in this absolute vacuum; and (3) mechanical necessity. On the basis of an extant text it may be stated that L. was the first to establish both the law of causality (q.v.) and the principle of sufficient reason (q.v.). "Nothing arises without cause, but everything arises on some grounds and by force of necessity."

Lévy-Brühl, Lucien (1857-1939), French sociologist and ethnologist. His sociological views were formed under the influence of Durkheim (q.v.) While studying primitive peoples, L.-B. arrived at the conclusion that various social types had their corresponding patterns of thought. The thinking of primitive man differs from the logical thinking of modern man in that it ignores the law of contradiction and makes no distinction between the natural and the super-natural. L.-B. maintained that primitive man saw only the direct connection between first cause and final effect while failing to perceive the intervening relationships. This process he described as the operation of the law of participation. Some of L.-B.'s conclusions, though rather schematic, are of interest in the study of primitive thinking. Main works: *Les fonctions mentales dans les sociétés inférieures* (1910) and *La mentalité primitive* (1921).

Lévi-Strauss, Claude (b. 1908), French ethnographer, anthropologist and sociologist, representative of structuralism (q.v.). While studying the correlation between the biological (inborn) and the social in man's behaviour, he came to the conclusion that the main thing in relations between people is the existence of structures, the adoption of a definite language as a system for modelling public institutions. Most important in his structural anthropology is the interpretation of myths as the basic content of collective consciousness, the basis of stable social structures. The search for an extra-social origin of social life, efforts to formalise or even mathematise some methods of sociological analysis proper render L.-S.'s position methodologically vulnerable. Main works: *Mythologiques* (vols. 1-4, 1964-71), *Anthropologie structurale* (vols. 1-2, 1958-73).

Li, a basic concept of Chinese philosophy signifying the law, the order of things, form, and so on. The idealists interpreted it as a spiritual, immaterial principle in contrast to the material principle, *ch'i* (q.v.). Confucianism (q.v.) contained another concept of L., signifying a norm of conduct for various social groups.

Liberal Christianity, a trend in bourgeois theology, philosophy and ethics current in the 19th century, survivals of which (the "moral rearmament" movement and others) exist to this day. The representatives of L.C. (in the USA— Walter Rauschenbusch, Francis Peabody, in Europe—Albrecht Ritchl, Ernst Troeltsch, Adolf Harnack and others) advocated turning Christianity into a concrete programme for solving social and moral problems (the "social gospel" movement). L.C. differs from many other religious teachings by its optimistic view of the historical possibilities of man and society, of the "salutory" mission of social, scientific and technological progress. Its supporters strive to modernise Christianity in accordance with modern science, attach great importance to the logical proof of the rationality and social expediency of Christ's teaching, believing that the improvement of society will depend on the cogency of his preaching addressed to both the propertied and the poor. In ethics they try to approximate the biblical commandments to the modern concepts of secular morals, regarding service of society as the best form of service of God. They regard the "kingdom of God" as a social ideal to be achieved by mankind in the course of history, and the image of Christ as a moral ideal, a model for mortals. On the whole, L.C. is based on the still persisting illusions about the historical possibilities of the bourgeois society, which it defends from the liberal point of view. The general crisis of capitalism undermined the social basis of L.C., its ideas were sharply criticised from the right by neo-Protestantism (q.v.).

Libido, a concept introduced into philosophical, psychological and psychoanalytical literature by Freud (see Freudianism) and meaning sexual desire, the force of the sexual urge, the love instinct and psychic energy. Freud first perceived L. as energy in the form of which sexual desire manifests itself in man's spiritual life and used the so-called L. theory to account not only for nervous disorders but also for normal psychosexual development, scientific and artistic activity (see Sublimation). Later he interpreted L. as energy of desires connected with everything included in the notion of love (sexual love, self-love, love for parents and children, general love of mankind, etc.) and changed the theory of L. into the psychoanalytical teaching of desire for life or death. Carl Gustav Jung interpreted L. in a broader sense, that of psychic energy as such. The teaching on L. ignores the social aspects of man's existence and biologises its essence.

Life, a form of the motion of matter, qualitatively higher than the physical and chemical forms, possesses some specific features. It is realised in individual biological organisms and their combinations (populations, species, etc.). Each organism is an open self-organised system which is characterised by the processes of metabolism, control of growth, development and reproduction. A number of conceptions of the origin and essence of L. have been suggested by biologists and philosophers. One of them, Linnaeus, advocated creationism (q.v.)., that is, he admitted that all living creatures were brought into being by God by a single act of creation. As for Cuvier, he recognised repeated acts of creation maintaining that all the more perfect forms of life were created after the previous ones had been destroyed as a result of "cataclysm". Vitalism (q.v.), which goes back to the Aristotle's (q.v.) teaching of entelechy (q.v.), tried to explain life's processes through the action of some non-material "life force", "vital impulse". Similar ideas were expressed by the representatives of emergent evolution and holism (qq.v.). S. Arrhenius's hypothesis about the spores of life being brought to the Earth from the outer space and K. Baer's theory of eternal coexistence of animate and inanimate nature can be classified as metaphysical-materialist ones. A. Oparin's theory suggests the initial formation of protein-like complex colloid systems and then of first living bodies. According to modern scientific data, the combinations of amino acids resulted in the formation of a material system, which can be divided into two sub-systems: controlling and controlled (cell nuclei and cytoplasm). The cell nucleus contains molecules of nucleic acid (DNA), each of which consists of two chains of atoms, which are connected with each other by means of four bases that constitute the alphabet of the information (genetic) code; the order in which these bases are placed determines the sequence of all processes in the organism's life activity. It is, first of all, metabolism, by means of which the organism, being an open system, receives from the outside substances that serve as building materials; which ensures its growth and development, ensures its reproduction and provides it with energy. Thus, biosystems are always in a state of dynamic balance on the biological level of matter's

structure. Among the materialist theories explaining the mechanism of development of the organic world the most important are: J.B. Lamarck's (see Neo-Lamarckism) theory of exercise and non-exercise of organs as a source of new features of organisms, acquired by them in the process of individual life and supposedly inherited; and Darwin's (q.v.) theory of natural selection. According to modern genetics (q.v.), the influence of the natural environment (cosmic rays, changes of temperature, etc.) calls forth non-directed changes in the genetic code (mutations). The latter result in the creation of qualitatively new organisms, which of necessity become subject to natural selection: only those which are best adapted to the conditions of environment survive and produce posterity that gives birth to new biological species. The ramification of the genealogical tree, which has three main branches corresponding to protozoa, plants and animals testifies to the absence of predestination in the development of the organic world. No indications that living organisms exist on other planets of the solar system have been as yet found. The question whether life exists only on the Earth can be answered only after thorough experimental research is done; philosophical speculations are of no help here.

Linguistic Analysis in Ethics, a trend in modern bourgeois philosophy of morals, current in Britain (P. Nowell-Smith, R. Hare), the USA (H. Aiken) and other countries. The advocates of L.A. in E. criticise the most nihilistic conclusions of emotivism (q.v.), and try to prove the possibility of substantiating moral judgements, admitting that these contain special (prescriptive) shades of meaning. But in their conclusions on matters of principle they share the views of the emotivists, holding that moral judgements cannot be true or false, that they cannot be proved by theoretical or factual knowledge, that normative ethics (q.v.) is not scientific and scientific ethics (see Metaethics) is not normative, i.e., cannot have practical moral significance. In contrast to the emotivists, who deal mainly with analysis of moral statements, the supporters of L.A. in E. consider the logic of moral language as a whole. Their research in this field is of certain interest. They admit that particular moral judgments can be substantiated by more general propositions, moral principles and ideals. But ideals and principles themselves, they hold, cannot be substantiated by any means. This conclusion results from the use of false methodology in research into phenomena of moral consciousness, from considering morals as a field of specifically everyday language. Their method is purely empirically descriptive. As a result the logic of moral consciousness with its objective laws remains unexplained. Such a method leads to the assertion that the choice of a moral position is a matter for each individual and is carried out at will, depending on individual inclination or preference. The supporters of L.A. in E. hold that ethics cannot provide ideological and moral orientation and confine its social and practical function to teaching people the formal rules of moral language. Such formalism condemns man to ideological impotence in matters of morality.

Linnaeus, Carolus (1707-1778), Swedish naturalist. The service rendered to science by L. was his classification of the plant kingdom. Despite the fact that this system is artificial, his binomial nomenclature has retained its significance and is still in wide use. Though an adherent of creationism (q.v.), L. also made conjectures as to the hybrid origin of some forms and admitted a limited mutability of species resulting from the conditions of their existence.

Lobachevsky, Nikolai Ivanovich (1792-1856), Russian mathematician. L.'s geometry was based on the idea of close dependence of geometrical relations on the actual nature of material bodies. Assuming the independence of the fifth postulate of Euclidean geometry (see Euclid) in respect of its other postulates, he constructed a new geometry free of logical contradictions, whose fifth postulate states: through a point lying outside a straight line not one but at least two parallel lines may be drawn (K. Gauss and J. Bolyai arrived at the same conclusion independently of L., but only the latter of the two published his results in 1832). L. sought to prove the postulate on parallels by recourse to reality itself, to the nature of things. L.'s geometry was a convincing argument against Kant's (q.v.) a priori theory. Philosophically, L. was a materialist and considered our conceptions of the world the result of the impact of objective reality on human consciousness.

Locke, John (1632-1704), English materialist philosopher. The works of L. belong to the period of the Restoration. He joined the struggle of parties as a philosopher, economist, and political writer. In his major work *Essay Concerning Human Understanding* (1690) he developed the theory of knowledge of materialist empiricism (q.v.). Rejecting the Cartesian doctrine of innate ideas (q.v.), L. declared experience to be the sole source of all ideas. Ideas come into being either through the influence of external objects on the sense-organs (ideas of sensation) or through attention being directed on the condition and activity of the soul (ideas of reflection). The latter alternative was a concession to idealism. Through the ideas of sensation we apprehend in things either primary or secondary qualities (see Primary and Secondary Qualities). Ideas acquired through experience are only the material of knowledge, not knowledge itself. To become knowledge the material of ideas must undergo the process of reasoning, which differs both from sensation and from reflection. Through this activity simple ideas are transformed into complex ones. Following Hobbes, L. considered that universal knowledge depends entirely on language. He was convinced that our ability to know material and particularly spiritual substances is limited, but this does not mean that L. was an agnostic. According to L., our task is to know not everything but only what matters as far as our conduct and practical life are concerned, and to attain such knowledge our abilities are ample. In his doctrine on state power and law, L. developed the idea of transition from the natural to the civil condition and various forms of government. The purpose of the state, according to L., is to preserve freedom and property acquired through labour. Power cannot, therefore, be arbitrary. He divided it into (1) legislative, (2) executive, and (3) federative. L.'s doctrine of the state was an attempt to adapt theory to the political form of government that was established in England as a result of the bourgeois revolution of 1688 and the compromise between the bourgeoisie and the section of the aristocracy that had become bourgeois. His philosophy has had a great historical influence. The idea that people themselves should change the existing social system if it does not provide the individual with proper opportunities for education and development was of great importance in justifying the bourgeois revolution. One of the trends in French materialism takes its origin from L. His distinction between primary and secondary qualities was used by Berkeley (q.v.), the idealist, and Hume (q.v.), the agnostic.

Logic, see Logic, Dialectical; Logic, Mathematical; Logic, Formal.

Logic, Constructive, a trend in mathematical logic founded by L. Brouwer, H. Weyl and A. Heyting. Basically, it forbids the application to infinite sets of principles that are true for finite sets (e.g., the postulate that whole is greater than a part, the law of excluded middle, q.v., etc.). Classical logic and C.L. hold different views of the concept of infinity: the former regards it as actual, complete, and the latter as potential, becoming. Proceeding from the principles of C.L. attempts are being made to revise the basic results of modern mathematical logic and mathematics. A great contribution to the development of C.L. has been made by Soviet scholars A.N. Kolmogorov, A.A. Markov, and N.A. Shanin.

Logic, Dialectical, the logical teaching of dialectical materialism, the science of the laws and forms of the mental reflection of the development of the objective world, and of the laws governing the cognition of truth. Scientifically, D.L. arose as part of Marxist philosophy. However, its elements were already in evidence in antique philosophy, particularly the doctrines of Heraclitus, Plato, Aristotle (qq.v.), and others. For historical reasons, formal logic (q.v.) reigned for

a long time as the sole teaching on the laws and forms of thought. Approximately in the 17th century, developing natural science and philosophy revealed their insufficiencies and highlighted the need for a new teaching on the general principles and methods of thought and cognition (F. Bacon, Descartes, Leibniz, qq.v., and others). This tendency emerged most clearly in classical German philosophy (q.v.). Kant (q.v.), for instance, distinguished between general and transcendental logic, the latter differing from the former, i.e., formal logic, in that it examined the development of knowledge and did not abstract itself, as the former, from the content. Special credit in the development of D.L. goes to Hegel (q.v.), who produced the earliest comprehensive system which was, however, permeated with his idealistic outlook. The Marxist teaching on logic absorbed all the valuable elements of the preceding development, moulding the vast experience of human consciousness into a strict science of cognition. D.L. does not reject formal logic, but demonstrates its limits, its place and role in the study of the laws and forms of thought. While formal logic is the science of the laws and forms of reflection of constancy in thought and rest in the objective world, D.L. is the study of reflection in the laws and forms of thought of the processes of development (q.v.), of the internal contradictions (q.v.) of phenomena, their qualitative change, the passage of one into another, etc. As a science D.L. is possible only on the basis of dialectico-materialist method and at once it serves, as it were, as its concretisation by investigating the laws and forms of reflection in thought, the manifestation of infinite motion in the finite, the unity of the infinite and the finite in motion, the internal and the external, etc. The cardinal task of D.L. is to investigate how it is best to express in concepts the operation of the laws of dialectics in things, objects, etc. With this the other basic task of D.L. is associated, namely, the examination of the development of cognition itself. D.L. identifies the laws and forms of development of thought in the course of development of cognition and the historical social practice. The method of ascension from the abstract to the concrete (see Abstract and Concrete, the) is used by D.L. as a general logical principle. Another general principle of D.L. is the unity of the historical and logical (q.v.). Both principles are interconnected and interpenetrating. Thought goes from the surface of objects and things to their essence and then also comprehends its real manifestations. When examined logically, a process, a phenomenon, an aspect, etc., are taken in their developed, mature form, and this makes it possible to understand both the past existing in the present in a sublated form and the future, since it exists already in the present albeit in an undeveloped, embryonic form. Thus, by investigating the reflection of the processes of development in the laws and forms of thought, D.L. also investigates the development of thought and the system of its categories changes with the historical development of cognition and human practice. In contemporary science a big part is played by formalised logical systems and substantive formal logical theories which study the various aspects and tasks of thought. D.L. is the general logical basis of human cognition, the general logical theory which can and must be employed to explain all the particular and concrete logical theories, their significance and role.

Logic, Formal, a science which studies forms of thinking (concept, judgment, inference, and proof, qq.v.) as regards their logical structure, i.e., by abstraction of the concrete content of thoughts and singling out only the general means by which the parts of that content are linked. The main task of F.L. is to formulate laws and principles whose observance is a requisite for achieving valid results in obtaining knowledge by deduction. The foundation of F.L. was provided by the works of Aristotle (q.v.), who elaborated syllogistic (q.v.). Contributions to its development were made by the early stoics (q.v.), the scholastics in the Middle Ages—Duns Scotus, Occam (qq.v.), and others, and subsequently primarily by Leibniz (q.v.). At the turn of the century F.L. reached a new stage as a result of the rapid development of mathematical (symbolic) logic (q.v.). The latter has elaborated the logical theories of

mathematical reasoning and proof and enriched F.L. with new methods and means of logical analysis.

Logic, Inductive, the part of traditional logic concerned with logical processes of inferences from the particular to the general (see Induction). Traditional inductivists, Mill (q.v.), for example, saw the task of I.L. in analysing the processes of obtaining general theoretical knowledge from the single, empirical. In the history of logic there was also another conception of the subject-matter of I.L., limiting its tasks to analysing logical criteria for verifying scientific assertions within the framework of the hypothetico-deductive method (q.v.). This conception was formulated in the 19th century by W. Whewell, a British logician, and has become widespread in the modern logic of science. It stems from the inadequacy of the inductive methods for obtaining theoretical propositions, which require the identification of new thought-content and the formation of new scientific abstractions. The shortcoming of this conception is its unjustified renunciation of a logical study of the processes for obtaining scientific knowledge in general, i.e., their analysis as socially necessary processes, independent of individual consciousness and determined by the objective content of the cognitive processes. Modern I.L. widens the sphere of its application and examines not only inferences from the particular to the general, but all logical relationships in general when the truth-value of the knowledge we want to verify cannot be reliably established on the basis of the knowledge whose truth-value is known to us, when we can only determine whether it is confirmed by the latter knowledge, and if so, to what extent. Therefore, one of the central concepts of modern I.L. is the degree of confirmation, which is usually interpreted as the probability of a hypothesis (q.v.) with available empirical knowledge. Modern I.L. thereby utilises methods of the theory of probability (q.v.). and is being turned into probabilistic logic (q.v.).

Logic, Many-Valued, a logical system whose propositions are interpreted in more than two meanings (in the case of only two meanings—"true" or "false"—we have classical two-valued logic), but in the general case we have any finite or infinite multitude of meanings. Today there is a series of different systems of M.V.L. whose philosophical and structural aspects are under study. The works dealing with M.V.L. had the purpose of solving various problems, both general logical and specifically scientific ones. Other important applications of M.V.L. include attempts to validate quantum mechanics (works by G. Birkhoff, J. Neumann, Reichenbach, q.v.) and to elaborate the theory of relay-schemes (works by V.I. Shestakov, G. Moisil and others).

Logic, Mathematical (or symbolic logic) appeared as a result of the application of the formal methods of mathematics (q.v.) in the realm of logic, of the logical investigation of mathematical reasoning and proof. M.L. investigates logical processes through their reflection in the formalised languages, or logical calculi (q.v.). Besides its study of the formal structure of logical calculi (see Logical Syntax) M.L. also examines the relations between calculi and those substantive fields which serve as their interpretations and models (q.v.). This task describes the problems of logical semantics (q.v.). Logical syntax and semantics belong to metalogic (q.v.), the theory of the means of description, the premises and properties of logical calculi. To all appearance, the idea of logical calculi was first formulated by Leibniz (q.v.). As an independent branch of science M.L. established itself only in the mid-19th century, thanks to the works of Boole (q.v.), who founded the algebra of logic. Another trend of M.L., now a dominant one, appeared at the end of the 19th century, arising from the need of mathematics to provide a foundation for its concepts and methods of proof. The sources of this trend are to be found in the works of Frege (q.v.). A large contribution to its development was made by Russell and Whitehead, qq.v. (*Principia Mathematica*, 1910-13), and Hilbert (q.v.). Two fundamental logical systems—the classical propositional calculus (q.v.) and predicate calculus (q.v.)—were elaborated at the

time. Big results that determined the present-day state of M.L. were obtained in the 1930s by Gödel, Tarski (qq.v.) and A. Church. Today M.L. investigates the various types of logical calculi and takes interest in semantical problems and metalogic in general, as well as in the problems of special mathematical and technical application of logic. M.L. exerts great influence on contemporary mathematics. M.L. is applied in electrical engineering (the study of relay-contacts and electronic systems), in computers (programming), in cybernetics, q.v. (theory of automatic devices), in neurophysiology, and linguistics (structural linguistics and semiotic, q.v.).

Logic, Modal, a logical system which studies the structure of propositions that include such modalities (q.v.) as "necessity", "reality", "possibility", "chance", and their negations. Attempts to construct M.L. were undertaken by Aristotle, stoics (qq.v.) and scholastics, who formulated a number of its important definitions and principles. The study of modalities by means of mathematical (symbolic) logic (q.v.) was pioneered by C. Lewis and Lukasiewicz (q.v.).

Logic of Relations, a branch of mathematical logic (q.v.) dealing with relations (q.v.).

Logic, Probabilistic, logic that studies probabilistic statements no matter whether probability is regarded as a property of an individual statement (in this case probability is attributed to it as an intermediate between truth and falsehood) or as an appraisal of the relation between a pair of usual two-digit statements. As distinct from the theory of probability, L.P. does not require probability to be expressed by a precise number. The logical framework built on this basis is used to arrive at an appropriate judgment of hypotheses not by comparing them with reality but through other statements expressing the available knowledge. Thus, we can judge the degree of probability of the hypothesis "It will rain tomorrow" on the basis of its agreement with the weather forecast. Consequently the probability of a hypothesis is the function of two arguments: the hypothesis itself and the available information. The probability of complex hypotheses, when the probabilities of all the statements included in them are known, is calculated in all L.P. systems according to the rules of mathematical calculation of probabilities (see Probability, Theory of). Consequently, L.P. is one of the interpretations of this calculation. It would seem that the most fruitful application of L.P. is in inductive logic (q.v.). References to L.P. were made by Aristotle (q.v.) and the sceptics in ancient times, but Leibniz (q.v.) was the first philosopher to have serious ideas on the subject. The separation of L.P. from the theory of probability began in the mid-19th century, when the attention of the latter was concentrated on mass-scale random events. Even today, many attempts have been made to regard the teaching on probabilities as a single science with two branches, the theory of probability and L.P.

Logical Atomism, a conception formulated by Russell (q.v.) in *Our Knowledge of the External World* (1914), and other works, and by Wittgenstein (q.v.) in *Tractatus logico-philosophicus* (1921). According to L.A., the whole world is a totality of unconnected atomic facts (q.v.). The philosophy of L.A., as Russell himself admitted, is an extreme pluralism (q.v.), because it posits the existence of a multiplicity of individual things and denies them any unity or integrity. Historically, L.A. was a reaction to the neo-Hegelianism (q.v.) of F. Bradley, who held that only the absolute, the whole was real and that separate things were mere appearance. The formation of L.A. was greatly influenced by the logical model of the knowledge of the world described in particular by Wittgenstein, who regarded all knowledge as a totality of "atomic" propositions connected by logical operations and inferred the structure of the world by analogy with the logical pattern of knowledge. L.A. absolutised the discrete and the individual. The unsoundness of L.A. was ultimately acknowledged even by its advocates.

Logical Consequence, one of the basic concepts of logic expressing the relation between statements and depending on

their logical content. The concept "L.C." does not entirely correspond to intuitive use of the term "L.C." in the practice of scientific knowledge. This non-correspondence is manifest in the so-called "paradoxes" of consequence (any kind of statement can follow from contradictory statement and a logical truth can follow from any statement). A new trend in logic—relevant logic—appeared in the 1960s. Its aim is to elaborate a more exact concept of L.C. The concept of logical correctness of a judgment (see Correctness and Truth) is directly connected with the concept of L.C. L.C. is of great importance in defining a number of concepts in the logic of scientific knowledge (law of science, scientific explanation, etc.).

Logical Empiricism, a variety of analytical philosophy (q.v.) stemming directly from the logical positivism (q.v.) of the late 1920s and early 1930s. The main exponents of L.E. were Carnap, Reichenbach and Frank (qq.v.). As an "empirical language of science" L.E. suggested a so-called physical-object language expressing sensually perceptible physical phenomena instead of a language of the personal emotional experience of the subject. This does not mean, however, the adoption of materialist positions, since for L.E. the acceptance of a physical-object language did not involve recognition of the theoretical assertion of the objective existence of the world of things. Recognition of the fact that besides empirical content scientific knowledge has its own specific pretersensual content could not be conciliated with the basic epistemological ideas of the Vienna Circle, i.e., the principle of verification (q.v.), etc., to which L.E. sought to remain loyal. This gave rise to internal contradictions and eclecticism in its epistemological doctrine resulting in an acute internal crisis of L.E. in the mid-1950s, as is shown by its abandonment of the widely proclaimed programmes characteristic of early logical positivism and by its acceptance of watered-down compromise versions.

Logical Fallacies, mistakes caused by an incorrect step in the process of reasoning. They may arise through an erroneous interpretation of a proposition or through its incorrect use as a premise (e.g., a proposition which is true under certain circumstances is taken to be unconditionally true); or through violation of the rules of logic in the process of reasoning; or through drawing from a proposition a conclusion that cannot, in fact, be drawn, etc. L.F. may be divided into the unintentional (see Paralogisms) and deliberate sophisms.

Logical Forms, ways of constructing, expressing, and connecting ideas (and partial ideas) in the process of cognition, irrespective of their different concrete meaning. These forms have taken shape in the course of man's socio-historical practice and have a universally human character; they are forms of the reflection of reality in thought and themselves reflect the most general features of reality (e.g., the fact that every object has certain qualities, enters into certain relations with other objects, that objects form classes, that certain phenomena cause other phenomena, etc.). L.F., such as concepts, judgments, inferences, proofs and definitions (qq.v.), are studied in formal logic (q.v.). In cognition, the use of one or another L.F. is determined by the character of the content reflected in thought. In language, L.F. are expressed by the grammatical structure of the expressions involved and also by the use of special words denoted in mathematical logic by definite symbols: "and" ($\cdot$, $\triangle$, &), "no" ($-$, $\urcorner$, $\sim$), "or" (v), "if ... then" ($\flat$, $\rightarrow$), etc. In dialectical logic (q.v.), L.F. are studied from the point of view of how the changing and developing reality and the development of cognition itself are reflected in thought.

Logical Positivism 1. A variety of neo-positivism (q.v.). Originating in the 1920s with the Vienna Circle (q.v.) including Carnap, q.v., Otto Neurath and others. By the early thirties it had become widespread as the ideological basis of the neo-positivist "philosophy of science" in bourgeois scientific circles. Since the late thirties the centre of L.P. has moved to the USA, where it is found in a considerably modified form as compared with the days of the Vienna Circle and is known as

logical empiricism (q.v.). L.P. succeeded to empirio-criticism (q.v.) and the generally subjective-idealist tradition originating from Berkeley and Hume. According to L.P., a genuinely scientific philosophy is possible only as a logical analysis of the language of science. The function of this analysis is, first, to get rid of "metaphysics" (i.e., philosophy, in the traditional sense), and on the other hand, to investigate the logical structure of scientific knowledge in order to determine the empirically verifiable content of scientific concepts and assertions. The ultimate aim of this investigation was held to be the reorganisation of scientific knowledge within a system known as "the unity of science", which would eliminate the distinctions between the separate sciences— physics, biology, psychology, sociology, etc. Logic and mathematics are regarded as "formal sciences", not as knowledge of the world, but as a collection of "analytical" assertions which formulate the agreed rules of formal transformation. In the early thirties, L.P. attempted to free itself of some of the more unpleasant consequences of the principle of the "protocol-statement". It accepted the conception of physicalism (q.v.), but this did not change the subjective nature of its philosophy. The subjective-idealist essence of L.P. disposes of its claim to be a "philosophy of science". Nevertheless, some representatives of L.P. (Carnap, Reichenbach, and others) have achieved valuable results in the field of logical research. 2. In ethics, L.P. was an attempt to investigate moral judgments by means of formal logic (q.v.) and the methodology used by the neopositivists in the natural and exact sciences. This led to an extremely formal treatment of moral phenomena, to extreme simplification of their nature and to a number of scientifically inconsistent conclusions: such problems as the origin and historical development of morality were left uninvestigated, and its mechanism unexplained. The advocates of L.P. in ethics ignored the fact that morality is a special form of social relations and consciousness; they made only the "moral language" the object of their studies. Owing to this narrowing of the object of ethics, moral concepts and judgments themselves were falsely interpreted. For example, because good and evil are not perceived by the sense-organs or susceptible of empirical observation and experiment, they inferred that these concepts had no meaning at all. As moral judgments cannot be verified (see Verification, Principle of), the positivists deprived them of any sense, describing them as "meaningless", "pseudo-judgments". Such methodology further led to a number of nihilistic conclusions on morality (see Emotivism).

Logical Semantics, the branch of logic that studies the meaning of linguistic expressions, or more precisely, a branch of metalogic (q.v.) which studies interpretations (see Interpretation and Model) of logical calculi (see Formalised Language). Semantic analysis must be used when considering formalised languages from the standpoint of metatheory (q.v.) because many essential facts (e.g., those regarding the completeness and non-contradiction of the language) cannot be established within the framework of a purely syntactical examination (see Logical Syntax). Investigation of the semantic properties of the languages of science and the natural languages is increasingly applied in connection with the development of mathematical linguistics—machine translation, etc.

Logical Syntax, 1. A set of rules governing the construction and transformation of the expressions of a calculus (q.v.). 2. A branch of metalogic (q.v.) concerned with studying the structure and properties of uninterpreted calculi. The main problems arising from the syntactical examination of logical calculi are the problems of non-contradiction (see Axiomatic Theory, Non-Contradiction of), completeness (see Axiomatic Theory, Completeness of), independence (see Axiomatic System, Independence of), decision (see Decidability, Problem of), and provability. The concept of L.S. was introduced by Wittgenstein (q.v.) in 1919. Carnap (q.v.) gave a systematic exposition of the problems and concepts of L.S. in *Logische Syntax der Sprache* (1934), which shows the fruitfulness of syntactical investigation of the languages that formalise the various branches of the

natural sciences (see Formalised Language).

Logicism, one of the basic directions in providing a basis for mathematics by reducing the whole of mathematics to logic. Although this idea was originally advanced by Leibniz (q.v.), it was only at the end of the last century that Frege (q.v.) attempted to put it into practice. Frege set himself the aim of (1) defining the basic concepts of mathematics in terms of pure logic, and (2) proving its principles while restricting himself entirely to the principles of logic and employing only logical proofs. Further positive work in this direction (Russel and Whitehead, qq.v., 1910-13, F. Ramsey, 1926, W. Quine, 1940) failed, however, to produce the desired results due to the basically incorrect methodological assumption of L. that mathematics is independent of the material world and the tasks of its investigation. The development of mathematical logic (q.v.) has, on the contrary, led to the conclusion, as in Gödel's (q.v.) theorem, that the most basic branches of mathematics (e.g., arithmetic) cannot be reduced to logic.

Logistic, originally used to denote a logical calculus. Leibniz (q.v.) frequently spoke of mathematical logic as "Logistica". The use of L. as a synonym for symbolic or mathematical logic was accepted at the Geneva International Congress of Philosophy in September 1904 (see Logicism).

Logistic Method, in modern mathematics and logic, a method of constructing formalised systems (see Formalisation) and calculus (q.v.). Such systems are constructed on a purely formal basis, as arrangements and sequences of symbols disregarding the meaning of the expressions involved. Sometimes the L.M. includes interpretation as well as construction of a formal system (see Logical Semantics). This purely formal construction of a system does not, of course, imply complete disregard for content, particularly of the class of logical laws, which are always taken into account in one way or another when constructing a calculus.

Logos, a term whose original meaning was universal law, the basis of the world, its order and harmony. One of the main concepts of Greek philosophy. Heraclitus (q.v.) spoke of L. in this sense when he said that everything proceeds according to L., which is eternal, universal, and essential. The idealists (Hegel, Windelband, qq.v., and others) wrongly regarded the L. of Heraclitus as universal reason. Plato and Aristotle (qq.v.) understood L. as a law of being and a principle of logic. Among the stoics (q.v.) the term "L." denoted the law of the physical and spiritual worlds insofar as they merged in a pantheistic unity (see Pantheism). Philo of the Judaic-Alexandrian school (1st century A.D.) developed the doctrine of the L. as a creative divine force (reason) acting as mediator between God and the created world and man. We find a similar interpretation of L. in Neoplatonism (q.v.), among the gnostics (q.v.), and later in Christian literature in which L. was identified with Christ. Hegel in his philosophy described L. as an absolute concept. An attempt was made by representatives of religious idealist philosophy in Russia (Trubetskoy, q.v., V. Ern, and others) to revive the idea of a divine L. In oriental philosophy concepts analogous to L. are *tao* and, in a certain sense, *dharma*. The term "L." is not used in Marxist literature.

Lokāyata, a materialist doctrine in ancient India. The earliest information on L. is to be found in the Buddhist canonical texts known as the Vedas (q.v.) and in the Sanskrit epics. Traditionally, the origin of the L. has been connected with the mythical sage Brihaspati. Certain atheistic attacks on the Vedas are attributed to the legendary Chārvaka, and in a number of ancient texts this materialism is known as the Chārvaka. The teaching of L. about the nature of being is founded on the idea that everything in the Universe consists of four elements—earth, fire, water, and air (in some texts a fifth element—ether—is added). The elements are eternal and immutable. The properties of an object depend on the types of elements it consists of and in what proportion they are combined. The consciousness and sense-organs are also the result of a certain combination of elements; after the death of a living being this combination disintegrates into elements which join up those of the corresponding type existing in inanimate nature. Some texts contain a notion of evolution, treating certain elements as originating from others with earth as primordial. The epistemology of L. is sensationalist, the sole valid source of knowledge being sense perception. The sense-organs can apprehend objects to the extent that they themselves are composed of the same elements. L. denied the existence of extra-sensual and pretersensual objects, and in the first place of God, the soul, heaven and hell, and the like. The predominant feature of the ethics of L. is hedonism (q.v.). L. evidently exercised a certain influence on ancient Indian methods of government. Not a single text written by the followers of L. has come down to us in modern times. L. is most fully expounded in the philosophical treatises written by the idealist opponents of L., who upheld the Vedas between the 9th and 16th centuries.

Lomonosov, Mikhail Vasilyevich (1711-1765), Russian encyclopaedist, founder of materialist philosophy in Russia. Son of a peasant. As the best pupil of the Slavonic-Greco-Latin Academy in Moscow, which he entered in 1731, he was sent to the St. Petersburg Academy of Sciences in 1736, then abroad, to Marburg University. In 1741, L. returned to Russia. A thinker of immense versatility, L. made a great contribution to the development of physics and chemistry. He also did much for Russian philology, history, and poetry. The materialist tradition of Russian philosophy stems from L. As a materialist, he contested the various speculative views that dominated science in his day. In his treatise *O sloyakh zemnykh* (On the Strata of the Earth), 1763, he anticipated the theory of the evolution of the vegetable and animal worlds, stressing the need to study the causes of change in nature. Basing his explanation of natural phenomena on the transformation of matter, which, he held, consisted of minute particles or "elements" (atoms) united in "corpuscles" (molecules), L. always regarded matter as being in motion. He expressed this idea in his law of the conservation of matter and motion, which he formulated in a letter to Eiler of July 5, 1748 (see Conservation of Energy, Law of). In *Razmyshleniya o prichine teploty i kholoda* (Reflections on the Cause of Heat and Cold), 1749, he rejected the concept of heat as being caused by a special type of heat-giving matter (the thermogen) and showed that the cause of heat processes should be found in the movement of particles of matter. This led him to the assumption that the variety of natural phenomena was due to the various forms of the motion of matter. The basic properties of matter, according to L., are: extension, power of inertia, shape, imperviousness, and mechanical motion. L. considered a "first push" to be one of the causes of the development of nature; in this respect, too, he was following the interpretation given by mechanistic materialism. In epistemology L. was a materialist. Considering the effect of the external world on the sense-organs to be the source of knowledge, he opposed the theory of innate ideas (q.v.). Though he attached great importance to experience as a source of knowledge, L. postulated that only the combination of empirical methods and theoretical generalisations could reveal the truth. He was the first to provide evidence of the existence of an atmosphere surrounding the planet Venus. He also played a great part in the geological and geographical study of Russia and in setting up the porcelain, mining and metallurgical industries. As the founder of Moscow University (1755), L. was responsible for the emergence of eminent Russian scientists and scholars who carried forward the development of the natural sciences and materialist philosophy in Russia. In the field of social studies L. advocated enlightenment and moral improvement as the sole means of improving the life of society and pointed to the ignorance of the priests as one of the causes of the widespread ignorance of the people. In his struggle against the clergy he adopted rationalist positions, with a tendency towards deism (q.v.). His poetry and historical writing had a strong patriotic vein. In his *Drevnyaya Rossiskaya istoriya* (History of Ancient Russia), published in 1766, he refuted the falsification by foreign historians of the distinctly original character of the Russian people.

Lossky, Nikolai Onufriyevich (1870-1965), Russian idealist philosopher; professor at St. Petersburg University. Emigrated in 1922; professor at the Russian Orthodox Seminary in New York from 1947. He attempted to create a system of "integral" intuitionalism (q.v.) combining the ideas of Plato (q.v.), of the Russian personalist A. A. Kozlov and the mysticism of Solovyov (q.v.). L.'s objective idealist teaching on being was based on the idea that the world is an organic whole: the essence of reality lies in timeless ideal personalities (a notion similar to Leibniz's monad) connected with one another and also with the supramundane principle (God). These "agents" create all diverse material and psychic processes. Epistemologically, L. was close to immanence philosophy (q.v.). Objects are apprehended by means of sensual, mystical or intellectual intuition, q.v. (unlike Bergson, q.v., he also included reason in intuition). Present in the consciousness of the individual, he held, is not the image of the object but the object itself. L. never emerged from the framework of subjective idealism. He based ethics and aesthetics on recognition of "the kingdom of God" with its absolute values embodied in man's behaviour and creative activity. His *History of Russian Philosophy* (1951), besides being a complete distortion of the history of materialism, attempts to prove that the distinctive feature of Russian philosophy lies in its religiousness and contains many false charges against the Soviet system. Main works: *Obosnovaniye intuitivizma* (The Bases of Intuitionalism), 1906; *Dostoyevsky i yego khristianskoye miroponimaniye* (Dostoyevsky and His Christian World-View), 1953.

Lotze, Hermann (1817-1881), German philosopher. His philosophy was a compromise between materialism and idealism, in which the latter predominated. His best known work is *Mikrokosmos* (1856-64). L.'s ideas paved the way for the "phenomenology" of Husserl (q.v.). His logic influenced Karinsky (q.v.).

Lovers of Wisdom, members of a secret philosophical circle which existed in Moscow in 1823-25. It dealt with problems of philosophy, aesthetics and literature. Although its members held different political views, the circle tended in philosophy towards German idealism, mainly that of Schelling (q.v.), criticised French materialism and the aesthetics of classicism. The circle's significance for Russian philosophy lay in the fact that it developed and propagated the ideas of idealist dialectics in natural philosophy, epistemology, aesthetics, and social theory. It published the almanac *Mnemozina,* that carried philosophical articles and fiction. A. Pushkin and A. Griboyedov contributed to it. The chairman of the circle, V. Odoyevsky held conservative views and wrote mainly on questions of philosophy and aesthetics. On his initiative the circle was closed in connection with the Decembrists' insurrection and its papers were burnt. Radical views were held by Decembrist V. Kyukhelbeker, who ran the literary section of *Mnemozina;* the poet, philosopher and aesthete D. Venevitinov, who sympathised with the Decembrists, and A. Koshelev. After the radical members had been forced to withdraw from the circle (Kyukhelbeker was banished for being a Decembrist, Venevitinov left for St. Petersburg and soon died), during the period of reaction which followed the Decembrists' insurrection, some of its members adopted a conservative stand.

Lucretius, Carus (c. 99-55 B.C.), Roman poet, and materialist philosopher, continued the work of Epicurus (q.v.), author of *De Rerum Natura.* L. set out to reveal the path to happiness for the individual thrust into the vortex of social conflict and disaster and haunted by fear of the gods, death, and punishment after death. Release from fear was to be had through acceptance of the philosophy of Epicurus regarding the nature of things, man, and society. The soul, L. maintained, is mortal, for it is merely a temporary combination of special particles and, when the body dies, it disintegrates into atoms. Realisation of the mortality of the soul eliminates not only belief in an afterlife but also in punishment after death. It releases man from his fear of hell. The fear of death is similarly dismissed. While we are alive there is no death, when death comes we no longer exist. Lastly, even fear of the gods disappears as soon as we realise that the gods live not in this world but in the empty spaces between worlds; living a life of bliss in these regions, they can have no influence on the life of man. L. gave a vivid materialist picture and interpretation of the world and the nature of man, the development of material culture and technology. He was a great enlightener of the Roman world and his poem had an immense influence on the development of the materialist philosophy of the Renaissance (q.v.).

Ludwig Feuerbach and the End of Classical German Philosophy (1886), a philosophical work by Engels, which played a prominent role in substantiating and developing a dialectical and historical materialism. Engels begins with an analysis of the essence of the philosophy of Hegel (q.v.) and the contradictions in it and shows that Marxist dialectics and Hegelian dialectics are opposites. Engels gives a classical definition of the fundamental question of philosophy (q.v.), its two aspects and criticises agnosticism, q.v. (above all that of Hume and Kant, qq.v.), showing that practice is the most decisive refutation of it. Giving a scientific definition of materialism and idealism, Engels analyses the views of the 17th-18th century English and French materialists and of Feuerbach (q.v.), and proves that mechanistic, metaphysical materialism was limited and that its understanding of social phenomena was idealistic and inconsistent. Engels underscores the significance of Feuerbach's criticism of idealism, but at the same time criticises his attempt to create a new religion and his idealistic views on ethics. Having established the fundamental difference between dialectical materialism and all previous philosophies, Engels, in the latter part of his work, expounds concisely the essence of materialist conception of history. Developing the theory of historical materialism, he emphasises the idea that the superstructure is relatively independent. This was of great importance for the critique of economic materialism (q.v.), which sprang up at the time. Engels' analysis of the causes, content, and significance of the radical revolution wrought in philosophy by Marxism and his popular exposition of the essence of dialectical and historical materialism make this work (which Lenin placed on the same level as the *Manifesto of the Communist Party*) an indispensable manual for the study of the origin and history of the basic ideas of Marxist philosophy.

Lukasiewicz, Jan (1878-1956), Polish logician. He was one of the most eminent representatives of the Lvov-Warsaw school (q.v.) of logic. He elaborated the first system of many-valued (three-valued) logic, q.v., bracketless logical symbols, carried out original research into Aristotic syllogism, the logical teaching of the early stoics, the classical and intuitionist theory of deduction and modal logic.

Lully, Raymond (1235-1315), medieval mystic philosopher, theologian and missionary. Studied and taught in Paris. An orthodox representative of medieval realism (q.v.) going as far as panlogism (q.v.). L. fought against Averroism (q.v.) on twofold truth (q.v.), attempting to prove the possibility of a complete merger of philosophy and theology. In this dispute he solved scientific tasks by means of the "truth machine". Its operation consisted in mechanical rotation of concentric circles relatively to each other. On each circle 9 general concepts were written (e.g., heaven, god, man, virtue, truth, etc.) comprising, according to L., all fields of knowledge. When these circles rotated various combinations of these concepts were produced which L. regarded as new truths. In this way he tried to prove all the truths of Christianity. His attempt to create a logical machine contained a rational idea of formalisation of logical operations, which later influenced Leibniz (q.v.) and to some extent mathematical logic (q.v.) in general.

Lunacharsky, Anatoly Vasilyevich (1875-1933), Soviet statesman and public figure, propagator of Marxism-Leninism, writer on the theory of art, publicist and

playwright. Became a Bolshevik in 1903. In the years of reaction following the defeat of the Russian revolution of 1905-07 he turned away from Bolshevism and professed Machism and god-building, q.v. (*Religiya i Sotsialism* [Religion and Socialism], Part 1, 1908; Part 2, 1911). For this he was criticised by Lenin. In July 1917, he was readmitted to the Bolshevik Party, and from 1917 to 1929 was People's Commissar for Education. In 1930, he was elected a full member of the Academy of Sciences. L.'s early works *Osnovy pozitivnoi estetiki* (Fundamentals of Positive Aesthetics), 1904; *Etyudy kriticheskiye i politicheskiye* (Critical and Political Studies), 1905, etc., showed the influence of positivism, q.v. (Spencer, Avenarius, Bogdanov, qq.v.). But in his best pre-revolutionary writings, *Russkii Faust* (Russian Faust), 1902; *Dialog ob iskusstve* (Dialogue on Art), 1905; *Zadachi s.-d. khudozhestvennogo tvorchestva* (Tasks of Social-Democracy in the Arts), 1907; *Pisma o proletarskoi literature* (Letters on Proletarian Literature), 1914, he criticised decadence and attempted to elaborate from a proletarian standpoint such problems as partisanship (q.v.) in art, the influence of the revolution on the development of culture, the significance of art in the class struggle of the proletariat, the connection between the artist's world outlook and his art, etc. After the October Revolution, he was a prominent organiser of socialist culture, though he made certain mistakes (e.g., on the question of Proletkult); he contributed to the history of literature (his writings on the Russian and Soviet classics, on the revolutionary democrats, on West European writers, and so on), to aesthetics and the theory of art, e.g., *Klassovaya borba v iskusstve* (The Class Struggle in Art), 1929; *Lenin i literaturovedeniye* (Lenin and Literary Studies), 1932, and to theatrical and musical criticism. He paid particular attention to the elaboration of problems that were of great importance to the theory of art and creative work: Lenin's ideological legacy and scientific aesthetics, cultural revolution, the Communist party's guidance of the arts, the task of Marxist criticism, socialist realism (q.v.), the connection between proletarian art and the classical heritage, and the struggle against bourgeois modernism and vulgar sociologism (q.v.) in the study of art.

Luther, Martin (1483-1546), eminent leader of the Reformation (q.v.) and founder of Protestantism (q.v.). He influenced all spheres of spiritual life of Germany in the 16th-17th centuries. His translation of the Bible played an important role in the formation of the German language. L. was a supporter of moderate burgher reformation. He denied that the church and the clergy were mediators between man and God. He affirmed that the "salvation" of man does not depend upon the performance of "good deeds", mysteries, and rituals, but upon man's sincere belief. According to him, religious truth is based not on the "sacred tradition" (decrees of oecumenical councils, papal judgments, etc.), but on the Gospel itself. These demands reflected the conflict between the early bourgeois world outlook, on the one hand, and the feudal ideology and the church, on the other. At the same time L. opposed the doctrines which expressed the material interests of the German burghers, criticised the theory of natural law (q.v.), the ideas of early bourgeois humanism, and the principles of free trade. L. stood on the side of the ruling classes during the Great Peasant War (1525).

Lvov-Warsaw School, a group of Polish logicians and philosophers (Lukasiewicz, Tarski, qq.v., and others), who worked in the inter-war period mainly in Warsaw, Lvov, and Cracow. Its founder was K. Twardowski. Philosophically, the school was representative of widely varying trends (from the materialism of T. Kotarbinski to the neo-Thomism of J. Salamuja and I. Bochenski). Characteristic of the majority of its representatives were: (a) rejection of irrationalism (q.v.), concrete enumeration through mathematical logic (q.v.) of the basic ideas and principles of traditional rationalism (q.v.); (b) stress on precise research into the logic of scientific reasoning; (c) interest in logical semantics (q.v.). Representatives of the school made a considerable contribution to the development of mathematical logic, the foundations of mathematics, the methodology of the deductive sciences and the history of logic and logical semantics. The philosophers and logicians of socialist Poland continue to elaborate the progressive ideas of the L.W.S.

m

Mably, Gabriel Bonnot de (1709-1785), French historian and political thinker. M. expressed his approbation of the communist system which, in his opinion, existed at the dawn of human history and considered the rise of private ownership as the cause of all social evils. M. held that the system founded on private ownership contradicts natural equality and man's social instinct. But humanity strayed so far that it could not return again to the communistic order. M. favoured measures directed towards the equalisation of property. He recognised the right of the people to revolution whenever they realise that they are subject to unjust and irrational laws. He did not consider revolution, however, a prerequisite for the achievement of the communist ideal, believing that it was only a means for achieving more limited aims. M. was not a consistent utopian socialist; but many aspects of his social philosophy promoted the dissemination of socialist ideas. His main work: *De la législation ou principes de loi* (1776).

Mach, Ernst (1838-1916), Austrian physicist and philosopher, subjective idealist and one of the founders of empirio-criticism (q.v.). By acknowledging a thing to be a "complex of sensations", M. counterpoised his teaching to philosophical materialism. Proceeding from the philosophy of Hume (q.v.), he rejected the concepts of causality, necessity and substance, since these are not given in "experience". The description of the world should include only the "neutral elements of experience"; only these "elements" (which M. identified with sensations) and their functional connections are real. M. regarded concepts as symbols denoting "complexes of sensations" ("things"), and science in general as the totality of hypotheses which can be replaced by direct observation. Lenin's *Materialism and Empirio-Criticism* (q.v.) exposed and refuted M.'s subjective idealism and its inconsistent nature. Main works: *Die Analyse der Empfindungen und das Verhältnis des Physischen zum Psychischen* (1886), and *Erkenntnis und Irrtum* (1905). His philosophy influenced the shaping of neo-positivism (q.v.) and underlay the basic Machist revision of Marxism (F. Adler, V. A. Bazarov, Bogdanov, q.v., Yushkevich, q.v., and others).

Machiavelli, Niccolo di Bernardo (1469-1527), Italian thinker and ideologist of the rising bourgeoisie. Society, according to M., develops not by the will of God but owing to natural causes. The driving forces of history are "material interest" and power. He noted the conflict of interests between the masses of the people and the ruling classes. M. demanded the creation of a strong national state, free from feudal internecine conflicts and able to suppress popular riots. He considered permissible the employment of all means in the achievement of great goals in political struggle, the disregard for the rules of morality and justified cruelty and treachery in the struggle of rulers for power. The historical merit of M., to use Marx's words, was that he was one of the first to see the state through the human eyes and to deduce its laws from reason and experience and not from theology. Main work: *Il Principe* (1532).

Macrocosm and Microcosm, two specific spheres of objective reality, which differ in the level of the structural organisation of matter. The sphere of macrophenomena is the world in which man lives and acts (planets, terrestrial bodies, crystals, large molecules, etc.). The microcosm (atoms, nuclei, elementary particles, q.v., etc.) is qualitatively different. Here the measurements of objects are less than a thousand-millionth part of a centimetre, and time intervals are measured in thousand-millionths of a second. In other words, they cannot be directly observed. Both M.&M. are characterised by their peculiar structure of matter, spatial-temporal and causal relations, and law-governed movement. Thus, macrocosm material objects have a clearly discernible discontinuous, corpuscular structure, or a continuous wave structure, and their movement is subject to the dynamic laws of classical mechanics. Microcosm phenomena, on the other hand, are characterised by a close-knit connection between corpuscular and wave properties, this being expressed in the statistical laws of quantum mechanics (q.v.). A border dividing the macrocosm and microcosm has been established with the discovery of Planck's constant (see Planck). Modern "physical idealists" make absolute the distinctions between the macrocosm and the microcosm, the peculiarities of their cognition and deny the objectivity and knowability of the microcosm. In reality, however, science shows that there is a close link between M.&M. and reveals, in particular, the possible appearance of macroscopic objects in the collisions of microparticles of high energy. The penetration of physics into the world of atoms, and then into the atomic nucleus and elementary particles, was a brilliant confirmation and enrichment of the principles of dialectical materialism.

Magic, one of the forms of primitive religion, which imputes many of the incomprehensible phenomena to enigmatic forces; a set of rituals which aim to affect people, animals, imaginary spirits, etc. Primitive M. was most fully studied by Lévy-Bruhl (q.v.) and the Soviet researcher N. Marr (1864-1934), who saw in M. a specific form of thinking, following which man could not as yet draw a qualitative distinction between things and therefore transferred the properties of a phenomenon or thing to any other phenomena and things. The primitive man regarded such a transfer as immutable reality in which there is no place for the supernatural. M. as an action associated with the conception of a supernatural force appeared later, when "magic thinking" coexisted with logical thinking. Ordinary conception of M. was connected with the belief in the direct implementation of human desires without goal-oriented actions (e.g., recovery of a patient, fall of rain, death of a person, etc.).

Magnitude, a basic mathematical concept originating as an abstraction of the numerical characteristics of physical properties. The concept of M. may be regarded, like the concepts of set, continuity, etc., as a closer definition of the category of quantity. A distinction is made between scalar Mm. (characterised by number alone, e.g., length, area, volume, etc.) and vector Mm. (embracing, besides number, direction, e.g., force, speed, etc.). Mm. are also divided into constant and variable. The concept of the variable was introduced into mathematics by Descartes (q.v.) and played an important part in the development of modern mathematics and natural science.

Maimonides, or Moses ben Maimon (1135-1204), Jewish philosopher, adherent of the teachings of Aristotle (q.v.) and one of the leaders of the rationalistic school of Judaism (q.v.). M.'s philosophy is a synthesis of Judaistic theology and Aristotelianism; he tried to reconcile religion with philosophy by way of an allegorical interpretation of the Bible and isolated dogmas of Judaism. According to M., the ultimate aim of knowledge was to provide a rational basis for the supreme truth. M. was persecuted by religious fanatics for his rationalistic ideas. His main work *Moreh Nebouchim* (Guide for the Perplexed) gained wide popularity in Europe and exerted considerable influence upon later scholasticism (q.v.).

Makhayevism, a petty-bourgeois anarchist trend spread in Russia during the 1905-07 revolution. It preached a hostile attitude to the intelligentsia (q.v.). This trend was named after Social-Democrat V. Makhaisky who claimed that the intelligentsia is a parasitic class.

Malebranche, Nicolas de (1638-1715), French idealist and adherent to occasionalism (q.v.). From an idealistic position he attempted to eliminate dualism in Descartes' (q.v.) system. M.'s philosophy attributes an exclusive role to God, who not only creates all existing things but also contains all of them within himself. The permanent interference of God is the only cause of all changes; there are no "natural causes" and "interactions" between spatial and thinking substances. In the theory of knowledge, too, M. adhered to the idealistic position: man gets to know things not through their effect on the sense-organs; cognition is human perception of ideas about all existing things, while God is the source of these ideas. Main work: *Recherche de la vérité* (1674-75).

Malthusianism, an unscientific sociological theory founded by the English clergyman Malthus (1766-1834), who expounded his views in *An Essay on the Principle of Population*. These views were later accepted by the bourgeois social thought, especially the political economy of the late 19th century. M. formulated an extra-historical law of population (q.v.), according to which the population increases in geometrical progression, while the means of subsistence grow only in arithmetical progression. Hence, he held, contradictions in social development. M. believed that social contradictions could be overcome by preventing the population growth (by restricting marriages, and childbirth) and also by regulating it through hunger, epidemics, wars, etc. Contemporary Malthusians consider that their main task is to spread delusions about the possible removal of social contradictions only by demographic means. The recent period has seen the most active spread of different neo-Malthusian conceptions (the "optimum population" theory of J. Bonner and the statements by G. Taylor and P. Ehrlich to the effect that the growth of population is the only cause of the present ecological crisis). This spread is associated with the accelerated growth of the global population and the further exacerbation of capitalist contradictions. The regulation of population growth, one of the present global problems (q.v.), will be possible only with the consolidation of a new, socialist system, and the implementation of a demographic policy consonant with it.

Man, the subject of historical process, of developing material and spiritual culture on earth, a biosocial being (representative of the "homo sapiens" species) genetically linked to other forms of life, standing off from them due to his ability to produce instruments of labour, endowed with articulate speech, reasoning power and consciousness. Current bourgeois philosophical conceptions of man and those prior to Marxism form a ramified conglomerate of ideas (existentialism, philosophical anthropology, qq.v.), gravitating towards two poles: idealist, mystico-religious understanding of the essence of M. and naturalistic anthropologism relying on biologising approaches. Marxism associates the understanding of the essence of M. with the social conditions of his functioning and development, conscious activity (q.v.), through which M. becomes both a prerequisite and a product of history. Emphasising the significance of social relations and characteristics of M., Marxism is far from attempting to level off all individuals, to belittle their specific qualities as personalities, endowed with their own character, will, abilities and feelings. Quite the opposite, Marxism highlights the general laws in order to put personal qualities of M. in sharper relief and make them better suited for scientific definition. While examining the social essence of M., Marxism is well aware of the complicated interaction of social and biological factors and asserts the primacy of the former. M., as a biosocial being, does not possess a "dual nature", although biological factors are of major importance. Marxism rejects the biologising conceptions of M. and his future that spring up today, including those referring to ethology, genetics (q.v.) and other sciences. Marxist-Leninist theory relates the future of M. to his social development towards communism, when full, comprehensive, free development of each individual and of all members of society will become an "aim in itself". The M. of the future will be a reasonable, humane, wondering and active, capable of appreciating beauty, full of integrity, all-round developed personality, an embodiment of all essential human powers combined, of spiritual and physical perfection. Asserting himself as a social being, M. remains a personality, a personal "I", with its inimitable individuality, a social being.

"Man", one of the main concepts of existentialism (q.v.), introduced by

Heidegger (q.v.). The German term of "M." serves as a subject in the indefinite-personal sentences. According to Heidegger, the stay in the world of "M." is the way the individual exists when he or she thinks, feels and acts as anybody else without choosing his or her true path in different situations. "M." is manifested in the universally recognised principles of behaviour, moral standards, in congealed and materialised forms of language, thought, etc. "M.", according to Heidegger, is always inimical to the human being, obstructs his freedom of action and deprives him of his individuality. In order to break away from the power of "M." and become free, the human being, according to existentialism, should place himself in a border-line situation (q.v.) between life and death. The individual is able to break away from "day-to-day existence" only by fear of death; then he becomes free and can be responsible for his actions. The conception of "M." reflects the irrational solution to the problem of the interrelation between the individual and bourgeois society—the antagonism between the individual and society inherent in the capitalist system.

Mandeville, Bernard (1670-1733), English philosopher, moralist, author of *The Grumbling Hive* (1705), a sharp satire on the society of his time. It describes the life of a hive where vices thrive and every bee takes care only of its own interest. To punish the bees, Jupiter turns all of them into honest creatures with the result that the hive becomes ravaged. This book shows that M. was the first to advance the idea that evil is inevitable and even beneficial in the conditions of social inequality. This idea ran counter to the views of Shaftesbury (q.v.); later it was developed by Hegel (q.v.). M. saw clearly that the bourgeois nation's wealth rests on the poverty of workers. M. greatly influenced many succeeding philosophers and economists (Helvétius, q.v., Adam Smith, etc.).

Manifesto of the Communist Party, the first programmatic document of scientific communism, expounding the foundations of Marxism, written by Marx and Engels and published at the beginning of 1848.

The first chapter—"Bourgeois and Proletarians"—discloses the laws of social development, proves the inevitable and law-governed nature of the replacement of one mode of production (q.v.) by another. Proceeding from the fact that the history of all hitherto developing society, except the primitive-communal system, was the history of class struggle, Marx and Engels proved that the fall of capitalism and the formation of a new social system, communism, were inevitable. In this same chapter they elucidated the historic mission of the proletariat as the revolutionary transformer of the old society and the builder of the new, the champion of the interests of all toiling masses. In the second chapter—"Proletarians and Communists"—Marx and Engels highlighted the historic role of the Party of Communists as the vanguard of the working class. The immediate aim of the Communists is the "formation of the proletariat into a class, overthrow of the bourgeois supremacy, conquest of political power by the proletariat" (K. Marx and F. Engels, *Collected Works*, Vol. 6, p. 498). In this chapter Marx and Engels advanced the idea of the dictatorship of the proletariat, explained the relation of the Communists to the family, property, and the motherland and outlined the economic measures which the proletariat must take upon coming to power. In the third chapter—"Socialist and Communist Literature"—they made a profound criticism of bourgeois and petty-bourgeois trends masquerading under the banner of socialism and defined their own attitude to the systems of utopian socialism and communism. In the fourth chapter—"Position of the Communists in Relation to the Various Existing Opposition Parties"—Marx and Engels set forth the tactics of the Communists regarding various opposition parties. *Manifesto of the Communist Party* concludes with the immortal slogan: "Working Men of All Countries, Unite!" Of the invaluable historic significance of the work Lenin wrote: "This little booklet is worth whole volumes: to this day its spirit inspires and guides the entire organised and fighting proletariat of the civilised world" (Vol. 2, p. 24). Being the first programmatic document of scientific communism, this work contains the new philosophical doctrine of Marxism—consistent philosophical materialism, revolutionary dialectics and the materialist conception of history.

Marburg School, one of the trends in neo-Kantianism (q.v.). The main exponents of this school were Cohen (q.v.), Paul Natorp, Cassirer (q.v.) and Rudolf Stammler. Having discarded the materialist tendency in Kant's (q.v.) teaching, these thinkers subscribed to consistent subjective idealism. The exponents of the M.S. held that philosophy does not provide knowledge of the world, but consists only of the methodology and logic similar to those of special sciences. This methodology is but the insipidity in general principles, which are ascribed to special sciences. The most important of these principles is the so-called principle of obligation, which the school spread to sociology as well. The adherents of M.S. denied the objective existence of laws of social development and considered socialism exclusively as a moral phenomenon, as an "ethical ideal" standing above the classes. The theorists of the M.S. demanded that Marxism be "supplemented" with Kantianism, emasculated scientific communism of its economic and political content and denied the revolutionary struggle and the dictatorship of the proletariat. The sociological ideas of this school influenced "legal Marxism" (q.v.) in Russia and later served as the basis for the revision of Marxism by the opportunists of the Second International (Bernstein, Kautsky, qq.v., M. Adler, and others). In our days these ideas are being used by the Right Socialists to combat Marxism-Leninism.

Marcel, Gabriel (1889-1973), French philosopher and writer, chief exponent of the so-called Catholic existentialism (q.v.). Among the existentialists M. stands closest to the teaching of Kierkegaard (q.v.). He believed that philosophy is at variance with science, which studies the world of objects but does not touch upon existential experience, i.e., the inner spiritual life of the individual. For M., it was precisely through existential experience that one could comprehend God; for this reason it was necessary to renounce

rational proof of God's existence. M.'s ethics was built upon the Catholic doctrine of predestination and the freedom of the will. In politics he adhered to reactionary positions. His main works are *Journal metaphysique* (1927), *Être et Avoir* (1935), and *Les hommes contre l'humain* (1951).

Marcus Aurelius, Antoninus (121-180 A.D.), philosopher, stoic (q.v.), and Roman Emperor (161-180). His only work *Meditations* expressed his philosophy in the form of aphorisms. The impending crisis of the Roman Empire influenced M.A.'s philosophy. In his interpretation stoicism ultimately lost all materialistic features and became religious mysticism. For M.A. God, the prime basis of all that is living, is universal reason, in which all forms of individual consciousness are dissolved after physical death. His ethics was permeated with fatalism (q.v.), with preaching humility and asceticism. He appealed for moral perfection and purification through self-absorption and the cognition of the fatalistic necessity which rules the world. M.A.'s philosophy greatly influenced Christianity (q.v.), despite his harsh treatment of Christians.

Marcuse, Herbert (1898-1979), a prominent representative of the Frankfurt school (q.v.). He became widely known in the New Left (q.v.) movement by his critique of modern society. He presented this society as a maximally technicised and bureaucratised community, which integrates the working class by drawing it into the orbit of "false" requirements. Under these conditions, he held, the driving force of social change that involves the "great rejection" of all social values is the radical intellectuals and students, as well as the so-called outsiders (the unemployed, lumpens, etc.). In the early 1970s M. renounced his most nihilistic views on culture and art. This coincided with the loss of influence by the New Left, to which he owed his popularity in the 1960s. His main works: *Eros and Civilization* (1955), *The One-Dimensional Man* (1964), and *An Essay on Liberation* (1969).

Maréchal, Pierre Sylvain (1750-1803), representative of the plebeian-democratic wing of French materialism and atheism. M. recognised that existing nature was eternal, believing that only its concrete expressions, i.e., "forms" appeared or disappeared. God, to him, was synonymous with nature. Out of fear man invented a supreme being and endowed that being with the properties of nature. His atheism was more consistent than that of Encyclopaedists (q.v.). He associated the final removal of religion with a revolution, the overthrow of the exploiting system and the establishment of communism. M. joined the Babouvist movement (see Babouvism) and became a utopian communist. M.'s theory of knowledge was based on sensationalism (q.v.). His main work: *Manifeste des égaux* (1794).

Maritain, Jacques (1882-1973), French philosopher, leader of neo-Thomism (q.v.). The chief motive of his works was to renovate the social views of Thomas Aquinas (q.v.) and to adapt them to the modern epoch. M. created neo-Thomist personalism (q.v.), based on the idea of a personalist revolution aimed against "the spirit of money and capitalism". At the same time he opposed socialism as well, for it allegedly impinges upon man's spirit impulses. M. suggested the idea of "new humanism" which was to rally people around religious values. In other words, his conception of a moral revolution diverted the masses from the real struggle for the emancipation of man. In his various works he elucidated problems of psychology, sociology, aesthetics, ethics, and pedagogics from the standpoint of orthodox Thomism. His main works: *Antimoderne* (1922), *Humanisme intégral* (1936).

Marković, Svetozar (1846-1875), Serbian revolutionary democrat, materialist philosopher and utopian socialist, who studied in Russia. M.'s world outlook was developed at a time when Serbia was faced with the problem of completing her bourgeois-democratic revolution. He was greatly influenced by the ideas of the Russian revolutionary democrats. He severely criticised the capitalist system and came out openly in the defence of the Paris Commune. M., however, did not reach the level of dialectical and historical materialism and scientific socialism in spite of his knowledge of the main works of Marx and Engels and his participation in the work of the First International. He held the mistaken notion that, relying on the *zadruga* (a big patriarchal family) and the village commune, it was possible after the victory of a popular revolution to pass on to socialism, bypassing capitalism.

Marti, Jose (1853-1895), Cuban thinker, publicist, poet, the ideologist and leader of the national liberation movement. M.'s views have a pronounced revolutionary-democratic character. He regarded revolution as a path that leads not only to national independence, but also to social renovation, to a truly democratic system. The philosophical views of M., who tried at first to overcome the "extremes" of materialism and idealism, gradually tended towards materialism. He adhered to the basically materialist view on the origin of life and the emergence of man, and held that these processes had taken place under the impact of natural forces. M. spoke in favour of free thinking, not fettered by speculative and religious dogmas, upheld man's right to scientific knowledge and devoted much attention to a critique of spiritualism, scholasticism and clericalism. In the field of aesthetics he tried to lay the theoretical basis for the social and educational role of art.

Marx, Karl (1818-1883), founder of scientific communism, dialectical and historical materialism, and scientific political economy, the leader and teacher of the world proletariat. The starting point of M.'s spiritual evolution was Hegel's philosophy, its left trend (see Young Hegelians). Among the Young Hegelians he supported most consistently revolutionary democratic ideas both in theory and in practice. In his early work, his Ph. D. thesis on *Difference Between the Democritean and Epicurean Philosophy of Nature* (1841), M. drew, in spite of his idealism, very radical and atheistic conclusions from Hegel's philosophy. In the course of his practical activities and theoretical investigations M. clashed head-on with Hegelian philosophy, because of its conciliatory tendencies, conservative political conclusions, and of the discrepancy between its theoretical principles and the actual social relations and the tasks of transforming those relations. His knowledge of real economic developments, and the philosophy of Feuerbach (q.v.) played a significant role in the process of his switching to materialist positions. A final revolution in M.'s world outlook was wrought by the change in his class stand and his passage from revolutionary democracy to proletarian communism (1844). This transition was brought about by the development of the class struggle in Europe, by his study of political economy, utopian socialism, and history. His new stand found expression in "Contribution to the Critique of Hegel's Philosophy of Law. Introduction" and "On the Jewish Question", two articles published in the *Deutsch-Französische Jahrbücher* (1844). Here M. for the first time disclosed the historic role of the proletariat and arrived at the conclusion of the inevitability of the social revolution and the need of uniting the working-class movement with a scientific world outlook. M. and Engels had been drawn together by that time, and they began systematically elaborating a new world outlook. The results of scientific research and the main principles of the new theory were generalised in the following works: *Economic and Philosophic Manuscripts* (1844), *The Holy Family* (1845), q.v., and *The German Ideology* (1845-46), q.v., written in collaboration with Engels, *Theses on Feuerbach* (1845), q.v., and *The Poverty of Philosophy* (1847), q.v. Marxism was formed as an integral science, reflecting as it did the close unity of all its component parts: philosophy (dialectical and historical materialism), political economy and scientific communism. In 1847, M. joined a secret propaganda society called the Communist League and took an active part in the 2nd Congress of the League. At the Congress' request M. and Engels drew up the famous *Manifesto of the Communist Party* (1848), q.v., which on the basis of all their previous theoretical studies outlined "a new world-conception, consistent materialism, which also embraces the realm of social life; dialectics, as the most comprehensive and profound doctrine of development; the

theory of the class struggle and of the world-historic revolutionary role of the proletariat—the creator of a new, communist society" (V. I. Lenin, *Collected Works*, Vol. 21, p. 48). M.'s philosophy is the most adequate method of cognition and transformation of the world. The development of practice and science in the 19th-20th centuries have convincingly proved the superiority of Marxism over all forms of idealism and metaphysical materialism. M.'s teaching as the only form of the theoretical expression of the working-class interests was steeled in the fight against all sorts of unscientific, anti-proletarian and petty-bourgeois currents. Marx's activities are characterised by partisanship and irreconcilability with any digression from scientific theory. Being a revolutionary in science, M. took an active part in the liberation struggle of the proletariat. During the revolution of 1848-49 in Germany he was at the forefront of the political struggle. He resolutely defended the proletarian stand in his capacity as chief editor of the *Neue Rheinische Zeitung*, which he founded. Banished from Germany in 1849 he settled permanently in London. After the Communist League was dissolved (1852), M. continued his activities in the proletarian movement, working for the creation of the First International (1864). He was active in this organisation, followed closely the progress of the revolutionary movement in all countries, and to the very last day of his life was in the thick of contemporary events. This afforded him the indispensable material for the development of his theory. The experience of the bourgeois revolutions of 1848-49 in Europe was of great importance for the development by Marx of the theory of socialist revolution and class struggle, of the idea of the dictatorship of the proletariat, the tactics of the proletariat in the bourgeois revolution, the need for worker and peasant alliance (*The Class Struggles in France, 1848 to 1850*, 1850), the inevitable destruction of the bourgeois state machine (*The Eighteenth Brumaire of Louis Bonaparte*, 1852). Having examined the experience of the Paris Commune (*The Civil War in France*, 1871), M. discovered a state form of the dictatorship of the proletariat and profoundly analysed the measures adopted by the first proletarian state. In his *Critique of the Gotha Programme* (1875), q.v., M. further developed the theory of scientific communism. His main interest lay in the sphere of political economy, and his lifework *Capital* (q.v.): Volume I was published in 1867; Volume II was published by Engels in 1885, and Volume III, in 1894. The creation of Marxist political economy laid the scientific basis for communism. The philosophical importance of *Capital* and of the extensive preparatory manuscripts of 1857-59 and 1861-63 is unequalled. In these works M. comprehensively developed the major aspects and principles of Marxist philosophy (the dialectical method, the principle of unity of dialectics, logic and the theory of knowledge, etc.) and applied them in a brilliant form to the study of the capitalist system of economic relations. In his preface to *A Contribution to the Critique of Political Economy* (1859), one of his earlier works in economics, M. set forth, in a concise form, the essence of the materialist understanding of history. In *Capital* this understanding found a scientific application. M.'s correspondence contains much of what characterises his philosophy. Never before has any other doctrine been so confirmed in practice as that created by Marx. Lenin, his disciples and followers developed Marxism further under new historical conditions. It was embodied in the victory of socialist revolutions in a number of countries, and it now furnishes the scientific foundation for the activities of Communist and Workers' parties.

Marxism-Leninism, a scientific system of philosophical, economic and sociopolitical views, created by Marx and Engels (qq.v.) and creatively developed by Lenin (q.v.) in new conditions. Marxism was born in the mid-19th century, when capitalism's historical limits began to show and the working class (q.v.), its future grave-digger, made its appearance in the arena of history. Marxism was created through the critical reworking of achievements of classical German philosophy (q.v.), particularly of Hegel and Feuerbach (qq.v.), the political economy of A. Smith and D. Ricardo, and the utopian socialism of Saint-Simon,

Fourier and Owen (qq.v.). Lenin called these three teachings the sources of Marxism. The intrinsically connected component parts of M.L. are philosophy (q.v.) that covers dialectical and historical materialism, political economy and scientific communism (q.v.). M.L. not only scientifically explained the world, but also defined the conditions, ways and means of changing it. The application of the principles of Marxist philosophy, materialist dialectics (q.v.) to an analysis of society led to the discovery of the laws of its functioning and development. For the first time society was regarded as an integral organism, whose structure includes productive forces (q.v.), relations of production (q.v.) and the following spheres of social life which they determine: the state, politics, law, morality, philosophy, science, art, religion. Marx and Engels created a scientific political economy which disclosed the nature of capitalist exploitation, proved the historically transient nature of capitalism and substantiated the need for the transition to socialism. The principles and programme of building the new society known as scientific communism is a major component of M.L. It has shown that the transition from capitalism to socialism takes place as the result of the struggle of the working class whose historic mission is to win political power through revolution, to put an end to any exploitation of man by man and to build communism. The working-class movement can achieve victory only if it is combined with socialist theory, with M.L. This is effected by a Communist party, the vanguard of the working class, its organiser and leader. M.L. is a guide to the transformation of society and nature. It develops as a living and creative science, and is incompatible with any form of dogmatism and ready-made recipes. A new, important stage in the creative development of Marxism is associated with the name of Lenin, who enriched all its component parts in the period when proletarian revolution and socialist construction had become matters of immediate practice. He raised Marxist philosophy to a qualitatively new stage, generalised the latest achievements of science, comprehensively developed materialist dialectics by applying it to new conditions of social life. He produced a scientific theory of the imperialist stage of capitalism as its highest and last stage and developed the theory of the socialist revolution (q.v.). While guiding the world's first socialist revolution, Lenin defined the concrete paths of building the new society. Today M.L. is creatively developed by the collective effort of the CPSU and other Communist and Workers' parties, which have analysed the intensifying process of the general crisis of capitalism (q.v.) and also the basic contradiction of the current epoch— that between socialism and capitalism and its influence on world developments. The historical experience has confirmed that general regularities of socialist revolutions and the building of the new society manifest themselves in various concrete forms, depending on the stage of social development, the correlation of class forces inside a given country and in the international arena. These regularities form the objective groundwork for the international solidarity of the working class, of all the currents of the world liberation movement. Of great importance is the conclusion made by Communist parties that a new world war is not inevitable, the analysis of the interrelationship between peaceful coexistence and the class struggle (qq.v.), and the peace movement for social progress. The CPSU and the Communist and Workers' parties of other socialist countries have elaborated the conception of a developed, mature socialist society. With the building of this society in the USSR, the state of the dictatorship of the proletariat (q.v.) has turned into a state of the whole people (q.v.), and a new historical community—the Soviet people—has emerged. The Communist parties uphold the creative nature of M.L. by struggling against bourgeois ideology and against the revisionist and dogmatic distortions of this advanced theory. In the present epoch M.L. gives a great deal of attention to the problems of socialist and communist construction, of the struggle of the working class in capitalist countries and of the national liberation movement. The entire course of modern social development proves the strength and vitality of M.L., the correctness of its main conclusions

and propositions, demonstrates its growing impact on the forms and pace of social progress. M.L. has gripped the minds of progressive people and is being put into practice by millions of people struggling for a better life, for building socialism and communism.

Marxist Philosophical Thought Abroad (after the triumph of the October Revolution). The victory of the Great October Socialist Revolution in 1917 ushered in a new historical era, the era of the transition from capitalism to socialism. In capitalist countries people have shown more interest in Marxism-Leninism and its philosophy, particularly in works by Lenin (q.v.). The emergent Communist parties, united into the Third International in 1919, regarded dialectical and historical materialism (qq.v.) as their philosophical banner. Already in the 1920s Lenin's philosophical works were translated into the principal European languages. Philosophical problems were dealt with by G. Dimitrov, A. Gramsci, P. Togliatti, M. Thorez, E. Thaelmann, W. Foster and other Communist leaders. They sought to uphold the theory of the unity of Marxist theory and the proletariat's revolutionary practice. Bourgeois scholars intensified their attacks on Marxist-Leninist philosophy. Reformists continued their revision of dialectical and historical materialism from the standpoint of ethical socialism (q.v.). The 1918-23 revolutionary upsurge in some European countries was followed by the consolidation of the political positions of the Left in the European labour movement. However, some of its representatives showed theoretical immaturity and subjectivism and underestimated the role of the masses in history. Lenin's work "Left-Wing" Communism—an Infantile Disorder (1920) was of decisive importance for the exposure of Leftist views. The temporary economic boom in some capitalist countries (1924-29) and the growing activity of bourgeois and Right-socialist ideology caused by it facilitated the penetration into Communist parties (in the USA, Germany, Italy and other countries) of Right-wing opportunism and mechanistic philosophy, its ideological core. The Marxists united in the Third International opposed the Leftist and Rightist deviations on philosophical problems as well. The deepening general crisis of capitalism precipitated by the successes of socialist construction in the USSR and by the 1929-33 economic crisis resulted in the establishment of fascism (q.v.) in some capitalist countries. Ideologically, these developments manifested themselves in wider propaganda of irrationalism (q.v.), subjective idealist philosophy, voluntarism (q.v.), etc. The communist tactics of united popular fronts in the struggle against fascism contributed to the unity of the progressive intelligentsia round Marxists and accelerated the transition of some of its representatives to the side of dialectical materialist philosophy. The struggle of Marxist philosophers against intuitionalism, q.v. (works of G. Politzer), neo-Hegelianism, q.v. (works of A. Gramsci), pragmatism (q.v.) (works of W. Foster), the immanent school in philosophy, q.v. (works by Th. Pavlov), and against other trends in bourgeois philosophy in the 1930s raised the prestige of dialectical materialism and showed its role as a methodological principle of science and an effective instrument in combating fascist ideology. A new stage in Marxist-Leninist philosophy began soon after the Second World War. Several socialist states emerged after the defeat of German and Italian fascism and Japanese militarism and the victory of popular revolutions in Europe and Asia. Led by Communist and Workers' parties, the philosophers of these countries waged the struggle for the assertion of a scientific, communist world outlook among the popular masses. They did a great amount of work to overcome the reactionary bourgeois, reformist and revisionist ideology, to study the wide spectre of problems of dialectical and historical materialism, socio-philosophical problems of socialist society, philosophical problems of natural science, problems of the history of philosophy, ethics, aesthetics and of the propaganda of philosophical knowledge. Philosophers in socialist countries consistently defend the principles of proletarian internationalism (q.v.), hold joint scientific forums, and publish joint works on topical problems of Marxist-Leninist philosophy. Marxist philosophers in

capitalist countries actively defend progressive philosophical traditions and expose anti-communist propaganda and the latest methods of refined idealism. The works by M. Cornforth, J. Lewis (Britain), H. Wells, H. Selsam and H. Parsons (the USA), G. Besse, L. Sève (France), W. Hollitscher (Austria), R. Steigerwald (the FRG) and other authors reveal the inner contradictory nature and insolvency of the latest idealist trends—neo-positivism (q.v.), pragmatism, existentialism (q.v.) and neo-Thomism (q.v.). The deepening of capitalism's general crisis, the widening world revolutionary process, and the strengthened positions of existing socialism on the world arena are accompanied by the accute ideological struggle on the problems associated with the analysis of the laws governing the transition from capitalism to socialism in present-day conditions. Anti-communism (q.v.) tries to discredit the experience of existing socialism. All kinds of petty-bourgeois illusions make their appearance, numerous attempts are being made to justify ideological pluralism, to errode the ideological basis of the communist movement. Resolute struggle against anti-communism is closely linked with the striving to overcome petty-bourgeois illusions and to frustrate the attempts aimed at undermining the principles of proletarian internationalism.

Marxist Philosophy in the USSR. Marxist-Leninist philosophy became widespread in the country since the first years of Soviet power established in 1917. At that time it waged a struggle against the remnants of old, bourgeois philosophy and also against the philosophical theories of Menshevism, Russian Machism and so on. The year of 1922 witnessed the foundation of the first Marxist philosophical journal— *Pod znamenem marksizma* (Under the Banner of Marxism). It was published until 1944 and was succeeded in 1947 by the journal *Voprosy filosophii* (Problems of Philosophy). The third issue of the journal *Pod znamenem marksizma* carried Lenin's article "On the Significance of Militant Materialism", which formulated the tasks that faced philosophical science and exerted great influence on the subsequent work of Soviet philosophers. The first Soviet years saw the formation of a new generation of philosophers closely associated with the Communist Party and its efforts to reorganise the country on socialist lines. Soviet philosophers elaborated philosophical problems of socialist construction, the cultural revolution and interpreted the history of philosophy in Marxist terms; they allied with natural scientists and brought them to the side of dialectical materialism. In the late 1920s and early 1930s they criticised the relapses of mechanistic materialism and Hegelian revision of dialectical materialism. Engels' *Dialectics of Nature* (q.v.) and Lenin's *Philosophical Notebooks*, q.v. (published for the first time in 1925 and 1929 respectively) gave impetus to a profound study of problems of dialectical materialism. However, Soviet philosophical science like the other social sciences in the country fell under the negative influence of Stalin's personality cult. His work *On Dialectical and Historical Materialism* was declared the "acme" of Marxist philosophy without any foundation. The Communist Party of the Soviet Union strongly condemned the cult of Stalin's personality. The creative elaboration of Marxist theory by the 20th and subsequent congresses of the CPSU marked the beginning of a new stage in the development of Soviet philosophical science. This stage is a witness to the extension of the sphere of research and a broader approach to topical problems of modern philosophical science. Soviet philosophers overcame elements of dogmatism and wrote many fundamental scientific works, text-books and manuals, and also reference books and encyclopaedias, e.g., *Philosophical Encyclopaedia*. The results achieved by Soviet philosophical science in the 1960s, 1970s and early 1980s have shown the greater role of Marxist-Leninist philosophy in solving the tasks set by social practice and scientific knowledge. The resolutions of the 23rd, 24th, 25th and 26th CPSU congresses and the decisions of the CPSU Central Committee "On Measures to Develop Further the Social Sciences and to Enhance Their Role in Communist Construction" (1967) and "On the Further

Improvement of Ideological and Politico-Educational Work" (1979) helped to determine the main directions in the development of philosophical thought, strengthen its ties with social practice and ensure a creative atmosphere in the philosophical science. The country's philosophical institutions—the Institute of Philosophy of the USSR Academy of Sciences and the corresponding institutes in the Republican Academies of Sciences, the Philosophical Society of the USSR, the philosophical chairs at the Academy of Social Sciences under the CC CPSU and at universities and institutions of higher learning—are engaged in research into major trends of modern philosophical knowledge. These institutions study the problems of dialectical materialism—problems of the theory of materialist dialectics; the theory of knowledge, the theory of reflection, problems of dialectical logic, the methodology and logic of science (works by B. M. Kedrov, P. V. Kopnin and others). Considerable results have been obtained in the study of the philosophical problems of natural science. Soviet philosophers, e.g., M. E. Omelyanovsky, I. T. Frolov, and natural scientists, e.g., V. A. Ambartsumyan, A. I. Berg, V. A. Fok, interpret the latest discoveries in physics, cosmology, biology, cybernetics and other special sciences in the light of dialectical materialism. D. N. Uznadze, A. N. Leontiev, B. F. Lomov and others fruitfully elaborate the philosophical questions of psychology. Studies in this sphere of philosophical knowledge contribute to the closer alliance between Marxist philosophers and natural scientists. The greatest contribution to historical materialism has been made by the investigations of the socio-philosophical problems of developed socialist society, the dialectics of modern social development, the world revolutionary process, problems of management and of the development of the individual. F. V. Konstantinov, V. G. Afanasiev, P. N. Fedoseyev, Ts. A. Stepanyan and others analyse the nature of major socio-political processes of the present epoch, the regularities of socialist revolution, the dialectics of the general and the particular in socialist and communist construction, the role of the working class in the socialist and bourgeois societies. Wide research is undertaken into the scientific and technological revolution and its social consequences and the global problems of today. Soviet scholars conduct intensive studies of historico-philosophical problems, the problems of Russian and world history of philosophy. Especially great results have been obtained in the study of Lenin's stage in Marxist-Leninist philosophy. Soviet philosophers are active participants in the current struggle of ideas: they subject to a highly argumented and effective criticism the philosophical conceptions that are hostile to Marxism-Leninism and reveal the insolvency of modernised idealist and metaphysical trends. They attach great importance to problems of ethics (A. F. Shishkin and others), aesthetics (A. G. Yegorov, M. F. Ovsyannikov and others) and scientific atheism. Today we witness the growing synthesising, integrating role of Marxist-Leninist philosophy, which unites the efforts of the representatives of social, natural and technical sciences to solve vital problems in a comprehensive way. In the 1980s, the Soviet philosophers have to solve a number of important tasks—the comprehensive elaboration of the theory of materialist dialectics, analysis of the dialectics of scientific cognition and social practice, the study of socio-philosophical problems of existing socialism, the formation of a new culture, the philosophical interpretation of man's modern development, etc.

Masaryk, Tomáš Garrigue (1850-1937), Czech philosopher and political leader, founder of so-called Masarykism. M.'s philosophy (which he called "realism") is inconsistent. It combines positivist empiricism (chiefly characteristic of his early works) and irrational and religious ethical ideas. According to M., religion asserts itself when knowledge transcends phenomena and people are confronted with the question about the meaning of human being, the meaning of history. By religion he understood not usual orthodox theology but belief based on a "moral conviction". M. preached abstract humanism and upheld the programme of bourgeois reforms and class collaboration. M.'s views were thoroughly anti-Marxist and were a source of Right-opportunist distortions of Marxist-Leninist ideology and of revisionist attacks on it. His main works: *Modern člověk a náboženství* (1896-98) and *The Social Question* (1898).

Mass Communication, the process of spreading information (knowledge, spiritual values, moral and legal norms, etc.) through technical means (the press, radio, cinema, television) among numerically large and scattered audiences. Bourgeois sociologists hold that M.C. has a supraclass and non-partisan character. Marxists, on the other hand, recognise and stress that it is socially conditioned. In a capitalist society the main function of M.C. is to impose on man stereotypes of existing relations, to keep people within the framework of a dominant ideology. For this reason the means of M.C. operate in the first place as propaganda that imposes standards of bourgeois thought, suppresses man's critical abilities and cultivates a strictly limited set of standard actions, tastes and deeds. A fundamentally different situation exists under socialism where society sets itself the task of reaching a harmony of personal and collective interests (see Collective and Individual, the). In this society the principal task of M.C. is to assist the all-round and full development of the individual, to form his active stand in life and to spread a scientific world outlook. This difference entails different approaches and methods of a scientific analysis of the means of M.C. Most Western sociologists and social psychologists seek above all to study the impact of mass media on audiences and to determine the degree to which convictions change under the influence of propaganda. In socialist society, the main object of studies is the structure and the range of the audiences' needs and the degree to which they are met by means of M.C.

Mass Consciousness, the social consciousness of the masses (classes and social groups) in a society which reflects the conditions of their everyday life, needs and interests. M.C. includes people's ideas, views, notions, illusions and social sentiments spread in society. It is a fusion of the ordinary psychological and theoretico-ideological levels of social consciousness, although the real presence of theoretico-ideological elements and their share in M.C. depend on historical circumstances and the degree of the development of the masses as a social subject. M.C. reflects public opinion (q.v.), the sentiments and actions of the masses. In the antagonistic class formations, M.C. is formed in a spontaneous way, being the result of the impact by conditions proper and the pressure of dominant ideology which is imposed on M.C. by all the means of spiritual influence wielded by the economically and politically dominant class. Today, capitalist states make a wide use of mass media and resort to refined methods of manipulating M.C. for the benefit of the monopolies and the bourgeois state. Marxist-Leninist parties take into account the real condition of the M.C. of the working people and at the same time introduce into it scientific and revolutionary ideology, develop it by educating the masses on their own political experience. Under socialism the genesis mechanism of M.C. undergoes a qualitative change, the element of spontaneity in it diminishes and the significance and role of the active and goal-oriented principle increase. Communist parties direct the ideological and educational work along the channel of developing the consciousness of the masses, of moulding the new man. Greater volume of information and of competence of M.C. is a vital task in the context of involving the masses into the administration of social processes. Qualitative change in M.C. is an essential prerequisite for mass participation in conscious history-making.

Mass Culture, a typical product of "mass society", a specific form of functioning bourgeois culture. It represents a well-organised consumer industry and has a highly ramified network of means of mass communication (q.v.) exerting appropriate influence on individual and social consciousness and providing advertisement to ensure the demand for products of M.C. The latter is the instrument of maintaining bourgeois conceptions of man's purpose in life, his predestination in the world, of the ways of humanising

social being and also the means of the socialisation and education of man and his incorporation into the socio-economic and political institutions of state-monopoly capitalism. The main social functions of M.C. are: integration of people into the existing system of social relations; the switching of their attention from the interpretation of problems of real life to the perception of mass fads in entertainment establishments, to emotional relaxation and the freak of imagination that lead the man to the realm of fancy and illusion and create the semblance of his commitment to the solution of vital problems of today; psychological control of the people's minds, brainwashing and influencing them with the aim of forming standard needs, stereotyped patterns of thinking and acceptable forms of adaptation to the bourgeois world order; the reconciliation of man with the existing and ever growing contradictions of the present stage of social development. M. C. is a partial but, as a rule, distorted form of bringing cultural values within the reach of the broad masses. By and large, M.C. is fundamentally opposed to a genuinely democratic culture, the one aimed at mastering the world in spiritual and practical terms, at developing the cultural and historical process along humanist lines, at creatively increasing man's spiritual wealth and at moral perfection of the individual.

"Mass Society", Theories of. Bourgeois conceptions which regard societal tendencies and prospects from the angle of mounting industrialisation and urbanisation, standardisation of production and consumption, bureaucratisation of social life, the spread of mass media (the press, radio and TV) and mass culture (q.v.). The bourgeois sociologists who develop the theories of "M.S." (Mills, Fromm, Parsons, Bell, qq.v., and others) belong to different trends, ranging from those that criticise capitalism from the position of bourgeois humanism, liberalism and romanticism to direct apologia for it. Marxist-Leninist analysis of the theories of "M.S." demonstrates their untenability in the light of the real tendencies and perspectives of human development, noting at the same time their criticism of the bourgeois society and the formulation of some vital problems of the present-day reality (problems of correlation between the individual and social groups, problems of cultural development, the social role played by mass media, etc.).

Material and Moral Labour Incentives, conscious stimuli of human activity (q.v.) aimed at satisfying man's need for labour (q.v.). Material incentives are associated with the need for labour as a means of life, while moral incentives with the need for creative labour that finds satisfaction in the social importance of its results. Every socio-economic formation (q.v.) has its own system of labour incentives, which represents a totality of social phenomena (economic, moral, ideological and others). The nature and content of incentives are determined by social relations, the development level of productive forces (q.v.), the degree of the individual's spiritual perfection. Interests of private enterprise reign supreme under capitalism. This makes for the warped development of material incentives, the development to the detriment of moral incentives, whose sphere of operation is limited. Only under socialism is it possible to create a system of stimulation based on the dialectical unity of material and moral incentives. Under socialism, the first stage of communism, where labour has not as yet become life's prime necessity, personal material interest (payment according to the work done) is the basic form of drawing people into labour, improving their skills and raising their labour productivity. Lenin emphasised that the masses can be brought to communism, "not directly relying on enthusiasm, but aided by the enthusiasm engendered by the great revolution, and on the basis of personal interest, personal incentive and business principles" (Vol. 33, p. 58). The CPSU and the Soviet Government attach great significance to personal material stimulation and constantly improve its forms: extend the powers of enterprises to provide stimuli, promote cost accounting, bonus systems, etc. Along with material incentives, of great importance are the moral incentives (awarding government orders and medals, certificates of honour, celebrations in honour of fore-

most workers, etc.). Being relatively independent, the moral incentives exercise direct influence on material incentives. In their turn, the material incentives are closely connected with the moral ones. The organic combination of the two is achieved in socialist emulation and is a condition for the full employment of the socialist system's advantages. Under communism, where labour will become a life's prime necessity for all and everybody and people will work without any remuneration (see Communist Labour), moral incentives will be the main ones, and personal material interest will merge with society's material interest.

Material and Technical Base of Society, a totality of material conditions of production (implements and means of labour) necessary for the emergence and development of a socio-economic formation (q.v.). The M.T.B.S. is a component of productive forces (q.v.) and makes certain demands on their other elements—the workers and their cultural development, intellectual and volitional qualities. The M.T.B.S. of a socio-economic formation may differ in quantitative and qualitative terms from the previously existing base. Qualitative changes occur at a time when revolutions take place in the development of production. Every new leap in production enables the society to rise to a qualitatively new stage of labour and its productivity. The first qualitative leap took place in the primitive-communal system (q.v.) due to the discovery of the smelting of metals, above all iron, and to the making of metal tools. Like plant cultivation and domestication of animals the discovery of smelting made it possible to obtain surplus product and exploit other men. All this formed the basis for the emergence of the antagonistic socio-economic formations—the slave-owning system and feudalism (qq.v.). The implements individually used by labourers possessing certain habits of manual labour underlie the M.T.B.S. of both formations. The second qualitative leap in the development of the material conditions of production took place during the industrial revolution and gave rise to large-scale industry, which became the M.T.B. of capitalism (q.v.). The large-scale industry is based on machinery produced in the wake of discoveries in natural science. As Marx put it, the water-mill embodies feudal society and the steam-mill the capitalist society. At a certain level the large-scale industry creates conditions for a socialist revolution and serves as an economic basis for building a socialist society. Socialism differs from capitalism not so much by the material side of production as by the position of the worker who is freed from exploitation and is a co-owner of the socially owned means of production. The third qualitative leap in the development of the material conditions of production is taking place today. It is called current scientific and technological revolution (q.v.). Although the achievements of the scientific and technological revolution are also used by capitalism, the radical change it causes in the material side of production does not fit in with the narrow framework of capitalist relations, private ownership of the means of production. On the other hand, social ownership opens up a wide scope for their comprehensive application, for building the M.T.B. of communism. This entails the broad use of all the achievements of scientific and technological progress, of new sources and methods of obtaining and transforming energy, the creation and extensive application of new synthetic materials, comprehensive automation (q.v.) of production, the introduction of production processes that do not require man's direct interference, the development of electronics and computer technology as the necessary material conditions for the organisation of production and control of it. The M.T.B. of communism qualitatively changes the character of both mental and physical labour and secures their harmonious fusion. It implies the conversion of science (q.v.) into a direct productive force and of production into a practical application of science, and this makes labour creative and pleasant. The M.T.B. of communism creates the abundance of material and spiritual values, which makes possible the transition to the realisation of the basic principle of communism: "From each according to his abilities, to each according to his needs". The M.T.B. of communism is formed within the womb of socialist society, on the basis of the achievements of the scientific and technological revolution, through the labour of the members of society, their conscious and systematic activity directed by the Communist party. The CPSU congresses and the guidelines they adopt for the economic and social development of the Soviet Union for five years and for longer periods outline new stages of building the M.T.B. of communism. In fulfilling and overfulfilling five-year plan assignments, the Soviet working people make their contribution to the cause of building a communist society and prepare the development of socialism into communism (see Socialism and Communism).

Materialism, the scientific philosophical trend, opposed to idealism (q.v.). We distinguish two kinds of M., the spontaneous belief of all people in the objective existence of the external world, and the philosophical world outlook, which scientifically deepens and develops spontaneous M. Philosophical M. maintains that the material is primary and the spiritual, ideal, secondary. This implies that the world is eternal, not created by God, and is infinite in time and space. Maintaining that consciousness is a product of matter, M. considers it as the reflection of the external world, and thereby asserts the knowability of the world. In the history of philosophy M. was, as a rule, the world outlook of progressive classes and strata in society, who were interested in correctly understanding the world and in increasing man's power over nature. In summing up achievements of science, M. promoted the growth of scientific knowledge, the improvement of scientific methods; this, in its turn, favourably influenced man's practical activity and the development of productive forces. In the process of the interaction between M. and the special sciences M. and its forms underwent changes. The first materialist theories made their appearance with the rise of philosophy as a result of the progress of scientific knowledge in astronomy, mathematics and other fields in the slave-owning societies of ancient India, China and Greece. The general feature of ancient M., which for the most part was naive (Lao Tsû, Yang Chu, q.v., Wan

Chung, q.v., the Lokāyata, q.v., school, Heraclitus, Anaxagoras, Empedocles, Democritus, Epicurus, qq.v., and others), was recognition of the materiality of the world and its independent existence outside of man's consciousness. Representatives of M. tried to find in the diversity of natural phenomena the common source of origin of all that exists or takes place (see Element). It was the merit of ancient M. to create a hypothesis on the atomic structure of matter (Leucippus, q.v., Democritus). Many of the ancient materialists were spontaneous dialecticians, but most of them did not make a clear-cut distinction between the physical and the psychic, attributing all the properties of the latter to nature (see Hylozoism). The development of materialist and dialectical principles in ancient M. went side by side with the growth of the influence of mythological ideology. In the Middle Ages, materialistic trends appeared in the form of nominalism (q.v.), early pantheistic heresies and the teachings that nature and God are eternal. In the epoch of the Renaissance M. (Telesio, Bruno, qq.v., and others) took often the form of pantheism and hylozoism and regarded nature in its wholeness and in many respects resembled ancient M. M. developed in Europe in the 17th-18th centuries (Galileo Galilei, Hobbes, Gassendi, Spinoza, Locke, qq.v.). This form of M. developed on the basis of nascent capitalism, and the attendant growth of production, technology and science. Speaking for the then progressive bourgeoisie, the materialists combated medieval scholasticism and ecclesiastical authority, looking to experience as their tutor and to nature as the object of philosophy. The M. of the 17th-18th centuries developed in conjunction with the then rapidly progressing mechanics and mathematics, as a result of which it was mechanistic. Another of its features was a desire to analyse, to divide nature into more or less isolated and mutually unrelated fields and objects of investigation, and to study these without regard for their development. French M. of the 18th century occupied a special place in the materialist philosophy of this period (La Mettrie, Diderot, Helvétius, and Holbach, qq.v.). The French materialists maintained on the whole the mechanistic conception of motion, considering it as a universal and inalienable property of nature. Many elements of dialectics are to be found in Diderot's M. The organic link existing between all kinds of M. and atheism (q.v.) was particularly apparent in the French materialists of the 18th century. The peak in the development of this form of M. in the West was the "anthropological" M. of Feuerbach (q.v.). At the same time contemplation characteristic of all pre-Marxist M. was more manifest in Feuerbach than in any of his contemporaries. A further step in the development of M. was made in the second half of the 19th century in Russia and other countries of Eastern Europe by the philosophy of the revolutionary democrats (Belinsky, Herzen, Chernyshevsky, Dobrolyubov, Marković, Botev, qq.v., and others), a philosophy which rested upon the traditions of Lomonosov, Radishchev (qq.v.), and others. In some respects the revolutionary democrats rose above the limited horizon of anthropologism and the metaphysical method. The highest and most consistent form of M. was dialectical materialism created by Marx and Engels in the middle of the 19th century. It overcame not only the aforementioned shortcomings of the old M. but also the idealistic understanding of human society common to all its representatives. In its later development M. split into two main trends: dialectical and historical materialism, on the one hand, and a number of simplified and vulgarised varieties of M., on the other. The most typical variety was vulgar M. which gravitated to positivism (q.v.); and to this latter gravitated those varieties of vulgar M. which appeared at the turn of the century as a distortion of dialectical M. In the second half of the 19th century the mature forms of M. proved to be incompatible with the narrow class interests of the bourgeoisie. Bourgeois philosophers hold that adherents of M. are immoral and identify M. with its primitive varieties. Sometimes idealists present their theories as "genuine" and "the most modern" M. (see Carnap, Bachelard, Sartre). While concealing in some cases the antithesis between M. and idealism, bourgeois philosophers resort not only to positivism and neorealism (q.v.), but also to such amorphous and ambiguous constructions as modern American naturalism. Some leading scientists turn from natural-scientific to conscious M., and finally to dialectical M. (Langevin, Joliot-Curie, qq.v., and others). An important peculiarity of the development of dialectical M. is its enrichment with new ideas. The contemporary development of science demands that the natural scientist become a conscious adherent of dialectical materialism. At the same time socio-historical practice and science call for continued progress in M. philosophy and for its concretisation. The latter takes place in the constant struggle of M. against the latest varieties of idealist philosophy.

Materialism and Empirio-Criticism. *Critical Comments on a Reactionary Phylosophy,* Lenin's fundamental philosophical work, written in 1908 and published in May 1909. The book was written during the period of reaction brought about by the defeat of the first Russian revolution (1905-07). At that time the Marxists were confronted with the urgent political and theoretical task of defending dialectical and historical materialism against the attacks of revisionism and of refuting the reactionary philosophy of empirio-criticism (q.v.) which was being vigorously propagated by the revisionists. *M.&.E.* criticised thoroughly the subjective-idealistic philosophy of empirio-criticism and showed that dialectical and historical materialism is entirely opposed to the former in all problems of philosophy. Lenin pointed out that the Russian Machists, in their desire to "supplement and develop" Marxism through Machian philosophy, were in fact only echoing the reactionary ideas of subjective idealism and agnosticism (qq.v.). The experience of all mankind, the data of natural science, completely refute all the concoctions of these "latest" idealists. Lenin's book shows the sources of empirio-criticism and its ideological place in the development of bourgeois philosophy: beginning with Kant (q.v.), the Machists went from him to Hume and Berkeley (qq.v.) and were unable to go beyond their views. A typical feature of Machism

was its proximity to the most reactionary trends in bourgeois thought of the type of the immanent school in philosophy (q.v.). Claiming the role of philosophy in contemporary natural science empirio-criticism in fact adversely influenced the development of science, using and amplifying the idealist vacillations of some physicists brought about by the crisis in physics at the turn of the century. Lenin's discovery of the social roots and the class role of Machian philosophy is of exceptional importance. Resolutely and persistently pursuing the line of partisanship (q.v.) in philosophy, Lenin gave the lie to the claims of the Machists and of the whole trend of positivism (q.v.) to be above materialism and idealism, and pointed out that empirio-criticism served the forces of reaction, religion, and was hostile to science and progress. Apart from his comprehensive criticism of Machism and its Russian followers and fellow-thinkers, Lenin in his book substantiated and developed further the most important tenets of dialectical and historical materialism. He gave an all-round analysis of the fundamental question of philosophy (q.v.) and the most important categories of Marxist philosophy (e.g., matter, experience, time and space, causality, freedom and necessity, qq.v.), creatively developed the Marxist theory of knowledge (q.v.), especially the theory of reflection (q.v.), the role of practice in cognition, the place and role of sensations in cognition, objective truth (q.v.), the relation between absolute and relative truth (q.v.), and the basic problems of historical materialism (q.v.). Lenin's generalisation of new data accumulated by natural science is of particular importance. The outstanding discoveries in physics at the turn of the century marked the beginning of a revolution in natural science. These discoveries, however, gave birth to an acute crisis in the development of natural science, which was intimately connected with physical idealism (q.v.). Exposing the class and epistemological roots of physical idealism, Lenin proved that the new discoveries in physics, far from refuting materialism, supplied, on the contrary, further confirmation of dialectical materialism. Having summed up the latest scientific accomplishments,

Lenin convincingly showed the great importance of the method of materialist dialectics for progress in science and for the overcoming of the crisis in natural science. Lenin's work is a masterpiece of creative Marxism and even now serves as an ideological weapon in the struggle against bourgeois philosophy and revisionism and promotes the philosophical generalisation of the present state of the natural sciences.

Materialism, Dialectical, the scientific philosophical world outlook, a component of the Marxist doctrine, its philosophical basis. D.M. was evolved by Marx and Engels and further developed by Lenin and other Marxists. It originated in the 1840s and developed in intimate association with scientific progress and the practice of the revolutionary labour movement. Its emergence was a revolution in the history of human thought, the history of philosophy. But this revolution included continuity and critical acceptance of all the advanced, progressive elements already attained by human thought. The two mainstreams of preceding philosophical development merged in D.M. and were fructified by a new approach, a new, profoundly scientific outlook. There was the development, on the one hand, of materialist philosophy, which went back to the remote past, and, on the other, of the dialectical outlook, which also had deep-rooted traditions in the history of philosophy. The development of philosophical thought in close association with science and the historical practice of mankind led inevitably to the triumph of the materialistic outlook. But despite glimmers of dialectics, the doctrines of the old materialists were metaphysical or mechanistic, and combined materialism in their view of nature with idealism in their explanation of social phenomena. The philosophers who developed the dialectical outlook were essentially idealists, as is shown by Hegel's (q.v.) system. Marx and Engels did not merely borrow the teaching of the old materialists and the dialectics of the idealists. They did not merely synthesise the two, but proceeding from the latest discoveries in natural science and from the historical experience of mankind they proved that materialism can be scientific and consistent only if it is dialectical, and that dialectics, in turn, can be genuinely scientific only if it is materialistic. The development of a scientific outlook on social development and its laws (see Materialism, Historical) was a most essential element in the formation of D.M. It was impossible to defeat idealism in its last retreat, in the explanation of the essence of human society, without the dialectical materialist outlook, and just as impossible to create a consistent philosophical world outlook and explain the laws of human cognition without a materialist approach to society, without an analysis of socio-historical practice and, above all, of social production (q.v.) as the basis of human being. The founders of Marxism solved this problem. D.M. emerged, therefore, as a philosophical synthesis, embracing the intricate complexity of natural phenomena, the phenomena of human society and thought, and combining its philosophical method of explaining and analysing reality with the idea of a practical revolutionary reconstruction of the world. The latter fact distinguishes D.M. from old philosophy, which confined itself essentially to explaining the world. This reflected the class roots of Marxist philosophy as the world outlook of the most revolutionary class, the working class, with its mission of destroying the social system based on exploitation of man by man, and building a classless, communist society. The emergence of D.M. essentially was the culminating point in the historical process by which philosophy became a separate science with a specific object of research. This object comprises the more general laws governing the development of nature, society, and thought, the general principles and foundations of the objective world and its reflection in human consciousness, which yield the correct scientific approach to phenomena and processes, a method of explaining, cognising, and reconstructing reality. The teaching that the world is material, that there is nothing in the world besides matter and the laws of its motion and change, is the corner-stone of D.M. It is a determined and irreconcilable enemy of all conceptions of supernatural essences, no matter what garb they are clothed in by religion or idealist philosophy. Nature develops, attaining its highest forms, including life and thinking matter, through causes inherent in itself and in its laws, and not by any supernatural power. The dialectical theory of development (see Dialectics), which is part of D.M., defines the general laws governing the processes of motion and mutation of matter, the passage from lower to higher forms of matter. Contemporary physical theories concerning matter, space, and time, which recognise the mutability of all matter and the inexhaustible capacity of material particles for qualitative transformations, are in complete agreement with D.M. More than that, D.M. is the only possible source of the philosophical ideas and methodological principles which these physical theories require. The same applies to the sciences investigating other phenomena of nature. Contemporary historical practice confirms the principles of D.M., for the world is making an abrupt turn—from the old, outmoded forms of social life to new, socialist forms. D.M. combines the teaching on being, on the objective world, and the teaching on its reflection in the human mind, thus constituting a theory of knowledge (q.v.) and logic. The fundamentally new advance made by D.M. in this field, which provided the teaching on cognition with an enduring scientific foundation, consisted in practice (see Theory and Practice) being included in the theory of knowledge. D.M. has applied the dialectical theory of development to cognition, established the historical nature of human concepts; it revealed the interconnection between the relative and the absolute in scientific truths, and elaborated the question of the objective logic of cognition (see Logic, Dialectical; Cognition). D.M. is a developing science. Every major discovery in natural science and the changes in social life serve to concretise and develop the principles and propositions of D.M., which absorbs the new scientific evidence and the historical experience of mankind. D.M. is the philosophical basis of the programme, strategy, and tactics, and all activities of the Communist parties.

Materialism, French 18th-Century, an ideological movement representing a new

and higher stage in the development of materialist thought on a national, and also on a world scale as compared with 17th-century materialism. In contrast to English 17th-century materialism, which largely reflected a compromise between the bourgeoisie and the nobility, F.M. was the outlook of the progressive French bourgeoisie; its doctrine aimed to enlighten and arm ideologically a broad section of society—the bourgeoisie, artisans, bourgeois intellectuals, and the progressive part of the aristocratic intelligentsia. The leading French materialists — La Mettrie, Helvétius, Diderot, and Holbach (qq.v.)—expounded their philosophical views not in Latin treatises but in widely accessible publications written in French—dictionaries, encyclopaedias, pamphlets, polemic articles and so on. The ideological sources of F.M. were the national materialist tradition represented in the 17th century by Gassendi (q.v.) and mainly by the mechanistic materialism of Descartes (q.v.) and English materialism. Of particular importance were the doctrine of Locke (q.v.) on experience as a source of knowledge, criticism of the Cartesian doctrine of innate ideas (q.v.), and also a basically materialist understanding of experience as such. Locke's pedagogical and political ideas exerted no less influence. He held that the perfection of the individual is determined by education and the political structure of society. But F.M. did not simply assimilate Locke's theory of materialist sensationalism and empiricism (qq.v.) but discarded vacillations towards Cartesian rationalism (q.v.). Medicine, physiology, and biology, side by side with mechanics, which retained its leading significance, became the scientific basis for the French materialists. Because of this, the doctrines of the French materialists contained many new ideas as compared with 17th-century materialism. Elements of dialectics in Diderot's teaching on nature were the most important of them. The ethical and socio-political theories of F.M. were highly original. Developing the ideas of Hobbes, Spinoza (qq.v.), and Locke in this sphere, F.M. largely cleared their ethical doctrines and their socio-political views from the abstract, naturalist limitations: in contrast to Hobbes, who deduced man's striving for self-preservation from an analogy with the mechanical inertia of a physical body, Helvétius, and Holbach regarded this "interest" as a specifically human motive of behaviour. F.M. rejected the compromise forms of pantheism and deism (qq.v.) and openly preached atheism (q.v.) based on the conclusions of the natural and social sciences. In *Materialism and Empirio-Criticism* (q.v.) Lenin showed how great was the role of F.M. in elaborating philosophical principles for any materialism. He also demonstrated its theoretical limitations, its metaphysical methodology and idealism in explaining phenomena of social development and progress.

Materialism, Historical, a component part of Marxist-Leninist philosophy, the philosophical science about society which solves the fundamental question of philosophy (q.v.) in a materialist way, historically, and studies on this basis the general sociological laws of historical development and the forms of their application in the activity of people. H.M. is the theoretical and methodological basis of sociology (q.v.) and other social sciences. All the pre-Marxist philosophers, including materialists, were idealists in their understanding of social life, inasmuch as they did not go beyond noting the fact that, whereas in nature blind forces are in operation, in society people, intelligent beings, act guided by ideal motives. The development of H.M. caused a fundamental revolution in social thought. It made it possible, on the one hand, to formulate a consistently materialistic view of the world as a whole, society as well as nature, and, on the other, to reveal the material basis of social life and the laws governing its development. Marx elaborated his main idea of the natural historical process of social development by singling out the economic sphere from the different spheres of social life and the relations of production (q.v.) from all social relations as the main ones which determine all the others. Marxism takes its point of departure in what lies at the basis of every human society, namely, the method of obtaining the means of livelihood, and

establishes the connection between that method and the relations into which people enter in the process of production; it sees in the system of these relations of production the foundation, the real basis of every society, on which there rises a political and legal superstructure and different forms of social thought. Each system of production relations, arising at a definite stage in the development of the productive forces (q.v.), is subordinated both to general laws common to all socio-economic formations (q.v.) and to particular laws inherent only in one formation, which determine how that system arises, functions, and passes on into a higher form. The actions of people within each socio-economic formation—infinitely diverse and individualised and seemingly not susceptible of calculation and systematisation—were summed up and reduced to actions of big masses, and in a class society—to actions of classes who realise in their activities the pressing requirements of social development. The discovery of H.M. removed the two main shortcomings of all pre-Marxist sociological theories. In the first place, these theories were idealist, i.e., they limited themselves to examining the ideological motives of human activity but did not study what material causes engendered these motives. Second, they studied only the role of outstanding personalities in history, but did not examine the actions of the masses, the real makers of history. H.M. demonstrates that the socio-historical process is determined by material factors. In contrast to vulgar materialist theories which deny the role of ideas, political and other institutions and organisations, H.M. stresses their retroactive influence on the material basis which produced them, and shows the great role of the subjective factor—the actions of people, classes, parties, the consciousness and organisation of the masses. H.M. is opposed to both fatalism and voluntarism (qq.v.). People are the makers of their history but they cannot do it of their own will, as each new generation acts in definite objective conditions which had been formed before it. These conditions and laws which operate on their basis open up various possibilities for people's activities. The utilisation of these possibilities and consequently the real course of history depend on the people, on their activity and initiative, on the organisation and unity of the progressive forces. The main features of H.M. were expounded for the first time by Marx and Engels in *The German Ideology* (q.v.). As history develops and new experience is accumulated, H.M., like Marxism as a whole, is necessarily developed and enriched. Lenin cited a remarkable example of such development. H.M. is closely related to the tasks of the revolutionary class struggle of the proletariat, to the requirements of socialist and communist construction and the development of science. At present, H.M. is being developed by joint efforts of the CPSU and of the Communist and Workers' parties, by Marxist scholars in the world.

Materialism, Vulgar, a trend in mid-19th-century philosophy; it simplified the basic principles of materialism. Stimulated by the rapid development of natural science, V.M. arose as a positivist reaction to idealist, especially the classical German, dialectics, by the metaphysical materialism of natural science. Exponents of V.M., such as Vogt, Büchner and Moleschott, took pains to disseminate current natural science theories, which they opposed to what they styled as philosophical "chicanery". They set out to resolve all philosophical problems by concrete scientific investigations. They believed that consciousness (q.v.) and other social phenomena were the effect of exclusively physiological processes, that they depended on diet, climate, etc. They inferred that thought was a material secretion of the brain. Later, too, vulgar materialist interpretations appeared in different forms, especially in some philosophical interpretation of natural science, mostly in the field of physiology, with physiological phenomena being regarded as a spatial interaction of the organism with external objects. Vulgar materialists sought to reveal (decode) man's psychics in the traces of this interaction. But man lives in historical time as well as in space: his life activity and ability to realise it (consciousness) arise and function in historically developing forms of active intercourse, and their

content is at the same time the content of his consciousness.

Mathematics, the science of mathematical structures (sets between whose elements there are some relations). M. arose in the remote past to meet the requirements of practice. Initially, it had as its subject-matter the simple numbers and geometrical figures. This situation basically prevailed up to the 17th century, and right up to the second half of the 19th century M. developed mainly as mathematical analysis, discovered in the 17th century. M. was completely reconstructed with the discovery of non-Euclidean geometries (q.v.) and the creation of the set theory (q.v.). As a result of this, new branches of M. came into being. Mathematical logic (q.v.) assumed great importance in contemporary M. The mathematical methods are extensively used in the exact natural science. Until now the application of M. in biology and the social sciences was quite accidental. The development of such branches as linear programming, games theory, information theory under the direct impact of practice and the appearance of electronic computers have opened up entirely new prospects. The philosophical problems of M., the origin of mathematical abstraction and its peculiarities, have always been the venue of struggle between materialism and idealism. Of great importance are the philosophical problems that arose in the 20th century in connection with the problems of foundations in M. (see Formalism; Intuitionism).

Matriarchy, a form of the clan organisation in the primitive-communal system (q.v.), where woman occupied the dominant role in social production (upbringing of posterity, communal economic management, keeping the home fire burning and other important functions) and in the social life of gentile community (management of its affairs, regulation of relations among its members, religious rites, etc.). In the sphere of family relations M. was marked by matrilocality (the arrival of men in gentile community families) and by matriliny (tracing descent through the maternal line). Modern science has established that M. did not exist among all peoples. In the opinion of some scholars, M. was not a special stage in the development of the primitive-communal system.

Matter, objective reality, which exists outside and independent of consciousness and is reflected by it. M. is the infinite plurality of the world's existing objects and systems. M. is not created and cannot be destroyed, it is eternal in time and infinite in space, in its structure. It is indissolubly linked with motion and is capable of uninterrupted self-development, which, at definite stages and given favourable conditions, leads to the emergence of life and thinking creatures. Consciousness (q.v.) appears as the supreme form of reflection (q.v.) peculiar to M. The characteristic features of the material unity of the world are the universal and absolute nature of M. The world does not know anything that would not be a definite type or state of M., its property and form of motion, a product of its historical development. The recognition of the material unity of the world is a primary principle of philosophical materialism in contradistinction to all idealist conceptions, which accept the divine will, "absolute idea", spirit, energy (see Energism), etc., as the substance of all phenomena in the world. M. cannot be reduced to its concrete forms, e.g., to substances or atoms, since there are immaterial types of M.—electromagnetic and gravitation fields, neutrino of various kinds with a complex structure. M. is inexhaustible and its cognition is potentially unlimited. At the same time M. always has an orderly systemic organisation and is inseparable from different properties and forms of motion. From the standpoint of modern science the main forms of M. are as follows: 1) systems of inanimate nature (elementary particles, q.v., fields, atoms, molecules, macroscopic bodies, cosmic systems of different orders); 2) biological systems (all biosphere, from microorganisms to man); 3) socially organised systems (man, society). But M. does not resolve itself into these forms alone, since in the infinite world there exist qualitatively different types of M. as objective reality, e.g., quarks and other possible microobjects in the structure of elementary particles. The

philosophical understanding of M. as objective reality is concretised by the theories of natural science about the structure and properties of M. and the laws of its motion. It would be incorrect, however, to identify M. as a philosophical category with concrete physical or chemical conceptions of M., since they have a local character and do not encompass the endless plurality of the actually existing types of M. It is just as erroneous to identify M. with any of its properties, e.g., mass, energy, space, etc., since M. possesses an inexhaustible variety of different properties. The concept of M. is revealed in detail by dialectical and historical materialism, by its theory of the universal properties of M. and the laws of its development (see Matter, Forms of Motion of; Infinite and Finite; Universe; Substance; Unity and Diversity of the World).

Matter, Forms of Motion of, main types of motion and interaction of material objects expressing their integral changes. In accordance with the data of modern science three main groups of F.M.M. are distinguished: (1) in inorganic nature; (2) in animate nature; (3) in society. In each of these groups there are many F.M.M. owing to the inexhaustibility of matter. The F.M.M. in inorganic nature include: spatial displacement of various bodies; movement of elementary particles and fields (electromagnetic, gravitational), strong and slight interactions, processes of transmutation of elementary particles, etc.; motion and transformation of atoms and molecules, including the chemical F.M.M.; thermal processes, sound oscillations, etc.; the geological F.M.M.; changes in cosmic systems of various orders—planets, stars, galaxies and their conglomerations. In animate nature the F.M.M. include the aggregate of the vital processes in organisms and meta-organism systems: metabolism, processes of reflection, self-regulation, control and reproduction, interaction of the entire biosphere (q.v.) with the natural systems of the Earth and with society. All the biological F.M.M. within organisms are oriented towards preserving those organisms and maintaining their internal stability in the changing conditions of existence. The meta-organism F.M.M. express the relations between representatives of various species in ecosystems and determine their number, habitat (area) and evolution. The social F.M.M. include the various man-ifestations of man's conscious activity (q.v.), all the higher forms of reflection and purposeful transformation of reality. Historically, higher F.M.M. arise on the basis of relatively lower ones, embodying them in a transformed way—in conformi-ty with the structure and laws of develop-ment of a more intricate system. Unity and reciprocal influence exist between them. But the higher F.M.M. qualitatively differ from the lower and are not reduci-ble to them. Disclosure of the relationship between F.M.M. is of great importance for understanding the unity of the world and the historical development of matter, getting to know the essence of intricate phenomena, and for controlling them in practice.

Mayo, Elton (1880-1949), American sociologist, a founder of American indus-trial sociology. According to M., the relations between social groups, including the employer-worker relations, have an emotionally psychological character and for this reason no objective class con-tradictions exist in society. Hence, the workers should take interest not in improving their living and working condi-tions, but in establishing good personal relations with their superiors. In M.'s opinion, sociology must in practice contri-bute to such a "peace" and work out recommendations to influence conscious-ness, psychology and morality of working people so that they should put up with capitalism. M. was one of the creators of the theory of "human relations" (q.v.). His main work: *The Social Problems of an Industrial Civilization* (1945).

Means of Production, a concept denot-ing the aggregate of the material elements of the productive forces (q.v.), as distinct from the living element of production, i.e., the workers. The M.P. include, first, the objects of labour, i.e., the objects which man works on. In modern industrial processes (excluding the mining industry) these are mainly raw materials, i.e.,

natural objects which have already been changed to a certain extent by man's labour. Second, the means of labour—the aggregate of material elements which man uses to influence the objects of labour (work tools, workshops, transport, warehouses for raw materials and finished products, arable land). The most impor-tant means of labour promoting produc-tion and, consequently, the development of society, are the work tools, which enhance man's natural strength and serve as a criterion for assessing his production potential and the degree of development of the social productive forces, that is, as an indication of the social relations under which labour takes place. Therefore, Marx said, "it is not the articles made, but how they are made, and by what instru-ments, that enables us to distinguish different economic epochs" (*Capital*, Vol. I, p. 175).

Measure, a philosophical category ex-pressing the organic unity of quality and quantity of a given object or phenome-non. Every qualitatively distinct object has its own quantitative attributes, which are mobile and mutable. This very muta-tion, however, is of necessity bound by certain limits, beyond which quantitative changes lead to qualitative changes (see Transition from Quantity to Quality). These limits are M. itself. In its turn the qualitative change in a given object leads to a change in its quantitative attributes and M. The connection and unity of quantity and quality is conditioned by the nature of a given object. Once the de-velopment of this object is approached, the points of transition from one qualita-tively different stage of this process to another appear as nodal points in the change of M. Usually such a system of the nodal points is called the nodal line of measures. Hegel (q.v.) was the first to elaborate M. as a philosophical category.

Measurement, a cognitive procedure at the empirical level of scientific research, aimed at determining the characteristics (weight, length, co-ordinates, speed, etc.) of material objects by means of appro-priate measuring instruments (q.v.). In the final count, M. amounts to comparing the measured magnitude with some similar magnitude accepted as a unit. By means of one system of units or another M. gives a quantitative expression to the properties of bodies, which is an important element of knowledge. M. makes our knowledge more exact. Positivists wrongly interpret the increasing role of M. in the study of microphenomena and regard it as "preparation of the object by the subject" ("instrumental idealism") or reduce the content of physical concepts to separate operations of M. (see Operationalism).

Mechanism, a world-view which explains the development of nature and society by the laws of the mechanical form of matter's motion, which are regarded as universal and extend to all types of material motion. Historically, the emergence and spread of M. were associated with the achievements of 17th-18th-century classical mechanics (Galileo Galilei, Newton, qq.v., and others). Classical mechanics elaborated specific notions of matter, motion, space and time. These notions like M. as a whole played a positive role in the development of science and philosophy despite their limited nature conditioned by the then level of natural science in the 17th and 18th centuries. They provided a natural-scientific understanding of many natural phenomena and rid them of mythological and religious-scholastic interpretations. The absolutisation of the laws of mechanics led to the creation of a mechanistic picture of the world, according to which all the Universe (from atoms to planets) represented a closed mechanical system consisting of immutable elements whose motion was determined by the laws of classical mechanics. Brought into line with this level of scientific development was the metaphysical method of thinking (see Metaphysics). The subsequent progress of science, however, revealed the limitations of M. Attempts to explain electromagnetic, chemical, biological and even social phenomena from the standpoint of mechanics were bound to fail. The achievements of natural science in the 19th and 20th centuries destroyed the mechanistic picture of the world and insistently called for a new, dialectical materialist explanation of natural and social processes. Under these conditions the return to M. in any form becomes an obstacle to the progressive development of scientific knowledge. The term of M. used in a broad sense of the word denotes the abstract identification of the higher form of matter's motion with the lower one (e.g., the social form with the biological one and the biological form with the physical or chemical one, etc.).

Mechnikov, Lev Ilyich (1838-1888), Russian sociologist, geographer, and publicist; a democrat. M. took part in the national liberation movement in Italy and was a volunteer in Giuseppe Garibaldi's "Thousand". He contributed to Herzen's (q.v.) *Kolokol* and Chernyshevsky's (q.v.) *Sovremennik*. He planned a sociological work devoted to the history of the world civilisation, but had only time to write the introduction, which was published in 1889 under the title *Tsivilizatsiya i velikiye istoricheskiye reki* (Civilisation and the Great Historical Rivers). He was a partisan of a geographical school (q.v.) in sociology. Social development, he held, was determined by the physico-geographic, principally hydrospheric, environment. River, sea, and ocean routes created, in their time, ancient, medieval, and modern civilisations. M. opposed racism and came forward against the sociologists who extended the laws of biology to society. He considered the free co-operation of people who gradually change nature as a specific characteristic of society. M. was inconsistent in his views, for he found elements of social cooperation in the animal world as well. M. could not overcome idealist conception of history (q.v.) and saw the growth of solidarity and freedom in a society developing from oppression to anarchy as the criterion of social progress (he was influenced by Bakunin, q.v.). M.'s theory played a positive role in combating the religious-philosophical views on society.

Mediation, existence or definition of a thing (concept) by revealing its relation to another thing (concept). The properties of things are revealed in their interconnection with other things. Only through its relation to another thing can a thing be what it is, can it be defined as the given concrete thing. M. is a basic category in the philosophy of Hegel (q.v.). The category of M., in unity with the category of the immediate, expresses the universal interconnection of phenomena, and the universality of the development of diverse things and of the concepts that reflect them.

Medieval Philosophy (in Western Europe), the philosophy of the feudal society which developed from the fall of the Roman Empire (5th century) to the emergence of the early forms of capitalist society (14th-15th centuries). The collapse of antique slave-owning society was attended by a decline of philosophy. The philosophical heritage of antiquity was lost and was unknown to West European scholars until the latter half of the 12th century. Religion became the dominant ideology—the Muslim in Hither Asia, Arabia, and the Arab-speaking countries, and two varieties of Christianity (Roman Catholicism and the Eastern Orthodox Church) in Europe. The school and education fell into the hands of the church, whose dogmas formed the basis of all notions about nature, the world, and man. The development of lay and clerical schools, and the establishment of the first universities in the mid-12th century (in Italy, England, Bohemia, and France) made philosophers devise philosophical explanations, even justifications, for the religious dogmas. For a number of centuries, philosophy was thus the "handmaiden of theology". This is the role it played in the writings of the apologists, the champions of Christianity against heathens, and then in those of the "Fathers of the Church". The most prominent of these, St. Augustine (q.v.), introduced elements of Neoplatonism (q.v.) into the system of Christian philosophical doctrines. Johannes Scotus Erigena (q.v.) was also prominent in creating M.P. In elucidating religious dogmas, the medieval philosophers had to deal with complex problems concerning the relation of the individual to the general, and the reality of the general. Depending on the way these problems were handled, scholasticism (q.v.), the name under which school philosophy came to be known, developed several points of views, the most promi-

nent of which were the mutually antagonistic doctrines of realism (see Realism, Medieval) and of nominalism (q.v.). In the 12th century, Abélard (q.v.) opposed the extremism of both these schools of thought. From the mid-12th century onward, the main writings of Aristotle (q.v.) were translated into Latin. The church received them with hostility at first, but soon the Aristotelian doctrine was recognised as the philosophical foundation of Christianity. The scholastics became protagonists and interpreters of Aristotle. They adapted Aristotelian ideas to their own religious and philosophical concepts, turning the regressive aspects of his doctrine into dogma (e.g., the geocentric system, the principles of his physics) and rejecting all search for the new in science. The chief protagonists of scholasticism in the 13th century were Albert the Great, Thomas Aquinas and John Duns Scotus (qq.v.). Thomas Aquinas was most highly assessed and even canonised by the church, which declared his teaching its official philosophical doctrine (see Neo-Thomism) in the latter half of the 19th century. A prominent contemporary of the three 13th-century scholastic systematisers was R. Bacon (q.v.), who objected to the social basis of feudal society. The development in the 13th century of towns, the arts and crafts, commerce and trade routes, and the contacts with the East extended by the crusades, led to a certain rise of philosophy, particularly of nominalism, whose most prominent protagonists were Occam (q.v.) and his followers of the Parisian school of Occamism. The ideological struggle proceeded beyond the pale of scholasticism too. Opposed to the latter was mysticism (q.v.), which placed the authority of the church and its doctrines beneath the testimony of man's senses and subjective consciousness. In the spiritual life of feudal society, mysticism took often a form of opposition to the official and obligatory dogmas: the personal attitude of the believer to God grew into criticism of, and even struggle against, the feudal ideology and the feudal social system. But mysticism also had a reactionary wing, personified, among others, by Bonaventura (q.v.). A strong anti-scholastic movement emerged in the 13th century, fructified by the teaching of Averroës (q.v.) on the mortality of man's soul and on a reason common to all. The Dominican and Franciscan orders were founded in the early 12th century to fight against heresies, anti-clericalism, and the new philosophical ideas. Despite the relative rise of M.P. in the 13th century, the results of its more than one thousand years of development were meagre both for philosophy and for science, because even the great thinkers were less concerned with the truth than with ways and means of vindicating religion; the clerical regime of medieval society fettered the initiative and thought of those who were audacious enough to go beyond its hidebound framework. It was not until the appearance of the new, capitalist mode of production and the new appreciation of the practical and theoretical tasks of science that the thinking of the foremost minds of Western Europe was gradually freed from the bonds of M.P.

Megarian School, a philosophical trend which existed in Greece in the 4th century B.C. Euclid of Megara (c. 450-380 B.C.), disciple and friend of Socrates (q.v.), founded this school. After the death of Socrates the Megarians tried to synthesise the teaching of Parmenides (q.v.) on the eternal and immutable one being and the supreme concept of Socratian ethics—the idea of the good. Euclid asserted that there exists only one good, which is immutable and is identical to itself, and known also under the names of truth, reason, god, etc. The only virtue, of which the others are only varieties, is the knowledge of the good. A plurality and diversity of things are opposed to the one good, and are, therefore, non-existent and unreal. The exponents of the M.S. continued the traditions of Zeno of Elea and the sophists (qq.v.) by using dialectics and the heuristics (q.v.) as their main method of philosophising. The later Megarians were very close to the cynics (q.v.) in their ethical views. Together with the cynics Zeno (q.v.) the Stoic transformed the M.S. into the stoic school (see Stoics).

Mehring, Franz (1846-1919), leader of the working-class movement in Germany

and of the Left wing of German Social-Democracy, and one of the founders of the German Communist Party (end of 1918); historian, philosopher, literary critic, and publicist. M.'s Marxist outlook took shape in the late 1880s. He denounced the revisionist and reformist critics of Marxism (Bernstein, q.v., and others). His fruitful elaboration of problems of historical materialism, his tireless fight against bourgeois sociology (L. Brentano, P. Barth, and others), against neo-Kantianism (see Socialism, Ethical) played a big role in the defence of Marxist philosophy from the attacks of the ideologists of capital (*Über den historischen Materialismus,* 1893; *Kant und der Sozialismus,* 1900; *Kant, Dietzgen, Mach und der historische Materialismus,* 1910; and many others). He exposed the reactionary essence of the irrational conceptions of Schopenhauer, Nietzsche and E. Hartmann (qq.v.) fashionable at the turn of the century. The historical works of M. (like *Geschichte der deutschen Sozialdemokratie,* in 4 vols., 1897-98; *Karl Marx. Geschichte seines Lebens,* 1918), while containing some incorrect conclusions, are of great scientific value. M. published the earlier works of Marx and Engels. As a literary critic (*Aesthetische Streifzüge,* 1898-99; *Schiller,* 1905; and others), he lampooned Kantian aesthetics, the theory of "art for art's sake", and naturalism. But M. made some serious mistakes: he underestimated, for instance, the role of the Marxist party as the political leader of the masses; and he could not understand the importance of a principled break with opportunists. Under the influence of the October Revolution of 1917, which he welcomed, M. overcame many of his mistakes.

Mellier (Meslier), Jean (1664-1729), materialist philosopher, founder of a revolutionary trend in French utopian socialism (q.v.). His main work, *Le Testament,* is the first example of a teaching about society and its future. His exposure of religion and the church led him to consistently materialist and atheistic deductions; he criticised social injustices and at the same time appealed for the building of a society based on collective ownership. For him, insurrection by the united labouring people against their oppressors is the affair of the people themselves; it is the prerequisite of transition to a new society wherein there will be neither rich nor poor, neither oppressors nor oppressed, neither idlers nor people exhausted by backbreaking labour. Although *Le Testament* was published in full only in 1864, it was widely read in manuscript form in 18th-century France. Many representatives of French social thought from the deists of the first half of the 18th century and Voltaire (q.v.) to the materialist Enlighteners and the Babouvist Maréchal (q.v.) spread his ideas.

Memory (in psychology), preservation by the individual of the results of his interaction with the world, which makes it possible to reproduce and utilise these results in subsequent activity, process and combine them into systems; sum total of mental models of reality constructed by the given individual. The biological mechanisms of M. are today intensively studied by many sciences, including genetics (q.v.), biochemistry and cybernetics (q.v.). M. is connected with thought (q.v.) and derivative forms of activity as a product is with a process. The content of elementary non-speech memory consists of mental models of reality formed during the direct relations of the individual with his environment. In higher, speech M., the models of objective relations of things are fixed. Speech enables man to reproduce the formations of this type of M. without direct influence of the modelled objects, under the impact of a recognised aim, which ultimately leads to the subordination of M. to the objective logic of things, to meaningful memorising and reproduction.

Mendel, Gregor Johann (1822-1884), Czech natural scientist, a founder of modern genetics (q.v.). He set forth the results of his experiments in his lifework *Versuche über Pflanzenhybriden* (1866). He assumed that sexual cells have hereditary units which are subject to the laws of independent assortment and recombination of hereditary factors. These laws, subsequently called after M., now underlie the theory of the corpuscular, discrete nature of heredity that plays a great role in the development of genetics. M. provided a brilliant scientific solution to a major problem of biology by which religion and idealism profiteered and thereby contributed objectively to the development of materialism.

Mendeleyev, Dmitry Ivanovich (1834-1907), great Russian chemist, materialist and spontaneous dialectician. He fought against spiritism and energism (q.v.), upheld the connection between science and production. In 1869 he discovered the periodic law and deduced from it the periodic system of chemical elements. The modern formulation of M.'s law reads: the properties of elements are periodically dependent upon the ordinal number, or charge, of atoms. M.'s law expresses both the relations between the chemical elements and their actual transmutations. It is a law that governs the development of inorganic substances. In actual fact M. applied the basic laws of dialectics to chemical atomism. On the strength of his law, M. made a prognosis concerning the existence of three hitherto unknown chemical elements. The latter were discovered in 1876-86. Engels wrote that "Mendeleyev achieved a scientific feat by means of the—unconscious—application of Hegel's law of the transformation of quantity into quality" (F. Engels, *Dialectics of Nature*, p. 68). Main work: *Osnovy Khimii* (The Foundations of Chemistry), 1869-71.

Mêng Tzǔ (c. 372-289 B.C.), prominent follower of Confucius (see Confucianism). His views are expounded in the book *Mêng Tzǔ*. His philosophical theories were based on idealism. For him, the testimony of reason rather than sensory perception and sensations, formed the basis of the process of cognition. Morals and ethics, according to him, originate in man's inborn qualities, which he considered to be innately good. The ethical and moral principles peculiar to human nature derive from "Heaven", the highest guiding power. He also recognised the existence of "innate abilities" and "innate knowledge". In his socio-political views he advanced certain progressive propositions, emphasising the idea of the paramount role of the people and the subordinate role of the ruler, whom the people have the right to depose if he fails to meet their requirements. He called for a unification of the country. His teachings had a serious impact on the ideology of feudal China.

Mental and Physical Labour, the two interconnected modes of human activity. Unlike animals, which act out of instinct, man acts consciously, anteceding his actions with an ideal plan which forms the purpose of his activity. M. and P.L. were an undivided whole in the primitive-communal society. Given the low level of the productive forces, the development of M. and P.L. was possible only on the basis of the division of labour (q.v.) and the separation of mental from physical labour. With the emergence of private property, classes and the state, M.L. became the privilege of the ruling class. This was responsible for the antithesis (q.v.) between M.L. and P.L., which varied in different socio-economic formations. In slave-owning society, where all forms of labour fell to the lot of slaves, the latter were partly engaged in M.L., were trained as managers, physicians, and artists. In feudal society, the antithesis between M.L. and P.L. coincided in the main with the division into classes and was camouflaged by the division into social estates. The peasantry was doomed to P.L. as a lower estate, while M.L. was the privilege of the "noble estates"—the aristocracy and the clergy. Under capitalism, M.L. becomes to a considerable degree the professional occupation of the intelligentsia (q.v.)—a social group used by capitalists as a means of dominating over P.L. In capitalist society the division into mental and manual workers does not coincide with the division into classes because the larger part of the intelligentsia are professionals who earn their own living and are thus on the same footing as the working class and the peasantry. In conditions of the scientific and technological revolution (q.v.) an increasing part of the professionals play a direct role in the production process, their position being very much the same as that of white-collar workers, while the new complex technology demands a new kind of worker, in whose activity elements of mental

and manual labour combine. The antithesis between M.L. and P.L. cannot, however, be overcome under capitalism. It is overcome in socialist society through the abolition of private property and of the exploiting classes, and the emergence of a new intelligentsia. However, in socialist society there remain essential distinctions between workers, depending on the nature of their labour and their technical and cultural levels. These distinctions can be fully obliterated only with the achievement of communism. This does not mean that the specificity of various occupational activities will disappear, but it will mean that individuals will not be bound for life to a particular occupation. The two modes of labour will be socially homogeneous, and will become two complementary elements of the integrated activity of harmoniously developed man for whom participation in both physical and mental work will become a prime need.

Meritocracy, a concept used in bourgeois political science to designate a society ruled by a government of persons elected on the basis of their merits and abilities, a synonym for "post-industrial society", that follows "the consumer society". The term of M. was introduced in 1958 by M. Young, a British sociologist, in his novel-parable *The Rise of Meritocracy, 1870-2033* and was used at the outset to study the educational system and elaborate recommendations to streamline it. With the publication of Bell's (q.v.) book *The Rise of Post-Industrial Society* (1973) the concept of M. is used to denote a new principle in governing society, the one that allegedly makes it possible to remove bureaucracy and technocracy and also to change the class structure of the society as a whole. The purpose of the conception of M. is to play down the socio-class contradictions inside the bourgeois society, particularly the contradiction between the creative intelligentsia and state-monopoly capital, which is brought to a head during the scientific and technological revolution (q.v.).

Merleau-Ponty, Maurice (1908-1961), French philosopher, existentialist and phenomenologist (see Existentialism; Phenomenology). M.P. attempted to draw a "third line" in philosophy. In fact his assertion that the immediate data of perception are true reality means subjective idealism (q.v.). Moreover, M.P.'s philosophy was eclectic, for he tried to synthesise existentialism and Marxism. His main works are: *La Structure du comportement* (1942), *Phénoménologie de la perception* (1945), and *Les Aventures de la dialectique* (1955).

Merton, Robert King (b. 1910), American sociologist. In his works (*Social Theory and Social Structure*, 1949, is the chief one) M. tries to systematise the basic propositions of functionalism (see Structural-Functional Analysis). He draws a distinction between functions (human behaviour and its objective consequences favourable for the social whole) and disfunctions (all sorts of deviations from generally accepted norms, behaviour standards, conflicts, etc., that break the unity and wholeness of a system). According to M., the important task of sociological analysis is to reveal unwitting consequences of human activity. Disregard of "deviant behaviour" or its appraisal merely as "undesirable" leads, in the opinion of M., to the sociologist's neglect of changes in social life. Like other bourgeois sociologists M. classifies "deviations" among the phenomena primarily of a moral and psychological order and divorces them from socio-economic relations. M. is known for his elaboration of concrete sociological problems (the study of the means of mass communication, q.v., etc.).

Metaethics, the section of ethics which elaborated problems of the epistemological and logical nature of ethical language. The term was introduced into ethics by the logical positivists, for whom M. is a specific philosophical discipline, which, in contradistinction to normative ethics (q.v.), studies only the ethical language and which claims to be neutral to different moral views. Strictly speaking, there is nothing wrong in studying the logic of ethical judgement and in including methodological and logical problems of ethics into a special sphere, but the

positivists understand M. to be a purely formal study of ethical judgements regardless of their content. Such a study is not concerned with the questions as to what is good and what is evil, as to how morality depends on socio-historic conditions, and as to what importance morality has in man's life. However, unless these questions are solved M. cannot become a philosophical theory and turns into a variety of modal logic (q.v.). The positivists' claim that they have created ethics as a "non-party", "neutral" science is equally erroneous (see Logical Positivism). The sociological, historical and philosophical problems of ethics are organically connected with questions that have a direct bearing on man's choice of his moral position and behaviour in practice.

Metagalaxy, a cosmic system composed of milliards of galaxies (q.v.). The term was introduced by the American astronomer H. Shaply. In the past the term "Big Universe" (as distinct from the "Small Universe", which is our galaxy) was also used. A M. is the largest material system which can be observed by modern instruments.

Metalanguage and Object-Language, concepts in modern logic. If the object of study is a natural or an artificial language (for instance, a logical calculus, q.v., or the language of a concrete scientific theory), it is necessary to distinguish the language under study, called the object-language, from the language used for its study. The latter is called metalanguage in relation to the given object-language. In particular, a metalanguage is one in which a metatheory (q.v.) is formulated.

Metalogic, a theory studying the systems and concepts (see Metatheory) of contemporary formal logic. It elaborates the theoretical problems of proof, the definability of concepts and truth in formalised languages (q.v.), interpretation, sense, etc. M. is divided into two parts: logical syntax (q.v.) and logical semantics (q.v.). The development of M. is associated with the construction and study of formalised languages (q.v.). The main works in this sphere are by Frege (q.v.), by the Polish logicians of the Lvov-

Warsaw school (q.v.), Hilbert, Gödel, Carnap (qq.v.), and others.

Metamathematics (theory of proof), a theory which studies the different properties of formal systems and calculi, q.v., (non-contradiction, completeness, etc.). Hilbert (q.v.) introduced the term M. in connection with his conception of the foundations of mathematics (see Formalism).

Metaphysics. 1. The term of M. came into usage in the 1st century B.C. to denote part of the philosophical heritage of Aristotle (q.v.). He called this most important part of his philosophical doctrine the "First Philosophy", that which studies the "highest" principles of all that exists, which are inaccessible to the senses, comprehensible only to speculative reason, and indispensable for all sciences. In this sense the term of M. was current in subsequent philosophy. In the philosophy of the Middle Ages M. was used to substantiate theology philosophically. Approximately from the 16th century on the term of M. was used in the same sense as the term "ontology" (q.v.). With Descartes, Leibniz, Spinoza (qq.v.) and other philosophers of the 17th century M. was still closely connected with the natural and humanitarian sciences. This connection was broken in the 18th century, particularly in the ontology of Wolff (q.v.). This term is now widely used in bourgeois philosophy. 2. In the period of modern history there arose the understanding of M. as an anti-dialectical method of thinking, owing to its one-sidedness in cognition; it regards things and phenomena as immutable and independent of one another; denies that intrinsic contradictions are the source of development in nature and society. Historically, this was explained by the fact that in ancient times and during the Renaissance scientific and philosophical knowledge regarded nature as a whole, in motion and development; subsequently, due to the deepening and differentiation of scientific knowledge, the latter divided nature into a number of isolated spheres, being investigated outside the connection with one another. Hegel (q.v.) was the first to use the term of M. in its anti-dialectical sense. While generalising the data of science and social progress, Marx and Engels demonstrated the scientific bankruptcy of metaphysical thinking and counterpoised to it the method of materialist dialectics (q.v.). Lenin showed that absolutisation of any aspects of cognition is metaphysical.

Metatheory, a theory whose subject-matter is some other theory. It studies the system of propositions and concepts of a given theory, designates its limits and the means of introducing new concepts and proof of its propositions, etc.; it makes it possible to construct a given theory in a more rational way. M. is formulated in metalanguage (see Metalanguage and Object-Language). In our days the most developed are the M. of logic (see Metalogic) and the M. of mathematics (see Metamathematics), in the development of which the works of Hilbert, Gödel (qq.v.) played an exceptional role. Creation of M. for non-mathematical disciplines has just begun. The central task of M. is to study the conditions for formalising scientific theories, and the syntactical (see Logical Syntax) and semantic (see Logical Semantics) properties of formalised languages (q.v.). Such studies are of particular significance in connection with the development of cybernetics (q.v.) and computer technology.

Method, in its most general meaning, a means of achieving an aim, a definite way of ordering activity. As a means of cognition, M. is a way of getting a mental reproduction of the subject under study. The most essential condition for obtaining new knowledge is the conscious application of scientific M. Scientific thought has evolved the following general principles in the process of cognition: induction, deduction, analysis and synthesis, analogy, comparison, experiment, observation (qq.v.), etc. At the base of all Mm. of cognition lie the objective laws of reality. That is why M. is inseparably linked with theory. There are special Mm. for the concrete sciences, since these have their specific objects of study. As distinct from the concrete sciences, philosophy works out the general M. of cognition: materialist dialectics (q.v.). The most general laws of the development of the material world form the objective basis of the dialectical M. This M. does not replace the Mm. of other sciences, but is their common philosophical foundation and serves as an instrument of cognition in all spheres. Dialectics is at the same time the M. for transforming the world. The dialectical-materialist M. is opposed to idealist dialectics and metaphysics.

Methodology 1. The aggregate of the ways of investigation used in a given science. 2. The doctrine on the method (q.v.) of scientific cognition and the transformation of the world. The need for a theoretical foundation of the methods of scientific cognition arose from the rapid advance of science, and this theoretical foundation was developed mostly in new philosophy beginning with F. Bacon and Descartes (qq.v.). Pre-Marxian materialist philosophers sought to substantiate the methods of cognition by the laws of the objective world. The idealist systems attempted to explain these methods by the laws of the spirit, or the idea, or regarded them as an aggregate of rules arbitrarily created by human reason. At the same time the general method of cognition was often related to the laws of one of the concrete fields of knowledge (mechanics, mathematics, biology, etc.) and reduced to the method of a particular science. An important contribution to M. was made by Hegel (q.v.), who was the first to emphasise the specific character of the philosophical method, its distinction from the methods of the concrete sciences and its irreducibility to them. He also stressed that method is the motion of the content itself, and that is why it cannot be examined in isolation from the content. However, his idealism led to the absolut-isation of the role of method and reduced the laws of the objective world to the laws of cognition. The Marxist M. proceeds from the fact that the methods of cognition are based on the objective laws of nature and society. A method of cognition can be scientific only when it reflects the objective laws of reality itself. For this reason the principles of the scientific method, its categories and concepts are not the sum total of arbitrary

rules created by human reason, but an expression of laws both of nature and of man. At the same time, Marxist M. takes into account the specific laws of the activities of the mind and, what is particularly important, connects these laws with the practical action of the social subject upon the objective world. The significance of the M. of scientific knowledge is growing in modern conditions as a result of the tremendous advance of science, particularly of such branches as physics, mathematics, biology, cybernetics (qq.v.), etc. The great interest in problems of M. is borne out by the extensive development of metatheoretical investigations (see Metatheory), by the close link between concrete research and problems of M.

Methods of Concrete Sociological Investigation, ways and means used by sociologists in collecting primary information and analysing it. There are three groups of such methods. The first group includes the ascertainment of singular facts and the accumulation of primary data. Facts are ascertained by direct observation, analysis of documents or by inquiry. At this stage of investigation it is important to ensure the stability, authenticity and validity of primary data. This is accomplished by rechecking facts, control observations and inquiries, by a combination of different methods of information gathering. The second group of methods covers the monographic investigation (the study of various aspects of a social phenomenon or process by means of varied methods), general and selective observation or inquiry. Selective observation presupposes the statistically valid selection of such facts from the general body of the object under observation (e.g., the share of newspaper readers in the investigation of a reading audience) that would be sufficiently representative to enable the investigator to properly assess the tendencies relating to the entire body of this kind. The third group includes methods used in processing the primary data: description and classification, generalisation, systems analysis, etc. Of great importance in the processing of data apart from logical methods (see Analysis and Synthesis) is the search for a statistical regularity. An important method of analysis is the social experiment in the course of which the investigator tests the hypotheses concerning the causal nexuses in the phenomena under observation. The selection of this or that method of investigation depends chiefly on the nature of the object under study and the theoretical premises of the investigation. The latter are formulated in advance in the shape of a study programme that sets forth the aim of investigation and the main concepts that relate to the analysis of data and assumptions concerning possible connections and dependencies between the essential characteristics of the process (hypothesis) under study. Marxist concrete sociological investigation (q.v.) rely on historical materialism. The methodological principles of the study programme make it possible to determine such a combination of methods in collecting and processing primary data that would ensure the objective nature of information and the consideration of facts in their totality in a concrete social situation.

Microsociology, a department of sociology (q.v.) which studies the so-called small groups (social groups with stable personal contacts among their members). The small groups include the family (q.v.), primary work, scientific, sports, military and other collectives, the school form, religious sects, etc. M. sprang up in the 1930s as a trend in bourgeois sociology. Its methodological basis is the philosophical principles of positivism (q.v.) and its theoretical basis is the works of Durkheim (q.v.), F. Tennis and others, while its empirical basis is the data of research into the bourgeois society's social problems (the need for resolving inter-class, inter-national and inter-racial conflicts, the search for reserves of boosting labour productivity, propaganda efficiency, combating crime, desintegration of the bourgeois family, growth of mental diseases, etc.). The theoretical M. is represented by the works of Moreno of the USA, Gurvitch of France (qq.v.), R. König of the FRG, and others. Applied M., closely connected with social psychology, synthesises different trends: the sociometric trend influenced by psychiatry (Moreno's school), the psychological trend, or "group dynamics" (K. Lewin's school) and the behaviourist trend (Mayo's, q.v., school). Scholars belonging to these trends have elaborated appropriate methods and research techniques for the study of small groups and contact collectives: observations of various kinds, polls, interviews, sociometric techniques (drawing up scales, producing matrices, graphical presentation of small groups' structures, etc.). Methodologically, the drawback of microsociological research within bourgeois sociology lies in the futile attempts to transfer conclusions arrived at in the study of small groups, regarded as society's basic element, to large social groups and society as a whole. The main cause of such errors is the idealist absolutisation by bourgeois sociologists of the primary nature of psychological factors in analyses of social phenomena. Marxist sociology acknowledges both the existence of small groups and the social conditionality of their formation and activity. The study of the problems of small groups (the microenvironment, the interaction between the collective and the individual, the collective and society, psychological interrelations in groups, i.e., a psychological climate, special group values and norms of behaviour, i.e., a moral climate, etc.) is of great importance for the development of sociological theory and social practice.

Middle Level (or "middle range"), Theory of, a concept introduced in bourgeois sociology by Merton, q.v. (USA). Like many other bourgeois sociologists, Merton understands that empirical sociology has reached an impasse and is in need of a general sociological theory. However, as a proponent of positivism, he recognises only such generalisations as can be reduced to direct sense data. He therefore derives his main generalisations, which become the concepts of the T.M.L., from the empirical observation of uniformities in human behaviour. A case in point is the theory of small groups advanced by G. Homans (USA), which attempts to generalise group processes under the names of interplay, norms of behaviour, stimuli, and the like. Soviet sociology employs the concept of particular sociological theories which, as distinct from the positivist-oriented T.M.L., are directly linked with the primary propositions of the general sociological theory—historical materialism (q.v.)—and adapt these propositions to particular spheres of research (social structure of labour activities, personality, spiritual life, and the like).

Mikhailovsky, Nikolai Konstantinovich (1842-1904), Russian sociologist, publicist, ideologist of Narodism (q.v.). In the early 1870s, he turned to reformism. In 1877, he came to the conclusion that it was necessary to radically reorganise Russia's political system. In 1879, he drew closer to the People's Will organisation. Lenin considered him "one of the finest spokesmen of Russian bourgeois democracy in the latter third of the last century" (Vol. 20, p. 117). From 1892 he was one of the leading editors of the *Russkoye Bogatstvo* (Russian Wealth) journal, which led the fight of liberal Narodism against Marxism. In philosophy, M. criticised Spencer's (q.v.) theory of society's "organic development" because it was apologetic towards capitalism. Contrary to Spencer M. advanced his own "formula of progress" and justified it by means of the subjective method (q.v.) in sociology, according to which history is "something moral, just and inevitable". This method ignored the objective logic of historical development, the real social forces capable of putting into practice the socialist ideal. Since M. emerged as a theoretician in the period of the political immaturity of the people, he in fact excluded the possibility of a mass revolutionary movement in Russia. His theory of "the hero" and "the crowd" which regarded mass movements as basically unconscious and imitative reflected his polemics with "people of revolution" who "pinned their hopes on a popular uprising". M.'s views were subjected to profound criticism by Lenin and Plekhanov (qq.v.).

Milesian (Ionic) School, the most ancient materialist philosophical school in Greece; the first of its exponents date back to the 6th century B.C. Miletus was then a major centre of commerce, navigation, and culture, this determining the broad horizon and scientific interests of prominent Milesians. Among them were Thales, Anaximander and Anaximenes (qq.v.). The Milesians made scientific discoveries in mathematics, geography, and astronomy. According to them, the common basis of infinite phenomena was something material—water, air, etc. These philosophers were also spontaneous dialecticians.

Military Democracy, a form of political organisation of society during the decline of the primitive-communal system (q.v.), and the formation of the state (q.v.). The term was coined by Morgan (q.v.). M.D. was practised by the Greeks in the Homeric age (12-9th centuries B.C.) and by the Romans in the period of the kings (8-6th centuries B.C.). It was also practised by the Scythians, the Celts, the ancient Germanic tribes, and the Normans. Its characteristic feature was increasing concentration of power in the hands of leaders, generals, and priests, and its gradually becoming a hereditary institution. War became a permanent occupation, its purpose being plunder and the capture of slaves. A military caste enjoying various privileges, made its appearance. The organs of the gentile system were thus "transformed from instruments of the will of the people into independent organs for ruling and oppressing their own people". (Marx, Engels, *Selected Works* in 3 vols., Vol. 3, p. 322).

Mill, John Stuart (1806-1873), English bourgeois philosopher, logician, and economist, exponent of positivism (q.v.). In philosophy he was a follower of Hume, Berkeley, and Comte (qq.v.). Examining materialism and idealism as two "metaphysical" extremes M. considered matter as permanent potency of sensation, while spirit as permanent potency of feeling. Things do not exist outside their perception. Man perceives only "phenomena" (sensations) and cannot go beyond them. In logic M. was a most typical exponent of inductivism. Denying deduction (q.v.) as a method of acquiring new knowledge, he metaphysically exaggerated the role of induction (q.v.). He elaborated the method of inductive investigation of causal connections. In ethics M. was influenced by Bentham's (q.v.)

utilitarianism (q.v.). In political economy, he replaced the classical labour theory of value by the vulgar theory of cost-price; he also defended Malthus' theory of population (see Malthusianism). M. was a bourgeois liberal in his socio-political views. Main works: *System of Logic* (1843), *Principles of Political Economy* (in 2 vols., 1848), *Utilitarianism* (1863).

Mills, C. Wright (1916-1962), American sociologist and publicist. His works, written in the spirit of bourgeois liberalism, drew a clear picture of the decadence of bourgeois democracy in the USA, showed the all-powerful oligarchy of corporations, government, bureaucracy, and the military, exposed the militarisation of the USA and its preparation for war. He severely criticised the various trends in contemporary American sociology, showing its methodological weakness, formalism, and subordination to monopoly interests. The world-view of M. was limited because he failed to see the true ways of reorganising society, denied the world historic role played by the working class and treated Marxist philosophy from the wrong position. Main works: *The Power Elite* (1956), *The Causes of World War Three* (1958), and *The Sociological Imagination* (1959).

Milyutin, Vladimir Alexeyevich (1826-1855), Russian economist, exponent of socialist thought in Russia in the 1840s. He was a member of the Petrashevsky's group (q.v.). At the end of the 1840s he said that bourgeois economics was in a state of crisis. According to M., only the exact sciences can lead to the discovery of the laws of human and social development. Hence it is necessary, on the one hand, that economic and social doctrines should master the methods of the natural sciences; and, on the other, that economic doctrines should be brought nearer to socialism. In defining his positive ideal, M. leaned towards the sociology of Comte (q.v.) in the field of scientific philosophy. In the socio-political sphere he inclined towards reformistic hopes of peacefully transforming the whole land into indivisible means of labour and of maintaining the class of small proprietors (peasants) united in producer associations.

Mimansa, one of the major orthodox systems of Indian philosophy. The exponents of M. thought that the Vedas (q.v.) are not a revelation in the full sense of the word; the religious and philosophical tenets in them required a logical substantiation. This system attaches great significance to the Brahmanas and Upanishads (q.v.). The M. doctrine is based on the belief that the final salvation cannot be rationally explained and achieved by knowledge or any conscious effort. Attention must be chiefly directed to the strict observance of public and religious duty, which consists in the fulfilment of rituals and in obedience to all kinds of limitations and prohibitions imposed upon the Indian by his caste. M. holds that the observance of duty by the individual can lead him to final emancipation. Like Sankhya (q.v.) M. admitted the existence of the spiritual and material principles in the Universe. Later commentators strengthened the theological aspect of M. and developed the idea of a personal godship. M. is a doctrine closely related with religion. At the same time the utmost realistic and rationalistic nature of the methodology of M. provides grounds for its convergence with Old Indian materialism.

Mobility, Social, a sociological concept denoting the movement of social groups in a social structure. There is a "horizontal S.M." (i.e., the transfer of an individual from one social group into another at the same social level) and a "vertical S.M." (i.e., the transfer of an individual into another social stratum or class). The variability and mobility of a social structure takes place in actual fact. But bourgeois sociologists distort the nature of this phenomenon and claim that in capitalist society it serves to soften the class contradictions and to introduce social homogeneity. According to them, the "vertical S.M." affords the possibility to a man in the "lower class" to rise up the social ladder to join the "upper class", or to become a millionaire. The fact is, that the "road to the top" in bourgeois society, i.e., the change in the social status of individuals and families is an exception and does not alter the position of the class as a whole in the system of production. The main direction of S.M. in bourgeois society is not "upward" but "downward". It reflects the impoverishment of the petty bourgeoisie in town and country, leading to the sharpening, not to the softening, of the class contradictions of capitalism. Under socialism, S.M. has a different nature. Profound changes in the social structure of developed socialism are caused by the gradual abolition of essential distinctions between mental and physical labour, between town and country. They make for the society's full social homogeneity under communism.

Modality (in logic), a characteristic of a statement (q.v.) according to the degree of assertion: a statement can be necessary, possible, accidental, impossible, etc. In traditional logic statements are divided into necessary, possible, and real statements. Modern logic provides the possibility of analysing the property of M., considering it as a certain "metalogic" appraisal of a statement. M. may be logical and descriptive. Logical M. of statements is determined from purely logical considerations. Descriptive Mm. include above all the physical (causal) ones. The latter depend upon whether the statement expresses something necessary, possible or accidental due to some physical laws.

Mode of Life, one of the most important spheres of society's life, inseparably connected with the reproduction of man himself; material and cultural environment where man's needs for food, clothing, housing, rest, recreation, and preservation of health, etc., are satisfied. The character of the M.L. and the means and forms of satisfying people's requirements depend on the mode of production (q.v.) and the changes to which it is subject. At the same time the M.L. is deeply influenced by customs, morals (qq.v.), national traditions, class differences, distinctions between town and country (q.v.), the status of women in society, national characteristics, and the ideology and culture of society in question. Being part of the way of life (q.v.) the M.L., in its turn, influences the society's economics, politics and culture. The family (q.v.) is a very important form of organisation of the personal mode of life. In a socialist society, the working people's mode of life improves with the growing level of material and spiritual production, with the steady advance of the material and cultural standards of the people. In the society of mature socialism the service industries develop into a mechanised branch of the national economy.

Mode of Production, a concept characterising a concrete manner of producing the necessities of life (food, clothing, housing, tools of labour) relevant to historically conditioned forms of social relations. The M.P. is one of the most important categories of historical materialism, since it characterises the main sphere of social life—the sphere of material production—and in general determines the social, political, and spiritual processes. The structure of any historical society, its functioning and development depend on the M.P. The history of social development is above all the history of development and change of the M.P., which determines the change of all other structural elements of society. The M.P. represents the unity of two closely interrelated elements: the productive forces and the relations of production (qq.v.). Production begins with the development of its determinative aspect—the productive forces—which, once they have reached a certain level, come into conflict with the relations of production within which they have been developing. This leads to an inevitable change in the relations of production, since in the obsolete form they cease to be an indispensable condition of the production process. In its turn, the change in the relations of production, which means the substitution of a new economic basis for the old one, leads to a more or less rapid change in the superstructure, i.e., the whole of society. Therefore, the change in the M.P. comes about not through people's volition, but by virtue of the general economic law of correspondence of production relations to the character and level of development of productive forces (q.v.). Due to this the development of society takes the form of the natural historical change of socioeconomic formations (q.v.). Conflict between the productive forces and the relations of production is the economic basis of social revolution carried out by the progressive forces of society. Under the communist M.P., contradictions between the productive forces and the relations of production do not reach conflict point, since public ownership of the means of production makes the whole of society interested in changing the relations of production whenever these cease to correspond to the new level of production. Cognisant of the laws governing the development of the communist M.P., the Communist party and the state are in a position to detect the germinating contradictions in good time and to work out concrete measures to resolve them. The historical stages in the development and change of Mm.P. find expression in the concepts of the primitive-communal, slave-owning, feudal, capitalist, and communist Mm.P. To reflect the historical peculiarity of the variants of one and the same M.P. (e.g., ancient Greek and Oriental slavery, Prussian or American way of capitalist development in agriculture, specific features of socialism in different countries, specific features of the non-capitalist development of some countries, etc.) each of the foregoing concepts characterising one M.P. needs to be further concretised.

Modelling, reproduction of an object's characteristics in its analog, specially constructed for their study. This other object is called a model. The need for M. arises where it is impossible, difficult or expensive to study real objects directly, or where this process requires too much time, etc. There must be some analogy between the model and the object that evokes the researcher's interest. It may be expressed either in the similarity of the physical properties of the model and the object or in the similarity of functions (q.v.), performed by the model and the object, or in the identical mathematical description of the behaviour of the object and its model. In each concrete case the model may perform its role if the degree of its correspondence to the object is defined strictly enough. Today M. is in wide use in computers and electronic simulation devices. The principal merits of this type of models are their universality, convenient use, quick and cheap

research. The recent period has witnessed the development of global M., whose purpose is to produce with the aid of computers the models of solving global problems (q.v.). While recognising the heuristic significance of some methods of global M. suggested by bourgeois scientists (see Club of Rome), the Marxist sociologists focus their attention on the analysis of social, economic, political and ideological aspects of these problems. In a scientific-technical investigation M. is only one of the methods of scientific cognition as a whole. The main regularities in the process of building sensory and logical models are studied by different departments of the theory of knowledge, q.v. (primarily by the teaching of truth, q.v.), whose achievements underlie the scientific-technical theory and practice of M. In their turn, these theory and practice are very important for the further development and concretisation of the dialectico-materialist theory of knowledge.

Modus, a philosophical term which was used in pre-Marxist philosophy and denoted the object's property that was implicit in it only in certain states as distinct from the attribute (q.v.). In Spinoza's (q.v.) philosophy M. expressed the endless plurality of things and their transient qualities, in which the singular, eternal and infinite material substance was manifested.

Monad, a philosophical term denoting the structural, substantial unit of being. It is interpreted in different ways by different philosophical systems. According to the Pythagoreans (q.v.), for instance, the M. (a mathematical unity) is the basis of the Universe. According to Bruno, q.v. (*De Monade, Numero, et Figura,* 1591), the M. is the sole source of being, which is but spiritualised matter (see Pantheism). In this source, he held, the opposites coincide—the finite and the infinite, the even and the odd, etc. The M. is one of the main concepts of Leibniz's (q.v.) philosophy (*Monadology,* 1714). He regarded the M. as a changeable substance (q.v.). The Mm., endowed with the ability of clear perception, are called souls. The rational soul of man, Leibniz held, is a spirit, M. Taking note of Leibniz's view that the whole world is reflected in the M., that it, as an individuality, contains infinity in itself as in embryo, Lenin wrote: "Here is dialectics of a kind, and very profound, *despite* idealism and clericalism" (Vol. 38, p. 383). Lomonosov (q.v.) employed the term "physical M." to designate a particle (corpuscule) of matter. Goethe (q.v.) regarded the M. (calling it entelechy, q.v.) as an active spiritual principle which is peculiar to matter and which contributes to the individualisation of objects. The concept of M. is applied in one form or another in modern idealistic systems of pluralism and personalism (qq.v.).

Monism, a philosophical doctrine which holds that the underlying basis of all existence is one source. The materialists consider matter (q.v.) to be the foundation of the world, while the idealists consider the spirit, the idea (qq.v.). Hegel's (q.v.) philosophy is the most consistent trend of idealist M. Scientific and consistent materialist M. is typical of dialectical materialism, which proceeds from the fact that the world is by its nature material, that all phenomena in the world are but various forms of moving matter. In Marxist philosophy, materialism is extended also to social phenomena. The opposite of M. is dualism (q.v.).

Montaigne, Michel de (1533-1592), French philosopher of the Renaissance. A point of departure of M.'s philosophy is scepticism (q.v.). According to him, man has the right to doubt anything. He doubts the scholasticism (q.v.) of the Middle Ages, the dogmas of Catholicism and the Christian idea of God himself. M. rejected the religious teaching about the soul's immortality and regarded consciousness as a specific property of matter. As distinct from agnosticism (q.v.) the scepticism of M. does not deny the knowability of the world. His main moral principle is that man should not passively wait for his happiness, which religion promises him in heaven; he has a right to strive for happiness on earth. Main work: *Essais* (1580).

Montesquieu, Charles Louis de (1689-1755), French philosopher of the Enlightenment, political thinker, sociologist and historian. He was an adherent of deism, severely criticised the church and theology, although ascribed to religion a role in maintaining social morality. M. developed the idea of universal regularity governing natural and social phenomena. While accepting the general premises of the theory of natural law (q.v.), M., in contrast to consistent rationalism, held that it was impossible to construct in accordance with this theory a universal system of social laws, since the conditions for the existence of peoples were different. This, according to M., accounted for a diversity of laws and forms of government. M. was a founder of the geographical school in sociology (q.v.). He attached special importance to climate, soil, terrain, etc., but at the same time emphasised the role of social environment which he identified with the political system and law. He subjected to scathing criticism the feudal and absolutist orders, but, being an ideologist of political compromise between the bourgeoisie and the nobility, upheld the idea of a moderate constitutional monarchy and the principle of the separation of powers. Main works: *Lettres persanes* (1721), *Considérations sur les causes de la grandeur et de la décadence des Romains* (1734), *L'Esprit des Lois* (1748).

Moore, Georg Edward (1873-1958), English idealist philosopher, exponent of neo-realism (q.v.). Criticising subjective idealism, M. counterposed it with the concept of common sense that induces us to recognise the objectivity of the surrounding world. According to this philosophy of "common sense" there exist in the Universe material objects and conscious actions associated with only certain material objects. At the same time "common sense" does not preclude the possible spiritual nature of the Universe, and the existence of a divine reason, its actions, and an after-life. M. developed methods of logical analysis and influenced neo-positivism. His ethics is based on the recognition that good and evil are undefinable concepts. His main works: *Principia Ethica* (1903), *A Defence of Common Sense* (1925) and *Some Main Problems of Philosophy* (1958).

Moral Judgment, approval or disapproval of various aspects of social reality and the behaviour of individuals depending on their moral value. In contrast to moral norm (q.v.) which obliges people to behave according to definite moral requirements, M.J. determines whether the latter are honoured or not. A general M.J. is made in the categories of good and evil (q.v.). It is based on the objective criterion of morality which is historical and changes according to the social system, the class struggle, etc. Assessment of the social significance of people's behaviour serves as the basis of M.J., and people's behaviour can, therefore, be regulated with its help. Marxist ethics requires that the motives (q.v.), as well as the social consequences of the people's actions, should be taken into account.

Moral Norms, a form of ethical standards which regulate people's conduct through general prescriptions and bans as regards actions of the same type. In contrast to legal norms, M.N. are sanctioned not by the state authority but by the force of habit and public opinion; they are formed in the moral consciousness of society spontaneously and not as a result of a specially promulgated law. M.N. as such are not sufficient to control human behaviour; being general and abstract, they do not provide the possibility of various exceptions stemming from special circumstances. That is why the question of application of these or other M.N. in particular situations must be solved on the basis of more general in content and at the same time more specific moral principles. By their social content M.N. may be both of a general human and of a historically limited, class character. In the latter case the transition from one social formation to another takes place over a long period and sees the breaking up of the old and the creation and establishment of the new M.N. (for example, the struggle between communist and bourgeois M.N. in the life of a socialist society).

Moral Sense, Theories of, subjectivist ethical theories which explain the origin and the nature of morality by special human senses of approval and disapproval. T.M.S. were advanced in England in the 17th-19th centuries by A. Smith, Hume, Shaftesbury (qq.v.). These theories were further developed in the 20th century by E. Westermarck (Finland), W. McDougall (USA), and A. Sutherland (Great Britain). The main tenet of T.M.S. is that the moral notions, which help people in evaluating events and choosing their line of conduct, are based on their senses of approval or disapproval as regards various phenomena. In other words, the proponents of T.M.S. think that the information, contained in moral judgments, covers not proper or evaluated objects as such but only moral senses aroused in man by these objects. With their researches limited to mainly psychological phenomena and dissociated from the objective laws of society's development, these theoreticians fail to reveal the laws of the development of moral consciousness. This explains the relativistic interpretation of moral notions by these theoreticians. In general, T.M.S. have all the drawbacks of approbative ethics (q.v.), the type of ethics they belong to.

Morality, a form of social consciousness, a social institution that regulates people's conduct in all spheres of social life without exception. M. differs from other forms of regulating mass activity (law, rules of administrative procedure, government decrees, popular traditions, etc.) by the method of giving substance to its requirements and of their implementation. M. expresses the social requirements (q.v.) and interests of society or classes in the shape of spontaneously formed and generally recognised injunctions and evaluations supported by the force of mass example, habit, custom and public opinion (q.v.). For this reason the requirements of M. take the form of impersonal obligation, injunction equally addressed to everybody but issued by nobody. These requirements are of a relatively stable nature. They differ from a common custom or tradition, supported by force of the established order, in getting the ideological justification in the form of conceptions of man's mode of living and conduct. As for law, M. differs from it in two respects: first, the compliance with moral requirements by each individual is supervised by all people, the moral authority of an individual not being bound up with official duties; second, the observance of moral requirements is sanctioned only by the forms of spiritual influence (public appraisal, approval or condemnation of deeds performed). This makes for a relatively greater part of consciousness in M. than in other forms of social control, consciousness being expressed both in the rational form of concepts and judgments and in the emotional form of feelings, urges and inclinations. Individual consciousness plays a no small role in M. than social consciousness. Relying on moral conceptions produced by society, assimilating them in the process of education, the individual may independently regulate his behaviour to a considerable extent and judge about the moral significance of all developments taking place around him. Thanks to this the individual acts in the sphere of M. not only as the object of social control, but also as its conscious subject, i.e., as an ethic personality. Being a complex social formation, M. includes the following components: moral activity from the standpoint of its content and motivation (what actions are accepted in a society, what norms of behaviour are adopted for people, what morals, q.v., are spread), moral relations which regulate this activity and manifest themselves in different forms of obligation and demands made on man (see Moral Norms; Duty; Responsibility; Conscience); moral consciousness that reflects these relations in the shape of relevant notions (norms, principles, social and moral ideals, q.v., concepts of good and evil, justice and injustice, qq.v.). All these forms of moral consciousness are united into a logically ordered system which can prescribe, motivate and appraise moral actions in some way. Conformably to different spheres of social life M. formulates special rules (labour M., professional and party ethics, everyday and family M.), which constitute only relatively independent fields of M. with one common justification. M. appeared in the early stages of society's formation and has undergone a long development under the impact of economic and other social relations, the progress of humankind's

material and spiritual culture. In addition to general human elements M. incorporates historically transient and class norms, principles and ideals. In a society split into classes, M. is bound to bear a class nature, reflecting as it does the class struggle. In every antagonistic class society, the system of M. that sanctions the existing social relations and asserts the interests of the ruling exploiting class is paralleled by M. that denies the former M. The latter is produced by the exploited class, which rises to the struggle for changing the society, emancipates from the spiritual power of the ruling M. and creates its own M., the basis for forming the M. of a future society. In this respect communist morality (q.v.) has fundamentally different specifics. It emerges as a class morality of the proletariat and subsequently becomes, in a socialist society, the M. of the whole people and in the final analysis, in a communist society, the general human M.

Morality, Christian, the morality preached by the Christian religion. Theologians seek to present the standards of C.M. as common to all mankind, and C.M. itself as the loftiest and most humane, putting in the forefront the commandment of love for one's neighbour. At the same time they have to recognise that C.M. is unrealisable due to man's sinfulness. In their view only God is absolutely moral and he is also the only competent moral judge. Unconditional trust in divine grace is regarded as the supreme moral virtue of man. Another important virtue is forgiveness which is also deduced from man's sinfulness. Christianity (q.v.), which arose historically as a religion of the oppressed, reflected the aspirations of the masses (particularly the idea of brotherhood of all the destitute, love for one's neighbour, etc.). The church, while preaching universal love, humility and submission, turned these commandments against the masses themselves. The church links the reward of the oppressed for their suffering and the triumph of justice with the "kingdom of God", the advent of which depends upon God's will.

Morality, Communist, the aggregate of principles and standards of conduct based on the ideals of communist society. The objective criterion of C.M. is what contributes to the establishment of communist society and the realisation of the communist ideal. The following main principles of C.M. make up the moral code of the builder of communism: devotion to the cause of communism; increase of social wealth by labour; a high sense of public duty, collectivism, humanism, internationalism (qq.v.). The initial historical form of C.M. was the revolutionary morality of the working class, which formed within the capitalist society. Although this morality was subordinate to the proletariat's class struggle and was opposed to the prevalent morality of the exploiters, proletarian morality included basic universal moral norms elaborated by the popular masses throughout millennia in the struggle against the social yoke and moral evils. At the same time the working class has put forward its own ethical standards, such as class solidarity, internationalism and collectivism. With the victory of socialism C.M. transforms from the proletarian class morality into the morality of the society as a whole; its principles are enriched with a new content and spread to all spheres of social life. Thus, C.M. is the highest degree of moral progress of humanity. The standards of C.M. are not confined to people's behaviour; they are active factors in transforming society; they influence the formation of communist social institutions and the whole course of social development. When the standards of C.M. become universal, man's behaviour in line with the recognised public duty will gradually make superfluous many links in the legislative and administrative regulation of the relations between the individual and society and will lead to full freedom of the individual. The natural replacement of the code of laws and forms of sheer administration by the standards of C.M. will be a revolution in the history of morality. As the standards of C.M. spread and assert themselves, they are confronted today with non-communist morality along two lines: inside socialist society, where the old and obsolete standards exist as survivals of the past (q.v.), resulting from non-compliance with, and violation of, the laws obtaining in society, this giving birth to amoral actions and crime; outside socialist society, where C.M. is opposed to the morality of bourgeois society. C.M. is being formed in the complicated struggle and construction as the future morality of the whole of humanity (see Morality; Ethics).

Morals, the concept reflecting the actual behaviour of members of big or small social groups as well as what do members of these groups allow or prohibit themselves to do. M. are the models and the standards of conduct people adhere to. M. as the actual being of good and evil in human behaviour are distinct from ideals as due to be. M. taken as a whole bear on the morality of a social community. M. differ inasmuch as there is difference between the being of different classes and social strata, their places in the system of social production, and their cultural levels.

Morelly, French "rationalistic" communist of the 18th century. His main work *Le Code de la nature* (1755) was a treatise which substantiated the principles of a society where collective ownership dominates. According to M., the system of his time was irrational, being the outcome of errors. By the rational system M. had in mind a centralised economic commune managed on the basis of a single economic plan which regulated production and distribution of goods. M. formulated three basic laws of society, meeting the demands of nature and reason: (1) abolition of private property, (2) the right of every person to existence and the right to labour, and (3) the obligation for all citizens to work. M. was a typical representative of the so-called vulgar egalitarian communism. He advocated petty regulation of life, including marital relations. M. exerted considerable influence upon many utopian socialists of the 18th and 19th centuries: F.N. Babeuf, Cabet, Blanqui (qq.v.), and others.

Moreno, Jacob (1892-1975), American psychiatrist and sociologist, founder of sociometry (q.v.). M. studied the psychological aspects of the behaviour of small social groups: children up to school age, apartment neighbours, office employees, air crews, etc. (see Microsociology). By concentrating attention on emotional relations among people, for instance, on the feelings of sympathy, antipathy, or indifference to one another, M. tried to present these emotions and inclinations of men as the primary and decisive factor of social progress. Acknowledging the crisis of capitalism in the USA, M. considered the regulation of relations among people and their organisation into groups according to their inclinations and sympathies to be the basic means of solving all social problems. The measures suggested by M. to "rally" American society do not affect the main pillars of capitalism: private ownership, the rule of monopolies, and the exploitation of the working people. Main works: *Who Shall Survive?* (1934), *Foundations of Sociometry* (1954).

More, Thomas (1478-1535), one of the founders of utopian socialism (q.v.), humanist-rationalist of the Renaissance (q.v.). He was brought up in a bourgeois family; between 1529 and 1532 M. held a high government post—Lord Chancellor of England. He was beheaded by order of the king. M. described a journey into Utopia, the unknown land (literally, a non-existent place) in his book *A fruteful and Pleasant Worke of the best state of a Publyque Weale, and of the newe Yle called Utopia* (1516). M. criticised extensively the system based on private property, the sociopolitical relations in England at his time. He portrayed a system in which public property dominates. He gave the first systematical enunciation of the idea of socialisation of production, linking it with the idea of a communist organisation of labour and distribution. The chief economic unit in the ideal, free state of Utopia is the family; production is based on handicrafts. The Utopians live under democratic administration and enjoy equality in labour. People work six hours a day, the rest of the time being devoted to science and the arts. Great importance is attached to the all-round development of the individual, to the fusion of theoretical education with labour. This idea is a rudiment of the socialist view of education. M. did not understand that realisation of the socialist ideal necessitated a high development of technology. He dreamed of a peaceful transition to a new system.

Morgan, Augustus de (1806-1871), English mathematician and logician. In modern mathematical logic (q.v.) his name is borne by the following fundamental laws of algebra of logic (q.v.): the negation of conjunction (q.v.) is tantamount to the disjunction (q.v.) of negations; the negation of disjunction is tantamount to the conjunction of negations.

Morgan, Lewis Henry (1818-1881), American scientist, ethnographer, and archaeologist. He studied the American Indians' way of life and collected an enormous amount of factual material on the history of primitive-communal society. He generalised these facts in his book *Ancient Society* (1877). M. attempted at making the periodisation of the history of the pre-class society by linking each of the historical periods with the development of production techniques. M. was among the first to establish that the family (q.v.) is a historical phenomenon which changes with the development of society. Engels wrote that M. rediscovered "in his own way, the materialist conception of history that had been discovered by Marx" (K. Marx and F. Engels, *Selected Works* in three volumes, Vol. 3, p. 191). Engels used M.'s discovering in his work *The Origin of the Family, Private Property and the State* (q.v.). He, however, not only enunciated M.'s materials, but interpreted them along Marxist lines.

Morgan, Thomas Hunt (1866-1945), American biologist, the founder of the chromosome theory of heredity which disclosed the cytological mechanism of Mendel's (q.v.) laws. Having shown the connection between the genes and intracellular processes M. laid the groundwork for the theory of genetic determination of the organism's development. He was a convinced materialist in his philosophical views, took up an irreconcilable position with regard to idealism and all kinds of mysticism. In his polemics with the representatives of neo-vitalism, holism (q.v.) and the adherents of the emergent evolution (q.v.) conception, M. advanced and developed the idea that "metaphysical speculations" are meaningless and matched them with his strictly scientific approach. However, his chromosome theory of heredity contained some simplified mechanistic conceptions. These drawbacks were overcome in the subsequent development of genetics (q.v.).

Morris, Charles (b. 1901), American philosopher, who combines the ideas of pragmatism (q.v.) with some concepts of logical empiricism (q.v.). His main works, based on the tenets of behaviourism (q.v.) analyse man's social and biological behaviour. While developing the views of Peirce (q.v.), he was the first to formulate the fundamental concepts and principles of a new science—semiotic (q.v.). Main work: *Foundations of the Theory of Signs* (1938).

Morris, William (1834-1896), English socialist, poet, fiction writer, and artist. He hated and severely criticised the bourgeois system. Initially, he shared the utopian views on art, which he regarded as the principal means for the peaceful transformation of society. He took an active part in the labour and socialist movements in the 1880s. The description of a future communist society (*News from Nowhere*, a utopian novel, 1891) was idyllic and therefore not scientific. In his creative and political activity M. championed revolutionary principles. He made a valuable contribution to English democratic literature.

Motion, the key attribute and mode of existence of matter (q.v.). M. denotes all processes occurring in nature and society. Loosely, M. is change (q.v.) in general, any kind of interaction (q.v.) of material objects. No more can there be matter in the world without M. than M. without matter. The M. of matter is absolute, while the state of rest is relative and just a moment of M. A body at rest in relation to the Earth moves with the Earth round the Sun, and with the Sun round the centre of the galaxy, etc. Since the world is infinite, every body participates in an infinite number of forms of M. Qualitative stability of bodies and of their properties is also the result of the interaction and M. of

minute objects. Thereby M. predicates the properties and structure of matter and the nature of its existence. M. of matter is diverse in its manifestations and multiple in form (see Matter, Forms of Motion of). Qualitatively new and more complex forms of M. appear in the process of the development of matter. Yet, even mechanical M. is not absolutely simple. A body in motion interacts all the time with other bodies through the electromagnetic and gravitational fields, and changes in so doing. The theory of relativity (q.v.) indicates that any increase in velocity of M. causes an increase in the mass of a body, while linear dimensions decrease in the direction of M. and the rhythm of processes occurring in bodies becomes slower. At velocities approaching that of light, electrons and other particles are able to radiate electromagnetic quanta in the direction of M. Thus, all M. includes the interaction of different forms of M. and their mutual transformations. M. is just as inexhaustible as matter. The M. of matter is a process of the interaction ("struggle") of opposites comprising the inner content of various changes, and the reason for the change of specific qualitative states. Thus, electromagnetic, nuclear and gravitational M. is based on the unity of the opposite processes of absorption and radiation by minute objects of quanta of the electromagnetic, nuclear and gravitational fields. Chemical M. implies, among other things, association and dissociation of atoms. Vital processes are based on the unity of the assimilation and dissimilation of substances, stimulation and inhibition of cells, etc. The endless self-motion of matter in the Universe is also the result of the unity of the opposite processes of the dispersion of matter and energy (in the evolution of stars) and their reverse concentration which, in the ultimate, leads to the origination of stars, galaxies and other forms of matter. All forms of the development (q.v.) of matter occur in M. Development is the overall, irreversible, structural change of systems in a definite direction. This direction is the resultant force of the composition of diverse inner trends of change impelled by the laws of motion of the system and the outer conditions. Matter develops in diverse forms, depending on the complexity of the system, its forms of M., the velocity and rate of change, the character and direction of change, etc. In ascendant development the connections, structure and forms of M. of material objects become more complex, constituting progressive transformations from lower to higher states. Descendant development, on the other hand, constitutes degradation and disintegration of the system, a simplification of the forms of its M. M. is a more general concept than development, because it connotes all changes, including external and accidental, which do not conform to the internal laws governing the development of the system.

Motive, a conscious urge prompting to action in order to satisfy man's certain requirements (q.v.). M. is a definite justification of man's volitional action, revealing his attitude to a society's demands. Mm. play an important part in the appraisal of human actions and deeds, since on them depends what a subjective meaning this or that action has for a given man.

Motive Forces of the Development of Society, essential, necessary and lasting factors securing society's functioning, progress, development. Idealists identify M.F.D.S. with ideal motives and incentives of man's historical activity, see their origin in immutable human nature, in outside nature or supernatural powers, or in mechanical combinations of various factors. The classics of Marxism-Leninism proved that man's historical activity is impelled by material factors. They proved that the latter are primary and determining in relation to political and intellectual factors, that they are active and relatively independent. They showed that the working masses are the real makers of history. M.F.D.S. in a broad sense include social contradictions as an ultimate condition of self-development and self-motion; the progressive activity of social subjects, which resolves these contradictions; the motivations for this activity (needs, interests, etc.). According to their composition and function, M.F.D.S. are divided into natural (demographic and geographic) and social factors; the social into material and economic, socio-political and spiritual, objective and subjective. The major general historical motive force is the mode of production (q.v.) of material goods. The main specific motive force for all antagonistic socio-economic formations is the class struggle (q.v.). In history, the effectiveness of M.F.D.S. grows. Their highest type takes shape in the communist socio-economic formation. In a developed socialist society the nucleus of M.F.D.S. are non-antagonistic contradictions; the motive force here is the socio-political and ideological unity of society (q.v.) headed by the working class, with the Communist Party playing the vanguard role; the increasingly effective material and moral incentives for work and the socialist emulation movement spread on a mass scale; the role of the working masses increases in all spheres of social activity; socialist patriotism and internationalism, criticism and self-criticism (qq.v.), and other spiritual motive forces are in evidence. As a result there is an ever higher rate of social progress and ever fuller use of its achievements for the benefit of the working people.

Mo Tzŭ, or **Mo Ti** (479-381 B.C.), founder of a school of philosophy (Moism) in ancient China which drew numerous followers. An opponent of Confucianism (q.v.), he considered predetermined fate non-existent, a man's fate depending on the manner in which he practised the principles of "universal love" which are based on the "will of Heaven". He exorted people to help one another, follow a useful occupation, reject the use of force and war, and appoint the wise and worthy to govern the country regardless of the position they occupy in society. Though leaning towards mysticism (q.v.), his teachings contained some elements of materialism. Thus, he maintained that our knowledge was a direct product of our investigation of reality. His followers — Moists — subsequently developed his rational ideas into a naive materialistic theory of knowledge, which was destined to play an important role in the evolution of philosophy in ancient China. The school of M.T. ceased to exist as an independent ideological trend in the 2nd century B.C.

Münzer, Thomas (c. 1490-1525), church preacher, one of the leaders of the Great Peasant War in Germany (1525), ideologist of the radical peasant-plebeian wing of the Reformation (q.v.). Unlike Luther (q.v.), the moderate reformer, M. energetically opposed not only the Catholic Church but Christianity and feudalism as a whole. For M., the basic task of the Reformation was a socio-economic revolution of the peasants and the urban poor, rather than a reformation of the church and its teachings. M.'s philosophy, which was formed under the influence of medieval peasant-plebeian heresies and mysticism (qq.v.), was pantheistic (see Pantheism). M.'s political programme was very close to equalitarian utopian communism.

Mysticism, a religious-idealistic view of the world based on belief in the supernatural. M. owes its origin to secret rites conducted by the religious societies of ancient Orient and Occident. The underlying feature of these rituals was contact between man and God, or some other mysterious being. Communion with God is supposedly achieved through ecstasy or revelation. Elements of M. are peculiar to many ancient philosophico-religious doctrines, e.g., Confucianism, q.v., Brahmanism, Pythagoreanism, Platonism and Neoplatonism (see Plato) and to the philosophy of the Middle Ages. To a greater or lesser degree M. is a feature of practically all idealist philosophies of modern times (particularly neo-Thomism, personalism, qq.v., and

some forms of existentialism, q.v.). In Russia, religious-mystical philosophy was developed by the Slavophiles, Solovyov (qq.v.) and his adherents (Berdyayev, Trubetskoy, qq.v., and others). Mystic philosophers believe that the highest form of cognition is some mystical intuition in which God appears as the primary basis of the world. M., as a rule, is preached by the ideologists of reactionary classes, although there are cases when progressive ideas or revolutionary opposition and political protest (for instance, by Münzer, q.v.) appeared in the religious-mystical form.

Mythology 1. Fantastic reflection of reality in primitive consciousness, which was embodied in oral folklore characteristic of the antiquity. Myths were narratives born in the early stages of history, whose fantastic images (gods, legendary heroes, big events, etc.) were but attempts to generalise and explain different phenomena of nature and society. M. was a peculiar form of the world-view of people in the ancient society. It has elements of religion (q.v.) insofar as it contains the concepts of the supernatural. But at the same time it reflects man's moral views and aesthetic attitude to reality. That is why images of M. have been often employed in the arts in various interpretations. The concept of myth is used in the ideology of the 17th-20th centuries to designate different kinds of illusions influencing mass consciousness. 2. The science that studies myths, their origin and the reflection of reality in them.

n

Naigeon, Jacques André (1738-1810), French materialist philosopher and atheist, opponent of the Catholic Church. N.'s world outlook was shaped under the direct influence of Diderot (q.v.), who enlisted him to work on the *Encyclopedie*. In the theory of knowledge N. adhered to materialist sensationalism (q.v.). In 1768, he published *Le Militaire philosophe* (in translation *The Soldier-Atheist*), in which he proved that all religions were false and based on fear. God had been invented solely to intimidate slaves. N. took part in editing Holbach's (q.v.) *Le Système de la nature* and jointly with him wrote a *Theologie portative*, a dictionary giving a witty criticism of religion.

Nalbandyan, Mikael Lazarevich (1829-1866), Armenian materialist philosopher, revolutionary democrat, utopian socialist, enlightener, poet and publicist. In the theory of knowledge he proceeded from the unity of the sensory and rational, deduction and induction (qq.v.), and criticised the idealist understanding of the nature of general concepts and ideas. N. criticised the philosophy of Kant, Fichte, and Hegel (qq.v.), especially their political views. In aesthetics he shared the views and further developed the ideas of the Russian revolutionary democrats. A prominent writer and poet, he embodied these ideas in his artistic work. His main works: *Two Lines* (1861), *Agriculture as a True Road* (1862), *Hegel and His Time* (1863) and others.

Name, in logic, a linguistic expression denoting some object understood in the broadest sense, as everything we can name and not only as a material object. Logical semantics (q.v.) usually deals with the so-called semantic triangle; (1) name; (2) object designated by it (denotat, or designatum); (3) meaning of name (see Denotation and Sense). As distinct from the ordinary word usage, contemporary logic regards as names not only terms (words) but also sentences. The denotat of a term is the object it denotes, the meaning of the term is the property it expresses. The denotat of a sentence is its truth-value (i.e., truth or lie) and the meaning is the judgment (q.v.) it expresses.

Narodism, a system of views held by petty-bourgeois peasant democrats in Russia. The specific features of N. are: the combination of agrarian democracy with peasant utopian socialism, the hope of bypassing the capitalist road of development. N. is characteristic of countries that have taken the road of the bourgeois-democratic revolution at a relatively late period, when capitalism has already revealed its intrinsic contradictions and has given rise to the socialist movement of the proletariat. Herzen and Chernyshevsky (qq.v.) were the founders of N. in Russia. They were the first to raise the question of a possible direct transition to a higher, communist form of society through the peasant community. In the 1870s, the N. became predominant in the Russian democratic movement, acquired new features, making a peasant revolution its immediate practical task. Bakunin, Lavrov, and Tkachyov (qq.v.) and others were the most prominent ideologists of the N. of the 1870s. Being the socio-political ideology of militant revolutionary democracy, the N. of the 1870s made a step backward in theory as compared with Chernyshevsky. The Narodniks sympathised with the historic struggle of the international socialist proletariat, but exposed the evils of capitalism in romantic terms; they fought against big landownership and tsarism, and sincerely believed in a special path of Russia's development. They rejected the central idea of Chernyshevsky's sociological conception—the idea of historical necessity in social development—under the pretext that this idea allegedly justified the bourgeois road of development, unacceptable to the revolutionaries. In philosophy the Narodnik theoreticians of the 1870s preached positivism (q.v.). They did not accept materialist philosophy and its theory of knowledge, which they treated as "a metaphysical generalisation" that transcends the limits of science. In the mid-1880s N. entered the period of deep crisis caused, on the one hand, by the failure of the socialist propaganda, carried on by the Narodniks among the peasantry, and the rout of the People's Will, and on the other hand, by such changes in the country's class structure as the bourgeois evolution of the peasantry, the growth of the proletariat and the intensification of its struggle. A group of revolutionaries (Plekhanov, q.v., and others) broke with N. and adopted the positions of Marxism. A liberal trend (Mikhailovsky, q.v., S. Yuzhakov, and others) prevailed in N.; they abandoned the struggle for the revolutionary overthrow of the existing order. The main thesis advanced by N. in the 1880s-1890s was: small peasant farming is the antipode of capitalism. Some Narodniks were compelled to recognise Russia's capitalist evolution and the process of differentiation among the peasantry. But their admission was accompanied by all kinds of utopian petty-bourgeois schemes of "people's production" to be protected from capitalism. The liberal Narodniks waged an active fight against Marxism, but this struggle ended in their ideological fiasco. The upsurge of the peasant movement in the early 20th century and the Russian revolution of 1905-07 made for the appearance of a number of Narodnik groups and parties, including the Socialist-Revolutionary Party. Its ideology was of an eclectic nature, combining the old dogmas of N. with some distorted tenets of Marxism. In the course of the revolution the Socialist-Revolutionaries constantly vacillated between submission to the leadership of the liberals and a struggle against the landowners. Lenin (q.v.) and Plekhanov made a profound critique of N.

Nation, a historically formed community of people which succeeds nationality (q.v.). The N. is distinguished first of all by common material conditions of life: common territory and economic life; common language and certain traits of national character, manifested in the national peculiarity of its culture. The N., a broader than nationality form of community, comes into being with the appearance and development of the capitalist formation. Liquidation of feudal disunity, the consolidation of economic ties between regions within a country, the merging of local markets into a national market served as the economic basis for the formation of Nn. The bourgeoisie was the leading force of Nn. in that period, which fact left a definite imprint on their socio-political and cultural aspects. As the bourgeois Nn. develop, their social contradictions grow increasingly sharp and the antithesis between the classes becomes apparent. Seeking to cover up these contradictions, the bourgeoisie fans antagonisms between Nn. It advocates the ideology of nationalism (q.v.) and national selfishness. In opposition to the bourgeois nationalism the proletariat puts forward the ideology and policy of internationalism (q.v.). With the abolition of capitalism the make-up of Nn. radically changes. The old, bourgeois Nn. are transformed into new, socialist nations with no class antagonisms but with the alliance of working class and working peasantry forming their social basis. The relations between these socialist Nn. are basically different, with the remnants of the former distrust between them vanishing and friendship of the peoples developing. The abolition of national oppression and the establishment of equality between the peoples, their mutual assistance, and the elimination of the economic and cultural backwardness of peoples who had been retarded in their development have created all the requisites for the thriving of the socialist Nn. in the Soviet Union. In a socialist society, Nn., on the one hand, develop and flourish, and on the other, they draw closer together. On this basis a new historical community, the multinational Soviet people, has formed in the Soviet Union. After the complete victory of communism, the all-round convergence of nations will ultimately bring about a gradual disappearance of national distinctions. A new form of historical community of people, broader than the N. and uniting the whole mankind into one family, will arise in a fully developed communist society. But such a community will come into being only as a result of prolonged social progress and, moreover, much later than the time when full social homogeneity is attained.

National Question, the question of nations' liberation and of the conditions for their free development. The N.Q. should be approached historically, because its content and importance are not the same in different epochs. In the period of the emergence of nations, the N.Q. involved the overthrow of feudalism and their liberation from foreign national oppression. In the epoch of imperialism, the N.Q. has become an interstate problem, has merged with the general problem of liberating the colonial peoples. It is closely linked with the peasant question, because the majority of participants in the national movements are peasants. In the present epoch of the spreading national liberation struggle and abolition of the colonial system the international communist movement is faced with a task—to oppose the aggressive neocolonialist policy of the imperialist powers and to assist peoples in upholding their national independence and sovereignty. The countries of a socialist orientation, which have chosen the non-capitalist road of development, are the vanguard of the national liberation movement of today. According to bourgeois ideologists, the only way to solve the N.Q. is to isolate nations, which actually leads to greater enmity between them and to the subordination of some nations by others. Meanwhile, the October Socialist Revolution and the practice of the socialist construction in the Soviet Union demonstrated the possibility and expediency of a different, revolutionary way of abolishing national oppression, and establishing friendship of the peoples. The Soviet system has not limited itself to proclaiming the legal equality of nations, it has eliminated their actual economic and cultural inequality inherited from the old system. Drawing on fraternal assistance, all Soviet republics have built up a modern industry, trained their own skilled workers and intellectuals, and developed culture, national in form and socialist in content. The building of communism leads to still greater unity of the Soviet peoples. The obliteration of the distinctions between classes and the development of communist social relations make for a greater social homogeneity of nations and contribute to the development of common communist traits in their culture, morals, and way of life, and to a further strengthening of their mutual trust and friendship. Based on the drawing together of all the social groups, nationalities and nations, a new historical community—the Soviet people—has been formed in the Soviet Union. This is not a national but an international community. The formation and successful development of the Soviet people testify to the triumph of the principles of socialist internationalism (q.v.), which has become firmly established in the life of the peoples of the USSR in the fight against various manifestations and survivals of nationalism (q.v.).

Nationalism, a principle of bourgeois ideology and politics expressed in the advocacy of national isolation, the exclusiveness of individual nations (q.v.), of mistrust and enmity among nations. N. came into being in the process of nations' formation and is determined by capitalism's specific features of development. While reflecting the nature of interrelationship of nations under capitalism, N. appears in two forms: great-power chauvinism of a dominant nation, marked by contempt for other nations, and local N. of an oppressed nation stamped by the striving for national seclusion and mistrust of other nations. Speculating on the slogans of "nationwide" interests, bourgeois and reformist ideologists utilise N. as a refined means for stifling the class consciousness of the working people, splitting the international working-class movement, and justifying colonialism and wars between nations. N. is unacceptable in any form to the working people, whose true interests are expressed only by proletarian, socialist internationalism (q.v.). But at a definite stage of the national liberation movement, Communists consider it historically justified to support the N. of an oppressed nation, which has a general democratic content (anti-imperialism, striving for political and economic independence). This variety of N., however, has another side, expressing the ideology and interests of the reactionary exploiting top group, which leans towards compromise with imperialism. Communists, no doubt, reject this side. As a feature of the world outlook N. is most widespread and tenacious in a petty-bourgeois environment; it is typical of the social groups and political parties marked by petty-bourgeois ideology. Under socialism, which establishes real equality of nations, the social roots of N. are wiped out and its manifestations merely represent the survivals of the past in the minds and behaviour of people.

Nationality, one of the forms of community of people, which follows historically the clan and tribal community; it is formed in the period of the consolidation and merging of separate tribes, of the replacement of the relations inherent in primitive-communal society by those of private ownership and of the emergence and development of classes. The formation of N. is characterised by the changeover from blood relationship to territorial community, from a variety of tribal languages to a common language with a number of local dialects still in use. Each N. receives a collective name and accumulates elements of common culture. Nn. existed both under slavery (the Egyptian, Grecian Nn., and others) and feudalism (the Old Russian, French Nn., and others). The nation (q.v.), a new historical form of the community of people, comes into being on the basis of developing capitalist relations. Since under capitalism pre-capitalist relations still remain along with the capitalist ones, not all nationalities grow into nations. As a rule, the consolidation of nationalities and their growth into nations are hindered in the dependent countries oppressed by the monopoly capital of the imperialist countries. Under socialism, the transformation of nationalities into socialist nations takes place in the context of free and all-round social, political and cultural development of all nations. The N., however, still exists as an ethnic formation. Some socialist Nn. do not grow into nations mainly because they are not big enough in size. By their social nature the socialist nations and Nn. radically differ from the similar ethnic formations in capitalist countries.

Natural-Historical Materialism (natural-scientific materialism), the concept used by Lenin to imply the spontaneous "philosophically unconscious conviction shared by the overwhelming majority of scientists regarding the objective reality of the external world" (Vol. 14, p. 346). Great popularity of N.H.M. among natural scientists proves that the admission of the materiality of the world logically follows from man's cognition of nature. However, if N.H.M. does not evolve to become a coherent philosophical theory, it does not exceed the limits of one-sided mechanistic and metaphysical materialism and invariably degenerates into vulgar empiricism and positivism (qq.v.). The limitations of N.H.M. are best of all exposed in the period of breaking scientific theories. N.H.M. proves to be insufficient to explain new accomplishments of knowledge, which contradict the old generally recognised conceptions. That is why, natural scientists, confronted with difficulties in interpreting new phenomena, often come to renounce their spontaneous materialist views and yield to idealism (see Idealism, Physical). A proper philosophical generalisation of the results achieved by specific sciences can be made only from the standpoint of dialectical materialist philosophy.

Natural Law, a doctrine of ideal law which is independent of the state and is held to be derived from the reason and nature of man. Ideas of N.L. were put forward in ancient times by Socrates, Plato (qq.v.), etc. In the Middle Ages N. L. was considered a variety of the law of God (see Aquinas, Thomas). The ideas of N.L. were taken up most widely in the period of Western bourgeois revolutions (17th-18th centuries) and its chief advocates (Grotius, Spinoza, Locke, Rousseau, Montesquieu, Holbach, Kant, Radishchev, qq.v., and others) used it to criticise feudalism and affirm the "naturalness" and "reasonableness" of bourgeois society. In the period of imperialism the ideas of N.L. are often used to defend capitalism.

Natural Philosophy, the name given to philosophy, distinguished by the predominantly speculative interpretation of nature taken in its entirety. The boundaries between natural science and N.P. and also the place of N.P. in the system of other philosophical sciences have undergone changes in the course of the history of philosophy. In antiquity, N.P. merged with natural science and in ancient Greek philosophy was usually called physics. Ancient N.P. gave a spontaneous and naive dialectical interpretation of nature as an integral and living whole, and asserted the identity of man and nature (see Hylozoism). Cosmology and cosmogony (qq.v.) were also an integral part of N.P. Elements of N.P. were present even in medieval scholasticism (q.v.). They consisted chiefly in the adaptation of some principles of Aristotelian N.P. and cosmology to the geocentric picture of the world. In the course of the struggle against the scholastic picture of nature the N.P. of the Renaissance (q.v.) preserved in the main the concepts and principles of ancient N.P., though it was based on a higher level of natural scientific knowledge, and developed a number of profound materialist and dialectical ideas, e.g., the idea of the infinity of nature and the countless number of its constituent worlds, the idea of the coincidence of the opposites in the boundlessly great and the boundlessly small (see Cusa, Nicholas of; Bruno). In the 17th century, a number of natural sciences, first of all mathematics and mechanics, emerged from N.P., but the latter was still regarded as closely connected with them. In the 18th century, the philosophers of the French and European Enlightenment and materialism, put forward the idea of the encyclopaedic interconnection of all the sciences, which had been extended and deepened as compared with the preceding century. Schelling's (q.v.) N.P. played a big part at the end of the 18th and the beginning of the 19th centuries. Although it rested on an idealist foundation, it formulated the idea of the unity of nature's forces and summed up a number of essential natural science discoveries of that epoch. L. Oken, a follower of Schelling, suggested the idea of the development of the organic world. Characterising N.P., Engels wrote that it "put in place of the real but as yet unknown interconnections ideal, fancied ones, filling in the missing facts by figments of the mind and bridging the actual gaps merely in imagination. In the course of this procedure it conceived many brilliant ideas and foreshadowed many later discoveries, but it also produced a considerable amount of nonsense, which indeed could not have been otherwise. Today, when one needs to comprehend the results of natural scientific investigation only dialectically, that is, in the sense of their own interconnection, in order to arrive at a 'system of nature', sufficient for our time, when the dialectical character of this interconnection is forcing itself against their will even into the metaphysically-trained minds of the natural scientists, today natural philosophy is finally disposed of. Every attempt of resurrecting it would be not only superfluous, but a *step backwards*" (K. Marx and F. Engels, *Selected Works* in three volumes, Vol. 3, pp. 364-65). Subsequently, at the turn of the 20th century such a step backwards was taken by W. Ostwald, Avenarius (q.v.) and some other idealist philosophers, who attempted to overcome the crisis in natural science by means of N.P. Certain elements of N.P. are to be found in the theory of emergent evolution (q.v.) or in N. Hartmann's (q.v.) theory of critical ontology.

Natural Science, science of nature, the natural sciences taken as a whole; one of the three basic divisions of human knowledge (the other two being the social sciences and the sciences concerned with thought). N.S. forms the theoretical basis of industrial and agricultural technology and medicine; it is the scientific foundation of philosophical materialism and the dialectical comprehension of nature. It studies the various forms of matter and forms of their motion, how they operate and manifest themselves in nature, their connections and regularities. N.S. may be either empirical or theoretical, depending on its content and methods of investigation; depending on the nature of the object of its study, it may be either non-organic, i.e., studying forms of motion in inanimate nature (the mechanical, physical, and chemical, etc., forms of motion), or organic, where the object studied are the phenomena of life. These subdivisions indicate the inner structure of N.S., the classification of sciences (q.v.). Since it helps to provide a natural scientific or "physical" picture of the world, N.S. is closely associated with philosophy, mainly through its theoretical part (concepts, categories, laws, theories, hypotheses) and also through the elaboration of ways and methods of scientific research; it has a direct influence on the development of philosophy and determines changes in the forms of materialism brought about by great scientific discoveries. On the other hand, N.S. is closely linked with technology, with the process of production. N.S. acts as a kind of direct productive force; moreover, in the process of building communist society this social function of N.S. shows itself more and more fully. In the course of its development N.S. has passed from the immediate contemplation of nature (among the ancients) through the period of analytical dissection (15th to 18th centuries), which in its absolute form became the metaphysical view of nature, to the synthetic reconstruction of nature in its comprehensiveness, wholeness and concreteness that has been achieved in the 19th-20th centuries. The spontaneous penetration of N.S. by dialectics in the 19th century was complicated in the 20th by the crisis of N.S., the causes of which, as well as ways of overcoming it, were revealed by Lenin in his *Materialism and Empirio-Criticism* (q.v.). Up to the mid-20th century N.S. was dominated by physics (q.v.), which sought the ways of using atomic energy and penetrating into the microcosm, the atom, its nucleus and elementary particles. Physics stimulated the development of other branches of N.S.—astronomy (q.v.) (cosmonautics), cybernetics (q.v.), bionics, chemistry, biology (q.v.), etc. Physics in company with chemistry, mathematics (q.v.) and cybernetics helps molecular biology to solve the theoretical and experimental task of biosynthesis; it also contributes to the discovery of the material nature of heredity, to the cognition of the nature of chemical connections, to the solution of the problems of cosmogony and cosmology (qq.v.). In modern N.S. the leading role belongs not only to physics but to a whole group of sciences, such as molecu-lar biology, cybernetics, macrochemistry. Modern N.S. raises a number of philosophical problems, which require a serious study. Solution of these problems is necessary to develop materialist dialectics and to combat various religious idealist doctrines, which since the turn of this century have been nourished by the continuous revolution in N.S. The growing part played by N.S. in the life of contemporary society is strongly manifested in the scientific and technological revolution (q.v.).

Naturalism 1. In philosophy, the methodological principle used by some pre-Marxist theories to explain the development of society by the laws of nature (climatic conditions, geographical environment, biological and racial distinctions between peoples, etc.). N. is close to anthropologism (q.v.), which also fails to see the specific laws governing social life. In the 17th and 18th centuries philosophical N. played a positive part in the struggle against spiritualism (q.v.); subsequently, it degenerated into a reactionary idealist trend. 2. A system of aesthetic views on art and a corresponding artistic method which took shape in the second half of the 19th century. Positivism (q.v.) represented by Comte, Spencer (qq.v.) and others, formed the philosophical foundation of N. N. does not try to fathom the essential, deep-going processes of reality and reduces artistic portrayal to copying accidental, singular objects and phenomena. The contradictory nature of the aesthetic conception of N. was strikingly displayed in the works of E. Zola, which were often at variance with his statements on the identity of social and biological phenomena, the independence of art from politics and morality, etc. Concentration on physiological aspects of life, striving for primitive entertainment, sentimentality and melodrama, ostentatious embellishment are characteristic features of N. expressed in diverse genres of "mass culture" in capitalist countries. The ideas of passivity, renunciation of social struggle, indifference to the joys and suffering of people, particular interest in the base sides of human life, preached (directly or indirectly) by the proponents of N., bring the latter closer to formalistic trends in art (see Formalism). 3. In ethics, the methodological principle of giving substance to morality. This principle was characteristic of many ethical theories of the past, especially of 20th-century bourgeois conceptions. According to it, moral standards (in particular, the concept of good) are deduced not from the laws of man's social being, but from a kind of natural principle (the laws of space, the organic world, biology, or human psychology). Ethical N. includes hedonism, eudaemonism, utilitarianism, evolutionary ethics (qq.v.), and others. The majority of trends of the modern bourgeois ethics continue to derive moral concepts from various notions and data of anthropology and psychology. Among these trends are ethics of cosmic teleology, theories of moral sense, theory of interest (qq.v.) and others. Moore (q.v.) was the first among the bourgeois theorists of morality to criticise N. According to Moore and his followers, moral standards cannot be derived from "natural" concepts (they considered this a "naturalistic mistake"). Meanwhile, having a broader understanding of the "natural", they placed within this category everything that is outside morality, including social phenomena. In the result both morality and ethics are separated from the social sciences and the actual knowledge of man. This is the drawback typical of the whole formalistic trend of the modern bourgeois ethics. In the 1940s and 1950s the authors of a number of studies conducted in Western countries, defended the principles of N. against formalism and neo-positivism (qq.v.). This criticism, levelled by naturalists against formalism and idealism in ethics, and the elements of materialism contained in their theories are by and large progressive. Their drawback is the lack of a clear understanding of the basic differences between the socio-historical laws of the development of morality and those of anthropology and psychology. Marxism has proved that morality (q.v.) is a specific social phenomenon, whose essence cannot be grasped without complete abandonment of the survivals of N. in ethics.

Nature, the world surrounding us in the endless diversity of its manifestations.

N. is the objective reality (q.v.) existing outside consciousness and independently of it. It has neither beginning nor end, it is endless in time and space, and it is in a constant state of movement and change. Sometimes the term of N. denotes only one part of it, the biosphere (q.v.), and the latter, engendered by the preceding development of N., prepared all the necessary conditions for the appearance of man. However, the decisive factor in the process of the appearance of man is labour (q.v.). The emergence of society considerably changed N. itself (see Noosphere). Cognising the objective laws of N., acting on it by means of specially created tools and implements of labour, people utilise the substances and energy of N. for creating the material wealth necessary for mankind. In this way the natural habitat is supplemented by an artificial one, the so-called second nature, i.e., the sum total of things not found in nature in ready form and created in the process of social production. But in acquiring ever greater power over N., in actively transforming it, people do not cease to belong to it, to be its organic part. In transforming N. in a desired direction people are guided by the laws of N. and use natural forces and processes. The character of productive forces (q.v.) is the basic yardstick for gauging the relations between society and N. The problem of N. conservation and protection, and of rationally combining the society's production activity with global natural processes has acquired utmost importance in the conditions of the current scientific and technological revolution (q.v.).

Nebular Hypothesis, a cosmogonic hypothesis, according to which the solar system (or celestial bodies in general) evolved from a rarefied nebula. The term was applied to the hypothesis voiced by Laplace (q.v.), who assumed that planets arose from an incandescent gas nebula, and more seldom to the hypothesis of Kant (q.v.), who assumed that planets originated from a dust nebula; at times it is also applied to modern hypotheses. The idea underlying the N.H., the natural origination of cosmic bodies and other forms of cosmic substance (gas, dust), has not lost its importance to this day (see Cosmogony).

Necessity and Chance, philosophical categories which reflect relation between the essence (q.v.) of phenomena and their manifestations. Any phenomena that are the realisation and development of their essence are necessary, while solitary and unique phenomena are fortuitous. In other words, N. is that which necessarily must occur in the given conditions. On the contrary, C. is rooted not in the essence of phenomena but in the influence of other phenomena on the given phenomenon; C. may or may not occur, it may take this or that form. A metaphysical, rational-empirical approach to interconnection and development of phenomena leads one to an insoluble contradiction. On the one hand, all phenomena, events, etc. are caused by some reason and, therefore, could not but emerge. On the other hand, their emergence depends upon an infinite number of various conditions, which make the given reason effective; an unpredictable combination of such conditions makes the emergence of these phenomena, events not necessary or chance. Unable to solve this contradiction, the metaphysical thinking comes either to fatalism (q.v.), where any event happens to be predetermined from the very beginning, or to relativism (q.v.) and indeterminism (see Determinism and Indeterminism), where events are in the final analysis a chaos of chance occurrences. In both cases any conscious human activity is useless. Comprehension of internally interconnected N. and C. is possible only through the dialectical understanding of the process of development as becoming in unique forms of individual events, through a certain way of resolving the primary contradiction (q.v.). Any process is resolving a mature contradiction in time and space. The contradiction that has reached a point of maturity must be of necessity resolved, but this process may take different forms, which may be accidental, as at a given moment and under given conditions various events and phenomena, having a broader basis, are involved in this process. Thus, N., i.e., the inevitable resolution of a contradiction, makes its way through chance, while

the latter serves as a complement and form of the manifestation of N. It is the goal of any conscious human activity to correlate various solitary, chance events and circumstances with their common basis, to change these circumstances by identifying certain ways of resolving existing contradictions. Marxist philosophy proceeds from the assumption that in each event it is always possible to single out the essential (necessary) and inessential (chance) properties. N. and C. are dialectical opposites, which do not exist without each other. Behind chance there is always N., the necessary basis of all phenomena, which determines the course of development in nature and society. As Engels put it, "where on the surface accident holds sway, there actually it is always governed by inner, hidden laws and it is only a matter of discovering these laws" (K. Marx and F. Engels, *Selected Works* in three volumes, Vol. 3, p. 366). The task of science is to reveal the necessary basis of phenomena behind chance connections. However intricate a given phenomenon, however numerous the chances on which it depends, it is ultimately governed by objective laws, by N. Dialectical materialism helps to see not only the connection but also the interpenetration of N. and C. Contemporary science enriches the dialectico-materialist conclusions concerning the essence of N. and C. (see Probability, Theory of; Laws, Statistical and Dynamic).

Negation 1. In materialist dialectics N. is regarded as a necessary moment of development, a condition for qualitative change of things (see Negation of the Negation, Law of). 2. A logical operation with the help of which a new proposition is inferred from a given proposition (so-called negation of the initial proposition). If the initial proposition was true, its N. is false, and vice versa.

Negation of the Negation, Law of, a basic law of dialectics first formulated in the idealist system by Hegel (q.v.). L.N.N. expresses continuity (q.v.) of development, the connection of the new and the old, and repetition at a higher stage of development of some properties of the lower stage. It proves the progressive character of development. In dialectics the concept N. means the transformation of one object into another and the simultaneous "elimination" of the former. But this "elimination" gives scope for further development and serves as a link with the previous stages in that it preserves the positive content. Dialectical N. is engendered by the intrinsic laws of a phenomenon, and manifests itself as a self-negation. The characteristic feature of development expressed in the double negation (or negation of the negation) derives from the essence of dialectical negation. The self-development of an object is generated by its inherent contradictions (see Unity and Conflict of Opposites, Law of), by the presence in it of its own negation. The contradiction is resolved through the motion of the object (and of cognition), which means emergence of a "third" negation in relation to the two antitheses. As long as the two antitheses not only exclude but also penetrate each other, the "third" negation appears as a preserving factor (see Sublation). The conditions and prerequisites that gave rise to the object do not disappear as it develops, but are reproduced by it. In thinking, too, this is expressed through the negation of the negation, through a better understanding of the already achieved truths at the new stage of theory. It follows from the principle of the unity of dialectics, logic and epistemology that only through L.N.N. as the law of practical and theoretical activity (q.v.) it is possible to interpret its universality. Since practice (see Theory and Practice) forms the basis of human relations with the external world, its characteristic features also determine the theoretical (cognitive) relation. This relation consists in that the reproduction of the developing object occurs only through the history of the object's cognition, through theories and concepts that dialectically negate each other. The development of general knowledge and the negation of one theory by another take place in this movement, showing the laws of the motion of the material world to be the negation of one of its states by another state. This explains the fact that the negated state is not eliminated but is retained and transformed. Any one-sided

approach to the object will, after all, reveal something constant in it, which is preserved in the process of negation. That is why the development of scientific theory is only possible when the positive content of the rejected knowledge is retained and included in the new theory. In natural science this relation between the new and the old theory is expressed in the correspondence principle (q.v.), revealing the dialectics of the objective world. Hence, L.N.N. is both a law of cognition and a law of the objective world.

Neo-Freudianism, a trend in modern bourgeois philosophy which studies man, his place and role in the structure of social institutions by using the principles of psychoanalysis. N. arose in the late 1930s as a result of revision of some of the principles of Freudianism (q.v.) which revealed their limitations and lack of promise. Representatives of N. (K. Horney, H. Sullivan, Fromm, q.v.) criticised a number of initial assumptions and final conclusions of the classical psychoanalysis (q.v.) regarding its interpretation of intrapsychic processes responsible for conflict situations, its understanding of the structural levels of psychics and the mechanism of functioning of the unconscious (q.v.). At the same time N. accepts the major schemes of the classical psychoanalysis, including its ideas of the irrational motives of human activities, which are alleged to be inborn in every individual, and the psychoanalytical method of study of personal and social structures. With their attention focussed on the social and cultural processes largely responsible for intra-personal conflicts of the individual, representatives of N. rely on the Freudian conception of unconscious inclinations, which, in their opinion, has extended the limits of cognition of man's inner world. The classical psychoanalysis gives no comprehensive answers to the questions as regards human existence—how man should live and what he should do. Neo-Freudians are willing to fill the gap. They criticise the modern Western society where man loses his uniqueness, alienates from the external world and himself and is deprived of the actual human dimension. In doing so they do not disclose the true reasons for the degradation of the individual and for the contradiction between social and personal interests. They hope to remedy various forms of human alienation (q.v.) by "humanistic psychoanalysis" alleged to be able to rouse critical elements in man's consciousness and transform his life values and ideals. Meanwhile, the procedure of healing society through the healing of the individual turns out to be utopian and the abstract-humanistic approach based on this procedure holds no promise, being unable to eliminate either the actual reasons for split personality in bourgeois society or the crisis of capitalist civilisation.

Neo-Hegelianism, an idealistic philosophical trend which appeared in Britain and the United States in the second half of the 19th century as a reaction to natural-historical materialism and positivism (qq.v.) and for the defence of religion and speculative philosophy (Th. Green, F. Bradley, J. Royce, J. McTaggart, and others). At the turn of the century N. assumed an anti-Marxist trend and spread in Italy (see Croce; Gentile), in Russia (I. Ilyin and others) and Netherlands (G. Bolland). German N. (H. Glockner, R. Kroner, Th. Litt) came to the fore on the eve of, and after, the First World War. After the Second World War N. spread in France, largely merging with existentialism, q.v. (J. Wahl, Hyppolite, q.v.). N. in general renounces dialectics or limits its application to the sphere of consciousness alone. A solution of the problem of contradiction by N. varies from "reconciliation" to denial of any possibility of resolving contradictions. In sociology, some representatives of N. utilise the reactionary aspects of Hegelian philosophy of the spirit for "justifying" the policy of the imperialist state and also of the fascist corporate state (q.v.) as a means of reconciling classes in society. In 1930, a centre of N. was set up under the name of International Hegelian Union.

Neo-Kantianism. an idealist trend which sprang up in Germany in the second half of the 19th century under the slogan "Back to Kant!" (Otto Liebmann, F. Lange). It also spread in France (Ch. B. Renouvier, O. Hamelin), Italy

(C. Cantoni) and Russia (Vvedensky, Chelpanov, qq.v., and so-called "legal Marxism", q.v.). N. reproduces and develops the idealist and metaphysical elements in the philosophy of Kant (q.v.), ignoring its materialist and dialectical elements. The thing-in-itself is either discarded or interpreted in a subjective idealist way. N. received full expression in two German schools: the Marburg school, q.v. (Cohen, Cassirer, qq.v.) and the Freiburg or Baden school, q.v. (Windelband, Rickert, qq.v). The former school paid particular attention to the idealist interpretation of scientific concepts and philosophical categories, regarding them as logical constructions. The second school focussed attention on justifying the contradistinction of the natural and the social sciences on the basis of the Kantian doctrine of practical and theoretical reason and on striving to demonstrate the impossibility of scientific knowledge of social phenomena. N. was utilised by revisionism (q.v.) in its struggle against Marxism and practically became the official philosophical conception of opportunists in the Second International (Bernstein, q.v., M. Adler). Crushing blows at this conception were struck by Lenin and Plekhanov (qq.v.). At present N. enjoys influence in some trends of axiology (q.v.).

Neo-Lamarckism, an unscientific trend in the theory of evolution, which derived its name from the French naturalist J. Lamarck (1744-1829) and which became widespread at the end of the 19th century. The characteristics of N. are an explanation of evolution only as a result of physiological processes, denial of the creative role of natural selection, recognition of primordial purposefulness of organisms. One of the varieties of N. was so-called mechanistic Lamarckism. It was most consistently elaborated by Spencer (q.v.) in his equilibrium theory, according to which the interaction of the organism and the environment led to their equilibrium. Spencer considered evolution to be the result of the continuous disturbance of this equilibrium. The inability of mechanistic Lamarckists to give a scientific explanation to the relative purposefulness of organisms led them to idealism.

So-called psycho-Lamarckism, founded by the paleontologist E.D. Cope (1840-1897), is an extreme idealist variety of N. According to psycho-Lamarckism, the source of evolution lies in primitive forms of consciousness and will, in some kind of "creative principle" interpreted in the spirit of vitalism (q.v.). Varieties of mechanistic Lamarckism and psycho-Lamarckism may be found today in the philosophical interpretation of biological processes.

Neoplatonism, a reactionary mystic philosophy in the epoch of the decline of the Roman Empire (3rd-6th centuries). Plato's (q.v.) idealist theory of ideas assumed the form of a doctrine of mystic emanation of the material world from the spiritual primordial element. Matter is only the lowest link in the hierarchy of the Universe, emanation of the "world soul", over which rises the "spirit" and still higher the "prime essence", or the "One". In this philosophy, idealism degenerated into theosophy (q.v.). N. first arose in Egypt. A Neoplatonic school was founded by Plotinus (q.v.) in Rome. The last Neoplatonic school, founded by Proclus (q.v.) in Athens, existed until 529. N. originally was hostile to Christianity and contained numerous elements of Oriental magic and mythology. Nevertheless it exerted a great influence on Christian patristics (q.v.) and on the development of philosophy in feudal society both in Christian and Muslim countries.

Neo-Positivism, one of the trends of bourgeois philosophy in the 20th century, the contemporary form of positivism (q.v.). N. deprives philosophy of its subject-matter. According to N., knowledge of reality is given only in everyday or concrete scientific thinking, while philosophy is possible only as an analysis of language, in which the results of these forms of thinking are expressed (see Philosophy, Analitical). Philosophical analysis, in the opinion of neo-positivists, does not extend to objective reality, it must be limited only to direct experience or language. The extreme forms of N., for example, the early neo-positivist Vienna Circle (q.v.), by limiting the sphere of philosophy to individual emotions, arrived directly at solipsism. Logical positivism (q.v.) is the most influential variety of N. The British analytical philosophers, followers of Moore, q.v. (L. Stebbing, A. Wisdom, and others) adhered to the general platform of N. Some members of the logical Lvov-Warsaw school, q.v. (K. Ajdukiewicz) were also neo-positivists. An ideological and scientific organisational merger of various groups and individual philosophers who adhered to neo-positivist views took place in the 1930s. These were the Austro-German logical positivists of the Vienna Circle (Carnap, Schlick, qq.v., and others) and the Berlin Society of Scientific Philosophy (Reichenbach, q.v., C. Hempel, and others), the British analysists, a number of American representatives of the "philosophy of science" who adhered to the positivist-pragmatic trend (O. Nagel, Bridgman, q.v. and others), the Uppsala school in Sweden, the Münster logical group in Germany headed by H. Scholz, and others. Since then international congresses have been regularly held and the ideas of N. are widely advocated in the press. N. calls itself "scientific empiricism", exerts substantial influence on scientific circles by giving rise to idealist conceptions in interpreting the discoveries of contemporary science. Mention should be made, however, of the positive significance of concrete results of studies in formal logic and methodology of science achieved both by the neo-positivists themselves and by scientists who are not neo-positivists but participate in the congresses and discussions they arrange, etc. Since the end of the 1930s the United States has become the main centre of N. At present this philosophy is represented above all by logical empiricism (q.v.). Linguistic philosophy (q.v.) is a specific variety of N. in Britain. Since the 1950s N. has been undergoing a deep ideological crisis, displayed in its inability to solve the real problems of scientific world-view and methodology of science and is being criticised by representatives of such trends in Western philosophy as postpositivism and critical rationalism (q.v.).

Neo-Positivism in Ethics, see Linguistic Analysis in Ethics; Logical Positivism; Emotivism.

Neo-Protestantism, the trend in modern bourgeois theology (q.v.), which after the First World War gained currency in Europe (K. Barth, E. Brunner) and in the 1930s — in the United States (Reinhold and Richard Niebuhr, P. Tillich, and others; see Dialectical Theology). N. sharply criticised the liberal Christianity (q.v.) and counterposed the absolute supreme God to man, limited in his potentialities. In contrast to neo-Thomism (q.v.), where God is understood as an eternal law, in the philosophy of N. God is a subject freely exercising his will. From the point of view of N. man in his earthly being is in antagonism with God, whose will he inevitably violates; this comprises basically unavoidable human sinfulness. N. declared illusory all human hopes for historical progress, for a development of society, science and enlightenment, criticising secular humanistic culture, in which it included the Renaissance, the philosophy of rationalism (q.v.) of the 17th-18th centuries, the Enlightenment and also Marxism. According to the proponents of N., social-historical being instigates man "to rebel against God", tempts him to view himself as an independent subject and creator of history. Proceeding from this viewpoint religion (and religious conscience) fulfils a purely critical function, i.e., exposes this sort of human sinful pretensions. In the ethics of N. secular morality is counterposed to Christian morality. Secular morality is alleged to subject to material and social interests, to fit a sinful human nature and to have a compromise character. Christian morality, however, is absolute and unconditional; it is beyond any expedience and is based on the principle of love. The proponents of N. think that Christian morality cannot be practised in social life and always remains "an impossible possibility". This morality cannot be expressed in any concepts or through a system of specific principles of behaviour. Christian morality consists merely in unconditional criticism of any human pretensions to be moral, in complete obedience to God's will, in making no attempts to conceive its essence or expedience.

Neo-Realism, a trend in Anglo-American philosophy of the 20th century. Its main representatives in Great Britain are Moore, Russell (in early period of his activities), Alexander (qq.v.) and in the United States—R. Perry, W. Montague, and others. The neo-realistic theory of knowledge, directed against the materialist theory of reflection and condemning the latter as "dualism", is based on the recognition that the cognisable thing can directly enter the mind, but at the same time does not depend on knowledge as regards its existence and nature. In ontology, N. recognises that general concepts which possess "ideal existence" are real and that things are independent of relations into which they enter. Epistemologically, N. results from the dissociation of the universal from individual things, and from ontologisation of logical connections and concepts. N. also has a "cosmologic" trend, which develops on the basis of an idealistically understood theory of development, universal philosophical systems (theory of emergent evolution, q.v., Whitehead's, q.v., philosophy of the process, and holism, q.v., of J. Ch. Smuts).

Neo-Slavophiles (or "late Slavophiles"), followers of Slavophiles (q.v.) in the second half of the 19th century. N. borrowed from their forerunners the proposition that the social development of the East and that of the West are antithetical and also the idea of the exceptional role of the Slavs (particularly of Russia) in history; they provided a new theoretical substantiation for the conservative sides of Slavophilism. N. Danilevsky (1822-1885), the main representative of the trend, used the falsely interpreted methods of natural science as the basis for his theory of "cultural and historical types". According to it, each nation has its own history, in which it passes through the tribal (youth), the state (maturity) and the civilisation (old age, decay) periods (*Russia and Europe*, 1869). From Danilevsky's viewpoint the "European type" (i.e., bourgeois Europe) was in the period of wasting away, while the Slavs entered the period of flourishing. Therefore, it was a Slav federative state with the autocratic Russia at its head that could foster the progressive development of mankind. Danilevsky's adherents were Leontyev (q.v.) and N. Strakhov (1828-

1896). The basic social contradictions of Russian society were viewed in the theories of N. as anomalous; these theories reflected the interests of the ruling classes and were directed against revolutionary democracy and socialism. The N.'s general philosophical views were an eclectic combination of religious idealism with elements of naturalism. N. denied the scientific value of Darwinism.

Neo-Thomism, the official philosophical doctrine of the Catholic Church based on the teaching of Thomas Aquinas (q.v.). An encyclical of Pope Leo XIII (1879) recognised N. the only true philosophy conforming to the Christian dogmas. In 1889, a Higher Institute of Philosophy was established in Louvain, Belgium. It is still the international centre of N. This doctrine is widespread in countries with a large number of Catholics (France, Italy, West Germany, the United States, and Latin American countries). Among neo-Thomists are Maritain (q.v.), E. Gilson (France), K. Rahner (Belgium), J. de Vries, F. Van Steenberghen (West Germany), G. Wetter (Austria), J. Bochenski, and others. Neo-Thomist philosophy serves as the ideological mainstay of clericalism (q.v.). The principle: "philosophy is the handmaiden of theology" is the basis of N. N. is a theological form of contemporary objective idealism. Neo-Thomists regard "pure being", understood as the spiritual, divine prime element, as the highest reality. Neo-Thomists widely utilise as proof of religious dogmas the falsified Aristotelian categories of form and matter, potential and action (possibility and reality) and also the categories of existence and essence. The neo-Thomist speculative constructions result in recognising God as the prime cause of being and the prime foundation of all philosophical categories. Religious interpretation of contemporary natural scientific theories holds a big place in N. The aim of the new policy of N., which shaped itself after the Second Vatican Council (1962-65), was to accustom N. to contemporary philosophy through a synthesis of Thomist principles with certain propositions of existentialism, phenomenology, philosophical anthropology (qq.v.), and other trends of modern philosophical idealism. According to N., the process of history depends upon supernatural forces, which govern every individual's behaviour. By this any possibility of man's active influence on world history is actually excluded. Neo-Thomist sociology is based on the utopian idea of an ideal society where the church will rule.

New Left, the movement of protest by a large part of students and intellectuals in Western countries against bourgeois society, its social, economic and political institutions, way of life, moral values and ideals. It has no common ideological guidelines or practical programmes and consists of many groups and organisations of different political orientations. The movement comprises elements of a spontaneous rebellion against the social reality but has no effective methods, ways and means for its practical change. The "left" radical moods, which arose in the early 1960s, spread over the wide strata of young people and intelligentsia. The majority of the N.L. members adhere to the general philosophy of "total negation" of the existing institutions, authorities, values of life. Nihilism, anarchism (qq.v.), spontaneity, a desire to violate the "rules of the game" and to withdraw from the bourgeois society's social, economic, political and cultural structures—these are the main attitudes of the N.L. movement, borrowed from the works by Marcuse, Sartre (qq.v.), R. Debray, and other "left" radical ideologists. All these attitudes proved abstract, utopian, actually unrealisable. Eventually, in the early 1970s the N.L. movement split into small groups as a result of inner differences and repressions by the official authorities. By and large, the movement contributed to the awakening of the conscience of the masses in capitalist countries. Meanwhile, representing petty-bourgeois radicalism, it could not effectively hold out against the state-monopoly capitalism because it stood apart from the working class and denied its leading role in revolutionary reorganisation of society.

New Philosophers, a heterogeneous group of French bourgeois philosophers that emerged in the 1970s to deny any philosophy or culture based on reason. In essence, the main ideas of the N.P. (A. Glücksman, B.-H. Lévy and others) echo the propositions put forward by Schopenhauer and Nietzsche (qq.v.). The N.P. are former active participants in the student unrest of the 1960s who subsequently opposed the theory of the revolution and existing socialism. This sort of opposition is used by the bourgeois ideologists and politicians to compromise and blacken the entire left movement. The denial of the revolutionary ideals is justified by the N.P. by their idea of man as an object of unconscious desires and social bans. From this viewpoint, a revolutionary is a rebel inimical to all human, for he is free from the burden of "flesh", desires and needs. Their disbelief in human mind and power, in the possibility of cognising the laws of development and transformation of society inevitably leads the N.P. to regeneration of the faith in God, in the "saviours" of the mankind. All this makes the N.P. allies of reactionary bourgeois ideologists, on the one hand, and of the leftist, anarchist groups, on the other.

Newton, Isaac (1642-1727), English physicist, founder of classical mechanics, who formulated the law of universal gravitation and exerted great influence on the development of philosophical thought. Newton's main work is *Philosophiae Naturalis Principia Mathematica* (1687). The law of universal gravitation completed the heliocentric conception of the solar system and, moreover, laid a scientific foundation for explaining many processes in the entire Universe, including physical and chemical processes. It became the foundation of an integral physical picture of the world (q.v.). Philosophically, N. adhered to positions recognising objective reality and the knowability of the world. In N.'s system inertia and gravitation explain the endless repetition of elliptical movements of celestial bodies, but the "prime impulse" is attributed to God. N.'s theological views and interests and also his unwillingness to analyse the internal causes of the phenomena described (his words: *hypothesis non fingo—*I do not make hypotheses—became the slogan of em-

piricism, q.v., in 18th-century science), did not prevent his system of a definitive and exact explanation of nature from exerting great influence on the development of materialism in Europe.

Nietzsche, Friedrich (1844-1900), German philosopher, proponent of voluntarism (q.v.), a founder of modern irrationalism (q.v.). The classical philosophical categories of matter and spirit were replaced by him by the category of life understood as the "will to power". Power, according to N., serves as a criterion for evaluation of the significance of phenomena. Cognition was alleged to be effective only as "an instrument of power". N.'s epistemological relativism (q.v.) led to "reassessment of all the values" in ethics and culminated in the opposition of current "slave" morality to "master" morality related to the idea of the "superman". N. denied the socialist ideal, for he viewed it as an "uprising of slaves in morality". The Christian religion was rejected by N. for its proclamation of men's equality before God as well as for the self-humiliation of man, killing in him the "will to power". N. substituted for religious myths the myths of "God's death" and "eternal return", regarding the latter as a substitute for the soul's immortality. The social foundation of N.'s philosophy is the reaction of the imperialist bourgeoisie to the developing revolutionary working-class movement. Some socio-critical ideas of N. exerted substantial influence upon certain outstanding writers and thinkers (Th. Mann, H. Ibsen, Schweitzer, q.v., and others). The basic reactionary conclusions of Nietzscheanism determined the main direction of its development and it became a source of the ideas of German fascism (q.v.). His main works: *Thus Spake Zarathustra* (1883-85); *Beyond Good and Evil*, 1886; *The Will to Power*, 1889.

Nihilism, absolute denial, a viewpoint rejecting any positive ideals. The term N., which was first used by Jacobi (q.v.), gained popularity in Russia thanks to I. Turgenev's novel *Fathers and Sons*. In Russia reactionaries called the revolutionary democrats nihilists, ascribing to them unconditional denial of all past culture.

Actually, the revolutionary democrats put forward their own positive programme. Lenin differentiated between revolutionary N. as a natural negative attitude to reactionary social orders (Vol. 4, p. 275) and N. of anarchist intellectualism (Vol, 17, p. 187), which finds its expression in bourgeois philosophy. Nietzsche (q.v.), for example, proclaimed the reappraisal of values, i.e., denial of the standards of culture, morality and justice elaborated by humanity. In present-day conditions N. is often used not only for criticising capitalism, but also for attacks against socialist society, its socio-economic foundations.

Nominalism, a trend in medieval philosophy. In contrast to medieval realism (q.v.) nominalists asserted that only individual things with their individual properties really exist. General concepts created by our mind, far from existing independently of things, do not even reflect their properties and qualities. N. was inseparably connected with materialist tendencies to recognise that things are primary and concepts secondary. N., according to Marx, was the first expression of materialism in the Middle Ages. But the nominalists did not understand that general concepts reflect the real qualities of objectively existing things and that individual things are not separate from the general but contain them within themselves. Roscelin, Duns Scotus, and Occam (qq.v.) were the most outstanding nominalists in the 11th-14th centuries. The ideas of N. were developed on an idealist basis in the doctrines of Berkeley and Hume (qq.v.) and more recently in semantic philosophy.

Nomothetical and Idiographical, the, the notions used by representatives of the Baden school (q.v.) of neo-Kantianism to denote methods applied in the natural sciences and the "sciences of spirit". The N. (generalising) method is applied in the natural sciences for the working out of general concepts and laws, while the I. (individualising) method is used by the sciences which study social phenomena, in which they reveal not the general but the particular. Opposition of these two methods stems from the metaphysical gap between the singular, the particular and

the general and leads to agnosticism (q.v.) in the social sciences, to schematism and formalism in the natural sciences.

Non-Contradiction, a basic condition which knowledge (in particular, scientific knowledge) must fulfil, and according to which a proposition and its negation cannot be simultaneously deduced within the bounds of a relatively separate system of knowledge. Failure to fulfil this condition makes a theory invalid, because it could prove any proposition. The dialectical law of the unity and conflict of opposites, which demands the disclosure of objective contradictions in objects, and the demand of the N. of knowledge are not mutually exclusive. The proposition of logical N. applies to the method of presenting knowledge and implies that our thoughts and arguments must be consistent (see Contradiction, Law of; Axiomatic Theory, Non-Contradiction of).

Non-Euclidean Geometries, all geometric systems differing from the Euclidean. Usually, however, N.G. are understood as the geometries of Lobachevsky (q.v.), J. Bolyai and B. Riemann. From the viewpoint of logical structure, Lobachevsky's geometry has the same axioms as that of Euclid (q.v.), except the axiom on parallels. It is accepted in Lobachevsky's geometry that through a given point not on a straight line *a* not less than two straight lines can be drawn parallel to *a* in a given plane, defined by this point and the straight line *a* (from this it follows that there is an infinity of such lines). The theorems of this geometry differ from the Euclidean. It is assumed in Riemann's N.G. that any straight line on a plane intersects any other straight line in the same plane (there are no parallel straight lines). N.G. play an important part in contemporary theoretical physics (see Relativity, Theory of; Quantum Mechanics). Their discovery is of philosophical significance, because they refute Kant's (q.v.) proposition about the a priori nature of the concept of space and the metaphysical view of space as an immutable essence. N.G. prove the dialectical view of space as a form of matter's existence capable of changing together with it.

Noosphere, the sphere of the planet embraced by rational human activity, a concept introduced in science by Teilhard de Chardin (q.v.) and E. Le Roy and developed by Vernadsky (q.v.). According to Vernadsky, with the emergence and development of human society the biosphere naturally turns into N., because mankind, as it masters the laws of nature and develops technology, increasingly transforms nature in line with its requirements. N. has a tendency continuously to expand as man penetrates outer space and reaches deep into the planet.

Notion, sensory, generalised image of objects and phenomena of the reality, retained and reproduced in the consciousness without immediate action of the objects and phenomena upon the sense-organs. What objectively becomes the property of individuals thanks to their practice takes shape and is retained in man's N. Although N. is a form of individual sensory reflection, in man it is inseparably linked up with socially-evolved values through the medium of language (q.v.), is of social significance and always comprehended and realised. N. is a necessary element of consciousness, since it permanently connects the denotation and sense (q.v.) of concepts with the images of things and at the same time enables our consciousness to operate freely with sensory images of objects.

Noumenon, a term signifying, in contrast to phenomenon (q.v.), the essence conceived only by reason. Plato (q.v.), who first used this term, understood it to mean reality as it exists in itself and an object of speculative knowledge. Kant (q.v.) examined N. in two aspects: being a negative, problematic concept, N. is an object of reason, of intellectual intuition (q.v.); Kant also pointed to the possibility of a positive concept of N. as an object of non-sensuous contemplation. In this sense N. is inaccessible to man, because his contemplation, according to Kant, can be only sensuous.

Nous, a basic concept of ancient philosophy denoting the concentration of all the existing acts of consciousness and thinking in the world. This concept appeared in a clear form for the first time in the philosophy of Anaxagoras (q.v.) where it was treated as a principle shaping and ordering formless matter. This concept was given an idealist interpretation by Plato (q.v.) and especially by Aristotle (q.v.) who considered it the form of all forms in a state of eternal self-contemplation. This concept acquired great importance with the Neoplatonists who, on the ground of Aristotelianism, treated it as a special kind of pretersensual being which imparts meaning and definite form to the world. Materialists also used this concept. Democritus (q.v.) understood N. as fire. Thales (q.v.) also attached cosmological importance to N. Ancient N. is always extra-personal and even impersonal in contrast to medieval doctrines which found a personal element in it.

Nyāya, an orthodox system of Indian philosophy. Logic and epistemology played a particularly big part in the doctrine of N. The origin of N. is associated with the name of the ancient mythical sage Gotama. *Nyāya sūtras* were recorded in the second century A.D. According to the doctrine of N., a material universe consists of atoms, the combinations of which form all objects. In addition, a countless number of souls exist in the Universe. They can be either in a free state or bound with the material atoms. The supreme spirit or God Ishwara is not the creator of the souls and atoms, but of the combinations of atoms, and links the souls with the atoms or releases the souls from the atoms. A syllogism (q.v.) theory, different from that of the ancient Greeks, was developed in India for the first time in N. The five members of the syllogism are premise, proof, illustration, application of proof, and conclusion. N. recognises four modes of knowledge: sensation, inference, analogy, and testimony of other people and books. N. also elaborated a detailed classification of the main categories of knowledge and a classification of objects of knowledge. The philosophy of N. blossomed forth in the early Middle Ages.

O

Object — see Subject and Object.

Objectification and Deobjectification, terms which designate characteristic distinctions of human activity (q.v.). O. means the passage of human active forces and capabilities from a form of motion to the form of an object in the process of the subject's activity; D. means the transition of an object from its own sphere into the sphere and form of human activity. These concepts were applied in Hegel's (q.v.) philosophy. But Hegel idealistically reduced man's labour activity solely to abstract spiritual labour, to thinking, and unhistorically identified O. with alienation (q.v.). These concepts have a fundamentally different meaning in the description of labour given in Marx's early works. Examining O. and D. in their unity, Marx revealed the place of labour in man's life, the fact that by his labour man actively remakes, humanises, the objective world, creating his own special "human reality", the world of culture (as a result of O., which expresses the active side of labour. At the same time man depends on the objective world, including the results of the preceding activity of mankind, utilising them in his activity and co-ordinating this activity with objective laws (as a result of D., which expresses the connection of man with the object of his activity). All this enabled Marx scientifically to characterise the process of labour, to open a way to the dialectical materialist understanding of the relationship between the subject and object (q.v.) and to solve problems of the theory of knowledge in the light of practice.

Objective, pertaining to an object or determined by it. As applied to real objects, this concept means that objects, their properties and relations, exist out-

side and independent of man. As applied to ideas, concepts or judgments, it indicates the source of our knowledge, its material basis.

Objective and Subjective Factors of History, two kinds of conditions of social development. O.F. are conditions which are independent of people and determine the direction, the bounds of their activity. Such, for example, are natural conditions, a given level of production, the historically urgent tasks and requirements of material, political, and spiritual development. S.F. are the purposeful activity of the masses, classes, parties, states, and individuals; their consciousness, will, ability to act, etc. O.F. always play a determining part, but their action is manifested only through the operation of S.F. The latter can play a decisive role only when the objective conditions for them have been prepared. The influence of S.F. on social development rises with the transition from one socio-economic formation (q.v.) to another, more progressive formation. The importance of S.F. particularly increases in socialist society where the possibility is created for planned development in all spheres of social life and the people are drawn into the building of socialism and communism.

Objective Idea, the concept in idealism which not only possesses objective reality but also determines sensory being. Dialectical materialism denies the primacy of the ideal principle. The idea is a reflection of matter, i.e., it has an objective content. Therefore, it is possible to speak of the real existence of ideas, which are recorded in different forms of social consciousness and are objective as regards their content and also in relation to the mind of the individual. But in this case, too, the O.I. is a subjective reflection of material reality, although it actively influences this material reality itself for the purpose of transforming and developing it.

Objective Reality, the material world in its entirety, in all its forms and manifestations. In terms of the fundamental question of philosophy (q.v.) O.R. is that which exists independently of human consciousness and is primary to it. The concept O.R. is relative. It is everything that exists outside the individual's mind and is reflected by it. But the individual himself with his mind will be O.R. in relation to other people, and so on. If abstraction is made of the individual view of the world, it may be said that O.R. coincides with reality in general. The latter includes diverse material objects, their properties, space, time, motion, laws, diverse social phenomena— relations of production, the state, art, etc. From this, however, we must not conclude that the concept of O.R. is broader than the concept of matter (q.v.). Such an idea can arise if matter is divorced from its multifarious properties and forms of manifestation, without which it does not exist. Motion, space, time, are all properties and interactions of various kinds of matter differing in degree of complexity, which in their sum total form the world as a whole or the entire O.R. (see Being).

Objectivism, an approach to reality according to which philosophical knowledge is incapable of making critical appraisals, drawing partisan conclusions or forming judgments on values (q.v.); philosophers must, therefore, abstain from this. O. limits the bounds of thinking and yields the solution of the main problems of social outlook to subjective ideology. That is why O. is always supplemented by subjectivism. According to O., science is neutral to values (see Scientism). Marxism has proved that world outlook cannot be neutral and, having overcome O. and subjectivism, has risen to scientific objectivity and partisanship (q.v.).

Object-relatedness, a concept denoting that a phenomenon, action, state, etc. is connected with objects or is (becomes) itself an object through its involvement into the subject's activity (q.v.). Human activity is of an object-related nature, since in this process men deal with objects and create objects. Knowledge also has an object-related nature, because its objective content is the reflection of the material world cognisable by man in the course of his activity. Recognition of the O. of man's activity, of the content of

his consciousness, etc., distinguishes materialist from idealist philosophy.

Observation, a purposive perception of the outside world which provides the primary data for scientific research. O. may be simple or complex, direct or indirect, combined with an experiment (q.v.). In the course of O., in contrast to experiment, the subject does not exercise a prevailing influence on the object. In certain cases (O. in psychology, sociology, etc.), the absence of such an effect is not a drawback, but an advantage. O. may imply the use of various devices and instruments to compensate for the natural limitation of human sense-organs.

Occam, William of (c. 1285-1349), medieval English theologian, scholastic philosopher, prominent representative of nominalism (q.v.). Tutor at Oxford University, he was accused of heresy and escaped from prison to Bavaria. He was an ideologist of the secular feudal lords who fought against the claims of the Catholic Church and papacy to world domination. Alongside Duns Scotus (q.v.), a leader of the scholastic opposition to Thomism (q.v.), O. asserted that the existence of God and other religious dogmas could not be proved by reason and were founded solely on faith. Hence philosophy must get rid of theology.

Occasion, external, often casual event, circumstance, providing an impulse for other events. O. differs from cause in that it may represent facts of various kinds, not connected of necessity with other events, effects (see Causality). O. may give rise to one or another phenomenon only because the latter has been prepared by a natural and necessary course of development.

Occasionalism, a religious idealist doctrine of the 17th century (J. Clauberg, A. Geulincx) which tried to explain the inexplicable interaction of soul and body inferred by the dualism of Descartes (q.v.), by referring it to the direct intervention of God. Malebranche (q.v.) carried O. to a point where he saw a divine act in every causality.

Occultism, a term denoting doctrines which admit the existence of supernatural phenomena and forces beyond scientific investigation and elaborate "practical" methods of interacting with them (magic, q.v., spiritism). In ancient times (for example, among Chaldeans and Hindus) and in the Middle Ages O., like other false conceptions of nature and man, was the consequence of the low degree of socio-economic and scientific development (we find O. in the works of R. Bacon, Lully, Paracelsus, qq.v., and others). Later O. became a means of struggle with the materialist world outlook. In theosophy (q.v.) occult ideas were zealously propagated by Rudolf Steiner ("The Way of Initiation", 1909; "Die Geheimwissenschaft im Umriss", 1910, etc.), who asserted that O. was an exact science based on experience. In fact, although some of the postulates of O. are expressed in terms of natural science, there is nothing scientific about them. At present in many capitalist countries there exist occult societies and occult literature is widespread.

Ogaryov, Nikolai Platonovich (1813-1877), Russian revolutionary democrat, philosopher, publicist, and poet. With Herzen (q.v.) he opposed serfdom, the reactionary ideology of the Orthodox Church, autocracy and official nationalism, and the liberalism of the landowners and bourgeoisie. The ideological co-operation of O. with Herzen, which began during their youth, continued to the end of their life. As students of Moscow University, Herzen and O. organised a clandestine circle whose members studied political literature, including socialist writings. In 1834, O., Herzen and other members of the circle were arrested and exiled, after nine months in prison. Herzen to Vyatka, and Ogaryov to Penza. In 1850, O. was arrested a second time, in 1856, he emigrated and, together with Herzen, organised the publication of Russian revolutionary periodicals — *Polyarnaya Zvezda* (Polar Star), *Kolokol* (The Bell), *Obshcheye Veche* (General Assembly), *Russkaya Potayonnaya Literatura* (Russian Secret Literature). O. and Herzen were the founders of Russian peasant utopian socialism, of Narodism (q.v.). The theory of communal socialism of O. and Herzen expressed the revolution-

ary demands of the peasant masses who strove for the complete abolition of big landownership and the overthrow of the rule of the landowners. O. was one of the founders of the underground revolutionary organisation Zemlya i Volya (Land and Freedom) in the 1860s. Prior to 1840, O. adhered to idealist positions. Knowledge of the achievements of 19th-century natural science and the philosophy of French materialism and Feuerbach (q.v.), enabled him to adopt philosophical materialism and atheism. Although O. paid tribute to anthropologism (q.v.), the speculative character of Feuerbach's philosophy did not satisfy him. Together with Herzen he critically assimilated the philosophy of Hegel (q.v.), especially his dialectics, drawing from it revolutionary conclusions and utilising it to justify a revolution in Russia. O. voiced many profound ideas on the origin and development of consciousness, the relationship between absolute and relative truth and problems of contradiction in the development of nature and society. He elaborated the principles of materialist aesthetics, emphasising the social role of art and its kinship with the people (q.v.), advocating lofty idea-content and resolutely rejecting the idealist theory of "pure art". O. was one of the predecessors of Russian Social Democracy. His main works are *Russian Questions*, 1856-58; *More about the Emancipation of the Peasantry*, 1858; *Clarification of Some Questions* (1862-64).

Old Hegelians, the conservative wing of the school of Hegel (q.v.) in Germany in the 1830s and 1840s; they endeavoured to interpret his teaching in an orthodox Christian spirit. At first, the O.H. (K. Göschel, F. Hinrichs, G. Gabler) took advantage of the conflicting and inconsistent delineation between philosophy and religion in the Hegelian system to infer the synthesis of reason and faith. Later on the O.H. (Ch. Weisse and I. Fichte, Jr.) developed their doctrine in opposition to radical Young Hegelians (q.v.). They also took a conservative political stand.

Olminsky (Alexandrov), Mikhail Stepanovich (1863-1933), a Russian revolutionary, Marxist historian and writer.

Arrested for revolutionary propaganda in workers' study-circles and exiled in 1898. In exile he disavowed Narodism (q.v.) and adopted Marxism. Articles by O. propagated Marxist ideas. As a historian, O. devoted his attention to the problem of the state, criticising bourgeois theories of the supraclass nature of the state (*The State, Bureaucracy and Absolutism in the History of Russia*, 1910). As a Marxist writer on aesthetics and a literary critic, O. defended realistic, humanistic and civic traditions in art, opposed decadence (*Shchedrinian Vocabulary* composed in 1897 in prison; *A Utopian Socialist as Appraised by Contemporaries*, 1906; *Overcoming Aesthetics*, 1911; articles on Fyodor Sologub, Leonid Andreyev, Mikhail Artsybashev).

On the Significance of Militant Materialism, an article by V. I. Lenin showing the most important trends in the development of Marxist philosophy in the new period of history and characterising the role of philosophy, like that of all Marxist theory, in the period of socialist and communist construction. Published in the journal *Pod znamenem marksizma* (1922, Issue No. 3), it is the continuation and further elaboration of Lenin's *Materialism and Empirio-Criticism* and *Philosophical Notebooks* (qq.v.). In fact, it is his philosophical testament. The main idea of the article is that of the Marxist partisanship in philosophy (q.v.) expressed in the concept of militant materialism. Explaining the meaning of this concept, Lenin defines the main tasks confronting philosophers: first and foremost, propagation of the dialectical and materialist world outlook among the masses, especially tireless atheistic propaganda using concrete material; further development of philosophy, first of all materialist dialectics, in the light of the problems posed by contemporary social development and scientific progress; active struggle against various trends in bourgeois philosophy. To fulfil these tasks it is necessary to unite the efforts of all Marxist philosophers and consistent materialists who do not belong to the Communist Party. Alliance of Communists and non-Communists in different spheres is indispensable. Also essential is alliance be-

tween philosophers and natural scientists. Philosophers cannot successfully develop the dialectical and materialist theory without using the achievements of natural science. In its turn, natural science cannot withstand bourgeois ideas without sound philosophical background. Lenin also examines the question of the philosophical heritage, opposes the nihilistic attitude towards it, and emphasises the necessity for using the best achievements of past philosophical thought in the contemporary struggle of ideas. The article has become an important theoretical guide for Marxist philosophers.

Ontology 1. In pre-Marxist philosophy O., or the "First Philosophy", was the doctrine of being in general. In this sense O. is equivalent to metaphysics (q.v.), a system of speculative universal definitions of being. In the late Middle Ages, Catholic philosophers utilised the Aristotelian idea of metaphysics to construct a doctrine of being which would serve as philosophical proof of the truths of religion. This tendency was most fully elaborated in the philosophico-theological system of Thomas Aquinas (q.v.). Since the 16th century O. has been understood as a special part of metaphysics, the doctrine of the supersensuous, non-material structure of everything existing. The term O. was coined by the German philosopher Rudolf Goclenius (1613). The idea of O. received its final shape in the philosophy of Wolff (q.v.) which lost all connection with the content of the specific sciences and constructed O. largely through abstract analysis of its concepts (being, possibility and reality, quantity and quality, cause and effect, etc.). An opposite tendency was displayed in the materialist doctrines of Hobbes, Spinoza, and Locke (qq.v.) and the French 18th-century materialists, inasmuch as the positive content of these doctrines, which were based on the experimental sciences, objectively undermined the concept of O. as a philosophical subject of the highest rank, as "First Philosophy" isolated from epistemology and logic. Criticism of O. by the German classical idealists (Kant, Hegel, qq.v., and others) was dual: on the one hand, O. was declared to be meaningless and tautological and, on the other, this criticism ended in the demand for a new, more perfect O. (metaphysics) or its replacement by transcendental idealism (see Kant, Schelling) or by logic (see Hegel). Hegel's system anticipated in an idealist form the idea of the unity of O. (dialectics), logic, and the theory of knowledge and indicated a way out of the framework of speculative philosophical constructions to real positive knowledge of the world. 2. Attempts to construct a "new ontology" on an objective idealist basis have been made in the 20th century as a reaction to the spread of subjective idealist trends (see Neo-Kantianism; Positivism). In the new ontological doctrines ("transcendental ontology" of Husserl, q.v.; "critical ontology" of N. Hartmann, q.v., and "fundamental ontology" of Heidegger, q.v.), O. is regarded as a system of universal concepts of being conceived with the help of supersensuous and superrational intuition. The idea of the "new ontology" has been taken up by a number of Catholic philosophers, who are trying to "synthesise" the "traditional" O. coming from Aristotle (q.v.) with Kantian transcendental philosophy and to put their own O. against the philosophy of dialectical materialism. 3. In Marxist philosophy the term "ontology" is not used systematically; in some cases it is used as a synonym of a doctrine on the most general laws of being.

Operational Definitions, definitions (q.v.) which indicate experimentally reproduced operations, the objective results of which are accessible to direct empirical observation or measurement (q.v.). Most often O.D. are used as a means for partial empirical interpretation of scientific concepts. Here is a simple example. "If a litmus-paper is placed in a liquid, that liquid is an alkali only if the paper turns blue." One and the same scientific concept can be given several O.D., indicating different empirical situations of applying the given concept (see Hypothetico-Deductive Theory). An exaggeration of the role of O.D. and their elevation into an absolute are characteristic of operationalism (q.v.).

Operationalism, a trend in contemporary bourgeois philosophy which is a synthesis of logical positivism (q.v.) and

pragmatism (q.v.). It was founded by Bridgman (q.v.). The main thing in O. is the idea of operational analysis, according to which the meaning of any concept can be determined only through a description of the operations employed in forming, using and testing this concept. Concepts not connected with any operations are considered meaningless. O. includes among them many concepts of materialism. Sentences are formed by combining operationally defined concepts, and sentences are combined to form theories. O. inevitably arrives at subjective idealist conclusions: if in concepts we cognise only the operations of measurement, then recognition of the objects themselves independent of the measurement procedures is meaningless.

Opinion, in ancient philosophy, imperfect, subjective knowledge, as distinct from authentic knowledge—truth. Already the Eleatics (q.v.) clearly differentiated between truth based on rational knowledge and O. based on sensory perception and implying only the appearance of things. For Aristotle (q.v.), O. was the empirical method of cognition whose subject-matter can change to become false, since it is classed among the accidental and individual. Aristotle distinguished O. from scientific knowledge, which has the essential and the universal for its subject.

Optimism and Pessimism, two opposite attitudes to the course of events. O. is belief in a better future, in the ultimate triumph of good over evil, of justice over injustice. P. is a depressive view that events go inevitably from bad to worse, and disbelief in the triumph of good and justice. In the history of philosophy the optimistic world outlook was advocated in one way or other by many thinkers: Aristotle and Epicurus (qq.v.) in antiquity, and Leibniz (q.v.) in the post-medieval period. The latter held that the existing world was the best of all possible worlds. The absolute O. of Leibniz eventually led to the justification of evil, misfortune and calamities. P. was posited by the German irrationalist philosophers Schopenhauer (q.v.) and E. Hartmann (q.v.). As a rule, classes that outlived their time, like the modern bourgeoisie, tend to adopt P. Attempts to overcome the extremes of O. and P. were made by the exponents of meliorism, a view that although evil was inevitable the world could be improved by human effort. This term was coined in the 19th century by the English novelist George Eliot and the French philosopher J. Sully. Meliorists think that the world can be improved only through the perfection of the individual, through enlightenment. Marxist theory asserts historical optimism, based on scientific foreknowledge of the future communist society, on the knowledge of the objective laws of social development.

Organic and Mechanical Systems, two ways of understanding and theoretically reproducing complex objects. Only an object regarded as complete is seen as a mechanical system. Investigation of such system was characteristic of the metaphysical mode of thinking (see Metaphysics) and was historically justifiable in the early stages of the natural and social sciences (reducing complex forms of movement to mechanical motion in space, and the conception of man as a machine—La Mettrie, etc.). In the early 19th century, however, belief in the need for a historical approach to natural and social objects as self-developing systems (O.S.) began emerging in philosophy (Hegel), natural (see Darwin) and social sciences. Marx worked out and examined the categories for studying these systems (for example, the capitalist mode of production). Theoretical reproduction of the history and genesis of O.S. is only possible by ascending from the abstract to the concrete (see Abstract and Concrete, the; Historical and Logical, the).

"Organic Growth", Theory of, a model for solving global problems (q.v.), a conception of the development of the "world system". It was presented in the second report of M. Messarovic and E. Pestel to the Club of Rome (q.v.) entitled "Mankind at the Turning Point" (1974). It opposed the concept of "zero growth" presented in the first report to the Club. The authors apply this term to the growth of the "world system" by analogy with the growth (development, to be more exact) of an organism, implying specialisation of its various parts and their

functional interdependence. The necessity of such an approach is determined, according to the authors, by the interdependence of crisis situations: the crisis of overpopulation, the ecological crisis, and the food, energy, raw materials, and other crises, which are said to become all-embracing. T.O.G. postulates that the world consists of various parts and regions, including national states, irrespective of their socio-economic and political systems. This approach, which overlooks class divisions and is deliberately abstract, ignores the concrete socio-economic, political and ideological factors that are essential in any scientific solution of these problems, makes it unrealistic and far removed from the effective ways that could help mankind to achieve its desired goals.

The Origin of the Family, Private Property and the State, the work written by F. Engels in 1884. Basing himself on the data of L. Morgan's (q.v.) book, *Ancient Society,* as well as on other data of science, Engels investigates in this work the essential features of the primitive-communal system (q.v.). He shows the changes in the forms of marriage and the family in connection with the economic progress of society, analyses the process of the decay of the gentile system (quoting as examples the Greeks, Romans, and Teutons) and its economic causes. The growth of the productivity of labour and the division of labour (q.v.) led to exchange, private property, the disintegration of the tribal system, and the formation of classes (q.v.). The appearance of class contradictions called into life the state (q.v.) as an instrument for defending the interests of the ruling class. Engels' book demonstrated that: (1) private property, classes, and the state did not always exist, but appeared at a certain stage of economic development; (2) the state, in the hands of the exploiter classes, is always an instrument of coercion and oppression of the broad mass of the people; (3) the classes will disappear as inevitably as they appeared in the past. With the disappearance of classes the state is bound to wither away. Engels' book is to this day an important manual for the study of historical materialism.

Orphists, followers of a religious movement in Ancient Greece in the 8th century B.C. The foundation of Orphism is ascribed to the semi-legendary poet Orpheus. The teaching of O., representing the world outlook of the ruined peasants and slaves, was opposed to mythology (q.v.), the world outlook of the hereditary aristocracy. In mythology, life in the other world was considered a continuation of life on earth. O., however, associated life in the other world with bliss, and life on earth with suffering. The body, they said, was sinful and mortal, while the soul was pure and eternal. Orphism rejected the idea of the primary unity of soul and body, characteristic of mythology; it considered cognition to be the means of contemplating God. O. expressed a protest against man's being made a slave, a speaking tool. A slave associated his liberation with the soul leaving the body, which belonged to the lord. Orphism exerted a great influence on the emerging philosophies, especially on ancient Greek idealism, but by the 5th century B.C. it lost its positive content and turned into mystic cults.

Ortega y Gasset, José (1883-1955), Spanish philosopher, subjective idealist; held an intermediate position between Nietzschean philosophy of life (q.v.) and contemporary existentialism (q.v.). He focussed attention on social problems. In his works, *La deshumanización del arte*, 1925, and *La rebelión de las masas*, 1929-30, O. was the first to expound the main principles of the theories of "mass society" (q.v.). O. gave the name of "mass society" to the spiritual atmosphere which formed in the West as a result of the degeneration of bourgeois democracy, bureaucratisation of social institutions, and the spread of money-exchange relations to all forms of contacts between individuals. A system of social ties arises in which each man feels himself to be an insignificant actor performing a role imposed on him from the outside, a particle of an impersonal element called the mob. O. criticises this spiritual situation "from the right". He considers it to be the inevitable result of the development of democratic activity of the masses and sees a way out in the creation of a new

aristocratic elite of men capable of making a voluntary "choice", guided solely by the direct "life impulse", a category close to the Nietzschean "will to power".

Orthodoxy, a variety of Christianity (q.v.) which spread mainly in the countries of Eastern Europe, the Balkans and the Middle East. O. took final shape as an independent trend in the 11th century as a result of the difference between the ways of development of feudalism in the West and in the East of Europe. The differences in dogmas are the following: recognition of the procession of the Holy Spirit from the Father alone, infallibility of the Church as a whole (but not of the head of the Church), immutability of dogmas, denial of purgatory, etc. Cult and canonical differences include the worship of icons, obligatory marriage for the secular clergy, a special (Byzantine) form of church hymn, etc. Unlike Catholicism (q.v.), O. has no single centre, but consists of fifteen independent (autocephalous) Orthodox churches. Conservatism is highly characteristic of O. Russian O. served the autocracy faithfully, was one of its pillars and completely dependent upon it. From the time of Peter the Great to 1917 the Russian Orthodox Church was part of the state machinery. It was hostile to the revolutionary movement. After the October Revolution (particularly since the 1930s and 1940s) this counter-revolutionary policy of the Russian O. changed, under the pressure of the believers, into loyalty to Soviet government. The ideologists of O. try to adapt it to present-day conditions, modernising its dogmas and cults. The religious philosophy of O. is represented by Khomyakov, Bulgakov, Florensky (qq.v.).

Osipovsky, Timofei Fyodorovich (1765-1832), Russian materialist thinker, professor of mathematics. He criticised Kant's assertion about the a priori origin of the truths of geometry. On the whole, his views did not go beyond metaphysical mechanistic materialism. The scientist was influenced by the idea of Descartes (q.v.), which made him exaggerate the methodological role of mathematics and overestimate the importance of the analytical method in cognition. O. actively fought against mysticism (q.v.) and highly valued the role of education and science. However, in his views on religion he remained an adherent of deism (q.v.). His main philosophical works: *On Space and Time*, 1807; *A Discourse on Dynamic System of Kant*, 1813.

Owen, Robert (1771-1858), Welsh utopian socialist. From 1791 to 1829 participated in capitalist enterprise and managed large factories. He therefore knew the negative aspects of the capitalist system better than other utopian socialists. O. engaged in philanthropic activity and was the father of factory legislation. Subsequently, his criticism was spearheaded against private property, religion which sanctifies it, and bourgeois marriage. He was a rationalist (see Rationalism) and atheist with some deviations towards deism (q.v.). O. held that the social system exerts decisive influence on man; interpreted history in an idealist way as gradual progress of human self-knowledge; saw the root of social evil in people's ignorance. O. attached exceptional importance to education as one of the measures preparing a "new moral [i.e., socialist] world". He introduced many valuable ideas in the theory and practice of pedagogy. By 1820, his main ideas had been shaped into a system which O. began to call socialist. Its principles were common ownership and labour, a combination of mental and physical labour, all-round development of the individual, equality of rights. He conceived the future classless society as a free federation of self-governing communities, each uniting from 300 to 2,000 people. O. laid the main emphasis on distribution. Failing to understand the need for a social revolution, he relied on bourgeois governments to transform society. He organised labour communes (New Harmony in the United States from 1825 to 1829 and Harmony Hall in Britain from 1839 to 1845) and also exchange markets, all of which failed. O. was the only great utopian who associated his activity with the destinies of the working class although he did not understand its historical role. Early in the 1830s he actively participated in the British trade union and co-operative movements; his ideas at that time anticipated syndicalism to a certain extent.

Ownership, the belonging of objects to a subject, which may be individuals, groups of people, the state, and society. Depending on the subject, property may be personal, private, co-operative, and social (state). The object of O. may be anything that is included in the vital activities of the subject, mainly in his productive activities (q.v.). A historically determined form of O. emerges within a specific mode of production (q.v.) as a corresponding system of relations between people geared to conditions of production and reproduction. These relations determine all relations of O. in society and are fixed in the superstructure (above all as law). As a social and historical institution O. passes through several stages of evolution and has two principal forms—social and private. O. comes into existence in the primitive society. The main production organism and, therefore, the subject of O., given a low level of development of the productive forces, is the community (q.v.), which predetermines the dominance of social (communal) property. The development of productive forces and the emergence of exchange give rise to private property, alongside which classes are formed. History enters the period of class antagonistic societies. After it has passed through all the stages of ascending development in these societies, the last of which is capitalism, private property in means of production and the exploitation of man by man based on it become outdated, creating prerequisites for the assertion of social property. Under socialism social property exists in two principal forms as state property and as the property of collective farms and co-operatives, and this is explained by the persisting differences in the levels of development of the productive forces in industry and in agriculture. In the USSR, socialist property also includes the property of social organisations which they need to perform the tasks formulated in their Rules. Ongoing development of socialist production and further socialisation of labour bring all forms of socialist property closer together up to their merging into uniform communist property (see Personal Property).

p

Panlogism, an objective idealist teaching on the identity of being and thinking according to which all development in nature and society is the realisation of the logical activity of the universal mind. Considering the laws of logic to be the only driving forces of all development, P. distorts the true relationship between being and consciousness. At the same time one can discern in this view the true idea that everything existing can be rationally, logically cognised. P. was most fully developed by Hegel (q.v.).

Panpsychism, an idealist view that all nature possesses life and psychics (q.v.); it is a philosophical reproduction of animism (q.v.). Many modern idealist philosophers (personalists, Whitehead, q.v., the critical realist Ch. Strong, the founder of analytical psychology K.G. Jung, etc.) are open proponents of P. The scientific understanding of psychic activity as a special property inherent only in highly organised matter rejects any kind of P. (see Hylozoism).

Pantheism, a philosophical teaching according to which God (q.v.) is an impersonal principle which is not outside of nature but identical with it. P. dissolves God in nature, rejecting the supernatural element. The term was introduced by Toland (q.v.) (in 1705). Whereas earlier P. often enough included essentially materialist views on nature (e.g., Bruno and especially Spinoza, qq.v.), it has now been transformed into a religious and idealist theory of the existence of the world in God and is an attempt to reconcile science with religion.

Paracelsus, Philippus Aureolus (real name: Theophrastus Bombastus von Hohenheim) (1493-1541), a Swiss born physician and natural scientist of the Renaissance (q.v.). According to P., the world created by God from the primary substance is the self-developing entity. Man (microcosm) as part of nature (macrocosm) is capable of cognising it in principle. P. was the first to proclaim knowledge obtained by experiment the basis of any scientific knowledge. P. believed in the omnipotence of human intellect and called upon physicians and scientists to study nature and not the Holy Books. He sharply criticised medieval "indisputable" authorities, scholasticism (q.v.), and religion. At the same time he was under the spell of the then dominant unscientific conceptions and explained the surrounding world from positions of anthropocentrism and panpsychism (q.v.). maintaining that everything in the world was permeated by a mysterious spirit. Though trying to make medicine and chemistry into real sciences he still believed in alchemistry and magic (q.v.).

Paradigm, a totality of theoretical and methodological premises defining a concrete scientific study, embodied in scientific practice at a given stage. P. is a basis for selecting problems and a pattern for solving research problems. The term "P." was introduced by the American scientist Th. Kuhn (b. 1922). According to Kuhn (*The Structure of Scientific Revolutions*, 1962), P. makes it possible to cope with the difficulties arising in research work, as well as record changes in the structure of knowledge taking place under the impact of the scientific revolution and linked with the assimilation of new empirical data. However, the concept of P. does not adequately reflect the worldview and social parameters of scientific development. The Marxist works on the science of sciences operate with notions of modes of scientific thought.

Paradoxes (in logic and the set theory), formal logical contradictions which arise in the set theory (q.v.) and in formal logic, while preserving the correct line of reasoning. P. arise when two mutually exclusive (contradictory) propositions are equally demonstrable. They can appear both in a scientific theory and in ordinary arguments (e.g., Russell's, q.v., rewording of his paradox about a set in all normal sets: "...Barber in a certain village shaves all and only those persons in the village who do not shave themselves. Does he shave himself?"). Since a formal logical contradiction destroys inference as a means of finding and demonstrating truth (in a theory in which P. appears, any proposition both true and false is equally demonstrable), the task arises of revealing the sources of P. and finding ways of eliminating them. A dialectical materialist analysis shows that P. are an expression of profoundly dialectical and epistemological difficulties associated with concepts of an object in formal logic, of a set (class) in logic and in the set theory, with the employment of the principle of abstraction, which makes it possible to introduce new (abstract) objects, and with methods of defining abstract objects in science, etc. That is why there can be no universal method of removing all P. The problem of philosophical understanding concrete solutions of P. is an important methodological problem of formal logic and the logical principles of mathematics (see Antinomy; Antinomies, Semantics).

Paralogism, unpremeditated violation of the laws and rules of logic, which deprives an argument of the force of proof and usually leads to false conclusions. A distinction must be made between P. and a deliberate violation of the rules of logic (see Sophistry).

Parapsychology, a field of study concerned with the investigation of the forms of sensuality which cannot be explained by the activity of the known sense-organs, as well as forms of psychokinesis (movement of living beings without use of physical means). The scientific study of these forms of sensuality, otherwise called extrasensory perception, is compounded by difficulties involved in localising, reproducing and selecting these phenomena. It is difficult to demonstrate such phenomena under an adequate experimental monitoring, and this does not exclude the possibility of many of them being a product of imagination, coincidence of circumstances or even a deliberate deception. However, the para-

psychological phenomena are not supernatural and their physiological and psychokinetic parameters can be explained from the materialist standpoint. While studying the phenomena of P., attempts are made, contrary to the spiritualist speculation, to explain them by subconscious actions and the effect of biofield (the electromagnetic energy of a living being). The biophysical and radioelectronic methods are used to study the electromagnetic field as a means of biological communication and vehicle of information. The materialist study of parapsychological phenomena almost unyielding to the experimental investigation helps to strip them of their mystical shrouds and expose the idealist and religious speculations attending them.

Parmenides, Greek philosopher (late 6th-early 5th centuries B.C.) from Elea (Southern Italy), head of the Eleatic school (see Eleatics). P. conceived the world as an immobile and completely filled sphere. He vigorously opposed the "doctrine of truth" (true being is single, eternal, immobile, indivisible, and free from void) to the "doctrine of opinion" (there exists a plurality of things—arising and transitory, moving, divisible into parts, and separated from each other by a void). The "doctrine of truth" is authentic, the "doctrine of opinion" is only seemingly true. P. deliberately directed the "doctrine of truth" against the dialectics of Heraclitus (q.v.) and his followers. In the "doctrine of opinion" P. expounded his astronomical, physical, and physiological hypotheses. His naive materialist "physics" proceeded from the assumption that there are two basic elements: an active one—fiery and bright, and an inert one—dark. Mistrust of the evidence of the senses and high appraisal of speculative knowledge introduced an element of rationalism (q.v.) into his teaching, while the denial of motion made P. the father of metaphysics (q.v.).

Parsons, Talcott (1902-1979), American sociologist, founder of the functional school. His name is associated with the "general theory" in modern bourgeois sociology. Now it is represented by the "theory of social action", which he expounded in his *Structure of Social Action* (1937), *Essays in Sociological Theory* (1949), *The Social System* (1951), etc. P. used the structural-functional analysis (q.v.) to construct the model of a social system the basic element of which is interaction of abstract individuals. The assimilation of the generally accepted standards of behaviour and their conversion into internal motives of their actions is the mechanism which co-ordinates their actions and through which they perform the functions they were entrusted with by society. Considering the state of equilibrium to be the most important characteristic of the social system's state, P. paid much attention to the processes of regulation and the means of social control to maintain this state (political and legal activity, response of social groups to actions of individuals, etc.), which, in his view, are to safeguard society from undesired conflicts and abrupt changes. In his work *Societies: Evolutionary and Comparative Perspectives* (1967) he makes use of some ideas of evolutionism by including analysis of their changes in the description of social systems. He regarded social processes from a conservative point of view, maintaining that social changes mean primarily internal differentiation of a system which promotes its adaptability, rather than its transformation into a fundamentally new system.

Part and Whole, philosophical categories reflecting the relation between a combination of objects (or elements of an object) and the connection between them that gives the combination new properties and regularities untraceable in the objects themselves when taken as isolated entities. That connection forms a W., in relation to which each object is a part. The categories of P. and W. also indicate the general process of cognition, which, as a rule, starts with an integral perception of the W., goes through a stage of analysis, when the W. is broken down into parts, and is completed by mental recreation of the object as a concrete W. The problem of P. and W. was raised in antiquity (by Plato, q.v., and especially by Aristotle, q.v.) and since then has been dealt with by all major philosophical schools. Materialist

trends, relying on science, mostly identified themselves with a mechanistic interpretation of W., borrowed from mechanics (later from classical physics). But idealist conceptions speculated on the fact that the W. cannot be reduced to the sum of its Pp. Mental products alone were allowed a character of true wholeness, while material entities were treated as inanimate, mechanical aggregates. The opposition of philosophic to scientific knowledge was in particular based on that premise. Classical German philosophy (Schelling, Hegel, qq.v.) distinguished inorganic (mechanical) and organic (self-developing) W. However, the latter was associated only with the development of spirit, not of matter. In the 19th-20th centuries, many idealist schools (neovitalism, holism, intuitionalism, qq.v., etc.) widely indulged in speculations over the problem of relations between P. and W. While critically reappraising the traditions of classical German philosophy, Marx formulated the principles for studying organic W.—a method of ascending from the abstract to the concrete, a dialectical approach to analysis and synthesis (q.v.), etc. Marx was also the founder of the methodology for the scientific study of society as a W. Furthermore, dialectical materialism summarises the findings of theoretical conceptions and disciplines that stick to wholeness as the basic approach to things. The new approach opens the way to a rational understanding of the dialectic of P. and W. The fact that a complex W. cannot be reduced to a mere sum of its parts was proved not only theoretically, but also experimentally. W. acquires new properties and qualities absent in its Pp. (elements) and appearing due to the interaction of the Pp. in a certain system of interconnections. This property of any W. entity, which can be referred to as the property of integrality, is the most important common feature of all such entities that clear the way to understanding all other specific features of W. Among them are: origination of new aspects in the process of development, origination of new types of wholeness, formation of new structural levels and their hierarchical interdependence, division of whole systems into organic and inorganic, the division being based on the fact that the properties of parts of an inorganic system (atom, molecule, etc.), though reflecting the nature of the W., are determined chiefly by the inner nature of the parts, while in an organic system (see Organic and Mechanical Systems), such as biological and social objects, the properties of parts are determined entirely by the properties of the W. The components of an organic W., as products of its development, cannot be singled out from the W. as outwardly independent parts, without their new nature being nullified. Modern cognition is able to solve the traditional cognitive paradox: how can a W. be cognised if a prior knowledge of parts is presupposed? The solution of this paradox rests on a dialectical understanding of the unity of analysis and synthesis. Cognising the W. and Pp. occurs simultaneously: setting off the parts, we study them as elements of the given W., which, when synthesised, appears as dialectically structural, consisting of parts.

The Part Played by Labour in the Transition From Ape to Man, a work by Engels (1876) studying the social laws of the origin of man and society. Generalising the material accumulated by biology, paleontology, and anthropology, Engels shows that the prerequisites for labour (q.v.) (erect gait, freeing of the upper limbs, higher development of the psychics of the anthropoid apes, the ancestors of man) were created in the process of biological evolution. Labour acquires the features of specific human activity with the beginning of instrument-making, and this led to the appearance of speech and thought, which developed as social forms of life asserted themselves. Man masters the forces of nature. He does not only use it as a consumer, as is the case with animals, but also makes it serve his pre-established purposes. Labour, speech, thought, and corporal organisation influence each other mutually. *The Part Played by Labour...* was first published in 1896 in German. Later it was included in *Dialectics of Nature* (q.v.).

Partisanship in Art, the fullest expression of the ideological trend of art, defence in artistic works of the interests of a definite social class. Lenin, in his article "Party Organisation and Party Literature" (1905) and other works, substantiated the principle of P.A. Anti-Marxist theoreticians of aesthetics counterpose freedom of creative endeavour to P.A. and declare them to be incompatible. But the tenet that art is non-partisan is a form of camouflaging bourgeois partisanship. In bourgeois society, so-called freedom of creation is intended to hide the fact that the creative endeavour of most artists is subject to the interests of capital. Only artists who realise what adverse effect this dependence of art on the exploiting classes has and who side with the people can really be free. It is they who link their creative endeavour with progressive movements, above all with the struggle and ideology of the proletariat. The principle of communist partisanship requires that the artist freely and consciously serve mankind's aims.

Partisanship in Philosophy, an objective social pattern (having class nature in a class society) of any world outlook (q.v.). Philosophy is never neutral, P.P. stems from the dialectic of social progress and the objective contradictions of social development. Subjectivist P.P. makes philosophy a means for attaining goals and establishing norms and principles that were brought into it from outside as ready-made propositions, rather than formulated on the basis of knowledge of the objective course of history. Subjectivism thus reduces philosophy to the status of a servant of dogmas and social forces and institutions behind them. Objective P.P., on the contrary, stems from the consistent cognition of truth; it requires that one follow only those conclusions and appraisals that were obtained by science itself and that everything without exception be judged by reason in the light of spiritual values (q.v.). That is why it is opposed to both subjectivism and objectivism (q.v.). P.P. can be equated with scientific objectivity only by a systematic study of reality, specifically its dialectical contradictoriness, and constant search for truth. Marxist, communist partisanship is consistently objective, for it is the most progressive, truly scientific, and is opposed to all kinds of subjectivism, voluntarism, irrationalism and dogmatism (qq.v.). Spearheaded against ideological pluralism (q.v.) inherent in capitalist society, communist P.P. upholds truth and variety in scientific quests and solutions. This does not contradict the establishment of socialist ideology as the only scientific one, because this variety is a *sine qua non* for the development of science, art and culture and expresses the wealth of results they bring. Therefore, communist P.P. in no way runs counter to the freedom of scientific debate. Moreover, it presupposes this debate, protecting the creative search for truth from sluggishness and dogmatism. It maintains that discussion or dialogue is a permanent state of creative thinking and stimulates vigorous criticism of bourgeois ideology. Communist P.P. is the most profound scientific and also the most revolutionary-critical and creative approach to reality.

Pascal, Blaise (1623-1662), French philosopher, mathematician and physicist, one of the founders of the theory of probability (q.v.). His philosophical views were contradictory. He vacillated between rationalism and scepticism (qq.v.) and was inclined to recognise the superiority of faith over reason. His logical views (teaching on induction and deduction, on types of authentic knowledge, etc.) continued Descartes' (q.v.) teaching on method and exerted influence on the logic of Port Royal. P.'s criticism of, and struggle against, the spiritual tyranny of the Jesuits, who were the mainstay of Catholic reaction, was supported by the advanced sections of French society. At the same time some of his ideas of man's place in the world are regarded as an anticipation of religious existentialism (q.v.). His main work: *Pensées* (published posthumously in 1669).

Patriarchy, a form of clan organisation in the primitive-communal system (q.v.), marked by the supremacy of the man in social production (hunting, fishing, stock breeding and other occupations vital for the survival of the collective) and in social life of the clan community, q.v. (running its affairs, regulating relations between its members, administering religious rites, etc.). Under P. women were taken into families of clan community (patrilocality) and descent was traced through paternal line (patrilineage). Modern science identifies early P. based on a pair marriage and late P. which arose at the end of the primitive-communal era in the form of large monogamous patriarchal families. Like matriarchy (q.v.), P. did not exist among all the peoples, and some scientists maintain that it was not a stage in the development of the primitive-communal system.

Patriotism, a moral and political principle and social feeling whose content is love of one's homeland, devotion to it, pride for its past and present, and readiness to defend its interests. Historically, the elements of P., such as attachment to one's native land, language and traditions, have their roots in hoary past. In antagonistic societies, P. acquires a class character, for every class expresses its own attitude to homeland through its particular interests. Under capitalism, as nations (q.v.) and nation-states are formed, P. becomes an organic component of social consciousness. As bourgeois society continues to develop and class antagonisms aggravate, the contradictory nature of P. comes to the fore: with the establishment of bourgeois domination P. ceases to reflect the aspirations of the whole nation, as was the case during the struggle against feudalism, it becomes reduced to the narrow interests of the exploiting class and fuses with nationalism (q.v.) and chauvinism. The petty-bourgeois P. is marked by its national narrow-mindedness and egoism, because the attitude of the petty bourgeoisie to its homeland is determined by narrow selfish interests and not by the requirements of social progress. In bourgeois society, the proletariat alone expresses the genuine national interests and is, therefore, the bearer of true P. A socialist revolution changes the social content of P., making socialism—the pride of all the working people—its central element. Accordingly, new, socialist P. of the whole people takes shape. Socialist P. is inseparably linked with internationalism (q.v.), its main features being loyalty and devotion to one's own homeland and to the entire socialist community, and also solidarity with the anti-imperialist struggle waged by the working people the world over.

Patristics, Christian theology of the 2nd-8th centuries, which upheld the dogmas of Christian religion against paganism and asserted the incompatibility of the religious faith with ancient philosophy; from the 3rd century, P. tried to adapt the philosophy of Hellenism (see Neoplatonism) to Christianity. P. was represented mainly by Tertullian (c. 150-222), Clement of Alexandria (c. 150-215), Origen (185-254), and St. Augustine (q.v.).

Pavlov, Ivan Petrovich (1849-1936), Russian natural scientist, founder of objective experimental study of higher nervous activity (q.v.) in animals and man by the method of conditioned reflexes (see Reflexes, Conditioned and Unconditioned). He developed the teaching of Sechenov (q.v.) on the reflectory nature of mental activity. The method of conditioned reflexes enabled P. to discover the basic laws and mechanisms of the activity of the brain. The phenomenon of "psychic saliva secretion" and numerous experimental investigations served as the basis for his conclusion about the signal function of the psychic activity. P.'s doctrine as a whole provides the natural-scientific foundation of materialist psychology and the dialectico-materialist theory of reflection, q.v. (the tenets on the connection between language and thinking, sense reflection and logical cognition, etc.). The works by P. and his school now serve as a basis for developing cybernetics. His main works: *Dvadtsatiletny opyt obyektivnogo izucheniya vysshei nervnoi deyatelnosti (povedeniya) zhivotnykh. Uslovniye refleksy* (Twenty Years of Objective Study of the Higher Nervous Activity [Behaviour] of Animals. Conditioned Reflexes), 1923; *Lektsii o rabote bolshikh polushary golovnogo mozga* (Lectures on the Work of the Large Hemispheres of the Cerebrum), 1927.

Pavlov, Mikhail Grigoryevich (1793-1840), Russian natural philosopher, graduate and later professor of Moscow University. He taught a number of subjects in natural science, including physics and agronomy. Initially he was a materialist, but not finding an answer to many questions in metaphysical materialism, P. became a follower of Schelling's (q.v.) natural philosophy. Thanks to the dialectical nature of his world outlook and his close ties with science P., though remaining an idealist, worked fruitfully on problems of the relationship between empirics and speculation, science and practice, and the classification of the sciences. His main work: *Osnovaniya fiziki* (Basic Principles of Physics), in two volumes, published in 1833-36.

Peaceful Coexistence, a principle of relations between states with the diametrically opposed social systems (socialism and capitalism) that implies renunciation of war as a means of settling controversial issues. According to the Marxist-Leninist theory of socialist revolution, socialism cannot triumph simultaneously in all countries. Hence, socialist states will coexist with capitalist states for a fairly long historical period. Lenin gave substance to the principle of P.C. and sought to implement it in the foreign policy of the Soviet state. The principle of P.C. stems from the nature of socialist society where private ownership—the economic basis of war—has been eliminated and, therefore, there are no social forces interested in war. It reflects the humane essence of communist ideology. The Leninist principle of P.C. guides the foreign policy of the socialist countries in the present conditions as well. P.C. implies non-interference in the peoples' internal affairs, respect for the sovereignty of all states, the development of economic and cultural relations between nations. P.C. does not mean, however, the renunciation of armed struggle in cases where the imperialist forces violate this principle and seek to impose by force of arms their dominance on other peoples. P.C. is not applicable to the relations between the exploiters and the exploited, between the colonialists and the victims of colonialism. Marxism-Leninism holds that any nation has the right to struggle against aggression and exploitation with weapons in their own hands (see War). The policy of P.C., far from excluding the class struggle, presumes this struggle. The main arena of this struggle is the economic competition of the socialist and capitalist countries on a world scale. The accomplishments of socialism in this competition exercise decisive influence on the course of world history. P.C. also presupposes political struggle on the international scene: support by the socialist states of all forms of the peoples' struggle for their social and national liberation, for democracy and socialism. P.C. does not extend to the sphere of ideology (q.v.).

Pearson, Karl (1857-1936), English mathematician, idealist philosopher, Machist. He is well known for his works in the field of the mathematical theory of statistics and its application in biology (biometry). His main philosophical work *The Grammar of Science* (1892) is devoted to the methodological problems of science. The task of science, in his opinion, is not to explain but to classify and describe facts. Like all other Machists he regarded material objects as a group of sense perceptions, and the natural laws, space and time as the products of the human mind. At the same time the subjective idealism of P. is distinguishable from Machism as a whole by its frankness and consistency as well as by the absence of any attempts to pass off as materialism. Comprehensive criticism of P. was given by Lenin in his *Materialism and Empirio-Criticism* (q.v.).

Peasantry, a class engaged in agricultural production and possessing the necessary means of production or using them on definite conditions. The P. as a class arose through the division of labour (q.v.), the separation of the crafts from farming and the antithesis between town and country (q.v.) in antagonistic socioeconomic formations. Under feudalism, the P. is the main class oppressed and exploited by the owners of the land—feudal lords. Working on the feudal lord's land, performing numerous services for him and being personally dependent on him, the peasants at the same time owned communal land in some countries as members of rural communities. The P. resisted oppression and struggled against the landowners, waging long and stubborn peasant wars. Under capitalism the P.

splits into various sections—the poor and middle peasants and rural bourgeoisie. It is no longer the main class and decreases in numbers, the bulk of it are ruined, lose their land and become agricultural proletariat, swelling the ranks of the urban proletariat. Being exploited by monopoly capital, the rural bourgeoisie and, in countries with survivals of feudalism, also by landlords, the P. is the natural ally of the working class (q.v.) in its struggle against social oppression. When the working class has won power the working P. acts as its ally in building socialism and chooses the path of co-operative farming. In socialist society the working class and P. are the two basic friendly classes. In the USSR the P. own the means of production requisite in agriculture as collective property, and the land is allotted to them for free use in perpetuity. The distinctions between the working class and the P. are gradually obliterated as agricultural labour becomes a variety of industrial labour and the essential distinctions between town and country are blurred out.

Peirce, Charles Sanders (1839-1914), American philosopher and logician, founder of pragmatism (q.v.). In his article "How to Make Our Ideas Clear" (1878) he introduced the so-called P.'s law: the value of an idea lies in its practical results. Having identified the latter with sensations, P. adopted the position of Berkeley. Contrary to the subjective-idealist epistemology, P. worked out an objective-idealist theory of development, based upon the principle of "chance" and "love" as the guiding force of development. His works on semiotic (q.v.) have significantly influenced mathematical logic (q.v.) and modern positivism (q.v.). He also dealt with the theory of probability (q.v.) and the logic of relations.

People, in a usual sense, the population of a state, of a country; in a strictly scientific sense, a historically changing community of people, including those sections and classes which, owing to their objective position, are capable of jointly tackling the tasks of the progressive development of the given country in the given period. "In using the word 'people'

Marx did not thereby gloss over class distinctions, but united definite elements capable of bringing the revolution to completion" (V. I. Lenin, *Collected Works*, Vol. 9, p. 133). The concept of P. as a sociological category reflects the change in the social structure of society: for the primitive-communal system the difference in the terms "population" and "people" was of no essential significance; but in antagonistic socio-economic formations (q.v.) this difference is very important, because there is an increasingly deeper chasm between the dominant exploiting groups and the mass of the people. It is in socialist society alone that the concept of P. again covers entire population, all its social groups. A major criterion for considering definite groups of the population a part of the P. is their objectively conditioned interest in society's progress and ability to participate in accomplishing its tasks. In the course of social development, as revolutionary changes are effected, the objective tasks themselves and the content of the revolution change, and, therefore, the social composition of the sections which at the given stage make up the P. is also inevitably altered. The concept of P. includes, as its main components, the direct producers—working people and non-exploiting groups of the population. Nevertheless it cannot always be reduced to these classes and sections. This should be especially borne in mind in present-day conditions, when wide popular movements against imperialism, for peace, democracy and socialism are under way. Marxism for the first time established that P., the masses, are the decisive force in history, that they create all the material and the bulk of the spiritual wealth, thereby ensuring the decisive conditions for society's existence. They develop production, which leads to change and development of all social life; they make revolutions, thanks to which there is social progress. A new historical community—the Soviet people—has formed in the conditions of developed socialism in the USSR. This community has emerged through the convergence of all classes and social groups, on the basis of the legal and actual equality of all nations and nationalities, and their fraternal co-operation.

People's Democracy, one of the forms of the dictatorship of the proletariat (q.v.) that reflects the distinctive development of socialist revolution at a time when imperialism is weakened and the balance of forces has tilted in favour of socialism. It also reflects the historical and national features of various countries. P.D. arose in the course of people's democratic revolutions in a number of East European and Asian countries. These revolutions resolved the contradictions between the foreign imperialists, internal big bourgeoisie and landowners, and a wide coalition of the other classes, and were carried out under the leadership of the working class and its vanguard, the Communist party. As the revolution deepened, it increasingly invaded the capitalist economy (nationalisation of means of production) and at the same time restricted the political influence of the bourgeoisie. Land reforms, which put an end to the feudal survivals and strengthened the alliance of the working class with the working peasantry, were of great importance for the development of people's democratic revolutions. Deep-going democratic reforms ensured the development of these revolutions into socialist revolutions. Accordingly, P.D., which at first acted as the democratic dictatorship of the people, began to discharge the functions of proletarian dictatorship. This general course of the revolution had its specific features in various countries. The form of P.D. is determined by the broad class basis of the people's democratic revolution (not only the proletariat and the peasantry, but also definite sections of the bourgeoisie), and the peaceful development of the people's democratic revolution into a socialist revolution, which made it possible to utilise some old forms of the representative system (parliament). The characteristic features of P.D. are: the existence of a multi-party system (in addition to the Communist party there are other democratic parties which adhere to the platform of socialism and recognise the leading role of the working class): the existence of a specific form of organisation of a people's front type, which unites political parties and mass organisations. Other characteristics of the period in which P.D.

is formed are the absence of restrictions in political rights, a longer period for the break-up of the old state machinery, etc. Experience has shown that P.D. is a powerful instrument in building socialism. At present the People's Democracies, which have created the foundations of socialist society, aim to build developed socialism.

Perception, a sensuous image of the external structural characteristics of objects and processes of the material world directly affecting the sense-organs. P. is based on sensations (q.v.). The classification of Pp. coincides with that of sensations. Most important for cognition are visual Pp., then tactile, auditory, etc. Manipulation of objects, in many respects determined by their structure, helps form a clearcut image. Motor components of P. formation are reduced to a minimum in adults (movement of the eyes). Pp. perform the following functions in the process of cognition: 1) reflect separate relations inherent in objects and processes of the external world; 2) make it possible to single out an integral object from the surroundings, reflecting, according to the laws of similarity and perspective, its form, size, surface texture and position in space (visual and tactile Pp.); 3) may serve as a sign of other properties of the object which are not observable, if we know beforehand the connection between the Pp. and these properties; 4) may serve as models of other objects not observable but similar in some respects to the one perceived; 5) may serve as a basis for forming complex conceptions (q.v.).

Peripatetics, the followers of the philosophy of Aristotle (q.v.). The name derives from the fact that in the philosophical school of Aristotle, founded in Athens in 335 B.C., instruction usually took place during walks. The peripatetic school existed for nearly one thousand years (up to 529 A.D.) and was a great centre of antique science. The most prominent leaders of this school after Aristotle's death were Theophrastus of Ephesus (c. 372-287 B.C.), particularly famous for his works in botany; Strato of Lampsacus (c. 305-270 B.C.), who developed the materialist trend in Aristotle's philosophy;

Andronicus of Rhodes (1st century B.C.), who published Aristotle's works; Alexander of Aphrodisias (end of 2nd century A.D.-beginning of 3rd century A.D.), who wrote commentaries on Aristotle's philosophy in terms of materialism.

Personal Property, ownership (q.v.) of the articles of personal use, earned income and savings, also certain means of production for use on personal subsidiary plots of land. P.P. differs essentially from private property, which serves as a means of exploitation of man by man, of appropriation of the results of other people's labour. Recognition of P.P. does not, however, mean recognition of its unlimited growth. Under socialism abuse of personal property to derive unearned income is still possible. Under communism the concept of P.P. will have no meaning, since personal requirements will be satisfied mainly from social funds and each will receive from society according to his needs.

Personalism, an idealistic trend stemming from Leibniz's (q.v.) theory of monads (q.v.), which spread in bourgeois philosophy at the turn of the century. The main feature of P. is recognition of the personality as the primary reality and the supreme spiritual value, the personality being regarded as the spiritual primary element of being. To the materialistic world outlook P. opposes the conception that nature is the sum total of personalities-spirits (see Pluralism). The "supreme personality" is God (theism). The founder of P. in the USA was B.Bowne (1847-1910). The chief exponents of P. in American philosophy were the leader of the Californian school R. Flewelling (1871-1960) and the leader of the Bostonian school E. Brightman (1884-1953). They associated P. with Protestant theology. In Britain the most prominent representative of P. was H. Carr (1857-1931), in Germany the psychologist W. Stern (1871-1938). In their teachings, however, there was no direct connection with theology, as is the case with the American personalists. According to P., the main social task is not to change the world but to change the personality, i.e., to promote his "spiritual self-perfection". A group of

French personalists occupies a special place; it was founded by E. Mounier (1905-1950) and J. Lacroix (b. 1900). This group of petty-bourgeois intellectuals, united round the journal *Esprit* (founded in 1932), represents the left Catholic circles who took part in the French Resistance and now advocate world peace and bourgeois democracy.

Petrashevsky's Group, members of a political circle which was organised by Butashevich-Petrashevsky, q.v. (1821-1866) and existed in St. Petersburg in 1845-49. Most prominent among them were N. A. Speshnev, A. V. Khanykov, P. N. Filippov, N. S. Kashkin, Dostoyevsky (q.v.), S. F. Durov, and others. In April 1849, the circle was routed by the tsarist government. The leaders of the group were sentenced to death, which was later commuted for hard labour in Siberia. P.G. was not homogeneous in composition. Besides the revolutionary democrats it included supporters of a liberal trend. The revolutionary-minded members of P.G. hated tsarist autocracy and serfdom in Russia, advocated revolutionary methods of struggle against tsarism. P.G. studied socialist literature; they highly valued the works of Belinsky, Herzen, Feuerbach, and Fourier (qq.v.). Their library contained Marx's *The Poverty of Philosophy* and Engels' *The Condition of the Working-Class in England*. The philosophical and sociological ideas of P.G. were fully expounded in Petrashevsky's *Karmanny Slovar Inostrannykh Slov* (Pocket Dictionary of Foreign Words), 1846. Adhering to the materialist positions, Petrashevsky, Speshnev, and some others criticised the idealism of Kant, Hegel, Fichte, and Schelling (qq.v.). They considered nature and its laws to be objective reality undergoing continuous change and development. They declared nature to be the prime source of life and human knowledge. P.G. maintained that "there is nothing in the world except matter", there is nothing that is supernatural, nothing that could not be included in the natural world and not developed from it. While highly assessing Feuerbach's philosophy, P.G., however, criticised his propagation of love as a new form of religion which "draws all men to

God" (Speshnev). Petrashevsky, Speshnev, Kashkin, and some others were atheists. The utopian socialist ideas of the revolutionary wing of P.G. were close to the ideas of the revolutionary democrats. In Siberian exile, members of P.G. carried out a vast amount of work to enlighten the masses and published articles in the local press.

Phenomenalism, a theory of knowledge based on the postulate that only sensations are the immediate object of knowledge. Extreme P. leads to subjective idealism: the world is a sum total of "ideas", of "complexes of sensations" (see Berkeley; Empirio-Criticism) or to agnosticism (q.v.): we cannot know what is concealed behind the sensations (Hume, q.v.). Moderate P., recognising the existence of objects manifested in sensations, leads either to inconsistent materialism, which considers objects as material things (see Locke), or to Kantian agnosticism if objects are regarded as unknowable "things-in-themselves" (see Kant, Mill, Spencer). In contemporary positivism P. assumes the linguistic form, inasmuch as its main thesis is reduced to the possibility of expressing experience in an "object" or "phenomenalistic" language. Acknowledging initially the complete possibility of reducing statements about things to statements about the content of consciousness, some neo-positivists have been lately realising the futility of these attempts. From the viewpoint of dialectical materialism, the initial thesis of P. is false, because it divorces knowledge from reality and practice.

Phenomenology, a subjective idealist trend founded by Husserl (q.v.) and his followers (L. Landgrebe, E. Fink, and others). It has exerted a great influence on contemporary bourgeois philosophy. The central concept of P.—the "intentionality" of consciousness (its being directed towards the object)—is intended to assert the subjective idealist principle: "There is no object without a subject." Philosophy is counterposed to the knowledge of real facts. The ideas of P. became the philosophical basis of existentialism, q.v. (see Heidegger, Sartre). M. Scheler and Merleau-Ponty (q.v.) based themselves on

P. when developing their own teachings. Catholic philosophers (Van Breda and others) combine P. with neo-Thomism (q.v.). The frankly idealist conclusions of P. have aroused opposition within the phenomenological school itself; its Left wing tries to protect P. from subjectivism, irrationalism and existentialism, by preserving only its supposed "rational kernel" (M. Farber, who tends towards materialist "naturalism", and partly R. Ingarden). The theoretical centres of the phenomenological trend are the Husserl Archives at the Catholic University of Louvain in Belgium, and the International Phenomenological Society, which since 1940 publishes the journal *Philosophy and Phenomenological Research* (Buffalo, New York State, USA).

Phenomenon, or appearance, an object of experience perceived by the senses. In Kant's (q.v.) philosophy, P. differs in principle from noumenon (q.v.), which remains beyond the bounds of experience and is inaccessible to human contemplation. Kant tried, by means of the concept of P., to discriminate between essence and appearance, regarding the first as unknowable (see Agnosticism). From the viewpoint of dialectical materialism there is no sharp boundary between essence and appearance (q.v.); the essence is perceived through the appearance.

Philosophers' Stone (stone of wisdom, elixir, tincture), according to ideas prevailing between the 4th and 16th centuries, a substance with the magical power to convert base metals into gold and silver, to cure all diseases, and rejuvenate people (see Alchemy). The basis for such ideas was provided by practical observation of transformations of some substances into others and natural philosophers' conjectures concerning the unity of matter. In the Middle Ages the idea of P.S. acquired a distinctly religious mystic tinge. Later it was rejected. At present the possibility of transmutation of chemical elements has been scientifically proved. The term of P.S. is often used figuratively to mean either a search for something non-existent or a decisive means of achieving desired results.

Philosophical Anthropology 1) A philosophical teaching on man which has gained currency in recent years. Some Marxist philosophers regard it as a philosophical discipline answering the question "What is man?" and synthesising the objective scientific and axiological view of man and the world. 2) A trend in modern bourgeois philosophy which took final shape in West Germany after the Second World War. The main ideas and methodological postulates of P.A. date back to the works of M. Scheler, *Die Stellung des Menschen im Kosmos* (1928) and H. Plessner, *Stufen des Organischen und der Mensch* (1928). Among the representatives of P.A. are H. Hengstenberg, A. Gehlen, P. Landsberg, and E. Rothacker. The scientific material adduced by the "anthropologists" is interpreted by them in an idealistic or eclectical way, ruling out the possibility of a scientific answer to the question of the essence and structure of man, of the human personality. Such an interpretation shows that modern P.A. has two branches: biological and functionalist. The advocates of the biological version replace the concept of human essence by that of a natural substratum viewed in terms of idealist naturalism and biologism. The proponents of the functionalist interpretation raise to the absolute man's alienation in the system of capitalist relations and interpret these relations in the spirit of idealist symbolism. The "anthropologists'" research into these problems provides an epistemological basis for several particular disciplines that have branched out from P.A. Among them are the "cultural anthropology" of Cassirer (q.v.) and the "medical anthropology" of P. Christian and W. Weizsäcker. An eclectic mixture of Husserl's phenomenology, philosophy of life and existentialism (qq.v.) in P.A. engenders an illusory model of man with its social links mystified and presented as depending on some "other-worldly" principle. Conclusions of this kind gloss over the real social and class antagonisms. The meaning of human life is usually deduced from the "extra-temporal" meaning and is often interpreted in overtly religious terms. The anti-scientific and politically reactionary ideas of P.A. have considerably influenced modern philosophical revisionism (q.v.). All varieties of bourgeois P.A. are opposed to the truly scientific conception of man in Marxist-Leninist philosophy.

Philosophical Communism, the term used by Engels to denote attempts at a theoretical substantiation of communism by the revolutionary bourgeous intellectuals in 1842-43. P.C. sought to link the theoretical views of the Young Hegelians (q.v.) and particularly Feuerbach (q.v.) with elements of the teachings of utopian socialists and also with tasks of social, chiefly anti-feudal, transformations. P.C. completely ignored the role of the proletariat and did not understand the class nature of communism. This, together with the inadequate level of concrete historical and especially economic studies, explains the speculative nature of P.C. Its rational element consisted in stressing the ties of communism with classical German philosophy. Subsequently, P.C. degenerated into "true socialism" (q.v.).

Philosophical Journals in the USSR reflect the condition of Marxist philosophical thought and promote its creative development. After the victory of the Great October Socialist Revolution in 1917, the following P.J. were among those published in the USSR: *Pod znamenem marksizma* (Under the Banner of Marxism) (1922-44), *Problemy marksizma* (Marxist Review) (1928-34). The leading journal *Voprosy filosofii* (Questions of Philosophy) has been published since 1947. The journal covers major aspects of the socio-political and ideological work of the CPSU and the Soviet state, pays special attention to the analysis of the fundamental principles of dialectical and historical materialism, and studies the social processes in the society of developed socialism, the global problems (q.v.) of our time, philosophical problems in the natural sciences, problems in the history of philosophy, Marxist-Leninist ethics and aesthetics and the theory of scientific atheism. The journal carries polemical articles on topical issues and combats bourgeois ideology and philosophy. The contributors to the journal include philosophers from the socialist and some capitalist countries, scholars of

the natural sciences and the humanities. An all-Union journal of higher educational establishments, *Filosofskiye nauki* (Philosophical Sciences), has been published since 1958. The Ukrainian-language journal *Filosofskaya dumka* (Philosophical Thought) has been published since 1969 in Kiev. The Moscow and Leningrad universities publish philosophical issues of the *Herald.*

Philosophical Notebooks, Lenin's notes on philosophy, which were published for the first time as a separate volume in 1933. The *P.N.* are extensive excerpts made by Lenin (mainly between 1914 and 1916) from various philosophical works. Besides summaries of their content Lenin made important critical remarks, conclusions and generalisations. Of great interest is the fragment "On the Question of Dialectics", in which Lenin gives a concise and profound exposition of the essence of materialist dialectics. The *P.N.* also deal with books on natural science and other subjects and contain many valuable ideas and statements on diverse problems in philosophy. The central subject of the *P.N.* is dialectics (q.v.). Lenin gave a definition of dialectics which reveals all aspects of its essence and elements; he formulated the basic principles of the Marxist understanding of logic and its categories, characterised the dialectical process of cognition and the doctrine of contradictions as the core of dialectics. Lenin's proposition on the unity of dialectics, logic, and the theory of knowledge (q.v.) and also his statements concerning the elaboration of dialectical logic (q.v.) are of great importance for the development of philosophy. Of particular significance in this respect are Lenin's ideas that the history of thought and the laws of thinking coincide in logic and that to elaborate a correct theory of knowledge it is necessary to sum up philosophically the history of technology, natural science, the mental development of children, animals, etc. Lenin gave much attention to the history of philosophy (q.v.), showing that it is the history of the struggle between materialism and idealism; he pointed to the importance of studying the history of dialectics, examined a number of methodological questions in the history of philosophy as a science and assessed the views of many philosophers, paying special attention to Hegel. In his notes on books dealing with the natural sciences Lenin highlighted dialectical materialism as the only scientific methodology. The *P.N.* are a model of creative development of materialist dialectics and provide a programme for the further elaboration of Marxist philosophy.

Philosophy, the science of the general laws of being (i.e., of nature and society) and human thinking, the process of cognition. P. is one of the forms of social consciousness (q.v.). It is ultimately determined by society's economic relations. Pythagoras was the first to use the term of P.; P. was developed as a special science by Plato (q.v.). It arose in slave-owning society as a science embracing the sum total of man's knowledge of the objective world and himself, which was natural, considering the low level of knowledge at the early stages in human history. As social production grew and scientific knowledge accumulated, individual sciences branched out from P., the latter being developed as an independent science. P. as a science arose out of the necessity to elaborate a general view of the world, to study its general elements and laws, out of the need for a rational method of thinking, for logic and a theory of knowledge. The fundamental question of P. (q.v.) as a separate science is the relation of thinking to being, consciousness to matter. Every philosophical system gives a concretely elaborated solution of this problem, even if the fundamental question is not directly formulated in it. This results in the polarisation of P. into two diametrically opposed trends, materialism (q.v.) and idealism with dualism (qq.v.) holding an intermediate position between them. The struggle between materialism and idealism lays its imprint on the entire history of P. and is one of its driving forces. This struggle is closely associated with the development of society, the economic, political, and ideological interests of the classes. Elaboration of P.'s specific problems and its development led to its various aspects being singled out as more or less independent and at times

sharply delineated sections. These are ontology, epistemology (see Theory of Knowledge), logic, ethics, aesthetics, psychology, sociology, and history of P. (qq.v.). At the same time, in view of the inadequacy of concrete knowledge, P. tried to replace the missing links and laws of the world by invented ones, thereby becoming a special "science of sciences", standing above all other sciences. In relation to nature it was natural philosophy (q.v.) and in relation to history, the philosophy of history (q.v.). The last system of this kind was Hegel's (q.v.) P. But as knowledge was accumulated and differentiated, all grounds for the existence of P. as a "science of sciences" disappeared. Marxism-Leninism for the first time clearly understood the social requirements giving rise to P. as a special science, and its place and role in spiritual culture, and consequently also the range of its problems, its subject-matter (see Materialism, Dialectical; Materialism, Historical). Theoretical knowledge of phenomena of the surrounding world is impossible without logically developed thinking. But it was P. that elaborated logical categories and laws because of the historically shaped division of labour between the sciences. Marxist-Leninist P. developed and consistently applied the materialist principle in understanding the objective world and thought, fructifying it by its dialectical outlook and constructing dialectical logic. Marxist P. considers logical forms and laws as forms and laws of development of natural and socio-historical processes cognised and tested by entire human experience. It has abolished the distinction between ontology, logic, and the theory of knowledge. The coincidence of all these is a fundamental principle of the P. of dialectical materialism. The philosophical theory of Marxism thus represents a dialectico-materialist solution of the fundamental question of P., a solution concretely expounded and elaborated in all details. Logical forms and laws appear here as universal forms and laws governing every natural and socio-historical process reflected in man's mind, as stages in the theoretical reproduction of objects in conformity with their real development. Based on such an understanding of its role, subject-matter, and tasks in the development of human culture, P. is a powerful instrument of man's knowledge and activity, an active factor in further developing knowledge and practice. With such an understanding of P. its parts, psychology, ethics and aesthetics increasingly turn into independent sciences, which are only traditionally regarded as philosophical. True, this tradition has its grounds, for these sciences are mainly connected with specific problems of P., especially the relationship of subject and object (q.v.). P. promotes man's self-awareness, his understanding of the place and role of scientific discoveries in the general development of human culture and thereby provides a criterion for assessing them and connecting separate links of knowledge into a single world outlook (q.v.). Anti-philosophical tendencies are inherent in contemporary bourgeois theories. They are especially characteristic of neo-positivism (q.v.), which declares the problems of P. to be pseudo-problems and tries to replace philosophical analysis of contemporary knowledge and practice by analysis of the "language of science", i.e., a linguistically semantic analysis of the "external forms of thought"—language, sign systems for expressing thoughts, etc. Thereby they hold that philosophy as a science is actually abolished. Dialectical materialism, which continues the finest traditions of world P., remains therefore the only way of developing P. as a special science.

Philosophy, Analytical, a broad and rather motley movement current in the 20th century that unites various groups, trends and philosophers who see the task of philosophy in an analysis of language (q.v.) so as to clarify the content of problems that have been traditionally philosophical. It is suggested that analysis must replace the vague expression of a problem in the language by a formula that would demonstrate its real essence. In this case the problem may prove to be either posed incorrectly, being a "pseudo-problem", or involve the use of particular linguistic forms, or, finally, be irrelevant to philosophy and solvable by methods of special sciences. A.P. has been spread chiefly in the USA and Britain, its indi-

vidual exponents and groups existing also in the Scandinavian countries, Australia and elsewhere. In Britain the dominant form of A.P. is linguistic philosophy (q.v.). In the USA, A.P., apart from several philosophers close to linguistic philosophy, is also represented by supporters of logical empiricism (q.v.) (Carnap, q.v., H. Feigl, and others) and neo-pragmatism (W. Quine, N. Goodman, M. White). There are also a number of "independent" American analysts who do not belong to any trend (W. Sellars and others). Denying the world-view character of philosophical knowledge A.P. expresses the trends of positivism (q.v.) in modern bourgeois philosophy. Most followers of A.P. lay emphasis on the concrete forms and means of linguistic analysis. A.P. either reduces philosophy to metaphilosophy, i.e., to an analysis of the forms and means of expressing philosophical problems in language, or in general replaces philosophy by logical or linguistic studies.

Philosophy, Arab, a set of philosophical doctrines developed in the Middle Ages by Oriental thinkers who adopted Islam and wrote in the Arabic. In the 9th century A.D. the Arabs familiarised themselves on a broad scale with the natural scientific and philosophical legacy of ancient Greece and Rome. They were especially keen on the philosophy of Aristotle (q.v.) and its prevailing interest in problems of natural science and logic. The assimilation of Aristotelian philosophy was mediated, however, by the knowledge of the works of its latest commentators who belonged to the Neoplatonic schools in Athens and Alexandria. The "Neoplatonicised" Aristotelianism formed the basis of theories developing in tune with the leading school in medieval A.P.—Oriental Peripateticism (see Peripatetics). This school is considered to have been founded by al-Kindi (q.v.), a philosopher who first used and popularised the main conceptions of Aristotelianism. The further development of Oriental Peripateticism is connected with the names of al-Farabi (870-950) and Ibn Sina (q.v.) who, unlike al-Kindi, argued for the eternity of the world. The cosmic and natural phenomena, they maintained, do not depend on

Providence, for God's knowledge only embraces the universal, rather than the singular. According to Ibn Sina, the universal (general ideas) has a triune being: in divine reason, in things, and in the human intellect. Matter is only predisposed to the acceptance of forms, but receives them from without; the "grantor of forms" for the "sublunary world" is the so-called active reason, which also generates immortal human souls. The supreme aim of human being is to cognise this reason. The Peripateticism of al-Farabi and Ibn Sina was paralleled by the development of certain philosophical trends inimical to orthodox Islam (q.v.), as represented, in particular, by the secret organisation Pure Brothers. Another form of opposition to orthodox Islam, as well as to rationalistic philosophy, was the mystical trend of the Sufis (see Sufism), whose teosophic doctrines betray the influence of gnosticism (see Gnostics), Neoplatonism (q.v.) and some Eastern religions. These doctrines are based on the belief in the possibility of contemplating the divinity and of man's final merger with Him, the man who has cast off the fetters of the material world. Representatives of late Kalam (rational theology)—Mutakallims, followers of al-Ashari (874-935), engaged in the apologetics (q.v.) of Islam with the help of rational arguments. To prove the dogmas on Providence, creation of the world and possibility of miracles, they used atomistics (q.v.). Al-Ghazali (1059-1111) was a representative of a religious-idealist school; he criticised naturalist and rationalist elements in the philosophy of Oriental Peripatetics through a synthesis of the conceptions of the Mutakallims and Sufis. A.P. was further developed in Andalusia and North Africa, where the Oriental Peripatetic school was represented by Ibn Tufail (1110-1185) and Ibn Rushd, q.v. (Averroës), whose work constituted the peak of medieval A.P. He did not only purify the Aristotelian doctrine from the latest Neoplatonic accretions, but also created an independent system leaning towards naturalist Pantheism (q.v.). Ibn Rushd substantiated the supremacy of reason over faith and argued against the theologists' right to engage in philosophical problems. At the same time he called on the philosophers not to divulge their doctrines to the "broad public", as this may rob it of religious convictions and hence moral principles. Ibn Rushd's doctrine greatly influenced philosophical free-thinking in medieval Western Europe (see Averroism). Subsequent centuries saw an increasing consolidation of dogmatic theology and mysticism in the spiritual life of the peoples of Muslim East. The struggle against these forces was only resumed in the late 19th century. The exception is the work of the North African historian Ibn Khaldun (1332-1406), who was one of the first to demand the study of the general regularities of historical phenomena and create his own sociological theory.

Philosophy, Fundamental Question of, the question of the relationship of consciousness (q.v.) to being (q.v.), of thought (q.v.) to matter (q.v.) and nature, examined on two planes, first, what is primary—spirit or nature, matter or consciousness—and second, how is knowledge of the world related to the world itself or, to put it differently, does consciousness correspond to being, is it capable of truthfully reflecting the world? A consistent solution of the F.Q.P. is possible only if both sides are considered. The philosophers who form the camp of materialism (q.v.) regard matter, being, as primary, and consciousness as secondary, and hold that consciousness is the result of influence exerted upon it by the objectively existing external world. The idealist philosophers accept the idea, the consciousness, as being primary and regard it as the only true reality. From their viewpoint cognition is not a reflection of material being but merely cognition of consciousness itself in the form of self-cognition, an analysis of sensations and concepts, cognition of the absolute idea, universal will, etc. A metaphysical approach to solving this question was inherent in pre-Marxian philosophy; it consisted either in underestimating the activity of consciousness or in reducing knowledge to passive contemplation (metaphysical materialism) and the identification of consciousness and matter (see Materialism, Vulgar), in exaggerating the activity of thought, elevating it to an absolute divorced from matter (see Idealism), or asserting their incompatibility in principle (see Dualism; Agnosticism). Only Marxist philosophy has given an all-round, dialectically materialist, scientifically-based solution of F.Q.P. It sees the primacy of matter in that: (1) matter is the source of consciousness, while consciousness is a reflection of matter; (2) consciousness is a result of a long process of development of the material world; (3) consciousness is a property and function of highly organised matter—the brain; (4) the existence and development of the human mind and thought (q.v.) is impossible without the linguistic material shell, without speech; (5) consciousness arises, develops and improves as a result of man's material labour activity; (6) consciousness is social and is determined by material social being. Noting the absolute antithesis of matter and consciousness only within the bounds of the F.Q.P., Marxism-Leninism simultaneously points to their interconnection and interaction. A derivative of material being, consciousness possesses relative independence and in its development also exerts retroactive influence on the material world, facilitating its practical mastery and transformation. The human mind, relying on practical experience, is capable of truthfully knowing the world. The relationship of matter and consciousness is the fundamental question of philosophy because, by virtue of its universality, it encompasses all philosophical questions, determines the solution not only of particular problems, but also the nature of the world outlook as a whole and provides a reliable criterion for differentiating the basic trends in philosophy. That is why a scientific formulation of the F.Q.P. makes it possible to consistently apply the principle of partisanship (q.v.) in philosophy, strictly to delimit and counterpose materialism and idealism and resolutely to uphold the scientific world outlook of dialectical materialism.

Philosophy, History of, a science which studies the origin and progressive development of philosophy (q.v.), the laws and phases of this development, and the struggle of philosophical schools and trends. Even in antiquity, philosophers (e.g., Aristotle, q.v.) turned to the views of their predecessors with the object of criticising or utilising them in their own conceptions. Diogenes Laertius, Sextus Empiricus (qq.v.) and others contributed compendiums of the opinions and biographies of philosophers. A more or less arbitrary list of "opinions" of philosophers is contained in the main works on the H.P. up to the 18th century. Historico-philosophical works were dominated by empiricism (q.v.) and they were primarily of an educative nature. Gradually, with the development of philosophy, elements of a scientific approach to its history appeared: H.P. was released from the grip of theology and attempts were made to apply the principle of historism (q.v.), to establish the connection between the development of philosophy and the general development of history and scientific knowledge; a critical attitude to the sources was adopted. Materialist philosophers (F. Bacon, Spinoza, qq.v.) and also thinkers who drew closer to the idea of historical laws (Vico, Herder, qq.v., and others) made an important contribution to the H.P. Hegel's conception of the H.P. is especially interesting. According to Hegel (q.v.), the H.P. is the process of development of thought in the apprehension of truth (absolute idea); truth can be uncovered only in the entire history of human thought. Hegel's conception contained valuable surmises: the idea of the necessary and natural development of philosophy, its dependence on the history of society and knowledge, of the H.P. as the developing apprehension of truth, etc. On the whole, however, this conception is inacceptable because of its idealist nature: Hegel conceived the H.P. as the self-development of the absolute spirit, which leads to a distortion of real history. Russian 19th-century thinkers, especially Herzen (q.v.), contributed valuable ideas towards the elaboration of a scientific H.P. Nevertheless, pre-Marxist philosophers could not transform the H.P. into a science. The bourgeois H.P. of the second half of the 19th and the 20th centuries made a considerable step backward in the area of methodology even in comparison with Hegel. A scientific approach to the H.P. is provided only by dialectical and historical materialism. Marxist philosophy, first, establishes the objective laws governing the development of all forms of social consciousness (q.v.) and, second, brings out the structure and characteristics of scientific knowledge, which alone makes it possible to study its history scientifically. The central place in the scientific H.P. is held by the study of the history of the formation, development of and the struggle between materialism and idealism (qq.v.), between dialectics and metaphysics (qq.v.). In the course of the development of philosophy, scientific, materialist views, based on the progress of knowledge and the practical activity of people, oust unscientific, idealist views. A Marxist analysis of the H.P. includes partisanship as an important element in the assessment of the various schools and trends (see Partisanship in Philosophy). Such an approach does not, of course, mean discarding the elements of positive knowledge achieved within the framework of idealist philosophy. A scientific analysis of the H.P. proceeds from the necessity to examine the development of philosophy as a process determined by the socio-economic and political advance of society, to evaluate philosophical ideas and systems (ultimately) as an expression of the interests and ideology of this or that class or social group, as a reflection of the requirements of society's historical experience and the development of scientific knowledge. It is necessary to determine why the given social system and the sum total of historical conditions have produced this philosophical system and not another. Otherwise it is impossible to avoid simplification and a vulgar materialistic view of the interrelation between economics and philosophy. The dialectico-materialist approach makes it possible to present the H.P. as a single process, to disclose the necessary connections between different schools and trends, the progress in the solution of philosophical problems. Since the H.P. is the process of philosophical cognition of the world, it must establish direct connections between the historical development of human knowledge and its internal structure and logic. Here we see clearly the dialectical principle of the unity of the historical and logical (q.v.): the history of an object (philosophy) is inseparably connected with its developed logical structure; the emergence of science can be properly understood only in terms of its developed state. It is this that opens up the way to comprehending the laws by which philosophy develops and helps to understand the real place and significance of conceptions and ideas that arise in the course of history. At the same time, the H.P. must not be separated from the history of the sciences and from society's historical experience. Philosophy must dialectically analyse and summarise the history of thought, science, and technology. The study of the H.P. is of great importance for the development of contemporary philosophy. Marxist philosophy has assimilated everything positive created by human thought for many centuries of its development and, therefore, the H.P. is an important component part of Marxist philosophy. The study of H.P. is necessary to develop the modern methods of scientific research and practical transformation of the world, to raise the level of philosophical culture.

Philosophy, Linguistic (also known as the "philosophy of linguistic analysis"), a trend in analytical philosophy (q.v.) widespread in the 1940s and 1950s mainly in Britain (Ryle, q.v., J. Austin, A. J. Wisdom, and others) and in the USA (M. Black, N. Malcolm, and others). There were two schools of L. P.: the Cambridge school which was influenced by Wittgenstein (q.v.), and the Oxford school strongly influenced by Moore (q.v.). Like the other schools of neopositivism (q.v.), L.P. denies that philosophy is a world outlook, and regards traditional philosophical problems as pseudo-problems arising owing to the confusing influence of language on thought. The supporters of L. P. maintain that it should show that philosophical problems are unreal and that they arise from the wrong use of words. Holding that the analysis of language is the sole possible aim of philosophical investigation, the supporters of L.P., particularly the representatives of the Oxford group, concentrated their attention not on artificial model languages but on the language of common speech. Here they proceeded from the generally correct assumption that the rich resources of the natural spoken language cannot be fully expressed within the framework of any "ideal language". But by refusing to analyse the philosophical problems of the relation of language and thinking. L.P. confines research to empirical description of various types of usage and closes the path to a true explanation of the essence of language, arriving ultimately at a merely conventionalist (see Conventionalism) interpretation. For L. P. language is a means of construing, not reflecting the world; it becomes a kind of independent, self-contained force. This shallow treatment of philosophical problems and refusal to tackle the vital problems of science and social consciousness, and the scholastic tendencies of L.P. led to violent criticism even from bourgeois philosophers (e.g., Russell, q.v.), though there is no denying a certain significance of the works of the representatives of L.P. for metaphilosophical research (see Metatheory). Lately the representatives of L.P. tend to reject the orthodox position of pure "analysis" and turn to vital philosophical problems.

Philosophy of Antiquity, the totality of philosophical theories developed in the Greek slave-owning society from the end of the 7th century B.C. and in the Roman slave-owning society from the 2nd century B.C. up to the beginning of the 6th century A.D. The P.A. is an original, but not isolated, phenomenon in the development of man's philosophical knowledge. It took shape on the basis of the rudiments of astronomical, mathematical, and other knowledge brought into Greek cities from the East as a result of attempts to remove from philosophical thought the mythological conceptions of the world and of man. Already in the 5th century B.C., philosophical and cosmological systems were developed in which myths were used as a means of figuratively expressing ideas rather than as the basic view. In the 6th and even in the 5th centuries B.C., philosophy and the knowledge of nature had not been separated. The number of hypotheses that occurred owing to the absence of experimental verification was enormous. As far as philosophy was concerned, this multiplicity of hypotheses meant a multiplicity of types of philosophical explanation of the world.

This multiplicity and the level of elaboration made P.A. a school of philosophical thinking for later times. "...The manifold forms of Greek philosophy," wrote Engels, "contain in embryo, in the nascent state, almost all the later modes of outlook on the world." (*Dialectics of Nature,* p. 44). The starting point for the development of the P.A. was philosophical materialism. Thales, Anaximander, Anaximenes, Heraclitus (qq.v.), despite the many differences between them, assumed that all things originated from some single material source. Those who held these naive materialist views, later advanced certain ideas that led to the appearance of idealism. Equally clear in the P.A. is the antithesis of the dialectical and metaphysical methods of thinking. Many of the early Greek philosophers were actually dialecticians, who studied nature as a single whole and, consequently, in the interaction and connection of its phenomena. In the more than a thousand years of the development of the P.A., materialism and idealism, dialectics and metaphysics, which took shape in early Greek philosophy, underwent an intricate evolution, reflecting as they do in the final analysis the dialectic of the development of the society of antiquity. The materialism of the P.A. was developed by Empedocles, Anaxagoras, Leucippus, and Democritus (qq.v.). In the teachings of Socrates (q.v.) and, particularly, Plato (q.v.) philosophical idealism took shape, counterposing itself, first and foremost, to the materialism of the atomists. From this time on there was a clearly marked struggle between the two main lines of development, materialism and idealism (or, as Lenin said, "the line of Democritus and the line of Plato"). Aristotle (q.v.), who wavered between materialism and idealism, also expressed his ideas in polemics with theories preceding and contemporary to him. Aristotle's criticism of the theory of "ideas", the central theory in Plato's idealism, was particularly energetic and witty. In the Hellenic period that marked the beginning of the crisis of the polis slave-owning system, the struggle between the different schools in the P.A. once again became more acute. Especially sharp was the struggle between the Epicurean school and that of the stoics (q.v.) into whose fundamentally materialist doctrines elements of idealism had made extensive inroads. Questions of ethics came to the forefront in philosophical problems, but this ethics had its basis in the theory of nature and the theory of knowledge and thought. Philosophical schools were shut off from the world, they became coteries of people united in their indifference to external events and their excessive interest in questions of ethics and education. In the epoch of the Roman Empire the crisis of the slave-owning society became more acute and the urge for religious self-oblivion and solace became stronger. A wave of religious cults, doctrines and mysteries spread from the East to the West. Philosophy itself became religious, even mystical in some doctrines. Examples of this were Neoplatonism (q.v.) and neo-Pythagoreanism, the first of which exerted considerable influence on the development of Christian philosophy. In 529 the Emperor Justinian issued a decree closing down the philosophical schools in Athens. But before this decree and quite independently of it, the basic ideas of P.A. had completed their course of development.

Philosophy of History, a field of knowledge which studies the meaning of history, its laws, and the main trends of man's development. Historically, P.H. dates back to antiquity. In the 17th-18th centuries it was elaborated by Vico (q.v.) and the philosophers of Enlightenment (Voltaire, Herder, Condorcet, Montesquieu, qq.v.). To combat the influence of theology on history, dating back to St. Augustine (q.v.), the Enlighteners introduced into P.H. the idea of causality, elaborated the theory of progress, voiced the idea of the unity of the historical process, and proved the idea of influence of the geographical and social environment on man. Hegel's (q.v.) P.H. was the peak in the development of bourgeois P.H. He regarded history as a single, law-governed, intrinsically necessary process of self-development of the spirit, the idea. The founders of Marxism noted the limitations of P.H., its speculative, a priori and idealistic nature. Their discovery of historical materialism (q.v.) provided the basis for a truly scientific philosophical generalisation of history and establishment of its main laws of development. In modern bourgeois P.H., the conceptions of Toynbee and Spengler (qq.v.) predicting the inevitable decline of Western civilisation enjoy a great influence. W. Rostow recently attempted to put forward an optimistic version of P.H. (see Stages of Economic Growth, Theory of). Still, the majority of bourgeois sociologists and historiographers reject any philosophical generalisation of history, regarding it as a chaotic succession of accidents and deny the concepts of causality, regularity, and progress.

Philosophy of Identity, a philosophical conception aimed at solving the question of the relationship of thinking and being, spirit and nature by acknowledging their absolute identity. The basic principle of P.I. is diametrically opposed to the principle of dualistic systems (see Dualism). P.I. as a definite philosophical conception is historically associated with the name of Schelling (q.v.), who tried to overcome the dualism of Kant's and Fichte's conceptions by advancing a new initial principle of monistic philosophy, the absolute identity of the subjective and the objective, the ideal and the real. The principle of the identity of thinking and being also underlies the Hegelian system. But this principle is realised by Hegel (q.v.) differently, because Hegel understood identity dialectically, not as an immobile absolute, an indefinite unity, facing with indifference the multiformity of the real world, but as a self-developing logical idea, whose definiteness and distinction are contained within itself as its immanent infinite form. What sets P.I. apart from other objective idealist conceptions is not recognition of the identity of thinking and being, but the metaphysical understanding of this identity. P.I. attempts to solve the fundamental question of philosophy (q.v.) by practically removing it and dissolving the difference between spirit and nature, thinking and being in immobile and absolute substance. At present the metaphysical identity of thinking and being is advocated by certain schools of neo-Thomism (q.v.). The truly scientific philosophy is Marxist philosophy, which bases its monism (q.v.) on the material unity and development of the world.

Philosophy of Life, a subjective-idealist trend of bourgeois philosophy which arose in Germany (Nietzsche, Dilthey, qq.v., G. Simmel) and France (Bergson, q.v.) at the turn of the century. The origins of this philosophy were connected with the rapid development of biology, psychology, and other sciences which revealed the falseness of the mechanistic picture of the world. P.L. tried to overcome the limitations of mechanistic materialism from idealist positions. Its appearance signified a crisis of bourgeois philosophy, its renunciation of science and transition to irrationalism and nihilism (qq.v.). P.L. was a distorted, idealist interpretation of the specific features of socio-historical process. The pivot of this philosophy is the concept of life as the absolute, infinite principle of the world which, in contrast to matter and consciousness, is active, multiform, and in eternal motion. Life cannot be understood with the help of the senses or reason, it is perceived intuitively and is accessible to emotion. In the 1920s and 1930s the ideas of P.L. were developed by Spengler (q.v.) and E. Spranger and were also used by the ideologists of fascism (q.v.). Certain ideas of P.L. served as ideological sources of existentialism (q.v.).

Philosophy, Subject-Matter, see Philosophy.

Physical Picture of the World, a term which denotes a conception of nature (at times, in a narrower sense, the inorganic world) based on certain general principles of physics. In this sense, ancient atomism (q.v.), the physics of Descartes (q.v.) and the system of Newton (q.v.) were a P.P.W. A feature of all attempts to construct a P.P.W. in the 17th and 18th centuries was the idea that complex natural phenomena are reducible to simple mechanical movement of discrete particles of matter. The idea of specific laws of complex forms of motion irreducible to the more simple forms became established in 19th-century natural science. This conception was voiced in the most profound and generalised manner in Engels' *Dialec-

tics of Nature* (q.v.). The 19th-century P.P.W. was based on a hierarchy of the forms of motion and their reciprocal transitions, and in this sense the law of conservation and transformation of energy was its most general physical principle. In the 20th century, the laws of Newtonian mechanics could no longer play the part of the most general laws. In the second quarter of the 20th century, attempts by Einstein (q.v.) and other physicists to construct a single theory of the field did not lead to the creation of a new, integral P.P.W. The theory of elementary particles (q.v.) and their transmutations, the rough outlines of which are now emerging in physics, could be the basis of such a picture.

Physicalism, a conception in logical positivism (q.v.), elaborated by Carnap (q.v.), O. Neurath, and others. The proponents of P. maintain that the only way to verify a scientific proposition is to translate it into the language of physics, into "physicalia". Propositions which cannot be translated are regarded as devoid of scientific meaning. The problem of the unity of all scientific knowledge and of its objective truth is thus replaced by the search for a single, or, to be more exact, the only language of science. Attempts to create a unified language and translate into it the whole system of accumulated knowledge failed to yield positive results, as was recognised both by the physicalists and their critics (see Critical Rationalism).

Physics, the science of the properties and laws of motion of material particles, matter and field, of the structure of atoms, gravitational, electric, magnetic, and other interactions, and of molecular processes. In antiquity, the word "physics" designated the sum total of knowledge about nature. Subsequently physics was understood as the study of the laws governing the motion of bodies (mechanics) and of the causes of sound (acoustics), of thermal, electric, magnetic, and optical phenomena. Classical physics sought to explain the causes of these phenomena by Newton's (q.v.) laws of mechanics. It was established in the 19th century that mechanical, thermal, and electromagnetic processes are connected by reversible transitions, the quantitative measure of all these forms of motion, energy, remaining constant. The principle of the conservation of energy (see Conservation of Energy, Law of) became the basic principle of P. At the turn of the century, many new, hitherto unknown physical phenomena were discovered — the origination and propagation of radio signals, X-rays, and radioactivity. At the same time the periodicity of the chemical properties of elements discovered by Mendeleyev (q.v.) held the focus of theoretical physics. Exploring the causes of these phenomena, P. branched out into atomic and nuclear physics and then the physics of elementary particles (q.v.). In the first half of the 20th century, theoretical physics departed from the basic classical concepts and ideas in connection with the appearance of the theory of relativity and quantum mechanics (qq.v.). Modern physics, which has registered striking successes, is exerting an unparalleled impact on technology and social life. Throughout its development P. has been closely connected with philosophy. In antiquity, physical knowledge and hypotheses were a component of various philosophical systems. Generalisation of physical knowledge, accumulated through the development of classical mechanics, formed the basis for the materialist ideas in the 17th-19th centuries. The analysis and summary of 19th-century discoveries in physics provided Marx and Engels with a basis on which the teaching of dialectical materialism was founded. In the 20th century, as in earlier periods, the idealist trends have been seeking to make use of the changes in the conceptions of physics in favour of idealist, positivist conclusions (see Idealism, Physical). Subsequent development of science has shown that P. provides irrefutable arguments in support of dialectical materialism and that the application of the philosophical ideas of Marxism in physical research gives fresh stimuli to the study of nature.

Piaget, Jean (1896-1980), Swiss psychologist, philosopher, and logician. Using vast experimental data, P. created in the 1930s and 1940s the theory of the intellect formation, which regards the intellect as a system of operations, i.e.,

the inner actions of the subject, derivative from the external object actions, and forming a certain structural unity. P. used mathematical logic (q.v.) as a formal apparatus to describe the intellect's operations. Great credit goes to P. for the development of experimental psychology: in a number of his works he analysed the mechanisms of forming basic psychic functions, notably those shaping major concepts and principles of human thought. P.'s psychological and logical ideas were synthesised in his "genetic epistemology", a theoretico-cognitive conception based upon a genetic and historico-critical approach to the analysis of knowledge. According to P., the development of a subject's knowledge of an object makes it more and more invariant, more and more stable in the changing conditions of experience, this invariance (q.v.) of knowledge being considered as a reflection of the object itself, its properties, and cognitive activity of man. In the last years of his life P. elaborated problems of genetic epistemology in the light of the vital problems of logic, psychology, biology, linguistics and cybernetics (specifically, the problems of interdisciplinary ties in psychology, its place in the system of sciences, the specifics of structural methods of cognition, etc.).

Pisarev, Dmitry Ivanovich (1840-1868), Russian materialist philosopher, literary critic, revolutionary publicist. He was a staff member and actual editor of the journal *Russkoye Slovo* (The Russian Word) from 1861. For defending Herzen (q.v.) he was imprisoned in the Peter and Paul Fortress from 1862 to 1867. In the years 1867-68 he was on the staff of the magazines *Dyelo* (Cause) and *Otechestvenniye Zapiski* (Notes of the Fatherland). P.'s democratic, revolutionary and socialist views, which took shape towards the end of 1861 subsequently changed significantly. The rapid decline of the revolutionary emancipation movement which arose in 1859-61 convinced P. of the lack in Russia of the conditions necessary for a revolution, of the peasantry's inability to emancipate themselves and build a free society. P. saw the main purpose of his activity in the solution of "the problem of the starving and destitute people"; he advocated the socialist ideal (it is true that P. was not satisfied with any of the existing socialist doctrines). Not rejecting in principle the use of revolutionary violence ("The Historical Ideas of O. Comte", 1865; "The Thinking Proletariat", 1865; "The Propagators of Negative Doctrines", 1866; "Heinrich Heine", 1867, and others), P. put forward the idea of a "chemical" path of revolution—gradual social changes, leading to public education, to the growth (due to the dissemination of knowledge) of the productivity of labour and to the improvement of the living conditions of the masses as the main prerequisites of a radical reconstruction of social institutions. He sought to entrust the progressive intelligentsia with the task of public education. His works written in 1867 and 1868, the last years of his life (e.g., "The French Peasant in 1789") testify to the growth of the radical tendencies in P.'s world outlook. He devoted much attention to philosophical problems. In particular, he regarded the progress of scientific knowledge as the basis of historical development. This determined P.'s incessant struggle against religion and "mysticism" in science that draw mankind away from the path of reasonable progress and conditioned P.'s negative attitude towards Hegel's (q.v.) "speculative philosophy". P. saw a counter-balance to idealism in the theories of the "vulgar materialists" J. Moleschott and K. Vogt, whom he assessed positively. P. was one of the first in Russia vigorously to propagate Darwinism ("Progress in the Animal and Plant Kingdom", 1864). Being inclined to sensationalism (q.v.) in epistemological problems, P. was, however, opposed to empiricism (q.v.) and pointed to the constructive role of creative vision. A confirmed adherent of realism, P. engaged in sharp polemics with the supporters of "pure art". P.'s appeal "to smash all that can be smashed" reflected both the nihilistic extremes of the democrats of the 1860s and their hatred of autocracy and serfdom, of social parasitism and liberal timeserving.

Planck, Max (1858-1947), German physicist-theorist. While elaborating the thermodynamic theory of thermal radia-

tion, P. introduced a new universal constant—quantum of action. He established that light was radiated and absorbed discretely, by definite portions—quanta ($h=6.62 \cdot 10^{-27}$ erg./sec.). This discovery marked the transition from macrocosm to microcosm, the new world of quantum phenomena. Thus, P. became the founder of the quantum theory, which established the fact of discreteness in the energetic processes and extended the idea of atomism to all phenomena of nature. Holding a materialist view on a number of cardinal problems of science, P. sharply criticised empirio-criticism (q.v.).

Plato (428/427-348/347 B.C.), Greek idealist philosopher, disciple of Socrates (q.v.), founder of objective idealism (q.v.), author of more than 30 philosophical dialogues (*Sophistes, Parmenides, Theatietus, Republic*, and others). In defending the idealist world outlook, P. actively fought against the materialist teachings of that time. He widely employed the teachings of Socrates, the Pythagoreans, Parmenides, and Heraclitus (qq.v.). To explain being, he developed the theory of the existence of immaterial forms of objects, which he called "forms" or "ideas" and identified them with being. To these "ideas" P. counterposed non-being identified with matter and space. According to P., the sensible world, which is the product of "ideas" and "matter", occupies an intermediate position. "Ideas" are eternal: they neither arise nor perish, they are irrelative and do not depend upon time and space. Sensible objects are transient, relative, and they depend upon time and space. Authentic knowledge is possible only of truly existent "forms". The source of such knowledge is the immortal human soul's reminiscence of the world of ideas, contemplated before its incarnation in the mortal body. We cannot have knowledge of sensible things and phenomena, but only a probable "opinion". Between "ideas" and sensible things P. placed the mathematical objects accessible to rational knowledge. The method of cognition is "dialectics", which P. understood as a two-way process: ascending by degrees of generalising concepts up to the highest kinds and descending again from the most general concepts to those of lesser and lesser generalisation. In this process the descent involves only "forms" ("ideas"), and not the sensible individual things. In politics, P. was a representative of the Athenian aristocracy. His teaching on society portrayed an ideal aristocratic state, the basis of which is slave labour *(Laws)*; the state is governed by "philosophers"; it is protected by soldiers; below these free citizens are the "handicraftsmen". P.'s teaching played a prominent role in the further evolution of idealist philosophy. To this day it is employed by the opponents of the materialist world outlook.

Plekhanov, Georgi Valentinovich (1856-1918), Russian revolutionary and thinker, founder of the Social Democratic movement in Russia, an eminent Marxist theoretician and publicist. P.'s world outlook and political activity underwent a complicated evolution. Initially P. was the leader of the Narodnik organisation Land and Freedom (later, General Redistribution); later (in 1880), having emigrated from Russia, he studied the works of Marx and Engels and established connections with the Social Democratic movement in Western Europe. As a result of this he broke off with Narodism (q.v.) and became a convinced adherent of Marxism, an active propagandist of its ideas in Russia; the Emancipation of Labour group which he founded in Switzerland (1883) played a great role in the dissemination and victory of Marxism in the Russian emancipation movement. P. himself greatly contributed to the development of the Marxist theory, combatting the ideology of Narodism, "legal Marxism", revisionism (qq.v.) and bourgeois philosophy. After 1903, P. became a Menshevik, although he adopted a correct, Marxist stand on certain issues. During the First World War P. sided with the social-chauvinists. He did not accept the October Revolution of 1917, but to the end of his life P. remained loyal to Marxism, to the cause of the working class. P.'s philosophical and sociological works were highly appreciated by Engels and Lenin. His works *The Development of the Monist View of History* (q.v.) 1895; *Essays on the History of Materialism*, 1896; *The Role of the Individual in History*, 1898, and many others brilliantly expounded the Marxist theory. P. assessed Marxism as a new stage in philosophy, showed its qualitative distinctions from all previous philosophical and sociological doctrines. P. developed the materialist understanding of history, showing what intricate relations exist between social being and social consciousness; he emphasised the role of social psychology in the struggle of ideas, which is the expression of the struggle between the antagonistic classes in a given society. P. was one of the founders of Marxist aesthetics and art criticism; he developed the Marxist teaching on the origin of art, regarding it as a specific form of reflection of social life and realism as the most fruitful method of artistic assimilation of reality that fully corresponds to the nature of art. P. laid the foundation of the Marxist history of Russian social thought. He disclosed the historic role of the Russian revolutionary democrats as the forerunners of Marxism in Russia. P. drew many valuable conclusions on the origin and development of religion, on the role of religion in social life, on its place among the other forms of social consciousness, on the attitude of a Marxist party towards religion. Dealing with philosophical problems, P. committed a number of errors: he underestimated the role of the subjective factor in historical development, made concessions to the theory of hieroglyphs (q.v.), etc. But these individual errors seem extraneous against the background of P.'s system of philosophical views as a whole and his lifelong defence of dialectical and historical materialism. P.'s philosophical works are rich and convincing, and the popularity and the captivating interest of their exposition make them even today valuable aids for the study of Marxist philosophy.

Plotinus (205-270), Greek idealist philosopher, who was born in Egypt and lived in Rome. P. was the founder of Neoplatonism (q.v.), which intensified the mysticism of Plato's (q.v.) teaching. According to P., the world process begins with the incomprehensible divine One, which is the eternal source of all being and emerges first as universal reason, then as the world-soul, and later as individual souls, as individual bodies, including matter, which P. considered as non-being. For P., the object of human life is to ascend to the One. This can be achieved by restraining the bodily attractions as well as by developing spiritual forces, including those of cognition. At its supreme stage of ascent the soul achieves the communion with God. P.'s teaching displays mystical dialectics: the principle of opposites and their unity determines harmony and beauty, evil and ugliness in the world. His main work: *Enneads*.

Pluralism, the conception opposed to monism (q.v.), which holds that all that exists consists of a multiplicity of equivalent isolated substances, irreducible to a single principle. P. was the basis of Leibniz's (q.v.) monadology. Modern idealists (pragmatists, neo-positivists, existentialists, and others) gravitate towards P. in their attempt to be above materialist and idealist monism. In sociology, P. serves as the basis for denying the existence of a single determining principle of society, for understanding history as a current of accidental events, and, consequently, for refusing to analyse the objective laws of social development. P. is employed to discredit the monistic foundation of Marxist-Leninist philosophy and the political system of socialism, and to justify bourgeois democracy.

Poincaré, Jules Henri (1854-1912), French mathematician, member of the French Academy of Sciences. His main works are devoted to mathematical physics, differential equations, celestial mechanics, etc. In 1905, simultaneously with Einstein (q.v.), P. arrived at the special theory of relativity (q.v.). He contributed greatly to the development of mathematics where, alongside discovering quantitative correlations, he established certain facts of a qualitative nature. P. maintained that the laws of science do not relate to the real world, but that they represent arbitrary conventions destined to promote a more convenient and useful description of corresponding phenomena (see Conventionalism).

Politics, activity linked with relations between classes, nations and other social groups, centred on the seizure, retention and use of state power. The relations between classes, and hence their policy, which expresses their fundamental interests, arise from their economic position. Political ideas and the institutions corresponding to them constitute the superstructure on the economic basis. This does not mean, however, that P. is the passive result of economics (see Economics and Politics). For P. to be a great transforming force it must correctly reflect the needs of the material life of society. The politics of the reactionary bourgeoisie hinders the progressive development of society, because it runs counter to its objective needs. The strength of the policies of the CPSU, the Communist and Workers' parties of other socialist states lies in the fact that they take into account these needs. The scientifically grounded P. is based on the knowledge of the laws of social development and directed to suit the interests of society. These policies answer the essential needs of the people, find permanent support among the working masses. According to the spheres of social life P. is subdivided into economic, social, national, agrarian, etc. Culture and ideology develop under the guidance and influence of the Communist Party's policy. Successful guidance of the building of communism in the USSR is secured due to the integration of correct P. with the corresponding organisational and ideological work. The internal policy of the Communist Party determines its foreign policy, whose object is to ensure peaceful conditions for building communism in the USSR, strengthen the world socialist community, support the national liberation struggle and resolutely oppose the imperialist policy of war and aggression.

Polysyllogism, a complex syllogism (see Syllogistic), which is a sequence, chain of syllogisms, in which the conclusions of preceding syllogisms (called prosyllogisms) are included in the premises of consequent ones (called episyllogisms). Formal logic lays down certain general conditions for the correctness of various kinds of P.

Polytheism and Monotheism, the worship of many gods or of one god. P. arose from totemism, fetishism, animism (qq.v.) in the period of the decay of the primitive community (q.v.). Belief in the plurality of equal fetishes and spirits was replaced by belief in gods who assumed concrete appearance, name, and cult. Social division of labour, earthly relations of supremacy and submission found a remote reflection in the hierarchy of gods. The consolidation of the slave-owning system, the creation of monarchies led initially to the worship of one God, with recognition of the existence of other gods. Then from the pantheon of gods one Almighty God was singled out—a copy of the earthly king; M. was thus established. Pure M., however, does not exist. Signs of P. are discernible even in such monotheistic religions as Islam and Judaism (qq.v.), to say nothing of Christianity (q.v.), with its Trinity, the Virgin, and a great number of saints.

Pomponazzi, Pietro (1462-1524), Italian philosopher of the Renaissance (q.v.). He developed Aristotle's (q.v.) view in a materialist and anti-scholastic spirit. In his main work *De Immortalitate Animi* (1516) P. stressed the elements of sensationalism (q.v.) in Aristotle's philosophy, and claimed that the soul, constituting the form of the body, is, nevertheless, mortal. This gave rise to indignation on the part of the clergy, and P.'s book was burned. Rejecting one of the main dogmas of religion, the immortality of the human soul, this theoretician of humanism stressed the fact that only refusal to believe this dogma corresponds to the real nature of man, because the object of his activity is found not in a life beyond, but here, in this earthly world. Adhering similarly to the conception of twofold truth (q.v.), P. aspired for the complete separation of philosophy and politics from religion.

Popovsky, Nikolai Nikitich (1730-1760), Russian enlightener, philosopher, and poet of the commoner background, disciple of Lomonosov (q.v.). He was professor of elocution and philosophy at Moscow University (since 1755), and founder of the newspaper *Moskovskiye Vedomosti* (Moscow Gazette), 1756. In philosophy P. took the standpoint of deism (q.v.), although his views could be assessed generally as

materialist. He translated into Russian some works by Locke (q.v.) and a number of works of Quintus Horace, Titus Livy, and others. He was the first in the University to lecture on philosophy in Russian, proving that philosophy must be independent of theology and is destined to satisfy the inquisitiveness of the human mind concerning nature and the structure of the worlds in the Universe. P. advocated enlightenment and the development of the sciences, reasonable legislation and good government, and wider civil rights. Shortly before he died, P. burnt all his manuscripts, regarding them not perfect enough to be left to the descendants.

Popper, Karl Raimund (b. 1902). Austrian philosopher, logician and sociologist. P. opposed his conception of critical rationalism (q.v.) to logical positivism (q.v.), despite the fact that he was influenced by the latter. He substituted the principle of falsification (q.v.) for the principle of verification (see Verification, Principle of), and the principles of organic connection between the theoretical and empirical levels of knowledge for narrow empiricism and inductivism propounded by logical positivists. P. maintains that all scientific knowledge is of a hypothetical character and is subject to errors. However, his conception of the growth of scientific knowledge encountered considerable difficulties which stemmed from P.'s making an absolute of the principle of falsification, from his denial of the objective truth of scientific knowledge, from relativism (q.v.) in interpreting its growth and conventionalism (q.v.) in treating the fundamentals of knowledge. In social philosophy P. criticised Marxism and historism, rejected the existence of objective laws of social development and upheld bourgeois reformism. His main works: *Logik der Forschung* (1935), *The Open Society and Its Enemies* (1945), *The Poverty of Historicism* (1957), *Conjectures and Refutations* (1963), *Objective Knowledge* (1972).

Population, the whole number of people living within distinct social communities: mankind as a whole, a group of countries, single countries, various regional subdivisions of these countries, and individual settlements. P. is viewed in philosophico-sociological terms as the subject and at the same time the object of social production. In political economy P. is the source of labour power and the subject of consumption; in demography (q.v.)—all human generations distinguished by their size, age and sex; in demogeography—the same generations in terms of their settlement and migration within a given territory. Population development is the main problem considered by all these sciences. The discrepancy between the needs of the national economy in manpower and the size of population and the imbalance between the population's needs in goods and services and the possibilities to meet these needs are the cause of contradictions in the development of P. as an economic category and a source of social problems. P. has its own specific laws that correspond to each mode of production (q.v.). For instance, the capitalist society is characterised by a relative overpopulation, which is the result of the existence of the army of unemployed (reserve working population). The socialist law of population consists in the systematic maintenance of full employment and rational use of manpower resources. In socialist society the policy of P. is aimed at using economic achievements to ensure that the work done by each member of the society should gradually become more interesting, creative, and all-round.

Poretsky, Platon Sergeyevich (1846-1907), Russian logician. He was the first in Russia to lecture on mathematical logic, q.v. (at Kazan University in 1887-88). P. contributed to the elaboration of the algebra of logic (q.v.). For this theory he found original and simple methods of solving the problem of finding a set of consequences following from a given system of premises and a set of hypotheses, from which these consequences are deducible. P.'s philosophical views can be described as natural-scientific materialism. His main work: *O sposobach resheniya logicheskikh ravenstv i ob obratnom sposobe matematicheskoi logiki* (On the Methods of Solving Logical Equations and the Inverse Method in Mathematical Logic), 1884.

Positivism, a trend in bourgeois philosophy which declares natural (empirical) sciences to be the sole source of true knowledge and rejects the cognitive value of philosophical study. P. emerged in response to the inability of speculative philosophy, q.v. (e.g., classical German idealism) to solve philosophical problems which had arisen as a result of scientific development. Positivists went to an opposite extreme and rejected theoretical speculation as a means of obtaining knowledge. P. declared false and senseless all problems, concepts and propositions of traditional philosophy on being, substances, causes, etc., that could not be solved or verified by experience due to a high degree of abstract nature. P. claims to be a fundamentally new, non-metaphysical ("positive") philosophy, modelled on empirical sciences and providing them with a methodology. P. is essentially empiricism (q.v.), brought to extreme logical conclusions in certain respects: inasmuch as any knowledge is empirical knowledge in one form or another, no speculation can be knowledge. P. has not escaped the lot of traditional philosophy, since its own propositions (rejection of speculation, phenomenalism, q.v., etc.) turned to be unverifiable by experience and, consequently, metaphysical. P. was founded by Comte (q.v.), who introduced the term of P. Historically, there are three stages in the development of P. The exponents of the first P. were Comte, E. Littré, and P. Laffitte (France), J. S. Mill and Spencer, qq.v. (England). Alongside the problems of the theory of knowledge (Comte) and logic (Mill), the main place in the first P. was assigned to sociology (see Comte's idea of transforming society on the basis of science, organic theory of society, q.v., by Spencer). The rise of the second stage in P.—empirio-criticism (q.v.)—dates back to the 1870s-1890s and is associated with Mach and Avenarius (qq.v.), who renounced even formal recognition of the objective real objects, which was a feature of early P. In Machism the problems of cognition were interpreted from the viewpoint of extreme psychologism, which was merging with subjectivism. The rise and formation of the latest P., or neo-positivism (q.v.) is linked up with the activity of the Vienna Circle, q.v. (O. Neurath, Carnap, Schlick, Frank, qq.v., and others) and of the Berlin Society for Scientific Philosophy (Reichenbach, q.v., and others), which combined a number of trends: logical atomism, logical positivism, semantics, qq.v. (close to these trends are operationalism and pragmatism, qq.v.). The main place in the third P. is taken by the philosophical problems of language, symbolic logic, the structure of scientific investigations, and others. Having renounced psychologism, the exponents of the third P. took the course of reconciling the logic of science with mathematics, the course of formalisation of epistemological problems.

Possibility and Reality, categories reflecting the development of the material world. P. expresses the objective tendency of development inherent in existing phenomena, the presence of the conditions requisite for their appearance or at least the absence of conditions that would impede their coming into being. R. denotes anything objective (object, condition, situation) which actually exists as a result of the realisation of a P. The conversion of P. into R. is based on the causal nexus of phenomena of the objective world. We distinguish real and abstract P. Abstract (or formal) P. expresses the absence of any conditions that would give rise to some phenomenon and at the same time the absence of any conditions that would obstruct it. It may also denote a poorly pronounced tendency in the phenomenon's development. Real P. means the presence of certain necessary conditions under which P. will turn into R. In certain circumstances abstract P. may become real P., and vice versa. The qualitative relationship between them may be expressed by the degree of probability of the phenomenon's appearance (see Probability, Theory of). Allowance for real Pp., steps to turn some of them into R., and removal of the danger of realisation and even appearance of undesirable Pp. constitute an important task of human activity. Such activity is promoted by theoretical analysis of P., particularly of its relation to necessity and chance (q.v.). P. becomes R. only when all the condi-

tions for the existence of a certain phenomenon either arise or are provided. The more there are of these conditions to hand and the more essential they are, the more real the P. becomes. Thus, the P. of an economic crisis under commodity production is already implicit in the acts of commodity exchange. But the conversion of this P. into R. requires a whole set of conditions and relations that does not exist within the framework of simple commodity production. These arise in developed capitalist society, and then crises and recessions in production become inevitable. By combining certain materials and forces of nature, man is able to bring into being such phenomena he desires (by providing a full set of conditions required for their appearance) and to remove phenomena he does not desire (by abolishing their cause). Such activity is limited by the objective laws of the world and develops in accordance with these laws. The same is true of social life. For example, the building of communist society is impossible unless people work consciously for it under the leadership of a Communist party, and this activity must comply with the objective laws of social development.

"Post-Industrial Society", Theory of, a conception of modern bourgeois futurology (q.v.) based on the principles of industrialism, according to which the development of every society is determined by the level of industrial development expressed in terms of gross national product (GNP). Accordingly, the low GNP typical of the most Asian, African and Latin American countries, regardless of their social system, means that they are at the stage of "pre-industrial society". The high level of GNP characteristic of the European and North American countries, signifies the various stages of "industrial society", while the still higher level expected at the close of the 20th-the beginning of the 21st centuries, will mark the advent of "post-industrial" society, qualitatively differing from the existing ones. Some bourgeois ideologists claim that the USA and other economically advanced capitalist countries are entering "post-industrial society". The architects of "post-industrial society" say that its characteristic feature is the predominant share of those engaged in the services industry and in spiritual production—up to 9/10 and more of all the gainfully employed population, and the decrease in the numbers of those engaged in industrial production—up to 1/10 and less, and in agricultural production—up to 1/100. Approximately the same ratio applies to workers of high, middle and low skills and levels of education. Another important feature of "post-industrial society" is the considerable reduction of working time in the year, zero population growth thanks to effective birth control and reorientation of the economy and culture on improving the quality of life, i.e., satisfying chiefly cultural requirements. The ideologists of P.S. W. Rostow, J. Galbraith, Bell, q.v., H. Kahn, R. Aron and others) oppose their conception to the theory of scientific communism (q.v.); they ignore the laws governing the development of society, the trends of development of the general crisis of capitalism, on the one hand, and the trends of socialist and communist construction in the countries of the world socialist system, on the other hand. During the crisis of bourgeois futurology that showed itself in the 1970s, the T.P.S. was sharply criticised by some bourgeois ideologists themselves who pointed out to its obvious discrepancy with the tendencies and prospects of mankind's development. The problems raised by the T.P.S., are solved by the theory of scientific communism.

Postulate, a principle or statement in a scientific theory, which is taken as the initial proposition, incapable of proof within the framework of that theory. In modern logic and the methodology of science the concept of P. is usually used as a synonym of the more widely used term of axiom (q.v.). Sometimes the difference in the meanings of these concepts derived from ancient philosophy is preserved: axioms signify the initial logical principles of a theory, and Pp.—initial special scientific propositions in this theory. In some cases Pp. denote axioms and rules for inferring a certain theory.

***The Poverty of Philosophy. Answer to the "Philosophy of Poverty"* by**
M. Proudhon, an early work by Marx, in which he set forth the fundamentals of scientific socialism. It was written in French in 1847 and was directed against the ideas of the anarchist Proudhon (q.v.), French petty-bourgeois philosopher and economist. Marx opposed Proudhon's "dialectical" verbiage by demonstrating that the latter had not exceeded the limits of bourgeois outlook. Marx gave much thought to criticising Hegel's dialectics and to working out the materialist dialectics (q.v.). *The P.P.* gave a scientific analysis of the capitalist mode of production and laid the foundations of Marxist political economy.

Power, one of the main functions of social organisation, an authoritative force having the real possibility to govern human activity by co-ordinating contradictory individual or group interests, to subordinate them to a single will either by persuasion or by coercion. The primitive-communal system had no special organ of P., its functions being discharged by all adult members of the tribe. In a society composed of antagonistic classes P. expresses the interests of the ruling class, is taken away from society and placed above it (see the State). In the period of transition from capitalism to socialism P. becomes an instrument for suppressing the exploiter classes and building social relations of a new type. In communist society P. will undergo a radical change, inasmuch as individual strivings will be co-ordinated on the basis of a voluntary recognition of the advantages of complying with necessity, which is identical for the whole of society (see Communist Public Self-Government).

Pragmatics, a branch of Semiotic.

Pragmatism, a widespread subjective idealist trend in modern bourgeois philosophy. The so-called principle of pragmatism is the core of pragmatic philosophy and determines the value of knowledge by its practical utility (see Peirce). By practical utility P. understands not confirmation of objective truth by the criterion of practice, but what meets the subjective interests of the individual. This explanation reflects the strictly practical approach of the American bourgeois. In explaining reality P. adopts the standpoint of "radical empiricism", which is closely related to empirio-criticism (q.v.). Objective reality is identified in P. with "experience", and the division of cognition into a subject and object is made only within experience. In logic P. comes to irrationalism (q.v.): in open form in James' (q.v.) works, and in disguised form in Dewey's (q.v.). P. regards the laws and forms of logic as useful fictions. In ethics P. subscribes to meliorism, that is the view about the gradual improvement of the existing order, while in sociology it varies from the cult of "outstanding individuals" (James) and apology for bourgeois democracy (Dewey) to an outright defence of racism and fascism, qq.v. (F.C.S. Schiller). At the present time P. appears in the form of "experimental naturalism", combining subjective idealism with anti-Marxism and anti-communism (S. Hook), or in the form of neo-pragmatism, combining P. with neo-positivism (q.v.), and semantic idealism. For a long time P. dominated the spiritual life of the USA, only recently has it given way to neo-positivism and religious philosophical conceptions.

Praxeology, a branch of sociology that studies methods of considering various actions or aggregates of actions from the standpoint of their effectiveness. P. is one of the methods of modern sociological investigations. The essence of this method consists of practical (and historical) investigation, description of various habits and methods of work, identification of their integral elements, and hence elaboration of various practical recommendations. P. studies the history of these categories, and undertakes concrete investigations of the work of collective bodies, analyses of forms of labour organisation, its specialisation, the subjective (less frequently objective) factors changing the organisation and degree of efficacy of labour. P. studies the interaction between individuals, and between the individual and the collective, in the process of production.

Predestination, Theory of, the teaching according to which everything in the world, including human life and be-

haviour, is predetermined by the will of God (see Providentialism; Fatalism). St. Augustine, Luther, Calvin (qq.v.) and other advocates of the T.P. used notions of man's "condemnation" or "salvation" to justify the moral principles established by the ruling classes of society. The dialectical nature of social development and the correlation of freedom and necessity (q.v.) in it bear out the untenability of the T.P.

Predicables, types of predicates in Aristotle's (q.v.) logic. Aristotle counted four P.: genus, species, property, and accident. P. are opposed to individual names, because the latter, as distinguished from P., cannot be used as predicates.

Predicate, in traditional logic one of the two elements of any proposition, which states something about the subject of the proposition. Until the end of the 19th century, the subject in logic, as a rule, was identified with the grammatical subject of the sentence, while P. with the nominal part of the compound predicate, expressed by, say, an adjective. Thus, the form of the predicate (predicative bond) was reduced to attributive connection only, signifying that object (subject) had a definite property. The development of mathematical logic (q.v.) led to a revision of this point of view. According to the contemporary conception of the logical structure of proposition, the traditional concepts of the P. and the subject are replaced by the exact mathematical concepts of function and its arguments, respectively. In keeping with this, Pp. are defined on the basis of sets (object-fields) whose elements are either arguments or meanings of corresponding variables. The new interpretation of P. makes, of necessity, the logical discourse more general, and this unites syllogistic and non-syllogistic inferences (q.v.), while the functional form of recording opens up broad opportunities for formalising (q.v.) statements of any scientific theory (see Function; Predicate Calculus).

Predicate Calculus, an extension of propositional calculus (q.v.) by formalising conclusions based on the inner structure of propositions. The P.C. formula is extended by introducing the concept of predicate (q.v.) from one or several variables of the object.

Pre-established Harmony, recognition of divinely ordained harmonic cause-effect nexuses, of universal concord between the material and spiritual spheres. The teaching of P.H. represents an attempt to overcome the dualism of spiritual and material substances. Hints of P.H. are to be found in Descartes' (q.v.) teaching, but it is explicit in the works of the occasionalists, viz., Malebranche (qq.v.). The concept of P.H. was somewhat revised by Leibniz (q.v.), who professed the P.H. of all monads in the Universe. According to Leibniz, the world and each one of the creatures inhabiting it develops by its own abilities, but these abilities are created and chosen by God in such a way as to predetermine the best possible order in the world. In his conception of eternal expedience of everything that exists, Wolff (q.v.) carried some aspects of Leibniz's teaching of P.H. to the point of absurdity.

Premises (in logic), propositions from which a new proposition, or inference (q.v.) is drawn. According to the kind of inference, the P. may be a great variety of propositions or their combinations. For the conclusion to be true the P. must be true and correctly (according to the laws of logic) combined in reasoning.

Pre-Socratics, name for the earliest Greek philosophers (7th to beginning of 4th century B.C.). The term is conventional because many of the notable P. made their contribution to philosophy after Socrates (q.v.). It is not conventional in the sense that the P. did not pose the problem of the purpose and designation of the individual, of the relation of thought to being, and confined themselves to the study of nature, the Universe, and objective reality as it was apparent to the senses. These problems were all treated from the standpoint of a sensual Universe consisting of a perpetual cycle of elements. To P. belong: Thales, Anaximander, Anaximenes, Heraclitus (qq.v.), Diogenes of Apollonia (5th to 4th centuries B.C.), Xenophanes (q.v.),

Pythagoras, Parmenides (q.v.) and his Eleatic pupils, Empedocles, Anaxagoras, Leucippus, and Democritus (qq.v.). The main object of study of pre-Socratic philosophy—the Universe—was believed to consist of the usual sensual elements—earth, water, air, fire, and ether, which constantly interchange by means of densification and rarefaction. The dialectic of the elements is a characteristic feature of the natural philosophy of the P., particularly Democritus and Heraclitus. These elements are sensual and imbued with an organising but purely material principle (logos in Heraclitus, love and enmity in Empedocles, the eternally moving atoms in the atomists, etc.). The classics of Marxism-Leninism gave a high appraisal of the spontaneous materialism of the P., which emerged from the attempts to refute mythology.

Priestley, Joseph (1733-1804), English scientist and materialist philosopher. He continued the traditions of F. Bacon and Hobbes (qq.v.). In P.'s opinion, all matter possesses the properties of extent, density and impenetrability, its characteristics being determined by the action of the forces of attraction and repulsion. Man's thought and sensations are the product of the complex organisation of matter. P. rejected Locke's (q.v.) dualism from the position of mechanism (q.v.). He demanded that experiments should be combined with theory and paid great attention to the problems of hypothesis and analogy. In sociology P. advocated the principle of determinism (q.v.), but opposed fatalism (q.v.); he criticised the atheism of French materialists from the standpoint of deism (q.v.). P. was an adherent of the ethics of eudaemonism. In his opinion, the greatest individual happiness is compatible with the happiness of other men.

Primary and Secondary Qualities, the terms used to distinguish the qualities (properties) of things according to their objectivity. The terms were introduced by Locke (q.v.), although this distinction was made earlier by Democritus, Galileo Galilei, Descartes, Hobbes (qq.v.). By primary, or objective, properties Locke meant motion, impenetrability, solidity, cohesion of particles, shape, volume, etc.

Secondary, or subjective, qualities were colour, smell, taste, sound. Thus, all properties that could not be explained by means of mechanics were declared by Locke to be secondary, definable only by the subject's organisation and state. Turning to account the inconsistencies of metaphysical materialism, the subjective idealists Berkeley, Hume (qq.v.), and others classed primary properties as subjective. Dialectical materialism denies the division of the properties of things into objective and subjective. At the same time, it draws a distinction between inherent properties of the thing that are a result (effect) of its internal interactions and external (potential) properties. The latter are realised only when the given thing enters into interaction with other things (e.g., salt dissolves in water).

Primitive-Communal System, the first (archaic) socio-economic formation characterised by the interaction of communal and kindred relations between people. The primitive man lived within the community (family, clan, village), which consisted of families, or cells reproducing people themselves. These families were centres of economic, religious and other activity, more or less dependent on the community. Since marriage was exogamous, the community included relatives in blood who made up its core and people from other communities. In terms of time, the P.C.S. covered the period from the origination of social relations to the appearance of a class society (6-5 millennia B.C.). In a broader sense, the P.C.S. began at the phase of the primitive horde, continued during the most structural development of the clan, and ended at a stage when the clan system disintegrated and the embryonic class differentiation emerged. The primitive-communal relations attained the peak of structural development in the period of clan system. Here production relations were based on common (collective) ownership of the means of production (instruments of labour, land, dwellings, agricultural implements, etc.). This property existed side by side with personal property in weapons, household articles, clothing, etc. As instruments of labour, forms of economy, the family, matrimonial and other relations developed further, the

new social relations that arose on this basis ousted the primitive relations which existed at the initial stages of mankind's technical development, collective ownership, and religious and magic beliefs.

Principal Co-ordination, a subjective idealist theory developed by Avenarius (q.v.) and his disciples (R. Willy, J. Petzoldt, and others). According to this theory, there is P.C. (inseparable link) between the "ego" and the environment. The objective world cannot exist without an "ego" which perceives it. This theory is incompatible with science, which considers man as the product of a long evolution of matter, and nature as existing before man and independently of him. Echoing Berkeley and Fichte (q.v.), the theory of P.C. leads to solipsism (q.v.). The criticism of P.C. is given in Lenin's *Materialism and Empirio-Criticism* (q.v.).

Principle, the principal element, the guiding idea, the basic rule of behaviour. In early ancient philosophy water, air, fire, earth, etc., were taken as the prime elements. The P. was considered as the expression of necessity or the law of phenomena. Logically, the P. is the central concept, the basis of a system, and the generalisation and extension of some proposition to all the phenomena in the field from which the P. is abstracted. The P. of activity (i.e., maxim), for example, means the ethical standard characterising the relations between people in society.

Probability, Theory of, the study of mass-scale random events, i.e., of random events that are equivalent to each other in some definite properties or may occur repeatedly under certain circumstances. Abstraction of m.s.r.e. can be applied to a wide range of natural and social phenomena, with importance attached not to individual, but to the most general properties which permit them to be regarded as equivalent to each other. Thus, it is the distribution of molecules according to speed, and not their individual "behaviour", that is important for a system's thermodynamic characteristics, say its temperature; the ratio of male to female birth is important for many biological species' characteristics, etc. The T.P. studies the properties of m.s.r.e. by building their mathematical models and then operating with them as with purely mathematical objects. The probability of m.s.r.e. is the principal property dealt with by the T.P. and it must be adequately describable by a constant number. This is the case, for example, when it is possible, first, to count the number of experiments n resulting in m.s.r.e. of the type studied (such experiments are described as random, e.g. the tossing of a coin), and, second, the number of experiments m resulting in m.s.r.e. of the desired type (e.g., coin landing heads). Then the relative frequencies of m.s.r.e., which may be regarded as the result of probability calculation, are grouped around this numerical characteristic. Thus it is possible to express numerically the probability of m.s.r.e., to describe in mathematical terms their most important property, the Large Numbers Law, according to which the compound action of a great number of random events leads to results quite independent of chance. J. Bernoulli was the first to do this (true, for a narrow class of m.s.r.e.), and later on many scientists considerably extended this class by their research. The T.P. makes it possible to discover objective laws in random phenomena of a statistical nature. The investigation of probabilistic events gives a fuller insight into the concept of regularity and also into the problem of the relations between necessity and chance (q.v.). The probability of any event is its objective property, not a result of our observations, as holders of the subjective views in the T.P. maintain. Probability is not a property exclusively of m.s.r.e. Other probabilities are studied, e.g. in probabilistic logic (q.v.). An extremely important role in the development of the T.P. has been played by the Soviet mathematicians S. N. Bernstein A. N. Kolmogorov, A. Y. Khinchin, and others.

Process, a regular, successive changing of a phenomenon, its transition into another phenomenon (see Development).

Proclus (410-485), founder of the school of Neoplatonism (q.v.) in Athens.

P. was the initiator of the dialectical notion of triadicism (see Triad). Because of his effort to fit the contents of ancient mythology in a single philosophical system, P. is characterised in historico-philosophical literature as a systematiser of heathenism. Proceeding from the idea of Plato (q.v.) that the singular is revealed in plurality, and that the latter strives to secure unity, P. recognised three stages in the development of all that exists: sojourn, aspiration forward, the reverse aspiration. His main works: *The Elements of Theology, Platonic Theology.*

Production, the process of man's active transformation of nature to create the necessary material conditions for his existence. In contrast to animals which satisfy their needs by what the nature provides, man produces everything he needs to live on—food, clothes, housing, etc. P., therefore, is the eternal natural condition of human life, the basis of human history. Three elements are necessary for every process of P.: the object of labour, the means of labour and the purposeful activity of man, his labour (q.v.). P. has always a social character and two sides to it: the relation of man to nature, expressed in the concept "productive forces", q.v. (reflecting the content of the process of P.) and the relations between men, expressed in the concept "relations of production", q.v. (reflecting the social form of the process of P.). The relationship between these two sides is determined by the law that production relations should correspond to the character and development level of productive forces (q.v.). P. always exists as a historically established mode of production (q.v.): as primitive-communal, slave-owning, feudal, capitalist and communist. P. in general is an abstraction which makes it possible to identify and describe certain elements common to every mode of production. P. is inseparably linked with distribution, exchange and consumption. P. and consumption are two diametrically opposed and, at the same time, closely interconnected poles in social life. The determinative factor in their relationship is P., which not only creates the object to be consumed and conditions the mode of consumption but is the basis on which human requirements (q.v.) arise and develop. In the process of P. people not only act upon and transform external nature but, at the same time, change their own nature, abilities, knowledge, needs and interests. P. is linked to consumption via the distribution of the products created, which depends on the character of production relations predominant in a given society. In the antagonistic class societies the owners of the means of production—slave-owners, landlords and capitalists—appropriate the surplus product and often part of the necessary product, while the working masses (slaves, serfs and proletarians), due to their complete or partial disposession of the means of production, receive the minimal share of the wealth they themselves produced. Socialist revolution does away with this injustice and establishes social ownership of the means of production. With the abolition of the exploiter classes P. is geared to satisfy the growing requirements of all the members of society. Under socialism the distribution of consumer goods is based on the quantity and quality of one's work, done for the benefit of society by its members. Under communism everything will be distributed according to one's needs.

Productive Forces, a category of historical materialism, characterising the main, determining factor of the historical process. "Just as material causes underlie all natural phenomena, so the development of human society is conditioned by the development of material forces, the productive forces" (V. I. Lenin, *Collected Works*, Vol. 2, p. 21). The development of the material and technical base of society (q.v.) and, in this connection, of the P.F. underlies the entire social development and the continuity of the historical process as a whole. The content of the category P.F. is the organic unity of the accumulated and living labour, i.e., the totality of material and personal elements of production necessary for the production of things to satisfy human requirements from the objects of nature. The material elements of production include implements of labour, production premises, railways, canals, highways, pipe-lines, etc., in other words all objects

and sets of objects which man uses as vehicles of his action on the object of labour. Personal elements include people who produce means of labour and set them in motion, having the necessary skills, experience and knowledge. The implements of labour, machines and sets of equipment are the determining material element of the P.F., by which the level of production is gauged. But even the most advanced technology is useless without men, for people are the basic P.F. Implements of labour, all means of labour are created by man and are the material result of his endeavour, of his accumulated experience and knowledge, an indicator of his success in harnessing nature. In improving means of labour, which he uses to transform nature, and thus in developing his P.F. and social relations, man simultaneously develops himself. The operation of the P.F. presupposes, first of all, the creation of means of labour and their subsequent use for producing consumer goods. Every social production includes the production of the means of production (group A) and the production of consumer goods (group B). The law of extended reproduction signifies the priority development of the group A, the creation of increasingly efficient means of labour based on the use of scientific advances and the re-equipment on this basis of all branches of the economy. Today, the utilisation of advances made by the scientific and technological revolution (q.v.) to develop the P.F. and total social production has become the sphere of the economic competition between socialism and capitalism. Socialism aims at accelerating scientific and technological progress in order steadily and systematically to create the material and technical base of communism. The comprehensive mechanisation and automation of entire social production, which constitute the foundation of communism, will help solve such social tasks as abolishing labour-intensive processes, making labour a prime vital requirement of people, increasing opportunities for an all-round development of the individual and creating an abundance of consumer goods as a condition for going over to the communist principle of distribution according to one's needs.

Prognostication, a variety of scientific prevision (q.v.), a special study of the prospects of a phenomenon. In the social sphere P. is a scientific foundation of social control, q.v. (target-setting, planning, programming, projecting, administrative decision-making). There are two types of P.: investigative and normative. The former is the projection to the future of tendencies under observation, assuming that they would not be subject to changes by managerial means. Its purpose is the identification of problems to be tackled in the future. The latter is concerned with determining the ways and means of solving problems in order to achieve the desired state of the object on the basis of pre-set criteria. The comparison of data obtained by both investigative and normative P. helps draw up recommendations to raise the efficiency of management. In a wider sense, P. can be subdivided into scientific-technical and socio-economic. Also, there is current, short-, medium- and long-term P. (in social sciences these types of P. embrace one year, 1-5, 5-10 and 10-15 years respectively). Another type of P. is superlong-term covering 15-20 years. The most widespread methods of P. include: extrapolation, interpolation, modelling (q.v.), experts' poll, historical analogy, forecast scenarios, matrices of interdependent factors of "input-output" kind, as well as methods based on drawing charts, "a problem tree", "a goal tree", use of patents, etc. In socialist countries, the theory of P. (prognostics as a science studying the laws of P.) is developed on the basis of Marxist-Leninist prevision and is opposed to bourgeois futurology (q.v.) as a theoretical foundation of P. under state-monopoly capitalism. P. is an organic part of the economic and social planning in the USSR and other socialist countries.

Progress and Retrogression in social development, opposite forms of social development as a whole or individual aspects of it, signifying respectively either the progressive development of society on an ascending line, its flourishing, or the reversion to the old, outlived forms, stagnation, and decay. The criterion of social P. is the degree of development of the productive forces (q.v.), of the

economic system, and the institutions of its superstructure determined by it, together with the development and dissemination of science and culture, the development of the individual, the degree of extension of social freedom. In individual historical periods essential significance for the description of social development from the point of view of P. or R. may, on the strength of their relative independence, attach to such social phenomena as political life, culture, education, etc., although they are secondary, derivative and determined by the economic system. The countries where a fascist dictatorial regime was established, or is established (see Fascism) may serve as examples of social R. determined by political factors. The development of antagonistic socioeconomic formations is extremely contradictory. Although in certain periods of history these formations serve as stages of P. they always possess the features of R., which become the dominant ones in the period of social decline. However, even in this period R. cannot be universal, inasmuch as the basic tendency in the development of mankind as a whole is not R. but P., which in the case in point is expressed in the emergence of the elements and prerequisites of a new society and in the development of certain aspects of social life. For example, the R. is observed in the development of bourgeois society in the imperialist era, but it is accompanied by P. in many branches of science and technology, as well as in a number of other social phenomena. However, to assess the vitality of a given society, its ability to show P. or R., it is important to determine the general tendency of its development, which aids the classes and social groups interested in social P. to cognise more deeply and apply the laws of social development. The concepts of P.&R. are interpreted differently in philosophy and sociology. The scientists in the period of the progressive development of capitalism (Vico, Diderot, Hegel, qq.v., and others) recognised P. and tried to find its rational foundation. Scientists in the period of the decline of capitalism, which began since the second half of the 19th century, have taken different approaches to history: a positivist approach that was founded by Comte (q.v.), a "historico-cultural" one introduced by the Russian Slavophil scientist N. Ya. Danilevsky and advocated by Spengler, Toynbee (qq.v.), and others, and a cultural-critical approach (Nietzsche, q.v., and later S. Freud, Husserl, q.v., and others). The positivists maintain that history should be just an empirical description of scientifically established facts and attempts should not be made to study the essence of history as a whole and to understand the phenomena of P.&R. According to the historico-cultural conception, the investigation of individual cultures or civilisations is the most important way of studying P.&R. in history. Its proponents see human history as the replacement of independent "types" of cultures or civilisations possessing their own periods of P.&R. by others. The advocates of the cultural-critical approach deny the concept of P. from positions of "natural anti-culture", eternal "will to life", spontaneous, unconscious inclinations (Freud) or "universal structures of consciousness" (Husserl). Marxism-Leninism gives a scientific explanation of P.&R. P. as a forward movement without relapses into R. is possible only in a non-antagonistic, communist society.

Proof, process of reasoning designed to establish the truth (or falsity) of an assertion. The assertion to be proved is called the thesis. The inferences on which the proof is built, and from which the thesis logically follows, are called arguments (q.v.). Arguments are assumed to be true and must not involve premises which assume the thesis to be proved, otherwise the result is the error known as circular evidence (q.v.). A P. which establishes the truth of the thesis is called simply P.; one which establishes the falsity of the thesis is called a refutation. P. may be direct, i.e., it may consist of a series of deductions whose premises are arguments or propositions inferred from arguments, or it may be arrived at by means of additional assumptions. Pp. are subject to various errors due to *ignoratio elenchi*, acceptance of unfounded or erroneous arguments, or due to the employment of incorrect methods. A P. containing an error is invalid. But the detection of a fallacy in P. does not constitute P. of

the falsity of the thesis. It is possible to have Pp. that establish the truth of a thesis not as a certainty but as a probability (see Logic, Probabilistic).

Proof of the Existence of God, logical arguments seeking to prove the main dogma of religion—the existence of God (q.v.)—put forward by idealist philosophers. The three basic arguments are as follows. The cosmological argument (found already in Plato and Aristotle, qq.v., and maintained by Leibniz and Wolff, qq.v.) states that God exists as the prime cause of all things and all phenomena. This argument is based on the unscientific assumption that the world must be finite in time, and that its prime cause is non-material. The teleological argument (proposed by Socrates and Plato, qq.v., subsequently developed by the stoics, q.v.) states that everything in nature has a purpose, and this can be explained only by assuming the existence of a supernatural rational being, which puts all phenomena in order. This argument was disproved by Darwin's (q.v.) evolution theory (q.v.), which proved the natural causes of purposefulness. The ontological argument was advanced by St. Augustine (q.v.), who asserted that all men conceive of God as the perfect being. This conception, he argued, could not arise unless a perfect being existed in reality. Therefore God exists. In the Middle Ages this argument was taken up and defended by Anselm of Canterbury (q.v.). Its weakness in assuming that what is thought must be real and objective was so obvious that it was criticised not only by the materialist philosophers but by many theologians, e.g., Thomas Aquinas (q.v.). Other arguments for the existence of God, epistemological, psychological, and moral, are advanced by various idealist philosophers. Arguments for the existence of God were disproved within the framework of idealism by Kant (q.v.), who asserted that God is a being above experience (transcendental) and known only by reason, and therefore the existence of God cannot be proved. Analysis of the arguments for the existence of God reveals that they all contain a logical mistake (see Circular Evidence) and rest ultimately on blind faith (q.v.).

Propaedeutics, preliminary exercise, preparatory, introductory course in some science, expounded in a systematised and concise form. P. precedes the more detailed study of a corresponding branch of knowledge. An introductory course of philosophy is sometimes called philosophical P.

Property, an aspect of an object which determines its difference from, or similarity to, other objects and is manifested in the interaction with them (for example, extention, elasticity, colour, electric conductivity, etc.). Every P. is relative. In relation to wood, iron is hard, in relation to diamond it is soft. Each individual thing possesses countless Pp., the unity of which constitutes its quality (see Quality and Quantity). Pp. inherent in all objects or connected with the very nature of matter are called universal (see Attributes). There are specific and general Pp., basic and non-basic, necessary and accidental, essential and non-essential, external and internal, compatible and incompatible, separable and inseparable, natural and artificial, etc. Dialectical materialism asserts that all Pp. of things are inherent in the things themselves, i.e., are objective. A study of individual Pp. of objects is a stage in cognising their qualities.

Propositional Calculus, the logical system which formalises reasoning based on true relations between propositions which are regarded in abstraction from their internal subject-predicate structure. Classical P.C. is non-contradictory (see Axiomatic Theory, Non-Contradiction of) and complete (see Axiomatic Theory, Completeness of). For non-classical P.C., see Logic, Constructive; Logic, Many-Valued.

Protagoras (c. 480-c. 410 B.C.), Greek philosopher, a leading sophist (q.v.), lived in Abdera; he was expelled from Athens for his atheism, and his book *On the Gods* was burnt. Bourgeois researchers interpreted P. as an absolute sceptic, translating extant fragments of his work as follows: "Man is the measure of all things: of those which are, that they are; of those which are not, that they are not." But the Greek word corresponding to "that" may be translated differently: "existing, so long as they exist", etc. With this interpretation P. is not a subjectivist and sceptic; his thesis contains an element of anthropologism (q.v.) of a materialist shade.

Protestantism, the third kind of Christianity (q.v.), after Orthodoxy and Catholicism (qq.v.), arising in the period of the Reformation (q.v.). P. is the name of a number of various independent religions or churches differing in dogmas and canonical principles. Protestants do not recognise the Catholic purgatory, reject Orthodox and Catholic saints, angels, the Virgin, worshipping only the divine Trinity. The main distinction between P., on the one hand, and Catholicism and Orthodoxy, on the other, is that P. professes an immediate link between God and man. In the Protestant view, grace is communicated to man by God, without the intermediary of the church and "salvation" is achieved only by man's own faith and God's will. This doctrine undermined the primacy of spiritual power over secular power and the dominant role of the Catholic Church and the Pope of Rome, liberating man from feudal chains and arousing in his soul the sense of personal dignity, and bourgeois individualism. As a result of the different relations between God and man in P., not only the clergy and the church but also the religious cult are assigned a secondary place. There is no worship of icons or relics, the number of sacraments is reduced to two (Baptism and the Eucharist), divine service consists, as a rule, of sermons, congregational prayer, the singing of psalms. Formally, P. is based exclusively on the Bible, but in practice every Protestant religion has its own symbols of faith, authorities and "sacred" books. Contemporary P. is spread mainly in the Scandinavian countries, Germany, Switzerland, Great Britain, Canada, Australia, and the USA. In the 20th century, the oecumenic movement has gained considerably in P., resulting in the creation of the World Council of Churches. P. has ties with various political trends. Some clergymen try to adapt it to new conditions, bringing it closer to progressive political aspirations shown by a part of Protestants (e.g., in the drive for peace and detente).

Proudhon, Pierre Joseph (1809-1865), French petty-bourgeois politician, philosopher, sociologist, and economist, one of the founders of anarchism (q.v.). In philosophy P. was an idealist, eclectic; he vulgarised Hegelian dialectics, transforming it into a rough scheme, into a teaching of the mechanical combination of "good" and "bad" aspects in every phenomenon. P. considered the history of society as the struggle of ideas. While declaring big capitalist property as "stolen", he was perpetuating small property. He defended the utopian and reactionary idea of organisation under capitalism of a "just exchange" between individual commodity producers. The founders of Marxism sharply criticised P. and his adherents. His main works: *Qu'est-ce que la propriété?* (1840), *La Philosophie de la misère* (1846).

Providentialism, a religious-philosophical doctrine, according to which the entire development of human society (both its motive forces and aims) is governed by mysterious extra-historical forces—Providence or God (q.v.). This approach to history inevitably leads to fatalism (q.v.). P. is inherent not only in all religions, but also in many idealistic doctrines of history. Even Hegel (q.v.), although with reservations, recognised that providence, and divine providence at that, governs the world development. The ideas of P., which was the dominant ideological conception under feudalism, found the most graphic expression in the works of religious philosophers and historians (e.g., St. Augustine, Thomas Aquinas and Slavophiles, qq.v.). In contemporary philosophy it is expressed by neo-Thomism (q.v.) and other religious trends. In a broader sense, the term of P. is applied to conceptions which view any changes in the world at large only in connection with the "will of providence" which determines them. Historical materialism has shown the apologetic and unscientific nature of P. and its idealist approach to history as a whole.

Psychics, the product and condition of signal interaction between a living system and the surrounding world. For man P. takes the form of phenomena of his subjective world: sensations, perceptions, notions (qq.v.), thoughts, feelings, etc. Speaking about the essence of P., it is necessary to identify it as a philosophical concept and as a concrete scientific concept. The philosophical concept of P. has a direct bearing on the fundamental question of philosophy (q.v.). In this respect the concept of P. is identified with the epistemological concepts "consciousness", "thought", "cognition", "mind", "idea", "spirit", etc., and is regarded by dialectical materialism as a special property of highly organised matter, which is the reflection of the objective reality in the form of ideal images. Matter and P. are diametrically opposed, but only within the limits of the fundamental question of philosophy, i.e., the question of the relation of consciousness to being, for P. cannot exist outside and independent of matter. In psychology the concept of P. is used to describe the specific signal interaction of a living system (animals, men) with the surrounding world. In the process of such interaction, psychic models are formed in the human brain to reflect the environment, man himself, including the organism's state. While reflecting reality, these models regulate the process of man's interaction with the surrounding world and allow him to find his bearings in it. The appearance of P. is connected with the development of life, with the complication of the forms of interaction between living beings and their surroundings. In the process of animal evolution the special organ of P. was formed, first the nervous system and, later, its higher department—the brain (q.v.). The P. of man developed in the process of social intercourse, of labour, inseparably linked with the development of speech. It differs qualitatively from the P. of animals, the product of biological development. A specific feature of human P. is awareness of reality, which ensures prevision of events and planning of actions. The transition to the higher form of the development of P. was the result of the reconstruction of the organ of P.—the brain: in the human phase, the mechanisms of the nervous activity of animals were complemented with the mechanisms of the second signal system (see I. Pavlov). From its very inception human P. has been a socio-historical product. In individual development the P. of man is formed in the process of his mastering the forms of activity developed in the course of history (see Psychology; Higher Nervous Activity).

Psychoanalysis, the general theory and method of treating nervous and psychical diseases proposed by S. Freud, and a theoretical tenet of Freudianism (q.v.). The main propositions of P. are the following: the unconscious (q.v.) which dominates the psyche is inhibited in the depths of the psyche by "censorship", a psychic instance formed under the influence of the system of social interdictions. In special "conflicting" cases the unconscious inclinations evade "censorship" and appear before the consciousness as dreams, slips of the tongue or of the pen, neurotic symptoms (the appearance of diseases), etc. Since the psychic cannot be reduced to the corporeal, it is necessary to investigate the psyche by special methods. One such method introduced by P. is the method of interpreting dreams, slips of the pen, etc. These methods are called upon to divine the "truth", i.e., the sexual condition which the apparent sense (or visible nonsense) of the manifestations of the unconscious conceal. P. is a glaring example of a "vicious circle": the supposed supremacy of the unconscious, which it is required to prove, "is proved" in every concrete case of P. by means of interpretations, based on this supposition itself. In the latter period of his activities Freud, and later his disciples and contemporary investigators, transplanted the methods of P. into social history, all the events of which they interpret as manifestations of complexes (inevitable collisions of unconscious inclinations with real life) both in the case of the individual and the nation as a whole. P. is the theoretical and methodological basis of a number of trends of the modern psychological school (q.v.) in sociology.

Psychological School in Sociology, a subjective idealist conception of society which arose at the end of the 19th century. The representatives of the P.S. sought the key to the understanding of social phenomena in the psyche of individuals or in the collective psyche (psychical interaction of individuals). The founder of the P.S. was the American sociologist L. Ward (1841-1913). Ward saw the qualitative peculiarity of society in the psychological character of social phenomena. Another prominent exponent of the P.S. was the French sociologist G. Tarde (1843-1904), who considered men's imitating one another (vogue, tradition) to be the main law of sociology. The beginning of the 20th century saw the decay of the P.S., the rejection of frank, straightforward psychologism. The psychological theories of society change under the strong impact of Dürkheim's (q.v.) "sociologism" and Weber's (q.v.) "institutionalism". Contemporary psychologism is not a special school, but is a peculiar methodological principle underlying almost entire bourgeois sociology. The application of psychologism to social phenomena is practised to a greater extent in the conception of social psychology (q.v.). Freudianism (q.v.) and neo-Freudianism (q.v.) are also widespread. Psychologism may be considered as a kind of social reformism, since it is based on the unscientific aspiration to improve the degenerating bourgeois society by means of psychology. Psychologism in sociology also provides some information on the means of influencing the masses.

Psychology, a science, dealing with the laws governing the origin and functioning of the psychic reflection of objective reality in the course of man's activity (q.v.) and in animals' behaviour. P. dates back to antiquity and it developed for long within the sphere of philosophy reaching a high level in Aristotle's (q.v.) works, who provided the first system of psychological concepts. Later Descartes (q.v.) discovered behavioural reflexes and French materialists promoted the thesis of the material nature of psychics and its dependence on social milieu. Representatives of the classical German philosophy, especially Hegel (q.v.), approached psychic phenomena from a historical position, based on idealism. The history of P. has been the arena of a struggle between materialism and idealism. The fundamental problem whose solution determines the materialist or the idealist positions in P. is the problem of the nature of psychics (q.v.): whether it is the product of the development of matter or is a substance independent of matter. In the middle of the 19th century, with the introduction of experimental methods in P., it became an independent field of knowledge. However, the false subjectivist methodological positions of many representatives of P. at that time plunged bourgeois P. into a crisis. In the 20th century, it split into a number of trends—behaviourism, *Gestalt* psychology, Freudianism (qq.v.), and others. Methodologically, Soviet P. is based on dialectical and historical materialism. Its natural scientific basis is the theory of the reflectory mechanisms of the brain (q.v.), propounded by Sechenov (q.v.) and developed by I. Pavlov (q.v.). P. is very much differentiated and besides general P., which investigates the nature of psychic activity and its laws, it includes child P., pedagogical P., labour P., engineering and cosmic P., and others. One of the basic problems of P. is the investigation of human labour, especially in connection with the appearance of modern technology, the elaboration of the theoretical foundations of instruction and of the communist education of the harmoniously developed individual, and the introduction of control processes.

Psychology of Creative Work, the field of psychology (q.v.) which investigates the laws of man's activity in creating what is new and original in science, technology, art, and other forms of labour activity (see Creative Work). The authors of idealist theories erroneously considered creative work as an inexplicable phenomenon, accessible only to the elect. Often enough the role of any labour or any activity (q.v.) whatsoever, including thinking, has been denied in the act of creation; it was considered that the discovery of the new comes about by itself or as a result of inexplicable unconscious work. Materialist psychology, while not denying the certain role played by the unconscious actions in the process of creation, proceeds from the fact that creative work in its developed forms, is a result of labour. The motives and aims of creative activity arise from the requirements of society, and the possibility of solving a given creative problem in the sphere of science or art appears when the conditions necessary for it are provided in the course of social development. Scientists, inventors, artists make use of the knowledge and the means which have been worked out and stored in the course of the development of science, technology, and the arts. However, the creative element proper often presupposes the discovery of a new mode, means or method of action, reflecting the properties and relations of objects and phenomena hitherto unknown. Creative activity demands the maximum application of the initiative, knowledge, and abilities of man. Such application is reflected in the will and the particular emotional conditions depicted in detail by many writers and philosophers.

Psychophysical Parallelism, a trend in philosophy first represented by occasionalism, q.v. (Malebranche, q.v.), offering a solution to the psychophysical problem (q.v.), which inevitably arises in the mechanistic opposition of the incorporeal soul to the body which possesses extent (see Descartes). The adherents of P.P. (Wundt, q.v., T. Lipps, and others), who follow the logic of mechanism (q.v.) and, therefore, cite the arguments of occasionalists almost word for word, regard the psychical and the physiological as mutually independent, parallel, cause-effect lines. P.P., as a rule, is supplemented by the theory of psychophysical interaction (O. Külpe, and others). Here, as in the vulgar materialist conception, the very principle of the correlation of the content of the psychics (q.v.) and physiology is erroneous. The physiological processes constitute the necessary, but far from adequate, mechanism that ensures the vital activity of man. Moreover, they do not determine the content of the psychic processes. The human life activity which is only possible in the people's intercourse includes the psychic activity as well (the psyche, consciousness) and, at the same time, constitutes the content of the latter. That is why the soul (the psychic) must not be contrasted to the body (the physiological) but must be regarded in correlation with the object world of human activity. In the last analysis, P.P. necessarily leads to idealistic conclusions.

Psychophysical Problem, the problem of the relation between the psychical and the physical. The P.P. became particularly acute in the 17th century, when Descartes (q.v.) affirmed the existence of two substances, q.v. (matter—the substance which has extent but does not think, and the soul—the substance that thinks but has no extent) and counterposed the soul and the body. The advocates of occasionalism (Malebranche, q.v.) tried to close this gap by their proposition of God's interference into the relationships between the psychic and physical (physiological) phenomena. In bourgeois psychology there have always been tendencies towards a false solution of the P.P., e.g., the theory of psychophysical parallelism (q.v.) and its varieties. The dialectico-materialist approach to the P.P. is based on the principle of monism (q.v.), according to which the psychic is a product of the development of matter.

Public Opinion, a specific mode of existence of social consciousness in the form of the unofficial mass consciousness of social groups or associations of people with common interests which registers their relation to events or phenomena of social life, to the activity of parties, institutions and persons. It is expressed in the form of recommendations and demands, and the approval or condemnation of the actions of some social institution, an individual or a group of people. P.O. is formed purposefully by class organisations and institutions and also spontaneously when people are guided by practical experience and tradition. That is why P.O. reveals not only a difference of interests, but also an unequal degree of social awareness. In an antagonistic society two mutually exclusive P.O. always exist as a reflection of the interests of the exploiters and the exploited. In socialist society P.O. differs radically in both its nature and its features. Here, by virtue of common fundamental interests, the struggle of opinions is not antagonistic and the differences are resolved through the growth of the communist consciousness of society's members, stimulated by criti-

cism and self-criticism (q.v.) and ever growing consideration for the interests of the people. This is promoted by the activities of the Communist Party armed with knowledge of the laws of social development.

The development of socialist statehood in the direction of communist public self-government (q.v.) is increasing the role of P.O. as a means of communist education (q.v.) and as a specific regulator of people's behaviour.

Purpose, a visualised result of the effort being made. As an immediate motivation, P. directs and controls man's actions, imbues human activity as an inner law, to which man's will is subordinated. While representing the active side of human consciousness, P. must remain in agreement with the objective laws, real possibilities of the surrounding world and the subject itself. The dialectical relation between freedom and necessity (q.v.) is evident in the realm of human rational activity. P. can become a force capable of transforming reality only when combined with certain means required for its realisation. Pp. may be classified into remote, close and immediate, general and specific, intermediate and final.

Pyrrho of Elis (c. 365-275 B.C.), Greek philosopher, founder of antique scepticism (q.v.). His teaching was expounded in the works of his disciple Timon. P. concerned himself chiefly with ethics, the problems of happiness and its achievement. He regarded happiness both as imperturbability (see Ataraxia) and as the absence of sufferings (see Apathy), scepticism being the means of achieving it. According to P., we cannot know anything about things, and, therefore, it is best to refrain from judging them, the moral value of this action lying in the achievement of a peace of mind. P.'s teaching influenced the New Academy (see Academy of Plato) and Roman scepticism.

Pythagoreans, followers of the Greek philosopher Pythagoras of Samos (c. 580-500 B.C.). The Pythagorean school enjoyed especially great influence in the 4th century B.C., making a valuable contribution to the development of mathematics and astronomy. However, by absolutising abstract quantity and divorcing it from material objects, the P. arrived at the conclusion that quantitative relations constitute the essence of things. This teaching gave rise to Pythagorean mathematical symbolism and mysticism of numbers, which was full of superstitions and combined with P.'s faith in the soul's transmigration. As the school developed, its idealistic and mystical tendency grew. Five hundred years later, in the epoch of the decline of the antique slave-owning system, the Pythagorean mysticism of numbers was adopted and revived in Neoplatonism (q.v.) and neo-Pythagoreanism.

q

Quality and Quantity, philosophical categories reflecting important aspects of objective reality. The world does not consist of ready, finished things, it represents a sum total of processes in which things are constantly coming into being, changing, and undergoing destruction. But from this it does not follow that they do not have a definite form of existence, are absolutely unstable, and are indistinguishable from one another (see Relativism). However much an object changes, for a time it remains a given qualitatively definite object, and not another. The qualitative definiteness of objects and phenomena is what makes them stable, what differentiates them, and makes the world boundlessly diverse. Quality is the definiteness of an object by virtue of which it is that object and not another, and differs from other objects. The quality of an object is not reducible to its separate properties. It is bound up with the object as a whole, embraces it completely, and is inseparable from it. That is why the concept of quality is associated with the being of an object. While remaining itself, an object cannot lose its quality. Any object, in relations with other objects, reveals its diverse properties or groups of properties; in this sense we may say that objects and phenomena possess a multitude of qualities. Besides qualitative definiteness, all objects also possess quantitative definiteness: a definite magnitude, number, volume, speed of their processes, degree of development of properties, etc. Quantity is that definiteness of a thing, owing to which it can be (really or mentally) divided into homogeneous parts or assembled from these parts. Homogeneity (similarity) of parts or objects is a distinctive feature of quantity. The differences between dissimilar objects are qualitative, the differences between similar objects are quantitative. In contrast to quality, quantity is not associated so closely with the being of an object; quantitative changes do not at once lead to the destruction or essential change of an object. Only after reaching a definite limit for each object do quantitative changes cause qualitative changes. In this sense quantitative definiteness in contrast to qualitative definiteness is characterised by an external relation to the nature of the objects. That is why, in the process of cognition (for example, in mathematics, q.v.) it can be separated from the content as something indifferent. The exceptionally wide applicability of mathematical theories to spheres of natural science and technology differing in their concrete content is explained by the fact that mathematics studies quantitative relations. Quality cannot be reduced to quantity, as metaphysicians try to do. No object possesses only qualitative or only quantitative properties. Each object represents the unity of a definite quality and quantity (see Measure); it is a qualitative magnitude (quantity) and a quantitatively definite quality. Disturbance of the measure leads to a change of the given object or phenomenon, to its conversion into another object or phenomenon (see Transition from Quantity to Quality).

Quantification of the Predicate, ascertainment of the logical quantity of the predicate (q.v.) of a proposition. In traditional formal logic, propositions are divided according to the scope of the subject (q.v.) into two kinds: universal propositions (for example, "all squares are rectangles") and particular propositions (for example, "some students are athletes"). Hamilton (q.v.) proposed also to take into account the scope of the predicate. Thus besides two kinds of affirmative propositions in which the predicate is not taken in its full scope and which Hamilton calls universal-particular and particular-particular, two more kinds are singled out: universal-universal (for example, "all equilateral triangles are equiangular triangles") and particular-universal (for example, "some trees are oaks") in which the predicate is taken in its full scope. Such Q.P. makes it possible to consider a proposition as an equation.

Quantifiers, operations in mathematical logic (q.v.) which are applied to logical expressions and characterise the scope of the objects (or scope of the predicates, q.v.) with which those expressions deal. The most common are universal Q. and existential Q.

Quantum Mechanics, the branch of physics that studies phenomena of the microcosm. Q.M. was founded, developed and interpreted by Planck, Broglie, Bohr, Heisenberg (qq.v.) and others. Soviet scientists Vavilov (q.v.), V. A. Fok, I. E. Tamm, L. D. Landau, D. I. Blokhintsev and others contributed substantially to the scientific elaboration and interpretation of the physical and philosophical problems of Q.M. Q.M. has made it more apparent that a researcher cannot have adequate knowledge of a system of interacting objects without active interference in it. Although in the new conditions the basic principle for the interaction of man and the outside world, i.e., that the object is primary and the subject secondary, is still valid, they are linked more closely. Acute polemics developed around these philosophical issues which became, especially at the inception of Q.M., the object of various unscientific, in particular positivistic, speculations, connected to a certain extent with the views expressed by supporters of the so-called Copenhagen school. Erroneous interpretation of the specific features of the microcosm resulting from peculiarities in the process of cognition and measurement exclusively, led to exaggeration of the role of the "observer" and to assertions of a "collapse of causality", "free will of the electron", etc. The retraction of such assertions, and the evolution in the views of some members of the former Copenhagen school, as also the situation as a whole in modern physics, are evidence that "the basic materialist spirit of physics" (V. I. Lenin, *Collected Works*, Vol. 14, p. 306) is gaining the upper hand. Today Q.M. has not only made possible a scientific explanation of a vast range of phenomena in physics, chemistry, and biology, it has also become a branch of engineering. This has once again borne out the boundless potentialities of human reason, aided by advanced methodology, for getting to know the secrets of the microcosm.

Question, a statement (q.v.) that fixes unknown elements of a situation or task or those subject to elucidation. In ordinary language it is expressed by an interrogative sentence or phrase. The Q. has a complex structure, including both a problematic and an assertoric aspect. The latter describes the subject of the Q. and singles out something the existence of which is implied, although its characteristic features are as yet unknown, and outlines the class of possible meanings of the unknown. This aspect of the Q. is sometimes in the forefront and has an independent significance (rhetoric, prompting, provocative Qq.). From the viewpoint of truth-value Qq. are divided into intelligible (satisfying syntactical, semantic, and pragmatic criteria of intelligibility), or more or less correctly posed, and unintelligible. Intelligibility and precision of Qq. are important features of correct, clear thinking.

Quietism, a theological and ethical trend which arose in Catholicism (q.v.) in the 17th century. Q. preached a passive contemplative attitude to life, renunciation of vigorous activity, indifference to good and evil, resignation to all suffering, implicit submission to the "divine will". Q. is a consequence of fatalism (q.v.) which is inherent to a certain extent in all religions. Impassivity and indifference to suffering were advocated by Schopenhauer (q.v.)

r

Racism, a reactionary theory, justifying social inequality, exploitation, and wars by the fact that people belong to different races. R. reduces the social nature of people to their biological, racial features and arbitrarily divides races into the "higher" and "lower" ones. In nazi Germany R. was the official ideology which served to justify aggressive wars and mass annihilation. Racial prejudices are explicitly manifested in the USA in respect of the Black population, which is treated as a "lower", "inferior" category of people. The rapid development of formerly backward peoples, particularly in the socialist countries, and the absence of racial antagonism among them have convincingly refuted R.

Radishchev, Alexander Nikolayevich (1749-1802), Russian writer, materialist philosopher, father of revolutionary thought in Russia; his ideas took shape under the influence of the political and sociological ideas of Rousseau, Helvétius, Mably, and Diderot (qq.v.). He condemned autocracy as "the condition most alient to human nature". In "A Letter to a Friend Living in Tobolsk" (1782) R. affirmed that the kings never waived their power for the sake of the liberty of the people. The ode of R. *Liberty* (1783) glorified the "great example" of the English and American revolutions—the execution of the king by order of Oliver Cromwell and the armed struggle of the American colonists for national liberation. R. declared that an uprising of the people driven to extremity was the earnest of liberation and he cursed those who tried to alleviate the lot of the people by appealing to monarchs. The conception elaborated by R. in these works was thoroughly substantiated by the data on Russian life, cited in R.'s main work— *Puteshestviye iz Peterburga v Moskvu* (A Journey from St. Petersburg to Moscow), 1790. This work shows the futility of attempts to help the people by means of liberal reformism and sets the task of instilling revolutionary ideas in the people as a condition for the future popular revolution. R.'s political ideas reflected the most important events of the 17th-18th centuries: the victorious bourgeois revolutions in the West and the fiasco of Catherine II's policies of "enlightened absolutism", which showed (with particular evidence after the peasant war of 1773-75) the futility of the peasants' hopes in those at the top. For the publication of *A Journey* R. was condemned to death, the sentence being commuted to exile to Siberia (up to 1797). In exile R. wrote the philosophical treatise *O cheloveke, yego smertnosti i bessmertii* (On Man, His Mortality and Immortality), 1792, in which, examining the problem of the supposed immortality of the soul, he contrasted two diametrically opposite systems of views, those of the French and English materialists of the 18th century (Holbach, Helvétius, Priestley, qq. v.) and the German idealists of the 17th-18th centuries (Leibniz, Herder, qq. v.). Describing the arguments of the former as founded upon experience and proof, and considering the assertions of the latter to be speculative, R. at the same time tried to apply dialectical ideas in the materialist system of proofs of the mortality of the soul, particularly Leibniz's idea that the "present is pregnant with the future". He adduced proof that nothing in man's life on earth indicates the possibility of the existence of the soul after his death. However from the position of limited metaphysical materialism R. could not reinterpret the activity of human cognition, on which the representatives of German idealism capitalised. Towards the end of his life he was disappointed with the outcome of the French Revolution. As he supported the idea of the rotation of freedom and slavery R. interpreted the Jacobinian dictatorship as a new example of freedom turning into autocracy. Seeing the sinking of the "ship of hope" which was to have brought people "happiness and freedom" and witnessing the repetition of Catherine II's ostentatious liberalism in the administration of Alexander I, R. committed suicide. As a whole, the evolution of the socio-political views of

R. mirrored what was typical of the latest generation of Enlighteners and leaders of the French Revolution (G. Raynal, Th. Paine, Condorcet, q. v., Desmoulins and others) and the sharp upsurge of bourgeois-democratic radicalism as well as its decline caused by the aggravation of class antagonisms in the course of the revolution.

Ramakrishna (1836-1886), public figure in India, reformer of Hinduism (q.v.). R. advocated a single religion true for all mankind, the philosophical prerequisites of which were taken from the Vedānta (q.v.). He tried to reconcile the different schools of Vedānta, representing them as different stages of the spiritual experience of yoga. Acknowledging as the supreme principle of being the absolute free from any internal distinctions, he at the same time rejected the concept that the world is illusory and defended the importance of public activities. He understood the latter in a very narrow sense and reduced them essentially to philanthropy and concern for universal "spiritual perfection", in which he saw the key for overcoming the disasters of the "iron age", the features of which were the omnipotence of money, the dominance of foreign invaders, etc. In his pronouncements he exposed the evil consequences of the British colonial administration and maintained a naive belief in the revival of the nation by means of faith. R.'s preaching did not go beyond a passive protest against colonial rule. Yet his preaching of a single religion in the India of those days with her numerous religious sects and dogmas—all of the survivals of feudal ideology—was in its way an appeal for national unity.

Rationalism 1. A teaching in the theory of knowledge, according to which universality and necessity—the logical attributes of true knowledge—cannot be deduced from experience and its generalisation; they may be deduced only from the mind itself: either from concepts innate in the mind (theory of innate ideas, q.v., of Descartes, q.v.), or from concepts existing only in the form of the predispositions of the mind. Experience exerts a certain stimulating influence upon their appearance, but the character of absolute universality and absolute necessity is given to them by a priori judgements of the mind or a priori forms absolutely independent of experience. In this sense R. is in opposition to empiricism (q.v.). R. came into being as an attempt to account for the logical peculiarities of mathematical truths and mathematical natural science. Its representatives in the 17th century were Descartes, Spinoza, Leibniz (qq.v.); in the 18th century, Kant, Fichte, Schelling, and Hegel (qq.v.). The limitation of R. lies in its denial of the thesis that universality and necessity of authentic knowledge came into being through experience. R. absolutises the indisputable nature of these logical attributes, does not recognise the dialectics of transition of knowledge from the lesser universality and necessity to the greater and absolute ones. This limitation of R. was overcome by Marxism, which examines knowledge in its unity with practice (see Cognition: Theory and Practice). R. is widely manifested in various spheres of knowledge, where it means belief in reason, in the reality of rational judgement, in the force of argument. In this sense R. is opposed to irrationalism (q.v.). 2. In theology, R. is a trend, according to which only those dogmas of faith are acceptable which are considered to be in conformity with logic and sensible arguments.

Reactology, a mechanistic conception, regarding the psychics (q.v.) of highly developed animals and man as an arithmetical sum of reactions to external influences. It was current in Soviet physiology and psychology in the 1920s-30s. The term "R." was introduced by K. N. Kornilov, *Ucheniye o reaktsii cheloveka s psikhologicheskoi tochki zreniya* (Teaching on the Reaction of Man from the Psychological Point of View), 1922. Like behaviourism (q.v.), R. left out of account the dependence of the external influences upon the internal situation, upon the whole system of the organism's higher nervous relations. R. played a certain positive part in the struggle against idealist psychology and physiology. R.'s mechanism (q.v.), however, often grew into idealism.

Realism, an artistic method which provides for the most complete embodiment of the objective, cognitive and aesthetically transformative nature of art. R. is characterised by true reflection of the human personality in its multiple relations with reality, and demonstration of the logical and typical in life by means of illustration. R. implies, besides truth of detail, truth in reproducing typical characters under typical circumstances. The elements and tendencies of R. manifested themselves at the early stages of the history of art. R. as a specific artistic method took shape in the epoch of the Renaissance, q.v. (Servantes, Shakespeare, Rabelais, etc.) and continued to develop in the Enlightenment period (Swift, Lessing, q.v., Voltaire, q.v., Beaumarchais, etc.). It assumed its final form by the mid-19th century in the art of critical realism. The pathos of the works of critical realism (Stendhal, Balzac, Dickens, Gogol, Saltykov-Shchedrin, Nekrasov, Tolstoy, q.v., Shevchenko, q.v. Repin, and others) unmasked the evils of feudal and bourgeois societies, played an important part in shaping the ideas of man's social and spiritual emancipation, and helped to cultivate democratic social ideals. Critical R. is alive at present in the works of many progressive writers and artists in capitalist countries and is opposed to modern bourgeois formalist and naturalist art. The artistic achievements of R. are used to advantage by socialist realism (q.v.).

Realism, Medieval, a trend in medieval scholasticism (q.v.), maintaining that universal concepts (see Universals) possess real existence and precede the existence of singular objects. M.R. continued Plato's line in the solution of the problem of the relation between the concept and the objective world, between the universal and the singular. M.R. served as a philosophical basis of Catholicism (q.v.). Its prominent exponents were Anselm of Canterbury (q.v.) and William of Champeaux. Thomas Aquinas (q.v.) was close to this trend as well. Exponents of nominalism (q.v.) fought against M.R. This struggle was a reflection of the two trends in philosophy—materialist (nominalism) and idealist (realism).

Realism, Naive, a spontaneous materialist understanding of the world inherent in every person, the conviction that all objects exist independently of human consciousness. But N.R. is not a consistent, theoretically conceived scientific world outlook. A false interpretation of N.R. is given by subjective idealists (Berkeley, Mach, qq.v. and others). The Machists, for example, claim that N.R. is a world outlook, according to which man deals only with his sensations and the existence of the material world is of no importance to him.

Realism, Socialist, an artistic method ensuring a truthful, historically concrete reflection of reality taken in its revolutionary development and presented in the light of the communist aesthetic ideal (q.v.). The emergence and assertion of S.R. was concomitant with the appearance on the world scene of a new progressive and revolutionary social force, the working class, which is a true producer of human values. The first works of S.R. were created at the beginning of the 20th century, in the conditions of the crisis of capitalism, the upsurge of the proletarian class struggle and the preparation of socialist revolution in Russia (M. Gorky's novel *Mother* and his play *Enemies,* poems by D. Bedny and other proletarian poets). The method of S.R. which, after 1917, spread to all genres of Soviet art (V. Mayakovsky, M. Sholokhov, Eisenstein, K. Stanislavsky, A. Deineka, D. Shostakovich and many others), became a world-wide phenomenon and was adopted by many outstanding progressive art workers in bourgeois countries and in socialist countries (H. Barbusse, M. Andersen-Nexö, B. Brecht, L. Aragon, Marie Pujmanova, L. Kruczkowski, G. Karaslavov and others). Being a logical continuation and development of the finest realist traditions of art in the past, S.R. is a new stage in man's artistic progress. Its essence is fidelity to the truth of life, this being expressed in artistic images from the position of the communist world outlook, which enables artists to understand the historical meaning of the events they deal with and truthfully to reproduce in art the past and the present, as well as tendencies of social development. The communist aesthetic ideal is embodied in a new type of positive hero — the working man and fighter, the builder of communist society. The chief ideological and aesthetic principles of S.R. are commitment to communist ideology, service to the people and adherence to partisanship, close bonds with the working people's struggle, socialist humanism and internationalism, historical optimism, rejection of formalism (q.v.) and subjectivism, and of naturalistic primitivism. In the course of its development, S.R. has worked out a number of specific features pertaining to the ideological-aesthetic content and artistic form of works of art. These are a source of such aesthetic feelings as rejoicing at the progressive development of life, joy at understanding the noble aims and lofty prospects unfolding before the builders of the new society. This is why S.R. is a powerful instrument of communist education (q.v.). S.R. stimulates artists' creative endeavours and helps them choose forms and styles consistent with their individual inclinations.

Reason and Intellect, concepts which express two mutually necessary aspects of development of scientific knowledge, and also moral and artistic thinking, two mutually helping abilities. The intellectual ability is characterised by the fact that notions within it are not in the process of transformation and remain stable, and act as ready-made theoretical "yardsticks" for empirical material and for constructing results. Hence, the abstract character of intellectual operations and their results, which gives ground for the cult of abstractions and for ascribing to them an independent creative role. Armed with I. alone man makes his life increasingly more intellectual—a sphere of rationality. On the contrary, reasoning ability is characterised by the fact that notions enter the process of transformation. Aims and values are seen in the process of their change, and the theoretical process is directed to a specific ideal, leading to the development of the subject of knowledge, of values, etc. If scientific research based on intellectual ability alone is contrary to morality and art, R. creates the atmosphere of their communion. The problem of R.&I. is present in all European history of philosophy, passing from their distinction by Plato and Aristotle (qq.v.) to the understanding that they are stages of cognition by Nicholas of Cusa, Bruno and Spinoza (qq.v.). Leibniz (q.v.) made the problem a subject of study of German classical philosophy (q.v.). Hegel (q.v.) was very critical of I. but only in order to deify R. Nihilist criticism of I. is a popular subject of irrationalism (q.v.). In his theoretical investigation *(Capital)* Marx used the dialectically reasonable method of rising from the abstract to the specific. Marxism solves the problem of R.&I. by taking man as an integral whole and a unity of diverse manifestations of man's activity (q.v.).

Reasonable Egoism, Theory of, a theory in ethics advanced by the Enlighteners of the 17th and 18th centuries, based on the following principle: correctly understood private interest should coincide with social interest. In the ethics of Helvétius, Holbach, Diderot (qq.v.) and later Feuerbach (q.v.) T.R.E. expresses the interests of the rising bourgeoisie in its struggle with the ascetic feudal Christian morality and served as an ideological preparation for bourgeois revolutions. They proceeded from the possibility of a harmonious combination of private and social interests while preserving private property. The T.R.E. reflected the practice of the revolutionary bourgeoisie, free enterprise, idealised private initiative. The "social interest" was in fact the class interest of the bourgeoisie. The capitalist reality destroyed the illusion about the validity of the bourgeois society. Chernyshevsky and Dobrolyubov (qq.v.) rejected some ideas of the French 18th-century materialists about the possibility of combining social and private interests on the basis of "reasonable" laws to be established by enlightened monarchs or wise law-makers. In their ethics private interest as the motive of human behaviour was filled up with social content. They saw the significance of life and the criterion of man's action in unselfish service to the people, in their emancipation from the chains of serfdom, in the revolutionary transformation of reality. Although the Russian revolutionary democrats added some rational content to T.R.E. it failed to give a scientific explanation of the laws of morality or man's behaviour in society, for it addressed itself to man in general, to man's abstract "eternal" nature.

Reduction, a methodological device consisting in reducing data and problems to the form suitable for their analysis or solution and in making the complex simpler; it is applied in logic, mathematics, biology, philosophy, linguistics, etc. Making R. absolute leads to reductionism, a concept that it is possible to completely reduce higher phenomena to lower, basic phenomena. Although higher forms of the development of matter arise from lower forms and retain them in a sublated form (see Sublation), they are not reducible to them. Reductionism may be seen in mechanism (q.v.), the tendency to consider the psychic only as a result of physiological, etc., processes and to biologise the phenomena of social life. In neo-positivism (q.v.) reductionism is manifested in the tendency to "free philosophy from metaphysics" and to reduce scientific knowledge to propositions about sensations or to physical experiments and measurements (see Phenomenalism; Physicalism).

Reflection 1. A term meaning reflection and investigation of an act of cognition. In different philosophical systems it had a different content. For Leibniz (q.v.), R. is nothing more than attention to what happens in man himself. For Hegel (q.v.), R. is a mutual reflection of one in another, e.g., in the essence of a phenomenon. The term "to reflect" means to apply consciousness to one's self, to ponder upon one's own psychic state. 2. A basic concept of the materialist theory of knowledge and its core—the theory of reflection (q.v.). The dialectical-materialist theory of reflection distinguishes between R. in inorganic nature, on the one hand, and in living nature and social life, on the other, where it is active and is exercised by highly organised systems possessing an independent force of reaction, such as biological metabolism at the lowest level and the deliberate, creative, anticipative and transformative activity (q.v.) of man at the highest. In

inorganic nature R. is the property of things to reproduce, under the influence of other things, such traces, imprints, and reactions whose structure accords with some quality of the things that exercise the influence. But these imprints are not utilised by the things themselves. In living nature they are used for self-preservation and self-adaptation, e.g., the irritability of plants and simple organisms. Psychic R. (see Sensation; Perception) develops with the appearance and evolution of the nervous system and brain, through which the higher nervous conditioned reflex and psychic activity is exercised, securing the behavioural orientation and regulation of a subject-organism in the environment. The psychic R. of men and animals has two sides: 1) content and 2) form, i.e., the mode of existence, expression and transformation of this content. Human knowledge differs in quality from the psychic R. of animals because it is social by nature.

Reflection, Theory of, in Marxist philosophy, constitutes the basis of dialectico-materialist theory of knowledge (q.v.). The T.R. has its specific tasks: the revelation of the more general features and laws, which are common to all levels and forms of reflection (q.v.); the study of the emergence and development of forms of psychic reflection, including the questions of the origin of consciousness and special scientific proof of man's ability to cognise; the explanation of the essence of reflection in inanimate nature; the correlation and connection between man and cybernetic devices. The starting point for the T.R. and Marxist epistemology as a whole is the dialectical-materialist principle of reflection, which postulates that the results of cognition must be relatively adequate to its original source. They are obtained by means of two interrelated demands and the processes corresponding to them: active extraction of necessary and exclusion of unnecessary, collateral information about the original. Reflection as an epistemological principle was also acknowledged in pre-Marxist materialism, but the main shortcoming of old materialism was its failure to apply dialectics (q.v.) to the T.R., which resulted in reflection being regarded as passive "photographing" of the external world. Marxist philosophy understands reflection dialectically, as a complex and contradictory process coordinating sensory and rational cognition, mental and practical activity, as a process in which man does not passively adapt himself to the external world, but acts on it, changing and subordinating it to his purposes. Therefore, all attempts to criticise the Marxist T.R. as a "conformist" theory which allegedly dooms the cognising subject to passive and inactive contemplation of the surrounding world, are completely groundless. On the contrary, man's active material activity is only possible on the basis of the reflective function of consciousness, which ensures an adequate cognition of the world and its influence on it in conformity with the objective laws.

Reflexes, Conditioned and Unconditioned, adaptive reactions of man and animals determined by the stimulation of receptors and the activity of the central nervous system. U.R. are inborn responsive reactions of the organism, and are the same among all individuals of the given species. They are characterised by a constant and regular connection between the action on a receptor and a definite responsive reaction, ensuring the adaptation of the organism to stable conditions of life. U.R. are effected, as a rule, by means of the spinal cord and the lower parts of the brain. Intricate complexes and chains of U.R. are called instincts (q.v.). C.R. are reactions in response to the stimulation of receptors acquired in the course of the organism's life; in higher animals and man C.R. are developed by the formation of temporary connections in the cerebral cortex and serve as a mechanism of adaptation to the intricate changing conditions of the environment. Sechenov (q.v.) was the first to prove that the psychical activity has a reflectory nature. The objective method of C.R. evolved by I. Pavlov (q.v.) underlies the doctrine of higher nervous activity (q.v.), in particular the doctrine of the two signal systems. This doctrine is one of the scientific foundations of materialist psychology and the dialectical materialist theory of reflection.

Reformation, a widespread anti-feudal and anti-Catholic movement in Europe in the first half of the 16th century, ushering in the beginning of Protestantism (q.v.). The R. was the first immature bourgeois revolution in human history when the bourgeoisie in alliance with part of the noblemen came out against the ruling Catholic church as the pillar of the feudal system. Starting in Germany, the R. spread to a number of European countries and brought about the defection from the Catholic system of England, Scotland, Denmark, Sweden, Norway, the Netherlands, Finland, Switzerland, partially Germany, Bohemia, and Hungary. The R. cheapened, simplified and democratised the church, raised internal personal faith above the external manifestations of religiosity, imparted divine sanction to the standards of bourgeois morality. In the countries where the R. triumphed, the church, on becoming dependent upon the state, had less power than in Catholic countries, and this facilitated the development of science and secular culture as a whole. The national character of the new religion was in keeping with the process of formation of bourgeois nations. In the R. the Christian-plebeian camp existed alongside with the noblemen's and burghers' camps. Its representatives came out not only against the clergy but also against the nobility; not only against the inequality of the social estates, but also against inequality in property status. In this they based themselves on certain evangelical principles dating back to early Christianity (see Münzer). The Catholics' answer to the R. was counter-Reformation, which managed to prevent the further spread of Protestantism in Europe and to eradicate it in Poland and France.

Reformism, a political trend inside the workers' movement, which denies the necessity of class struggle and the socialist revolution, professes class collaboration and hopes by mere reforms to transform capitalism into a "welfare society". R. appeared in the last quarter of the 19th century. Its social basis is the upper stratum of the working class, the so-called labour aristocracy, representatives of the "middle section", and the trade union bureaucracy. R. is closely connected with revisionism (q.v.). It has no single integral world outlook. Eclectic combination of the ideas of neo-Kantianism, positivism, anthropologism, and Christianity (qq.v.)— that is the palette of ideas which hides the spiritual poverty of the theorists of R. They maintain that dialectics is obsolete, advocate smooth evolutionism; reject materialism and declare the natural-historical and economic inevitability of socialism a myth. The atheistic traditions of socialism are betrayed; alliance with clericalism and conciliation of science with religion have become the policy of Right Social Democracy. The adoption of new programmes (1958-61) marked the end of the postwar evolution of R., its integration in the system of capitalist relations. Many leaders of Social-Reformism openly defend state-monopoly capitalism from their position of anti-communism (q.v.). R. holds up the development of the proletariat's class consciousness. Struggle with R., overcoming of the split in the working class, is one of the urgent tasks of the communist movement. No reforms can create socialism without the revolutionary transformation of society, i.e., without the liquidation of capitalism. While criticising the Right opportunist practices and the ideology of R., Communists actively advocate cooperation with the Socialist and Social Democratic parties in the struggle for peace, democracy, and social progress.

Reichenbach, Hans (1891-1953), German philosopher and logician. In the 1920s R. was one of the organisers of the Society of Scientific Philosophy in Berlin, which, with the Vienna Circle (q.v.) formed the basis for the movement of logical positivism (q.v.). He engaged in the analysis of causality, regularity, the relations of causality and probability, statistical and dynamic laws, etc. As a logician R. was well known mainly for his contribution to probabilistic logic (*The Theory of Probability*, 1935).

Reification, as distinct from objectification (q.v.) stands for the transformation of social relations from relations between persons to relations between things; it is historically transient and characteristic of commodity production and especially of capitalist society. Accordingly, there takes place a depersonification of man and a personification of things. R. finds its reflection in fetishism (q.v.). Man's activity (q.v.) becomes a derivative of the prevailing conditions, is squeezed into them and is reduced to non-creative functions. Man himself is no more than a performer of a ready-made role, a functional means of producing things.

Relation, a necessary moment in the interconnection of all phenomena. The R. of things is objective; things do not exist outside R. and the latter is always the R. of things. The existence of each thing, its specific features and properties, and its development depend on the sum total of its Rr. to other things of the objective world. The properties themselves, necessarily inherent in one process or another or in a thing, are manifested only in their Rr. to other things and processes. Development of a phenomenon leads to a change in its Rr. with other phenomena, the disappearance of some Rr. and the appearance of other Rr. On the other hand, changes in the sum total of Rr. in which the given object exists may lead to a change in the object itself. Rr. are as diverse as things and their properties. It is necessary to differentiate internal Rr. of different, particularly opposite sides of an object and its external Rr. with other objects. Account should be taken, first, of the relative nature of differences in internal and external Rr., second, the passage of one into another, and, third, the fact that external Rr. depend on internal Rr., manifest and reveal them. Social Rr. are of a special nature. Relations are divided into essential and inessential, necessary and accidental, etc. The essential general R. between phenomena amounts to a law that governs their development or functioning. Man enters into Rr. with the things he creates, the objective world, and other people. As a result, in the world he is mastering he contemplates himself and begins to treat himself as a man (gains self-consciousness, q.v.) only by treating another man as his own likeness. This is what explains, on the one hand, the social nature of human consciousness, and, on the other, the necessity of studying social Rr. in order to know history. In dialectical logic (q.v.), "the relations (=transitions=contradictions) of notions=the main content of logic, *by which* these concepts (and their relations, transitions, contradictions) are shown as reflections of the objective world" (V. I. Lenin, *Collected Works*, Vol. 38, p. 196). In mathematical logic (q.v.), Rr. are opposed to properties like multiple predicates are to singular predicates (see Predicate). "More", "equal" are the examples of dyadic Rr. "Among" and others are triadic Rr. In formal logic, the theory of Rr. was developed by de Morgan and Peirce (qq.v.). The logical theory of Rr. studies the general properties of Rr. and the laws governing them. A calculus of Rr. related to a theory of classes forms an essential section of the theory of Rr. This studies the connections between Rr. and operations with them and establishes the laws by which some Rr. can be deduced from others.

Relations of Production, one of the most important concepts of Marxist science concerning human society, reflecting the objective material relations that exist in any society independently of human consciousness, relations that are formed between people in the process of social production, exchange, and distribution of material wealth. The R.P. are an indispensable aspect of any mode of production (q.v.), for men cannot produce without uniting for joint activities and mutual exchange of their activities. The basis of the R.P. is the ownership (q.v.) of the means of production. With social, collective ownership the members of society are equal as regards the means of production, and in the process of production, relations of co-operation and mutual help are formed between them. If property is private, relations of domination and subjection are established between men. Throughout history social property appeared in the form of the property of the clan, the tribe, the community, public or state property, co-operative and collective-farm property; private ownership appeared in history in three basic forms: slave property, feudal property, and capitalist property, to which correspond the three main types of exploitation of man by man. Private ownership of pro-

ducers, based on their labour, has existed and still exists today, but this form is always subordinated to the R.P. dominating in the society in question and gradually disappears under their determinative influence. Besides the two main forms of R.P., in periods of the fall of one and the rise of another socio-economic formation (q.v.) there emerged transitional R.P. The peculiarity of these relations is that they combine in one economic structure economic relations of different types. For example, in the period of the decay of the primitive-communal system the remnants of tribal relations were combined in the patriarchal family with the rudiments of slave-owning relations. In the period of the decay of the slave-owning relations there arose in a number of countries the colonate, combining in itself the elements of slave-owning and feudal relations; in the period of the transition from capitalism to socialism some economic forms combine in themselves relations based on collective and private ownership (state capitalism, joint state-private enterprises, semi-socialist forms of the co-operatives in the village, etc.).

Relativism, an idealist theory of relativity, conventionality, and subjectivity of human cognition. Asserting the relativity of knowledge, R. denies objective cognition, maintaining that our knowledge does not reflect the objective world. R. is common to the agnostic and subjective-idealist systems. It was, for example, one of the epistemological sources of physical idealism (q.v.). Dialectical materialism recognises the relativity of cognition only in the sense that its every historical stage is limited by a given level of development of the productive forces and of science, and not in the sense of negating objective truth. In contemporary bourgeois philosophy R. manifests itself in the negation of objective historical laws and is used as a means of struggle against materialist philosophy (see Truth, Absolute and Relative).

Relativity, Theory of, a physical theory of space and time formulated by Einstein (q.v.) in 1905 (the special theory) and in 1916 (the general theory). The development of optics and electrodynamics led to the rejection of the concept of absolute time, absolute simultaneity and absolute space. According to the special T.R., the course of time depends on the movement of a system, and the intervals of time (and also space dimensions) change in such a way that the velocity of light in the given system does not change according to its movement. A large number of physical conclusions were drawn from these premises. Usually they are called "relativist", i.e. based on T.R. Of great importance is Einstein's conclusion that the mass of a body is proportional to its energy. This correlation is widely applied in modern nuclear physics. By developing and generalising the special T.R. Einstein arrived at the general T.R., which is essentially a new theory of gravitation. It is based on the assumption that the four-dimensional space-time continuum in which the forces of gravity operate is subject to the correlations of non-Euclidean geometry. Einstein conceived the deviation of geometrical correlations in the four-dimensional space-time continuum from Euclidean correlations as a curvature of space-time. He identified such a curvature with the action of the forces of gravity. This assumption was borne out in 1919 by astronomical observations, which showed that the ray of a star, the prototype of a straight line, is curved in the vicinity of the Sun under the influence of gravitation. Unlike the special T.R., the general T.R. has not so far acquired the nature of a complete and incontestable physical concept. The philosophical conclusions of T.R. fully confirm and enrich the ideas of dialectical materialism. T.R. showed the indissoluble link between space and time (it is expressed in the single concept of the space-time interval), and also between the material movement, on the one hand, and the space-time forms of its existence, on the other. Definition of the space-time qualities as depending on the characteristic features of the movement of matter ("slowing" of time, "curving" of space) has revealed the narrowness of the views of classical physics on absolute space and time and the mistaken assumption that these concepts are separate from the concept of moving matter. T.R. has become the rational generalisation of classi-

cal mechanics and extends its principles to the field of physics dealing with velocities close to that of light. The idealist and positivist trends in bourgeois philosophy have tried to use T.R. to substantiate their claim that science is subjective and that physical processes depend on observation. However, the T.R., or relativist mechanics should not be confused with philosophical relativism (q.v.) which denies the objective nature of scientific knowledge. T.R. is a more exact reflection of reality than classical mechanics.

Religion, a specific form of social consciousness whose characteristic feature is a fantastic reflection in people's minds of external forces dominating over them, a reflection in which earthly forces assume unearthly forms. Marxism-Leninism considers R. a historically transient phenomenon of social consciousness and shows the main factors that determine its existence at different stages of society's development. The appearance of R. in primitive society was conditioned by man's impotence in face of the forces of nature because of the low level of the productive forces. The existence of R. in antagonistic class societies may be traced to class oppression, unfair social relations, the poverty and rightless status of the masses, which breed despair and a sense of hopelessness thus turning people's hopes to supernatural forces. By giving people false bearings and placing the solution of the vital problems of being in the other world, R. strengthens and perpetuates man's dependance on external forces and dooms him to passiveness, holding down his creative potential. In the society of antagonistic classes it diverts working people from active participation in the struggle for changing the world and impedes the formation of their class consciousness. Marx called R. "opium for the people". A scientific analysis of R. rests on the premise that it is a complex social phenomenon, a system of specific ideas, feelings and religious rites, and in a class society also of institutions that bring together professional clergymen. The above aspects are directly related to, and change with the social relations. This is distinctly seen in the present conditions when R. is being modernised under the influence of social, scientific and technological progress which has led to a crisis of R. The essence of R., however, remains unchanged and its disappearance, as predetermined by the course of social development, is inevitable. Marxism-Leninism provides convincing proof that the social roots of R. are being undermined by the economic and social changes brought about in the course of socialist construction, and will disappear altogether in a developed communist society.

Renaissance (Philosophical), a term denoting the sociological and philosophical doctrines that developed in Europe (primarily in Italy) at the time of the decline of feudalism and the emergence of bourgeois society (15th to early 17th centuries). While scholasticism (q.v.) remained the official philosophy in that period, the rise of humanist culture (see Humanism), the revival of the philosophical legacy of antiquity, and a series of important discoveries in the natural sciences enabled the progressive philosophy of the R. to break free of theology and develop anti-scholastic trends. These first showed themselves in ethics, bringing about a revival of the ethical doctrines of stoicism (Petrarch) and epicureanism (Laurentius Valla), which struck at the prevailing Christian morality of the time. The major role in the philosophy of the R. was played by natural philosophical conceptions (Bruno, Nicholas of Cusa, qq.v., Cardano, Telesio, Paracelsus, qq.v., etc.), which testified to the collapse of the scholastics' picture of the world and their methods of explaining nature. Although the transitional character of the R. was evident in some of these conceptions (preoccupation with astrology, magic, alchemy, and other unscientific interpretations of the world), the general line of development of natural philosophy (q.v.) came to mean the increasing supremacy of the materialist understanding of the world (Bruno, the heliocentric system of Copernicus, q.v.). The most important results of the scientific trends in the philosophy of the R. were the methods of experimental mathematical investigation of nature, philosophically generalised in the works of Leonardo da Vinci and particularly Galileo Galilei (q.v.), the determinist interpretation of reality, as opposed to its teleological interpretation by the scholastics, and the formulation (by Kepler in astronomy and Galileo in mechanics) of genuinely scientific laws of nature free of anthropomorphism (q.v.). The determining features of the philosophy of R. were: metaphysical understanding of the elements of nature as absolutely void of any quality and inanimate; absence of a historical view of nature and, consequently, a deistic inconsistency, which sets a place apart for God in the infinite world (Galileo Galilei and, to a certain extent, Francis Bacon, q.v.). The vast socioeconomic changes that took place in the R. were also reflected in many of the sociological conceptions of the time, which viewed society as a conglomeration of isolated individuals, since they expressed the growing individualism of the bourgeoisie. The emergence and consolidation of national states were reflected in the new conceptions of state power as something completely independent of religious sanction and the authority of the church (Machiavelli, q.v., Jean Bodin, and Andrzej Modrzewski). The R. also saw the appearance of utopian teachings, such as those of Münzer (q.v.), who demanded the socialisation of property on the basis of the "holy scriptures", and the first attempts of a utopian nature to outline a communist social system (see More and Campanella).

Renan, Josef Ernest (1823-1892), French philosopher, philologist and historian of religion, famous for his works on the history of Christianity (*La vie de Jésus*, 1863, *Histoire des origines du christianisme*, 1863-1883). Inclining towards positivism (q.v.), R. denied that philosophy is an independent science. According to R., the purpose of the development of the universe, governed by the laws of nature, is God, whom he saw as the domination of reason in the world. This principle, as he saw it, is personified in the perfect man, a man of genius. According to R., all other people are a necessary condition for the existence of the elite. An adherent of reactionary views, R. was hostile to the Paris Commune.

Requirement, the state of the organism whose demands necessary for its normal functioning are not satisfied that is aimed at removing this dissatisfaction. The R. implies the need for the object required. The R. is realised in the process of its satisfaction, active assimilation of the object required in the process of consumption. The unsatisfied R. of the organism may result in a change of its normal functioning or even in its death. Before it is realised, the R. exists as the arising and growing sensation of deficiency in something. In the course of its realisation the tensions that have arisen subside and die away. Rr. emerge as new products appear; they change along with changes in the objects required and in the course of consumption. The animals use the ready-made objects given by nature, while people produce them. Human Rr. develop in the process and on the basis of development of the mode of production (q.v.). Typical of man are social Rr. engendered by the development of society, namely, the R. of work, communication with other people, etc. Human biological Rr. are preserved in a transformed form; they cannot exist in isolation from social Rr. The richer, more varied and developed the life of society, the more varied and developed are human Rr. In a pre-class society human Rr. were very poorly developed and not differentiated. In the class antagonistic societies human Rr. develop and differentiate, they become more varied and rich in content. But they develop in an antagonistic way: the growth of wealth, including the richness of Rr., and the increasing poverty, including that of Rr., engender each other. With the transition to the communist formation, the richness of Rr. created in the world of private property, is preserved, but they cease to be antagonistic, and broad vistas are opened up for developing human Rr. and making them more "elevated". Everyone will have an opportunity to utilise all objects created by people to satisfy their material and spiritual Rr., and, consequently, to develop comprehensively all their Rr., above all, the requirement to work and create things for the benefit of the whole society and establish disinterested relations with all its members. Comprehensive develop-

ment of human Rr., creation of objects to satisfy these Rr. becomes a social imperative, a requirement for all.

Responsibility, an ethical and legal concept reflecting the individual's special social, moral and legal attitude to society (mankind as a whole), characterised by the fulfilment of his moral duty (q.v.) and legal norms. R. embraces philosophical and sociological problems of relations between the ability and the possibility of man's being a subject (author) of his actions, and more concrete problems as well: the ability to consciously (deliberately, voluntarily) fulfil certain requirements and to carry out set tasks; the ability to take correct moral options, to achieve a definite result. It also dwells on the questions of the rightness or guilt of a person, the possible approval or disapproval of his actions, reward or punishment. In all ethical and legal doctrines the problem of R. is seen in connection with the philosophical problem of freedom. In non-Marxist works it is, as a rule, solved abstractly, and made dependent on the answer to the question whether man can be at all considered free in his actions (see Freedom and Necessity). In Marxism, R. gains a concrete historical character and is solved by analysis of the obtaining freedom of man in the given historical conditions. The building of a society without exploitation and antagonistic classes, introduction of conscious planning in social life, and the involvement of the masses in self-government of society and the making of history greatly increase the measure of personal freedom and at the same time of the social and moral R. In socialist jurisprudence the civil, administrative and criminal R. of a delinquent is established not formally by defining the corpus delicti, but with consideration for the latter's upbringing, and life activity, the awareness of being culpable and the possibility of correction in future. This brings legal R. closer to moral R. In communist morality R. includes not only the actions committed but also awareness of the interests of society as a whole, i.e., in the final analysis, the realisation of the laws of the progressive march of history.

Revelation, a fundamental concept of theology and idealist religious philosophy expressing supersensible perception of supernatural reality in the act of mystic enlightenment. In religion R. is mainly represented by the Holy Writ (the Bible, Koran, etc.). Contemporary theology endeavours to modernise the idea of R. by maintaining that it is not contradictory to reason. The idea of R. in religious schools of modern bourgeois philosophy is responsible for the increasing role of irrationalism (q.v.) in the philosophical apology of theism (q.v.).

Revisionism, an opportunist trend in the revolutionary working-class movement which flies in the teeth of science to revise the principal proposition of Marxism-Leninism. Right R. is close to bourgeois reformism while Left R. is characterised by anarchist and voluntarist conceptions. R. appeared in the late 1870s, and at the turn of the century became a distinct trend in the Social Democratic movement of Germany, Austria-Hungary, France, Russia and other countries (Bernstein, Kautsky, qq.v., O. Bauer, E. Vandervelde, F. Scheidemann, S. Prokopovich, L. Martov, L. Trotsky, and others). Declaring that socialist views are independent of philosophical views, revisionists tried to combine scientific socialism with neo-Kantianism (q.v.) and Machism. The Marxist theory of class struggle was declared outdated because bourgeois democracy and universal suffrage had allegedly destroyed its basis. For this reason there is no need for the revolutionary overthrow of the bourgeoisie and for the establishment of the dictatorship of the proletariat (q.v.). According to R. new trends in the development of capitalism (q.v.) take the edge off its contradictions. The views of the revisionists were subjected to strong criticism by Lenin and other Marxists. After the collapse of the Second International and the victory of the Great October Socialist Revolution the workers' movement split into the reformist trend (see Reformism), which fully departed from Marxism, and the revolutionary trend—the international communist movement. Various "Left" and Right tendencies (the right deviation in some Communist parties, "Left" Communism, etc.) appeared in the communist movement whenever social contradictions grew sharper. Under the slogan of the creative development of Marxism and struggle against dogmatism (q.v.), and on the assumption that the scientific and technological revolution (q.v.) led to a qualitative change in the social structure of capitalist society, Right R. rejects the necessity of a socialist revolution and advocates improvement of capitalism through reforms. Revisionists say that the working class (q.v.), affected by the rising standard of living, has integrated in the capitalist system, relinquishing its leading role to the intelligentsia. Raising to an absolute the national and historical features in the transition of different countries to socialism, R. disregards the general laws of the building of socialism and the international importance of Leninism. R. denies the socialist nature of real socialism and makes an ideal of the principles of abstract and non-class democracy, and of the free play of political forces. R. rejects the principle of democratic centralism, which it portrays as suppression of "free discussion" in Communist parties. In reality, it tries to destroy the revolutionary organisation of the working class. The principles of internationalism (q.v.) are also under attack of the revisionists. The contemporary "Left" R. is manifested in the activities of "Left" extremist groups, exponents of petty-bourgeois revolutionism. The struggle against R. is an important condition for strengthening the Communist parties and the workers' movement as a whole, and for the success of the liberation struggle of the working people.

Revolutionary Situation, the sum total of objective conditions expressive of an economic and political crisis in a given social system and determining the possibilities of social revolution (q.v.). As pointed out by Lenin, R.S. is characterised by the following principal symptoms: 1) impossibility for the ruling classes to maintain their rule without any change. For a revolution to break out it is usually not enough that the "lower classes do not want" to live in the old way; another condition is that the "upper classes" cannot live in the old way. In other words, revolution is impossible without a nation-wide crisis (affecting both the exploited and the exploiters); 2) the want and misery of the oppressed classes must be more than usually oppressive; 3) there must be a considerable rise in the activity of the masses, who allow themselves to be robbed quietly in "peace time", but in stormy times are drawn to independent historical action both by all the circumstances of the crisis and by the "upper classes" themselves (see V. I. Lenin, *Collected Works*. Vol. 21, p. 214, Vol. 31, p. 85). The mere existence of a R.S. is not enough to ensure victory of a social revolution. Besides the objective conditions there must also be subjective conditions, i.e., the revolutionary class must be ready to fight bravely and selflessly, there must be an experienced revolutionary party, offering correct strategic and tactical guidance.

Revolution, Bourgeois, a type of social revolution concerned mainly with resolving the contradictions between the developing capitalist mode of production and the feudal or semi-feudal economic and political system. The historical function of B.R. is to get rid of the obstacles to capitalist development. The fact that revolutions of this type may carry out certain anti-capitalist measures does not alter their general character, since these measures leave intact the foundation of bourgeois society, namely, private ownership of the means of production. History has recorded many bourgeois revolutions in various countries at various times. The process of liquidating feudalism, which began in the 16th century (the Great Peasant War in Germany, the bourgeois revolution in the Netherlands), has not yet reached completion (hence numerous bourgeois revolutions in the colonies and dependent countries of Africa, Asia, and Latin America). There is bound to be, therefore, a great variety of specific forms of B.R. and of the forces that motivate it. Whereas in the period that preceded the rise of monopoly capitalism the leading role in B.R. belonged entirely to the bourgeoisie, in the period of imperialism the influence of the proletariat on the course and results of B.R. has sharply increased; in a number of cases the leadership passes to the proletariat (e.g., the Russian revolution of 1905). The most general way of classifying B.Rr. is to divide them into upper-crust bourgeois and bourgeois-democratic revolutions. The upper-crust B.R. is carried out under the leadership of the bourgeoisie without any wide participation by the people and does not lead to deep-going social changes, for example, the 1867-68 revolution in Japan, the Young Turk Revolution and various contemporary revolutions in Asian and African countries, which have proceeded no further than the winning of national sovereignty. A special form of B.R. is found in the bourgeois-democratic revolution. Its features are active participation of the proletariat and the peasantry, a link-up with the agrarian revolution and the peasant movement for a radical reform of land relations, and action by the masses with their own demands differing from those of the bourgeoisie. There are several types of bourgeois-democratic revolutions, each with its distinctive historical role and motive forces: (1) the bourgeois-democratic revolutions of the period of struggle against feudalism which took place under the leadership of the bourgeoisie and ensured its economic and political domination, e.g., the French Revolution of 1789-94; (2) the bourgeois-democratic revolutions of the early period of imperialism and the first stage of the general crisis of capitalism. The proletariat acting in alliance with the peasantry becomes the leader of this type of bourgeois-democratic revolutions, which create the conditions for their development into socialist revolutions, e.g., the February 1917 revolution in Russia; (3) the bourgeois-democratic revolutions of the second stage of the general crisis of capitalism (the revolutions in the East-European countries); (4) the bourgeois-democratic revolutions in the colonies and dependent countries during the third stage of the general crisis of capitalism, known as the national-democratic revolutions. Successful revolutions of this type lead to the setting up of socialist-oriented states taking up a non-capitalist development.

Revolution, Social, a turning point in social life, signifying the overthrow of the obsolete and the establishment of a new progressive social system, an instrument and means of transition from one socio-economic formation (q.v.) to another. In contrast to the theorists of the liberal bourgeoisie and opportunism, who regard social revolution as fortuitous, Marxism-Leninism teaches that revolutions are a necessary, natural result of the development of class struggle in antagonistic formations. S.R. completes the process of evolution, the gradual ripening in the womb of the old society of the elements or prerequisites of a new social system. S.R. resolves the contradiction between the new productive forces (q.v.) and the old relations of production (q.v.), destroys the obsolete relations of production and the political superstructure which entrenches them and makes way for the further development of the productive forces. The old production relations are strengthened by their bearers—the ruling classes, who safeguard the obsolescent order by means of state authority. Hence, to clear the way for social development, the progressive classes must overthrow the existing political system. The basic problem of every social revolution is the problem of political power. Revolution is the highest form of the class struggle. During revolutionary epochs the broad masses who formerly stood aloof from political life, rise to a conscious struggle. That is why revolutionary epochs greatly accelerate social development. Revolutions must not be confused with so-called palace coups, putsches, etc. The latter forcibly change the top governing section, replace individual persons or groups within the same class in power. The problem of power does not exhaust the content of S.R. In a broad sense, it includes all those social transformations which are performed by the revolutionary class. The character of revolutions is determined by the social tasks they accomplish and by the social forces that participate in them. The socialist revolution (q.v.) is the highest type of S.R. as it differs radically from all previous revolutions and produces more profound changes in the life of the people. Previous revolutions replaced one form of exploitation by another; the socialist revolution abolishes the exploiting classes and eradicates all forms of exploitation of man by

man. The uneven economic and political development of the capitalist countries in the period of imperialism leads to revolutions breaking out at different times in different countries. This makes inevitable the historical epoch of transition from capitalism to socialism on a world scale. During this period one country after another falls away from the capitalist system and this further deepens the crisis of that system. The national liberation revolutions and various kinds of democratic liberation movements are of great significance during this epoch. However, in each individual country the possibilities for a revolution to erupt and develop depend upon a number of objective conditions (see Revolutionary Situation), and on the degree of ripeness of the subjective factor.

Revolution, Socialist, a radical, qualitative transformation of society, marking the transition from capitalism to socialism. S.R. replaces the production relations of domination and subjugation based on private ownership by relations of cooperation and mutual assistance, and thereby abolishes the exploitation of man by man. The fundamental principles of S.R. were formulated by K. Marx and F. Engels, who discovered the laws of social development. They proved that S.R. is a logical result of society's development and demonstrated the world-historic mission of the working class (q.v.) as the maker of S.R. They showed the necessity of establishing the dictatorship of the proletariat (q.v.) to build socialism. The seizure of power by the working class is only the beginning of revolutionary transformation. The building of the new society involves fundamental social reforms which take up a whole historical period, described by Marx as the special period of transition from capitalism to communism (to its first phase). While analysing the imperialist stage of capitalism, Lenin developed Marxism further, enriching this revolutionary theory with some highly important, fundamentally new propositions: on the possibility of S.R. being victorious first in one or several countries, which necessitates the co-existence of countries with different socio-economic and political systems; on S.R. first breaking the weakest links in the world system of the capitalist economy; on the hegemony of the proletariat in bourgeois-democratic revolutions and on their growth into S.Rr.; on the alliance between the working class and the peasantry being a decisive factor for the victory of a revolution; on the link between the struggle of the workers in the advanced capitalist countries and the national liberation movements; on the revolutionary situation (q.v.); on the interaction of objective and subjective factors; on the multiformity of S.R., and a number of other propositions. Socialist construction in the USSR and other countries has shown that the chief regularities of S.R. are: political leadership by the working class and the assumption of state power for the benefit of the working people, the alliance of the working class and the peasantry, the abolition of capitalist property, the socialist transformation of agriculture, planned economic development, cultural revolution, abolition of national oppression, defence of socialist gains, and proletarian internationalism. Depending on the level of development of the productive forces, the particular combination of national peculiarities, the general cultural level of the people, their historical traditions, and the alignment of class forces in the country and in the world, these regularities are manifested in different ways, determining the specific nature of the transition from capitalism to socialism in the country concerned. Thus, depending on these conditions, the revolution may be peaceful or non-peaceful. Marxism-Leninism holds that the sharpness and intensity of the class struggle depend on the strength of resistance offered by the reactionary bourgeoisie to the majority of the people, on the degree of violence the bourgeoisie resorts to. In our time the theory of S.R. has been developed further, being enriched with a number of new conclusions: on the availability of conditions favouring a peaceful revolution in various countries; on the possibility of non-capitalist development in backward countries and the establishment of the state of national democracy; on the possibility of transitional stages in the struggle for the socialist transformation of society; on the need to unite all democratic movements opposing the financial oligarchy. Being a relatively lengthy and multifaceted process, S.R. calls for consolidation of all democratic forces, the interlacing of socialist and general democratic tendencies in one mighty anti-monopoly movement, and for a socialist orientation of developing countries.

Rickert, Heinrich (1863-1936), German idealist philosopher, who, together with Windelband (q.v.), was the leader of the Baden school of neo-Kantianism (q.v.). He considered the object of philosophical investigation to be the study of the possibilities and methods of cognition. He devoted special attention to the methodology of the historical sciences and philosophical investigations. R. classified sciences according to two methods: generalised abstraction in the natural sciences, and individualised abstraction in the historical sciences. The first method, ignoring the infinite variety of characteristics of objects, allows the formulation of a system of universal concepts and laws; the second makes it possible to focus attention on the individual characteristics of a historically important object. According to R., history is the sum total of phenomena (events), each one with its inimitable face and thus with a place in history. However, any attempt to apply the generalised method inevitably leads to failure in understanding the laws of history. The ethical views of R. exerted considerable influence upon contemporary sociology. His main works are: *Der Gegenstand der Erkenntnis* (1892), *Die Grenzen der naturwissenschaftlichen Begriffsbildung* (1896).

Robinet, Jean-Baptiste (1735-1820), French philosopher whose materialist views contained some elements of deism (q.v.). The main sources of his views were the teachings of Locke and Condillac (qq.v.), but he was also influenced by Leibniz (q.v.). R. held that material substance which is infinite in space and time underlies the world. The diversity of nature is ruled by the principle of universal unity and harmony determined by the causal relation of things. R. was a proponent of hylozoism (q.v.) in explaining the facts of the consciousness. According to his theory of knowledge, sensations are the only source of knowledge. He considered ideas as a concentration of sensations, as copies of objects, criticised Plato's (q.v.) idealism and was convinced in the unlimitedness of human cognition. His main work: *De la nature* (1761-66).

Romantic School, the first mature expression of romanticism (q.v.). Its efflorescence was in the years 1798-1800 when a close collaboration was established in Jena between the literary critics Friedrich and August Schlegel, Karoline Schlegel, the poets Tieck and Novalis, the philosophers Schelling and Schleiermacher (qq.v.). The journal *Athenaeum* was published during this period. R.S. came out against the rationalism of the Enlightenment, opposing to it the cult of feeling and creative ecstasy, which, they maintained, reveals the mysteries of nature more profoundly than the tedious work of the scientist. The romanticists saw as the motive force of cognition the experience of the contradiction between the finite and the infinite, the frustration born of the unattainability of the infinite, an ironical attitude towards oneself and one's creation. Exponents of R.S. maintained love, a mystical cult of nature, artistic creative work, and religious experience, to be the means of possible access to the infinite. They idealised the feudal-Catholic past, some of them became ideologists of the Restoration. R.S. later appeared in France, Poland, Italy, Spain, Denmark, and the USA.

Romantic Sociology, a trend in sociology which emerged in the middle of the 19th century in Britain and Germany. Originally, R.S. was interwoven with feudal socialism (see Carlyle), later its ideas were developed by the ideologists of German fascism (E. Krieck, A. Rosenberg and others). Exponents of R.S. criticise civilisation and reject bourgeois democracy. In their opinion, the only way out of the impasse in which mankind has found itself, is to change the existing world by means of "world expansion".

Linking their ideas with racist theory, exponents of R.S., from J. Gobineau on, maintain the cult of the heroic past of the Aryan tribes, call for a return to the "law of the jungle", and proclaim the supremacy of "the superior Aryan race" over other peoples.

Romanticism, an ideological and artistic movement in European culture which replaced classicism (q.v.) in the early 19th century. R. as an artistic method expresses the artist's attitude to the depicted phenomena, which makes his works elevated and gives them a certain emotional colouring. One of the trends was the conservative reaction to the victory of the bourgeois system, expressing at the same time fear of revolutionary and popular movements. This trend was manifested in the creation of illusory ideals and was an apology for the medieval past. Another basic trend of R. had a progressive revolutionary direction, expressing the protest of wide social circles against reactionary politics (Byron, Hugo, Mickiewicz, Ryleyev, Chopin, Berlioz, Liszt and others). Although some of the aesthetic ideals of this trend of R. were utopian, while romantic images were often distinguished by their duality and inherent tragicalness, the artists nevertheless expressed a certain understanding of the contradictions of bourgeois society and interest in the life of the broad masses of people, and were oriented towards the future. Revolutionary romanticism as an artistic form of historical prevision and the embodiment of the artist's dream is a component of socialist realism (q.v.).

Roscelin, Joane (c. 1050-c. 1112), scholastic from Compiègne (France). He is known for his polemics with Anselm of Canterbury and Abélard (qq.v.) and for his heretical interpretation of the Trinity as a complex of three separate gods. This tritheist teaching was condemned by the church and R. was compelled to renounce it. He was one of the founders of the nominalist tradition in medieval philosophy (see Nominalism). According to Anselm, R. affirmed that general concepts are only "vibrations of the air" (*flatus vocis*). In reality, according to R., there exist only single sensorily perceptible things. Out of his works only a letter to Abélard is extant.

Rousseau, Jean-Jacques (1712-1778), member of the Left wing of the French Enlighteners, philosopher, sociologist and aesthetician, one of the theoreticians of pedagogy. He advocated deism (q.v.). Alongside the existence of God R. also recognised the immortal soul. He taught that matter and spirit are two eternally existing principles (see Dualism). In the theory of knowledge he adhered to sensationalism (q.v.), although he also maintained that moral ideas are innate. As a sociologist R. took a radical position. He severely criticised feudal class relations and despotism, and supported bourgeois democracy and civil liberties, the equality of people irrespective of their birth. R. saw the cause of inequality in the establishment of private property. At the same time he stood for the perpetuation of small property. Being an exponent of the theory of social contract (q.v.), R. held, in opposition to Hobbes (q.v.) that in the "natural state" there was not only no war of all against all, but that friendship and harmony reigned among people. R. severely criticised the old feudal system of education and demanded that education should aim at the training of active citizens who respected labour. Marx, Engels and Lenin thought highly of the historical role of R., noting at the same time his idealism and bourgeois limitations Main philosophical and sociological works: *Discours sur l'origine et les fondements de l'inégalité parmi les hommes* (1755) and *Le contrat social* (1762).

Rural Community, a social community belonging to the type of primitive communities (q.v.). The early R.C. was a territorial unity of large family communities, characterised by relations of hierarchic domination and subordination, most often on the principle of genealogic closeness to the historical progenitor. Traditionally, the office of chief of the early R.C. was inherited by one of the family communities: the heads of large families were elected by their members. The R.C. was concerned with economic, military, and political matters. Ownership of the land was common, each family holding its allotted share. The basis of the R.C. was formed by its nucleus of blood relatives which continued to play a leading role in the religious life of the communities, in the matrimonial relations of its members, and in determining inheritance rights. The R.C. was composed of the nobility, freemen and churls; property and social differentiation gave rise to the more or less vigorous process of class formation. The R.C. could be a basis or an important element of pre-capitalist social systems which replaced the primitive-communal system (q.v.). All peoples known in history passed through the R.C. stage, and its survivals persisted in a class society (e.g., in Russia it was retained till the end of the 19th century).

Ruskin, John (1819-1900), English art critic, aesthetician and journalist. His idealist outlook was greatly influenced by Carlyle (q.v.). From the position of conservative romanticism R. criticised bourgeois society, its parasitism and depraved morals; he saw "the main root" of unjust wars in social inequality, avarice and the evil will of the capitalists. R.'s ideal was utopian by nature—it was a system based on free labour and patriarchal handicraft production which he sought to revive. R. considered universal education and moral upbringing of people a means of deliverance from social troubles, assigning a great role to art. Perfect art reflects the high moral values of a nation, reproduces the beauty of reality and through it man is morally uplifted. Such, in his opinion, was the art of the Middle Ages. R. exerted a strong influence on the cultural life of England. His main works: *The Stones of Venice* (1851-53, in three volumes), *Lectures on Art* (1870), *The Art of England* (1883).

Russell, Bertrand (1872-1970), English philosopher, logician, public figure. R. contributed considerably to the development of modern mathematical logic (q.v.). He developed the logic of relations, perfected the language of logical symbols. At the beginning of the 20th century, R., together with Whitehead (q.v.), following Frege (q.v.), made attempts to elaborate the logical basis of mathematics (see Logicism). He wrote a large number of philosophical works on natural science problems. R. maintained that philosophy draws its problems from natural science, and that its task is the analysis and explanation of the principles and concepts of natural science, that the essence of philosophy is logic, the logical analysis. R. is the founder of English neo-realism (q.v.) and neo-positivism (q.v.). In the solution of the fundamental problem of philosophy R.'s outlook underwent evolution from objective to subjective idealism. Man, according to R., has to do with sense data. What man perceives is a "fact". Facts cannot be considered either physical or psychical: they are neutral (neutral monism). According to R., what is empirically corroborated should be ascribed not to physics, but to physics plus psychology. Psychology is an essential component of every empirical science. R. rejected the materialist theory of reflection.

He opposed religion and defended atheistic convictions. As an active participant of the struggle against fascism, for peaceful co-existence, R. together with Einstein, Joliot-Curie (qq.v.) and other scientists was among the initiators of the Pugwash movement, and of international meetings of scientists fighting for peace and scientific co-operation.

Ryle, Gilbert (b. 1900-1976), English philosopher, a leader of the so-called linguistic philosophy (q.v.), professor of philosophy at Oxford. For R. the task of philosophy was merely to solve problems arising from the imperfect understanding of our means of cognition. In his main work, *The Concept of Mind* (1949), R. advanced a conception very close to behaviourism (q.v.).

S

Saint-Simon, Claude Henri (1760-1825), French utopian socialist. During the French Revolution he was close to the Jacobins; took part in the War of Independence of the United States. S.S. subscribed to the views of the French materialists, opposed deism (q.v.) and idealism and put up against them the study of nature. He resolutely upheld determinism, extending it to the development of human society, and paid special attention to the idea that history is governed by laws. S.S. held that history was to become as positive a science as natural science. Each social system is a step forward in history. The driving forces of social development are the progress of scientific knowledge, morality and religion. His idealist approach to history did not prevent S.S. from expounding the idea that social progress is an objective process, and advancing surmises on the role of property and classes in the development of society. Moreover, his sociological conception helped to show that every new social system springs naturally from preceding historical development. According to S.S., the society of the future will be based on scientifically organised and planned large-scale industry, but private property and classes will survive. The dominating role in it will be played by scientists and industrialists. Among the latter S.S. included the factory owners, workers, merchants, and bankers. All must he given the right to work; each man works according to his ability. The future society, rather than ruling over people, will administer things and manage production. The utopian nature of the views of S.S. stands out in his failure to understand the historic role of the proletariat as the builder of a new society, and of revolution as the means of transforming the old society, in the naive hope that by propaganda of a positive philosophy it will be possible to achieve a rational organisation of people's life. After his death, his social doctrine had a great influence on Comte (q.v.). Before long, however, the school of Saint-Simonists degenerated into a religious sect, which highlighted the weak sides of the doctrine. Main works: *Lettres d'un habitant de Genève à ses contemporains* (1802), *Mémoire sur la science de l'homme* (1813-16), *Travail sur la gravitation universelle* (1813-22), *Du système industriel* (1821), *Catéchisme des industriels* (1823-24), and *Nouveau christianisme* (1825).

Sankhya 1. A conception enunciated in the ancient Indian epic *Mahabharata*, which is premised on the idea of the supreme intuitive knowledge of man's soul and psychology. It is complemental to yoga (q.v.). 2. An orthodox system of ancient Indian philosophy dating back to approximately the 1st century A.D. S. recognises the existence of two prime elements in the Universe: material (matter, nature) and spiritual (consciousness). The latter is neither the supreme God, the creator, nor the universal spirit. It is the eternal immutable principle of individuality, consciousness which contemplates both the life of the living being in which it finds abode and the evolution of the Universe taken as a whole. The material element is in constant change and development and is subject to the law of causality. The foundation of the S. system is attributed to the legendary sage Kapila, but the first systematic exposition of S. was given by Ishvara-Krishna in the early centuries A.D.

Santayana, George (1863-1952), American philosopher and writer, proponent of critical realism (q.v.). Admitting the objective existence of the material world, S. held that only "essences" could be cognised, i.e., real or possible qualities of things which appear in cognition as signs of objects. In his understanding of the "essences" S. was close to Plato and Husserl (qq.v.). S. regarded consciousness as an epiphenomenon (q.v.): cognition is a passive reflection of reality. In aesthetics he defined the beautiful as "objectified pleasure". In ethics he supported escapism: happiness should be sought in liberating the spirit from the flesh, from the world and knowledge. In sociology (*Dominations and Powers*, 1951), S. put forward a theory which explains the development of society by the operation of man's instincts—that of self-preservation and the striving for material benefits, etc. In political science S. opposed democracy and favoured the power of the elite. Rejecting theological dogmas, S. recognised religion. Main works: *The Life of Reason* (5 vols., 1905-06), *Realms of Being* (4 vols., 1927-40).

Sarasvati, pseudonym of **Dayananda, Mulshankar** (1824-1883), Indian idealist philosopher and religious reformer, founder of Arya Samaj (Bombay, 1875), a reformist Hindu society, preaching "return to the Vedas" and revival of the ancient religion of the Aryans. He attacked idolatry, polytheism, domination of the priests, superstitions, retrograde customs, etc., and strove to "cleanse" Hinduism (q.v.) from medieval superimpositions. Religious reformism combined quaintly in S. with his ideas of enlightenment. While advocating universal scientific education, he at the same time sought to present science as a projection of the Vedas (q.v.). In philosophy S. was a follower of Advaita-Vedānta, on the basis of which he sought to "conciliate" all the six main "orthodox" philosophical systems of antiquity. S. advocated independent national development for India.

Sartre, Jean-Paul (1905-1980), French philosopher and writer, the leading proponent of French atheistic existentialism (q.v.). His philosophical views were contradictory. They were a peculiar combination of ideas of Kierkegaard, Husserl (qq.v.) and S. Freud. While emphasising the progressive nature of Marxist philosophy, S. sought to "complement" Marxism by basing it on existentialist anthropology and psychoanalysis. However, on the whole the conception of S. was eclectic. It sought a middle way between idealism and materialism, in an attempt to transcend both. Proceeding from the main precept of existentialism—

existence precedes essence—S. built his "phenomenological ontology" on a radical antithesis of being and consciousness. The separation of being from consciousness leads to dualism (q.v.). S. called his concept dialectical, but used dialectics as a method for substantiating indeterminism. His dialectics was purely negative. Its sphere was confined by consciousness, and it was completely banished from nature. In ethics S. adhered to the position of pure subjectivism, with freedom being the main category here. Regarded from the point of view of individual consciousness, freedom appeared as the essense of man's behaviour, the source of activity, and the only possible mode of his existence. S. denied the objective principles and criteria of morality and the objective determinateness of human behaviour. Each person has to "design" himself, to choose his own morality. In *Critique de la raison dialectique* (1960) S. sought to overcome the subjectivist limitations of his conception and build a new theory of social relations and historical development. But, forcing as he did objective economic and social structures into the background and proceeding from individual human action and logic, he substituted anthropological analysis for socio-historical. S.'s literary work was closely linked with his philosophical views. His social and political stand was inconsistent. He was in the ranks of the French Resistance, incisively criticised the evils of capitalist society, was active in upholding peace and democracy, spoke in support of the national liberation movement and condemned the US aggression in Vietnam. In his later years S. was increasingly close to the ultra-leftist movement, and shared leftist and revisionist ideas. Main works: *L'Imaginaire* (1940), *L'Être et le Néant* (1943), *L'Existentialisme est un Humanisme* (1946), *Situations* (6 vols., 1947-64).

Scepticism, a philosophical conception questioning the possibility of knowledge of objective reality. Consistent S. is close to agnosticism and nihilism (qq.v.). S. is most widespread in periods of social development when the old social ideals are already tottering, while new ones have not yet asserted themselves. As a philosophical doctrine, S. emerged during the crisis of antique society (4th century B.C.) as a reaction to the preceding philosophical systems which had tried to explain the sensual world by means of speculative reasoning and in so doing had often contradicted one another. S. reached its peak in the teachings of Pyrrho, Arcesilaus, Carneades, Aenesidemus, Sextus Empiricus (qq.v.) and others. Following the traditions of the sophists (q.v.), the first sceptics drew attention to the relativity of human knowledge and its dependence on various circumstances (living conditions, the state of the sense-organs, the influence of traditions and habits, etc.). Doubt as to the possibility of any generally recognised and demonstrable knowledge underlay the moral conception of antique S. The sceptics of old preached abstention from judgments for the sake of achieving complete peace of mind (see Ataraxia) and thereby happiness, the objective of philosophy. But the sceptics themselves by no means refrained from judgments. They wrote works criticising the speculative philosophical dogmas and putting forward their arguments in support of S. S. played an important role in refuting the dogmas of medieval ideology. The works of Montaigne, Charron, Bayle (qq.v.) and others questioned the arguments of the theologians, thus preparing the ground for the adoption of materialism. On the other hand, the S. of Pascal, Hume, Kant (qq.v.) and others restricted the possibilities of reason in general and cleared the way for religious faith. In modern philosophy, the traditional arguments of S. have been adopted for its own aims by positivism (q.v.), which considers all judgments, generalisations, and hypotheses pointless if they cannot be tested by experience. Dialectical materialism recognises S. as an element of knowledge (doubt, self-criticism, and the like) but does not absolutise it to the point of agnosticism.

Schelling, Friedrich Wilhelm Joseph (1775-1854), German philosopher, the third (in point of time) of the famous classical German idealists (after Kant and Fichte, qq.v.). In the 1790s he wrote a number of essays on problems of the philosophy of nature. Using Kant's ideas and Leibniz's (q.v.) teaching on living monads and nature's rational forces, S. introduced the idea of development into the conception of nature. In his *System des transzendentalen Idealismus* (1800), he tried to combine Fichte's subjective idealism with objective idealism in his own system. According to S., philosophy must supply answers to two questions: how does the development of unconscious-spiritual nature lead to the birth of consciousness, and, inversely, how does consciousness, being only a subject *per se*, become an object? The first question is answered by the "philosophy of nature" and the second—by the teaching of "transcendental idealism". By the subject S. understood not an individual's consciousness, but the mind's direct contemplation of the object itself, or "intellectual intuition". In developing this doctrine, S. joined the reactionary wing of the Romantic school (q.v.) according to which intuition was the lot of just a few select. The regular process in which spirit and nature, subject and object, freedom and necessity are combined is manifested and operates necessarily through the individuals' free activity. However, to S., this process was not open to knowledge, but only to faith, and the guarantee of historical and moral process lay in God alone. S.'s doctrine, conceived as dialectic of necessity and freedom in history but developed on the basis of idealism and mysticism, in fact wounded up as fatalism (q.v.) by denying any historical prevision. From his "philosophy of nature" and the system of "transcendental idealism", S. came over to philosophy of identity (q.v.), a new form of objective idealism. The idea of identity of object and subject became the central problem of S.'s teaching, the law of identity of the indivisible mind and itself was proclaimed the supreme law. S.'s teaching of freedom was further developed in his *Philosophische Untersuchungen über das Wesen der menschlichen Freiheit* (1809). Like Fichte, S. understood freedom as recognised necessity and viewed it not as an individual's heroic deed, but as an achievement of society. However, contrary to this view, S. mystified the problem of freedom by associating it with the problem of evil in the world. The ultimate root of freedom was declared to be a purely personal principle, its source transcending into the other world. From about 1815, S. entered his new, and final, evolutionary phase, the mystical "philosophy of mythology and revelation". His teaching of that period was marked by the extremely magnified mystical elements in his world outlook. He then smeared any philosophy based on reason, counterposing to it a "philosophy of revelation", which seeks the truth beyond the boundaries of reason, in "religious experience". S.'s open propaganda of his "philosophy of revelation" failed. Young Engels, in his brilliant pamphlets, explained to his contemporaries the reactionary content of that philosophy.

Schiller, Ferdinand Canning Scott (1864-1937), English pragmatist, professor at Oxford and Los Angeles. S. called his variety of pragmatism (q.v.) "humanism". He regarded truth as man's creation and declared all human knowledge to be subjective. He understood "reality" as "experience", as a plastic, amorphous mass, subject to the influence of man's will. Thus S. arrived at solipsism (q.v.), declaring it to be theoretically possible, although inconvenient in everyday life. His metaphysics was a mixture of subjective idealism and the evolution theory, which he regarded as a purposive process directed by divine power. S. interpreted formal logic pragmatically, replacing it with "logic of application". He considered the laws and forms of logic to be postulates and convenient fictions. From the position akin to that of Nietzsche (q.v.) he acclaimed fascism as a means of creating the "superman". His main work: *Humanism* (1903).

Schiller, Friedrich (1759-1805), German poet and aesthete. S.'s views were formed under the influence of the ideas of Rousseau, Lessing (qq.v.) and the movement Sturm und Drang. He acclaimed the French Revolution, but later became disappointed with it. His dramas *Die Räuber* (The Robbers), *Kabale und Liebe* (Love and Intrigue), and others and philosophical lyrics are imbued with humanism, hatred of tyranny and are marked by great profundity

in portraying human feelings and characters. However, in a number of his works the poet departed from reality in search of an abstract aesthetic ideal. In the 1790s, S. became a follower of Kant's (q.v.) philosophy and aesthetics, though not without reservations (for instance, he criticised the formalism of Kant's categorical imperative, q.v.). S. regarded art as an instrument of forming the harmoniously developed human personality, uninhibited in creating good. He believed that art alone was to help man attain real freedom. S.'s quest for freedom was of a purely moral nature, yet it was a form of protest against the feudal regime. His main philosophical works: *Philosophische Briefe* (1786), *Über Anmut und Würde* (1793), *Briefe über die ästhetische Erziehung des Menschen* (1795), *Über naive und sentimentalische Dichtung* (1796).

Schleiermacher, Friedrich Ernst Daniel (1768-1834), German Protestant theologian and philosopher. He was for many years a preacher, a professor of Berlin University. S.'s views are a combination of ideas of Spinoza, Kant, Fichte, Schelling, and Jacobi (qq.v.). His philosophy was dominated by Romantic, anti-Enlightenment trends (see Romantic School). He derived religion and morality from the inner disposition of the subject. Infinite being, according to S., rests on the unity of the world, or God, in which all contradictions are reconciled and which is open to immediate knowledge. His ideas stimulated further criticism of all sources of Christianity (see Young Hegelians). None of these criticisms, however, went beyond the limits of a religious world outlook. His philosophico-religious views had a strong influence on the ideology of Protestantism (q.v.) of the 19th century, though his treatment of religion is criticised by representatives of contemporary Protestantism (see Dialectical Theology). His main works: *Reden über die Religion* (1799), *Monologen* (1810).

Schlick, Moritz (1882-1936), Austrian philosopher and physicist, one of the leaders of logical positivism (q.v.) and founder of the Vienna Circle (q.v.). In his book *Allgemeine Erkenntnislehre* (1918), he formulated ideas which were later

adopted by logical positivists as the basis
for their doctrine, particularly the teaching of the analytical nature of logic and
mathematics and the principle of verification (q.v.). Besides defending the general
conception of logical positivism (*Positivis-
mus und Realismus*, 1932), S. attempted,
from the neo-positivist positions, to analyse specific philosophical problems (space
and time, causality and probability) and
ethics (value of moral judgments, free will).
He criticised Carnap's (q.v.) and O.
Neurath's conventionalism (q.v.).

Scholasticism, the name given to
medieval "school philosophy" whose exponents—the scholastics—sought to give
a theoretical substantiation and systematisation to the Christian dogma. S. rested
on the ideas of ancient philosophy (Plato,
q.v., and especially, Aristotle, q.v.,
whose views S. adapted to its own
purposes). The dispute over universals
(q.v.) was prominent in medieval S. Historically, S. is divided into several
periods: early S. (9th-13th centuries) was
under the influence of Neoplatonism
(q.v.) (Erigena, Anselm of Canterbury,
Averroës, Avicenna, Maimonides, qq.v.),
"classical" S. (14th-15th centuries) was
dominated by "Christian Aristotelianism"
(Albert the Great, Thomas Aquinas,
qq.v.). The disputes between the Catholic
and the Protestant theologians, which
took place later (15th-16th centuries) were
ultimately a reflection of the struggle
waged by the Catholic Church against the
Reformation (q.v.). Some bourgeois authors contend that this struggle of ideas
was responsible for the efflorescence of
scholastic philosophy. In subsequent centuries S. lost its erstwhile influence under
the impact of progressive philosophical
doctrines of the period of modern history
(Descartes, Hobbes, Locke, Kant, Hegel,
qq.v., and others). The 19th century saw
a resuscitation of S., which united various
schools of Catholic and Protestant
philosophy.

Schopenhauer, Arthur (1788-1860),
German idealist philosopher, taught in
Berlin University (1820-31). His main
work *Die Welt als Wille und Vorstellung*
appeared in 1819. S. became famous only
after the revolution of 1848, when the
bourgeoisie, frightened by the people's
revolutionary upheaval, turned to reaction. S.'s influence especially increased in
the epoch of imperialism. S. was an
enemy of materialism and dialectics;
counterpoised metaphysical idealism to
the scientific understanding of the world.
S. rejected Kant's (q.v.) uncognisable
"thing-in-itself" and maintained that blind
and irrational will was essence of the
world. His voluntaristic idealism (see Voluntarism) is a form of irrationalism (q.v.).
The will which rules the world excludes
any natural or social laws and, in fact,
any scientific cognition. Denial of historical progress is another peculiarity of S.'s
voluntarism. His world outlook, permeated, as it were, by hate of the
revolution and the people, is thoroughly
pessimistic. S.'s aesthetic views had great
influence. Fighting against progressive,
realistic art, S. preached aestheticism
which scorns reality and is alien to people's
vital interests. He set off aimlessness and
passive contemplation of artistic intuition
(q.v.) against ideologically committed,
creative art. S.'s philosophy was culminated by borrowing from Buddhism (q.v.)
the mystic ideal of "nirvana", absolute
serenity, killing the "will to live".

Schrödinger, Erwin (1887-1961), Austrian physicist, foreign member of the
Academy of Sciences of the USSR (from
1934), one of the creators of quantum
mechanics (q.v.). In 1926, he discovered
the basic (the so-called wave) equation of
quantum mechanics. His central idea in
physics was the wave theory of matter.
To him goes the credit for his attempt
(contrary to vitalism) at a materialist
interpretation of natural phenomena based
on physics. These ideas of S.'s have been
fruitfully applied in modern molecular
biology.

Schweitzer, Albert (1875-1965), Ger-
man-French philosopher, humanist, Protestant theologian, a progressive-minded
public figure. He was a missionary physician at Lambaréné (Gabon, Equatorial
Africa), where he devoted himself to
advocating humanist ideas. He took the
very phenomenon of life, rather than
knowledge of the world, as the basis for
his philosophical doctrine (new rational-

ism). He considered this main principle a filter to screen off the negative effects of civilisation and saw a promise of mankind's moral perfection in it. However, the true path to realising humanist ideals, according to S., was not social transformations, but men's personal efforts directed at bettering "human nature". S.'s optimistic view of man's future had a religious colouring and was paralleled with an ethical approach to the image of Christ. On the whole, S.'s world outlook was not a coherent system, embracing diversified philosophical conceptions. S. denounced war and spoke repeatedly in favour of banning nuclear weapons. He was a Nobel Peace Prize laureate. His main works: *Philosophie der Kultur* (in 12 vols., 1923-29), *Kultur und Ethik* (1960).

Science, the field of research directed towards obtaining further knowledge of nature, society and thought. It comprises all the conditions and elements of research: scientists with their knowledge and abilities, skills and experience, whose work is based on the principles of the division and co-operation of their scientific efforts; scientific institutions, test and laboratory equipment; methods of research, a system of concepts and categories, a system of scientific information, and the sum of scientific knowledge acquired as a prerequisite, means or result of this research. This result may be also treated as a form of social consciousness (q.v.). Contrary to positivists' viewpoint, S. is not limited to natural or exact sciences. S. is an integral system with its components flexibly correlated in history: study of nature—study of society, philosophy—natural science, methods—theory, theoretical research—applied research. S., the necessary outcome of social division of labour (q.v.), comes to being after mental work is separated from physical work and cognitive activities become the occupation of a specific, initially limited group of people. Prerequisites for S. arose in Oriental countries, such as Egypt, Babylon, India and China, where the empirical knowledge of nature and society was accumulated and comprehended, and rudiments of astronomy, mathematics, ethics and logic were created. This heritage of the Oriental civilisations was assimilated and shaped into a coherent theoretical system in Ancient Greece, where there were thinkers who dissociated themselves from the religious and mythological tradition and took up S. From that time on, up to the industrial revolution the principal function of S. was that of explanation; its main task was cognition for the purpose of gaining a wider outlook on the world and nature with man as an integral part of the latter. The appearance of large-scale machine production makes S. an active factor in it. Cognition for the purpose of changing and transforming nature became its main task. As a result of this technological orientation of S. the leading place in it was taken up by physics and chemistry with corresponding applied branches. In the context of the scientific and technological revolution (q.v.) a new basic reconstruction of S. as a system takes place. For S. to comply with the requirements of modern production, scientific knowledge must be acquired by a whole army of specialists, engineers, production managers and workers. The character of work in automated production sections requires that the workers should have a wide scientific and technological outlook, acquire the fundamentals of scientific knowledge. S. is increasingly becoming a direct productive force. Hence S. must be oriented not only on technology but also on man himself, on the unlimited development of his intellectual and creative abilities, efficiency of thought, and the creation of material and spiritual conditions for his all-round and integral development. For this reason modern S. is not merely following the development of technology but outstrips it, becoming the leading force in the progress of material production, shaping itself into an integrated system. The sum total of researches (both in natural and social sciences) gives impetus to social production. Being earlier an isolated element in the domain of social life, S. begins to penetrate all its spheres; scientific knowledge and scientific approach are indispensable in material production, the economy, politics, management, and the system of education. That is why the rate of development of S. is higher than that of any other sphere of activity. In socialist society the successful development of S. and the introduction of its results in production are of paramount importance for speeding up scientific and technological progress, building the material and technical base of communism; this means fulfilment of the task of combining scientific achievements with the advantages of the socialist economy. To attain the state of full flourishing S. needs the establishment of communist public relations. Communism in its turn needs S.; without S. communism can neither win nor successfully develop, because communist society is a scientifically governed society; it implies complete domination of man over his environment.

Science of Science, the, a discipline which studies the laws governing the functioning and development of science (q.v.), the structure and dynamics of scientific knowledge and scientific activity, the interaction of science with other social institutions and with the material and intellectual life of society. In the 1960s, the S.S. became an independent comprehensive discipline which embodies diverse researches in history, sociology, economics, logic, psychology of science, scientometrics, and in a number of other fields. The aim of the S.S. is to work out a theoretical interpretation of science, to specify ways and criteria for its rational application in life and development of society. The S.S. studies the problems of scientific organisation, policies in the field of science, information processes of forming and functioning of scientific knowledge, structure of the scientific potential, prediction in science and technology, application of science in global and regional scientific programmes. The Marxist S.S., which has dialectical materialism as its methodological basis, widely uses modern computer technology, mathematical modelling of the objects of study, methods of systems research (see Systems Analysis; Systems Approach).

Scientific and Technological Revolution, the fundamental qualitative transformation of the system of modern science and technology, covering all sides of technological relations and marked above all

by automation (q.v.), a new stage in the development of technology. Machine production, in which the worker directly participates in the production process, performing various technical functions, gives way to automated production, in which the object is machined entirely by a technical system operating without the worker's direct participation. Advanced forms of automation include cybernetic devices attached to automatic lines to perform the computing and controlling functions. Cybernetic technology is being introduced not only in material production but also in management, public services, science, and education. The technological methods of production undergo changes in the course of the S.T.R. Mechanical methods formerly prevalent in material production, are replaced by more effective methods, which alter not only the shape of objects but also the molecular and atomic structures of substance, transforming it into a new substance with preset properties. Examples are the chemical methods for the production of synthetic materials, the methods of nuclear power generation, application of lasers, high and low-temperature technologies, biochemical and biophysical methods applied in agriculture, light industry, and medicine. Technological changes are accompanied by changes in materials and raw materials, with ever wider use of man-made materials and a sharp increase in the amount of electric energy consumed by industry. All these processes bring about fundamental changes in the productive forces of society and are based on modern scientific achievements, the fusion of science and technology, science and material production. In present-day conditions, especially under socialism, this is an all-round process as science becomes a direct productive force, materialising not only in technology but also in the producers of material goods by raising their cultural and technical level, developing their intellectual and creative potential. As the S.T.R. develops, an increasingly wide range of researches, not particular "vanguard" sciences, exert influence on production. These include not only the natural sciences but also social sciences: economics and organisation of production, scientific organisation of labour, elaboration of principles of scientific control, concrete sociological investigations, social psychology (qq.v.), industrial aesthetics, forecasting of social, scientific and technological progress. The social essence of the S.T.R. is that it changes the place and role of man in production. Automation, far from diminishing this role, on the contrary, increases it because as man is relieved of mechanical, technical functions he is able to devote himself to more interesting and more creative work. The redistribution of functions between man and technology necessitates changes in the content of labour, in the professional composition of the workforce, cultural and technical standards of the workers. As a result of higher labour productivity the relative share of those engaged in material production falls and the non-productive sphere, particularly science, education and medical service, expands. Under capitalism, these requirements of the S.T.R. are distorted by antagonistic social relations. For example, changes in the professional composition of the workforce result in the representatives of traditional professions losing their jobs. The application of new technologies is accompanied by intensification of labour. The expansion of the non-productive sphere comes about primarily through the growth of the public services, advertising, administrative-bureaucratic machinery, police, etc. It is only in the context of socialism that the S.T.R. assumes the direction meeting the interests of man and society. Under socialism, the progress of science and technology resulting from the fusion of the S.T.R. and the advantages of the socialist system of economy is the principal way and means for the creation of the material and technical base for communism. Under socialism, the S.T.R. contributes to the solution of major socio-political tasks and to the triumph of socialism in the economic competition with capitalism.

Scientific Communism, one of the three component parts of Marxism-Leninism (q.v.), which studies the social movements seeking to eliminate capitalism and build a socialist and then communist society. Inasmuch as the main driving force and the leader of this movement is the working class, who unites all the oppressed and exploited people and has sympathies of progressive mankind, the main question of S.C. is that the proletariat performs its world-historic mission. This tenet is defined concretely in the theory of proletarian, socialist revolution (q.v.) and in the theory of the dictatorship of the proletariat (q.v.), which are the instruments of building socialist society. Thus, S.C. shows the real, scientifically grounded way to the abolition of exploitation of man by man and the introduction of a new form of organisation of society, free from contradictions of capitalism, of which the utopian socialists dreamed. As a component part of Marxism-Leninism, S.C. bases itself on the conclusions of the other two component parts—dialectical and historical materialism and political economy. The theory of class struggle (q.v.) and the theory of surplus value are particularly important for S.C. By making theory tackle the practical problems of the reorganisation of society, S.C. stimulates dialectical thinking, the discovery of historical and social laws, the further development of economics, including the political economy of socialism. As a world outlook and political ideology S.C. expresses the interests of the proletariat, the class responsible for a revolutionary reorganisation of society. S.C. is closely connected with the liberation movement. It is a generalisation of the experience of not only the class struggle of the proletariat, of the socialist revolution and proletarian dictatorship but also of the mass democratic movements and the bourgeois-democratic and national liberation revolutions. In contrast to utopian socialism (q.v.), S.C. is practically applied in the policy of the Communist Party of the Soviet Union and other Communist and Workers' parties; in life, in the practice of socialist and communist construction it finds all the new created by the broad masses, shows the theoretical and practical significance of such sproutings of communism, and contributes to their growth and spread. On the basis of the generalised experience of the international communist and working-class movement, the practice of socialist and communist construction in the Soviet Union and other socialist countries S.C. formulates the general laws of development for each country taking the road of transition from capitalism to communism (see Socialism and Communism). Compliance with these laws, combined with the diverse ways and means of solving practical problems, due consideration being made for the specific conditions and peculiarities of each individual country, with the search of new forms and methods, not only contributes to practical success but also creates favourable conditions for the further development and enrichment of the theory of S.C.

Scientific Prevision, prediction of natural and social phenomena, not yet observed or not yet established experimentally, based on a generalisation of theoretical and experimental data and consideration of the objective laws governing development. S.P. can be of two kinds: 1) it may concern existing phenomena which are relatively unknown or have not yet been observed experimentally (for example, prediction of antiparticles, new chemical elements, deposits of minerals, etc.); 2) it may bear on phenomena which must arise only in the future given certain conditions (for example, the prediction by Marx and Engels of the inevitable downfall of capitalism and victory of communism, Lenin's conclusion on the possibility of building socialism in one country). S.P. is always based on the extension of cognised laws of nature and society to a sphere of phenomena which are unknown or have not yet arisen, a sphere in which these laws should preserve their force. S.P. must also contain elements of supposition, especially as regards concrete future events and their dates. This is determined by the emergence, in the course of development, of qualitatively new causal nexuses and possibilities, which did not exist previously and, insofar as society is concerned, by the special complexity of its development. Practice is always the final criterion of the correctness of S.P. Denial of the objective laws of reality (see Agnosticism; Scepticism) also leads to denial of S.P., as the unavoidable outcome of the idealist theories of social development. On the other hand, recognition of S.P. is based on a materialist understanding of history.

Scientism, a conception which absolutises the role of science (q.v.) implying the natural and exact sciences, within culture and ideology. In its capacity of an ideological trend, rather than a formal system of views, S. may manifest itself in different ways and with varying amplitude, ranging from outward imitation of exact sciences—far-fetched use of mathematical symbols, deliberate application of the technique current in these sciences (axiomatic structure, a system of definitions, logical formalisation, etc.) to the analysis of philosophical, ideological, social and humanitarian problems—to the absolutisation of the natural sciences as the only scientific knowledge, or rejection of the sphere of the world outlook and ideological problems as devoid of any cognitive meaning and significance (see Neo-Positivism). Philosophical S. underestimates the identity of philosophy as compared with other sciences and denies it the status of a specific form of social consciousness, which has distinctive features of its own as compared with specialised scientific knowledge. Sociological S. denies that the object of social analysis has individual peculiarities distinguishing it from the objects studied by the natural sciences. It ignores the need to take into account value factors, is given to empirism and descriptiveness, is hostile to any theories having a bearing on socio-philosophical problems, and absolutises the importance of quantitative methods in social studies. Modern bourgeois culture has produced various trends of anti-scientism, some of which claim that science's potential for solving the key problems of human existence is limited, while its extreme varieties assess science as a force hostile to the true essence of man. Consistent anti-scientism regards philosophy as something basically different from science, which, it holds, is purely utilitarian, and is incapable of rising to the understanding of the genuine problems inherent in the being of the world and man. While upholding the principles of a scientific approach to any ideological, philosophical, social or humanitarian problem, and rejecting the anti-scientist attempts at downgrading the role of science, Marxism-Leninism is equally opposed to vulgar S. with its disregard for the complicated questions concerning the place and function of science in the system of culture, and the interrelation between different forms of consciousness.

Sechenov, Ivan Mikhailovich (1829-1905), Russian natural scientist, founder of Russian physiology and materialist psychology. His philosophical and socio-political views were greatly influenced by the Russian revolutionary democrats, particularly Chernyshevsky (q.v.). S. initiated experimental physiological investigations of the central nervous system, in particular the brain (q.v.). His major achievements were in the physiology of the nervous system, notably the discovery of central inhibition and the "inertness" of nerve tissue. The extention of the reflectory principle to the activity of the brain (in his articles "Reflexes of the Brain", 1863, and "Who and How Should Elaborate Psychology", 1873) marked the beginning of the reflectory theory of the mental activity of animals and man, which served as a point of departure for Pavlov (q.v.) in creating the doctrine of higher nervous activity (q.v.). S. made an important contribution to the natural scientific treatment of such problems of materialist epistemology as the nature of sensory reflection and its cognitive function, as the transition from sensory reflection to thinking, as the nature of thought processes, and the role of practical activity in shaping images and mental abilities.

Self-Consciousness, the process of man singling himself out of the objective world, awareness of his relation to the world, awareness of himself as a personality, of his behaviour, actions, thoughts, feelings, desires, and interests. The animal is identical with its activity, it changes nature only by virtue of its presence, i.e., is related to it directly. Man, however, mediates his relation to nature by his social practical activity and above all by the use of tools. Thanks to labour he transcends the direct nexus with nature. By changing nature, he changes himself.

By creating products in the process of labour, man, as it were, doubles himself, and in the object of his activity perceives his handiwork. He differentiates himself as producer from the objects of his activity. But since labour is always social, man begins to be aware of himself as a member of a given historical system, while regarding other men as similar to himself. Language (q.v.) plays an important part in the shaping of S.C. S.C. (as a predisposition) arises simultaneously with consciousness (q.v.) as derivative from it, but becomes manifest at a considerably higher stage in the development of mankind. At first man only differentiates himself from the object. Then S.C. is manifested as a generic, collective element; man is still fully absorbed by the gens which carries human essence. With the decline of the gentile system, the rise of civilisation and the emergence of the individual, the S.C. of the personality as such arises. Philosophers at different times treated S.C. as an active principle and tended to reduce man's practical activity (q.v.) to a mere manifestation of this principle (see Fichte; Hegel; Young Hegelians). Moreover, S.C. was frequently regarded as creating the objective world itself. In reality S.C., being an active principle, can only be understood as a result of man's productive activity in society.

Self-Motion, motion (q.v.) which has its source and cause in the moving thing itself. The conception of S.M. is the opposite of that of "external impulse" as the sole cause of change in nature. In the history of philosophy the origin and development of the category of S.M. was associated, first, with the question of the "beginning" of the world, the prime cause of world processes and, second, with difficulties in explaining the actual processes of development. Ancient materialists tried to explain movement by forces and properties inherent in nature itself: combination and division of the primary elements (Ionian philosophy), "love" and "hate" (see Empedocles), atoms and empty space (see Leucippus, Democritus). Deduction of change from an ideal transcendental element was characteristic of idealist systems (see Plato). The problem of understanding the cause of movement became especially topical with the appearance of the Christian dogma of the creation of the world. To prove the S.M. of the world it was necessary to reveal the source and mechanism of its movement within itself, but theology placed this source outside of it (the activity of God). The mechanistic conception of change is theoretically untenable because it cannot oppose the idea of the "prime impulse" (Newtonian mechanics) and is incapable of explaining real processes of development. A radical transformation of the method of thinking was required for a scientific explanation of S.M.: dialectics had to come to the aid of materialism. The Spinozian idea of *causa sui* (cause of itself), the Leibniz principle of the monad (q.v.) as the self-moving and self-determining substance, the Kantian ideas of the development of the heavens, earth, and man, the evolution idea in Schelling's (q.v.) philosophy, and, lastly, Hegel's (q.v.) idealist dialectics—all were landmarks in developing the S.M. conception. Marxist philosophy, upholding the materialist approach to S.M., emphasises that this category has a dialectical content, is incompatible with a metaphysical and evolutionist understanding of development, q.v. (simple decrease, increase, repetition) and is inseparably connected with the dialectical conseption of development as the unity and conflict of opposites.

Self-Realisation, Ethics of, a trend in the bourgeois ethical theory which emerged in the late 19th century. Among its proponents are philosophers of different schools such as objective idealists (F. Bradley, J. McTaggart in Britain; J. Royce in the USA), American and French personalists (B. Bowne, M. Calkins, E. Mounier), the Italian neo-Hegelian Croce (q.v.) and others. According to E.S.R., the aim of moral activity consists in each individual realising his unique "inner Ego". Hence the conclusion that the ethical value of human actions lies in their originality and specific personal quality. Making individualism the basic criterion of morality leads to voluntaristic conclusions. The theorists of E.S.R. include the many individual

"Egos" in an all-embracing system of the "absolute Ego" (sometimes interpreted as God), in relation to which the former are parts of a single whole. This system allegedly helps establish a harmony of interests: in being guided only by the inducements of his individual self, man serves the whole, i.e., society. The apologetic purport of E.S.R. is evident in its justifying the all-round submission of the individual to the laws of bourgeois society, which is made to appear as a non-historical, suprasocial system.

Semantics, a branch of Semiotic.

Semiotic, a science which engages in the comparative study of sign systems (see Sign), from the simplest signal systems to natural languages and formalised languages (q.v.) of science. The main functions of a sign system are: (1) the function of transmitting communications or expressing meaning (see Denotation and Sense); (2) the function of intercourse (q.v.), i.e., ensuring understanding by the listener (reader) of the communication transmitted, and also a motive to action, emotional influence, etc. The performance of any of these functions presupposes a definite internal organisation of a sign system, i.e., the presence of different signs and laws of their combination. In conformity with this, three main divisions are singled out: (1) syntactics, or the study of the internal structure of the sign systems regardless of the functions they perform; (2) semantics, which studies the sign systems as a means of expressing meaning; (3) pragmatics which studies the relation of sign systems to those who use them. The biggest role in the development of S. methods is played by the study of systems possessing, on the one hand, a sufficient variety of means for expressing meaning, and on the other, a sufficiently articulated structure. Up to now such systems have been above all the formalised languages of mathematics and particularly of mathematical logic (q.v.). Metalogic (q.v.) is the most developed branch of S. Its studies promote the formalisation (q.v.) of new spheres of science (cf. the developing calculuses in mathematical linguistics, experiments in formalising certain concepts of pragmatics, the concepts of "verse metre" etc.). The concepts and methods of S. acquire great importance in view of the development of the theory and practice of the rational storage and automatic processing of information (q.v.); in this sphere S. comes in close contact with cybernetics (q.v.). The main principles of S. were first formulated by the American logician and mathematician Peirce (q.v.); subsequently they were expounded and systematised by the philosopher Ch. Morris (q.v.) (*Foundations of the Theory of Signs*, 1938). Questions of S. were in fact considered as early as the 1920s by scholars of the Lvov-Warsaw school (q.v.).

Seneca, Lucius Annaeus (c. 4 B.C.-A.D. 65), exponent of Roman stoicism (see Stoics), the tutor of Emperor Nero, committed suicide at the latter's order. His numerous works (*Epistolae morales ad Lucilium* and others) have been preserved in the original. His doctrine reflected the conflicts of his epoch and was extremely contradictory. S. adhered to the pantheism (q.v.) of the Greek stoics, i.e., regarded the world as a single material and rational whole, and elaborated chiefly moral problems which, when properly solved, enable man to attain calm and undisturbed spirit (see Ataraxia). He sought to link his ethics, individualist in the main, with the tasks of society and the state. The ethics of S. exerted a great influence on the Christian ideology.

Sensation, an elementary psychical phenomenon appearing as a result of the direct influence of objects of reality on the sense organs of men and animals. Subjectively, the objects are perceived as red, green, warm, cold, etc. as if they possessed these qualities in themselves (see Primary and Secondary Qualities). Diverse factors of the environment (light and sound waves, molecules of chemical substances, etc.) act upon the peripheral part of the sense organs, are coded there and then transferred as electro-chemical impulses by nerves to the centre—the cortex, where S. occurs. Vision and the corresponding system of S. are most highly developed in man followed by tactile, auditory, gustatory and other Ss. Each group of Ss. has its own characteris-

tics—a totality of qualities continuously passing one into another, and incomparable with the qualities of other groups of Ss. Colours do not resemble sounds, tastes or smells. S. also differs in intensity. In the process of cognition the Ss. are the basis for the shaping of elementary notions (q.v.).

Sensationalism (also called sensationism), a doctrine in epistemology (q.v.) which considers sensations (q.v.) the sole source of knowledge. If sensations are regarded as a reflection of objective reality, consistent S. under certain conditions leads to materialism (see Holbach; Helvétius; Feuerbach). But if sensations are regarded only as subjective, behind which nothing exists or the unknowable "thing-in-itself" is posited, S. leads to subjective idealism (see Berkeley; Hume; Kant; Mach; Avenarius; Bogdanov). Therefore, S. by itself is not yet a materialist line in philosophy, and its exponents are often powerless in the struggle against idealism. Sensations can become a necessary side of cognition only given their organic unity with the other sides of the cognitive process: practice and abstract thinking (see Contemplativeness; Empiricism; Cognition; Rationalism; Theory and Practice).

Sentimentalism, an artistic method which emerged in England in the mid-1700s and spread mainly to the European literatures (S. Richardson and L. Sterne in England; Rousseau, q.v., and L. S. Mercier in France; Herder, q.v., and J. P. Richter—pseudonym Jean Paul—in Germany; N. N. Karamzin and early V. A. Zhukovsky in Russia). As the last stage of the Enlightenment, S. in its ideological content and artistic peculiarities opposed classicism (q.v.). S. expressed the social aspirations and sentiments of democrats belonging to the "third estate", their protest against feudal survivals, growing social inequality and the standardisation of human personality in the evolving bourgeois society. However, these progressive tendencies were substantially restricted by its aesthetic creed: idealisation of simple life in the lap of nature, which was supposedly free from any coercion and oppression, and devoid of the evils of civilisation; by its anti-rationalism and the cult of intimate feelings.

Set Theory, a branch of mathematics dealing with one of the main categories of philosophy, logic, and mathematics—the category of the infinite—by exact methods (see Infinite and Finite). It was founded by G. Cantor. The subject of the S.T. is the properties of sets (sum totals, classes) which are for the most part infinite. The fundamental principle of the S.T. is the establishment of different "orders" of infinity. The classical S.T. proceeds from the recognition of the applicability of the principles of logic, unquestionable in the sphere of the finite, to the infinite sets. However, as early as the end of the 19th century the development of the S.T. brought to light difficulties, such as paradoxes (q.v.), connected with the application of the laws of formal logic, particularly the law of excluded middle (q.v.), to the infinite sets. In the polemics that started in connection with this, some important epistemological problems of mathematical cognition were formulated: the nature of mathematical concepts, their relation to the real world, the concrete content of the concept of existence in mathematics, etc. In the course of these polemics there arose such trends in philosophy and mathematics as formalism, intuitionism, logicism (qq.v.). The constructive trend in Soviet mathematics deserves special attention. The methods of the S.T. are largely employed in all fields of modern mathematics. They have significance as a matter of principle in the problems of the substantiation of mathematics, particularly for the modern form of the axiomatic method (q.v.). All the problems of validating mathematics by logical means are nothing but problems of substantiating the S.T. However, efforts to substantiate the S.T. itself encounter difficulties which have not been overcome up to now.

Sextus Empiricus (c. 200-250), Greek philosopher and physician, follower of Aenesidemus (q.v.). The extant works of S.E., *Elements of Pyrrhonism, Pros mathematicus,* sum up the arguments used by ancient sceptics (see Scepticism) to refute the conception of "dogmatic" philosophy about the possibility of demonstrably correct, indisputable knowledge. Arguing against the existence of universally valid scientific, theological, ethical, and other truths, S.E. advised philosophers to refrain from categorical judgments and knowledge in order to achieve complete peace of mind and bliss, this being the aim of philosophy. S.E. taught that man should be guided in life by natural requirements, inclinations, habits, laws, traditions, and above all by common sense.

Shaftesbury, Anthony Ashley (1671-1713), English philosopher and moralist, wrote a number of essays on ethics, collected in *Characteristics of Men, Manners, Opinions, Times* (vols. 1-3, 1711). S.'s leading theme is his conception of the self-determining character of morality, its independence of social conditions. To S., moral cause is not related to religious sentiment, is innate in man and makes the latter advance supreme moral aims. Virtue is what brings supreme bliss, rational enjoyment. Man is stimulated to strive for virtue by "enthusiasm", due to which all contradictions are reconciled. The criterion for assessing the moral value of man's deeds lies in the motives, not in the results. Man, according to S., must seek balance between altruistic and egoistic motives. S.'s moral ideal is the harmoniously developed personality. All that is virtuous is simultaneously aesthetically beautiful, since beauty resides in harmony. S.'s moral teaching is marked by eudaemonism (q.v.). Many thinkers were greatly influenced by S.'s views: French materialists, Hume, Kant, Herder, Friedrich Schiller (qq.v.).

Shelgunov, Nikolai Vasilyevich (1824-1891), Russian revolutionary democrat, public figure, follower of Herzen, Belinsky and Chernyshevsky (qq.v.). He wrote essays on history, politics and economics, also engaged in art criticism and popularisation of natural science. In his pamphlets "To the Young Generation", "To the Soldiers", he severely criticised the peasant reform of 1861 and called for a peasant revolution. He was arrested a number of times for his articles against serfdom. He assisted in introducing Marxism into Russia. In his article "The Working Proletariat in England and France" (1861), he enunciated the main ideas of Engels' book *The Condition of the Working-Class in England*, referring to the author as "one of the best and noblest of Germans", to whom "European economic literature owes its best writing on the economic life of the English worker". In his social views S. did not rise up to materialism, although he spoke of the role of the masses in history and of the significance of production for social progress. He believed that transition to socialism was possible in Russia via the peasant community. S. criticised the teaching of innate ideas (q.v.) from the positions of materialist sensationalism (q.v.). As an adherent of Chernyshevsky's aesthetic views, S. opposed the "art for art's sake" theory. His works, *Usloviya progressa* (Conditions of Progress), 1863, *Zemlya i organicheskaya zhizn* (The Earth and Organic Life), 1863, *Ubytochnost neznaniya* (The Disadvantage of Ignorance), 1864, *Pisma o vospitanii* (Letters on Education), 1873-74, were devoted to philosophical problems.

Shevchenko, Taras Grigoryevich (1814-1861), Ukrainian poet, artist, thinker, fighter against tsarism and serfdom, founder of a revolutionary democratic trend in the history of the Ukrainian social thought. S. was born in a family of serfs, ransomed in 1838. In 1846, in Kiev, he joined a secret political Kirill and Mefody Society and headed its revolutionary wing; he was also associated with the Petrashevsky's group (q.v.). In 1847, he was arrested, forced to serve in the army, and exiled to steppe Kazakhstan. After his exile term expired (1857), he came to St. Petersburg where he became close to Chernyshevsky, Dobrolyubov (qq.v.) and other staff members of the journal *Sovremennik* (The Contemporary), who exercised fruitful influence on him. S.'s poetical writings "The Dream", "The Caucasus", "The Will" and others and his activities were directed against the "gang of selfseeking landowners" and the "crowned hangman"—the tsar, and against the apologists of serfdom. Exposing the yoke of Russian land-

owners and the tsar, S. came out against the Ukrainian bourgeois nationalists, stood for the friendship between the Russian and the Ukrainian peoples and fought for the development of the Ukrainian language and culture. Owing to his materialist world outlook, S. maintained that spiritual power was unthinkable without matter. He never spoke of himself as a materialist, because he mistakenly identified materialism with its vulgar form. Foreseeing the inevitable downfall of serfdom, he viewed the masses as a decisive force of social development. He was sharply critical of religion and the church. He took a realistic stand in aesthetics and considered nature the source of beauty. He held that art should be true to life, close to people and carry progressive ideology. His *Diary* is a vivid reflection of these views. S. had a strong influence on the development of the Ukrainian revolutionary social thought and culture (I. Franko, M. Kotsyubinsky, Lesya Ukrainka and others).

Shintoism, a religion which emerged in Japan under the primitive-communal system and underwent considerable changes in the course of its development. The term *Shinto* (Jap. the way of the gods) first came into use in the 18th century to distinguish S. from Buddhism (q.v.), from which many of its rites and conceptions were borrowed. In 1868, S. was proclaimed the state religion, which it remained formally until 1945; actually it began to lose its significance since the end of the 19th century. The chief element of S. is worship of numerous spirits, which were originally personified by animals, plants, things, natural phenomena and the souls of the ancestors. According to S., contact between the gods and people is effected through the emperor (Mikado), the descendant of Amaterasu, the Sun goddess, and her representative on earth. The Mikado is considered to be the forefather of all the Japanese and is honoured as a god. Following Japan's defeat in the Second World War the divine origin of the Mikado began to be denied, although in some respects S. is resuscitated and updated.

Shulyatikovism, synonym for crude oversimplification and vulgarisation of

Marxism. This conception reduces the complicated process of development of philosophy, art, literature and natural science in a class society to a mere expression of "class interest". The term of S. is derived from the name of V. M. Shulyatikov (1872-1912), a Russian Social Democrat, literary critic, whose book *Opravdaniye kapitalizma v zapadnoevropeiskoi filosofii* (The Justification of Capitalism in West European Philosophy) (1908) was an example of such vulgarisation. Proceeding from the philosophy of Bogdanov (q.v.), S. attempted to prove that all philosophical systems were but the theoretical justification of bourgeois interests, alien, as such, to the proletariat, and that Marxism, therefore, had nothing to do with them. Shulyatikov denied the existence of any element of objective truth in the philosophical views of Descartes, Spinoza, (qq.v.), the French materialists, Hegel (q.v.) and other pre-Marxist philosophers, since they gave the "picture of a class structure of society". Typical of S. is direct inference of ideological phenomena from the forms of production organisation, denial of a relative independence of science, literature and philosophy, the desire to find a vulgarly understood "class equivalent" for every philosophical category or artistic image. S. found its way to the conceptions of modern dogmatism (q.v.). Lenin sharply criticised S. (Vol. 38, pp. 486-502)

Sign, a sensorily perceptible material object, action or event, which indicates, denotes or represents another object, event, action, subjective formation in the process of cognition. The analysis of this concept plays an important part in philosophy, logic, linguistics, psychology, etc. Ancient philosophers (Plato, Aristotle, stoics, qq.v.) and 17th- and 18th-century thinkers (Locke, Leibniz, Condillac, qq.v.) gave much of their attention to the analysis of the epistemological functions of S. In the 19th century linguistics and mathematical logic (q.v.) contributed to the study of S. A special science, the subject of which is S., semiotic (q.v.), took shape in the 20th century (Peirce, Ch. Morris, qq.v., modern structuralists). To understand the nature of S. it is most important to single out particular social situations (so-called sign situations), in which the S. is used. Such situations are closely linked with the formation of speech (language) and thought (qq.v.). Ss. are usually divided into linguistic and non-linguistic, the latter are subdivided into signs-copies, signs-symptoms, and signs-signals. The connection of S. with the process of transmission of information (q.v.) is extremely important. From the definition of S. follows its most important property, that is: the S. being a certain material object serves to denote something else. Thus, it is impossible to understand what S. is without realising its meaning: objective (object denoted by S.), semantic (image of denoted object), and expressive (feelings, etc., expressed by means of S.) (see Denotation and Sense). In semiotics one should differentiate between relations of Ss. to each other (syntax), relations of Ss. to what they denote (semantics), and relations of an individual who uses Ss. to the corresponding S. systems (pragmatics). The study of formalised S. systems, which is conducted within the bounds of mathematical logic and metamathematics (q.v.), is of great importance for the creation of the theory of S. In spite of the intensive researches in all aforementioned directions, the problem of constructing a synthetic conception of S. has not yet been solved. This can be explained by the fact that S. belongs to complex structural formations, whose methods of research have not been sufficiently worked out. To create a synthetic theory of S. one should make detailed analysis of the structure and functions of social and production activity, which gives rise to a number of S. systems, first of all, to natural languages. The study of S. systems includes: 1) ascertainment of actions which are performed with them; 2) description and depiction of connections established between S. and other elements of human activity; 3) description of properties-functions of S. which arise thanks to these connections. The meaning of S. can be deduced from the fixation of all these components.

Sigwart, Christoph (1830-1904), German logician, was close to neo-Kantianism (q.v.). Known for his *Logic* (1873-78). According to S., logic is based on psychology and is the technical, normative doctrine of thinking. The criterion of truth, in his opinion, is necessity and universal significance, for which there is no basis whatsoever in the objective world. Evidence, simply postulated with a reference to faith, is considered by S. to be the basis of necessary thinking. He elaborated in detail the theory of judgment (q.v.).

Skovoroda, Grygory Savvich (1722-1794), a Ukrainian enlightener, democrat, philosopher and poet. He was educated at the Kiev-Mogilyansky clerical academy. Renouncing a clerical career, he chose the life of a wandering preacher and philosopher. His outlook was influenced by the ideas of Platonism, stoicism, and patristics (q.v.), and the philosophers of his time (Leibniz, q.v., and others) and Lomonosov (q.v.). In solving the fundamental question of philosophy (q.v.), he vacillated between materialism and idealism, but his standpoint on many questions was materialist. Following Lomonosov, he came to the conclusion that matter is eternal and infinite, that nature is ruled by law-governed connections and is its own cause *Druzhesky razgovor o dushevnom mire*—(Friendly Conversation on the Spiritual World), 1775. S. tried to eliminate the contradiction between the material and spiritual principles by combining the concepts "God" and "nature", considering them identical, as is typical of pantheism (q.v.). He acknowledged the boundlessness of human knowledge, but associated the study of nature with the necessity for self-analysis. S. sharply criticised the official religion for its dogmatism and scholasticism and propagated the heliocentric teaching of Copernicus (q.v), which was inimical to the church. He ridiculed the vices and parasitism of the clergy. His moral teachings were couched in a religious form and were associated with the search for a "religion of love and virtue". He defended the interests of the people, called for an end to oppression and to ignorance among the working people, but his solution of social problems was utopian, inasmuch as he considered the moral principle to be the main factor in setting up a new society. S. put forward ideas which were progressive for his time, in particular that social life should be based on creative labour, community of property, and universal love and equality. S.'s works were not published during his lifetime, but were widely circulated in manuscript copies.

Slave-owning System, a socio-economic formation (q.v.) based on the exploitation by the class of slave-owners of slaves, who are bereft of the means of production and are themselves chattels and "speaking instruments of labour". S.S. was the first antagonistic class society, the result of a long period of disintegration of the primitive-communal system (q.v.) and the emergence of class-society institutions— private property and the state. S.S. reached its peak in Ancient Greece and Rome where it provided the framework for the then effective economy, and for advanced philosophy and art. The productive forces of S.S. consisted of manual instruments of labour and large masses of slaves. The production relations were those of inhuman exploitation and oppression. The slaves's needs were reduced to the minimum, allowing for a more considerable surplus product than the previous mode of production and leading to the consolidation of private property and the development of commerce, including barter of commodities, trade, etc. Wars of conquest were frequent providing a constant supply of new slaves. In S.S., the main classes (of slave-owners and slaves) existed along with merchants, usurers, free craftsmen and peasants, small property owners with curtailed rights and a large mass of declassé elements. Among the slave-owning states there were monarchies and republics; in the latter free citizens participated in democratic institutions (people's assemblies, etc.). Democracy did not apply to slaves. They revolted against the slave-owners. The biggest slave uprisings were in Ancient Rome (Spartacus). Aggravation of the class struggle and foreign invasions brought about the collapse of S.S.. and its replacement by feudalism (q.v.). Slavery existed in the most countries to varying degrees, but some peoples by-passed S.S. as a social formation, thus stepping directly from the

primitive-communal system to feudalism. In some countries slavery existed even under feudalism and capitalism.

Slavophiles, adherents of a conservative political and idealist trend in Russian social thought of the 19th century, who argued that Russia was destined to follow a special path of development as compared with that of Western Europe. In its objective purport this was a utopian programme for the transition of the Russian nobility to the bourgeois path of development with maximum preservation of their privileges. This programme was evolved at a time when the need for a departure from the old forms of exploitation and an adaptation of the ruling class to the new historical conditions had become obvious even to the most reactionary figures. The founders of Slavophilism were Kireyevsky and Khomyakov (qq.v.). The ideas of the movement were first given literary expression in 1839, were developed in the 1840s and 1850s and were subsequently adopted by the pan-Slavists and the intellectuals who emigrated from Russia after the October Revolution. The S. regarded Orthodoxy (q.v.), community life, which they idealised, the "submissiveness" of the Russian people and the absence in Russia of class divisions as special features of Russian history, which in fact was a distortion of historical truth. The S. sought to justify this conception sociologically, claiming that the religion of a people determines the character of its thinking and is, therefore, the foundation of its social life. Since the S. considered Orthodoxy the true religion, they held that only those peoples who professed it, first and foremost the Russians, could have any claim to progress, while other peoples could do so only to the extent to which they accepted Orthodox civilisation. The S. sought a philosophical justification of their teachings in religious and mystic systems.

Social Action, Theory of, one of the main trends in present-day bourgeois sociology, which traces its origin to Weber (q.v.) who put forward the concept of S.A. The latter, according to Weber, is human behaviour in its entirety, when the acting individual gives it a subjective meaning, taking his patterns from the behaviour of other individuals. (Therefore, an instinctive reaction will not be a S.A.) According to Weber, S.A. is the main element of social reality, whereas social institutions, groups, and other social communities are merely the results of and methods for organising definite actions by individuals. Later on, the concept of S.A. was elaborated mostly by sociologists of the socio-atomistic orientation (R. McIver and others). Parsons (q.v.) sought to combine it with the notion of a hierarchy of social systems which organise and control the S.A. of individuals. He singled out four main levels of organisation of S.A. (or levels of action systems): 1. the level of the biological organism; 2. the level of the personality; 3. the level of the social system; 4. the level of the cultural system. Central to his theory of S.A. is the problem of equilibrium, i.e., of maintaining the stability of existing social systems. From the Marxist standpoint, human activities cannot be reduced to following generally accepted patterns of behaviour, or performing certain social roles. People themselves create their history, and act in conditions and under circumstances shaped by society as a result of its previous development.

Social Being and Social Consciousness, two interconnected and interacting aspects, material and spiritual, of society's life. Marxism understands S.B. as the material relation of people to nature in the process of the production of material wealth and the relations (in class society, class relations) people enter into in the process of production. S.C. is the views, concepts, ideas, the political, legal, aesthetic, ethical, and other theories, philosophy, morality, religion, and other forms of consciousness. The relationship between S.B. and S.C. is part of the fundamental question of philosophy (q.v.) as applied to society. Prior to Marxism the view prevailed in philosophy that consciousness plays a determining role in the life of society. Actually, however, consciousness is a reflection of the people's S.B. in their spiritual life. The first formulation of this proposition, which lays a solid scientific foundation under social science, was given by Marx and Engels. In *The German Ideology* they said: "... Men, developing their material production and their material intercourse [i.e., relations of production.— *Ed*.], alter, along with this their actual world, also their thinking and the products of their thinking. It is not consciousness that determines life, but life that determines consciousness" (K. Marx, F. Engels, *Collected Works*, Vol. 5, p. 37). Marxism explained this fact of decisive importance for understanding the life of people and also demonstrated that the relationship of S.B. and S.C. is not simple but complex and fluid and that it grows more complex simultaneously with social life. At the initial stages of history, S.C. was formed as a direct product of the material relations of people; subsequently, with the division of society into classes and the appearance of politics (q.v.), law, and political struggle, S.B. acted in a determining way on the minds of people through a mass of intermediate links like the state and state system, legal and political relations, etc., which also exerted a great influence on S.C. In these conditions the direct deduction of S.C. from material relations leads to vulgarisation and simplification. The diverse forms of S.C., for all their dependence on S.B., possess relative independence. The latter is expressed in the fact that changes in the material life of society never create new products of S.C., because spiritual concepts—scientific, philosophical, artistic, and other ideas—depend on the data accumulated earlier and are also subject to a definite intrinsic logic of development. Moreover, changes in material relations cannot cause instantaneous automatic changes of the S.C. because people's spiritual concepts possess a considerable power of inertia, and only struggle between new and old concepts leads to the victory of those which are called into being by the main requirements of changed material life. At the same time it is necessary to understand and to consider the great role of S.C. and its influence on the development of S.B. itself. The absolute counterposing of these two sides of the people's life holds true only within the framework of the fundamental question of what is primary and what is secondary.

Outside of it, such absolute contrasting is meaningless. In certain periods the role of S.C. can and does become decisive, although ultimately it is determined and conditioned by S.B. The historical materialist approach to the problem of S.B. and S.C. is of great methodological importance; it helps to formulate problems of social life scientifically and to solve them in the course of practical activity.

Social Consciousness, Forms of, different forms of reflection in the minds of people of the objective world and the social being on the basis of which these forms arise in the course of practical activity. Social consciousness exists and manifests itself in the forms of political ideology, legal consciousness, morality, religion, science, art and artistic views, and philosophy. As distinct from the immediate reflection of reality in everyday consciousness, the F.S.C. are more or less systematised consciousness mediated by theoretical or artistic reflection of reality. The F.S.C. differ in their object and form of reflection, in social functions and specific laws of development. The diversity of F.S.C. is determined by the wealth and diversity of the objective world itself—nature and society. Different F.S.C. reflect diverse spheres and aspects of reality (for example, political ideas reflect relations between classes, nations, and states and serve as a basis for political programmes realised in the actions of classes and social groups; the sciences study the concrete laws of nature and society, religion reflects in fantastic images man's dependence on the natural and later social forces, which rule over him, etc.). Each form of consciousness has its own object of reflection and is also marked by a special form of reflection (for example, scientific concepts, moral norms, artistic images, qq.v., religious dogmas). The wealth and complexity of the objective world merely create the possibility for the various F.S.C. to appear. This possibility is realised on the basis of a definite social requirement. Science arises only when the simple accumulation of experience and empirical knowledge becomes insufficient for the development of social production;

political and legal views and ideas arise with the appearance of classes and the state to justify and consolidate the relations of domination and subordination, etc. In each socio-economic formation (q.v.) all forms of consciousness are interconnected and in their entirety constitute the spiritual life of the given society. The specific nature of a social requirement giving rise to one F.S.C. or another also determines the historically concrete role which they play in the life and development of society. With the victory of communism the need for political and legal ideology will disappear and they will wither away. On the other hand, such F.S.C. as morality, science, art and philosophy will flourish. They will not only serve various social needs, but will also mould the spiritual make-up of each individual, become a requisite for his all-round development and creative endeavour.

Social Contract, Theory of, an idealist doctrine of the state and law (qq.v.), being the result of a contract consciously concluded between people. According to this theory, complete anarchy and "war of all against all" or, by some views, idyllic freedom, precede the origin of society and the state. The general feature of the "natural state", in which mankind allegedly obtained for a long period, is unrestricted personal freedom which people consciously forgo in favour of the state to ensure their safety, private property, and other personal rights. The first concepts of the origin of the state by contract arose in antiquity (see Sophists, Socrates, Epicurus). The T.S.C. was given its ultimate form in the 17th-18th centuries (see Hobbes, Locke, Rousseau, and others) in connection with the struggle of the bourgeoisie against feudalism and absolute monarchy. It was the ideological justification of the bourgeoisie's claim to political power. The theory declares the "natural" right to private property and thus justifies economic inequality of people, which is a reflection of the limitations of bourgeois thinking. Enlighteners in Russia (see Radishchev), the United States (Thomas Jefferson), and other countries, accepted the postulates of T.S.C.

Social-Darwinism: a theory in sociology, which regards the struggle for existence (q.v.) and natural selection as the prime mover of social development. This theory, which won currency in bourgeois sociology at the end of the 19th century, was an ungrounded attempt at applying to sociology certain (wrongly interpreted) propositions of Darwin's (q.v.) biological theory (L. Gumplowićz, G. Ratzenhofer, A. Small and others). Some Social-Darwinists claim that natural selection and the struggle for existence continue in human society to this day. Others hold that natural selection in its pure form operated in society over 100 years ago, but that under the impact of progress in science and technology the struggle for existence subsided and a situation emerged in which not only the fittest could survive but also those who in earlier conditions were doomed to extinction. The exponents of such theories see the root of almost all social evils in the intensified propagation of such inferior people. At this point, S.D. merges with the racial anthropological school in sociology.

Social Ecology, the branch of knowledge studying various aspects of interaction between society and nature (other variations of this term being, e.g., the ecology of man, global ecology). At the time of the scientific and technological revolution (q.v.), the metabolism between man and nature is increasingly mediated by man-made technical devices and systems, as a result of which man finds himself in greater isolation from nature. There appear new forms of drawing natural resources into production, which becomes a powerful factor affecting the biosphere (q.v.). As a consequence, man's economic activities exert a growing influence, both direct and indirect, on the chemical composition and properties of the atmosphere, the Earth's heat balance, radioactive background, the World Ocean, etc. These activities lead to the erosion and exhaustion of the soil, water pollution, depletion of fresh water reserves and non-renewable sources of raw materials and energy, the discharge into the biosphere of biologically non-decomposable and toxic waste, and to the growing urbanisation of landscapes, which along with other ecological factors adversely affects man's physical and mental health and the gene pool of human populations. The aggregate effect is sometimes so impressive that it is referred to as the ecological crisis. Various conceptions of this crisis, worked out by bourgeois theorists, for the most part ignore the ultimate connection between the aforementioned phenomena and the profound socio-class conditions. Marxist theory sees their social sources above all in the peculiarities of the capitalist mode of production with its spontaneity, anarchy and antagonism of production relations. The bourgeois system of values determining man's activities and his orientation in the world dictates a predatory attitude to the environment. The capitalist society is incapable of working out adequate mechanisms for rationally regulating the metabolism between society and nature, which would allow to assess the effects, both direct and indirect, of man's economic activities. Socialism creates the prerequisites for placing the metabolism between man and nature under public control, this, above all, through abolishing the private ownership of the means of production, of the land and other natural resources. Under socialism, environmental protection and rational use of natural resources form a consistent governmental policy, which envisages both an ecological optimisation of existing and future industrial projects and production processes, and the adoption of a set of special economic measures. As distinct from the capitalist countries, where ecological measures are inevitably half-hearted and limited in scope, the socialist system permits to carry out comprehensive long-term programmes aimed at conserving and improving the habitat, and at overcoming or preventing the ecologically adverse effects of scientific and technological progress. Preservation of the environment is one of the most important global problems (q.v.) of our day and age, its solution necessitating close co-operation of all nations of the world.

Social Estates, a form of class division typical of the slave-owning and feudal societies. S.E. were social groups distinguished by their actual position in society and their legal status in the state. Membership of S.E. was hereditary. In feudal Russia, the nobility and the clergy were the only privileged S.E. The nobles were tax-exempt, not subject to corporal punishment, and could only be tried by a court of the nobility. They alone possessed the right to own landed estates and serfs. The non-privileged townspeople (chiefly petty artisans and tradesmen) and the peasants made up the lower S.E., subject to taxes. Survivals of the division of society into S.E. persist today in many of the capitalist countries, particularly where the outdated feudal relations have not been entirely eliminated. To retain its class domination, the contemporary bourgeoisie is prepared to sustain any estate prejudices (typical in this respect are the Nazi theories of the corporate state, advocating the restoration of S.E., and also the reactionary theories of elite, q.v., recommending the transfer of power to the select top of society). In Russia, S.E. divisions were abolished in November 1917.

Social Psychology 1. a sum total of emotions, wills, inclinations, habits, traditions manifesting themselves in the psychology of social groups, classes, and nations owing to the community of socioeconomic conditions of their life. 2. The science studying the objective laws governing the interaction of psychological and social factors in individual and group human activities. S.P. studies the psychological peculiarities of various social groups, strata and classes, the features (class, national, etc.) and laws governing the formation of socio-historical types of personality, the mechanism of socio-psychological relations in various social groups, and different forms of collective intercourse and reciprocal influences. Socio-psychological thought traces its origin to Plato, Aristotle, Hegel, Feuerbach (qq.v.) and other thinkers of the past. As a science in its own right, S.P. emerged at the end of the 1890s. Bourgeois S.P. divided into two main trends—one seeking to single out socio-psychological problems in the sphere of human behaviour (James, q.v., W. McDougall), the other working out conceptions of the human personality as a product of a definite system of social relations (Durkheim, Lévy-Bruhl, qq.v.), and creating theories of "social roles" (Parsons, Merton, qq.v.). In the 1920s, bourgeois sociology produced a number of empirical researches in the socio-psychological characteristics of social groups, public opinion, and the socialisation of the personality. Experimental research into the inner structures of the personality, the systems of motivation and orientation, social attitudes and reactions to social situations is conducted in the West by Gestalt psychology, q.v. (K. Lewin), behaviourism q.v., (F. Allport), and Freudianism, q.v. (K. Horney, Fromm, q.v., A. Kardiner). Different theoretical and experimental trends of S.P. in capitalist countries tend to ignore the determinative role of production relations in society and recognise the psychological factors as the moving force of social development. Western researchers have acquired certain positive experience in psychological techniques and achieved good results in empirical research, which are being used by Marxist social psychology. This science considers socio-psychological phenomena in the light of dialectical materialism and proceeds from the fact that these are dependent on socio-historical conditions. While making the evolution of personality and society dependent on the objective logic of historical development, this approach also takes into account the influence of subjective factors. Of great importance for the development of Marxist-Leninist S.P. were the works of Plekhanov and Labriola (qq.v.) and also V. M. Bekhterev, L. S. Vygotsky and other Soviet psychologists and pedagogues. At the present stage of its evolution, S.P. makes a wide use of methods accepted in sociology and general psychology (e.g., questionnaires, interviews, opinion polls, and the like). S.P. includes several applied departments such as psychology of material production, psychology of everyday life (the family, social service systems, leisure), psychology of politics, psychology of science, art, religion, and other forms of social consciousness.

Social Relations, relations between people established in the course of their joint practical and spiritual activity (q.v.); these are divided into material and ideological. The production of material wealth forms the basis for the existence and development of human society. That is why the relations of production, economic relations, are the most important of all the S.R. The relations of production (q.v.) determine the nature of all the other S.R.—political, legal, moral, religious, etc. Understanding of the dependence of all S.R. on the relations of production made it possible for the first time, on a scientific basis, to explain the common features of society's development from country to country.

Socialism, a social system which comes into being as a result of socialist revolution (q.v.) setting off the transition from capitalism to communism. S. is based on public ownership of the means of production, which precludes the existence of exploiter classes and of the exploitation of man by man, and provides for relations of comradely co-operation and mutual assistance in society. Under S. there is no social oppression or inequality of nations, and no antithesis between town and country (q.v.), between mental and physical labour, q.v. (although considerable distinctions between them continue to exist). Socialist society consists of two friendly classes—the working class and the peasantry—and the social stratum of the intelligentsia. The distinctions between the two classes and also between them and the social groups are gradually obliterated. A prominent feature of the relations between all the social groups is their socio-political and ideological unity, while the relations between socialist nations are marked by friendship, co-operation and fraternal mutual assistance. By virtue of public ownership, S. develops its economy and entire society on a planned basis. The development of social production serves to satisfy the people's growing material and cultural requirements to an ever fuller degree. Social life is based on broad democracy: all working people are encouraged to take an active part in it. Socialist democracy ensures the social rights—the right to labour, rest and leisure, health protection, to security in old age, to housing, free education, equality of all the citizens before the law etc.—and political freedoms—freedom of speech, freedom of conscience, freedom of the press, freedom of assembly, meetings and demonstrations, freedom of participating in administering the state and public affairs. Under S., the productive forces are not yet developed enough to secure an abundance of products and labour is not yet a prime vital necessity for all members of society. For this reason, material wealth is distributed here according to the principle, "From each according to his ability, to each according to his work". In the Soviet Union, S. has triumphed fully and irreversibly, and a society of developed socialism has been built, this constituting the highest stage in the first phase of the communist social formation. At present, developed S. is being built in a number of socialist countries. The mature socialism existing in the USSR has a powerful material and technical base, which expands in step with the scientific and technological revolution (q.v.); socialist property rises to a higher level of socialisation; the people's requirements are met ever more fully and steadily; the social structure is characterised by the indestructible alliance of the workers, peasants and the intelligentsia. The development of social and national relations has led to the formation of a new historical community of people—the Soviet people—characterised by ideological and political cohesion, the leading role of the working class, and the rallying of the people around the Communist Party. The development of the political system and socialist democracy has resulted in the establishment of a state of the whole people (q.v.). Higher educational standards, the development of culture, and the prevalence of the scientific world outlook and Marxist-Leninist ideology reflect the people's rich spiritual life. In this society, S. develops on its own basis; the restructuring of all social relations is being completed; all advantages, potentialities and laws of S. are realised most fully and comprehensively; the conditions are maturing for S. to grow directly into communism.

Socialism and Communism, the two phases of the communist socio-economic formation, socialism being the first, or lower, phase, and communism the higher phase. They differ in degree of economic, social and spiritual maturity. Both are based on co-operation and mutual assistance of people free from exploitation. These relations are dominant in the economy and correspond to the social nature of the productive forces, As S. is being built, social property is created through the expropriation of capitalist property and the co-operation of the peasants and craftsmen. As a result two forms of socialist property emerge—the property of the whole people, and the property of the collective farms and cooperatives—and, correspondingly, two main classes, the working class and the collective-farm peasantry. S. is also characterised by the fact that, while abolishing the historical antithesis between town and country (q.v.), it does not yet abolish the distinctions between them in the level of material and spiritual development, the organisation of work, way of life (q.v.), in the medical care and cultural facilities, etc. S. does not yet abolish the considerable distinctions between mental and physical labour (q.v.), and therefore the intelligentsia remains and develops as a distinct social group. Finally, the still insufficient degree of economic and spiritual development necessitates a distribution of consumer goods according to the quantity and quality of work done, as well as the preservation of commodity and money relations in society. As the building of developed socialist society is completed, S. perfects itself on its own basis. The creation of the material and technical base of communism, improvement of all the social relations and their transformation into communist relations, the moulding of man possessing communist consciousness will lead to the communist formation entering its higher stage, when uniform ownership of the means of production by the whole people asserts itself, class distinctions disappear, essential distinctions between town and country, and between mental and physical labour are overcome, labour becomes the first vital necessity of everyone, and material wealth is distributed according to requirements. This process will cover a lengthy historical period. As C. asserts itself the world over, the state and the entire political and legal superstructure will wither away. C. is a highly organised society of free and socially conscious working people, functioning on the basis of self-administration and generally accepted norms of communist life, the observance of which will constitute an inner requirement and habit of the people (see Communist Public Self-Government). Nations will draw closer together and, ultimately, all distinctions between them will disappear. The social organisation which will emerge on the basis of the communist mode of production will be able to ensure, and, in fact, will ensure the all-round development and flowering of every individual, and provide for all his abilities to be used to the maximum for the good of society. C. is an association in which the free development of every individual becomes a condition for the development of all and, consequently, harmony between the individual and society is achieved.

Socialism, Christian, a teaching seeking to prove the possibility of blending the ideas of Christianity (q.v.) with the ideas of socialism on the grounds that the latter supposedly had been proclaimed in the Gospels. C.S. emerged in the first half of the 19th century and advocated class harmony, Christian love, ideas of social reforms through moral perfection. These tenets found expression in the social doctrines of a number of churches supporting the bourgeois regime, in the programmes of Christian parties, Christian trade unions and other organisations aiming to split the labour movement. Meanwhile, prompted by the growing authority of the communist ideology, a democratic trend originated in C.S. Its advocates reject capitalism, view socialism as a realisation of humanistic aspirations, attempt to adjust their religious beliefs to socialist ideals. The Communist parties show understanding towards those Christian leaders who voice genuine sympathy for socialism; they favour co-operation with the latter in the work for peace and social progress. However, this does not affect the overall attitude towards C.S. as a form of bourgeois ideology making it harder for

the working people to see the true path towards liberation, towards winning genuine happiness.

Socialism, Ethical, a theory claiming that socialism should be regarded chiefly as a totality of moral and ethical principles and norms. It is upheld by petty-bourgeois and liberal-bourgeois ideologists (mainly the right Social Democrats) who borrow arguments from various philosophical schools. Neo-Kantianism (q.v.) is its theoretical basis. Rejecting Marxist philosophy, the followers of Kant, q.v. (Cohen, q.v., P. Natorp, K. Vorländer and others) tried to marry scientific socialism to Kant's moral philosophy. They identified the concept "socialism" with a certain moral world outlook, they meant by ethics a kind of social pedagogics the aim of which was to exclude contradictions from social relations. They believed it was Kant who formulated the basic idea of socialism, the idea of solidarity. The substantiation of the doctrine of socialist transformation of society through the Kantian "extra-class" theory of morality actually denied that socialism is the result of the law-governed socio-economic development of society and turned this doctrine into a purely moral conception. The cardinal problems of Marxism (classes and class struggle, social revolution, etc.) were discarded, and moral values and the idea of man's gradual moral perfection were given the priority. In practice, the propositions of E.S. mean the renunciation of the fight for socialism. E.S. was propagated by M. Adler (Austria), by M. Tugan-Baranovsky (Russia), and others. A detailed exposition of E.S. is given in K. Vorländer's books, *Kant und der Sozialismus* (1900) and *Kant und Marx* (1911).

Socialism, Fabian, a reformist trend in Britain which arose as an antipode to scientific socialism. Its name is an allusion to the Roman army commander Fabius Cunctator (Procrastinator). The Fabian Society was organised in Britain in 1884, and in 1900 it became affiliated to the Labour Party as a literary-publicist group. F.S. was represented by B. and S. Webbs, M. Phillips, H. G. Wells, B. Shaw, and others. Officially, F.S. denies any connection with philosophy, but many of its proponents support religion, adhere in their views of history to the doctrine of the decisive role of ideas in society, and deny the class struggle. F.S., according to Lenin, "is the most consummate expression of opportunism and of Liberal-Labour policy" (Vol. 21, p. 260).

Socialism of the Chair, an ironical name given to a group of German liberal professors and politicians, members of the socio-ethical school, which in the second half of the 19th century was the first to "prove" theoretically that capitalism would peacefully develop into socialism. Following the teaching of the historical school in political economy, socialists of the Chair held that political economy must go beyond the study of economic phenomena in the narrow sense and merge with the other social sciences. They held that the state could regulate economic relations. S.C. was a kind of reaction to the growth of the working-class movement and expressed the desire of the bourgeoisie to retard the development of the proletariat's class consciousness. In 1872, soon after the suppression of the Paris Commune, the socialists of the Chair organised a Socio-Political Union which preached the need for social reforms and state intervention in economic relations. L. Stein, A. Wagner, G. Schmoller, L. Brentano, and Sombart (q.v.) were among the proponents of S.C.

Socialism, Utopian, a pre-scientific stage in the development of the teaching on society based on common property, labour obligatory for all members, and equal distribution of products. The term "utopia" as a designation of an ideal society was first used by More (q.v.) and was the name he gave to an imaginary island on which an ideal society was set up. Subsequently, this term was applied in describing imaginary and impracticable social systems. The utopian socialists, who criticised the existing system based on private property, painted pictures of an ideal future society and set out to prove theoretically the need for public ownership, voiced a number of brilliant ideas and conjectures. That is why U.S. (together with English political economy and classical German philosophy) is one of the

ideological sources of scientific socialism. Condemnation of private property and praise of common property can be found in the works of some ancient Greek and Roman authors, the medieval "heretics", in the programmes of some peasant uprisings in the epoch of feudalism, and in the views of peasant ideologists. That was a natural reaction to the inequality and exploitation of man by man in antagonistic societies. As capitalism developed and there appeared the predecessors of the proletariat U.S. acquired more of the features of historical realism, became more complex as a theory and branched out, forming various schools and trends. The systematic development of U.S. began in the period of capitalism's birth, the Renaissance and Reformation (qq.v.)—J. Hus in Bohemia, Münzer (q.v.) in Germany, More (q.v.) in England, Campanella (q.v.) in Italy, and others. It was further developed in the period of bourgeois revolutions in Europe, being at that time the ideology of the proletariat's predecessors (Mellier, Mably, Morelly, qq.v., and Babouvism in France, J. Lilburne and Winstanley, q.v., in England). U.S. reached its apex during the rapid development of capitalism, when the illusions of the ideologists of bourgeois revolutions vanished and the contradictions of capitalist society became increasingly apparent (see Saint-Simon, Fourier in France and Owen in England). No utopian socialist, however, succeeded in attaining a materialist understanding of history or discovering the real driving forces behind the socialist transformation of society. Besides this, there was a lack of understanding of the real ways for transforming the existing social relations, renunciation of revolution and naive faith that the existing order could be changed by spreading socialist ideas. Only the development of the productive forces, which makes a revolution in the mode of production inevitable, and the emergence of an industrial proletariat, sufficiently schooled and organised by the development of capitalist society itself, created the historical possibility of converting socialism from an utopia to science. Marx and Engels translated this possibility into reality by scientifically proving the inevitability of the transition to communism and discovering the force capable of effecting this transition, the proletariat, and by creating the doctrine of socialist revolution and the dictatorship of the proletariat as the instrument for translating the socialist ideals into reality. Marxism critically re-fashioned and assimilated everything valuable in U.S. With the rise of Marxism U.S. increasingly became a factor impeding the working-class and socialist movement. In individual countries, U.S., merging with the revolutionary democratic ideology, played a progressive part (Russian revolutionary democrats, Narodniks in the 1870s, and others) after the emergence of Marxism.

Socialist State, the political part of the superstructure that develops on the economic basis of socialism. The S.S. is a new type of state (q.v.) succeeding the bourgeois state as a result of socialist revolution (q.v.). Creation of the socialist superstructure embraces the whole period of transition from capitalism to socialism. In this period, the state takes the form of the dictatorship of the proletariat (q.v.). It is socialist in its aims and tasks, because it serves as a means of building socialism. As socialist society progresses, the functions of the S.S. change accordingly. With the abolition of the exploiting classes, the function of suppressing their resistance disappears, while the main functions of the S.S.—economic organisation, education and cultural development—are exercised to a greater extent. After the world socialist system (q.v.) was formed, the S.S. acquired a new external function, that of promoting fraternal co-operation with other socialist countries, in addition to the functions of upholding world peace and strengthening the country's defences. With the construction of mature socialism and the entering of society into the period of full-scale communist construction, the state of proletarian dictatorship turns into a state of the whole people (q.v.), which expresses the will of the entire people. The working people share in administering the state by participating in the work of the bodies of people's government (in the USSR these are the Soviets of People's Deputies) as well as of the organs of people's control. The withering away of the state in the course of building communism involves the gradual development of the S.S. and the entire political organisation of socialist society into communist public self-government (q.v.). The construction of a developed communist society and the victory and consolidation of socialism on a world scale are indispensable for the complete withering away of the state.

Society, Organic Theory of, a bourgeois theory of the second half of the 19th century which likens human society to a biological organism. Exponents of this school (Spencer, q.v., A. Schäffle) considered the structure of society to be analogous to that of an organism. Thus, class inequality and other features of bourgeois society were depicted as being natural and irremediable.

Socio-Economic Formation, a historical type of society based on a definite mode of production (q.v.), and appearing as a stage in the progressive development of mankind from the primitive-communal system (q.v.) through the slave-owning system, feudalism and capitalism (qq.v.) to the communist formation. The concept of S.E.F. was first elaborated by Marxism and is the cornerstone of the materialist understanding of history. It makes it possible, first, to differentiate one period of history from another and, instead of arguments about "society in general", to study historical events within the bounds of definite formations; second, to group the systems in different countries on the same level of production (e.g., in capitalist Britain, France, West Germany, and the United States) and to reveal the features common to these countries and, hence, to utilise in studies the general scientific criterion of repetition, whose application to social science the adherents of subjectivism deny; third, in contrast to the eclectic theories which regard society as a mechanical totality of social phenomena (the family, the state, the Church, etc.) and the historical process as resulting from the influence of diverse factors (natural conditions or education, development of trade, birth of a genius, etc.), the concept of S.E.F. makes it possible to examine human society in each period of its development as a single "social organism" incorporating all social phenomena in their organic unity and interaction on the basis of the mode of production.

And, fourth, it identifies individual aspirations and actions with the actions of large masses or classes whose interests are determined by their place in the system of social relations of a given formation. Each formation has its particular laws of emergence and development. At the same time, general laws operating in all formations bind them into a single process of world history. Replacement of one formation by another occurs as a result of social revolution (q.v.). Capitalist society is the last formation based on antagonism between classes. It completes the pre-history of mankind. The communist formation, of which socialism is the initial phase, for the first time in history provides conditions for the boundless development of mankind based on the abolition of social inequality and the accelerated growth of the productive forces. The communist formation begins the true history of mankind.

Sociology, a science studying the laws governing the development and function ing of social systems, both global (society as a whole) and particular. S. studies the connections between different social phenomena, and the general regularities in people's social behaviour. S. arose as an independent science in the 19th century. The growing complexity of social life and the differentiation of scientific knowledge were conducive to S. detaching itself from philosophy and becoming a science in its own right, one combining theoretical analysis of social relations with empirical research into social facts. Saint-Simon (q.v.) was the first to urge that the study of society should be raised to the status of science based on observation. However it was not before Marx and Engels that this aim could be achieved. Apart from providing the philosophical foundation for any scientific study of society, the materialist conception of history (see Materialism, Historical) they created contains a theoretical analysis of the structure of social life, of the interconnection between the most important social phenomena (the mode of production, clas-

ses, qq.v., political institutions, culture, q.v., forms of social consciousness, q.v., etc.) and the laws governing the evolution of socio-economic formations (q.v.). The classics of Marxism also attached great importance to empirical research of society (see Concrete Sociological Investigations). Marx's *Capital,* Engels's *The Condition of the Working-Class in England,* Lenin's *Development of Capitalism in Russia* and *A Great Beginning* are classical examples of how a theoretical investigation can be organically combined with an analysis of concrete social processes. In recent years, S. has registered an especially rapid progress in the USSR and other socialist countries. It studies general and specific regularities of socialist and communist construction, the scientific and technological revolution (q.v.), people's attitude to work, tendencies in the evolution of matrimony and the family, urbanisation problems, leisure time, ways and means of improving state administration, etc. Marxist S. is coming to play a greater part in solving practical problems, and ensuring scientific guidance to the development of society. Non-Marxist S., which traces its origin to Comte (q.v.), has passed through several stages of development. In the second half of the 19th century it was under the influence of positivism (q.v.) and engaged mainly in historical and evolutionary studies. Depending on which aspect of social life was considered to be the most important, S. fell into a number of trends: the geographical school (q.v.), the racial and anthropological school (J. Gobineau, H. Chamberlain), the bioorganic school (A. Shäffle), and Social-Darwinism (q.v.). At the end of the 19th century, a position of pre-eminence in S. was occupied by several variations of the psychological school (q.v.)—instinctivism, behaviourism (q.v.), introspectionism. There appeared theories that concentrated on collective and social, rather than individual, consciousness (F. Giddings, Durkheim, q.v.), or on abstract forms of social interaction (F. Toennis). Another theory to gain currency was so-called economic materialism (q.v.). From the early 1900s on, Western S. has been under a strong influence of idealistic philosophical trends, such as neo-Kantianism, the philosophy of life (qq.v.), etc., and Freudianism (q.v.). In the 1920s, empirical research began to play an increasingly greater part in S., which was mostly a theoretical science in the 19th century. This brought about improvements in sociological techniques and extended the scope of its practical application. Bourgeois S. serves the ruling classes ideologically, by providing theoretical justification of their interests, and practically, by helping them perform a number of concrete tasks (public opinion polls, propaganda campaigns, establishment of "human relations" in industry, optimisation of managerial methods, etc.). Due to the wide range of social phenomena coming within the scope of S., it increasingly specialises. In addition to general S. and sociological theory, there are numerous relatively autonomous branches such as industrial S., urban S., S. of the family, S. of crime, etc.). However, a purely descriptive S. does not provide answers to the vital problems of social life, and easily degenerates, under capitalism, into a senseless registration of facts. This has led of late to the crisis of sociological empiricism. A growing number of sociologists come to the conclusion that it is imperative to work out a generalising sociological theory. More interest has been shown in philosophy, and naturalistic, positivist theories come under sharp criticism. Sociologists evince greater interest in "humanistic sociology", phenomenology, historical method and interdisciplinary research. The ideological foundations of non-Marxist S. are not homogeneous. Along with diehard reactionaries and anti-Communists, there are, in the West, quite a few scientists who are critical of capitalism and try to get to the heart of its contradictions. In recent years, many of them have shown a greater interest in Marxism and Marxist S. This calls for a thoughtful differentiation in assessing various sociological ideas and their authors. In accordance with Lenin's instructions, Marxist sociologists use the positive experience amassed by bourgeois S., but, in doing this, they should "*be able* to lop off their reactionary tendency, to pursue our *own* line and to combat the *whole line* of the forces and classes hostile to us" (Vol. 14, p. 343).

Sociometry, applied microsociology (q.v.). Applying the usual methods of empirical sociology (questionnaires, interviews, etc.), S. studies psychological relations within what are called small groups in some specific place (a factory shop, a school-room, a volleyball pitch, an apartment, etc.). As a specific trend in microsociology, S. is represented by the Moreno (q.v.) school. There is a specialised centre of S. in the USA—the Moreno Institute—and the *Sociometry* magazine is published. Moreno and his followers hold that S. can help achieve social harmony by reshuffling small groups in such a way as to reconcile the wishes and feelings of their members. This idea of a psychological restructuring of society, termed as the "sociometric revolution", is no more than a utopia, since it leaves intact the most important thing, the economic and political foundations of bourgeois society.

Socio-Political and Ideological Unity of Society, the community of the objective position, vital economic and political interests, ideological and moral principles of all social groups, inherent in socialist society and constituting one of its essential features, and an important motive force of its development. Economically, this unity is based on the public ownership of the means of production and socialist relations of production; politically it is based on the political system centred on the Communist Party and the socialist state, while the main direction of its development is the perfection of socialist democracy; its ideological basis is Marxist-Leninist ideology. One of the indispensable conditions and an intrinsic feature of such unity is the solution of the national question (q.v.) and the establishment of friendly relations between socialist nations and nationalities. Since Soviet society entered the stage of mature socialism, its unity has acquired a new dimension corresponding to the greater degree of maturity of social life and manifesting itself in the fact that the CPSU has become a party of the whole people, and the socialist state—an organisation of the whole people, the social basis of which is the alliance of the workers, peasants, and the intelligentsia; a new social and international community—the Soviet people—has come into being. The unity of society widely manifests itself in the social practice of the working people, who, guided by the CPSU, work in an organised manner to attain the tasks common to all society.

Socrates (469-399 B.C.), Greek philosopher, whose doctrine initiated the turn from materialist naturalism to idealism. He lived and taught in Athens, and his many pupils included Plato, Antisthenes, and Aristippus (qq.v.). S. wrote nothing and his doctrine is known through the writings of Plato and Aristotle (q.v.). The structure of the world and the physical nature of things are unknowable; we can know only ourselves. This understanding of the object of knowledge was expressed by S. in the formula: "know thyself". Knowledge, according to S., is an idea, a concept of the universal. Concepts are revealed through definitions and summed up through induction. S. himself provided examples of definitions and generalisations of ethical concepts (e.g., valour, justice). Definition of a concept is preceded by conversation, in the course of which questions bring out contradictions in the interlocutors' thinking. Disclosure of contradictions leads to the elimination of sham knowledge, while the state of unrest generated in the mind stimulates the search for real truth. S.'s method of question-and-answer reasoning, which presupposed a critical attitude to dogmatic assertions, came to be known as Socratic "irony". The ethics of S. is rationalistic: evil actions are only produced by ignorance, and no one is ever bad of his own free will.

Solipsism, a subjective idealist theory, according to which only man and his consciousness exist, while the objective world, including people, exist only in the mind of the individual. In principle, every subjective idealist philosophy inevitably arrives at S. Berkeley and Fichte (qq.v.) and the supporters of the immanent school (q.v.) drew closest to this outlook. The viewpoint of S. deprives human activity and science of all sense. For this reason subjective idealist philosophers seek to avoid extreme S., for which

purpose they posit the existence of a divine consciousness. Epistemologically, S. stems from the view that sensation (q.v.) is the absolute source of knowledge. Lenin gave a criticism of S. in his *Materialism and Empirio-Criticism* (q.v.).

Solovyov, Vladimir Sergeyevich (1853-1900), Russian idealist philosopher, theologian, publicist, and poet. His views were greatly influenced by Christian literature and also the ideas of Buddhism, Neoplatonism (qq.v.) and other religious and philosophical systems. He borrowed a great deal from German philosophy (Kant, Schelling, Hegel, Schopenhauer, qq.v., and others). S. was especially close to the Slavophiles (q.v.). Central to his doctrine is the idea of "all-embracing being", which is defined as the sphere of the absolute, the divine, while the real world is its self-determination and embodiment (with the so-called universal soul acting as an intermediary between them). Unqualified "all-embracing being" (as perfect synthesis of truth, goodness and beauty) is conceived only by "integral" knowledge, which is a synthesis of mystical, rational (philosophical) and empirical (scientific) knowledge, with mystical knowledge playing the main role. According to S., theology, philosophy and science form a unity which he calls "free theosophy". In society the idea of "all-embracing being" reveals itself as a theo-human union of people ("free theocracy"), or as the oecumenical church which unites all nations and determines the absolute goal of mankind—the establishment of the "kingdom of God" on earth in which all social contradictions will be resolved. A "free theocracy" can result from a merger of the Western (Catholic) and Eastern (Orthodox) Christian churches within the framework of a theocratic monarchy conceived as a union of the spiritual and the temporal powers of the high-priest and the tsar; in this respect a "special role" belongs to the Russian state. At the end of his life he became disillusioned with theocratic utopia and espoused the idea that the world was bound to end in catastrophe, i.e., the idea of eschatology (q.v.). According to S., the main purpose of philosophy is rationally to vindicate the socio-religious ideal and, therefore, it must serve theology. S. also based ethics on religion: man is moral if he freely submits to God, and strives for "absolute goodness" and the establishment of the theo-human kingdom. Although S. was against "art for art's sake" (he believed that art must serve mainly religious education and theurgic purposes), his poetry and aesthetics became one of the ideological well-springs of Russian symbolism. The theory of S., which objectively reflected the interests of the reactionary circles of the bourgeoisie and the nobility, exerted a great influence on Russian religious-idealist philosophy at the turn of the century. Main works: *Kritika otvlechonnykh nachal* (Critique of Abstract Principles), 1880; *Chteniya o bogochelovechestve* (Lectures on Theo-Humanity), 1877-81; *Istoriya i budushchnost teokratii* (History and the Future of Theocracy), 1885-87; *Rossiya i vselenskaya tserkov* (Russia and the Oecumenical Church), 1889; *Opravdaniye dobra* (Vindication of Good), 1897-99; *Tri razgovora* (Three Conversations), 1900, and others.

Sombart, Werner (1863-1941), German sociologist and economist. Studied capitalism as a social phenomenon and also problems of social mobility and social stratification (q.v.). At first S. considered himself a Socialist and Marxist, but later turned anti-Marxist. His central idea is the peaceful evolution of capitalism into a society of "social pluralism" where capitalism and socialism will co-exist for a long time. The historical content of S.'s doctrine, which had a great influence on modern bourgeois and reformist ideology, is the perpetuation of capitalism, denial of its general crisis and of the historical inevitability of its replacement by socialism. Neo-Kantianism of the Baden school (q.v.) furnished the philosophical basis of his sociological views. Main works: *Sozialismus und Soziale Bewegung im 19. Jahrhundert*, 1896; and *Die Zukunft des Kapitalismus*, 1932.

Sophistry, the deliberate application of sophisms, i.e., superficially plausible specious arguments, in disputes or in reasoning. Typical instances of S. are consideration of events out of context, application of laws peculiar to one set of phenomena to another set, and of one historical period to the events of another. S. plays a reactionary role in science and in politics.

Sophists, Greek philosophers who were professional teachers of "wisdom" and "eloquence" (5th century B.C.). Though not constituting a school, they agreed in rejecting religion, giving a rational explanation to natural phenomena, and taking a relativist approach to ethics and social phenomena. The main group of S. ("the older" S.) advocated slave-owning democracy. Generally speaking, they had a materialist understanding of nature. The proponents of this group— Protagoras (q.v.), Hippias of Elis, Prodicus of Ceos, Antiphon of Athens—were the first enlighteners and encyclopaedists of antiquity. Their attention was focussed on problems of cognition. Some S. arrived at sceptical conclusions regarding being and knowledge (Gorgias, q.v.). S. belonging to the aristocratic camp—Critias, Hippodamus—gravitated towards philosophical idealism. In disputes S. resorted to methods which later became known as sophistry (q.v.). This tendency was particularly pronounced among the late S. (4th century B.C.), who, in the words of Aristotle (q.v.), turned into teachers of "imaginary wisdom".

Sorites, a chain of syllogisms in which the conclusion of each preceding syllogism forms a premise of the next, one of the premises being mutely implied.

Soul, a term used sometimes as a synonym for the psychics (q.v.). Primitive people regarded the S. as something material (blood, breath, etc.). In religion, the S. is viewed as an incorporeal and immortal immaterial force, capable of existing separately and independently of the body in the other world. In idealist philosophy, the S. is identified with various elements of consciousness. Plato (q.v.) called it the eternal idea, Hegel (q.v.) regarded it as the lowest, sensory manifestation of the spirit in its connection with matter (sentient and active S.). In dualistic doctrines the S. was looked upon as something that has an independent existence, that exists alongside the body (see Descartes, Spencer, Wundt, and James). Pre-Marxian materialism (Democritus, q.v., metaphysical materialism) regarded the S. as something secondary to, and dependent on, the body, while reducing its activity to mechanical or physico-chemical processes. Materialist philosophers were often prepared to recognise the universal animation of matter (see Hylozoism). A genuinely scientific explanation of the human psyche was provided by dialectical materialism, unscientific, idealistic notions of the S. being refuted on the basis of data provided by modern natural science.

Space—see Time and Space.

Species and Genus (in logic), categories expressing relations between classes (in particular, the extension concepts). Objects of class B constitute a species of objects of class A, if they have all the properties common to A objects and at the same time some specific properties distinguishing them from other A objects; in this case A objects are the genus of B objects. Concepts that make general A objects and B objects are called in relation to each other generic and specific respectively. For example, animals are a S. of organisms; organisms are the G. that includes animals. G. represents something general in the objects of a class, S., something particular (specific) within this general; properties characteristic of G. and S. are abstractions to be found only in individual objects.

Speculation, a method of cognising truth theoretically on the basis of abstract logical constructions often divorced from science-proven facts of observation and experiment (qq.v.). S. may therefore be unscientific. Speculative in character were the original philosophical constructions of many ancient Greek thinkers, medieval scholastic theories, 18th-19th-century natural-philosophical theories advanced, among others, by Schelling and Hegel (qq.v.) and by some natural scientists. As scientific knowledge makes further progress, speculative ideas are gradually discarded and replaced by scientific theories. Sometimes S. is treated as specifics of philosophical cognition.

Speculative Philosophy, philosophical systems based on speculative knowledge, i.e., knowledge derived without reference to experience, through reflection (q.v.). Relying on the "sheer power of the intellect", S.P. creates a set of speculative principles with which it seeks to embrace all objective reality. This type of knowledge is possible owing to insufficient natural scientific and experimental knowledge, to the fact that consciousness contains an integral picture of the world which precedes experimental knowledge, and to man's striving to synthesise all available scientific knowledge. Originally S.P. took the form of metaphysics (q.v.), a teaching on the pretersensual elements of things. However, if in the works, e.g., of Aristotle (q.v.) this teaching was a peculiar form of cognising the specific features of philosophical knowledge, in the Middle Ages, speculation was characteristic above all of scholasticism (q.v.) which was subordinate to theology (q.v.). In the 17th and 18th centuries philosophy oriented itself to exact sciences (mechanics, mathematics), which gave rise to anti-speculative trends. In Hegel's (q.v.) system, the speculative is viewed as the positive and reasonable, which can be achieved through the dialectical resolution of contradictions and which is opposed to the rational (see Reason and Intellect). By virtue of this, Hegel, while remaining within the sphere of speculation, often "gives a *real* presentation, embracing the *thing* itself", although at the same time speculation "falls into the most irrational and unnatural *bondage* to the object, whose most accidental and most individual attributes it is obliged to construe as absolutely necessary and general" (K. Marx, F. Engels, *Collected Works*, Vol. 4, p. 61). The generally speculative character of Hegel's philosophy can give rise to idealistic contemplativeness and undisguised theology. Feuerbach (q.v.) submitted the "philosophy of drunken speculation" to sharp criticism. Later on the struggle against S.P. degenerated into a struggle against philosophy as such (see Positivism). In emphasising the untenability of S.P., one should, nevertheless, take into account its rational results and its striving to understand the specific features of philosophical thinking. Connected with the special study of the universal forms of man's relation to the external world, these specific features are interpreted by Marxist philosophy, not in a speculative way, but through an analysis of objective activity (q.v.).

Speech, man's activity by which he communicates with his fellow men, expressing and conveying his thoughts by means of a language (q.v.). S. is the process of using language. Thanks to S. the consciousness of the individual constantly reflects the world, being enriched by what is reflected in social consciousness and associated with the achievements of the social productive practice of mankind. In this intercourse, constant exchange of thoughts takes place: on the one hand, the comprehension of another's thoughts and their mastery, and on the other, the formulation and utterance of one's own thoughts. In this connection S. is divided into passive (sensory) speech as perception and comprehension of the S. of others, and active (motor) speech as the utterance of one's own thoughts, feelings, and desires. What is divided between the speaker and the listener is united psychologically by the internal structure of S. into an integral whole: speaking, man hears and comprehends; hearing and understanding, he speaks. The main kinds of speech are oral, i.e., spoken and heard, and written. The latter appeared in human history much later than the oral and developed through a number of stages from pictography (the transmission of thought by conventional schematic pictures) to contemporary phonetic writing. S. is the object of linguistics, psycho-linguistics and psychology, which study the process of mastering language, the formation of S. in the process of man's individual development, the conditions of the influence of S., of its perception, comprehension and pronunciation.

Spencer, Herbert (1820-1903), English philosopher and sociologist, one of the founders of positivism (q.v.), a spokesman of the liberal bourgeoisie on the eve of the epoch of imperialism. His philosophical views were strongly influenced by Hume, Kant, and Mill (qq.v.).

The teaching about the "unknowable" held an important place in his system. Every scientific concept, S. held, was contradictory and, therefore, incomprehensible. The contention that science is based only on the limited experience of the individual, that is, on a false foundation, was another proof S. advanced for his view that science is unable to penetrate into the essence of things. Recognition of the "unknowable" is also one of the corner-stones of religion, which gave S. cause to maintain that science and religion were contiguous. Subjective idealism and agnosticism (q.v.) combined in the teaching of S. with elements of objective idealism (recognition of "absolute reality" as the source of human sensations and impressions) and a spontaneous materialist interpretation of the problems of specialised sciences. The spontaneous materialist approach was most prominent in S.'s teaching on evolution. S. extended the idea of evolution from living beings to all things and phenomena. However, he conceived evolution in a mechanistic way, as redistribution of matter and motion in the world, and thereby blotted out the distinctions between different spheres of the material world. S.'s conception of evolution lay at the root of his reactionary sociology, the organic theory of society (q.v.), as he called it, which attempted, quite unscientifically, to analyse social life in biological terms. S. was strongly opposed to socialism. His main work: *System of Synthetic Philosophy* (1862-96).

Spengler, Oswald (1880-1936), German idealist philosopher who belonged to the philosophy of life (q.v.) school, theorist of culture and history, and publicist. His main work, *Der Untergang des Abendlandes* (in 2 vols., 1918-22), expounding his philosophy of history, was published soon after the defeat of Germany in the First World War and was met with acclaim. S. extolled the "old Prussian spirit", the monarchy, nobility and militarism. War for him was an eternal form of human existence. S. set off fatalism (q.v.) against the materialist understanding of history and denied the concept of historical progress. S. was a follower of historical relativism (q.v.). He rejected the notion that world historical development is governed by laws. According to him, history falls into a number of independent, unique, closed cyclic "cultures", following their own individual destinies through periods of birth, efflorescence and demise. According to S., Western culture beginning from the 19th century, i.e., with the advent of capitalism, had entered the period of decline, the foregoing "culture" having deteriorated into "civilisation". A philosophy of history, theoretically akin to that of S., was propagated by Toynbee (q.v.).

Spinoza, Baruch or Benedict (1632-1677), Dutch materialist philosopher; excommunicated for his free-thinking by the Jewish community of Amsterdam. S. was the founder of the geometrical method (q.v.) in philosophy. S.'s doctrine originated in a historical environment which made the Netherlands a foremost capitalist country after its liberation from the yoke of the Spanish feudal monarchy. Like the leading thinkers of his age, F. Bacon and Descartes (qq.v.), S. considered mastery over nature and the perfection of man to be the main purpose of knowledge. S. supplemented the doctrines of his forerunners with a teaching on freedom: he showed how human freedom was possible within the bounds of necessity. In solving this problem, S. built his teaching on nature. In contrast to the dualism (q.v.) of Descartes, S. maintained that only nature exists, being the cause of itself *(causa sui)* and needing nothing else for its existence. As "creative nature", it was substance (q.v.), or, as he called it, God. S. differentiated between substance and the world of individual finite things, or modes, both corporeal and thinking. Substance is one, while the modes are infinitely many. Infinite mind could apprehend infinite substance in all its forms or aspects. But finite human reason apprehends the essence of substance as infinite in two aspects alone: as "extension" and as "thought". These are attributes (q.v.) of substance. S.'s teaching on the attributes of substance is, on the whole, materialistic, but metaphysical, because he does not consider motion an attribute of substance. These are the propositions S. based himself on in creat-

ing his teaching about man. According to S., man is a creature in whom the modus of extention, the body, is coupled with the modus of thought, the soul. By token of either modes, man is part of nature. In his teaching about the modus of the soul S. reduced the complexities of the psyche to intellect and passions, or affects,—joy, grief, and desire. He identified will with intellect. Man's behaviour, S. maintained, is motivated by his striving for self-preservation and personal advantage. S. repudiated the idealistic notion of freedom of the will and defined the will as always dependent on motives. At the same time, he believed freedom to be possible as a behaviour based on the knowledge of necessity. However, according to S., only a sage, and not the mass of people, can be free. This interpretation of freedom is abstract and unhistorical. In his theory of knowledge S. adhered to rationalism (q.v.). He elevated intellectual knowledge based on reason above the lower order of knowledge derived from the senses, and belittled the role of experience. S. did much to promote atheism (q.v.) and free-thinking. The purpose of religion, he held, was not the comprehension of the nature of things, but merely inculcation of high moral principles. Neither religion nor the state should encroach on freedom of thought. S.'s teaching on society makes him a successor to Hobbes (q.v.). Unlike the latter, S. considered democratic government, not monarchy, the highest form of power and restricted the omnipotence of the state by the prerogatives of freedom. S. exercised a strong influence on 17th- and 18th-century metaphysical materialism, and his free-thinking stimulated the development of atheism. His main works: *Tractatus theologico-politicus* (1670), and *Ethica* (1677).

Spiral in Development, a figurative description of the process of development (q.v.) employed by Engels and Lenin in elucidating the law of the negation of the negation (q.v.). Development produces in phenomena an apparent return to the old in the course of change: some features of a lower level are repeated at a higher level. This may be depicted graphically as a S. in which each new coil repeats the preceding one, but at a higher level.

Development in a spiral forms a contrast to the typically metaphysical idea of development as being motion along a closed circle without any new elements.

Spirit, a concept broadly associated with concepts of the ideal (q.v.), and of consciousness (q.v.), the non-material entity, as distinguished from the material one; in the more restricted sense, synonymous with the concept of thought (q.v.). In pre-Marxian philosophy, a distinction was made between the subjective S. (the subject, individual), the absolutisation of which leads to subjective idealism (q.v.), and the objective S. (consiousness, divorced from man and mystified as an independent force), admission of the primacy of which leads to objective idealism (q.v.). The ancient philosophers regarded S. as the activity of abstract thought (e.g., for Aristotle, q.v., the highest activity of S. was the thought about thought, delight in theory). S. was also regarded, however, as super-rational principle, apprehended directly, intuitively (see Plotinus). This point of view is outwardly close to religion, according to which S. is God, a supernatural being, which can be known only through faith. Classical German idealism stressed the active quality of the S., regarding it as the activity of self-consciousness (q.v.). Hegel (q.v.), for example, conceived of S. as the unity of self-consciousness and consciousness achieved in reason, and as the unity of practical and theoretical activity: S. exists insofar as it is active, although its only activity is cognition. According to Hegel, S. overcomes the natural, sensuous and achieves selfhood in the process of self-cognition. Materialist philosophy regards S. as secondary in relation to nature. For the ancient materialists S. was the most reasonable part of the soul, and it pervaded the whole body. The materialists of the 17th and 18th centuries (Hobbes, Locke, La Mettrie, qq.v.) regarded S. merely as a combination of sensations, as a form of sense knowledge. Dialectical materialism does not reduce the spiritual to a simple sum of sensations and rejects the conception that it is something existing independently of matter. The spiritual is the function of highly organised matter, the result of the material socio-historical

practice of human beings. The spiritual life of society—social consciousness—is the reflection of social being. At the same time it actively influences social being and the practical activity of mankind.

Spiritual Production, a concept used by Marx to denote the ultimate dependence of the immaterial sphere on the development of society, on material production and social relations, and also the inner dialectic of cultural production, the interconnection of creative endeavour and continuity. Works of culture and art produced in material form or in language must be reproduced by new generations and used in their activity (q.v.). Reproducing and re-evaluating the cultural legacy, men become able to create. They generate ideas and notions and reproduce them, thereby assuming responsibility for their future. S.P., according to Marx, expresses dominant material relations and has a class character. Two forms of S.P. are distinguished: functionally preset and universally successive. In the first case the individual is solely a bearer of a certain function; in certain social conditions the sphere of his cultural activity is distorted and limited by ready-made, predetermined premises. In the second case the individual is involved in development as a "general productive force" and performs, according to Marx, "the free spiritual production of this particular social formation" (K. Marx, *Theories of Surplus-Value*, Part I, p. 285). The latter form of S.P. will predominate under communism.

Spiritualism 1. An idealist teaching asserting the spiritual origin of the world. For some spiritualists the material world is a medium for the manifestation of God and his attributes, while for others it is an illusion of human consciousness. Exponents of S. maintain that the soul exists independently of the body. Consistent spiritualists ignore the evidence of modern science and seek to replace it by blind faith in spirits and divine providence. 2. The term used by some bourgeois philosophers to denote idealism (q.v.).

Spontaneity, self-action; processes impelled by internal rather than external impulses; also, ability to act on intrinsic motives. The philosophical conception of S. was first analysed by the ancient atomists in relation to the problems of necessity and chance (q.v.), possibility and reality (q.v.), probability, and free will. Recognition of S. does not by itself rule out faith in predestination, or a teleological interpretation of reality. Thus, while each monad (q.v.) in Leibniz's (q.v.) monadology is absolutely spontaneous and constitutes a self-sufficient world, all the monads form a world of pre-established harmony (q.v.). Dialectical materialism defines S. as a specific property of matter, a manifestation of its self-movement. Recognition of spontaneous motion and development does not rule out the need for considering external influences on the developing object, and its interrelation with the objective world as a whole. The idealistic conception of S. as non-determinate "free will", independent of the objective world is untenable and conflicts with the facts of science.

Spontaneity and Consciousness, categories of historical materialism describing the relation between the objective historical regularity and the purposeful activity of men. By spontaneity is meant a process of social development whose economic and social laws are not cognised by men and are, therefore, beyond their control, operating often with the devastating force of a natural calamity, while the conscious efforts of men do not lead to the achievement of the set goals and even bring about results entirely unexpected by them. Historical activity is said to be conscious when people are engaged in it in accordance with cognised objective laws of social development and direct it purposefully towards the achievement of the set goals. All pre-socialist socioeconomic formations developed, as a rule, spontaneously. Transfer of power to the working class headed by the Communist party and the substitution of public ownership of the means of production for private ownership ushered in a new period in history, a period of conscious history-making. But the difference between the historical activity of men under socialism and in the previous formations is not absolute. Previously, too, men based

themselves to some extent in their activity on the objective laws of history and gradually cognised individual manifestations of historical necessity. This was especially manifest at the turning points of social development, under the impact of objectively ripe tasks (e.g., in bourgeois revolutions). A characteristic feature of the working-class movement and its Party is its ability to foresee the main trend of development by relying on the laws of history discovered by Marxism, and to act purposefully in accordance with it, to achieve its goals. Socialism witnesses the growing role of the conscious factor. On the other hand, elements of spontaneity still survive under socialism, because various problems of social science have not yet been exhaustively elaborated or because of a lack of skill in utilising the objective laws to the full, or again because of some lag of social consciousness behind social being. The question of S. and C. is both of theoretical and practical political importance, being related to the Communist party's leadership of the masses. Marxism-Leninism wages struggle, on the one hand, against opportunism and revisionism (q.v.) with their inherent bent for spontaneity, and underestimation of the role of conscious, organisational activities by the party of the working class, and, on the other, against voluntarism (q.v.) and subjectivism, which ignore objective laws and the level of mass consciousness, and rely only on voluntarist decisions and actions.

Stages of Economic Growth, Theory of, the conception of US sociologist W. Rostow, a variant of the theory of the "integrated industrial society", set out in his book, *The Stages of Economic Growth. A Non-Communist Manifesto* (1960). According to it, history is divided into five stages: (1) "the traditional society", which includes all societies short of the capitalist; it is marked by a low productivity of labour and the predominance of agriculture; (2) "the preconditions for take-off", which roughly coincides with the transition to pre-monopoly capitalism; (3) "the take-off", marked by industrial revolutions and the beginning of industrialisation; (4) the stage of "maturity", completion of industrialisation and emergence of industrially developed countries; (5) "the age of high mass consumption", claimed to be attained, as yet, only in the United States. In his subsequent works Rostow attempts to substantiate one more, the sixth, stage, that of the "quality of life", at which global problems, such as environmental protection and world government, will be tackled. Unlike empirical sociology, which lacks broad generalisations, the T.S. aspires to the status of a universal philosophical and sociological theory capable of offering a challenge to historical materialism. For the relations of production (q.v.), the real basis of historical development, T.S. eclectically substitutes the interaction of a variety of factors—technical, economic, psychological, political, cultural, historical, and the like. The T.S. endeavours to identify phenomena which are qualitatively different in social substance by placing them under the common head of "industrial society" (e.g., the attempts to identify socialist and capitalist industrialisation). To vindicate capitalism, the T.S. denies the need for socialist revolution and maintains that the whole world is moving towards an "integrated industrial society" as exemplified by the United States.

Stankevich, Nikolai Vladimirovich (1813-1840), Russian idealist thinker; founder and leader of a circle frequented, at different times, by Belinsky, Bakunin (qq.v.), K. S. Aksakov, and others. S. concentrated on questions of ethics as the key to the solution of social problems. He was opposed to serfdom and attacked the corruption and egoism of the Russian gentry. He appealed for moral improvement and enlightenment, and for the union of people on the basis of "the principle of love", which had religious overtones. Despite the utopian nature of his conception of social progress, his ideas had a beneficial effect, because he criticised the Russia of his day and called for civic dedication. The philosophic views of S. were coloured strongly by idealist dialectics. In the last years of his life, S. arrived at the conclusion that philosophy had to be brought closer to reality and approved of the ideas of

Feuerbach (q.v.). The work and personality of S. were highly commended by Belinsky, Herzen, and Dobrolyubov (qq.v.).

State, the political organisation of the class dominant in the economy; its purpose is to safeguard the existing order and to suppress the resistance of other classes. It appeared when society broke up into classes as a tool of the exploiting class for the suppression of the exploited population. The emergence of the S. consisted in the formation of a special public authority having an army and police, prisons and various institutions of coercion. In a society based on private ownership of the means of production, the S. is always a tool of the ruling exploiting class, a dictatorship, a special force for the suppression of the exploited masses regardless of the specific form of government. While revealing the essence of any exploiter S., Marxists are not indifferent to its form, stressing the need to maintain democracy and to fight against the tendency of the bourgeois S. towards fascism. In its effort to preserve and extend the rule of the monopoly bourgeoisie, modern imperialist Ss. seek to suppress the liberation movements of peoples, and the struggle of the masses for peace, democracy and socialism. The proletarian S. is different in principle. It is an instrument of the dictatorship of the proletariat (q.v.), it operates in the interests of all working people, in the interests of the vast majority of the people, and suppresses the exploiters. After the Second World War, Ss. of people's democracy sprang up in a number of European and Asian countries. They, too, like the Soviets in the USSR, are a specific form of socialist S. Engels wrote that the proletarian S. is not a S. in the full sense of the word. Whereas the imperialist S. is a force that alienates itself more and more from the people, opposes the people and is intended to keep the people in submission to the exploiting class, the proletarian S. essentially expresses the interests of the people. Hence its other distinctive feature, which Marxist theory describes as the withering away of the S., will not exist eternally. In the future it will give place to communist public self-government (q.v.). The S. of the whole people (q.v.) is a phase which brings us nearer to a stateless society. This type of S. develops from the state of the working-class dictatorship in the course of the building of communist society.

The State and Revolution. The Marxist Theory of the State and the Tasks of the Proletariat in the Revolution, a book by V. I. Lenin written in August-September 1917 and published in May 1918. When the socialist revolution was being prepared in Russia questions concerning the attitude of the proletariat to the state were of keen theoretical and practical political significance. In his book, Lenin dealt with the main aspects of the Marxist theory of the state, and with its development by Marx and Engels on the basis of the experience of the 1848-51 revolutions and particularly of the Paris Commune of 1871. Lenin substantiated the Marxist conclusion that the main task of the working class in revolution with regard to the state is to smash the bourgeois state machine and to establish dictatorship of the proletariat (q.v.). In describing the two phases of communist society, Lenin analysed the economic reasons for the withering away of the state during the communist formation (q.v.) and outlined the chief ways of developing socialist statehood: extending democracy, giving the masses a growing share in state administration, etc. Lenin's book contains devastating criticism of anarchism and opportunism, the trends which distorted the Marxist teaching on the state and emasculated its revolutionary content (chiefly by rejecting the dictatorship of the proletariat). Lenin's main ideas on the socialist state (q.v.) were developed further in the Programme of the CPSU and in the 1977 Constitution of the USSR.

State of National Democracy, a form of political organisation of society which arises in the course of the development and deepening of the national liberation revolution. The basic features of the S.N.D. are: consistent struggle for political and economic independence, against imperialism and neo-colonialism; existence of broad democratic rights and freedoms; participation of the people in determining the government's policy; revolutionary social changes, a land reform in the first place. The political basis of the S.N.D. is the bloc of all the progressive, patriotic forces fighting to win complete national independence, broad democracy to bring the anti-imperialist, anti-feudal, democratic revolution to fruition. The S.N.D. is formed through the active participation of the working class in a national liberation revolution. Socially, the S.N.D. is not a socialist state, though under certain conditions it may become a political form of the transition of individual newly-free countries to socialism, bypassing the capitalist road of development.

State of the Whole People, a special type of socialist state expressing the interests and will of all the people, an instrument for building communism. It succeeds the state of the dictatorship of the proletariat (q.v.), after the latter fully discharges its historical tasks and society enters the period of building communism. The main features of S.W.P. are that it is not an instrument for the suppression of some class, that it rests on a single social foundation and is a stage in the transition to communist public self-government (q.v.). As a result of the complete and final victory of socialism, the peasantry and intelligentsia assume the positions of the working class, and the goal of the revolutionary proletariat becomes the goal of the whole people. S.W.P. pursues an internal and foreign class policy that is in the interests of all the working people. At the same time the leading role in the administration of society remains with the working class. The USSR Constitution of 1977 has legally entrenched the political system of developed socialism, the principles of organisation, functions and aims of S.W.P. It says that all power in the USSR belongs to the people and is exercised through Soviets of People's Deputies, the system of public organisations and work collectives. The leading and guiding force of Soviet society, the core of its political system, state and public organisations is the Communist Party. S.W.P. is the highest stage in the development of the socialist state.

Statement — in modern formal logic, a sentence in a particular language (q.v.) considered in connection with appraisals of its truth (true, false) or modality (probable, possible, impossible, necessary, etc.). A S. which contains other Ss. is said to be compound. Otherwise, it is called simple. Every S. expresses an idea. This idea constitutes its content and is said to be the meaning of S. The appraisal of the truth of a S. is said to be its truth-value. That about which a S. is made is called its object. Sometimes a S. is referred to as a "proposition" or a "judgement".

State-Monopoly Capitalism, a form of the capitalist economy in which the state (q.v.) intervenes in the economic life of the country on a large scale. In the epoch of imperialism (q.v.), there are sharply increasing possibilities for the state to intervene in the economy and social life. The growing concentration and socialisation of production, and centralisation of capital allow the monopolies to control the country's economy through the intermediary of the state. S.M.C. takes shape with its characteristic fusion of the major monopolies, finance capital and the bourgeois state machinery in order to extract high monopoly profits and to combat crisis phenomena. Under S.M.C., the state regulates the capitalist economy in various ways: through state-owned property, state enterprise, mixed state and private operations, the programmed target-oriented method, regulation of capital investment, stimulation of consumer demand, subsidising of research, financing of nature conservation measures, etc. The public sector in the economy grows, among other things, through nationalisation of some branches of the economy either because of these industries becoming unprofitable, or under the pressure of the class struggle. The increasingly socialised character of production within the world capitalist system has led to the formation of international economic organisations such as the EEC, Euratom, TNCs, etc. Under S.M.C. the role played by the managers of corporations grows, and the forms of exploitation are such that in its struggle the working class often confronts both the whole class of capitalists and the state. The working people's struggle for their rights and interests becomes more and more politically motivated. In its turn, S.M.C. uses the entire armoury of methods to suppress the struggle of the working people and to disunite them. Wide use is made of a ramified system of ideological propaganda to support the illusion that the state plays a supra-class role. Political integration of the major states (e.g., the European Parliament) pursues the same purpose. The state intervenes in the economic and social life mainly in the interests of finance capital, and at the expense of the working class, although this does not exclude conflicts between the state and private monopolies. The general crisis of capitalism (q.v.) grows deeper. The characteristic features of S.M.C. are chronic inflation, unemployment, crises affecting the economy and other aspects of the life of society such as energy, currency, etc. Leading to further concentration of production, S.M.C. aggravates to the extreme the basic contradictions of capitalism, namely, the contradictions between the productive forces and the relations of production, between labour and capital, and thus brings closer the end of the capitalist system. "...State-monopoly capitalism is a complete *material* preparation for socialism, the *threshold* of socialism, a rung on the ladder of history between which and the rung called socialism *there are no intermediate rungs*" (V. I. Lenin, *Collected Works,* Vol. 25, p. 363).

Stirner, Max (pseudonym of Johann Kaspar Schmidt), (1806-1856), German idealist philosopher, founder of anarchistic individualism; he was close to the Young Hegelians (q.v.). In 1845, he published his book *Der Einzige und sein Eigentum,* where he developed the system of anarchism (q.v.). The sole reality, according to S., is "I", the egoist, and the whole world is his possession. The concepts of morals, justice, law, etc., were declared "phantasms" and discarded. S. believed he thereby cleansed individual consciousness. Each individual is himself a source of morality and justice. An individual should be guided by the sole principle: "there is nothing above myself". Private property, according to S., must be preserved, as it is an expression of the unique character of "I". S.'s social ideal was the "union of egoists", wherein each viewed others only as a means of achieving his own ends. Regarding history as a product of ideas, S. believed that social relations could be changed by getting over the dominant concepts. He fiercely opposed communism and the revolutionary struggle of the proletariat. S.'s outwardly "rebellious" slogans were merely the cover for the interests of the petty bourgeois who tried to preserve his enterprise from bankruptcy. Marx and Engels criticised all aspects of S.'s speculative idealism and revealed its loss of touch with actual social relations.

Stoics, exponents of a philosophical school that appeared on the basis of Hellenistic culture in the 4th century B.C. under the impact of cosmopolitan and individualistic ideas and technical developments impelled by the expansion of mathematical knowledge. Zeno of Citium and Chrysippus (qq.v.) were the most prominent exponents of the school in the 4th and 3rd centuries B.C. The role of the sciences treated by the S. was defined by them as follows: logic is the fence, physics the fertile soil, and ethics its fruit. The chief task of philosophy concerned ethics; knowledge was no more than a means of acquiring wisdom and skill of living. Life, the S. held, had to be lived according to nature. That was the ideal of every wise man. Happiness lay in freedom from emotion, in peace of mind, in imperturbability. Fate preordained everything in life. He who consented was led on by fate; he who resisted was dragged along. The S. were materialists in their conception of nature, but their materialism combined with nominalism (q.v.). In contrast to predicate logic (see Aristotle), S. created propositional logic as a teaching about transforming simple propositions into complex ones, and used it as a basis for evolving a propositional theory of inference. The S. established the varieties of the connection of judgments which modern logic designates as conjunction, disjunction (qq.v.) and material implication (q.v.). S. appeared on Roman soil in the first centuries A.D.; they applied themselves to the moral and religious ideas of the stoic school; prominent among them were Seneca, Epictetus and Marcus Aurelius (qq.v.).

Stratification, Social, a bourgeois sociological doctrine of society's structure, which holds that society is divided into social layers or strata; these are identified on the strength of a wide range of criteria, including economic, political, biological, racial, religious, and others, there being no agreement among bourgeois sociologists as to which of these criteria are decisive. S.S. also includes the division of society into classes but this is often based on arbitrary and inessential criteria (e.g., occupation, housing, residential area, size of income, etc.). According to bourgeois sociologists, S.S. is in a state of flux, for it depends on social mobility (q.v.), that is, the movement of men between various strata. The S.S. theory substitutes secondary and derivative structures for the class divisions dependent on production relations, and therefore serves to play down class inequality and exploitation. By establishing the true criterion of class division—people's relation to the means of production—Marxism-Leninism has created a scientific theory of the class structure of society. At the same time Marxist sociology studies intra-class divisions (social strata, social groups) which are a consequence of the social division of labour (q.v.).

Structural-Functional Analysis, a method used in the study of objects constituting systems, above all social systems (q.v.). S.F.A. of various forms of social life is based on identifying within social systems structural components and ascertaining their roles (functions) in respect of each other. The foundations of S.F.A. in modern bourgeois sociology have been laid by Parsons and Merton (qq.v.) whose works expounded the ideas of early functionalism which emerged as a specific methodological trend within general anthropology. The principle of Parsons's analysis is to distinguish between structural categories (the system of values, social norms, the types of communities and the roles of those comprising them) and functional categories (self-preservation, integration, attainment of objectives, and adaptation). Keeping as he does to the idealistic view of society, he holds that the system of values and norms, which performs the function of cementing the social structure, is the main regulator of social relations. Merton asserts that there is no rigid connection between structural elements and definite functions in society. He differentiates between functions according to whether they have favourable or unfavourable effect on the system, and whether they are clearly perceived by members of the system (obvious and latent functions). On the one hand, such views are a reaction to empirism of modern American sociology. On the other hand, functional explanation of a social system is put in opposition to Marxist social science. Metaphysical, antihistorical and idealistic nature of these views is a consequence of recognition of the balance of social system (Parsons) being accepted as an initial concept, of rejection of the historical process, and of seeking to ignore the deep-going social conflicts of bourgeois society. The sociological ideas of Parsons and Merton, being removed as they are from social reality and speculative in nature, have been criticised even by bourgeois sociologists. Marxist science does not stop at mere criticism but reveals the epistemological and class roots of these sociological conceptions. At the same time, to criticise the views of Parsons and Merton does not mean to reject the analytical technique of S.F.A. as one of the means of investigating systems (see Systems Analysis; Systems Approach). Marx's *Capital* is a classical example of structural (systems) and functional analysis of the capitalist economy and capitalist society as a complex developing system. The main structural categories of Marxist sociology are socio-economic formations, the division of labour (qq.v.), and others. S.F.A. is an especially effective means in studying social phenomena when there is a need to pass from theoretical formulation to concrete social research. In Marxist sociology, this analysis is not opposed to historical approach; it combines with the latter, which allows of a comprehensive concrete study of the objects under investigation.

Structuralism, a concrete scientific methodological trend setting research the task of revealing the structure (q.v.) of objects. S. was evolved by some humanities (linguistics, literary criticism, psychology, etc.) at the beginning of the 20th century as a reaction to positivist evolutionism. It uses the structural methods of research produced by mathematics, physics and other natural sciences. It is characteristic of S. to focus on describing the actual state of the objects under investigation, to reveal their intrinsic timeless properties, and to establish relations between facts or elements of the system under investigation. Departing from the set of facts observed initially, S. proceeds to reveal and describe the inner structure of the object (its hierarchy, and interrelations between elements at each level), and further on to create a theoretical model of the object. Among the factors promoting the development of S. within several sciences were the creation of semiotic (q.v.), the ideas of F. Saussure in linguistics, those of Lévi-Strauss (q.v.) in ethnology, and L. S. Vygotsky and Piaget (q.v.) in psychology, as well as the emergence of metalogic (q.v.) and metamathematics, q.v. (Frege, Hilbert, qq.v.). Applied to individual sciences, structural methods produced positive results: e.g., in linguistics these helped to make a description of unwritten languages, to decode inscriptions in unknown languages by means of inner reconstruction of language systems, etc. The ideas of S. are also of definite methodological importance in promoting the interdisciplinary study of cultural phenomena, and in bringing the humanities and natural sciences closer together, their specific nature remaining inaffected. However, the widespread introduction of structural methods in different spheres of knowledge has given rise to futile attempts to raise S. to the status of a philosophical system, and, as such, to oppose it to other philosophical systems, particularly Marxism. These attempts, ignoring as they do the cognitive limits of S. as a concrete scientific method, are absolutely unwarranted and have been criticised by Soviet scholars and foreign Marxist philosophers. Marxist philosophy counterposes the methodological principles of dialectical analysis to anti-historical approach to structure and rejection of inner contradictions as the source of development and change of the objects' structures.

Structure, inner organisation of a system (q.v.), constituting a unity of stable interrelations between its elements, as well as laws governing these interrelations. S. is an inalienable attribute (q.v.) of all actually existing objects and systems. There are no, nor there can be, bodies lacking a S. capable of inner change. Each material object has an inexhaustible variety of internal and external ties and a propensity for changing states. Owing to the variety of structural levels of matter, each material system is polystructural. For example, there are economic S., political S., socio-class S., etc., in society. Depending on the level of knowledge attained or the goals of a research, different components of S. may be revealed in theory. The S. of a system is more stable than its individual properties. However, S. is not an immutable, invariant aspect of a system. When quantitative changes in a system exceed the limits of measure (q.v.) and call forth qualitative changes, the latter are always the changes in the S. of the system. Connection between elements in a S. is subordinate to the dialectic of the interrelation of part and whole (q.v.). At the same time, structural relations in a system bring about changes in the qualities of elements which obey the general laws governing the development of a system as a whole. In scientific theory, the transition from phenomena to the essence is concurrent with the cognition of the S. of systems and processes under investigation, with the transition from some structural levels to other deeper ones. Therefore, systemic and structural research and corresponding methods have been widely developed in modern science and technology. The philosophy of dialectical materialism studies the more general, universal laws governing structural organisation and development of all material systems, and also reveals the relations between the systemic-structural and other concrete methods of scientific knowledge.

Struggle for Existence, resistance of organisms to the factors of animate and inanimate nature unfavourable to their life and propagation. As a result of this struggle the species best adapted to their environmental conditions survive and produce the most abundant and viable progeny. The struggle for existence is one of the forms of relationship between organisms within one species and between different species and is a factor in the evolution of plants and animals. Application of the idea of the struggle for existence to human society has given rise to one of the most reactionary theories in bourgeois sociology—Social-Darwinism (q.v.).

Struve, Pyotr Berngardovich (1870-1944), Russian bourgeois economist, philosopher and publicist. In the 1890s he was the leader of "legal Marxism" (q.v.). Later he became an ideologist of the right wing of the bourgeois liberal movement, one of the leaders of the Constitutional Democratic Party (from 1905 on). After the 1917 October Revolution he went into emigration and engaged in activities inimical to the Soviet state. In the sphere of economics, he adhered to vulgar political economy and rejected the labour theory of value. As a philosopher, he started off as an exponent of positivism and neo-Kantianism (qq.v.) to evolve towards religious and idealistic metaphysics. He sought to substantiate the existence of unconditional ideal being which could not be cognised "by experiment or science" ("Apropos of Characterisation of Our Philosophical Development" in the collection *Problemy idealizma* [Problems of Idealism], 1902). Hence his idea about the irrational historical process. He criticised the "atheistic socialism" of the Russian democratic intelligentsia in his articles ("Intelligentsia and Revolution", "Historical Meaning of the Russian Revolution and National Tasks") published in the collections *Vekhi* (see Vekhism) and *De Profundis* (1918). He assessed social revolution as a "negative and destructive" phenomenon, setting it off against the idea of gradual changes in society whose strata and classes are united by national consciousness. Lenin referred to Struve as a counter-revolutionary liberal who "played at Marxism from 1894 to 1898" (Vol. 17, p. 167).

Lenin analysed S.'s views in several of his works, especially in *The Economic Content of Narodism and the Criticism of It in Mr. Struve's Book*. Main works: *Kriticheskiye zametki po voprosu ob ekonomicheskom razvitii Rossii* (Critical Notes on Russia's Economic Development), 1894; *Patriotica* (1911), *Khozyaistvo i tsena* (Economy and Price) (2 parts, 1913-16), and others.

Style in Art, a historically formed integrity of an imaginative system, the means and methods of artistic expression predicated by the sameness of the ideological, aesthetic and social content. This sameness is achieved by applying a definite creative method. S. reflects the socio-economic conditions of society, as well as the peculiarities and traditions of the nation concerned. Take archaic, Hellenistic, Roman, Gothic, Renaissance, Baroque, Rococo, Empire, modernist and other Ss. Each S. gains its fullest expression in a definite type of art. A new S. appears in order to express deep-going social changes whenever a fundamentally new correlation emerges between the artistic form and the ideological content. Formalistic bourgeois aesthetics produces either an exaggeratedly broad conception of S., identifying it with the artistic method (which reduces, say, realism to one of the Ss.), or an exaggeratedly narrow conception, identifying it with the artistic manners of this or that artist. The concept "the S. of the epoch" is also wrong, for it divorces S. from the world outlook and from the artistic method. There is always a variety of artistic methods in every epoch, and it is within the framework of these methods that various Ss. develop, which, in turn, embrace artists of different artistic manners and approaches. Multiplicity of Ss. and mannerisms is a typical feature of socialist realism (q.v.).

Subconscious, a characteristic of the active mental processes which, not being at the time the centre of conscious activity, influence the course of conscious processes. Thus, that which man does not directly think about at a given moment, but which he knows in principle and which is associated with the object of his thoughts, may influence the train of thought and accompany it in the context of its meaning, etc. In exactly the same way the perceptible (though unrealisable in fact) influence of the condition, situation, automatic actions (motions) are present as the subconscious perception in all conscious actions. A definite semantic role is played by the context of language, an idea unexpressed but implied by the very structure of the sentence. There is nothing mystical or unknowable in the S. These phenomena are the by-product of conscious activity, and they include the mental processes which have no direct part in the comprehension of the objects on which man's attention is concentrated at a given moment. For the idealist distortions of the concept of the S. see Unconscious, Freudianism (qq.v.).

Subject and Object, philosophical categories. The S. was initially (e.g., by Aristotle, q.v.) taken to be the repository of certain properties, states and actions, and in that context was identified with the concept of substance (q.v.). Beginning from the 17th century, the O., like its correlative, the S., was used chiefly in the epistemological sense. Today, the S. is taken to be an active and cognising individual or a social group, endowed with consciousness and will; the O. denotes that on which the S.'s cognitive or other activity is directed. The S.&O. relationship is a problem that is connected with the fundamental question of philosophy (q.v.), and has, accordingly, been given a different interpretation by materialists and idealists. Before Marx materialists regarded the O. as existing independently of the S., and took it to be the objective world, and in a narrow sense, the object of cognition, with the S. being something passive and receptive of external influences. The S. was understood to be an isolated individual, whose peculiarities were determined by his origin, since the regularities of object activity (q.v.)—the true foundation of the activity of the S.—were not discovered at the time. The idealists deduced the S. and O. interaction and the very existence of the O. only from the activity of the S. understood as God, idea, and the like, trying to explain the S.'s active role in cognition on that basis. The subjective idealists took the view that the S. is the unity of the individual's psychic activity; this virtually eliminated the O., for it was held to be nothing but the aggregate of the states of the S. The objective idealists, notably Hegel (q.v.), made some valuable suggestions on the role of practice in the S.&O. relationship, on the dependence of this relationship on history and the social nature of the S. Dialectical materialism holds that the O. exists independently of the S., but the two are regarded as a unity. The O. is not an abstract opposite of the S., since the latter actively transforms the O. and their interaction is based on man's socio-historical practice. It is in this practice that various aspects and properties of reality are turned into the O., whose transformation in the process of practical and theoretical activity of the S. permits one to reproduce in human mind the content of objective reality. In accordance with this, one should differentiate between objective reality, the O., and the cognitum (q.v.). From these positions one can understand the activity of the S., which forms itself and changes along with the transformation of the external world. This means that man becomes the S. only in history, in society, and is for that reason a social being whose capacities and potentialities have been shaped by practice. Therefore, Marxism regards the subjective not as the inner (psychic) state of the S. contrary to the O., but as derivative from the S.'s activity, which reproduces the content of the O. in the forms of this activity. Man, being the active force in the S.&O. interaction, nevertheless depends on the O. in his activity, for the latter sets definite limits to the S.'s freedom of action. This produces the need for cognition of the regularities of the O. for the purpose of adapting the S.'s activity to them, since his goals are shaped in conformity with the logic of the object world's development and are objectively conditioned by his requirements and the level of production. Depending on this and also on the level of his knowledge of the objective laws, man sets himself conscious goals, in the attainment of which both O.&S. undergo change.

Subjective Method in Sociology, idealistic interpretation of historical knowledge, which is based on the tenet that the researcher's ethical ideal (q.v.) determines historical knowledge. Adherents of the S.M. in S. claim that the task facing sociologists and historians is to elaborate a true ethical ideal and in adapting the factual material to fit this ideal. Realisation of it in the life of mankind is the only law of social progress. While justly stressing the importance of a socio-political stand for historical research, S.M. in S. denied the objective, in the long run socio-class, basis which gives rise to this or that point of view. For the S.M. in S., any "ethical ideal" in social science is equally subjective and relative. Its attainment is determined by the will, rather than objective reality. For this reason, the S.M. in S. gave a subjective and idealistic solution to the problem of the criterion of true historical knowledge. The epistemological basis of the S.M. in S. is the positivist interpretation of the historical process (see Positivism). Marxism opposes to the S.M. in S. the principles of objectivity and partisanship of historical knowledge.

Sublation, a term which was widely used by Hegel (q.v.). It stands for a simultaneous cancelling and preservation of something. Hegel used the term of S. to characterise the movement of the absolute idea. Each of its given states is "sublated" by a superior one, which accounts for the continuity of stages in development (q.v.). Thus, in the triad (q.v.), the supreme category (synthesis) of the thought process both cancels the antithesis and retains in a processed form the entire content of previous development. Hegel discerned in the idea of S. an objective regularity of the development of the material world, and peculiarities of human (theoretical and practical) activities. At the same time the S. as it appears in his writings is of an abstract and logical nature. In dialectical materialism the term of S. is used with reference to continuity in development and for the characterisation of relations in which a phenomenon of a lower order stands to a phenomenon of a higher order (e.g., the proposition that mechanical movement is included in the biological form of the motion of matter in a "sublated" form).

Sublimation, transfer of energy from socially unacceptable (lower, base) goals and objects to socially acceptable ones (higher, lofty). According to S. Freud, S. is a process of the sexual urge (libido, q.v.) converting into objectives other than sexual, with the energy of instincts being transformed into one which is socially acceptable and morally commended. Freud explained the emergence of religions, rituals, arts, social institutions, science and the development of mankind in terms of S. According to bourgeois philosophical anthropology, q.v. (M. Scheler), the ability to S. is inherent in all forms of organisation of the natural world, with man as the final act of S. in nature. Scheler introduces the term of "supersublimation" to denote "the excessive intellectualisation" of present-day culture, which induces in man destructive inclinations. The S. theory, which holds that the spiritual is the transformed energy of primary urges, ultimately reduces the social to the biological, and is incapable of explaining the complexities and specific features of the cultural and historical process.

Sublime, the, an aesthetic category expressing the essence of phenomena, events and processes of great social significance, having an impact on people's lives or/and the destiny of humanity. Events and phenomena regarded as the S. are aesthetically perceived by man as the opposite of everything base and commonplace. The S. evokes special sensations and feelings, elevating man above the trivial and mediocre, and inspires him to fight for lofty ideas. The S. is closely connected with the beautiful (q.v.), being, like the latter, an incarnation of an advanced aesthetic ideal (q.v.). A distinctive feature of the S. (as compared with the beautiful) is its intrinsic readiness to explore boundless possibilities and accomplish grand tasks facing man in mastering the surrounding world. This implies that the possibilities are so vast and the tasks so elevated that they cannot be accomplished by a momentary act, but only as a result of a long historical

process. Idealist theories attribute the S. to the subject or to ideas of divine infinity, eternity, etc. Marxist aesthetics sees the roots of the S. in objective reality, and in man's attitude to it involving its revolutionary transformation, and regards the S. itself as a concentrated manifestation of the beauty of man's exploit, the grandeur of the achievements of creative work. In this sense the S. is close to the heroic. The arts show the S. in man's loftiest aspirations and feats of daring and in the admiration and inspiration they evoke.

Substance, objective reality viewed as the inner unity of all forms of its self-development, the diversity of natural and historical phenomena with man and his consciousness included, and therefore, a fundamental category of scientific knowledge. In the history of philosophy, S. was initially understood as matter, of which all things are made. Later on, in the context of the quest for the foundation of all being, S. began to be viewed as a specific designation of God (see Scholasticism). Later on the problem of S. acquired an added topicality owing to the works of Descartes (q.v.). Spinoza (q.v.) managed to overcome dualism (q.v.) along the lines of materialist philosophy. Holding that extent and thinking were attributes (q.v.) of the integral corporeal S., he viewed it as a cause of itself. However, Spinoza failed to substantiate the inner activity, the "self-activity" of S. This task was attained (if inconsistently) by classical German philosophy (q.v.). Hegel (q.v.) defined S. as an integrity of changing, transient aspects of things. This added to the understanding of S., presenting it as a subject, i.e., as an active autogenetic and self-developing principle. At the same time, Hegel gave S. an idealistic interpretation by describing it as a mere moment in the development of the absolute idea. Marxist philosophy critically refashioned these ideas on the basis of materialism. S. is understood both as matter (q.v.) and as a subject of all its changes, i.e., an active cause of all of its own forms, and therefore it does not need to be acted upon by some external "subject" (God, spirit, idea, "Ego", consciousness, existence, q.v., etc.). The concept of S. presents matter not as something opposed to consciousness, but in the light of the inner unity of all forms of its movement, and of all differences and opposites, including the opposition of being and consciousness. Anti-substantialism in philosophy is upheld by positivism (q.v.), which describes S. as an imaginary and, therefore, scientifically harmful category. Rejection of the category of S., the loss of the "substantialist" viewpoint, leads theory to disintegration, to eclecticism, and artificial unification of irrelevant views and propositions.

Substance and Field, fundamental concepts of physics, denoting the two basic forms of matter at macroscopic level. S. is an aggregate of discrete formations possessing rest mass (atoms, molecules and their combinations), while F. is a form of matter characterised by continuity and having zero rest mass (electromagnetic field and gravitation field). The discovery of the F. as a form of matter was of enormous philosophical importance, because it showed the fallacy of the metaphysical identification of matter with S. At the subatomic level (i.e., the level of elementary particles, q.v.) the distinction between S. and F. becomes relative. The fields (electromagnetic and gravitation) lose their purely continuous character; to them necessarily correspond discrete formations, the quanta (photons and gravitons). The elementary particles of which S. is composed (protons, neutrons, electrons, mesons, etc.) operate as quanta of respective nucleon, meson and other fields and lose their purely discrete character. In modern physics, fields and particles form two inseparably connected aspects of the microcosm and express the unity of the corpuscular (discrete) and wave (continuous) properties of minute objects. Conceptions of F. also form the basis for the explanation of the processes of interaction (q.v.).

Substratum, the basis of unity, uniformity of different objects and diverse properties of an individual singular object, thing and their sum total (see Substance).

Sufficient Reason, Principle of, a general principle of logic according to which a proposition is considered true only if sufficient reason can be formulated for it. S.R. is a proposition (or a set of propositions) which is known to be true, and from which a conclusion may be logically derived. The truth of the reason may be demonstrated by experiment, in practice, or derived from the truth of other propositions. The P.S.R. characterises provableness, one of the essential features of logically correct thinking. The P.S.R. was first formulated by Leibniz (q.v.), though it was implied in many earlier systems of logic (e.g., in Leucippus and Aristotle, qq.v.). The P.S.R. is a fairly general methodological principle.

Sufism, a mystical religious teaching in Islam (q.v.) which arose in the 8th-9th centuries and spread in the countries of the Arab khalifate. Early S. is characterised by pantheism (q.v.) with some materialist elements. Subsequently, under the influence of Neoplatonism (q.v.), Indian philosophy, and Christian ideas, asceticism (q.v.) and extreme mysticism (q.v.) dominated S. The followers of S. accepted the existence of God as the only reality, with all things and phenomena being his emanation. The supreme goal of life, they said, was the soul's mystical communion with the deity, demanding estrangement from earthly life. Believers' communion with God, according to them, takes place through ecstasy. Among the prominent exponents of S. were al-Ghazali (1059-1111), the Central Asian philosopher Sufi Alayar (d. 1720), and others.

Sun Yat-sen (1866-1925), Chinese revolutionary democrat. Received medical education at Hongkong. In 1894, set up China's first revolutionary organisation. Under the influence of the Russian revolution of 1905-1907 Dr. Sun Yat-sen rallied the revolutionary forces for the overthrow of the ruling dynasty by advancing a programme based on three political principles: nationalism (China's national independence), democracy (establishment of a republic), and people's welfare (elimination of social inequality). S.'s revolutionary-democratic programme was given a high evaluation by Lenin, who criticised, however, S.'s utopian idea that capitalism in China could be averted. The victory of the Great October Socialist Revolution had a great impact on S. He drew close to the Communist Party of China, reorganised the Kuomintang and supported demands for a new democratic revolution. In the new conditions, he restated his programme of the three principles and adopted the threefold policy of alliance with the USSR, alliance with the Communist Party of China, and support for the peasants and workers. His economic programme included the demand to "restrict capital", i.e., nationalise big foreign and national capitalist enterprises. He was a great friend of the USSR, and highly appreciated the Soviet support of the revolutionary movement in China. His philosophical views were the theoretical basis of his revolutionary democratism. He took a materialist view of the relationship of consciousness and matter. He regarded the process of cognition in connection with man's practical activity, and held that the results of cognition, ideas and principles, were an active force helping to remodel the world. In the interpretation of social phenomena he remained, on the whole, an idealist. His main philosophical work: *The Doctrine of Sun Wen.*

Superstition, a term denoting false faith (q.v.). In theological and bourgeois writings, S. is usually contrasted with true faith and is associated with primitive magic (q.v.). The adherent of any religion (q.v.) tends to regard the dogmas and rituals of all other religions as S. Marxist atheism denies both religious faith and various Ss.

Survivals of the Past, remnants of socio-economic relations, views, ideas, morals and traditions inherited from the old society. Under socialism, the question of overcoming the S.P. is especially acute, since all of them (bourgeois, patriarchal and feudal) are the result of the development of the socio-economic formations based on private property and exploitation and therefore at variance with the socialist social relations and socialist ideology. In the socialist social structure, the bearers of the S.P. are usually individuals or groups of people and not classes. That is why the contradiction between the main content and trends of the development of social relations in a socialist society, on the one hand, and the S.P., on the other, shifts from the sphere of relations between classes into the sphere of interaction between society and the individual. Most clearly the S.P. are manifest in anti-social behaviour, violation of the rules of socialist law and the norms of communist morality: indifference to interests of society (nihilism, lack of principles and ideals, philistinism, formal attitude to social duty), violation of the norms of social life (bureaucracy, careerism, disregard for the interests of the collective or the individual, indiscipline, irresponsibility, etc.); direct hostility (the crime, parasitism). All these manifestations of the S.P. run counter to the nature and the main trends of the development of socialist society. The S.P. still have certain objective ground, inasmuch as socialist society is not yet totally homogeneous and its members possess varying levels of culture and morality, and do not display the same activity and consciousness. One reason for the preservation or a temporary revival of the S.P. (private-ownership psychology, localism or individualism) is the violation of those principles of socio-economic management which characterise socialist social relations (material incentives, correlation between the personal and the social, democratic centralism, etc.). The existence of the capitalist system and the impact of bourgeois propaganda on the most backward sections of the population in socialist countries also contribute to the preservation of the S.P. The complete overcoming of the S.P. is a programmatic goal set by the Communist Party in forming communist consciousness, the goal which can be attained through the improvement of social relations and the socialist way of life.

Swedenborg, Emanuel (1688-1772), Swedish natural scientist who subsequently became a mystic and theosophian. S. is known for his works in mathematics, mechanics, astronomy, and mining. He was an honorary member of the St. Petersburg Academy of Sciences. His philosophical works were permeated with the spirit of rationalism (q.v.). As a result of nervous shock and hallucinations S. lapsed into mysticism and proceeded to write an allegorical commentary to the Bible "on a mission from Christ himself". The theosophical doctrine of S. was influenced by the gnostics (q.v.). The mystic doctrine and occultism (q.v.) of S. were criticised by Kant (q.v.). S. had followers in Germany, France and Russia, especially among members of Masonic lodges. Main works: *Arcana Coelestia* (1749-56) and *Heaven and Hell* (1758).

Syllogism, see Syllogistic.

Syllogistic, a doctrine of inference (q.v.), historically the first logical system of deduction (q.v.) formulated by Aristotle (q.v.). The following is an example of syllogism: "If every metal is electroconductive, and some liquids are metals, then some liquids are electroconductive." Every syllogism consists of three terms which, arranged in pairs, form three propositions of the subject-predicate structure: two premises and a conclusion. The main purpose of S. is to ascertain the conditions under which a definite conclusion follows or does not follow from given premises. The use of means and methods of mathematical logic (q.v.) makes it possible to construct S. as a formalised theory: it is strictly axiomatised, and its non-contradictory nature and decidability are demonstrated.

Syntactics, a branch of Semiotic.

Synthetic and Analytic, concepts denoting different methods of ascertaining the truth of propositions (statements). All propositions in a logically ordered system of knowledge, which is fixed in terms of ordinary language or a formalised language of science, fall into two types: analytic, or those whose truth can be established only by the rules governing the given system, without recourse to extralinguistic facts, and synthetic, or those whose truth cannot be ascertained by the rules alone but requires recourse to empirical data. In the history of philosophy, the problem of the S. and A. is closely associated with the distinction between empirical knowledge and theoret-ical knowledge. A strict distinction between S. and A. is relevant only within a given formalised language. Its propositions are divided into logical truths (analytic statements) and factual truths (synthetic statements). Logical truths do not communicate any immediate information about extralinguistic reality; they constitute the content of formal logic. Factual truths are based on experience and constitute the content (including the laws) of specific sciences. Unlike neo-positivism (q.v.), which interprets analytic propositions as language conventions (see Conventionalism) dialectical materialism proceeds from the premise that every statement of every science is determined in the last resort by objective reality. The division of propositions into S. and A. depends on the place they hold in a definite system of knowledge.

System, an aggregate of elements which are related to and connected with each other, forming a unified whole. The concept of S. plays an important part in modern philosophy, science, technology and practical activities. An intensive research in the systems approach (q.v.) and the general theory of systems (q.v.) has been pursued since the 1950s. The concept of S. has a long history. The thesis that the whole is more than the sum of its parts was formulated in antiquity. The stoics interpreted S. as the world order. As philosophy evolved since antiquity (see Plato; Aristotle), a great deal of attention was given to revealing the specific features of the S. of knowledge. The systemic nature of cognition was emphasised by Kant (q.v.); this line was further elaborated in the works of Schelling and Hegel (qq.v.). Specific types of S. (geometrical, mechanical and others) were explored by specialised sciences in the 17th-19th centuries. Marxism formulated the philosophical and methodological principles of cognition of integrally developing Ss. In this connection, a most important part is played by the dialectico-materialist systems principle. In the mid-20th century a great contribution to better understanding of the mechanisms of control Ss. (large, complex Ss.) was made by cybernetics (q.v.) and a number of sciences associated with it. The concept of

S. is organically linked with the concepts of wholeness (q.v.), element, subsystem, connection, relation, structure (q.v.) and others. The S. is characterised not only by the ties and relations existing between its constituent elements (a definite organisation), but also by its inseparable unity with the environment, in the interaction with which the S. manifests its integrity. Any S. may be regarded as an element of a S. of a higher order, while its own elements may appear as Ss. of a lower order. Most Ss. involve the transfer of information and control (qq.v.). The most complicated types of Ss. are purpose-oriented Ss., whose conduct is subordinated to attaining definite objectives, and self-organising Ss. capable of adjusting their structure in the process of functioning. In addition, many complicated Ss. (living, social and others) are characterised by the existence in them of multi-level, and often differing, objectives, their conciliation and conflict. The rapid development, in the 20th century, of systems research and its wide practical application in science and technology (e.g., for the analysis of various biological Ss. and the Ss. of man's influence on nature, for the building of transport control Ss., space flight control Ss., various managerial Ss., global development modelling Ss., etc.) necessitated the elaboration of strict formal definitions of the concept of S., which are constructed with the aid of the set theory, mathematical logic, cybernetics (qq.v.), etc., and supplement each other.

Systems Analysis, a sum of methods and means used to investigate and design complex and supercomplex objects, above all methods involved in elaborating, making and substantiating decisions while designing, creating and controlling various social, economic, man-machine and technical systems (q.v.). S.A. emerged in the 1960s as a result of progress in the study of operations. The systems approach (q.v.) and the general theory of systems (q.v.) form the theoretical and methodological basis of S.A. The latter is used mainly in investigating artificial (largely man-made, man-influenced systems). According to the S.A. principles, a complicated problem facing society (above all, the control problem) should be regarded as a certain whole, as a system of all its components which interact among themselves. To take a decision on how to control this system, it is necessary to determine its purpose (q.v.), the objectives of its individual subsystems and many alternative ways of achieving these objectives, which are compared according to definite efficiency criteria, whereafter the most suitable control method is chosen. An important stage in S.A. is the construction of a general model (or a number of models) of the system in question, which should take into account all its essential variables. Owing to the multitude of components (elements, subsystems, blocks, ties, etc.) comprising socio-economic, man-machine and other systems, S.A. requires modern computer facilities, both for constructing general models of such systems and for operating them (e.g., by playing out on such models the scenarios of the systems' functioning, and by interpreting the data thus obtained). S.A. widely uses methods of the games theory, heuristic programming, imitation modelling, programmed target control, etc., which have been developed in the last two or three decades. An important feature of S.A. is the unity of formalised and non-formalised means and methods of research used in it.

Systems Approach, a methodological trend in science concerned with elaborating methods of research into and designing of complex objects—systems (q.v.) of different types and classes. The S.A. is a definite stage in the development of methods of cognition, research and designing, and methods involved in describing and explaining the nature of objects which are being analysed or artificially created. In terms of historical process, the S.A. came to replace the conceptions of mechanism (q.v.), which were widely current in the 17th-19th centuries, and in terms of its tasks is directly opposed to these conceptions. S.A. methods are most widely applied in investigating complex developing objects—multilevel, hierarchic, self-organising biological, psychological, social, etc., systems, large technical systems, man-machine systems, etc. The systems principle of dialectical materialism forms the theoretical basis of such methods. Marx and Lenin produced a profound analysis of the most complex developing object—the system of economic relations of capitalism—and formulated a number of principles basic to systems research. The systems research concentrates on revealing the manifold ties and relations both existing within the object under investigation and extending beyond it to the environment. The properties of the object as an integral system are determined not so much by the summed up properties of its individual elements, as by properties and system-forming ties of the object under consideration. Much importance in the S.A. attaches to predicting the probable behaviour of the objects under consideration. As a rule, systemic objects are not indifferent to the process of investigation, and in many cases may exert considerable influence on it. The mounting scientific and technological revolution (q.v.) is conducive to a further specification of the content of the S.A.—a minute elaboration of its philosophical basis, perfection of logical and methodological principles, and further progress in evolving a general theory of systems (q.v.). The S.A. is the theoretical and methodological foundation of systems analysis (q.v.)

Systems, General Theory of, special scientific, logical and methodological conception of the study of objects which represent systems (q.v.). G.T.S. is closely connected with the systems approach (q.v.) and is a concrete logical and methodological expression of its principles and methods. The first variant of G.T.S. was put forward by Bertalanffy (q.v.). He studied open systems which constantly exchange matter and energy with the environment. In the 1950s to 70s some other approaches to the G.T.S. were suggested. Much attention was paid to constructing the logical, conceptual and mathematical apparatus of systems investigations. G.T.S. is important for the development of modern science and technology: it formulates basic methodological principles of systems investigation without substituting for special systems theories and conceptions that analyse definite classes of systems.

t

Tai Chen (1723-1777), Chinese materialist philosopher. Of the interconnection between the ideal *li* (q.v.) and the material *ch'i* (q.v.), the two fundamental concepts of the neo-Confucian philosophy of nature, T.C. said that *ch'i* was primary and *li* secondary. The world, he said, is in a state of continuous becoming and development. He described motion as the interaction of opposite forces—the positive *yang* and the negative *yin* (see *Yin and Yang*). The action of these forces is eternal, indestructible and inseparable from nature. All phenomena and things are subject to natural necessity. T.C. believed sensations to be the basis of cognition, denied the existence of "innate knowledge" and advocated experimental verification of general conclusions. As for his social and political views, he maintained that the liberation of the people depended on the development of education and the moral self-improvement of the individual.

T'ai Shih, or the "Great Ultimate", one of the basic concepts of the ontological and natural philosophical systems in the history of Chinese philosophy. It is first mentioned in *The Book of Changes*, where this concept denotes the initial stage, the cause of origin and development of all phenomena and things. The term of T. is of primary importance in neo-Confucian philosophy. For instance, in his work *Explanation of the Diagram of the Great Ultimate*, Chou Tun-i (1017-1073) shows the process of world development. Initially, nature was in the state of chaos, or the "unlimited Great Ultimate". The self-motion of the "Great Ultimate" through the connections of *yin* (q.v.) and *yang* (q.v.) and the five primary elements generates and develops the entire multiformity of reality. Chu Hsi (q.v.) interpreted T. from an idealistic point of view, and identified it with *li* (q.v.), the absolute law.

Tan Ssŭ-tung (1865-1898), Chinese philosopher, ideologist of the bourgeois reformation movement towards the end of the 19th century. He expounded his philosophical views in his book *Jên-hsüeh* (A Study of Benevolence), which played a big role in developing the bourgeois-revolutionary movement in China. T.S. sought to justify the demands of the reformers' movement theoretically. His teaching was but a combination of the ideas of Chinese traditional philosophy with certain natural scientific conceptions held in Western Europe. The main concept of his teaching—*Jên*—means both an ethical standard and a metaphysical principle. *Jên* is the unifying factor in the interaction of all phenomena and things in "ether". T.S. professed the dependence of ethics and morality on social regulations. Philosophically, he was not consistent, his scientific conceptions being interwoven with religion, materialism with idealism, and dialectics with metaphysics.

Tantrism, a religious and philosophical teaching in ancient India, originally linked with the cult of female deities and magic land fertility rites. Historically, T. changed its form several times under the impact of the religions which developed later: it was Buddhist, Shivaist, Shaktist and Vishnuist. In the Middle Ages, T. admitted the reality of the world and its evolution out of the spiritual primary principle. The Tantrists held that the structures of the microcosm and the macrocosm were identical and tried to find a key to the knowledge of nature in man's knowledge. Their teaching on the human body contains much information that enables us to judge of the development of chemistry and medicine in ancient and medieval India. An important feature of T. is its appeal to all Indians, irrespective of their caste, sex or age. This is due to the fact that T. preserves a number of essential features of primitive-communal ideology. T. greatly influenced Indian philosophy, in particular, the ideas of the early Sankhya (q.v.). Among those influenced by T. in the 19th and 20th centuries were Ramakrishna, Vivekananda, Ghose (qq.v.), and R. Tagore.

Tao, one of the key categories in classical Chinese philosophy. Originally, T. denoted "the way", and was later used in philosophy to denote the "path" of nature, the laws governing nature. T. also connoted the purpose of life and the "ethical standard" (*tao te*). T. also means logic, reason and argument (*tao li*). The concept changed in step with the development of Chinese philosophy. Such materialist philosophers as Lao Tzŭ, Hsün Tzŭ (q.v.), Wang Chung (q.v.), and others, interpret T. as the natural way of things and the law that governs things. The idealists interpret T. as an "ideal principle", "true non-being" (Wang Pi and others), a "divine way" (Tung Chung-shu and others).

Taoism, the doctrine of *tao* (q.v.) or "the way" (of things), originated in China in the 6th-5th centuries B.C. Lao Tzŭ (q.v.), who is considered its founder, urged people to live a natural life. In the epoch of Tan (7th-9th centuries B.C.) Lao Tzŭ was canonised. He set out his basic ideas in the book *Tao Tê Ching* (The Canon of Reason and Virtue). He maintained that all things originate and change due to their own "way", or *tao*. All things are mutable and turn into their opposites in the process of mutation. Man should adhere to the naturalness of things, without philosophising. T. opposed domination and oppression, and urged a return to the primitive community of the ancients. Yang Chu (q.v.), Yin Wen and Chuang Tzŭ were prominent exponents of T. in the 4th and 3rd centuries B.C. Yang Chu contended that by observing the natural laws of life (*tao*) man would "preserve his nature intact", while Yin Wen believed that adherence to *tao* would yield every man wisdom and knowledge of the truth. The latter averred that man's soul consists of delicate material particles, which come and go depending on the "purity" or "pollution" of our "thought organ" (*hsin*). Chuang Tzŭ saw the object of cognition in the dialectic of the single and the plural, the absolute and the relative, the constant and the changing. Chuang Tzŭ strove, however, to absolutise the single in the

plural and rest in motion, and to separate *tao* from things. This served as the ideological basis of his theory of "inaction", subsequently one of the pillars of the Taoist religion, which originated at the dawn of the new era (T. as a philosophy is to be distinguished from T. as a religion).

Tarski, Alfred (b. 1902), logician and mathematician, an eminent representative of the Lvov-Warsaw school (q.v.). Since 1939 has been at Berkeley (USA). T. is the founder of formal semantics (q.v.) concerned with the meanings of concepts and judgments in logic. He also worked on problems of constructing deductive theories, metalogic, semiotic (qq.v.), etc. His main works: *Logic, Semantics, Metamathematics* (1956), *Logic, Methodology, and Philosophy of Science* (1962).

Taste, Aesthetic, man's ability acquired through social practice to appreciate different aesthetical properties, above all the beautiful (q.v.) and the ugly (q.v.). When works of art are appraised A.T. is called artistic taste. Good A.T. implies the ability to enjoy something truly beautiful, the need to perceive and create the beautiful in one's work, everyday life, behaviour, and art. On the contrary, bad A.T. distorts man's aesthetic appreciation of reality, renders him indifferent to genuine beauty and sometimes even leads him to enjoy ugly things. The degree of appreciation of aesthetic values in everyday life and the arts indicates the level of development of one's A.T. Development of good A.T. is one of the main aims of aesthetic education in socialist countries.

Tautology 1. In mathematical logic (q.v.), the equivalent of the identically true statements (q.v.). 2. In traditional logic, a definition in which the definitive is a simple repetition in different words of what is implied in the notion to be defined.

Technocracy, Theories of, a sociological trend which came into being in the USA on the strength of the ideas of the bourgeois economist T. Veblen. It gained popularity in the 1930s (H. Scott and others). Technocratic societies have sprung up in a number of capitalist countries. Adherents of T.T. claim that anarchy and instability of contemporary capitalism are the result of the administration of state affairs by politicians. They hold that capitalism may be cured provided that economic life and state administration are taken over by technical experts and businessmen. Their demagogic criticism of capitalist economy and politics camouflages their striving to justify the direct subordination of the state machinery to industrial monopolies. The contemporary scientific and technological revolution (q.v.) has revived some ideas of T. There emerged numerous theories of the "industrial" (R. Aron, W. Rostow), "post-industrial" (Bell, q.v.), "technotronic" (Z. Brzezinski) society, the theory of convergence, q.v. (J. Galbraith). Closely associated with T., but even more reactionary, is managerism, a doctrine of the leading role of the managers. The latter theory has acquired an anti-communist character in the works by J. Burnham, whose "managerial revolution" is the apologia of the open dictatorship by US monopolists. In the 1970s, Bell coined a notion of meritocracy (q.v.), which allegedly replaces bureaucracy and technocracy in what he calls "society of knowledge".

Teilhard de Chardin, Pierre (1881-1955), French paleontologist, philosopher and theologian, one of the discoverers of the Sinanthropus. The philosophical conception of T. was Christian evolutionism, a variety of idealistic pantheism (q.v.). According to T., God is present in every particle as special type of spiritual energy, which is the driving and directing force of evolution. The development of the Universe ("cosmogenesis"—"Christogenesis") was presented by T. as a sequence of stages of spiritual evolution by means of gradual complexification of matter. His conception of development contained important elements of dialectics (up-and-down movement, contradictions, etc.). According to T., science plays an important role in the process of perfecting the world, which with the emergence of man (the top of the evolution arrow directed towards the future) is carried out through

the consciousness and activity of men themselves. Unjustly considering science as a variety of religious approach to reality, T. sought to remove the antithesis between faith and knowledge. Problems of modernisation of Christianity (q.v.) occupied a considerable place in the works of T. His ideas (that are known as Teilhardism) have gained popularity in the West. Because of inherent contradictions in T.'s conception, his ideas are used by representatives of different social groups, sometimes adopting opposite political positions. Religious and idealistic premises distort the actual picture of the development of reality in T.'s conception, yet it contains some elements of optimism and humanism. This distinguishes Teilhardism from other trends in modern bourgeois philosophy. His main work: *Le phénomène humain* (published posthumously in 1955).

Teleology, a religious-philosophical doctrine of the existence of objective extra-human purposes and expediency (q.v.). T. finds expression in idealistic anthropomorphisation (see Anthropomorphism) of natural objects and processes. It associates them with the action of the target-setting principles in order to implement the pre-determined purposes. This thesis assumes the existence of a super-intelligent creator and underlies the teleological proof of God's existence. According to transcendental-anthropocentric T., the target-setting principle, or God, is outside the world, introduces purposes in nature created for man (Wolff, q.v.); according to immanent T., every object in nature has in itself an intrinsic vital purpose, a purposive cause, which is the source of the movement from the lower to higher forms (Aristotle, q.v.). In its different forms T. is present in stoicism (see Stoics), Neoplatonism (q.v.), in the conception of pre-set harmony of Leibniz (q.v.), in Schelling's (q.v.) theory of the "world soul", in Hegel's (q.v.) objective idealism, neo-Kantianism, neo-Thomism, personalism (qq.v.), etc. Contemporary fideism, holism (qq.v.), and the like, employ the idealistically interpreted data of genetics, cybernetics and psychology (qq.v.) to modernise T. In the period of modern history the natural sciences (physics, mechanics, astronomy) destroyed the geo- and anthropocentric religious picture of the world and explained the processes of motion in the Universe by natural causes. Darwinism enabled men to understand the natural character of expediency in the organic world. Later it was deepened by genetics, molecular biology and cybernetics. Marxist philosophy scientifically explained the expediency of social activity of people in different forms by their actions in conformity with the objective laws and overcame T. in the field of social life.

Telesio, Bernardino (1509-1588), Italian natural philosopher of the Renaissance (q.v.), materialist. He urged philosophers to study nature by means of experiments and emphasised the importance of the sense-organs, which he held to be the main source of human knowledge. He opposed the speculative method specific to scholasticism (q.v.). T. exerted a great influence on Bruno and Campanella (qq.v.) and was a predecessor of F. Bacon (q.v.). In his interpretation of nature T. proceeded from the fact that matter, filling up all the space, is as eternal as God. Like all other natural philosophers of his time, T. adhered to hylozoistic ideas (see Hylozoism). T.'s system of cosmological views implied that heat and cold as the antithetical and animated elements aspiring to self-conservation are in combat for matter, heat being concentrated on the Sun and cold on the Earth. His main work: *De Rerum Natura juxta Propria Principia* (1565).

Temperament, the sum total of the individual qualities of the person characterising the dynamics of his or her psychic activity. T. is manifested in the strength of man's feelings, their depth or superficiality, the speed with which they are displayed, their stability or variability. T. is similarly manifested in the peculiarities of the individual's movements. The basis of T. is man's higher nervous activity. A strong, balanced and mobile type corresponds to the sanguine T., distinctive features of which are quickly arising but easily changeable emotions, and vivacious movements. A strong, balanced, but im-

mobile type corresponds to the phlegmatic T., which is characterised by the stability of feelings, by calm movements. A strong, unbalanced type corresponds to the choleric T., whose distinctive features are suddenly changing emotions, emotional excitability, impetuous movements. A weak type corresponds to the melancholic T. with deep and lasting feelings, to which little outward expression is given. It should be noted that T. depends not only on the inborn qualities of the nervous system, but also on the conditions of man's life and work. T. is not invariable throughout an individual's life. No type of T. is necessarily a hindrance to the development of all socially essential qualities of the person. However, every T. requires special ways and means of forming these qualities. T. is one of the prerequisites of man's original character.

Term 1. A word having only one meaning, fixing a definite concept of science, technology, the arts, etc. T. is an element of the scientific language whose introduction is determined by the necessity for exact and unambiguous designation of the data of science, especially those data which have no corresponding names in everyday language. As distinct from words used in everyday language T. is devoid of emotional connotation. 2. In logic, T. is an essential element of a judgment (subject and predicate) or a syllogism.

Thales of Miletus (Asia Minor) (c. 624-547 B.C.), the first historically known Greek philosopher. In ancient tradition he was considered one of the "seven wise men". According to legend, T.M. mastered the mathematical and astronomical knowledge of Egypt and Babylon. He is credited with predicting the solar eclipse of 585-584 B.C. T.M. was the founder of the spontaneous-materialist Milesian school (q.v.). He sought a primordial principle in the diversity of things and regarded it as a corporeal substance perceptible by the senses. He held water to be the primary element of all that exists.

Theism, a religious philosophy which acknowledges the existence of a personal

God as a supernatural being endowed with reason and will and mysteriously influencing all the material and spiritual processes. According to T., all that occurs in the world is the implementation of divine Providence, on which, it holds, the laws of nature depend. As distinct from deism (q.v.), T. postulates a direct intervention of God in all world events, while, as distinct from pantheism (q.v.), it postulates the existence of God outside and above the world. T. is the ideological basis of clericalism, theology and fideism (qq.v.). T. is hostile to science and the scientific world outlook.

Theodicy, "vindication of the justice of God", a term used to designate philosophico-religious treatises which strive to justify the glaring and irreconcilable contradiction between belief in an almighty, wise and good God and the existence of evil and injustice in the world. In the 17th and 18th centuries T. became an independent branch of philosophical literature. Leibniz's (q.v.) essay on evil, *Théodicée* (1710), which was famous at the time, was subjected to scathing criticism by Voltaire in his satirical philosophical novel *Candide* (1759). By its social content T. was an attempt at philosophico-religious justification of the evil and injustice reigning in a society based on exploitation. Today many theological works deal with this subject.

Theogony, a system of religious myths concerning the origin and descent of the gods. The first known poetical collection of ancient Greek myths in European literature was *Theogony* by Hesiod (8th century B.C.).

Theology, or the study of God, the system of dogmas in a given religion. Christian T. is based on the Bible, the decrees of the first oecumenical councils and the "Holy Fathers", the Holy Scriptures and the sacred traditions, and is divided into basic theology (fundamentalism and apologetics, q.v.), dogmatic theology, moral theology, church history, etc. The prominent features of T. are extreme dogmatism, authoritarianism, and scholasticism. Closely related to T. is religious philosophy, which tries to prove that T. is compatible with science. T. has been severely criticised by progressive thinkers of all times. Criticism of T. is an inseparable part of scientific atheism (q.v.).

Theorem, in modern formal logic and mathematics, any proposition in a strictly built deductive (e.g., axiomatic) theory, which is proved by applying the permissible rules of deduction to its initial propositions (see Axiom). The concepts of axiom and T. are relative: the same propositions of a given theory may be regarded in some cases as axioms, and proved in others as Tt. For this reason axioms are often regarded as Tt.

Theory, a system of generalised authentic knowledge which gives an integral picture of the regularities and essential ties of reality. The term of T. has different connotations: as opposed to practice or a hypothesis, q.v., (unverified, suppositional knowledge). T. differs from practice, since it spiritually or mentally reflects and reproduces reality. At the same time it is inseparably linked with practice, which places pressing problems before knowledge and requires it to solve them. For this reason practice and its summarised results are part and parcel of every T. Both natural-scientific and social Tt. are determined by the historical conditions in which they originate, by the historically given level of production, technology, experiment and science, and also the dominant social order, which may favour or, contrariwise, hamper the creation of scientific Tt. Thus, only in the mid-19th century, with the emergence of Marxism, sociological views turned into a scientific T. of the laws of social development. Tt. may and actually do play a big role in scientific knowledge and the transformation of society by revolutionary means. Thus, while appearing as a generalisation of the cognitive activity and results of practice, T. is conducive to transforming nature and social life. The criterion of the truth value of T. is practice (see Criterion of Truth).

Theory and Practice, philosophical categories denoting the spiritual and material aspects of the socio-historical activity of people: cognition and transformation of nature and society. T. is the result of social spiritual production, which forms the purposes of activity and determines the means of their achievement. This result exists in the form of developing concepts of objects of human activity. As distinct from empiricism and positivism, Marxist philosophy regards P. not as the sensuous subjective experience of the individual and not as an experiment of the scientist, etc., but as the activity of people to sustain the existence and development of society, and above all, as the objective process of material production, which constitutes the basis of human life, and also as the revolutionary and transforming activity of classes and all the other forms of social activity which bring about changes in the world. P. is the basis of cognition and the criterion of truth (q.v.). Human activity is always purposeful. At the dawn of human history, the labour of our ancestors, who only knew its division according to sex and age, was also purposeful. At that time, there existed neither special theoretical activity nor T. The social division of labour (q.v.) into agriculture and cattle-breeding led to the emergence of productive labour, which for the first time separated the production of the means of production (cultivation of land for sowing and sowing itself) from the production of the means of consumption (gathering, storage, and processing of crops). This division of labour resulted in the separation of mental from physical labour, and in the class stratification of society. Along with that, the prerequisites arose for the emergence and separation of T. from P. The production of the means of production did not satisfy immediate vital needs. It served as a basis for accomplishing of the final social goals, while its own goals required organisation and management of labour. For instance, planning future work on an unploughed field meant seeing its borders which did not yet exist in reality, separating ideally the field from uncultivated land. The activity dealing with the generally significant ways and means of the purposeful change of objects, which emerged in the course of social division of labour, was divorced from material-practical activity proper, from P., and was transformed into special spiritual produc-

tion where mental labour prevailed. With the division of labour into mental and physical, came the real separation of T. from P., their transformation into relatively independent forms of social activity. The development of "pure" T. as a relatively independent special field of activity was one of the greatest leaps in the history of mankind. It enabled people to penetrate deeply into the essence of natural phenomena, to create a constantly changing scientific picture of the world. On the other hand, the unity of T. and P. became less obvious. On this basis and alongside the individualistic world outlook characteristic of societies where private ownership dominated, there arose various illusions: beginning from the view of T. as the result of individual passive contemplation of the surroundings by a "theorist" and ending with the idealist philosophical systems which regarded theoretical consciousness (ideas) as the creator of reality. The capitalist mode of production which socialised labour and developed productive forces on an unprecedented scale, creates objective premises for overcoming the separation of T. from P. The role of T. becomes increasingly greater not only in the process of production. The practical movement of masses aimed at abolishing the bourgeois system is being combined with progressive, Marxist theory, which reveals the objective laws of society and directs the proletarian party's activity towards the achievement of a scientifically realised goal— communism. Objective conditions for the separation and opposition of T. and P. disappear with the emancipation of labour, the abolition of class antagonisms, and the removal of the antithesis between mental and physical labour. Socialism and communism cannot be built without establishing organic links between T. and P., without constant theoretical generalisation of the practical experience of the masses, without introduction of the progressive scientific T. into P.

Theory of Knowledge, or epistemology, a department of philosophy concerned with the relation of subject and object in the process of cognitive activity, the relation of knowledge to reality, the possibility of man's cognition of the world, the criteria of the truth and authenticity of knowledge. The T.K. studies the essence of man's cognitive attitude towards the world. Therefore, any T.K. inevitably proceeds from a definite solution of the fundamental question of philosophy (q.v.). All varieties of the T.K. are divided into materialist and idealist. The materialist dialectics is a philosophical teaching on cognition, the Marxist logic and theory of knowledge. The laws and categories of materialist dialectics, being the reflection of the universal laws of development of the objective world, are thus the universal forms of cognoscitive thought. Therefore, the Marxist T.K., as distinct from the epistemology of the past, is not only the theory of specific laws of cognition but is also the result of the history of the cognition of the world. This means that in Marxist-Leninist philosophy the specific epistemology of the relation of consciousness and matter, the ideal and the material, the criteria of authentic knowledge, the relation of the sensuous and the logical, reflection, etc., is studied on the basis of the method of materialist dialectics and in close connection with the teaching of historical materialism, which allows to reveal the essence of man's cognition of the world by means of analysing his practical transforming activity. Strictly speaking, the history of the T.K. begins with the question of what knowledge is being put before philosophy (see Plato), although the term of T.K. appeared much later. In the history of philosophy, the problems of the T.K. have always played a significant part, and sometimes even occupied the central place. A number of trends in bourgeois philosophy (Kantianism, Machism) reduce philosophy to the T.K. The rapid development of special scientific methods of research (e.g. mathematical logic, semiotic, psychology, qq.v.) leads, in the opinion of certain positivists and scientists sharing positivist views, to the liquidation of the T.K. as a philosophical science. Dialectical materialism, however, maintains that the development of special scientific methods of research cannot in principle whittle away the philosophical problems of the T.K. On the contrary, this development stimulates it, setting ever new problems before the

T.K. (for instance, the study of the possibility of automation of mental labour). The dialectical-materialist T.K. uses in its development the data provided by modern special sciences of cognition and constitutes their philosophico-methodological basis.

Theosophy, the concept sometimes identified with theology (q.v.) or with some forms of mysticism (q.v.). T. proper is the teaching of E. Blavatskaya (1831-1891), who founded the Theosophical Society in New York in 1875 (shortly afterwards its centre shifted to India, where it is still functioning). Until 1913 R. Steiner, the father of anthroposophy (q.v.), was an active member of the Society. Blavatskaya set forth the tasks of the Society and her own ideas in *The Secret Doctrine* (1888), *The Key to Theosophy* (1889), and other books. T. claims to cognise by "scientific" methods divine wisdom, make it the property of man, and finally to ensure "heavenly bliss" for him after death. Only "masters" of T., possessing secret knowledge (see Occultism), can attain this goal by revealing "hidden powers", the spiritual divine nucleus in the individual. By combining eclectically the elements of various Eastern and Western religions and idealist systems (mainly Buddhism, q.v., and other trends in Indian philosophy), T. collects unscientific, mystical and fantastic ideas about the world and man.

Theses on Feuerbach, eleven theses written by Marx in the spring of 1845. They were first published by Engels in 1888 as an appendix to his work *Ludwig Feuerbach and the End of Classical German Philosophy.* As Engels put it, *Theses on Feuerbach* are "invaluable as the first document in which is deposited the brilliant germ of the new world outlook" (Marx, Engels, *Selected Works,* in three volumes, Vol. 3, p. 336). In their content, *Theses* are close to *The German Ideology.* In his *Theses* Marx concisely formulated the cardinal principles of a new philosophy. Their central idea is the elaboration of a scientific understanding of practice. This task required a materialist understanding of history, the basic propositions of which Marx expounded.

These are: that all social life is essentially practical, that man is the product of his own labour, that he is essentially social by nature, that ideological phenomena (for instance, religion) depend on the conditions of society's existence and development. From this viewpoint Marx criticised the historical idealism of Feuerbach (q.v.) and utopian socialism. Proceeding from the unity of theory and practice, Marx raised the problems of epistemology in a new light, criticised all "previous" materialism, noting that its chief defect was its contemplative character (see Contemplativeness). Marx exposed the defects of the idealist understanding of practical activity. Marx's theses substantiated the essence and tasks of the philosophy of dialectical materialism, and its role in the revolutionary transformation of society.

Thing, any part of the material world possessing relatively independent existence. One thing is distinguished from another by its qualitative definiteness (see Quality). The problem of identity (q.v.) and difference (q.v.) of things, as well as that of distinctness of the T. from the object are important from the epistemological and scientific viewpoints.

"Thing-in-Itself" and "Thing-for-Us", philosophical terms, the former meaning things as they exist by themselves, independently of us and our knowledge, the latter denoting things as they reveal themselves to man in the process of cognition. These terms acquired particular significance in the 18th century, when it was stated that it was impossible to know "things-in-themselves". First stated by Locke (q.v.), this proposition was developed in detail by Kant (q.v.), who claimed that we are concerned only with the phenomenon which is completely removed from the "thing-in-itself". For Kant, the "thing-in-itself" also means essences which are preternatural, unknowable, inaccessible to experience: God, freedom, etc. Dialectical materialism, which proceeds from the premise that it is possible to acquire exhaustive knowledge of things, regards cognition as the process of turning the "thing-in-itself" into the "thing-for-us" on the basis of

practical experience (see Cognition, Theory and Practice).

Thomism, the leading trend in Catholic philosophy started by Thomas Aquinas (q.v.). T. was most widely accepted in the various schools of the Dominican Order. In the Middle Ages T. was opposed by the adherents of Duns Scotus (q.v.) who grouped around the Franciscan Order. The earlier bourgeois revolutions, the Reformation (q.v.), and the resultant loss by the Catholic Church of its former supremacy were responsible for a certain renovation of T. by the Spanish Jesuit F. Suarez. The mid-19th century saw the last revival of T. (see Neo-Thomism), the prominent representatives of this trend being A. Stöckl (Germany), N. de Wulf (France), D. Mercier (Belgium), J. Newman (Britain), M. Liberatore (Italy), and others. The main tendency of contemporary T. is to falsify modern natural science theologically and to "synthesise" Thomas Aquinas' system with the philosophical ideas of Kant, Hegel, Husserl, Heidegger (qq.v.) and other bourgeois philosophers.

Thoreau, Henry David (1817-1862), American idealist philosopher and writer; a member of the club of transcendentalists (q.v.) headed by Emerson (q.v.). T.'s views took shape under the influence of European romantics (especially Carlyle, q.v.) and Rousseau (q.v.), as well as of oriental thinkers. He criticised the exploiter system of capitalism and its culture from petty-bourgeois positions. According to T., any state is "imbecile" and is an evil. His individualistic socio-ethical ideal—a free individual, independent of society and worshipping nature—was the consequence of his negative attitude towards the bourgeois system. T.'s pantheism (q.v.) had a flavour of mysticism. He opposed slavery in the USA and was one of the first to come out with the idea of civil disobedience; he welcomed John Brown's activity in defence of the Blacks.

Thought, an active process through which the objective world is reflected in concepts, judgments, theories, etc. and which is linked with the solution of problems; the highest product of a specially organised matter—the brain (q.v.).

T., being inseparably linked with the brain, cannot be fully explained by the activity of the physiological system. The inception of T. is associated not only with biological evolution, but also with social development. T. emerges in the process of people's productive activity and provides a mediate reflection of reality. It has a social nature as regards its specific origin, the way of functioning and its results. The explanation of this is to be found in the fact that T. is inseparably linked with such activities as labour and speech, which are peculiar only to human society. Hence, man's T. occurs in closest association with speech and its results are expressed in language (q.v.). T. comprises such processes as abstraction, analysis and synthesis (qq.v.), the formulation of definite tasks and the discovery of their solutions, the advancement of hypotheses, ideas (qq.v.), etc. The process of T. invariably produces some idea. The fact that T. is capable of generalised reflection of reality finds expression in man's ability to form general concepts (q.v.). The formation of scientific concepts is associated with the formulation of corresponding laws. The fact that T. is capable of mediate reflection of reality finds expression in man's ability to arrive at inferences (q.v.), logical conclusions and proof (q.v.). This ability greatly increases the range of cognition. It enables man to proceed from an analysis of facts which may be directly perceived to cognition of that which cannot be perceived through the sense-organs. Concepts and systems of concepts (scientific theories) record (generalise) the experience of mankind, represent the sum total of man's knowledge, and serve as a point of departure for further cognition of reality. T. is the object of study of various disciplines (physiology of higher nervous activity, logic, cybernetics, psychology, epistemology, qq.v., etc.) by various methods. Prominent among experimental studies in the field of T. has lately been modelling (q.v.) in the shape of various cybernetic devices. Idealism has always striven to dissociate T. from matter (the human brain, language, society's practical activities), and when it did recognise such an association, it strove to present T. as something derived from certain spiritual

principles superior to matter and the consciousness of individuals (e.g., Hegel, q.v.). Denial of T. as something really existing is taught by modern bourgeois philosophy, including neo-positivism (q.v.). Reducing mankind's entire range of experience to facts directly observed, as does behaviourism (q.v.), neo-positivism declares T. to be a fiction, just like matter (unlike language, which is invariably regarded as a fact perceived through the sense-organs). Neo-positivism ignores the fact that language is a means of expression, a form of the existence of thought. In actual fact language analysis is used in the study of those properties of the brain which are known as thought.

Time and Space, basic forms of existence of matter (q.v.). Philosophers are mainly concerned with the relation of T.&S. to matter, i.e., whether T.&S. are real or pure abstractions which exist only in men's consciousness. The idealist philosophers deny the dependence of T.&S. on matter and regard them either as forms of individual consciousness (Berkeley, Hume, Mach, qq.v.) or as a priori forms of sense contemplation (Kant, q.v.) or as categories of the absolute spirit (Hegel, q.v.). Materialism stresses the objectivity of T.&S. T.&S. are inseparable from matter, this being a manifestation of their universality. S. expresses the distribution of simultaneously existing objects, while T. expresses the sequence of existence of phenomena which replace one another. T. is irreversible, i.e., every material process develops only in one direction—from the past to the future. Dialectical materialism proceeds not from the simple external connection of T.&S. with matter in motion, but from the fact that motion is the essence of T.&S., and that, consequently, matter, motion, time and space are inseparable. This idea has been confirmed in modern physics. The natural science of the 18th and 19th centuries, while recognising the objective nature of T.&S., followed Newton (q.v.) in regarding them as divorced from each other, as something self-dependent, existing completely independently of matter and motion. Following the atomistic views of the ancient natural philosophers (Democritus, Epicurus, qq.v.) natural scientists right up to the 20th century identified space with vacuum, which they considered absolute, always and everywhere the same and motionless, with T. running always at the same pace. Modern physics has discarded the old conceptions of S. as an empty receptacle of bodies and of T. as something uniform for the boundless Universe. The main conclusion in Einstein's theory of relativity (q.v.) is precisely the establishment of the fact that T.&S. do not exist by themselves, in isolation from matter, but are part of a universal interrelation in which they lose their independence and emerge as aspects of a single and diverse whole. The general theory of relativity has proved that the elapse of time and the extent of bodies depend on the speed at which these bodies move, and that the structure or properties of the four-dimensional continuum (space-time) change according to the accumulation of masses of substance and the field of gravitation to which they give rise. The ideas of Lobachevsky (q.v.), Riemann, Gauss, and Bolyai contributed much to the present-day theory of T.&S. The discovery of non-Euclidean geometry refuted Kant's teaching on T.&S. as forms of sense perception outside the range of experience. The researches of Butlerov (q.v.), Y. Fyodorov, and their followers revealed the dependence of spatial properties on the physical nature of material bodies, and the dependence of the physico-chemical properties of matter on the spatial distribution of atoms. The changes in people's views on T.&S. are used by the idealists as an excuse for denying their objective reality. According to dialectical materialism, human knowledge produces as it develops a more profound and correct conception of objectively real T.&S.

Timiryazev, Kliment Arkadyevich (1843-1920), Russian scientist, follower of Darwin (q.v.), founder of plant physiology in Russia. T.'s world outlook was shaped under the impact of the ideas of the Russian revolutionary democrats. His basic experimental work in plant photosynthesis played a considerable role in laying the theoretical basis for the unity of living and inanimate matter. T. did not confine his research within the narrow framework of experimental methods; he made broad philosophical generalisations and fruitfully applied the historical method, which in many respects coincides with the dialectical-materialist method. T. strove to place biology at the service of the people. He was the first among the prominent Russian scientists to accept the Great October Socialist Revolution of 1917. His political and philosophical views are expounded in the collection of articles *Nauka i democratia* (Science and Democracy), 1920.

Tkachyov, Pyotr Nikitich (1844-1886), one of the theoreticians of revolutionary Narodism (q.v.) and publicist. T.'s views formed under the influence of the revolutionary democrats of the 1860s. Unlike, for instance, Lavrov (q.v.), T. held that a social revolution must be carried out in Russia immediately, before the establishment of bourgeois relations that could, for a considerable time, postpone the revolution in the country. Like Bakunin (q.v.), T. regarded the Russian people, above all the peasantry, with the prevailing communal land ownership, as instinctively traditional socialists. According to T., the revolutionary spirit of the people is manifested chiefly in the destruction of the old world, while the constructive tasks are tackled by "the revolutionary minority" that possesses strength, power and authority, that is by the state. Therefore, the "seizure of political power" by a group of well-organised revolutionaries through a conspiracy was considered by him an indispensable condition for the implementation of socio-economic and spiritual ideals of socialism. In this respect T. differed from the Bakuninists and assumed the position of the Blanquists. T. believed in terror and disorganisation of the existing state, which in Russia, he alleged, did not express the interests of any class and was not rooted in the country's economy. Although T. recognised some tenets of historical materialism (he, for example, acknowledged the determinative role of "economic life"), he failed to overcome his idealistic, voluntarist view on history. T.'s socio-political ideas were criticised by Engels in his work *The Emigrant*

Literature (1874-75). Main works: *Zakon obshchestvennogo samosokhraneniya* (The Law of Social Self-Preservation), 1870; *Zadachi revolyutsionnoi propagandy v Rossii* (The Tasks of Revolutionary Propaganda in Russia), 1874; *Otkrytoye pismo gospodinu Fridrikhu Engelsu* (An Open Letter to Mr. Friedrich Engels), 1874; *Nabat* (The Bell), 1875; *Revolyutsia i gosudarstvo* (The Revolution and the State), 1876, and others.

Toland, John (1670-1722), English materialist philosopher, advocate of free thinking. Having begun with deistic criticism of religion (see Deism), T. adopted atheism (q.v.): he denied the immortality of the soul, retribution in another life, the creation of the world and miracles, and tried to prove the secular origin of "sacred" books and to explain that religion was the outcome of developments on earth. His book *Christianity not Mysterious* (1696) infuriated the clergy and was burnt; T., however, managed to escape. To him goes the credit for creating the theory of the unity of matter and motion. Motion, he held, is an essential and indispensable property of matter. He criticised Spinoza (q.v.), who did not regard motion as the basic property of matter, and also Newton and Descartes (qq.v.), who believed that God is the source of motion. According to T., matter is eternal and indestructible, and the Universe is infinite. However, he adhered to mechanistic materialism, denied contingency, regarded thought as a purely physical movement of the cerebrum, and held that the motion of matter does not undergo qualitative changes. By his socio-political views, T. was a representative of the bourgeois-democratic circles in England. His main work: *Letters to Serena* (1704).

Tolstoy, Lev Nikolayevich (1828-1910), Russian writer and thinker. His works of art and his teaching reflected the epoch between 1861 and 1904, that is, the epoch of the accelerated growth of capitalism and the ruin of the patriarchal peasantry in Russia. As Lenin said, T. embodied in his works "the specific historical features of the entire first Russian revolution"—"a peasant bourgeois revolution"—"its

strength and its weakness" (Vol. 16, p. 324). Hence the "crying" contradictions in his viewpoints: on the one hand, we see ruthless criticism of capitalism and the official church, and exposure of the anti-popular essence of the state and, on the other hand, the preaching of submissiveness, the doctrine of non-resistance to evil, and a refined form of religion. T.'s philosophico-religious views were influenced by Christianity, Confucianism, and Buddhism (qq.v.), and also Rousseau, Schopenhauer, and the Slavophiles (qq.v.). The basic concept of T.'s teaching is the concept of faith, which he interpreted chiefly in terms of rationalist ethics: faith is the knowledge of what man is and the meaning of his life. According to T., the meaning of human life consists in overcoming the alienation of people, in uniting them on the basis of love and communion with God, on the basis of realising their divinity. In this T. saw the ideal of a "true" Christian religion, the one that is freed from historical distortions and can be achieved through personal self-perfection. T. held that the state, private property, church, and modern civilisation, which is hostile to the people, prevent the implementation of this ideal and give birth to all social vices. As a result, he came to reject the state (see Anarchism), the achievements of science and culture, and called upon people to take to plain living, idealised the peasants' work and the community. According to T., man is only free when he serves God (the good); the socio-historical process is guided by God (see Providentialism) and is exercised through the activity of the masses; the individual, even a tsar, is a slave of history (see Fatalism). In his works on aesthetics *Chto takoye iskusstvo?* (What Is Art?), 1897-98, and others, he opposed decadence and official culture. T. defined art as activity that must unite people and help them implement their ideals. But since T. saw the supreme goal of mankind in the establishment of "God's kingdom on earth", he came to the conclusion that the moral-religious idea must be a guiding idea in art. T. is known as a great realistic writer, as the author of *War and Peace, Anna Karenina, Resurrection,* and other works, as a thinker and humanist, who supported the mass protest against social inequality and oppression. His main philosophico-religious works are: *Issledovaniye dogmaticheskogo bogosloviya* (Investigation of Dogmatic Theology), 1880; *Ispoved* (Confession), 1880-84; *V chom moya vera?* (What Do I Believe In?), 1882-84; *Tsarstvo bozhiye vnutri nas* (God's Kingdom Inside Us), 1891, and *Put zhizni* (Path of Life), 1910.

Totalitarianism, a socio-political system characterised by the all-embracing despotic intervention of the authoritarian-bureaucratic state in the life of society and individuals. Totalitarian features were observed in absolute monarchies, but especially in the Bonapartist regimes of the 19th century (e.g., Louis Bonaparte's regime). The typical examples of T. in the 20th century were or are the fascist regimes in Germany, Italy, Chile, etc. The notion of T. is being employed by anti-communist propaganda for slandering the social system in the socialist countries. The anti-communists try to ignore the truly democratic essence of the reforms taking place in these countries and slur over the principle of democratic centralism underlying the activities of the Communist parties and socialist states.

Totemism, one of the early forms of religion in primitive society. As a term it was used for the first time by J. Long at the end of the 18th century. The main feature of T. is belief in common origin, blood relationship and association of a group of people with a definite kind of animal, plant, object or phenomenon. The emergence of T. was conditioned by the primitive economy (hunting, fruit-gathering, etc.) and the lack of knowledge of the other ties in society besides consanguinity. The primitive conception of the totem is the animal-ancestor, its emblem or symbol, and also a group of people. The totem, the powerful protector of people, supplies them with food. T. is widespread among the aboriginal tribes of Australia, North and South America, Melanesia, Polynesia, and Africa. The survivals of T. are preserved in developed religions (God is the father of believers; pure and impure animals) and in folklore (tales of marital and blood relationships between people and animals).

Town and Country, two relatively isolated forms of human settlement and association. T. and C. first emerged during the transition from pre-class to class society, and are mutually contradictory in the antagonistic socio-economic formations. The separation between T. and C. was objectively necessitated by growing material production, which at a certain stage in its development inevitably gives rise to a social division of labour (q.v.), the separation of industry from agriculture, manifested at first as the separation of the crafts from the cultivation of the land and of mental work from physical labour. The specific relations between T. and C. vary from one socio-economic formation to another. In Asiatic-type communities, in which craft production had not yet been singled out, the nascent Tt. were mainly military, bureaucratic, administrative and religious centres, organisers of public works and supracommunal exploiters of the C. In the slave-owning formation, T. is the place where the slave-owning class is concentrated, and at the same time becomes both the administrative, military, and cultural centre, and the craft production centre dominating the C. With the appearance of feudalism, the centre of economic life moves to the C. A considerable portion of the ruling class is concentrated in rural estates and domains. However, this does not cancel out the role of the T. as the link between them. As feudalism develops, T. plays an increasingly important role not only administratively, but also as a centre of the crafts, trade and culture. This is accompanied by a growth of the urban population. The T. intensifies its exploitation of the C. through monopoly prices for articles of guild production, taxation as well as outright cheating by merchants and usury. Under capitalism, the contradiction between T. and C. constitutes the basis of their mutual relations, and becomes particularly acute at the imperialist stage. The emergence and development of capitalism was universally accompanied by the ruin of the immediate producer and the expropriation of the peasants. The working people in the C. are subjected to double oppression—from the rural and from the urban bourgeoisie, who have their hands on all the economic and political levers for exploiting the C. When under imperialism the whole world was drawn into a single economic system, the industrially developed capitalist states sought to turn the colonial and dependent countries into appendages supplying them with raw materials and agricultural produce. The collapse of the colonial system has not yet brought complete economic independence to most of the formerly dependent countries. Only socialist-oriented countries helped by socialist states obtain the possibility to achieve economic independence from the imperialist states. Already under socialism, the first phase of the communist formation, the antithesis between T. and C. is being eliminated. The elimination of private property and the exploiting classes, and subsequently the socialist co-operation of the peasantry allow the socialist T. to organise the improvement of the economic and cultural standards and the everyday life of the C. Although it eliminates the antithesis between T. and C., socialism does not eliminate the substantial distinctions between them, such as the difference in the development levels of the material and technical basis and culture, the existence of two forms of property (state-owned in T. and collective-farm and co-operative in the C.), the different organisation of labour, everyday life, leisure, etc. The socialist T. retains its leading role in the building of communist society and manifests it in the development of the productive forces in the C., the raising of collective-farm property to the level of property of the entire people, in the conversion of farm work into a variety of industrial work, and in the improvement of the rural population's welfare and cultural standards. Only communism can resolve the problems, engendered by capitalism and intensified by the scientific and technological revolution, of unrestricted urban-isation (q.v.), of the transformation of the Tt. into megapolises stretching for hundreds of miles, suffering from lack of fresh air, vegetation and sunlight, and having a destructive effect on the entire environment. The experience of the Soviet Union shows that it is possible to find a solution to the problems of urbanisation and to overcome the former contradictions between T. and C.

Toynbee, Arnold Joseph (1889-1975), English historian and sociologist. His philosophy of history replaced the concept of social progress by the "theory of cycles". He held that world history is a sum total of various civilisations, which pass through the same phases: birth, growth, downfall, disintegration, and destruction. In treating the problem of the driving forces of history, T. combined the hopes of communion with God with the cult of "creative" individuals and regarded this as the meaning of history. T. differed from Spengler (q.v.) in trying to prove that it was possible to save "Western civilisation" by means of clericalism (q.v.). His main work: *A Study of History* (1-12 vols., 1934-61).

Tradition, historically shaped customs, rites, social precepts, ideas, values, rules of conduct, etc., handed down from generation to generation; elements of socio-cultural legacy preserved in society or its social groups for a considerable period of time. T. can be progressive, if it is connected with the creative development of culture, and reactionary, if it is linked with defunct survivals of the past. In science T. means continuity of knowledge and methods of research, in art it means continuity of style and skill. Under socialism, the development of progressive (revolutionary, patriotic, working) Tt. is combined with the elimination of reactionary Tt. in work, everyday life, culture, the entire way of life of the people.

Traduction, a sort of indirect inference (q.v.) in which the premises and conclusions are propositions of equal degree of generality. Analogy (q.v.) is an example of traductive inference.

Tragic, the, a category of aesthetics expressing the dialectic of freedom and necessity (q.v.), the contradictions of social development, the individual and society, the struggle between the beautiful (q.v.) and the ugly (q.v.). The T. reflects the contradictions which are unresolvable at a given time, the contradictions between the historically necessary requirements and the practical impossibility of implementing them. As distinct from the idealistic interpretation of the essence of the T., which was seen in the hopelessness of human existence, Marxist aesthetics sees the main cause of tragic developments in the collision of social forces, which is due to the laws of social development. Marxists draw a distinction between the tragic nature of new, progressive forces, opposing the old, obsolescent order and unable to score a victory in the given conditions, and the tragic nature of the departure from the scene of the historically obsolescent class, which has not yet exhausted its potentialities. In this case, certain representatives of the old social order realise the doom of their class, but cannot sever their ties with it and adopt the positions of a new class to whom the future belongs. T. contradictions lead to painful emotions, suffering, and even to the death of a hero. But they evoke in people's hearts not only grief, but also aesthetic emotions (see Catharsis), which purify man's feelings and consciousness, foster in him hatred for vile motives and steel his will and courage. Herein lies the so-called paradox of the T. The era of the socialist revolution and the building of a new society has given rise to a new type of tragic heroes who display revolutionary optimism and purposefulness, realise the aims of their struggle, believe in the forces of the people and in the triumph of progressive ideals, and are ready to face the most difficult trials and even death for the sake of communism. Expressing and postulating the aesthetic ideal, the T. is a form of the manifestation of the beautiful, of the sublime (q.v.).

Transcendent, a term denoting that which is beyond consciousness and cognition as opposed to the immanent (q.v.). This term is of vast importance in the philosophy of Kant (q.v.), who held that man's knowledge is unable to penetrate into the T. world, the world of the "things-in-themselves". On the other hand, man's behaviour is dictated by the T. standards (free will, immortal soul, God).

Transcendental means the supercategorical in scholasticism (q.v.). The T. definitions of being, or transcendentals, are broader in scope than the traditional categories of scholastic philosophy: form and matter, act and potentiality, etc.; they express the universal, super-sensuous properties of being which are cognised through intuition, prior to any experience. According to scholasticism, three principal transcendentals (there are six of them in all) denote: unity, the relation of being to itself, or the identity of being; truth, the comparison of being with the infinite spirit; blessing, the comparison of being with the infinite will. Transcendentals were mentioned for the first time by Alexander of Hales (12th-13th century Franciscan scholastic and realist), Albert the Great and Thomas Aquinas (qq.v.). The term of T. was introduced later, in the 16th century. In the 17th-18th centuries, the theory was criticised from the standpoint of nominalism (q.v.). Spinoza and Hobbes (qq.v.) called it "naive" and "senseless", and Kant (q.v.) "sterile" and "tautological". The modern scholastics hold that the theory of Tt. is independent of experience and the concrete sciences, and thereby seek to prove the "eternal value" of metaphysics and the philosophical justification of the theological truths. By its objective content the theory of the T. definitions is but an attempt to create a purely contemplative theory of being.

Transcendental Apperception, a term introduced by Kant (q.v.), denoting a priori, that is non-empirical, initial, pure, and invariable consciousness, which, he claimed, determines the unity of the world of phenomena, from which it receives its forms and laws. According to Kant, the identity "ego", i.e., the fact that the thesis "I think" is included in any conception, forms the basis of this unity. Basing himself on this idealist postulate of Kantianism, Fichte (q.v.) created his own system of subjective idealism.

Transcendental Idealism, a term denoting a special kind of philosophical idealism whose representatives were Kant (q.v.) and his followers. In scholastic philosophy it was used to designate concepts which rise above all the thinkable categories. According to Kant, all idealism that preceded him developed the theory of being in a "dogmatic" way, that is, failed to investigate beforehand the conditions and the very possibility of universal and necessary truths. Kant held that theoretical philosophy ("metaphysics") should explain how these truths are possible in science (mathematics, natural science) and whether they are possible in philosophy. In his opinion, explanations of this kind are supplied by transcendental idealism (also known as "critical"), which tries to prove that the a priori forms of consciousness are the condition for such truths, and studies the possibility of applying these forms both within the framework of experience and beyond it. In accordance with this approach, a number of theories enunciated in Kant's *Critique of Pure Reason* was called transcendental (e.g., transcendental aesthetics, transcendental logic).

Transcendentalists, a group of US idealist philosophers and writers who set up a Transcendental Club in Boston in 1836. This group included Emerson (q.v.), G. Ripley (1802-1880), Thoreau (q.v.) and others. The T. highlighted their negative attitude towards sensationalism (q.v.) and their connection with the philosophy of Kant and Fichte, Jacobi and Schleiermacher (qq.v.). Their world outlook was influenced by the socio-ethical ideas of American puritanism, by the views of Plato, Carlyle and Rousseau (qq.v.). They criticised the inhuman nature of capitalism from the standpoint of romanticism and petty-bourgeois democracy, set great store by spiritual self-perfection in resolving social conflicts and called upon people to draw nearer to nature. Many of the T. opposed slavery in the USA. In 1841, G. Ripley, N. Hawthorne and others set up a colony near Boston, based on Fourier's ideas and known as Brook Farm, which existed till 1847. The T., whose views were most fully expressed in Emerson's *Nature* (1836), left its mark on the development of American literature and philosophy.

Transition from Quantity to Quality, one of the basic laws of dialectics (q.v.), explaining how motion and development take place. This universal law of development states that the accumulation of imperceptible, gradual quantitative changes leads of necessity at a definite moment for each process to radical changes of quality, to a leap-like transition from the old to a new quality (see Quality and Quantity; Measure; Leap). This law holds true in all processes of development in nature, society, and thought. It is important for understanding the dialectical conception of development and its difference from all kinds of metaphysical conceptions which reduce development and motion to quantitative changes alone, without the abolition of the old and the emergence of the new. The development of every branch of knowledge—physics, chemistry, biology, etc.—and the world historic experience in carrying out social transformations, gained in recent decades, corroborate and enrich the dialectical theory of development as a process of qualitative changes taking place as a result of quantitative changes. Quantitative and qualitative changes are interconnected and interdependent: there is not only transition from quantity to quality, but also an opposite process—change of quantitative characteristics as a result of a change in the quality of objects and phenomena. Thus, the transition from capitalism to socialism involved a considerable change in quantitative indications: acceleration of economic and cultural development, growth of national income, etc. Quantitative and qualitative changes are relative. A change may be qualitative in respect to some (less general) properties, and only quantitative in respect to other (more general) properties. Thus, the transition from the pre-monopoly to the monopoly stage of capitalism is not an absolute change of quality: the quality of capitalism changed only in the sense that certain new essential features and properties have appeared, but its essence remains unchanged. Any process of development is at the same time both continuous and discrete. Discreteness appears in the form of a qualitative leap, and continuity in the form of a quantitative change (see Evolution and Revolution). Marxism has proved the unscientific character of the views of the bourgeois ideologists and Right revisionists, who reduce the development of society to slow evolution and minor reforms, deny leaps and revolutions, and of the anarchists and "Left"-wing adventurists who disregard the long and painstaking work of accumulating strength and organising and preparing the masses for decisive revolutionary actions. Hegel, who was the first to formulate this law, mystified it like other laws of dialectics. In his teaching the categories of quantity and quality and their mutual passage initially appeared in an abstract form—in the absolute idea—and only later in nature. Marxist philosophy considers this law not as a prerequisite for constructing the world, but as a result of the study of it, as the reflection of what happens in reality. Being a most important law of the objective world, it is also a vastly important principle for knowing the world and consciously transforming it in practice. In changing conditions of social development the laws of dialectics also undergo change as regards the forms of their manifestation. Thus, under socialism the passage from quantity to quality (leaps) does not take the form of political revolutions; social changes take place here gradually, through the dying away of the old and the emergence of elements of the new. This is the basic law of the development of socialism into communism.

Trendelenburg, Friedrich Adolf (1802-1872), German metaphysician, opponent of Hegel (q.v.). The rational kernel of his criticism of Hegel was his striving to show that Hegel tacitly used the concept of the external world in deducing his categories, and only because of this can these categories be considered as having imaginary independence, insofar as they are isolated from the material world. But having revealed the illusiveness of dialectical transitions in a purely idealistic understanding, T. proved to be anti-dialectic in principle. In actual fact he was an eclectic, an adherent of teleology (q.v.). T. was a prominent connoisseur of Aristotle (q.v.) and translater of his works. His main work: *Logische Untersuchungen* (1840).

Triad, trinity, three-phase development. The concept of T. was introduced by Plato (q.v.) and the Neoplatonists. It was widely used by German classical philosophers, especially Hegel (q.v.). According to Hegel, every process of development passes through three phases: thesis, antithesis, and synthesis. Every next phase denies the previous one, turning into its opposite, while synthesis not only denies antithesis but also combines in a new way certain features of both previous phases of development. In its turn synthesis begins a new T., and so on. T. reflects one of the peculiarities of development, in which the original starting point is reached again, but on a higher plane owing to the experience accumulated. Hegel made an absolute of T. and, contrary to his own statements, transformed it into the artificial scheme of the three-phase development of the concept. Marxist philosophy applies the rational content of T. to characterise the process of development (see Negation of the Negation, Law of).

Tribe, a form of human community peculiar to the primitive-communal system (q.v.). The T. is premised on gentile relations, resulting in the territorial, linguistic, and cultural disunity of the Tt. Only the individual's attachment to a T. made him co-owner of the common property, gave him a definite share of the produce, and the right to participate in communal life. The replacement of gentile relations by commodity-exchange relations led to the disintegration of the Tt. and united them in nationalities (q.v.).

Tropes, principles with the aid of which the ancient sceptics (see Scepticism) formulated the thesis that it is impossible to attain objective knowledge of what exists. It was Aenesidemus (q.v.) who gave the greatest number of T. in the most consistent form. The first four T. deny the possibility of attaining knowledge of things on the strength of the fluidity, indefiniteness, and contradictoriness of man's sensuous perception. Four other T. proceed from the state of the object. The ninth T. generalises all the other eight T., since it deals with the relativity of perception in connection with the infinite variety of relations between the perceiver and the perceived. The tenth T., unconnected with the previous nine T., deals with the impossibility of acquiring objective knowledge owing to the variety of people's opinions, moods, actions, intentions, etc. (for instance, some people have their own laws, other people have different laws; some people hold that the soul is immortal, others that it is mortal). The falseness of all T. is seen from the following: in order to affirm the relativity of cognition of objects, one must have an idea of the autonomous and independent existence of those objects; that is, if a sceptic does not know what the independently existing object is, he can neither prove the relativity of cognition of it nor even know of its existence.

Trubetskoy, Sergei Nikolayevich (1862-1905), Russian idealist philosopher. In 1900-05, he edited the journal *Problemy Filosofii i Psikhologii;* in 1905, was elected Rector of Moscow University. T.'s world outlook was formed under the influence of Platonism, German classical philosophy and the Slavophiles (q.v.), in particular Solovyov (q.v.). According to T., space and time are forms of sensitivity of some universal soul which dwells in God. Cognition of material and ideal objects of reality proceeds in empirical (scientific) and speculative (philosophical) forms. Faith is also a source of knowledge as a precondition of experience and speculation. It enables man to perceive supersensuous reality and establish its objectivity. Experience, reason, and faith provide, according to T., a concrete and integral picture of the world. The "concrete idealism" of Trubetskoy (who sought to reconcile empiricism, rationalism and mysticism, qq.v.) is closely connected with the recognition of God. Being a moderate liberal, T. advocated the system of representative institutions and the autonomy of universities. At the same time, he was a supporter of monarchy, an opponent of socialism and revolutionary methods of struggle. His main works: *O prirode chelovecheskogo soznaniya* (On the Nature of Human Consciousness), 1890; *Osnovaniya idealisma* (Principles of Idealism), 1896, and *Ucheniye o logose v yego istorii* (The Theory of Logos in Its History), 1900.

"True Socialism", a variety of petty-bourgeois socialism which arose in Germany in the mid-1840s (K. Grün, Hess,

q.v., H. Kriege, O. Lüning, and H. Püttmann). The philosophical views of the "true Socialists" were an eclectic combination of the ideas of French and English utopian socialists and Young Hegelians (q.v.) with Feuerbach's (q.v.) ethics. "True Socialists" considered socialism as a supra-class theory, declaring it to be the realisation of some kind of general human essence. They denied the class struggle, preached reconciliation of social contradictions, non-participation in politics and in the struggle for bourgeois-democratic freedoms, and urged the proletariat not to take part in political revolutions. Marx and Engels resolutely fought against the ideology of "T.S." and its influence on the working-class movement. In their works *The German Ideology* and *Manifesto of the Communist Party* they criticised "T.S.", demonstrating the reactionary role it played during the period when the revolution was maturing in Germany. Under the influence of Marx and Engels a number of "true Socialists" (J. Weydemeyer and others) broke with their old views. During the 1848-49 revolution many "true Socialists" discarded their pseudo-socialist phraseology and joined the ranks of petty-bourgeois democrats. Some ideas of "T.S." are now utilised to falsify Marxism in a spirit of idealist ethics.

Truth, the true, correct reflection of reality in thought, which is ultimately verified by the criterion of practice. The characteristic of truth is applied to thoughts and not to things themselves or the means of their linguistic expression. Marxism was the first to provide a consistently materialist basis for the understanding of T. and to indicate new, dialectical aspects of its study (see Criterion of Truth; Truth, Absolute and Relative; Concreteness of Truth; Truth, Objective; Theory and Practice).

Truth, Absolute and Relative, categories of dialectical materialism characterising the development of knowledge and revealing correlations between: (1) that which has already been known and that which will become known in the process of science's development; (2) that part of our knowledge which may be changed, made more precise or refuted as science develops, and that which is irrefutable. The theory of A. and R.T. answers the question: "...can human ideas which give expression to objective truth, express it all at one time, as a whole, unconditionally, absolutely, or only approximately, relatively?" (V. I. Lenin, *Collected Works*, Vol. 14, p. 122). A.T. is therefore understood both (1) as complete, exhaustive knowledge of reality and (2) as that element of knowledge which will not be refuted in the future. At every stage of development our knowledge is conditioned by the level achieved in science, technology and production. As knowledge and practice develop, man's conception of nature is deepened, made more exact and perfect. Scientific truths are, therefore, relative in the sense that they do not give complete, exhaustive knowledge of the objects under study and contain elements that will be changed, made more exact and profound and replaced by the new ones as knowledge develops. At the same time every R.T. is a step forward in the cognition of A.T. and will contain, if it is truly scientific, elements or grains of A.T. There is no impassable barrier between A. and R.T. A.T. is composed of the totality of R.T. The history of science and social experience confirms that knowledge develops in this dialectic way. As it develops, science reveals the properties of objects and relations between them which become known more fully and profoundly, coming close to the cognition of A.T., which is confirmed by the application of theory in practice (in social life, in production, etc.). On the other hand, the earlier developed theories are constantly being made more precise and developed; some hypotheses are refuted (e.g., the hypothesis of the existence of ether), others are confirmed and become proved truths (e.g., the hypothesis of the existence of the atom). The theory of A. and R.T. is opposed to metaphysics (q.v.), which declares every truth to be eternal and immutable ("absolute"), and to the various idealist conceptions of relativism (q.v.), which maintain that all truth is only relative, that the development of science is only evidence of a series of errors that replace each other in sequence so that

there cannot be any objective truth. In actual fact, to use Lenin's words "human thought ... by its nature is capable of giving, and does give, absolute truth, which is compounded of a sum-total of relative truths. Each step in the development of science adds new grains to the sum of absolute truth, but the limits of the truth of each scientific proposition are relative, now expanding, now shrinking with the growth of knowledge" (Vol. 14, p. 135).

Truth, Eternal, the term denoting the irrefutability of certain truths throughout the development of knowledge. In this respect it is analogous to absolute truth. In the process of cognition, however, man is mainly concerned with relative truths, which contain only grains of absolute truth. Metaphysics and dogmatism, which consider truth as being independent of conditions, overestimate the role of the absolute factor in truth, thus providing epistemological grounds for elevating all truths to the rank of eternal and irrefutable. Religion, being an expression of extreme dogmatism, regards all its postulates as irrefutable E.Tt.

Truth in Formalised Languages, a basic concept of logical semantics (q.v.) which specifies the Aristotelian concept of truth as applied to propositions in formalised languages. Attempts to define the concepts of a "true proposition" in a spoken language inevitably lead to antinomies of the type of "liar" (see Antinomies, Semantic). The first strict and non-contradictory definition of the concept "true proposition" was obtained by Tarski (q.v.) in 1931 for a language of some calculus of classes with the help of the concept of decidability in a specially constructed metalanguage (see Metalanguage and Object-Language). A substantial result of his studies was the establishment of the fact that every demonstrable proposition is true, but not every true proposition is demonstrable. The existence of true non-demonstrable propositions in a formalised language is proof of its incompleteness and non-contradictoriness (see Logical Syntax; Axiomatic Theory, Completeness of). There are also other methods of defining the concept of truth in formalised languages.

Truth, Logical and Factual, logical concepts dating from Leibniz (q.v.), who distinguished between necessary truths, or "truths of reason", and incidental truths, or "truths of fact". The truth of the former is derived from the laws of logic, the truth of the latter, from correspondence with the actual state of things. Leibniz, who regarded the laws of logic as absolute, held that "truths of reason" are true in all possible worlds (i.e., worlds that are not contradictory to logic), whereas truths of fact are true only in some worlds (including the world we live in). A similar distinction was made by Hume and Kant (see Synthetic and Analytic). Modern logic maintains this distinction without regarding it as absolute.

Truth, Objective, content of human knowledge which does not depend on the will and desire of the subject. Truth is not constructed by the will or desire of people, but is determined by the content of the object reflected and this is what determines its objectivity. The doctrine of O.T. is directed against all possible subjective idealist conceptions of truth, according to which truth is arbitrarily constructed by man and is a result of conventions between people. Such understanding of truth is unscientific, inasmuch as it allows all kinds of superstitions, religious beliefs, etc., to be regarded as truth because they are shared by many people. As a rule, contemporary bourgeois philosophy opposes the objectivity of truth. This leads to a subjective approach to scientific knowledge, thereby undermining and discrediting science. Pragmatism (q.v.), for example, holds that a proposition is true if its acceptance ensures success in life; neo-positivism (q.v.) declares mathematical and logical truths to be conventions (see Conventionalism).

Tsiolkovsky, Konstantin Eduardovich (1857-1935), Russian scientist and thinker, one of the founders of astronautics. He used his own "cosmic philosophy" as a basis for discussing ideas of a possible exploration of the outer space or populating it. He believed atom associations to constitute the entire variety of the world, including the human organism, the atoms being special particles of matter, indestructible "primitive spirits". However, man can control the course of their development and even create basically new biological creatures, revamp his own biochemical structure. T.'s conceptions included the so-called "cosmic ethics", stemming from his natural philosophy and involving elaboration of ethical guidelines for contacts with creatures from other planets, necessitating co-operation in the work for transforming space, etc. Despite some naturalistic and utopian elements in his world outlook, T. came to be one of the first theorists of space exploration by man. He advanced the theory of rocket propulsion (rocket dynamics), including the idea of their employment in space, the theory of multistage rockets, the theory of inter-planetary travel, including ideas of a man-made earth satellite, orbital stations, etc., important ideas in the field of rocket construction. His main works: *Gryozy o zemle i nebe* (Dreams of Earth and Heaven), 1895; *Issledovanie mirovykh prostranstv reaktivnymi priborami* (Space Exploration by Rocket Devices), 1903; *Obshchestvennaya organizatsia chelovechestva* (Social Organisation of Mankind), 1928; *Nauchnaya etika* (Scientific Ethics), 1930, and others.

Turgot, Anne Robert Jacques (1727-1781), French economist, sociologist and statesman. He shared the materialist views of Holbach, Diderot and Helvétius (qq.v.). In his philosophico-historical studies he (along with Voltaire and Condorcet, qq.v.) laid the foundation of the bourgeois theory of progress. He recognised the importance of economic growth, the progress of science and technology in social development. He put forward the idea that social development is closely connected with the changing forms of economic life. He joined the economic school of the Physiocrats, who in contrast to mercantilists held that *"produit net"*, i.e., surplus value, is created in the sphere of production, not in the sphere of exchange. T. advanced some conjectures about the class division of society and the

essence of wages. He made a step towards a scientific definition of the class.
Main work: *Réflexions sur la formation et
la distribution des richesses* (1776).

Turing, Alan (1912-1954), English logician and mathematician. In 1937, he
suggested a definition of an abstract
computer ("the Turing Machine"), with
the aid of which it would be possible in
principle to perform any calculation or
logical process according to an exactly
formulated instruction. "The T. Machine"
was one of the first exact concepts of the
algorithm (q.v.), anticipating a number of
features common to universal numerical
computers that came into existence later.
T. was one of the first to emphasise the
importance of creating teaching machines,
i.e., machines which could accumulate the
necessary experience and improve. their
behaviour in the process of interaction
with the environment.

Twofold Truth, the term denoting the
mutual independence of the truths of
philosophy and theology. The theory appeared in the Middle Ages, when science
strove to shake off the trammels of
religion. The notion of T.T. was set out
most clearly in Arab philosophy (q.v.).
Ibn Rushd (q.v.), for instance, believed
that philosophy contained truths unacceptable to theology, and vice versa. The idea
of T.T. was propounded by exponents of
Averroism and nominalism (qq.v.), such
as Duns Scotus and Occam (qq.v.), and
by Pietro Pomponazzi (q.v.) and others at
the time of the Renaissance.

Types, Theory of (the Hierarchy of
Types), a method of building formal
(mathematical) logic, by which a distinction is made between objects of various
levels (types); it aims at excluding
paradoxes (q.v.), or antinomies (q.v.)
from logic and the set theory. E. Schröder
was the first to develop T.T. and to apply
it to the logic of classes (1890). In
1908-10, Russell (q.v.) built a detailed
system of T.T. and applied it to the
predicate calculus (q.v.).

**Typification and Individualisation in
Art,** a specific method of reproducing
reality whereby the artistic generalisation
and penetration into the essence of depicted phenomena are effected by revealing their individual peculiarities. The individual in art is not a single fact, but a
means of revealing the general; therefore,
I. is an element of artistic T. In conformity with his ideological design, world
outlook and poetical manner, the artist
selects and picks out the most characteristic features of a given social phenomenon.
Through creative imagination he embodies
his generalisations in individualised, original characters acting in concrete circumstances. Any attempt to divorce T.
from I., to counterpose them, tells nega-
tively on creative work. Devoid of I.,
characters do not look human beings with
their peculiar features, but represent some
lifeless schemes or allegories. On the
other hand, I. without T. is not capable of
creating a truthful realistic image: unable
to penetrate into the essence of depicted
phenomena, it turns into a mere recording
of separate and accidental facts. The
correlation between T. and I. depends, in
the final analysis, on the artistic method
applied. It is only the harmonious unity of
T. and I., which is characteristic of the
realistic method, that makes it possible to
truthfully reproduce the world in art.

Typology, see Classification.

u

Ugly, the, an aesthetic category denoting phenomena inimical to the beautiful (q.v.), and man's negative attitude to these phenomena. In society ugliness, as opposed to beauty, finds expression, for example, in social conditions being inimical to the free manifestation and flowering of man's vital energy, in its restricted and grotesquely one-sided development and in the consequent collapse of the aesthetic ideal (q.v.). In the U. man's essence contradicts itself, appears in a distorted, inhuman way. In bourgeois society, the U. often prevails over the beautiful: this is particularly expressed in the fact that the art of critical realism is preoccupied more with negative rather than with positive characters and criticises and exposes the inhuman sides of life that destroy the beauty of man. In true art the portrayal of what is aesthetically ugly is a peculiar way of asserting the ideal of beauty. The task of the communist education of man is inseparably connected with the struggle against the U. in the form of the survivals of the past (q.v.) that impede the building of a new society.

Unamuno, Miguel de (1864-1936), Spanish philosopher and writer, exponent of existentialism (q.v.). Arrived at his philosophy under the influence of Pascal, Kierkegaard, and Nietzsche (qq.v.). His sense of impending tragedy as the world was nearing a war (*Del Sentimiento Trágico de la Vida,* 1913), his refusal to accept the military dictatorship established in Spain in 1923 and then the 1931 revolution, his efforts to retain faith in immortality coupled with doubts about the tenets of religion (*The Agony of Christianity,* 1931) explain the underlying pessimism of U.'s philosophy and literary works. Hence his quixotism as a sort of spiritual revolt (that is, struggle for an unattainable ideal, struggle contrary to reason), and an aesthetic utopia (*Vida de Don Quijote y Sancho,* 1905). U.'s philosophy had a considerable influence on bourgeois aesthetics and culture and the philosophical anthropology (q.v.) of the Madrid school.

Uncertainty Principle, one of the principles of quantum mechanics (q.v.) formulated by Heisenberg (q.v.) in 1927. This principle posits the impossibility, due to the contradictory, corpuscular-wave nature of micro-objects (see Corpuscular-Wave Dualism), of simultaneously determining their precise coordinates and impulse. The U.P. is expressed in the form of quantitative correlations between what are called uncertainties of conjugate variables: coordinate and impulse as well as time and energy. The less the uncertainty of a particle's coordinate, the greater the uncertainty of its impulse, and vice versa. The same correlation exists between definitions of the moment of time and a particle's energy. The U.P. is an objective characteristic of statistical regularities observed in the motion of micro-particles, one which depends on their corpuscular-wave nature; "uncertainties" are inherent in the actual state of a micro-object and by no means impose any limit to cognition. The U.P. led some physicists and philosophers to conclusions in the spirit of positivism (q.v.). They deny the causal determinateness of the states of elementary particles, as well as the objective nature of the microcosm, its independence of cognition (so-called "instrumental" idealism—see Instrument).

Unconscious 1. Qualifying an action, unconscious means performed automatically, by reflex, before the reason for it has reached the consciousness, e.g., defensive response, etc., or when consciousness is naturally or artificially switched off (sleep, hypnosis, intoxication, sleepwalking, etc.). 2. Active mental processes that are outside the range of the subject's awareness of reality and which are not therefore realised at the moment (see Subconscious). 3. In non-Marxist philosophy and psychology the term of the U. is used to denote a special region of psychic activity in which are concentrated eternal and immutable desires, motives and aspirations determined by the instincts and incomprehensible to consciousness. This conception of the U. was most fully developed in Freudianism (q.v.). It divides the psyche into three layers—the unconscious, the subconscious, and the conscious. The U. is the deep foundation of the psyche that determines the whole conscious life of the individual and even of whole nations. Unconscious desires for pleasure and death (instinct of aggression) form the core of all emotions and emotional experiences. The subconscious is a special frontier zone between the conscious and the unconscious. This zone is invaded by unconscious desires and here they are strictly censored by a special psychical instance born of man's social life, his "supra-ego" (or conscience). Consciousness is a superficial manifestation of the psyche at the point of contact with the real world and it is largely dependent on unconscious forces. The U. figures in the theories of Herbart, Schopenhauer (qq.v.), and other idealists as the mystical basis of all conscious actions.

Unity and Conflict of Opposites, Law of, a universal law of reality and its cognition by the human intellect, expressing the essence, the "core" of materialist dialectics. Every object contains opposites. By opposites dialectical materialism means elements, "aspects", etc., that (1) are in indissoluble unity, (2) are mutually exclusive, not only in different respects, but in one and the same respect, i.e., (3) interpenetrate each other. There are no opposites without their unity and there is no unity without opposites. Their unity is relative, temporary, their conflict is absolute. The law of the U. and C. of O. explains the objective inner "origin" of all motion without calling in any external forces and allows us to understand motion as self-motion (q.v.). Dialectical thinking does not dissect the whole by dividing it into opposites, in an abstract way, but assimilate it as an organic system, in which the opposites interpenetrate each other, thus making possible the process of development. This law expresses in the most concentrated form the antithesis

between dialectical and metaphysical thinking, which interprets the "origin" of motion merely as something different from, and external to, motion itself, and unity as something existing parallel to diversity. Metaphysics (q.v.) leads one to substitute for motion and the concrete unity of diversity a mere description of the external results of motion and the aspects of an object compared purely externally. The history of dialectics is the history of the controversy surrounding these problems and the attempts to resolve them. The founder of the dialectics of contradictions was Heraclitus (q.v.). The Eleatics (see Zeno of Elea) converted contradiction into something purely subjective and reduced it to a means of denying motion and diversity ("negative dialectics", aporia, q.v.). In the Renaissance the idea of the "coincidence of contraries" was developed by Nicholas of Cusa and Bruno (qq.v.). Kant (q.v.) "eliminated" antinomies only by dualistically separating the subject from the object. Attempts to overcome this separation led to the idea of dialectical contradiction (see Fichte, Schelling and Hegel). Particularly great credit for the elaboration of this idea goes to Hegel who did all that was possible towards solving the problem of contradiction within the framework of idealism. In modern bourgeois philosophy the characteristic tendencies are, on the one hand, to irrationalise contradiction as something insoluble ("tragic dialectics"), and, on the other hand, to attempt to dismiss this category altogether and replace it by terminological distinctions (see Positivism). Marxism has interpreted and defined the law of the U. and C. of O. materialistically, as a law of cognition (and a law of the objective world). Materialist interpretation, based on the principle that dialectics, logic, and the theory of knowledge coincide, prevents the law being reduced to a "sum of examples" and presents it as a universal law of being and thinking. The objective universality of the law forms the foundation of its methodological functions in the process of cognition. The solution of contradictions (q.v.) carries the investigation forward in accordance with the logic of the object itself and provides a rational means of evolving new concepts and their synthesis. Dialectical contradiction in the process of cognition is not merely a matter of setting thesis and antithesis against each other; its purpose is to arrive at their solution. To understand dialectical contradiction means to understand how it develops and is resolved. The process of development proceeds through the clash of internal and external opposites. Dialectics regards external opposites not as primordially distinct essences but as the result of the bifurcation of unity, and ultimately as derivatives of internal opposites. The Marxist doctrine of social development rests on the application of this law, on investigation of the contradictions in society; it substantiates the thesis of the class struggle as the motive force in the development of a class society and draws upon this thesis for its revolutionary conclusions. Socialism is the natural result of the development and solution of the contradictions of capitalism through a social revolution. There are various kinds of contradictions and various ways of resolving them. Socialism also develops by means of contradictions, but these contradictions are of a specific nature (see Antagonistic and Non-Antagonistic Contradictions). The category of dialectical contradiction is also important methodologically for modern natural science, which is more and more often confronted with the contradictory nature of objects. Marxism-Leninism made the category of contradiction a part of the system of views which are based on the integrated assimilation of the world by man, who has no reasons to be afraid of contradictions or to prevent them from being settled. The ideological and educational significance of this law finds expression in the fact that it teaches to recognise no stage of historical development as something finite and orients towards endless multiformity.

Unity and Diversity of the World. The unity of the world lies in its materiality, in the fact that all things and all phenomena are various forms or properties of matter in motion. There is nothing in the whole world that is not a concrete form of matter, its property, or the manifestation of its properties and interrelations. The unity of the world is expressed in the objective reality of matter as a substratum of various forms and properties of motion, its uncreatedness and nondestructibility, in its eternity and infinity. Besides, the unity of the world is expressed in the universal connection of phenomena (q.v.) and objects, in the fact that all forms of matter possess such universal attributes (q.v.) as motion, space, time, the ability to develop, etc., in the existence of universal dialectical laws of the motion of matter, in its historical development and also in the processes of transformation of some forms of matter and motion into other. Locally, the unity of the world is manifested in the fact that different objects are made up of the same physical and chemical elements, of the same atoms and elementary particles and fields, that the same physical and chemical laws operate on the Earth and in space systems, and in the similarity of the forms of motion. But the unity of the world should not be understood as uniformity and homogeneity of its structure, as the simple repetition of what already exists on all possible spatial and temporal scales. In accordance with the universal law of transition from quantity to quality (q.v.) in the process of the endless self-development of matter there emerged an infinite number of qualitatively different levels in the structural organisation of matter, at each of which matter possesses different properties and forms of motion. We now know several of these levels, from elementary particles (q.v.) to metagalaxy (q.v.), which are only a small part of the diversity and infiniteness of the world. But this diversity presents no insuperable barrier to acquiring authentic knowledge of matter. Proceeding from the unity of natural phenomena and the universal qualities and laws of material motion, the human mind discovers in every finite phenomenon elements of the infinite. The unity and diversity of the world are perceived through the universal and absolute in the properties and laws of material being.

Universal, see Individual, Particular, and Universal.

Universal Connection of Phenomena, the most general law governing the existence of the world; the result of the universal interaction (q.v.) of all things and phenomena. It expresses the inherent structural unity of all elements and properties in every integral system and the infinite multiformity of connections and relations between one system and other surrounding systems or phenomena. The universal interaction of bodies determines the existence of concrete material objects and all their specific features. U.C.P. reveals the unity of the material world, the determination of all phenomena by other material processes. Without U.C.P. the world would be a chaotic conglomeration of phenomena rather than the integral, law-governed process of the motion and development of matter. Every objective law expresses a certain order of connections and relations between phenomena. U.C.P. is infinite in its manifestations. The connections between objects and phenomena may be mediate or immediate, permanent or temporary, essential or unessential, necessary or accidental, functional or non-functional (see Functional Dependence), etc. U.C.P. is manifested through causal relations, through the dependence of every system's present on its past, on the influence of its surroundings, near and distant, through the connection between each body's properties and the various laws governing its changes, feedback (q.v.) in all self-regulating systems. Connections between phenomena are not to be reduced to the merely physical interaction of bodies. There also exist incalculably more complex biological and social relations, governed by their own specific laws. The development of matter and the conversion to more highly organised forms produce more complex types of interaction between bodies, creating qualitatively new types of motion. This also applies to the development of human society, where progress in the mode of production and the development of civilisation result in more complex relations between individuals and between states, producing a growing multiformity of political, economic, ideological and other relations. The concept of U.C.P. has great cognitive significance. Knowledge of the objective world is possible only through comprehensive and systematic investigation of any ob-

jects, through identification of all essential connections and relations, and the laws governing these connections. Cognition proceeds through motion of thought from reflection of the less profound and less general connections to the determination of more profound and more general connections and relations between phenomena and processes. The structure and classification of the sciences is a reflection of U.C.P. This explains why the connections and relations between sciences become continuously closer, keeping pace with the progress of scientific cognition. "Marginal" sciences appear, which connect formerly remote fields of knowledge (e.g., biochemistry, astrophysics, etc.).

Universality, in subjective idealist philosophy a verification of the truth of human knowledge. In reality, however, the propositions on U. merely disguise the idea of solipsism (q.v.) built on subjective idealist premises. Not everything, which is universal, is true. Everything true becomes, sooner or later, universally recognised. Thus, U. is but one of the effects of the veracity of knowledge, rather than a criterion of the truth.

Universals, the name given to general ideas in medieval philosophy. The dispute about U. centred on whether they are objective, real or merely names of things; whether, on the one hand, they exist "before things", ideally, as held by extreme realism (q.v.) and Erigena (q.v.) or "in things" as held by moderate realism and Thomas Aquinas (q.v.); or, on the other hand, whether they exist only in the mind, "after things", in the form of mental constructions, as professed by conceptualism (q.v.) or are even mere words as held by extreme nominalism, Roscelin, and Occam (qq.v.).

Universe, in the traditional conception, the material world, the sum total of material objects and of qualitatively different forms of matter. This conception has now been given greater precision: the U. is the object of cosmology (q.v.), the part of the material world which, at the present level of science, is accessible to astronomical (observational and theoretical) investigation. Up to the 18th century the object of cosmology was the Solar system (actually nothing was known about the nature of the stars and the distance between them); up to the 1920s, the stellar U., i.e. the galaxy (q.v.); at present, the metagalaxy (q.v.).

Upanishads, ancient Indian religious and philosophical commentaries on the Vedic hymns compiled over many centuries, the concluding part of the Vedas (q.v.). The oldest U. date back to the 7th-3rd centuries B.C. The Vedic gods and rites are invested by the U. with philosophical content. They are interpreted as the allegorical portrayals of man and the Universe. Belief in the transmigration of the soul receives a moral foundation. U. raise the question of what is supreme reality, the knowledge of which gives knowledge of everything else. The answer is idealistic: that from which everything existing is born, in which it lives after birth, and to which it returns after death is *brahman,* the spiritual basis of the world; *brahman* is identical with the spiritual essence of man, *ātman.* To rid himself of the cycle of new births on earth, man, according to the U., must dedicate himself to contemplation of the unity of his soul *(ātman)* with *brahman.* The U. also reflected materialist ideas which the authors of the U. opposed. According to these ideas, one of the material elements—water, fire, air, light, space or time—was the primary foundation of the world and denied the existence of the soul after man's death. Commentaries on the U. written by Bādarāyana (2nd century) and later Samkara (8th century) became the foundation of the Vedānta (q.v.).

Urbanisation, a historical process of the spread of the urban way of life caused by the growing proportion and role of cities in human settlement; it also encompasses changes in the location of the productive forces, in the social, demographic and cultural structure of society, and so on. Under capitalism, U. is spontaneous, seeing the growth of giant cities and agglomerations—megapolises— accompanied with changes in the economic and social structure of society

and causing acute social problems, such as unemployment, crime, demoralisation, environmental pollution, and other social ills. Hence the growing "anti-urbanisation" sentiment in Western countries. Socialism offers effective solutions to socio-economic problems, creates conditions for regulation of U., for overcoming the negative aspects and consequences of U. and for the all-round development of its enormous economic, social and cultural potential. In socialist society, U. promotes the historically progressive obliteration of the essential distinctions between town and country (q.v.).

Utilitarianism, a bourgeois ethical theory which considers the usefulness of an action the criterion of its morality. It was founded by Bentham (q.v.), who formulated its basic principle as the "greatest happiness of the greatest number" through the satisfaction of their individual interests. The morality of an action can be mathematically calculated as a balance between pleasure and suffering resulting from it. Mill (q.v.) introduced into U. the principle of qualitative assessment of pleasures and the demand that mental pleasures be preferred to physical ones. U. also underlies the understanding of the functions of state and law. The application of the principle of utility to the theory of knowledge gave rise to pragmatism (q.v.). In the 1960s, U. tended to regain influence on societal conceptions that vindicate capitalism.

Utopia and Anti-Utopia, an imaginary society which embodies an arbitrarily constructed social ideal. Being impracticable, the concept of U. became a metafor and synonym for any scientifically unfounded scheme (social, technical, etc.). Utopian ideas have been attending the entire history of social thought, starting from the conceptions of the "Golden Age" of the ancient Greek Hesiod (8th-7th centuries B.C.). Certain features of utopianism can be traced in the works of Plato and St. Augustine (qq.v.). The term of U. was introduced by More (q.v.). It reflects certain specifics of the social system which engendered it. At the same time it contains direct or indirect criticism of the existing system, a striving to eliminate its shortcomings by attaining other socio-political ideals. The ideal of a socialist society (see Socialism, Utopian) developed as an U. till the middle of the 19th century. The victory of the socialist revolution, first in Russia and then in a number of other countries, the successes scored in building a new society and the general crisis of capitalism led to the re-evaluation of the concept of U. in bourgeois ideology and culture. Then appeared the so-called anti-utopias in the form of "novels of warning" (*1984* by G. Orwell and *The Brave New World* by A. Huxley), satirical parables, science fiction (novels by I. Asimov, R. Bradbury and others). As a rule, A. expresses the crisis of hope in the future, declares the revolutionary struggle senseless, stresses the indestructibility of social evil; it regards science and technology not as a force which facilitates solving global problems and building a just social order, but rather as a means of enslaving man, which is alien to culture. Thus, in bourgeois consciousness the idea of U. arrives at its logical self-denial, though alongside pessimistic Aa. there exist quasi-optimistic technocratic Uu. At the same time, U. may, in a way, forecast social relations in the shape of science fiction.

V

Vairasse, Denis (c. 1630-c. 1700), author of the novel *Histoire des sevarambes* (1677-79), the first work in French literature propagating ideas of utopian socialism (q.v.). V. describes social reforms carried out in the imaginary Sevarambie society by Sevaris, its legislator. The description of society before Sevaris' reforms makes V. a forerunner of the theorists of natural law (q.v.) and the utopian socialists of the 18th century. The reformed land of Sevarambie, where all privileges of birth and private property are abolished, the land and all its riches belong to the people and labour is compulsory for all except the old and the sick, is divided on the production principle. Children are given an education combining general and vocational subjects. The Sevarambes elect their monarch, whose power is restricted by elective bodies, and the Sun is worshipped as the supreme ruler and divinity. The novel became widely known and gave rise to many imitations.

Vaisesika, a system of ancient Indian philosophy, first expounded by Kānada (Vaisesika-Sūtra, 6th-5th centuries B.C.). V. displayed strong materialist tendencies. Everything that exists is divided into seven categories: substance, quality, movement, generality, particularity, inherence, and non-existence. The first three exist in reality. The second three are logical categories, products of mental activity. An important role in cognition is played by the category "particularity" (hence the system's name), which expresses the real variety of substances. The world consists of substances possessing quality and movement. Of these there are nine: earth, water, light, air, ether, time, space, soul, and mind. All material objects are formed of atoms of the first four substances. Atoms are eternal, indivisible, and invisible. They have no extension, but in combination with other atoms they make up all extensive bodies. The combination of atoms is controlled by the world soul. Owing to the perpetual motion of the atoms the world, which exists in time, space, and ether, is periodically created and destroyed. Atoms are divided according to quality into four types depending on their origin, and produce four senses: touch, taste, sight, and smell. The epistemology of V. is similar to that of nyāya (q.v.) and distinguishes four types of true and four types of false knowledge. The truth is arrived at through perception, deduction, memory, and intuition.

Values, socially accepted evaluations of objects of the surrounding world revealing their positive or negative meaning for man and society (boon, good and evil, the beautiful, the ugly, qq.v., inherent in natural and social phenomena). On the face of it V. act as the properties of objects and phenomena. However, they belong to them because objects are involved with the social being of men and have become bearers of certain social relations, rather than because of the nature of the objects or by force of their own internal structure. In relation to the subject (man), V. represent the objects of his interest, while in his consciousness they serve as reference points in the daily substantive and social realities and as symbols of his various practical attitudes to surrounding objects and phenomena. E.g., a glass, an instrument for drinking, lends that useful property as use-value, a utility. As a product of labour and an object of trade exchange, a glass serves as an economic value. If a glass is a work of art, it is given an added aesthetic V., beauty. All these properties signify its various functions in the realm of human activity and serve as substantive symbols of the existing social relations involving man. Alongside such object V., with human interest addressed to them, some elements of social consciousness may also serve as V. with that interest assuming an ideal form (notions of good and evil, just and unjust, ideals, moral standards and principles). Such forms of consciousness do more than just provide a description of some real or imaginary phenomena. They give an appraisal of them, approve or denounce them, demand their realisation or elimination. Behind the collision of opposite spiritual V. on the ideological scene, one must perceive the struggle of socio-political platforms, class interests represented by integrated systems of views on society, its development, and eventually—the objective logic of historical process. A conscious perception of the objective laws of history gives Marxist world outlook the force of science, while a purely axiological approach to events and phenomena of social life usually does not transcend the boundaries of commonplace or moral consciousness.

Vavilov, Nikolai Ivanovich (1887-1943), one of the founders of Soviet genetics (q.v.) and modern scientific selection, geographer and plant breeder, author of the teaching on world centres of origin of cultivated plants. He attached great importance to the philosophy and methodology of science and pointed to the benefits derived from applying the dialectico-materialist method in genetics, and the need to criticise idealism and mechanism from those positions. He gave a dialectical interpretation of the law of homologous series in hereditary variation, according to which similar types of hereditary variation are typical of genetically like species. Developing the systems approach (q.v.) to species, V. insisted that in studying the complex interconnection between modifications in living systems more account should be taken of the fact that they form an organic whole. V. linked genetics closely with farming, and this promoted the development of the science of heredity and variation itself and also of Darwinism, its broader biological foundation.

Vavilov, Sergei Ivanovich (1891-1951), Soviet physicist, President of the Academy of Sciences of the USSR (1945-51). His main works were devoted to physical optics, particularly the investigation of the nature of photoluminescence. He gave a dialectico-materialist interpretation of a number of revolutionary discoveries in modern physics. He developed the idea of field as a particular form of matter, made an important contribution to the elaboration of a consistent materialist interpretation of corpuscular-wave dualism (q.v.) and highlighted mathematical hypothesis (q.v.) as the principal research method in modern physics. V. was one of the initiators of large-scale research conducted in the USSR into the philosophical aspects of the natural sciences.

Vedānta, one of the orthodox systems of Indian philosophy, a philosophico-religious doctrine based on the teaching of the Upanishads (q.v.). Even today V. holds an important place in the philosophy of Hinduism (q.v.). Its first basic propositions were expounded by Bādarāyana in the Vedānta-Sūtras. Further development took the form of commentaries on this work and on the Upanishads. There are two trends in the V. One is the *advaita* (absolute non-dualism), founded by Samkara in the 8th century. According to this trend, the world contains no other reality than brahman, the only supreme spiritual essence, indefinable, non-conditioned, unqualifiable. The conception that the Universe contains a variety of objects and phenomena results from lack of knowledge; in fact, everything except God is a pure illusion. In *advaita* the path to knowledge is through intuition and revelation, whereas deduction and sensation play only a secondary role. The aim of individual effort is to comprehend the divine unity underlying the apparent diversity of things. The teaching that man's psychic states condition external reality played a considerable part in Samkara's V. The second trend in the V. is the *Viśistadvaita* (differential non-dualism), founded by Rāmānuja (11th to 12th centuries). According to Rāmānuja's teaching, there are three realities: matter, soul, and God. They are mutually dependent on one another: the individual soul rules the material body and God rules them both. Without God, soul and matter can exist only as abstract concepts, not as reality. The aim of individual effort is to free oneself from material existence and this is achieved through spiritual activity, knowledge, and love of God, this last being of particular importance. *Advaita* was closely connected with the worship of the God Shiva, and *Viśistadvaita* with the God Vishnu.

Vedas, the four principal sacred books of ancient India: the Rig Veda, Atharva Veda, Sāma Veda, and Yajur Veda, produced between the 12th and 7th centuries B.C. The term of V. includes also the Brāhmanas (ritual treatises), the Āranyakas (the "forest treatises"), explaining the mystical meaning of the Vedic ritualism and symbolism, and the Upanishads (q.v.), treatises, composed later, in which the worship and mythology of the V. are provided with a philosophical basis and first place is given to discussion of God, man, and nature. The term of V. is also used in the sense of "sacred book" or "supreme wisdom". Besides ancient religious conceptions, the V. contain sections dealing with the causes and purposes of the world's existence and man's actions.

Vekhism, an ideological trend followed by the Russian bourgeoisie, whose political movement emerged against the background of the developed democratic and proletarian movement in Russia. As a result the Russian bourgeoisie quickly manifested its counter-revolutionism. In 1902, the former "legal Marxists" (see "Legal Marxism"), Struve, Berdyayev, and Bulgakov (qq.v.) collaborated with avowed mystics in producing the *Problemy idealizma* (Problems of Idealism), a collection of articles aimed against materialism and positivism in its materialist interpretation. Subsequent collections and the setting up of philosophico-religious societies culminated in the publication of the programmatic collection *Vekhi* (Landmarks) in 1909. This "encyclopaedia of liberal renegacy", as Lenin called it, covered three subjects: (1) the struggle against the ideological principles of the whole world outlook of Russian and international democracy; (2) repudiation of the liberation movement; (3) open proclamation of "flunkey" sentiments and a correspondingly "flunkey" policy in relation to tsarism. *Vekhi* attempted to set off the Russian philosophico-religious tradition represented by Yurkevich, Solovyov, and Dostoyevsky (qq.v.) against materialism and atheism. Their alternative to the class struggle was defence of the individual in his search for "inward", "spiritual" liberation. They blessed the tsarist government, because it protected them from popular fury. On the outbreak of the First World War the supporters of V. became chauvinists, and the October Revolution found them in the camp of the monarchist counter-revolution (collection *De profundis,* 1918; Berdyayev's *Philosophy of Inequality,* and others). As émigrés, the former *Vekhi* supporters opposed the tendency among certain émigré intellectuals ("smenovekhovtsy") to abandon the counter-revolution. Characteristic features of V., also typical of modern bourgeois philosophy, are the use of subtle forms of religion in the struggle against Marxism, the defence of extreme individualism in ethics, antiintellectualism and subjectivism in philosophy. V. ideas are widely used by modern Sovietologists in their struggle against Marxism.

Vellansky (Kavunnik), Danilo Mikhailovich (1774-1847), Russian doctor and idealist philosopher, follower of Schelling (q.v.). V. studied at the St. Petersburg Medico-Surgical Academy (1796-1802) and taught there in 1805-37, and in Germany (1802-05). In his *Prolyuziya k meditsine* (Prolusion to Medicine), 1805, V. evolved his idealist natural philosophy, thus pioneering in Russia the concepts of idealist dialectics.

Verification (Verifiability), Principle of, the basic principle held by logical positivism (q.v.), according to which the truth of every statement about the world must ultimately be ascertained by comparing it with sense data. The principle, as formulated in the Vienna Circle (q.v.), is based on the thesis that knowledge in general cannot extend beyond the limits of sense experience. A distinction is made between direct verification of assertions specifically describing the data of experience, and indirect verification, by logical reduction of a proposition to directly verifiable statements. The obvious philosophical and methodological speciousness of the P.V., which reduces knowledge of the world to "direct evidence" and deprives of cognitive significance all scientific statements not verifiable by direct experience, compelled the logical positivists to accept a watered-down version of this principle that demanded partial and indirect experimental verification of scientific statements; in this form it merely expressed the general methodological requirement that theoretical propositions should correspond to empirical facts, a requirement which must be combined with other factors and criteria of the acceptability of theoretical knowledge (its heuristic force, logical simplicity, etc.).

Vernadsky, Vladimir Ivanovich (1863-1945), naturalist whose field of research took in geology, biology, and the study of the atom; member of the USSR Academy of Sciences. He contributed to the emergence of geochemistry as a science and founded the new branch known as biogeochemistry. He developed the theory of the noosphere (q.v.) (*The Biosphere*, 1926, Vols. 1 and 2) and was one of the founders of genetic mineralogy and radiogeology; he also worked in the field of crystallography, soil science, meteoritics, and the history and methodology of natural science. His standpoint was materialist and he was spontaneously guided by some of the ideas of dialectics. He emphasised the importance of philosophy in scientific research and stressed the need for systematic elaboration of the logic and methodology of natural science. He wrote a number of substantial works on the history and theory of science, e.g., *O nauchnom mirovozzrenii* (On the Scientific World Outlook), 1902-03 and others, regarded scientific thought as "a tool for achieving something new".

Vico, Giambattista (1668-1744), Italian bourgeois philosopher and sociologist. He advanced the theory of the historical cycles (q.v.). Though he recognised the existence of a divine principle from which the laws of history originated, V. nevertheless pointed out that society must develop according to certain inner laws. According to V.'s theory, every nation passes through three phases: the divine, the heroic, and the human, which are analogous to the periods in the life of man—childhood, youth, and maturity. The state, which arises only in the heroic period, represents the domination of the aristocracy. This is replaced in the human

period by a democratic state, in which freedom and "natural justice" are triumphant. The peak in the development of humanity, its maturity, is followed by decline. Society returns to its primary state, then upward movement is resumed and a new cycle begins. V. extended his principles of historical development to language, law, and art. His main work: *Principii d'una scienza nuova* (1725).

Vienna Circle, a group which formed the ideological and organisational centre of logical positivism (q.v.). Developed out of a study group organised in 1922 by Schlick (q.v.) at the department of the philosophy of inductive sciences, Vienna University. Its members included Carnap (q.v.) from 1926, F. Waismann, H. Feigl, O. Neurath, H. Hahn, V. Kraft, F. Kaufmann, and Gödel (q.v.). Associated with the group were P. Frank (q.v.), E. Kaila, A. Blumberg, J. Jörgensen, and Ayer (q.v.). The V.C. inherited the ideas of Machism. It also accepted many ideas of Wittgenstein (q.v.), particularly the conception of logical analysis of knowledge, the doctrine of the analytical character of logic and mathematics, and the criticism of traditional philosophy as meaningless "metaphysics". Having achieved something in the nature of a synthesis between a Machist type of positivism and the ideas of logical analysis of knowledge, the V.C. formulated the basic proposition of logical positivism in its fullest and clearest form. In 1929, Carnap, Neurath, and Hahn published a manifesto entitled *Wissenschaftliche Weltauffassung: Der Wiener Kreis*. The V.C. thus acquired a definite organised form and established international ties with other neo-positivist groups (see Neo-Positivism). In 1930, the V.C. began publishing the magazine *Erkenntnis*, and in the 1930s its members worked the ideas of logical positivism. Towards the end of the 1930s, the V.C. ceased to exist. It was succeeded by logical empiricism, q.v. (Carnap, Feigl, and others).

Vitalism, an idealist trend in biology, which accounts for all the processes of life activity by special immaterial factors said to be present in living organisms. The roots of V. go back to the teaching of

Plato (q.v.) on the soul, which is supposed to spiritualise the animal and vegetable kingdoms, and to the teaching of Aristotle (q.v.). As a conception V. took shape in the 17th and 18th centuries. It was advocated by G. Stahl, J. J. Uexküll, H. Driesch and others. Citing the qualitative individuality of animate nature and absolutising it, V. dissociates the life processes from material physico-chemical and biochemical laws. Exaggerated stress on the antithesis between animate and inanimate nature leads V. to deny the possibility of the emergence of the animate from the inanimate. When the problem is posed in this way there is nothing for it but to ascribe the origin of life to divine causes or to assume its existence as eternal. V. makes capital out of the as yet little investigated problems of biology, the chief objects of its attention being the problems of the origin and essence of life, the integrity and purposefulness of structure and functions, embryogenesis, regeneration, etc. For example, the process of the embryonic development is regarded by V. as the urge of the embryo to realise a preset aim. The history of the development of science is the history of the refutation of V. and the assertion of the materialist interpretation of life (q.v.).

Vivekananda (real name—Narendra Nath Dutta, 1863-1902), Indian idealist philosopher, pupil of Ramakrishna (q.v.). Studied philosophy at Calcutta University (1880-84). In 1893, took part in the USA in the World Congress for propagation of the ideas of Vedānta (q.v.). Founded the religious Ramakrishna Mission in 1897. V. attempted to bring the ideas of the Advaita Vedānta closer to the scientific principles of his day. Like Ramakrishna, he advocated a "single religion" based on the Vedānta. His public activities, however, went beyond the narrow limits of religious reform. He became a prominent public figure, advocated the struggle for national independence and condemned the Indian liberals' policy of appealing to the British authorities. He was thus the direct predecessor of the extreme left ideological leaders of the Indian national liberation movement at the beginning of the twentieth century. Although he condemned imperialist oppression of nations, racism and militarism, his ideas were utopian and petty-bourgeois.

Voltaire, François Marie Arouet de (1694-1778), French writer, philosopher, and historian, one of the leaders of French Enlightenment. His view of the world was contradictory. Though a supporter of Newtonian mechanics and physics, he recognised the existence of God as the prime mover (see Deism). V. held that the motion of nature proceeds according to eternal laws, but God is inseparable from nature, is not a special substance but rather the principle of action inherent in nature itself. V. was actually inclined to identify God with nature. He criticised dualism (q.v.) and rejected the idea of the soul as a special kind of substance. Consciousness, according to V., is a property of matter inherent only in living bodies, but to prove this correct proposition he produced the theological argument that God endowed matter with the ability to think. In contrast to the theological metaphysics of the 17th century, V. insisted on scientific investigation of nature. Rejecting the teaching of Descartes (q.v.) on the soul and innate ideas (q.v.), V. regarded observation and experience as the source of knowledge and preached the sensationalism of Locke (q.v.). The task of learning was to study objective causality. At the same time V. recognised the existence of "ultimate causes" and maintained that experience pointed to the probable existence of a "supreme reason" and "architect" of the Universe. His sociopolitical views were distinctly anti-feudal. V. fought against feudalism, advocated equality before the law, and demanded proportional taxation, freedom of speech, etc. But he rejected criticism of private ownership on the grounds that society must of necessity be divided into rich and poor. The most reasonable form of state, according to V., was a constitutional monarchy ruled by an enlightened monarch. Towards the end of his life he tended to the view that the best form of state was a republic. In his historical works he criticised the Christian biblical view of the development of society and outlined the history of mankind. The "philosophy of history" (the term was of his coining) was based on the idea of the progressive development of society independently of the will of God. But he interpreted historical change idealistically, as due to changes in ideas. He struggled against clericalism and religious fanaticism, the chief target of his satire being Christianity and the Catholic Church, which he regarded as the arch-enemy of progress. Nevertheless V. did not accept atheism, and though he denied the possibility of any incarnation of God (Christ, Buddha, etc.), he considered that the idea of a vengeful God should be maintained among the people. His main works: *Lettres philosophiques* (1733), *Traité de métaphysique* (1734), *Eléments de la philosophie de Newton* (1738), *Essai sur les moeurs et l'esprit des nations* (1756).

Voluntarism, an idealist trend in philosophy which regards will as the prime basis of all that exists. There are two types of V., depending on whether it is a form of objective or of subjective idealism. Schopenhauer and E. Hartmann (qq.v.) were typical representatives of the former. Criticising Kant's (q.v.) agnosticism from the right, Schopenhauer asserted that the thing-in-itself, forming the basis of phenomena (conceptions), is primary, entirely indeterminate "world will". According to Schopenhauer, spontaneous, instinctive "will for life" is the motive force of all living beings. Conscious will is derivative of blind, instinctive individual will. In the spirit of Buddhism (q.v.), Schopenhauer advocated the fatalistic doctrine of renouncing individual will for life and dissolving the individual in the cosmic world will. The subjective-idealist form of V. was typical of Stirner and Nietzsche (qq.v.). The free individual will, the ego, is the motive force in their teachings. Thus they rejected the principle of universal objective regularity. As distinct from Schopenhauer's pessimistic and fatalistic V., Nietzsche's V. is aggressive, extolling "will for power" as the supreme will potential. In its vulgar form Nietzsche's doctrine served as a theoretical source of fascist ideology. In both its forms V. is an irrational version of idealism that considers the spiritual primordial principle of being as unknowable rationally and scientifically, not as

logical, rational and law-governed. Although the term "V." was introduced in philosophy in the late 19th century (F. Tönnies, 1883, F. Paulsen, 1892), voluntarist ideas, in fact, date back to the distant past, starting with the theological dogmas of divine will as the creative primordial source of being. Voluntarist motives were most pronounced in the teachings of St. Augustine (q.v.) and of Duns Scotus (q.v.), V. influenced considerably the bourgeois psychology of the 19th century (Wundt, q.v., H. Münsterberg), which considered will primary to the rest of psychic functions. In idealist logic and the theory of knowledge (see Pragmatism) V. is manifested in the attribution to the will of the decisive role in judgment and knowledge generally, which is considered as a function of interests and aspirations. In socio-political theory and practice V. means negation of scientifically based social activity that relies on the knowledge of the objective laws of history, and also its reduction to the subjective arbitrary will of political leaders. Political V. assumes various forms of anarchist adventurism, on the one hand, and fascist aggression and dictatorship by the "Führer", on the other. The scientific, Marxist conception of the world is incompatible with unscientific, irrational idealism in the understanding of nature, society and the process of cognition. Marxism-Leninism rejects V. and relies in all spheres of social activity on the scientifically based knowledge of the objective laws and trends of social development and on the principles of broad socialist democracy which are alien to voluntarist arbitrary rule.

Vorovsky, Vatslav Vatslavovich (1871-1923), Marxist publicist, revolutionary, and, after the October Revolution, Soviet diplomat. In his works he spread and popularised Marxist ideas and fought against their distortion. His biographical works on Marx, *Pismo iz Berlina* (Letter from Berlin), 1908; *Karl Marx*, 1917, and others, expounded the philosophical, economic and political views of the founders of Marxism. In *"Kommunistichesky Manifest" i yego sudba v Rossii* (The "Communist Manifesto" and Its Destiny in Russia), 1907, and *K istorii* *marxisma v Rossii* (On the History of Marxism in Russia), 1908, he showed how the Marxist teaching was spread in Russia. A number of his articles dealt with the problem of spontaneity and consciousness in the working-class movement, the attitude of the Party to the trade unions, the agrarian problem and the history of the revolutionary movement in Russia, and a critical analysis of neo-Kantian, Machist, and religious mystical ideology "The Rebels and the Reckless" (1906), "Was Herzen a Socialist?" (1920), and others. V. was one of the first Marxist literary critics. He revealed the role of revolutionary ideals in art and the class essence of social pessimism and decadence ("On the Bourgeois Nature of the Modernists", 1908, etc.).

Vulgar Sociologism, a simplified interpretation of social phenomena; distorts historical materialism by exaggerating such factors of social development as machines, forms of production management, economics, politics, ideology. V.S. ignores the significance of man's biological nature. In a narrow sense it is a simplified conception of the class purport of ideology. In philosophy, as represented by Bogdanov (q.v.) and V. Shulyatikov and in aesthetics and literary criticism, as represented by V. Pereverzev and V. Frieche, V.S. denied the relative independence of ideology and inferred all ideological forms directly from the mode of production. The contention that language was a class and superstructural phenomenon was a variety of V.S. in linguistics. Lenin described V.S. as an example of extreme vulgarisation, a caricature of materialism in history.

Vvedensky, Alexander Ivanovich (1856-1925), Russian bourgeois philosopher and psychologist, neo-Kantian. Describing his philosophy as logicism and carrying Kant's ideas a stage further, he deepened the dualism of faith and knowledge, soul and body. In his work *O predelakh i priznakakh odushevleniya* (On the Limits and Characteristics of Animation), 1892, he asserted that the spiritual life of others has no objective distinguishing characteristics and cannot, therefore, be known ("V.'s psycho-physical law"). In *Psikhologiya bez vsyakoi metafiziki* (Psychology Without Metaphysics), 1914, he attempted to justify a psychology that confined itself merely to describing mental phenomena. His logic is consistently idealist (*Logika kak chast teorii poznaniya* [Logic as Part of the Theory of Knowledge], 1909). After the October Revolution he opposed atheism and materialism (*Sudba very v boga v borbe s ateizmom* [The Fate of Faith in God in the Struggle Against Atheism], 1922).

Wang Chung (27-104), Chinese materialist philosopher. In his main work *Animadversions* (Lun Hêng) he resolutely opposed mysticism and idealism and the Confucian doctrine of "heaven" as the supreme guiding force that controls the origin and development of things and phenomena. According to Wang's teaching, everything in the world has its source in the basic material elements, the *ch'i* (q.v.). Man is part of nature and comes into being as a result of the concentration of the *ch'i*. Dispersal of the *ch'i* leads to death and destruction. Wang taught that the process of cognition began with man's sense perception, and rejected the idea of "innate" knowledge. He opposed the theory that the life of society depends on natural elements. History, he said, develops in cycles; periods of greatness are followed by decline, and then the process is repeated.

War, organised armed struggle between states (or classes), which in its socio-political essence is the continuation of these states' (classes') policy by force of arms. The scientific explanation of W. was provided by Marxism. Marx and Engels disproved the theory that W. is eternal and inevitable and showed that Ww. are typical of society with antagonistic classes and break out because of the domination of private property and the policy of the exploiting classes. In Marxism-Leninism a distinction is made between two kinds of Ww. Unjust Ww. continue the policy of the exploiting classes, consolidate their rule, and add to their wealth, bar the way to social progress and defend what is old and outdated. Just Ww. are aimed at liberating the people from class and national oppression. The nature of a W. may, however, change during its course: just Ww. may turn into unjust ones and vice versa. The working class and the Communist or Workers' party make the concrete appraisal of the nature of a W. a theoretical basis for their attitude towards it. The proletariat, and indeed all progressive mankind, condemn W. in general, making an exception only for just Ww. of liberation and defence, which are waged by nations that have become victims of aggression. With the onset of imperialism world Ww. occurred owing to contradictions within the world capitalist system of economy and the striving of the bourgeoisie to capture markets and sources of raw material. Only since the formation of the world's first socialist state, the USSR, have the forces of W. been opposed by the organised forces of peace. As a reasonable alternative to W. Lenin evolved the principle of the peaceful coexistence (q.v.) of states with different social systems. When socialism became a world system and the balance of forces in the world was changed radically in favour of socialism, world Ww. ceased to be inevitable. The problem of W. and peace is the fundamental issue of our time; in the age of missiles and thermonuclear weapons it is a question of life or death for all mankind. The Soviet Union and other socialist countries have put forward a broad and realistic programme for preserving and strengthening universal peace, and are implementing it in their foreign policy. The ability of the peace-loving forces to prevent a new world W. does not mean, however, that all possibility of W. is now excluded. Imperialism has not changed its aggressive nature, and therefore the danger to the peace, freedom and independence of nations still remains. Only with the victory of socialism on a world-wide scale will the social and national roots of W. be destroyed for ever. It is the historic mission of communism to do away with Ww. and to establish eternal peace on earth.

Way of Life, a philosophical and sociological concept embracing the totality of the typical modes of the life activity of an individual, a social group, including class and nation, or society as a whole, together with the conditions of life that determine it. It provides for comprehensive study of the main spheres of the life activity of people—their work, everyday life (with family and marital relations), education, culture (q.v.), social life (with national relations), and helps to determine the value orientations of people and their behavioural motivations (lifestyles) conditioned by the socio-economic system, standard (material well-being) and quality (spiritual well-being) of life. The socialist way of life, in contrast to the bourgeois, is characterised by collectivism (q.v.), true democratism and humanism (q.v.), social optimism, human dignity, sense of public duty (q.v.), comradely mutual assistance, internationalism and patriotism (qq.v.), respect for work and for the working man, social equality and justice, concern for culture and spiritual values (q.v.), public consciousness, intolerance of shortcomings, social activity based on the sense of responsibility for the affairs of one's collective and of society as a whole. W.L. of present-day Soviet society is characterised by the predominance of the features of the socialist W.L. However, there are remnants of the W.L. seen in previous stages of the historical development of society. These are being combatted. Signs of the future communist W.L. keep arising and are encouraged to develop in the process of communist construction.

Weber, Max (1864-1920), German sociologist. Associated with neo-Kantianism and positivism (qq.v.). According to W., the essence of any socio-economic phenomenon is determined not so much by its objective aspects as by the viewpoint of the investigator, the cultural significance attached to any given process. Proceeding from the assumption that the social sciences study only individual aspects of various phenomena, W. tried to substitute for scientific abstraction the arbitrary notion of an "ideal type". This "ideal type", he claimed, had no basis in reality, but was merely a device for systematising and comprehending individual facts, a concept to which the historian compares reality. The weight of W.'s ideas was directed against the Marxist teaching on socio-economic formations (q.v.). His theory of "ideal types",

his conception of the "plurality" of historical factors and the idea of "rationality" as the basis on which bureaucratic institutions function had considerable influence on contemporary bourgeois sociology. His main works: *Der Nationalstaat und die Volkswirtschaftspolitik* (1895), *Agrarverhältnisse in Altertum* (1901), *Die protestantische Ethik und der Geist des Kapitalismus* (1905), *The Economy and Society* (1921), *The Theory of Social and Economic Organisation* (1947), *The Sociology of World History* (1964), *The Sociology of States* (1966).

Weitling, Wilhelm (1808-1871), first German theoretician of communism; utopian communist, active agitator, propagandist and organiser of the workers. He took part in the work of the secret Bund der Gerechten (League of the Just) for which in 1838 he wrote its manifesto *Die Menschheit wie sie ist und wie sie sein sollte*. His main work was *Garantien der Harmonie und Freiheit* (1842). W.'s aim was to organise a communist society, which would ensure harmony between the abilities and strivings of every individual and of society as a whole. The structure of such a society takes into account the difficulties of the transition period, for which the best form of government would be dictatorship. The useful sciences would play a leading part in the new society and all the sciences would be guided by philosophy. W. divided the sciences into three types: (1) philosophical medicine, embracing all manifestations of man's physical and spiritual life; (2) philosophical physics; (3) philosophical mechanics. W. made no secret of his dislike of abstract philosophy and particularly Hegel's (q.v.) philosophy. While criticising religion, he used the Gospels to propagate the idea of communism. He was imprisoned from 1843 to 1844 for writing and publishing his *Das Evangelium des armen Sünders*.

"Welfare State", a bourgeois reformist theory which was most current in the 1960s alleging that since the middle of this century capitalism has become "people's capitalism" and consequently has created the "W.S." as a supra-class power capable of overcoming the anarchy of production and economic crises, putting an end to unemployment and ensuring the welfare of all working people. The facts repudiate the "W.S." myth. Persistent unemployment, inflation and falling living standards among the working people remain a social reality in the most developed capitalist countries. Social security measures are, as a rule, enacted there at the expense of the working people themselves. Democratic reforms are half-hearted and are often reduced to nought by the dominant political regime. In substance, the "W.S." is a system of state-monopoly measures designed to strengthen capitalism and weaken the determination of the working class to aspire for socialism.

Westerners, proponents of a trend of Russian social thought in the 1840s. They called for the elimination of feudal relations and Russia's development along the "Western", i.e., bourgeois road. In the mid-1840s the Moscow group of W. included, among others, Herzen, Granovsky, Ogaryov (qq.v.), V. Botkin, and Kavelin (q.v.). Belinsky (q.v.) was closely associated with it. I. Turgenev, P. Annenkov, and I. Panayev also subscribed to the views of the W. The W. held some common views: condemned the autocratic feudal system, developed the ideas of Enlightenment, and advocated the Europeanisation of Russia. These views had an objectively bourgeois content. Nevertheless there were differences among the W. At first the polemic (on aesthetical, philosophical and then sociopolitical questions) did not go beyond the groups of Westerners. But towards the end of the 1840s two main trends crystallised: Belinsky, Herzen and Ogaryov came forward as materialists, revolutionary democrats and socialists; Kavelin, Botkin and others defended idealism and carried on the line of bourgeois-landowner liberalism in political questions. Some of the W. (e.g., Granovsky) adhered to the positions of Enlightenment standing above classes. The present-day falsifiers of the history of Russian social thought use the term of W. to misrepresent the history of Russia. They claim that the Constitutional-Democrats and Mensheviks continued the traditions of Belinsky and Herzen and call them W., while declaring the Bolsheviks to be the ideological heirs of the Slavophiles (q.v.).

Whitehead, Alfred North (1861-1947), logician, mathematician, and philosopher, professor of London and Harvard universities. Jointly with Russell (q.v.), W. wrote a fundamental book on mathematical logic (q.v.), *Principia Mathematica* (1910-13). Attempts to overcome the crisis in physics by recognising the changeability and constancy of nature, led W. to understand nature as a "process". Defining nature as "experience", W. arrived at neo-realism (q.v.) which combines elements of materialism and idealism. Later on W. went over to objective idealism (q.v.). In sociology, W. combined recognition of ideas as the guiding force of history with raising to an absolute the role of outstanding personalities ("men of science") who must govern the world. His main works: *Process and Reality* (1929), *Adventures of Ideas* (1933).

Wholeness, an inner integrity of an object, as well as the object itself considered outside the environment. The latter circumstance should be viewed in a relative, rather than absolute term, inasmuch as the object is related to the environment in a multitude of ways and exists in close unity with the latter. Besides, any notions of an object's W. are historically transient and depend on the level of scientific thinking. Thus, in biology, the notion of W. is inadequate with regard to certain organisms, making it necessary to introduce such Ww. as "population", "biocenosis", etc. The history of philosophy reveals two tendencies in the interpretation of the term: W. as completeness embracing all the properties, aspects and relations of an object (in this sense W. approaches the notion of concreteness) and W. as an inner definitiveness of the object, that which determines its specific, unique character (in this sense W. approaches the notion of essence, q.v.). In later years attempts have been made to apply the term of W. not only to objects, but to processes occurring in complex systems as well.

Wiener, Norbert (1894-1964), American mathematician. His early works are mainly concerned with the foundations of mathematics. He was also interested in theoretical physics and achieved important results in mathematical analysis and the theory of probability. The study of the functioning of electronic control and computing machines and his research (in collaboration with the Mexican physiologist Dr. A. Rosenblueth) into the physiology of the nervous system led W. to formulate the ideas and principles of cybernetics, q.v. (*Cybernetics, or Control and Communication in the Animal and the Machine,* 1948). His general philosophical views were eclectic; he regarded himself as belonging to existentialism (q.v.) with its pessimistic view of society. W. opposed war and advocated international co-operation among scientists.

Will, a person's conscious determination to carry out a given action or actions. Idealism regards W. as independent of external influences and circumstances and not connected with objective necessity, and men's actions and behaviour as manifestations of the idealistically conceived free will. In fact, the objective world and man's practical activity are the source of his will aimed at transforming the world and based on objective laws of nature. Seen through the prism of the subject's internal conditions (needs, interests, desires, knowledge, etc.), the objective world enables him to set himself various aims, take decisions and act in one manner or another. The W. that chooses merely on the basis of subjective desires (see Voluntarism, Existentialism) is not free; that W. is free which chooses correctly, in accordance with objective necessity. The volitional character of an action is shown most clearly when a person has to overcome external or internal obstacles to achieve his aim. The first stage of a volitional action is the posing and apprehending of the aim; this is followed by the decision to act and the choice of the most expedient means of acting. An action can be described as an act of will only if it is the execution of a decision. Will-power, though determined genetically to a certain degree, is not exclusively a gift of nature. Skill and ability in taking correct decisions and carrying them out, completing what has

been begun, are the fruit of knowledge, experience, education, and self-education. In the philosophy of Schopenhauer (q.v.) and his followers W. is a blind, irrational and aimless world primordial principle, similar to Kant's "thing-in-itself".

Winckelmann, Johann Joachim (1717-1768), German enlightener, historian and theorist of art. His main work, *Geschichte der Kunst des Altertums* (1764), was the first attempt at scientific research into the history of art. The development of art, according to W., is determined both by natural factors (climate) and by social factors (influence of the "state system and administration and the pattern of thought which they call into being"). The "noble simplicity and sublime majesty" of ancient Greek art, born of freedom, formed his aesthetic ideal, which he called upon others to follow. His aesthetic views had a great influence on the subsequent development of aesthetics and art.

Windelband, Wilhelm (1848-1915), German idealist philosopher, founder of the so-called Baden school (q.v.) of neo-Kantianism. He studied the history of philosophy, logic, ethics, and the theory of values. W. treated the history of philosophy from the standpoint of Kantianism, attempted to substantiate the difference between the methods of the natural and the socio-historical sciences. According to W., the natural sciences postulate general laws, while the historical sciences deal with the particular, the individual. Based on a mistaken counterposition of the general to the particular, this distinction was aimed against the Marxist teaching on the objective laws of historical development. His main works: *Geschichte der alten Philosophie* (1888), *Geschichte der neuen Philosophie* (two vols., 1878-80), *Präludien* (1884), and *Geschichte und Naturwissenschaft* (1894).

Winstanley, Gerrard (b. 1609-d. after 1652), English 17th-century utopian, ideologist of the extreme Left trend in the English bourgeois revolution; one of the first to champion the interests of the expropriated masses. In substantiating his social and political ideal, W. was not quite free from theology (q.v.), but in the main adopted the positions of rationalism (q.v.). He held that the theory of natural law (q.v.) was a negation of private property and treated in a materialist way questions of ethics and morality. His main work, *The Law of Freedom* (1652) was permeated with the ideas of egalitarian communism which W. wanted to realise by peaceful means. W. combined features of the mode of production existing in England at that time with the communist principle of distribution through direct exchange of products. His political ideal was a consistently democratic republic.

Wittgenstein, Ludwig (1889-1951), Austrian philosopher and logician, one of the founders of analytical philosophy (q.v.). In his *Tractatus logico-philosophicus* (1921) he proposed the idea of a "logically perfect", or "ideal", language, the prototype of which he saw in the language of mathematical logic as expounded by Russell (q.v.) and Whitehead (q.v.) in their *Principia Mathematica*. This idea is an unjustified attempt to apply limited logical formalism to all knowledge of the world and to conceive it as a sum of elementary assertions interconnected by the logical operations of conjunction and disjunction (qq.v.), etc. W. justified the logico-epistemological conception ontologically by a premise in the form of the doctrine of logical atomism (q.v.). Everything that does not come within the pattern of the "ideal" language—traditional philosophy, ethics, etc.—was declared by him void of scientific meaning; philosophy was considered possible only as "criticism of language". Refusing to accept the idea of objective reality existing independently of "language", of consciousness, W. arrived at solipsism (q.v.). The ideas of the *Tractatus* were taken up by logical positivism (q.v.). Some of W.'s ideas on logic (use of the tabular, or matrix, method of defining the meaning of truth, probability, etc.) influenced the development of modern logic. His views, as summed up in *Philosophical Investigations* (published posthumously in 1953) have influenced linguistic philosophy (q.v.).

Wolff, Christian, von (1679-1754), German idealist philosopher, enlightener, who systematised and popularised the philosophy of Leibniz (q.v.). Having strip-

ped Leibniz's teaching of its dialectical elements, W. developed metaphysical teleology, according to which the general connection and the harmony of being are explained in accordance with the aims set by God. W. also revived scholasticism (q.v.) in a peculiar form. He founded his system on the method of rationalist deduction (q.v.), which derived all the truths of philosophy from formal logic's law of contradiction. Politically, he advocated enlightened absolutism. His main work was *Vernünftige Gedanken von den Kräften des menschlichen Verstandes* (1712).

Working Class, one of the principal classes of modern society, the main motive force of the revolutionary process in the transition from capitalism to socialism and communism. Under capitalism the working class is a class of employed workers deprived of the means of production and selling their labour power to be exploited by capitalists; under socialism it is a class of workers of socialist state enterprises, the leading force of society. Marxism-Leninism has proved that the historic mission of the working class in alliance with all other working people is to overthrow capitalism by revolutionary means and to build a classless, communist society. This role of the working class derives from its objective place in the system of large-scale social production, whose development leads to the growth of the numbers, organisation and solidarity of the working class and helps it to understand its own interests, which means that the working class is transformed from "the class in itself" into "the class for itself". The activities of its vanguard—the revolutionary political party that secures the merging of socialism with the workers' movement—play a decisive role in the formation of the working class, its organisational, political and ideological development. The class struggle of the working class against the bourgeoisie passes various stages—from passive resistance to conscious political struggle—and assumes economic, political and ideological forms. Despite the conceptions of bourgeois ideologists, proponents of reformism and revisionism (qq.v.) who claim that the proletariat is either disappearing, being absorbed by the middle class or is integrating in the capitalist system and relinquishing its revolutionary role, the ranks of the working class are growing, and its strength and prestige increasing in the struggle for the interests of the working people and for the true interests of the nation. Growth of production, especially under the scientific and technological revolution (q.v.), and the social gains of the working class tend to raise the level of its needs, interests, culture and activity. The working class is rendering an ever increasing influence on the development of society. Technological and scientific progress is diversifying the composition of the working class, bringing into its ranks along with the industrial and agricultural workers the mass of distributive and service staff, and the intelligentsia. In the capitalist countries, the working class fights for democratic changes in the economy and in politics. This calls insistently for unity of the various segments of the working class, for pooling the efforts of all the working people in the anti-monopoly struggle and for strengthening international proletarian solidarity. In socialist society the position of the working class changes radically; the proletarian conditions for its existence are eliminated and it becomes the main force of socialist and communist construction. The activities of the working class, in close alliance with other working people, are guided by the Marxist-Leninist party. The professional, cultural and educational level of the working class is rising steadily. So is its political consciousness. This strengthens its role in all spheres of social life. In developed socialist society the alliance of the working class, peasantry (q.v.), and intelligentsia (q.v.) grows more solid, based on their socialist nature, the common world outlook, common aims and increasing social homogeneity. The working class of the socialist countries plays a vanguard role in the liberation struggle waged by the international working class, whose various detachments are united by the identity of basic class interests.

World Outlook, a system of principles, views and convictions which determine the trend of activity and the attitude of an individual, social group, class or society as a whole towards reality. W.O. consists of elements that belong to all forms of social consciousness (q.v.). It comprises man's philosophical, scientific, political, moral, aesthetic and sometimes religious views. Scientific knowledge which forms part of W.O. gives man or a group of people a direct practical orientation in the surrounding social and natural reality. Moral principles and norms regulate the mutual relations and behaviour of people and together with aesthetic views determine their attitude to the environment, forms of activity, its purposes and results. Philosophical views and convictions constitute the foundation of the entire system of W.O.: it is philosophy that theoretically interprets the total data of science and practice and expresses them in the form of the most objective and historically determined picture of reality. The pivotal problem of W.O. is the fundamental question of philosophy (q.v.). Depending on its solution, there are two main types of W.O.: materialist and idealist. W.O. is a reflection of social being. In a class society it bears a class character, and the W.O. of the ruling class is usually dominant there. In a developed socialist society W.O. retains its class character because of the class struggle waged on an international scale. However, in this society the W.O. of the working class begins to represent the W.O. of the whole society: Marxism-Leninism becomes its theoretical, ideological and political basis. Under socialism, the conscious and purposeful cultivation of communist W.O. is one of the principal tasks of the Communist party and the state. Bourgeois ideologists and revisionists claim that the communist social system allegedly leads to the complete unification of W.O. The dominance of the communist W.O. under socialism implies only the acceptance of the scientific, Marxist-Leninist ideology by all members of society. Given the unconditional unity of ideology, the W.O. of people in socialist society presupposes the wealth of individual distinctions and realises them in its components, since the W.O. of the individual, expressing his specific life experience, is not a simple projection of the society's W.O. The presence of both knowledge and conviction is essential for a qualitative characterisation of W.O. It is the convictions that appear on the basis of knowledge that are the source of the activities of a person, group or class. This explains the overriding importance which is attached in socialist society to the conversion of the fundamental principles of the Marxist-Leninist W.O. into convictions in the process of the communist education (q.v.) of the individual.

World Socialist System, the social, economic and political community of the free, sovereign nations which have taken the road of building socialism and communism (qq.v.). The formation of the W.S.S. is a natural result of the objective historical process of internationalising the productive forces and the entire life of human society, of its advancing along the path of socio-economic and political progress. The objective prerequisites for the formation and development of the W.S.S. is the same type of the economic foundation in the member-countries—public ownership of the means of production and socialist relations of production, and this is responsible for the operation of the specific laws of socialist production in these countries; the same type of the state system—government for and by the people with the working class at its head; the unity of the ideological foundation—Marxism-Leninism; the common interests in the defence of the revolutionary gains and national independence against the encroachments of the imperialist forces and in the struggle for peace; the common final goal—the building of communism. The formation of the W.S.S. is a qualitatively new stage in the establishment of the communist formation, which is marked by the rise and development of a fundamentally new type of international relations, based on the close economic, political and cultural co-operation of socialist countries linked by bonds of international socialist solidarity (see Internationalism). These relations gave birth to such new phenomena in international life as the world socialist economy, the socialist international division of labour, socialist economic integration, the world socialist market, international organisations of socialist states, etc. The setting up of the Council for Mutual Economic Assistance (CMEA) in 1949 promoted the expansion

and improvement of various forms of economic, scientific and technical co-operation of socialist countries, the establishment and development of the socialist international division of labour. The collaboration and mutual assistance between socialist countries and their joint efforts contribute to a more rational and fuller use of economic resources and potentialities for rapidly advancing the productive forces, improving social relations, raising the people's living standards, gradually evening out the development levels of the member-countries of the W.S.S. An important role in defending the socialist gains, in consolidating the political unity and cohesion of the socialist countries is played by the Warsaw Treaty Organisation which was set up in 1955 and which today is a centre of coordinating the foreign policies of socialist countries. Being the decisive force in the anti-imperialist struggle, the W.S.S. greatly contributes to the prevention of a new world war. In the mid-1960s, the W.S.S. entered upon a new stage of development, which is stamped by the construction of developed socialist society in the USSR, by the completion of building the foundations of socialism and the transition to the stage of building a mature socialist society in a number of socialist community countries. In the process of improvement and advance, the socialist social system is revealing ever fuller the advantages of its economic and socio-political organisation. This is promoted by the elaboration and introduction of streamlined economic and political forms and methods of guiding the socialist society, including the improvement of the economic mechanism with the aim of raising efficacy and other qualitative indicators of socialist production. These problems are to be solved by the Comprehensive Programme for the Further Extension and Improvement of Co-operation and the Development of Socialist Economic Integration, which was adopted by the 25th CMEA Session in 1971. The W.S.S. is still a young and growing social organism, in which not all problems have been settled. Its improvement and the timely resolution of contradictions that arise depend in many respects on taking due note of the general regularities governing all socialist countries and the forms in which these regularities manifest themselves in concrete historical conditions of each country, that is, on the proper combination of the general and the specifically national in the development of the W.S.S. The formation and strengthening of the W.S.S. has opened up new prospects for human development.

Wundt, Wilhelm (1832-1920), German psychologist, physiologist and idealist philosopher, founder of experimental psychology. He regarded it as a science standing above materialism and idealism. W. based his psychological studies on the theory of psychophysical parallelism (q.v.). W.'s philosophical conceptions are an eclectical combination of the ideas of Spinoza, Leibniz, Kant, Hegel (qq.v.), and others. W. divided the process of cognition into three stages: first, sense perception of everyday life; second, rational cognition of special sciences representing different points of view on the same object of investigation; third (cognition by reason), philosophical synthesis of knowledge, which is the subject of metaphysics. W. defined being, the subject of metaphysics, as a volitional system of spiritual values. Lenin advanced strong arguments against W. in his book, *Materialism and Empirio-Criticism* (q.v.).

X

Xenophanes of Colophon (6th-5th centuries B.C.), Greek philosopher, founder of the Eleatic school (see Eleatics), elegiac poet and satirist. He is known as one of the first critics of anthropomorphism and mythology (qq.v.). He asserted that people create gods only in their own image, and that any animal, if it believed in gods, would picture them as animals. Although X. himself did not approach the problems of the singular and multiple, the identical and the changeable, his views facilitated the formulation of the problem of dialectical relationship between these categories. In his theory of knowledge X. attempted to prove the inadequacy of sense data.

y

Yang Chu (c. 395-335 B.C.), Chinese philosopher, exponent of naive materialism. He severely criticised religious views and the belief in immortality. As he saw it, all events and phenomena of nature and society are subject to the law of natural necessity, which he defined as fate. Hence his views are not free from elements of fatalistic determinism. Y.C. asserted that everything has to perish or to be destroyed. Of natural necessity life gives way to death, destruction follows birth. In ethics he laid much stress upon the individual with his desire for the maximum satisfaction of his feelings and wishes. He urged people to enjoy the present and not to bother about what will happen after death. However, Y.C. did not carry his hedonism and eudaemonism (qq.v.) to the extreme. His individualism was a response to the ethical and social gradation of people in Confucianism (q.v.).

Yin and Yang, basic concepts of ancient Chinese philosophy. In *The Book of Changes* they served to express lightness and darkness, hardness and softness, the male and female principles in nature. As Chinese philosophy developed the Y.-Y. concepts increasingly symbolised the interaction of the extreme, diametrical opposites: light and darkness, day and night, sun and moon, heaven and earth, heat and cold, positive and negative, etc. The Y.-Y. concepts acquired exceptionally abstract meaning in the speculative schemes of neo-Confucianism, especially in the doctrine of *li* (q.v.), the absolute law. The conception of interaction of the polar forces, regarded as the main cosmic forces of motion and the prime causes of constant change in nature, formed the main content of most of the dialectical systems of Chinese philosophers. The doctrine of dualism of the Y.-Y. forces is an indispensable element of the dialectical constructions of Chinese philosophy. The Y.-Y. conception has also found diverse applications in elaborating the theoretical principles of Chinese medicine, chemistry, music, etc.

Yoga, a Hindu philosophico-religious teaching. Patanjali is believed to be its founder (c. 1st century B.C. or A.D.). Y. shares the main principles of Hinduism (q.v.), but believes that the main thing on the way to the fusion of the individual soul with deity is a system of exercises for attaining a mystical ecstasy and complete trance where reality ceases to exist. The exercises originated in ancient times when they, allegedly, helped people to acquire or to subordinate the supernatural forces. Patanjali only made a system of these exercises and described them in his Yoga Sutras (Yogasutras). The lower level of Y. is the Hatha Yoga, physical methods aimed at achieving such body control that would allow to proceed to Raja Yoga, a system of psychic exercises leading to complete departure from reality. Yoga allegedly allows one to become infinitely small and invisible, to grow to enormous proportions, to fly on one's own will to any place, to "see" objects thousands miles away, to read other people's thoughts, to know the past and the future, to talk to the deceased. Y. exercises have gone into most religions of India (incl. Buddhism, q.v.) as a way of "salvation". Hatha Yoga is presented without any serious justification as a universal method of cure for all diseases and of extraordinary improvement of body health, although some of its methods (i.e. breathing technique) have found certain application in physical therapy.

Young Hegelians (or Left Hegelians), a radical wing of Hegel's (q.v.) philosophical school. In the conditions prevailing in Germany at that time their interpretation of Hegelian philosophy and their criticism of Christianity were but a specific form of bourgeois-democratic thought and political interest in general. D. Strauss' book, *Das Leben-Jesu* (1835), which critically analysed the Gospel dogmas, promoted the formation of the Hegelian left wing.

Strauss considered Jesus as an ordinary historical personality, whose supernatural entity was a product of a myth. The next step in the criticism of religion as a false form of consciousness was made by B. Bauer, who regarded the Gospel dogmas as deliberate inventions and the person of Jesus as fiction. The theories of the Y.H. were but the first attempt, modelled on religion, to analyse social consciousness as ideology. Their attention was centred on the question of how false concepts of society appear and acquire the force of compulsion. Strauss explained this by the traditional persistency of mythological views. Bauer saw the source of this phenomenon in the "alienation" of the products of individual "self-consciousness", in that the products of the human mind were considered as abstractions independent of it. The critical analysis of the idealist doctrine of the Y.H. laid bare the limited nature of their analysis of social consciousness and pointed to the necessity for investigating material social relations, for deducing from them the spiritual life of society. To a certain extent this necessity was grasped by Feuerbach (q.v.). The task was fulfilled by Marx and Engels, who joined the Y.H. movement at the beginning of the 1840s. But they arrived at a radically new understanding of social development—the theory of historical materialism. The bankruptcy of the Y.H. movement as bourgeois radicalism is seen most clearly in its underestimation of the role of the masses in history. The ideas of class struggle, of the objective laws of social development, and of the role of economic relations in the life of society were alien to Y.H. Their characteristic feature was revolutionary phraseology containing only liberal threats to the ruling classes who were trying to arrest the bourgeois de-velopment of Germany. Marx and Engels criticised the ideas of the Y.H. in their works, *The Holy Family* and *The German Ideology* (qq.v.).

Yurkevich, Pamfil Danilovich (1826-1874), Russian idealist philosopher and theologian. In his article "On the Science of the Human Spirit" (1860) he tried to refute the works of Chernyshevsky (q.v.) on the anthropological principle in philosophy from the standpoint of idealism. Y. rejected the materialist explanation of man's psychic life, counterposing to it the Christian notion of the unity of the body and the soul. Science should not interfere in the explanation of spiritual life because it does not possess the means necessary for such cognition. In his article "Polemical Gems" (1861), Chernyshevsky showed that Y.'s religious idealism was untenable.

Yushkevich, Pavel Solomonovich (1873-1945), Russian publicist and translator of philosophical literature, Social Democrat and Menshevik, who retired from political activity in the 1920s. In the book *Materialism i kritichesky realism* (Materialism and Critical Realism), 1908, he criticised the philosophy of Marxism from the standpoint of Machism and subjective idealism. He preached empirio-symbolism (q.v.). His work *Mirovozzreniye i mirovozzreniya* (The World Outlook and World Outlooks), 1912, attempted to justify idealistic myths by the specific character of philosophical creativity. According to him, philosophy was not a science but a result of semi-artistic, intellectual-emotional vision. This brought him close to James, Dilthey, and Nietzsche (qq.v.). Lenin criticised Y.'s views in his *Materialism and Empirio-Criticism* (q.v.).

Z

Zen Buddhism, a trend in Buddhism (q.v.); originated in China in the 6th century and became most widespread in Japan; postulated a single essence of Buddha and of all creatures, and the natural way, *tao* (q.v.), which supersedes all theoretical methods. Unlike other Buddhistic schools, Z.B. preaches "sudden awakening", the comprehension of truth. The irrationalism and intuitionism of Z.B., its exotic rites have been rousing great interest among West European and American philosophers, especially in recent decades.

Zeno of Citium (c. 336-c. 264 B.C.), founder of the stoic school born in Citium on Cyprus. In 308 B.C. he founded in Athens his own school which was called stoic (from *stoa poikile,* portico decorated with frescoes). Only a few fragments of Z.'s writings are extant. He divided philosophy into three parts—logic, physics and ethics. He introduced the term "catalepsis" (concept). According to Z., the idea is the imprint of things in the mind. He regarded the image as the criterion of truth, inasmuch as it is associated with the apprehension of reality (see Stoics).

Zeno of Elea (490-430 B.C.), Greek philosopher, a representative of the Elea school (see Eleatics). He was the first to introduce the form of dialogue in philosophy; he is known for his logical paradoxes, which posed in negative form important questions of the dialectical nature of motion. Z. held that being is non-contradictory, therefore contradictory being is seeming being. His paradoxes amounted to proof that (1) it is logically impossible to conceive the plurality of things, (2) the assumption of motion leads to contradiction. His best known paradoxes against the possibility of motion are "Achilles and the Tortoise" and "The Flying Arrow" (see Aporia). Lenin, pondering over Z.'s arguments stressed that Hegel (q.v.) was right in raising objections to them: to move means to be in this place and at the same time not to be in it; it is the unity of the continuity and discontinuity of space and time, which makes motion possible.

Zhegalkin, Ivan Ivanovich (1869-1947), logician and mathematician, professor of Moscow University; one of the founders of the Soviet school of mathematical logic (q.v.). In 1927-28, he devised a logic of propositions in the form of an arithmetic of two figures—nought ("even") and one ("odd"), thus achieving great simplicity in the solution of logical problems. Unlike the usual logical operations, his logic employs not conjunctions, but disjunctions (q.v.), the latter being used in the same way as odd and even numbers in arithmetic.

Zoroastrianism, a dualistic ancient Iranian religion. Its creation is credited to the mythical prophet Zarathustra (Zoroaster in Gk.). Z. had been fully shaped by the 7th century B.C. The main thing in Z. is the doctrine of the constant struggle between two opposite elements in the world: good, personified by the god of lightness and evil, personified by the god of darkness. Its eschatological ideas (see Eschatology) on the end of the world, retribution in another world, the last judgment, resurrection of the dead and a future saviour born of a virgin exerted great influence on Judaism and Christianity (qq.v.). Exists now in the form of Parsism in India, which has preserved the old dualistic ideas but developed the concept of a single Almighty God.

GLOSSARY OF FOREIGN, MAINLY GREEK AND LATIN, WORDS AND PHRASES CURRENT IN PHILOSOPHICAL LITERATURE

A, a conventional sign in logic, designating a universal affirmative proposition. Abbreviation for *affirmo*.

Ab ovo (L.), from the beginning (literally: from the egg).

Ad absurdum (L.), to absurdity. See also *Reductio ad absurdum*.

Ad hominem (L.), see *Argumentum ad hominem*.

Ad oculus (L.), to the eyes, visibly.

Ad rem (L.), see *Argumentum ad rem*.

Agens (L.), from *agere*, to set in motion; driving force, acting entity.

Agere sequitur esse (L.), action follows from being (existence), action is determined by being. A tenet of scholasticism (q.v.).

A limine (L.), refute something straight away, from the outset.

Amicus Plato sed magis amica est veritas (L.), Plato is dear to me, but truth is dearer. A paraphrase of the saying attributed to Aristotle (q.v.).

Analogon rationis (L.), similar to reason. By this term Leibniz (q.v.) designated the lowest forms of consciousness inherent in animals.

An sich (Ger.), translated from Latin *in se* (in itself), introduced by Wolff (q.v.) to designate things, objects as such. After Kant (q.v.) idealists used it to denote the inherently unknowable "thing-in-itself".

Antecedens—consequens (L.), antecedent—consequent.

A posteriori (L.), from effects to causes.

A prima facie (L.), at first sight.

A priori (L.), from causes to effects.

Arbitrum liberum (L.), a free decision, freedom of the will.

Argumenta ponderantur, non numerantur (L.), the force of the arguments lies in their weight, not number.

Argumentum ad hominem (L.), an argument appealing to the emotions of the opponent.

Argumentum ad rem (L.), an argument based on the facts of the matter.

Argumentum ad veritatem (L.), objective proof.

Argumentum baculinum (L.), literally: the argument of the cudgel; figuratively: tangible proof.

Argumentum ex contrario (L.), proof from the contrary.

Argumentum ex silentio (L.), an argument based on suppressing something.

A tempo (L.), simultaneously.

Bellum omnium contra omnes (L.), war of all against all. According to Hobbes (q.v.), the natural condition of human society prior to the emergence of the state.

Bona fide (L.), in good faith, with sincerity; honest, sincere.

Causa activa (L.), an acting cause.

Causa corporalis (L.), a physical cause.

Causa efficiens (L.), an efficient cause.

Causa essendi (L.), cause of being, existence.

Causa finalis (L.), a final cause.

Causa formalis (L.), a formal cause.

Causa materialis (L.), a cause acting in substance, matter; a substratum of action.

Causa movens (motiva) (L.), a motive cause.

Causa occasionalis (L.), an accidental cause.

Causa sui (L.), cause of itself, its own

cause; a term used by scholastics to signify the necessity of God, as well as by Descartes, Schelling and Hegel (qq.v.). *Causa sui* was the main tenet of Spinoza.

Characteristica universalis (L.), universal language, a system of symbols projected by Leibniz (q.v.), who believed that it is possible to translate philosophical concepts into a language of symbols.

Circulus vitiosus (L.), also *circulus in probando,* vicious circle, giving as proof that which has to be proved.

Cogito ergo sum (L.), I think, therefore I am. Descartes' (q.v.) fundamental basis of philosophy.

Coincidentia oppositorum (L.), coincidence of opposites. Nicholas of Cusa (q.v.) used the term to denote removal of contradictions in the infinite.

Conditio sine qua non (L.), an indispensable condition.

Consensus gentium (consensus omnium) (L.), consent of the nations, general consent; a criterion of truth: that which is universal among men is accepted as truth. This argument was used by the stoics (q.v.), Cicero (q.v.) and the thinkers of the Scottish school.

Contradictio in adjecto (L.), contradiction in terms, in definition, e.g., a "square triangle".

Contrat social (F.), social contract (see Social Contract, Theory of).

Credo, quia impossibile (est) (L.), I believe it because it is absurd. This dictum is often attributed to Tertullian (160-220) and advocates blind faith and the primacy of faith over reason. Cf. *Sacrificium intellectus.*

Credo, ut intelligam (L.), I believe, so that I may understand. Attributed to St. Anselm (q.v.) who considered faith the basis of knowledge.

Cum principia negante non est disputandum (L.), it is impossible to conduct a dispute unless there is a consensus regarding the basic premises.

Definitio essentialis (L.), an essential definition.

De omnibus dubitandum (L.), doubt everything. A point of departure in Cartesian philosophy. Descartes (q.v.) declared that doubt was the only correct method of cognition.

Deus ex machina (L.), a god from a machine, i.e., an unexpected and fortunate occurrence.

Deus sive Natura (L.), God or nature, i.e., the identity of god and nature. A tenet of Spinoza.

Dictum de omni et nullo (L.), literally, said of all and of none (see Axiom of the Syllogism).

Differentia specifica (L.), a generic distinction, a characteristic feature.

Docta ignorantia (L.), learned ignorance, i.e., scientific apprehension of the immensity of the infinite, the divine, and of the incomprehensibility of God.

E, in logic, a universal negative proposition; E is the first vowel in the Latin word *nego.*

Elan vital (Fr.), life force, vital impetus, a term used by Bergson (q.v).

Ens (L.), being, in the most abstract sense; existence, essence, entity.

Ens a se (L.), being as such, existence thanks to itself, as distinct from *ens ab alio,* that which is dependent on something else, conditioned, created.

Ens cogitans (L.), the thinking being.

Ens entium (L.), the essence of essences.

Ens rationis (L.), an abstract logical entity.

Ens reale (L.), being which is independent of the mind.

Ens realissimus (L.), in idealist philosophy, the most real entity, i.e., God.

Eppur si muove! (It.), "And yet it does move!" An exclamation uttered by Galileo (q.v.) before the Court of Inquisition, which had forced him to renounce the theory of Copernicus (q.v.).

Esse est percipi (L.), to exist is to be perceived, the main postulate of Berkeley's (q.v.) philosophy.

Essentia (L.), essence, a basic concept of scholasticism (q.v.); *existentia*—existence—is the opposite concept.

Exclusi tertii principium (L.), the law of excluded middle (see *Excluded Middle, Law of*).

Ex nihilo nihil fit (L.), nothing can be made out of nothing; a proposition first advanced by the Greek philosopher Melissus (5th cent. B.C.) and developed by Lucretius (q.v.) in his poem *De Rerum Natura* in opposition to the idealist teaching that God is the creator of the Universe.

Experimentia est optima rerum magistra (L.), experience is the best teacher.

Experimentum crucis (L.), literally, the experiment of the cross, a crucial test.

Explicite (L.), explicitly.

Fundamentum divisionis (L.), the basis of division.

Generalisatio (L.), generalisation, proceeding from the individual to the general.

Genus proximum (L.), the nearest genus, i.e., a broader class of objects embracing the species under discussion.

Gnothi seauton (Gr.), know yourself. See also *Nosce teipsum* (L.).

Homo homini lupus est (L.), man is a wolf to man. The dictum belongs to Plautus, a Roman poet. According to Hobbes (q.v.), it expresses the essence of relations between people prior to the emergence of the state.

Homo sapiens (L.), rational man. The concept was introduced by Linnaeus (q.v.) to designate man as a biological species.

I, a conventional sign in logic, a partial affirmative proposition; *I* is the second vowel in the Latin word *affirmo*.

Idem per idem (L.), the same through the same; definition by what is to be defined.

Ignoramus et ignorabimus (L.), "we do not know and will never know", a formula of extreme agnosticism (q.v.).

Ignorantia non est argumentum (L.), ignorance is no argument; an expression used by Spinoza (q.v.) in his dispute with theologians.

Ignoratio elenchi (L.), ignoring the argument; the fallacy of refuting a proposition different from that set forth by one's opponent; hence, any irrelevant arguments.

Im Werden (Ger.), in the process of emergence, of coming into being.

Implicite (L.), implied.

In abstracto (L.), in the abstract, out of contact with reality.

In concreto (L.), in reality, in actual fact, in a definite case.

In statu nascendi (L.), in the state of inception, at the moment of emergence.

Ipso facto (L.), by that very fact.

Laissez faire, laisser faire (Fr.), let matters take their course; in a dispute, non-interference, unconcern, philosophic indifference.

Lumen naturale intellectus (L.), the natural light of reason; in Descartes' (q.v.) philosophy—intellectual intuition.

Medias res (L.), the gist of the matter.

Medicina mentis (L.), medicine of the mind; figuratively, logic.

Meditatio (L.), reflection, meditation.

Modus probandi (L.), a mode of proof.

Modus vivendi (L.), a manner of living, coexistence; an arrangement between two sides that effects a temporary compromise on issues in dispute.

Mundus intelligibilis (L.), the world of reason perceived by the intellect.

Mundus sensibilis (L.), the world of things perceived by human senses.

Natura naturans (L.), creative nature; *natura naturata*, created nature. The terms were introduced by Ibn Rushd (Averroës in Latin transcription) (q.v.). Erigena (q.v.) regarded God as *natura naturans;* with Spinoza (q.v.), *natura naturans* was substance, while *natura naturata* was the world of individual things, modes. Schelling (q.v.) saw in *natura naturans* nature as an active creative subject, an object of study by natural philosophy (q.v.).

Natura non facit saltus (L.), nature does not make leaps. The phrase was introduced by Linnaeus (q.v.). But the thesis on gradual development of nature goes back to Aristotle (q.v.).

Nervus probandi (L.), the sinews of the argument, the most conclusive and decisive proof.

Nihil est in intellectu, quod non prius fuerit in sensu (L.), there is nothing in the intellect which was not first in the sensations. The main tenet of sensationalism (q.v.) formulated by Locke (q.v.). Leibniz (q.v.) qualified it by adding, *nisi intellectus ipse,* i.e., except intellect itself, thus indicating that the intellect possesses its own laws independent of senses.

Nosce teipsum (L.), know yourself. These words carved in Greek on the pediment of the temple of Apollo Delphinius; are ascribed to Thales (q.v.).

Nota notae est nota rei ipsius (L.), a sign of a sign is a sign of the thing itself; an axiom of the syllogism (q.v.).

Notiones communes (L.), common notions supposedly given to man by nature and therefore innate in all men.

O, a conventional sign in logic designating a partial negative proposition. *O* is the second vowel in the Latin word *nego.*

Obscurum per obscurius (L.), an attempt to explain something obscure by reference to something even more obscure.

Omne verum omni vero consonat (L.), every truth agrees with every (other) truth; a proposition of scholasticism (q.v.).

Omnis determinatio est negatio (L.), "every definition is negation" (Spinoza, q.v.).

Ordo ordinans (L.), the organising principle, the organising universal reason. By this term Fichte (q.v.) designated God.

P, a conventional sign in logic designating the predicate of a proposition. *P* is the first letter of the Latin word *praedicatum.*

Per se (L.), in itself, through itself.

Petitio principii (L.), begging the question; the logical fallacy of using a premise which is either equivalent to or dependent on the conclusion.

Philosophia prima (L.), First Philosophy, the name given by Aristotle (q.v.) to metaphysics (q.v.), and by Wolff (q.v.) to ontology (q.v.).

Post hoc, ergo propter hoc (L.), later than that, therefore, because of that. The statement of the common fallacy that succession in time implies a causal relationship. It has given rise to many superstitions.

Prius (L.), preceding, primary.

Pro et contra (L.), for and against.

Profession de foi (Fr.), profession of faith, declaration of one's views and convictions.

Quaternio terminorum (L.), introducing a fourth term: violation of a rule in logic. It is most apt to arise through the use of an ambiguous term as middle term with one meaning in the major premise and another in the minor premise.

Qui nimium probat, nihil probat (L.), he who proves too much proves nothing.

Quid pro quo (L.), one thing in exchange for another; a confusion of notions.

Quod erat demonstrandum (L.), which was to be proved. The expression belongs to Euclid (q.v.).

Ratio (L.), reason, intellect, basis.

Ratio agendi (L.), a basis of action.

Ratio cognoscendi (L.), a basis of cognition.

Ratio essendi (L.), the basis of being.

Reductio ad absurdum (L.), reduction to absurdity; proof of a proposition by showing the falsity of its contradictory opposite.

Res cogitans (L.), a thinking thing; *res extensa* (L.), an extended thing. Terms introduced by Descartes (q.v.) to designate spiritual and material substances.

S, a conventional sign in logic denoting the subject of a proposition. S is the first letter in *subjectum* (L.).

Sacrificium intellectus (L.), "sacrifice of reason", rejection of one's own thinking. After the Catholic Church adopted the dogma of the infallibility of the Pope, this expression has come to mean sacrifice of one's convictions for the sake of the church authority.

Salus populi suprema (est) lex (L.), let the welfare of the people be the highest law. The expression belongs to Cicero (q.v.).

Semper idem (L.), always the same.

Sic et non (L.), so and not so. The title of the work by Abélard (q.v.), where he laid the foundations of the scholastic method based on the solution of problems through the conflict of diametrically opposed views (See *Pro et contra*).

Species (L.), in philosophy, a mental image; in logic and biology, a concept subordinate to a higher concept called a genus.

Sub specie aeternitatis (L.), (considered) in relation to the one eternal substance.

Sui generis (L.), belonging to a species, all its own, unique.

Summa summarum (L.), in the end, all in all.

Tabula rasa (L.), a blank tablet. The name given by the stoics (q.v.) and later by the sensationalists to the soul of the man at his birth. They maintained that only in the course of his development experience fills it with ideas.

Terminus (L.), limit, frontier; concept.

Terminus a quo (L.), point of departure.

Tertium non datur (L.), literally, a third is not given (See *Exclusi tertii principium*).

Totum pro parte (L.), the total instead of a part.

Tout est pour le mieux dans le meilleur des mondes possibles (Fr.), "all is for the best in the best of possible worlds", a maxim from Voltaire's (q.v.) *Candide*, where he ridiculed the theory of pre-established harmony (q.v.) advanced by Leibniz (q.v.).

Ultima ratio (L.), the final argument; hence, the use of force in preference to argument.

Universalia ante rem, in re, post rem (L.), universals (q.v.) existing before things, in things, after things, viewpoints of extreme realism (q.v.), moderate realism and moderate nominalism, q.v., (conceptualism, q.v.), respectively.

Universalia sunt nomina (L.), universals are only names, a viewpoint of extreme nominalism.

Veritas aeternae (L.), eternal truths.

Verum index sui et falsi (L.), truth is the touchstone of itself as well as of falsehood.

Vivere militare est (L.), to live means to struggle. The expression belongs to Seneca (q.v.).

Volonté generale (Fr.), the general will. According to Rousseau (q.v.), people who live in a natural state conclude a social contract in order to place their personality and property within the purview of the general will, which exercises supreme guidance in their interest.